PRINCIPLES OF WEB DESIGN

SIXTH EDITION

Joel Sklar

DISCARD

CENGAGE
Learning®

Australia • Brazil • Japan • Korea • Mexico • Singapore • Spain • United Kingdom • United States

Principles of Web Design, Sixth Edition
Joel Sklar

General Manager: Kathleen McMahon

Senior Product Manager: Jim Gish

Senior Content Developer: Alyssa Pratt

Developmental Editor: Lisa Ruffolo

Product Assistant: Gillian Daniels

Senior Content Project Manager:
  Catherine DiMassa

Senior Marketing Manager: Eric La Scola

Art Director: Jack Pendleton

Manufacturing Planning: Julio Esperas

Cover Photo: © Galyna Andrushko/
  Shutterstock.com

Compositor: Integra Software Services Pvt. Ltd.

For product information and technology assistance, contact us at
**Cengage Learning Customer & Sales Support,
www.cengage.com/support**

For permission to use material from this text or product,
submit all requests online at **www.cengage.com/permissions**
Further permissions questions can be emailed to
permissionrequest@cengage.com

Library of Congress Control Number: 2014937482

ISBN-13: 978-1-285-85264-5
ISBN-10: 1-285-85264-8

Cengage Learning
20 Channel Center Street
Boston, MA 02210
USA

Some of the product names and company names used in this book have been used for identification purposes only and may be trademarks or registered trademarks of their respective manufacturers and sellers.

Any fictional data related to persons or companies or URLs used throughout this book is intended for instructional purposes only. At the time this book was printed, any such data was fictional and not belonging to any real persons or companies.

Cengage Learning reserves the right to revise this publication and make changes from time to time in its content without notice.

The programs in this book are for instructional purposes only.

They have been tested with care, but are not guaranteed for any particular intent beyond educational purposes. The author and the publisher do not offer any warranties or representations, nor do they accept any liabilities with respect to the programs.

Cengage Learning is a leading provider of customized learning solutions with office locations around the globe, including Singapore, the United Kingdom, Australia, Mexico, Brazil and Japan. Locate your local office at: **www.cengage.com/global**

Cengage Learning products are represented in Canada by
Nelson Education, Ltd.

To learn more about Cengage Learning, visit **www.cengage.com.**

Purchase any of our products at your local college store
or at our preferred online store **www.cengagebrain.com**

Printed in the United States of America
2 3 4 5 6 7 20 19 18 17 16 15

BRIEF
CONTENTS

PREFACE XXI

CHAPTER 1   HTML5 1

CHAPTER 2   WEB SITE DESIGN PRINCIPLES 47

CHAPTER 3   SITE PLANNING 98

CHAPTER 4   CASCADING STYLE SHEETS 138

CHAPTER 5   WEB TYPOGRAPHY 180

CHAPTER 6   BOX PROPERTIES 237

CHAPTER 7   PAGE LAYOUTS 291

CHAPTER 8   GRAPHICS AND COLOR 341

CHAPTER 9   SITE NAVIGATION 402

CHAPTER 10   DATA TABLES ···································· 457

CHAPTER 11   WEB FORMS ······································ 492

CHAPTER 12   RESPONSIVE WEB DESIGN ····················· 542

APPENDIX A   HTML5 REFERENCE ·························· 602

APPENDIX B   CSS REFERENCE ······························ 622

APPENDIX C   PRINT STYLE SHEETS ····················· 630

                INDEX ·· 636

CONTENTS

	Preface	xxi
CHAPTER 1	HTML5	1
	Creating Web Pages with HTML	2
	HTML Syntax	3
	Structure of a Basic Web Page	4
	Activity: Building a Basic HTML5 Document	5
	HTML in the Browser	11
	Adding Style with CSS	13
	CSS Syntax	15
	Activity: Using Cascading Style Sheets	16
	Organizing Information with Hypertext	19
	Understanding the History of HTML	19
	A Need for Standards	20
	XML and XHTML: A New Direction	22
	Problems with XHTML	23
	A Proposal for HTML5	23
	Working with HTML5	24
	HTML5 Loose and Strict Syntaxes	26

Choosing the Correct Syntax   27

Choosing the Correct Document Type and MIME Type   28

Creating Syntactically Correct Code   29

Element Categories   30

New Elements in HTML5   32

Attributes in HTML5   33

Obsolete Elements in HTML5   33

Using HTML5 Elements for Page Structure   33

Interactive Capabilities in HTML5   36

Using Good Coding Practices   **37**

Stick to the Standards   37

Use Semantic Markup   38

Validate Your Code   38

Chapter Summary   **40**

Key Terms   **40**

Review Questions   **42**

Hands-On Projects   **42**

Individual Case Project   **44**

Project Proposal   45

Team Case Project   **45**

Project Proposal   46

CHAPTER 2   **WEB SITE DESIGN PRINCIPLES**   **47**

Understanding the Web Design Environment   **48**

Browser Compatibility Issues   48

Connection Speed Differences   50

Browser Cache and Download Time   51

Device and Operating System Issues   52

Designing for Multiple Screen Resolutions   53

Desktop and Laptop Displays   53

Mobile Devices   57

Suggestions for Solving the Screen Resolution Dilemma   62

Crafting the Look and Feel of the Site   63

Balance Design and Content   63

Plan for Easy Access to Your Information   64

Plan for Clear Presentation of Your Information   64

Creating a Unified Site Design   65

Plan Smooth Transitions   66

Use a Grid to Provide Visual Structure   67

Use Active White Space   71

Designing for the User   72

Design for Interaction   74

Design for Location   76

Keep a Flat Hierarchy   81

Use Hypertext Linking Effectively   82

How Much Content Is Too Much?   84

Reformat Content for Online Presentation   85

Designing for Accessibility   87

WCAG 2.0 Guidelines   90

Chapter Summary   93

Key Terms   94

Review Questions   94

Hands-On Projects   95

Individual Case Project   96

Team Case Project   97

CHAPTER 3   SITE PLANNING   98

Understanding the Web Site Development Process   99

Requirements and Specifications   100

Information Design and Taxonomy Creation   101

Graphic Design and Page Template Creation   101

Construction and Content Development   103

Quality Assurance and User Testing   104

Publishing and Promotion   104

Ongoing Maintenance   104

Creating a Site Specification   104

Identifying the Content Goal   105

Analyzing Your Audience   107

Using Web Analytics   109

Identifying Technology Issues and Accessibility Constraints   111

Identifying Software Tools   112

Building a Web Site Development Team   113

Creating Conventions for Filenames and URLs   114

Naming Files   114

Using Complete or Partial URLs   116

Setting a Directory Structure   117

Using a Single Folder Structure   118

Using a Hierarchical Folder Structure   118

Creating a Site Storyboard   120

Organizing the Information Structure   121

Publishing Your Web Site   126

Choosing a Web Hosting Service Provider   127

Registering a Domain Name   128

Web Hosting Service Comparison Checklist   129

Uploading Files with the File Transfer Protocol   129

Testing Your Web Site   130

    Testing Considerations   130

    Usability Testing   131

Chapter Summary   133

Key Terms   134

Review Questions   135

Hands-On Projects   136

Individual Case Project   137

Team Case Project   137

CHAPTER 4   CASCADING STYLE SHEETS   138

Recognizing the Benefits of Using CSS   139

    CSS Style Rules   140

    Writing Clean CSS Code   144

Activity: Building a Basic Style Sheet   145

Using Inheritance to Write Simpler Style Rules   147

Examining Basic Selection Techniques   149

    Using Type Selectors   149

    Grouping Selectors   150

    Combining Declarations   150

    Using Descendant Selectors   150

    Using the Universal Selector   151

Activity: Applying Basic Selection Techniques   151

Using class and id Selectors   155

    Using the class Selector   155

    Using the id Selector   158

Using the <div> and <span> Elements   159

    Working with <div> Elements   159

Working with <span> Elements   161

Using Other Selectors   162

Using Attribute Selectors   162

Using Pseudo-Class and Pseudo-Element Selectors   163

Understanding How the Cascade Affects Style Rules   170

Advanced Selectors   172

Chapter Summary   174

Key Terms   174

Review Questions and Exercises   175

Hands-On Projects   176

Individual Case Project   178

Team Case Project   179

CHAPTER 5   **WEB TYPOGRAPHY**   **180**

Understanding Type Design Principles   181

Choose Fewer Fonts and Sizes   182

Use Common Web Fonts   183

Proprietary Web Fonts   185

Design for Legibility   186

Avoid Creating Text as Graphics   188

Understanding CSS Measurement Units   188

Absolute Units   189

Relative Units   190

Using the CSS Font Properties   193

Specifying Font Family   193

Using the @Font-Face Rule   196

Specifying Font Size   197

Specifying Font Style   199

Specifying Font Variant   199

Specifying Font Weight   200

Using the Font Shortcut Property   201

Using the CSS Text Properties   202

Specifying Text Indents   202

Specifying Text Alignment   204

Specifying Line Height   205

Specifying Vertical Alignment   207

Specifying Letter Spacing   209

Specifying Word Spacing   209

Controlling White Space   210

Specifying Text Decoration   212

Specifying Capitalization   213

Specifying Text Shadow   213

Currently Unsupported CSS3 Properties   214

Activity: Building a Font and Text Properties Style Sheet   216

Adding the <style> Section   217

Styling the Headings   218

Styling the Paragraphs   219

Making the Second-Level Headings More Distinctive   220

Capitalizing Key Words   221

Customizing Bulleted and Numbered Lists   223

Specifying the list-style-type Property   224

Specifying the list-style-image Property   227

Specifying the list-style-position Property   227

Using the list-style Shorthand Property   229

Chapter Summary   230

Key Terms   230

Review Questions and Exercises   231

Hands-On Projects   232

Individual Case Project   236

Team Case Project   236

CHAPTER 6   BOX PROPERTIES   237

Understanding the CSS Visual Formatting Model   238

Specifying the Display Type   239

Using the CSS Box Model   240

Measurement Values   244

Applying the Margin Properties   244

Specifying Margins   244

Negative Margins   246

Collapsing Margins   247

Zeroing Margins   248

Applying the Padding Properties   249

Padding Property Shorthand Notation   251

Applying the Border Properties   253

Specifying Border Style   254

Specifying Border Width   257

Specifying Border Color   259

Using the Border Shorthand Properties   261

Specifying Rounded Borders   262

Using the Page Layout Box Properties   265

Setting Element Width   265

Setting Sizing Type   267

Setting Element Height   269

Floating Elements   270

Clearing Elements   272

Controlling Overflow 274

Creating Box Shadows 276

Activity: Creating a Simple Page Layout 278

Chapter Summary 285

Key Terms 285

Review Questions and Exercises 286

Hands-On Projects 286

Individual Case Project 289

Team Case Project 290

CHAPTER 7 PAGE LAYOUTS 291

Understanding the Normal Flow of Elements 292

Creating Content Containers 295

Choosing the Correct Content Element 296

Creating Floating Layouts 298

Solution 1: Using a Normal Flow Element 300

Solution 2: Using the Clear Property 302

Floating Elements Within Floats 303

Fixing Column Drops 305

Clearing Problem Floats 306

Building a Flexible Page Layout 307

Controlling Flexible Layout Width 310

Activity: Creating a Flexible Layout 311

Building a Fixed Page Layout 318

Controlling Fixed Layout Centering 321

Activity: Creating a Fixed Layout 322

Chapter Summary 334

Key Terms 334

Review Questions 335

Hands-On Projects 335

Individual Case Project 339

Team Case Project 340

CHAPTER 8	GRAPHICS AND COLOR	341

Understanding Graphics File Formats 342

GIF 342

JPG 344

PNG 346

SVG 346

Using Interlacing and Progressive Display 346

Where You Can Find Images 347

Choosing the Right Format 348

Choosing a Graphics Tool 349

Using the Image Element 350

Specifying alt and title Attribute Text 351

Specifying Image Width and Height 352

Sizing Graphics for the Page 355

Using the Figure Element 356

Using the Canvas Element 356

Controlling Image Properties with CSS 357

Removing the Hypertext Border from an Image 357

Aligning Text and Images 358

Floating Images 359

Adding White Space Around Images 360

Creating Web Site Color Schemes 362

Warm and Cool Colors 364

Tints and Shades 364

Types of Color Schemes 365

Using Color Wisely 367

Specifying CSS Color Values 368

Understanding Element Layers 370

Controlling Color Properties with CSS 371

Specifying Color Values 371

Specifying Opacity 372

Setting the Default Text Color 374

Changing Link Colors 374

Specifying Background Color 375

Setting the Page Background Color 377

Creating a Text Reverse 378

Controlling Background Images with CSS 378

Specifying a Background Image 380

Creating a Page Background 381

Specifying Background Repeat 383

Creating a Vertical Repeat 384

Creating a Horizontal Repeat 385

Creating a Nonrepeating Background Image 387

Specifying Background Position 388

Positioning Repeating Background Images 390

Using Multiple Images in the Background 391

Chapter Summary 392

Key Terms 392

Review Questions 393

Hands-On Projects 394

Individual Case Project 400

Team Case Project 401

CHAPTER 9	SITE NAVIGATION	402

Creating Usable Navigation	403
Planning Site Navigation	403
Orienting the User	403
Limiting Information Overload	405

Designing Navigation for Mobile Devices	405

Using Graphics for Navigation and Linking	408
Using the alt Attribute	409
Using Meaningful Images	409

Activity: Building Navigation Structures	410
Linking with a Text Navigation Bar	411
Linking to Chapter Pages	415
Adding Internal Linking	417
Adding a Page Navigation Bar	419
Linking to External Document Fragments	422
Adding Page Turners	426
Adding Contextual Linking	429
Navigation Summary	430

Using Lists for Navigation	430
Removing Default Padding and Margin	431
Removing Default Bullets	431

Building Horizontal Navigation Bars	432
Customizing the Horizontal Navigation Bar	434
Controlling Navigation Bar Width	436
Controlling Navigation Button Width	437

Building Vertical Navigation Bars	438

Using Background Color and Graphics to Enhance Navigation	441
Indicating History	441
Indicating Location	443

Creating Hover Rollovers   444

    Changing Text Color and Background Color on Hover   444

    Changing Background Images on Hover   446

    Underlining on Hover   447

Chapter Summary   449

Key Terms   449

Review Questions   450

Hands-On Projects   450

Individual Case Project   455

Team Case Project   456

CHAPTER 10   DATA TABLES   457

Using Table Elements   458

    Collapsing Table Borders   461

    Spanning Columns   462

    Spanning Rows   462

Using Table Headers and Footers   463

    Grouping Columns   466

    Styling the Caption   468

Styling Table Borders   469

Applying Padding, Margins, and Floats to Tables   472

    Using Padding   472

    Using Margins and Floats   474

Styling Table Background Colors   476

    Specifying Background Color   476

    Creating Alternate Color Rows   477

    Creating Background Hover Effects   478

Activity: Applying Table Styles   480

Chapter Summary   486

Key Terms   486

Review Questions   486

Hands-On Projects   487

Individual Case Project   491

Team Case Project   491

CHAPTER 11   WEB FORMS   492

Understanding How Forms Work   493

Using the <form> Element to Create Forms   494

    Using get or post   495
    Using the mailto Action   496

Creating Input Objects   496

    Creating Text Boxes   498
    Creating Check Boxes   500
    Creating Radio Buttons   501
    Creating Submit and Reset Buttons   502
    Creating a Password Entry Field   504
    Using the <select> Element   505
    Using the <textarea> Element   509
    Creating Input Groupings   510
    Labeling Form Elements   512

Styling Forms with CSS   513

    Aligning Form Elements   514
    Styling <Fieldset> and <Legend> Elements   518

Activity: Building a Form   521

    Adding Check Boxes   523
    Adding a List Box and Radio Buttons   527

Adding Submit and Reset Buttons 529

Styling the Labels 530

Styling the Fieldsets and Legends 532

Chapter Summary 535

Key Terms 535

Review Questions 535

Hands-On Projects 536

Individual Case Project 540

Team Case Project 541

CHAPTER 12 RESPONSIVE WEB DESIGN 542

Recognizing the Need for Responsive Web Design 543

Content-First Designs 548

Measurement Units in Responsive Designs 549

Using Media Queries to Apply Conditional Styles 549

Applying Media Queries 550

Media Types 551

Media Features 552

Setting the Viewport Scale 554

Activity: Building a Basic Responsive Web Page 554

Creating Flexible Responsive Layouts 557

Creating Responsive Navigation Schemes 565

Using Responsive Images 570

Responsive Images for High-Resolution Devices 575

Building a Responsive Design 575

Creating the Design 575

Activity: Creating a Responsive Style Sheet 578

Chapter Summary   599

Key Terms   599

Review Questions   599

Hands-On Projects   600

Individual and Team Case Project   600

APPENDIX A   HTML5 REFERENCE   602

Alphabetical HTML5 Reference   603

Obsolete Elements   615

Global Attributes   615

Character and Numeric Entities   616

APPENDIX B   CSS REFERENCE   622

CSS Notation Reference   623

Alphabetical CSS Property Reference   623

CSS Measurement Units   629

APPENDIX C   PRINT STYLE SHEETS   630

Applying Print Styles   631

Creating Print Styles   631

Specifying Fonts and Color   632

Specifying Background Colors   634

Creating a Print Page Layout   634

INDEX   636

PREFACE

Principles of Web Design, Sixth Edition leads you through the entire web site creation process, from start to finish, while developing and enhancing your HTML, CSS, and visual design skills along the way. You will learn how to create accessible web sites that let users easily and quickly navigate through your information, regardless of browser type, connection speed, or browsing device. You will also explore the principles of responsive design, a new method of designing web sites that adapt to devices ranging from mobile phones to desktop monitors. Whether you are building a site from scratch or redesigning an existing site, the principles presented in this book will help you deliver your web content in a more responsive, accessible, and visually exciting way.

This edition reflects the latest in web design trends with expanded sections, plenty of new content, and an updated topic flow. The examples and activities emphasize building standards-based web designs using the latest web technologies including HTML5 and CSS3. You will learn how the smartphone and tablet revolution has changed the nature of web design and how to respond to those changes. You will examine current web design theories and view a variety of web sites, learning to focus on both the user's needs and the requirements of the content you want to deliver. In addition, you will learn about the web project design process and see how to turn an initial rough sketch into a finished layout. Through hands-on activities, you will gain experience controlling all web design aspects including typography, color, backgrounds, page layout, and navigation.

Updated illustrations and screen shots throughout the book reflect current browser, device, and web design trends.

Intended Audience

Principles of Web Design, Sixth Edition is intended for anyone who wants to learn how to design and build attractive, informative web pages. You may using this book because you are taking a college or high school web design course or you may be teaching yourself how to build web pages. A basic working knowledge of HTML is an advantage but not necessary to use this book. You should have a good working knowledge of using computers and be able to manage your file system, including copying, moving, and renaming files and folders.

Approach

As you progress through the book, you practice the design techniques by studying the supplied coding samples, looking at the example pages and web sites, and applying the principles to your own work. Each chapter concludes with a summary, individual and team project ideas, and a review section that highlights and reinforces the major concepts of each chapter. To complete a case project, you should complete each chapter in sequence.

Overview of This Book

The examples and exercises in this book will help you achieve the following objectives:

> Learn how to use HTML and CSS to create web pages.

> Learn about the latest release of HTML, called HTML5, and see how it can adapt to a variety of web design needs.

> Learn about the latest release of CSS, called CSS3, and see how you can control display and formatting characteristics for your web page designs.

> Understand the effects of browser and device type on your design choices.

> Learn to build portable, accessible, responsive web sites that present information with clarity and appeal.

> Gain a critical eye for evaluating web site design.

> Effectively use graphics, typography, and color in your work.

> Build user-focused navigation to help your users find content easily.

> Use CSS layout techniques to build responsive page layouts.

In **Chapter 1** you will explore how HTML is used along with CSS to create web pages, learn about the new elements and capabilities of HTML5, how to choose the best syntax for the web pages you are going to create, and how to create correct code. **Chapter 2** covers the design principles that you will apply to your web page design as you work through the book. You will look at a variety of web sites and learn to focus on both the user's needs and information requirements of your site. You will also consider strategies for adapting content to display on devices ranging from desktop computers to smartphones. In **Chapter 3** you will learn about the web development project lifecycle and the value of planning your web site before you start coding. You will also examine important file naming and directory conventions. After exploring how to create a flowchart that depicts the information structure of your site, you will learn how to publish your site to the web and plan for ongoing site maintenance and updates. **Chapter 4** introduces CSS, including its basic syntax and selection techniques, and explains how to control style information in a single file or across an entire web site. **Chapter 5** explains how you can use CSS as a potent style language to manipulate a variety of text properties to achieve professional, effective typographic design.

Chapter 6 introduces the CSS visual formatting model and the box model, which control the way content is displayed on a web page. You also explore the CSS box properties to set the margin, padding, and border characteristics of block-level elements and to enhance the display of content in the browser. **Chapter 7** expands on the concepts introduced in Chapter 6, and demonstrates how to use floats and other CSS layout techniques to create multicolumn web pages that can either be flexible based on the browser size and screen resolution, or fixed to a definite width. This chapter also explores how to use the HTML5 sectioning elements. **Chapter 8** explains the effective use of images and color on your web site, including image file formats, correct use of the <img> element, web site color schemes, and computer color basics. This chapter also discusses how to use CSS to control color properties and background images. **Chapter 9** focuses on navigation and how to help your users find content easily, know where they are at all times, and see where they can go within your web site whether it is displayed on a mobile device or desktop monitor. **Chapter 10** discusses how to use CSS to create attractive, legible data tables. In **Chapter 11**, you will learn how to work with HTML form elements to build interactive web pages that collect information from a user and process it on the web server. Finally, in **Chapter 12**, you will apply a wide variety of skills you learned in the book to build responsive web pages using navigation schemes and images that seamlessly adapt to the size of a user's device. The appendices provide reference information which may be useful as you use the book or work on your own. **Appendix A** provides a reference to HTML5, including a table of HTML5 elements listed in alphabetic order. **Appendix B** provides a reference to CSS, including a table of CSS3 properties listed in alphabetic order. **Appendix C** explains how to use print style sheets to let users print legible versions of web pages.

Features

Principles of Web Design, Sixth Edition contains many teaching aids to assist the student's learning.

> **Chapter objectives**: Each chapter in this book begins with a list of the important concepts to be mastered within the chapter. This list provides you with a quick reference to the contents of the chapter as well as a useful study aid.

> **Illustrations, tables, and screen shots**: Illustrations help you visualize common components and relationships. Tables list conceptual items and examples in a visual and readable format. Updated screen shots reflect the latest technology being used in web design.

> **Notes**: Chapters contain Notes designed to provide you with practical advice and proven strategies related to the concept being discussed.

> **Modern web design techniques**: All new content on HTML5 and CSS3-based layouts demonstrate the latest methods for creating web pages using standards-based design techniques.

> **Full color web page illustrations**: Web page figures and other illustrations are shown in full color so you can assess how color affects web page content and how designers use color effectively in sample web sites.

> **Activities**: Many chapters include step-by-step instructions for applying the principles and practicing the skills taught in the chapter. Sample files are provided to give students a head start on creating web pages.

> **Skills at Work sidebars**: Each chapter includes a short article on the skills students need to succeed as a professional web designer.

> **Chapter summaries**: Each chapter's text is followed by a summary of chapter concepts. These summaries provide a helpful way to recap and revisit the ideas covered in each chapter.

> **Key terms:** Each chapter includes a list of newly introduced vocabulary. The list of key terms provides a mini-review of the major concepts in the chapter.

> **Review Questions**: End-of-chapter assessment begins with a set of approximately 15 to 20 review questions that reinforce the main ideas introduced in each chapter. These questions ensure that you have mastered the concepts and have understood the information you have learned. Some questions have been updated for the Sixth Edition.

> **Hands-On Projects**: Although it is important to understand the concepts behind web design topics, no amount of theory can improve real-world experience. To this end, along with conceptual explanations, each chapter provides Hands-On Projects related to each major topic aimed at providing you with practical experience. Some of these include researching information from people, printed resources, and the Internet, as well as installing and using some of the technologies discussed. Because the Hands-On Projects ask you to go beyond the boundaries of the book itself, they provide you with practice implementing web design skills in real-world situations. Many projects have been updated for the Sixth Edition.

> **Case Projects**: The individual and team case projects at the end of each chapter are designed to help you apply what you have learned to business situations much like those you can expect to encounter as a web designer. Depending on instructor preferences, you can work on your own or with a team to independently synthesize and evaluate information, examine potential solutions, and make recommendations,

much as you would in an actual design situation. These have also been updated for the Sixth Edition.

Online Companion

The online companion to accompany *Principles of Web Design* has been an important component to this book since the First Edition. For the Sixth Edition, it offers greater enhancement to the textbook learning by providing updated information, web links for further research, and files containing the code used to produce the sample web pages shown in the figures. The URL for this site is *www.joelsklar.com/pwd6*.

Instructor Resources

The following teaching tools are available at *sso.cengage.com* to instructors who have adopted this book.

Instructor's Manual: The Instructor's Manual that accompanies this textbook includes additional instructional material to assist in class preparation, including Sample Syllabi, Chapter Outlines, Technical Notes, Lecture Notes, Quick Quizzes, Teaching Tips, Discussion Topics, and Key Terms.

Cengage Learning Testing Powered by Cognero is a flexible, online system that allows you to:

> Author, edit, and manage test bank content from multiple Cengage Learning solutions

> Create multiple test versions in an instant

> Deliver tests from your LMS, your classroom or wherever you want

PowerPoint Presentations: Microsoft PowerPoint slides are available for each chapter. These are included as a teaching aid for classroom presentation, to make available to students on the network for chapter review, or to be printed for classroom distribution. Instructors can add their own slides for additional topics they introduce to the class.

Data Files: Files that contain all of the data necessary for the Activities and Hands-On Projects are provided for students at *www.cengagebrain.com*.

Solution Files: Solutions to the Activities, end-of-chapter Review Questions, Hands-On Projects, and Case Projects are provided.

Read This Before You Begin

The following information will help you as you prepare to use this textbook.

To the User of the Data Files

To complete the steps and projects in this book, you will need data files that have been created specifically for this book. Your instructor will provide the data files to you, or you can obtain the files electronically from Cengage Learning by visiting *www.cengagebrain.com* and then searching for this book title. Note that you can use a computer in your school lab or your own computer to complete the steps and Hands-On Projects in this book.

Using Your Own Computer

You can use a computer in your school lab or your own computer to complete the chapters, Hands-On Projects, and Case Projects in this book. To use your own computer, you will need the following:

> **Web browser**, such as Microsoft Internet Explorer, Mozilla Firefox, Google Chrome, Safari, or Opera.

> **Code-based HTML editor**, such as Adobe Dreamweaver, one of the many shareware editors, or a basic text editor such as Notepad for Windows or SimpleText on the Macintosh.

To The Instructor

To complete all the exercises and chapters in this book, your users must work with a set of user files, called the data files, which are posted at *sso.cengage.com*. Students can also obtain them electronically at *www.cengagebrain.com*. Follow the instructions in the Help file to copy the user files to your server or standalone computer. You can view the Help file using a text editor, such as WordPad or Notepad.

After the files are copied, you can distribute the data files for the users yourself, or tell them where to find the files so they can make their own copies of the data files. Make sure the files are set up correctly by having students follow the instructions in the "To the User of the Data Files" section.

Cengage Learning Data Files

You are granted a license to copy the data files to any computer or computer network used by individuals who have purchased this book.

Acknowledgments

This book is dedicated to Jo, who helped.

Thanks Sammy for your enthusiasm and design advice.

As always, Lisa Ruffolo made this a better book.

Thanks to the team at Cengage Learning for their hard work and honest desire to produce the best book possible.

Thanks to Rob Shain for the use of his Seascapes Aquariums logo.

Thanks to the reviewers who provided plenty of comments and positive direction during the development of this book:

Jim McKeown, Dakota State University

Mark Merkow, Devry University

CHAPTER 1

HTML5

When you complete this chapter, you will be able to:

> Create web pages with HTML
> Add style with CSS
> Describe the history of HTML
> Work with HTML5
> Use good coding practices

In this chapter, you explore how HTML is used along with CSS to create web pages, and you learn the history of how HTML has evolved to its current state. As you will see, designing web pages has changed dramatically in the last few years. You will examine the latest release of HTML, called HTML5, and see how it can adapt to the future of the web. You will learn about the new elements and capabilities of HTML5, how to choose the best syntax for the web pages you are going to create, and how to create correct code. Finally, you will consider what type of software tool you can use to create your HTML code, and how to use good coding practices to make sure your work is useful now and in the future.

Creating Web Pages with HTML

In just 25 years since its inception, the World Wide Web (or web for short) has become an integral part of daily life for millions of people around the world. According to *internetworldstats.com*, the Internet had over 2 billion users as of June 2012, with more new users every day, most using mobile devices such as smartphones and tablets to access their preferred web sites. Imagine your daily life without access to your favorite social media, news, entertainment, and shopping sites. Most of us have integrated the web to such a degree in our lives that we cannot resist constantly checking email, Twitter feeds, Facebook, and the myriad of other online media that have become an essential part of our daily lives.

Despite the diversity of content, all of the web pages on the World Wide Web have one thing in common: They all must be created using some form of the Hypertext Markup Language (HTML). It is astonishing to think that the entire World Wide Web, used every day by millions, is based on a simple text-based markup language that is easy to learn and use.

HTML is a markup language, a structured language that lets you identify common sections of a web page such as headings, paragraphs, and lists with markup tags that define each section. For example, the <h1> element in the following code indicates that the text is a first-level heading:

```
<h1>What is HTML?</h1>
```

Web pages are simply text documents that use HTML to tell the browser how to display each document section. Figure 1-1 shows a basic web page and the code that is used to create it.

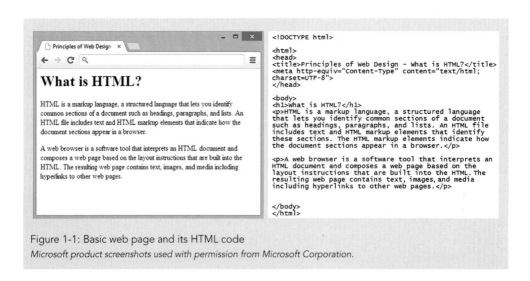

Figure 1-1: Basic web page and its HTML code
Microsoft product screenshots used with permission from Microsoft Corporation.

HTML Syntax

If you examine the HTML example in Figure 1-1, you see that the web page code is a mixture of the text the user sees in the browser surrounded by a variety of markup elements. In HTML, an **element** is a pair of HTML tags containing content. Figure 1-2 shows the syntax of an HTML element.

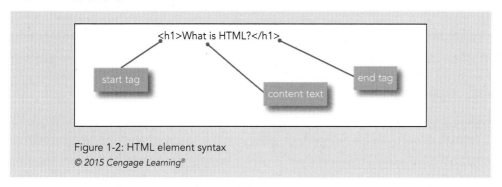

Figure 1-2: HTML element syntax
© 2015 Cengage Learning®

An HTML **tag** includes an opening bracket (<), an element name such as h1, and a closing bracket (>). Notice that the end tag has a slash (/) preceding the element. This indicates to the browser to end the <h1> element.

Many HTML elements let you build the structure for your web page content. For example, document headings are marked with one of a variety of heading tags, such as <h1> or <h2>, signifying a top-level or secondary-level heading. Paragraph content is marked with the <p> element. HTML offers many elements to expressly mark each section of a document. Appendix A contains a complete list of the HTML elements and their usage.

Some HTML elements contain only a single tag. These are known as **void elements** because they contain no content. Rather, they insert something onto the page, such as a new line using the <br> element. Void elements use only the opening tag, never an end tag. Void tags include the <br> element and <img>, the image element, which inserts an image that you specify. You will learn more about the <img> element in Chapter 8.

Each HTML element determines how the content will be organized and displayed in the browser. For example, the <h1> element creates a bold heading for any text it contains. Other HTML elements describe other types of text. The <p> element creates a paragraph of text as shown here.

```
<p>HTML is a markup language, a structured language that lets you
identify common sections of a document such as headings, paragraphs,
and lists. An HTML file includes text and HTML markup elements that
identify these sections. The HTML markup elements indicate how the
document sections appear in a browser.</p>
```

Some HTML elements support attributes that let you provide more information about an element. Here is an attribute (shown in bold) added to an <h1> element:

```
<h1 id="maintitle">Main Title of the Document</h1>
```

In the following example, the src attribute is added in bold to the <img> element to tell the browser which image to display.

```
<img src="prettypicture.jpg">
```

Attributes are always placed in the start tag of an HTML element. They are expressed in the form of a name and a value. The value should always be in quotes as shown in the two previous examples.

Structure of a Basic Web Page

An HTML file includes the text that the user sees in the browser, contained within HTML markup elements the user cannot see. The HTML markup elements identify document sections and elements as shown in Figure 1-3.

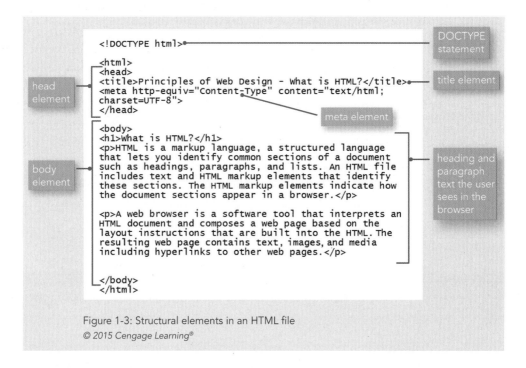

Figure 1-3: Structural elements in an HTML file
© 2015 Cengage Learning®

The HTML code in this example demonstrates the basic structure of an HTML document. First, the Document Type, or doctype for short, specifies the rules for the document language so the browser knows how to interpret the HTML code and display it properly.

After the doctype statement, the opening <html> tag and its closing </html> tag at the end of the page are the root element of the document. A root element is the container element for all other elements in the document.

After the root element is the <head> tag. The two main sections of an HTML document are the head and body sections, represented by the <head> and <body> elements. The head section is the container for all of the descriptive information about the document, including the document title, coding standards, links to external style sheets, and scripting code for interaction. None of the content in the head section appears in the browser window.

The head section includes the important <title> element. This element contains the title of the document, which is shown in the title bar or page tab of the browser and appears as the bookmark text when the user bookmarks the page. Document titles should clearly describe the page, contain key terms, and be understandable out of their web site context. The content of <title> is a primary source of information for search engines and is often the first text users see in a list of search results. The head section also contains the <meta> element, which defines the content type as type "text/html" and declares the character set for the document.

The body section includes the content that the user sees in the browser window. The body of the document can contain text, images, video or audio content, forms for gathering information, interactive content, and hypertext links to other web resources. Here is where all of the various structural elements that make up HTML come into play.

You should use the HTML elements properly to describe each section of the document based on the logical structure of the document. For example, mark headings as headings, long quotes as <blockquote>, paragraphs as <p>, and so on. In the earlier days of the web, HTML elements were often misused, selected for how they looked in the browser rather than for their structural meaning. Avoid using this type of markup, and express all display information with Cascading Style Sheets, which you will read more about later in this section.

Note

Once you are familiar with the HTML syntax, you will find that one of the best ways to learn new coding techniques is to find a web page you like and view the source code. All of the major browsers let you right-click a blank spot in the browser window and then choose View Page Source, View Source, or a similar command.

Activity: Building a Basic HTML5 Document

In this activity, you build a basic HTML file and test it in the browser. The new code to add is displayed in blue text in the following steps. Use a text editor such as Notepad or TextEdit to edit the HTML document.

To create a basic HTML5 document:

1. Copy the **ch1activity1.html** file from the Chapter01 folder provided with your Data Files to the Chapter01 folder in your work folder. (Create the Chapter01 folder, if necessary.)

2. In your text editor, open **ch1activity1.html** and examine the code. Notice that only the basic HTML elements are included to create the head and body sections of the document.

```
<!DOCTYPE html>
<html>
<head>
</head>
<body>
</body>
</html>
```

3. Add the <title> element with a title for your document and a <meta> element that defines the document type as shown in blue in the following code.

```
<!DOCTYPE html>
<html>
<head>
<title>Web Page Activity 1</title>
<meta http-equiv="Content-Type" content="text/html; charset=UTF-8">
</head>
<body>
</body>
</html>
```

4. Add an <h1> element with a heading for the document. The <h1> element must be contained within the <body> element.

```
<!DOCTYPE html>
<html>
<head>
<title>Web Page Activity 1</title>
<meta http-equiv="Content-Type" content="text/html;
charset=UTF-8">
</head>
```

```
<body>

<h1>The World Wide Web</h1>

</body>

</html>
```

5. Save your file, and view it in your browser. It should look like Figure 1-4.

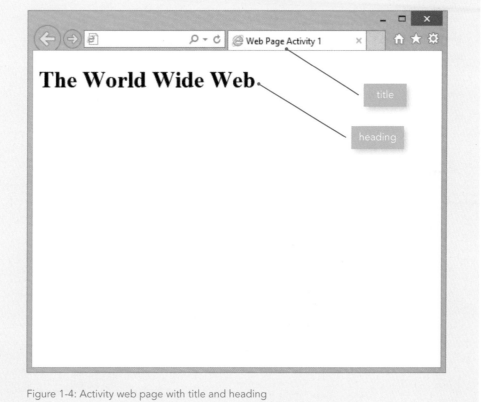

Figure 1-4: Activity web page with title and heading
Microsoft product screenshots used with permission from Microsoft Corporation.

6. Add two paragraphs of content immediately following the <h1> element as shown.

```
<!DOCTYPE html>

<html>

<head>

<title>Web Page Activity 1</title>

<meta http-equiv="Content-Type" content="text/html;

charset=UTF-8">

</head>
```

```
<body>
<h1>The World Wide Web</h1>
<p>The World Wide Web, abbreviated as WWW and
commonly known as the web, is a system of
interlinked hypertext documents accessed via the
Internet.</p>
<p>With a web browser, one can view web pages
that may contain text, images, videos, and other
multimedia and navigate between them by using hyperlinks.</p>
</body>
</html>
```

7. Save your file, and view it in your browser. It should look like Figure 1-5.

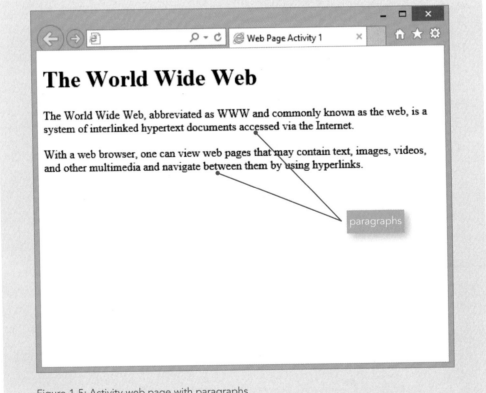

Figure 1-5: Activity web page with paragraphs
Microsoft product screenshots used with permission from Microsoft Corporation.

8. Add one more paragraph and a bulleted list as shown.

```html
<html>
<head>
<title>Web Page Activity 1</title>
<meta http-equiv="Content-Type" content="text/html;
charset=UTF-8">
</head>
<body>
<h1>The World Wide Web</h1>
<p>The World Wide Web, abbreviated as WWW and
commonly known as the web, is a system of
interlinked hypertext documents accessed via the
Internet.</p>
<p>With a web browser, one can view web pages
that may contain text, images, videos, and other
multimedia and navigate between them by using
hyperlinks.</p>
<p>There are many different types of web sites,
including:</p>
<ul>
<li>Social networking</li>
<li>Publishing</li>
<li>Wikis</li>
<li>Shopping and catalog</li>
<li>Search portal</li>
</ul>
</body>
</html>
```

9. Add a comment at the bottom of the page that includes your name where shown. Comments do not appear in the browser window.

```html
<html>
<head>
<title>Web Page Activity 1</title>
<meta http-equiv="Content-Type" content="text/html;
charset=UTF-8">
</head>
<body>
<h1>The World Wide Web</h1>
<p>The World Wide Web, abbreviated as WWW and
commonly known as the web, is a system of
interlinked hypertext documents accessed via the
Internet.</p>
<p>With a web browser, one can view web pages
that may contain text, images, videos, and other
multimedia and navigate between them by using
hyperlinks.</p>
<p>There are many different types of web sites,
including:</p>
<ul>
<li>Social networking</li>
<li>Publishing</li>
<li>Wikis</li>
<li>Shopping and catalog</li>
<li>Search portal</li>
</ul>
<!-- Web page activity #1 by Your Name -->
</body>
</html>
```

10. Save your file, and view it in your browser. It should look like Figure 1-6.

Figure 1-6: Activity web page with list
Microsoft product screenshots used with permission from Microsoft Corporation.

HTML in the Browser

The browser interprets the HTML markup elements and displays the results, hiding the actual markup from the user. Figure 1-7 shows the browser's rendition of the HTML code from Figure 1-3. Each HTML element contains basic display information to organize and present contents in the browser, such as heading elements that are displayed in a bolder and larger font than paragraph elements. Notice also that the title is displayed in the title bar of the browser.

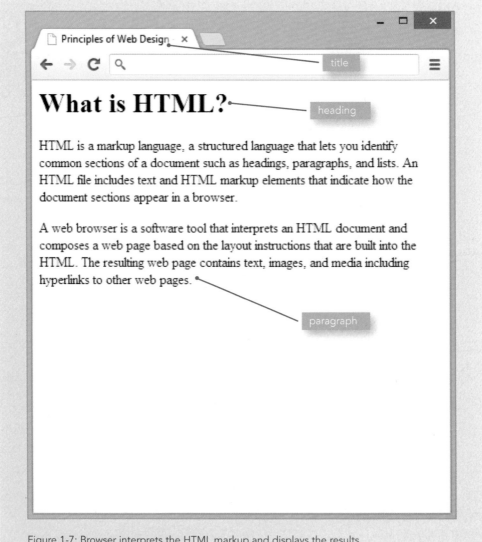

Figure 1-7: Browser interprets the HTML markup and displays the results
Microsoft product screenshots used with permission from Microsoft Corporation.

As you begin to design and build Web pages, remember that each browser interprets HTML in its own way, based on its **rendering engine**. A browser's rendering engine is software that reads the document's HTML code and associated CSS style information and displays the resulting formatted content in the browser window. Examples of rendering engines include Gecko, which is used in Firefox, and WebKit, used in Safari and Google Chrome. Although most of your web pages should look similar in most browsers, it is essential that you test your work in different browsers to make sure that your web pages are rendered as consistently as possible. You will learn more about browser differences in Chapter 2.

Adding Style with CSS

To add presentation information to web pages, web designers use a style language called Cascading Style Sheets (CSS). With CSS, you can display information for different devices, such as a smartphone, tablet, or computer screen, lay out page designs, and control typography, color, and many other presentation characteristics.

A style sheet is a set of style rules that describes the display characteristics of a document. Style rules express the style characteristics for an HTML element. With style sheets, the presentation properties are separate from the content. This accommodates the variety of devices and users that browse the web, as shown in Figure 1-8.

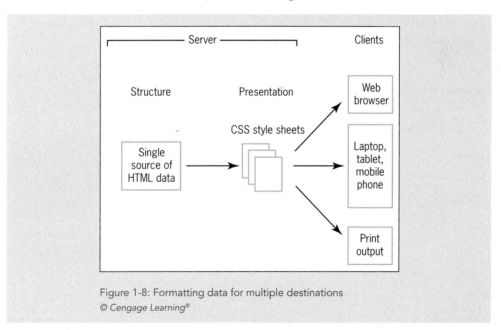

Figure 1-8: Formatting data for multiple destinations
© Cengage Learning®

CSS lets you control the presentation characteristics of an entire web site with a single style sheet document. For example, assume that you want all of your <h1> headings to appear green and centered everywhere on your web site. Using a CSS rule, you can express the style as follows:

```
h1 {color: green; text-align: center;}
```

You can place this rule in an external style sheet, and then link every page on your site to that style sheet; the single rule controls every <h1> element in your web site. Later, if you want to change the <h1> color to red, you simply revise the style sheet rule to change every page on your site.

Through much of web history, the adoption of CSS as a standard for style has been limited because of poor and uneven support by the major browsers. Modern browsers such as Internet Explorer, Chrome, Firefox, Opera, Safari, and others offer more complete and consistent support for CSS, freeing designers to work with this powerful style language. Modern web design requires CSS. You will learn about CSS in later chapters of this book.

Let's revisit the web page shown in Figure 1-7. Adding some simple CSS code adds style to the page. Notice the style section in Figure 1-9. The style rules specify that the body text for the page will be Arial, heading 1 will have a bottom border, and the paragraph will have a 30-pixel left margin. Figure 1-10 shows the result of adding style rules.

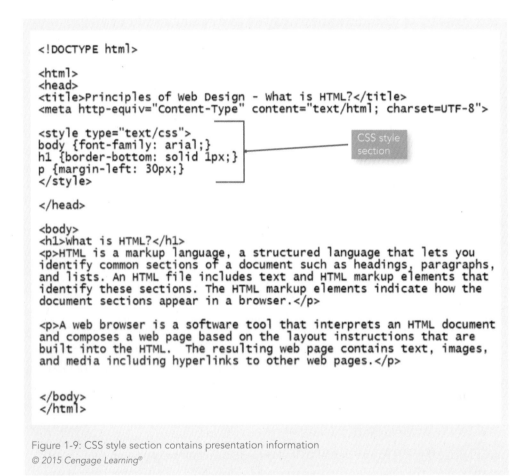

```
<!DOCTYPE html>

<html>
<head>
<title>Principles of Web Design - What is HTML?</title>
<meta http-equiv="Content-Type" content="text/html; charset=UTF-8">

<style type="text/css">                                          CSS style
body {font-family: arial;}                                      section
h1 {border-bottom: solid 1px;}
p {margin-left: 30px;}
</style>

</head>

<body>
<h1>What is HTML?</h1>
<p>HTML is a markup language, a structured language that lets you
identify common sections of a document such as headings, paragraphs,
and lists. An HTML file includes text and HTML markup elements that
identify these sections. The HTML markup elements indicate how the
document sections appear in a browser.</p>

<p>A web browser is a software tool that interprets an HTML document
and composes a web page based on the layout instructions that are
built into the HTML.  The resulting web page contains text, images,
and media including hyperlinks to other web pages.</p>


</body>
</html>
```

Figure 1-9: CSS style section contains presentation information
© 2015 Cengage Learning®

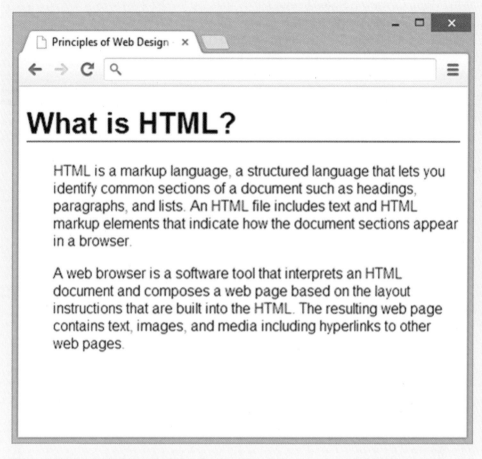

What is HTML?

HTML is a markup language, a structured language that lets you identify common sections of a document such as headings, paragraphs, and lists. An HTML file includes text and HTML markup elements that indicate how the document sections appear in a browser.

A web browser is a software tool that interprets an HTML document and composes a web page based on the layout instructions that are built into the HTML. The resulting web page contains text, images, and media including hyperlinks to other web pages.

Figure 1-10: Result of adding the CSS style rules

CSS Syntax

Recall that in CSS, style rules express the style characteristics for an HTML element, and a set of style rules is called a style sheet. Style rules are easy to write and interpret. For example, the following style rule sets all <p> elements in the document to blue text.

```
p {color: blue;}
```

A style rule is composed of two parts: a selector and a declaration. The style rule expresses the style information for an element. The selector determines the element to which the rule is applied; in this example, it is the <p> element. The declaration, color: blue, tells the browser how to display the paragraph. You will learn all about CSS syntax and how to write style rules in Chapter 4.

Activity: Using Cascading Style Sheets

In this activity, you add CSS style rules to a basic HTML file and test it in the browser. Use a text editor such as Notepad or TextEdit to edit the HTML document. Save your file, and test your work in your browser as you complete each step. The new code to add is displayed in blue text. Refer to Figure 1-12 as you work through the steps to see the results.

To add style rules to an HTML document:

1. Copy the **ch1activity2.html** file from the Chapter01 folder provided with your Data Files to the Chapter01 folder in your work folder. (Create the Chapter01 folder, if necessary.)

2. In your browser, open the **ch1activity2.html** file. It will look like Figure 1-11.

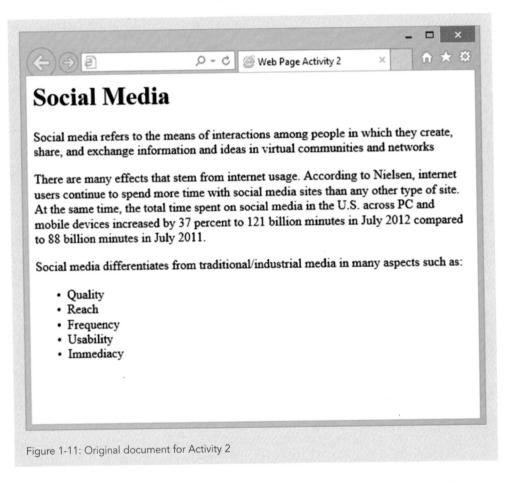

Social Media

Social media refers to the means of interactions among people in which they create, share, and exchange information and ideas in virtual communities and networks

There are many effects that stem from internet usage. According to Nielsen, internet users continue to spend more time with social media sites than any other type of site. At the same time, the total time spent on social media in the U.S. across PC and mobile devices increased by 37 percent to 121 billion minutes in July 2012 compared to 88 billion minutes in July 2011.

Social media differentiates from traditional/industrial media in many aspects such as:

- Quality
- Reach
- Frequency
- Usability
- Immediacy

Figure 1-11: Original document for Activity 2

3. In your text editor, open **ch1activity2.html** and examine the code. Replace "Your Name" in the comment at the bottom of the page with your first and last name.

4. Add a <style> element in the <head> section to contain your style rules, as shown in blue in the following code. Leave a line or two of white space between the <style> tags to contain the style rules.

```
<html>
<head>
<title>Web Page Activity 2</title>
<meta http-equiv="Content-Type" content="text/html;
charset=UTF-8">
<style type="text/css">

</style>
</head>
<body>
<h1>Social Media</h1>
<p>Social media refers to the means of interactions among people
in which they create, share, and exchange information and ideas in
virtual communities and networks.</p>
<p>There are many effects that stem from Internet usage. According
to Nielsen, Internet users continue to spend more time with social
media sites than any other type of site. At the same time, the total
time spent on social media in the U.S. across PC and mobile devices
increased by 37 percent to 121 billion minutes in July 2012 compared
to 88 billion minutes in July 2011.</p>
<p>Social media differentiates from traditional/industrial media in
many aspects such as:</p>
<ul>
<li>Quality</li>
<li>Reach</li>
<li>Frequency</li>
<li>Usability</li>
<li>Immediacy</li>
</ul>
</body>
</html>
```

5. Add a style rule that sets the font-family for the page as shown below. Notice the style rule contains both a specific style (Arial) and a fallback style (sans-serif) in case the user does not have Arial as an installed font.

```
<style type="text/css">
body {font-family: arial, sans-serif;}
</style>
```

6. Write another style rule that adds a solid thin bottom border to the <h1> heading element.

```
<style type="text/css">
body {font-family: arial, sans-serif;}
h1 {border-bottom: solid thin;}
</style>
```

7. Save your file, and view it in your browser. It should look like Figure 1-12.

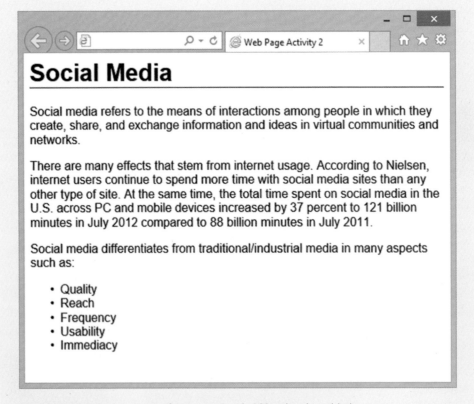

Figure 1-12: Finished document for Activity 2 with CSS style rules added
Microsoft product screenshots used with permission from Microsoft Corporation.

Organizing Information with Hypertext

The most engaging aspect of browsing the web is the linking of information on related topics using hypertext, a nonlinear way of organizing information. When using a hypertext system, you can jump from one related topic to another, quickly find the information that interests you, and return to your starting point or move onto another topic. As a web designer, you determine which terms to create as hypertext links and where users end up when they click a link.

On the web, clickable hyperlinks, which can be text or images, can connect you to another web page, for example, or allow you to open or download a file, such as a music, image, movie, or executable file. Although the basic one-way nature of a hypertext link has not changed since the web was developed, the nature of the destination content has changed greatly. The different types of linked content and media continually evolve as the web continues to grow into an increasingly rich and more interactive environment.

Understanding the History of HTML

Now that you've seen the basics of how HTML works, you should know how the web has evolved to its current state. As a web designer, you will encounter all types of HTML coding practices in the real world. Understanding the evolution of HTML will help you recognize various web design methods. You may encounter sites that completely comply with current standards, ones that still use design trends and code from years ago, and others that mix coding styles in improbable ways. Many sites still use table-based designs, which are outmoded and now rendered obsolete by CSS. Web design tools can create all different kinds of code. Proprietary software implementations manipulate code to get the exact result they want. Although it is easy to say that everyone should use web standards, to be a successful web designer you need to understand the past, present, and future directions of HTML, coding standards, and common practices, many of which may not match the standards you learn about in this book.

When Tim Berners-Lee first proposed HTML at the European Laboratory for Particle Physics (CERN) in 1989, he was looking for a way to easily manage and share information among scientific colleagues over the Internet. Until this time, the complexity of using the Internet for exchanging messages and sharing files limited its use to groups of specialists in defense, academia, and science.

Berners-Lee joined the ideas of a simple tool for reading the documents (the browser), rules for creating a document markup language (HTML), and a communications protocol that allowed hypertext linking through Uniform Resource Locators (URLs). This accessible, simple interface made using the Internet available to the public. Not only could people read documents, they could easily create them using the easy-to-understand HTML.

As Berners-Lee developed the idea of a web of documents connected by hypertext links and hosted by computers called hypertext servers, he created a simplified application of the Standard Generalized Markup Language (SGML), a standard system for specifying document structure, which he called the Hypertext Markup Language. HTML significantly reduces the complexity of using SGML to facilitate transmission of documents over the Internet.

When Berners-Lee created HTML, he adopted only the elements of SGML necessary for representing basic office documents such as memos and reports. The first version of HTML included roughly 20 elements that represented basic document structure such as titles, headings, paragraphs, and lists. HTML was originally intended for simple document structure, not for handling today's varied and complex information needs.

A Need for Standards

After the initial surge of interest in HTML and the web, a need arose for a standards organization to set recommended practices that would guarantee the open nature of the web. To meet this need, the World Wide Web Consortium (W3C) was founded in 1994 at the Massachusetts Institute of Technology (MIT). The W3C sets standards for HTML and provides an open, nonproprietary forum for industry and academic representatives. The various committees that make up the W3C look to expand and set standards for the many new web technologies that have emerged.

After the W3C was founded, the popularity of the web grew exponentially. By the mid-1990s, companies started to realize that having a web presence was vital. Publishing companies started reproducing their paper-based content on the web. Every advertisement contained a web address. More and more companies hired print designers to develop web sites. At this time, web design was a haphazard affair. HTML was a designer's nightmare, primarily because it was intended for basic page structure, not to create multicolumn print-type layouts. Most computer monitors used a 640 x 480 resolution and many only supported 256 colors, which limited design choices. Multiple browsers, each with their own proprietary elements, competed for market share, and many web sites were coded primarily for one browser or another. Web designers would manipulate the language in any way they saw fit to achieve a desired design result. After HTML tables were introduced, they became the designer's tool of choice, because they allowed the creation of multicolumn layouts. Although designed for data, designers manipulated tables as they needed to achieve the design they wanted.

As the web grew, designers learned they could get away with manipulating HTML because web browsers are very forgiving of nonstandard coding. Even if you coded your page incorrectly, you had a good chance that your results would look fine in the browser. If you left out closing tags, or used tags in the wrong order, the page would still be displayed. Web browsers did not display error messages if a page contained a coding error. If your web site worked with coding errors, you would have no reason to fix them, resulting in an Internet full of web pages with coding errors.

As development on the web continued to evolve into more data-based applications, such as shopping and banking, interoperability became an issue. If every organization coded and managed their web site content in their own way, exchanging data between organizations would become difficult. The more everyone followed the same standards, the easier it would be to write browser, application, and database software that "talked" to each other. Jointly developed standards, rather than ones dictated by a single vendor, would benefit everyone.

The 1999 release of HTML 4.01 attempted to address a number of these issues. HTML 4.01 supported CSS, which separated style information from HTML, as you read earlier. This separation of style information from the structure of the HTML document is crucial to the interoperability of HTML, as display information can be customized for the device viewing the web page, such as a tablet, smartphone, or desktop monitor, as you will learn in Chapter 12. HTML 4.01 also deprecated a number of display elements, such as the <font> element. A deprecated element means that the element would be removed from future releases of HTML. The W3C was recommending that web designers stop using these elements in favor of CSS. Many deprecated elements persist to this day, and it is not uncommon to find them in many web pages and in software programs that create web pages. Table 1-1 shows the history of HTML through its releases.

VERSION	RELEASE DATE	HIGHLIGHTS
HTML 1.1	1992	First informal draft
HTML 2	1995	First release supported by graphical browsers; documents written in HTML 2.0 are still viewable by all browsers
HTML 3.2	1997	Introduced forms and tables
HTML 4.01	1999	Added support for style sheets; increased support for scripting and interactivity
HTML5	Definition completed in 2012; should be nominated as a recommendation in 2014	Latest version adds page layout elements, audio/visual elements, enhanced animation, and graphic support
HTML5.1	Planned for 2016	New element and attribute refinements

Table 1-1: History of HTML
© 2015 Cengage Learning®

XML and XHTML: A New Direction

After the release of HTML 4.01, the W3C turned in a different direction for markup languages. In 1997, the W3C released XML, the Extensible Markup Language. Although not a direct replacement for HTML, XML has capabilities that are essential to software developers creating applications for the Web. Where HTML is a predefined set of elements that the browser understands, XML lets developers define their own markup language. Software developers can then create elements that match the data names in their databases or functions in their programs. For example, a developer can create a set of elements that describe customer information such as <name> and <city> that match the names in a database, easing the transition of data to the web. Additionally, XML is a stricter language than HTML. XML documents must be syntactically correct to be processed by a software application. This means that only one error in an XML document will keep the document from being processed. This is a very different model from HTML, where the syntax is less strict.

XML code looks similar to HTML code, with some syntactical differences that you will read about later in this chapter. The major difference between the two languages is that XML allows you to create elements that describe any type of information you desire. For example, consider that poets might want to create a markup language that expresses the different parts of a poem, as shown in the following code sample:

```
<poem>
<title>An Ode to the Web</title>
<stanza>
<line>So many web sites</line>
<line>So little time</line>
<line>And all I want to do</line>
<line>Is critique their design!</line>
</stanza>
</poem>
```

Notice that this code looks like regular HTML code, except that the tags are not standard, but specific to the type of content they contain. Unlike standard HTML, the browser does not know how to display this information unless CSS style rules are added to specify, for example, that the contents of each <line> element should be displayed in the browser on a separate line or in the color blue.

The W3C saw that XML syntax could provide a solution to the problem of widely varying HTML coding standards, and they started to move in this direction with the evolution of XML-based languages, trying to create a unified syntax under which the entire web could operate. Towards this end, the W3C reformulated HTML in XML, keeping all the same elements and attributes as HTML 4.01, and named it the Extensible Hypertext Markup Language, or XHTML 1.0.

XHTML follows the rules of XML, so it follows the markup rules for XML. In short, XHTML requires that documents conform to basic rules, stated briefly:

> Documents must be well formed.

> All tags must nest properly and not overlap.

> Use all lowercase for element names.

> Always use closing tags.

> Attribute values must be contained in quotation marks.

As you will see later in the chapter, these rules are good ones to follow when writing your HTML5 code.

Problems with XHTML

Web designers adopted the new XHTML language and syntax, hoping to standardize coding conventions. They adopted CSS to gain benefits in web site maintenance, interoperability, and adapting content to multiple destination media. The beneficial result is that a majority of commercial web sites have moved to much leaner, standardized code with all presentation and layout information described by CSS. At the same time, many web sites and software applications still use legacy style coding conventions. In many instances, relaxed rules had to be applied to projects with legacy content. Also, many web sites are still created by novices who want to put up a site quickly without learning the intricacies of XHTML.

As the W3C continued down the XML-based language path, dissatisfaction increased in the web developer community. When the W3C issued their first drafts of the XHTML 2.0 recommendation, they announced that XHTML 2.0 would not be backwards compatible with XHTML 1.0 or HTML 4.0. This meant that all of the content on the web, and all of the work that had been done to develop HTML to its current state would no longer be valid. Further, it dropped familiar elements such as <img> for images and the <a> element for hypertext links, and supported the unforgiving error handling of XML.

A Proposal for HTML5

These decisions moved sharply away from the existing direction of web development and the long-standing ease of use of HTML. In 2004, an independent group of browser vendors and representatives of the web development community reacted to the strictness of XHTML 2.0 and joined to create a proposal for HTML5. This independent group named themselves the Web Hypertext Application Technology Working Group (WHATWG). After a few years of wrangling over the direction of web languages, the W3C announced in 2007 that they would restart the effort to support HTML, and in 2009 they shut down the XHTML 2.0 working group completely.

The W3C's response to the development community's desires for the next generation of HTML highlights the unusual nature of the web, where standards are not dictated by one vendor, but rather decided upon and influenced by the people who work with HTML and web design day to day. As you will see later in this chapter, HTML5 supports standards-based coding, is compatible with both XHTML 1.0 and HTML 4.01, and supports new elements for better structuring of web pages. HTML5 is adaptable to the modern interactive web, where web pages are not just static documents, but applications. With the completion of a standardized definition for HTML5 in 2012, the W3C has created a stable cross-device environment for developers. As stated by W3C president Jeff Jaffe, "The broader the reach of web technology, the more our stakeholders demand a stable standard. As of today, businesses know what they can rely on for HTML5 in the coming years, and what their customers will demand. Likewise, developers will know what skills to cultivate to reach smartphones, cars, televisions, e-books, digital signs, and devices not yet known."

Working with HTML5

In this section, you learn about basic HTML5 markup and the two different syntaxes allowed within HTML5. You will learn how to choose the correct syntax for your web pages, and you will review the new elements in HTML5. You will see how the new HTML5 sectioning elements are designed to work and how HTML5 supports interaction in the browser.

HTML5 is the fifth major revision of HTML. It comes long after the last major revision, which was in 1999. HTML5 attempts to address the shortcomings of previous versions of HTML, while addressing the needs of modern web design and the application-based future of the web. HTML5 is intended to not only describe page structure and layout, but offers a variety of new features:

> Logical sectioning elements, such as <nav> (for a navigation bar), <section>, <header>, and <footer>

> Elements designed for different types of rich media, including <video> and <audio>

> Animations that play directly in the browser window without plug-ins using the <canvas> element

> Support for applications in the browser, including drag and drop, local data storage, and background data processing

HTML5 also removes the following features from previous versions of HTML:

> All display elements have been removed in favor of CSS for presentation.

> Framesets and frames have been removed because of their impact on accessibility.

HTML5 is compatible with older versions of HTML and XHTML and supports both the looser coding style associated with earlier HTML versions and a stricter syntax that is based on XML.

HTML5 looks almost exactly like previous versions of HTML. Figure 1-13 shows a sample of HTML5 code. Note two important conventions in this sample:

> The HTML5 <!DOCTYPE> statement is less complicated than in previous versions of HTML.

> The <meta> element specifies the document content type and character set. Many pages leave out this critical piece of information that tells the browser how to correctly interpret your HTML code.

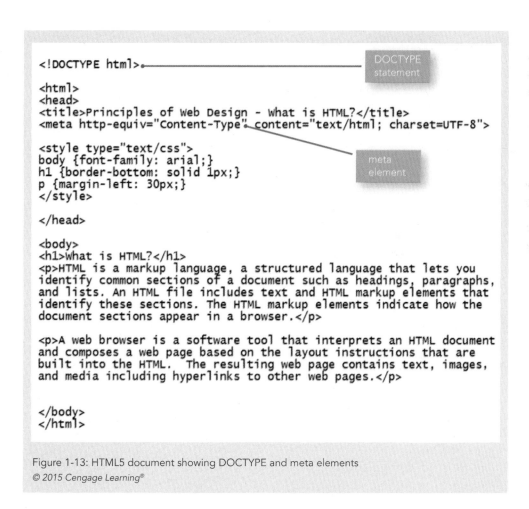

```
<!DOCTYPE html>                                          DOCTYPE
                                                         statement
<html>
<head>
<title>Principles of Web Design - What is HTML?</title>
<meta http-equiv="Content-Type" content="text/html; charset=UTF-8">

<style type="text/css">
body {font-family: arial;}
h1 {border-bottom: solid 1px;}                            meta
p {margin-left: 30px;}                                   element
</style>

</head>

<body>
<h1>What is HTML?</h1>
<p>HTML is a markup language, a structured language that lets you
identify common sections of a document such as headings, paragraphs,
and lists. An HTML file includes text and HTML markup elements that
identify these sections. The HTML markup elements indicate how the
document sections appear in a browser.</p>

<p>A web browser is a software tool that interprets an HTML document
and composes a web page based on the layout instructions that are
built into the HTML.  The resulting web page contains text, images,
and media including hyperlinks to other web pages.</p>

</body>
</html>
```

Figure 1-13: HTML5 document showing DOCTYPE and meta elements
© 2015 Cengage Learning®

HTML5 Loose and Strict Syntaxes

HTML5 offers two syntaxes. One is based on looser HTML syntax, and the other on stricter XML syntax rules.

Loose Version of HTML5

The HTML version of HTML5 is more relaxed and allows authors to use shortcuts in their code. Figure 1-14 shows the looser syntax with two examples of code shortcuts.

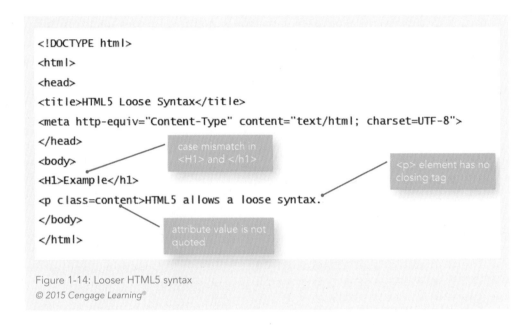

```
<!DOCTYPE html>
<html>
<head>
<title>HTML5 Loose Syntax</title>
<meta http-equiv="Content-Type" content="text/html; charset=UTF-8">
</head>
<body>
<H1>Example</h1>
<p class=content>HTML5 allows a loose syntax.
</body>
</html>
```

case mismatch in
<H1> and </h1>

<p> element has no
closing tag

attribute value is not
quoted

Figure 1-14: Looser HTML5 syntax
© 2015 Cengage Learning®

Notice in this code that the case of the <h1> tags does not match, the <p> element has no closing tag, and the class attribute has no quotes around the content value. Even though these seem like mistakes in the code, these loose conventions are allowed in HTML5.

Strict Version of HTML5

The stricter syntax rules of HTML5 are consistent with XML syntax, as shown in Figure 1-15. XML syntax rules are applied to the code and the two shortcuts removed.

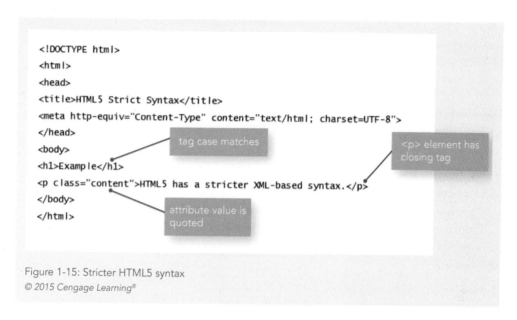

```
<!DOCTYPE html>
<html>
<head>
<title>HTML5 Strict Syntax</title>
<meta http-equiv="Content-Type" content="text/html; charset=UTF-8">
</head>
<body>
<h1>Example</h1>
<p class="content">HTML5 has a stricter XML-based syntax.</p>
</body>
</html>
```

tag case matches

<p> element has closing tag

attribute value is quoted

Figure 1-15: Stricter HTML5 syntax
© 2015 Cengage Learning®

Choosing the Correct Syntax

In a professional web development environment, it is a best practice to code using syntax that follows the stricter syntax rules, which are based on XML rules. With XML-based syntax, the code you create for web content can have multiple purposes and potentially be used in a variety of display and application environments.

For example, it is now commonplace in the publishing industry to repurpose content that was originally destined for web publication. This content can be organized and used in a content management system that allows output to be printed or displayed in different environments that meet users' individual needs. The multipurposing of content is often called single-sourcing, where one source of content is maintained but disseminated to different users or devices. Data in a single location can be maintained and updated more easily. The data also has greater value because it can be displayed and used in different ways.

Another reason for choosing the stricter syntax in your HTML5 code is to ensure consistent coding practices across an organization. Web site development should always formulate and apply consistent coding conventions across all web content to ensure uniformity. With stricter syntax, the coding conventions are already created and just need to be followed. Use a validator, software that checks an HTML document for syntax errors, to test for code compliance. You can use either an online validator or a built-in validator that is common to most HTML development tools. If you create coding conventions and stick to them, your web content will be more adaptable to different purposes, compatible with more software applications, and better prepared for future use.

Choosing the Correct Document Type and MIME Type

The key to displaying your web pages correctly in the browser is stating the correct <!DOCTYPE> and MIME type.

DOCTYPE Statement

The <!DOCTYPE> statement originated in SGML and was used to point to a Document Type Definition (DTD), which contained the elements, attributes, and syntax rules for a language like HTML or XML.

HTML5 is no longer based on SGML, so the <!DOCTYPE> statement primarily exists to make sure that browsers display the page in standards mode. When you include a document type, the browser operates in "standards mode," presenting the document using W3C rules. If the document type is not stated, the browser operates in "quirks mode," which renders the page like an older browser, allowing the "quirky" code from the earlier days of web development.

The standard doctype statement for HTML5 looks like this:

```
<!DOCTYPE html>
```

MIME Type

The Multipurpose Internet Mail Extensions (MIME) originated as a standard for email, but has grown to defining content types for the web. It is the MIME type that determines the type of document you are presenting. The browser relies on this information to know exactly how to interpret your markup code and content and display it correctly. For HTML web pages, specify a content type of text/html.

Every document should contain a <meta> element in the <head> section that specifies the content type and character set. The content value is the document's MIME type. The document's character set is specified as charset=utf-8, which is the standard character set for the web. Your <meta> element should look like this:

```
<meta http-equiv="Content-Type" content="text/html; charset=utf-8">
```

Putting all of this together, the beginning of all HTML5 documents should look like the following code, with the addition of a page name in the <title> element:

```
<!DOCTYPE html>
<html>
<head>
<title>Page Name</title>
<meta http-equiv="Content-Type" content="text/html; charset=UTF-8">
</head>
```

Creating Syntactically Correct Code

You should follow five basic rules to create syntactically correct HTML5 code. These are the same rules used for XML, applied in an HTML environment, and were listed earlier in the XML section.

> Documents must be well formed.

> All tags must nest properly and not overlap.

> Use all lowercase for element names.

> Always use closing tags.

> Attribute values must be contained in quotation marks.

Documents Must Be Well Formed

A **well-formed document** is one that adheres to the syntax rules described in this section.

All Tags Must Nest Properly and Not Overlap

You can nest HTML elements, but they must not overlap. Each set of opening and closing tags must completely contain any elements that are nested within the set. For example, the following is incorrect syntax:

```
<p><strong>some text... </p></strong>
```

The closing tag for the strong element must come before the closing tag for the paragraph element. The correct nesting syntax follows:

```
<p><strong>some text...</strong></p>
```

Use All Lowercase for Element Names

Even though HTML5 allows uppercase and lowercase element names, it is considered good coding practice to always use lowercase. Use all lowercase characters for element and attribute names when writing your code. This will ensure that your code can be XML compatible if it needs to be used in some type of content management or application-processing environment.

Always Use Closing Tags

In the looser HTML5 syntax, certain elements such as the <p> element are allowed optional closing tags. For example, the following two <p> elements do not have closing tags:

```
<p>This is the first paragraph.
<p>This is the second paragraph.
```

Even though HTML5 allows this, a much better practice is to always close all elements. The following example shows this syntax.

```
<p>This is the first paragraph.</p>
<p>This is the second paragraph.</p>
```

Attribute Values Must Be Contained in Quotes

In the looser HTML5 syntax, attribute values do not have to be quoted as shown in the following example:

```
<p class=copy>HTML5 is the newest web language.</p>
```

Even though HTML5 allows this, your code is more compatible when you always contain all attribute values within quotes. The preferred syntax follows:

```
<p class="copy">HTML5 is the newest web language.</p>
```

Element Categories

In HTML5, elements are divided into categories by use, as shown in the following list. Some elements may fall into more than one category.

> Metadata content

> Flow content

> Sectioning root

> Sectioning content

> Heading content

> Phrasing content

> Embedded content

> Interactive content

> Transparent

Metadata Content

These are the elements that reside in the head section of the document, such as <title>, <script>, and <style>. These elements contain the document metadata, which is information about the document itself, such as how to present the document or what other documents are related to this one, such as style sheets.

Flow Content

Flow content elements are most of the elements that are used within the body section of the document. This category includes all of the standard HTML tags, such as <p>, <div>, and <blockquote>, as well as the newer page layout elements introduced in HTML5 such as <article>, <header>, and <footer>.

Sectioning Root

Content on web pages is divided into sections. The <body> element is the root or parent element of all content sections, making it a sectioning root. Other elements in this category include <blockquote> and <td>.

Sectioning Content

Sectioning content divides a document into sections, each of which can have its own set of headings. These elements group sections of content on the page. Elements in this category include <section>, <article>, and <nav>. Sectioning elements are an exciting feature of HTML5, and they are supported by all modern browsers including mobile browsers. You will read more about this in Chapter 7.

Heading Content

This category includes the heading elements, <h1> thru <h6>, plus the new <header> element for creating heading sections.

Phrasing Content

Phrasing content includes elements that are used within lines of text in a document. These include <em>, <strong>, and <span>. These elements were called inline elements in HTML 4.01.

Embedded Content

Embedded content elements load external content into the web page. This content can be image, video, or audio files. The <img> element as well as the new <audio> and <video> elements are part of this category.

Interactive Content

Interactive elements let users interact with the web page content. Interactivity depends on the user's browser and input device, such as a mouse, keyboard, touchscreen, or voice input. Elements in this category include the <a> element, which creates clickable hyperlinks, plus the <audio> and <video> elements if the user can control the content, such as by using play or pause buttons. Flash animations and other content types, such as presentations or web-based learning, also accept user interaction. Form controls are also part of this category.

Transparent

Some elements have transparent content models, which means that their allowed content is inherited from their parent element. They may contain any content that their parent element may contain, in addition to any other allowances or exceptions described for the element. For example, the <a> element often occurs within a <p> element parent, and will usually follow the content rules of its parent element.

New Elements in HTML5

HTML5 has a number of new elements, as listed in Table 1-2. These new elements are supported in all modern browsers.

ELEMENT	DESCRIPTION
<article>	Contains a section for the main page content, such as a newspaper or magazine article, blog entry, or any other independent item of content
<aside>	Contains a section for side content such as a pull quote or other content related to the main article
<audio>	Contains sound, streaming audio, or other aural content
<canvas>	Lets scripting applications dynamically render graphics, animations, or other visual images
<command>	Defines a command action for interaction with the user
<datalist>	Contains drop-down list content for older browsers; used for legacy compatibility
<details>	Contains additional information or controls that the user can obtain on demand
<dialog>	Contains a conversation; used with the <dt> and <dd> elements
<embed>	Represents an insertion point for an external application or interactive content
<figure>	Contains an image or graphic with an optional caption using the <legend> element
<footer>	Contains the footer section of a web page, typically providing information such as who wrote the page, links to related documents, and copyright notices
<header>	Contains the header section of a web page, typically providing headings and subheadings that describe the page content
<keygen>	Provides client authentication and security information
<mark>	Contains a string of text in a document marked or highlighted for reference purposes
<meter>	Defines a measurement within a known range, or a fractional value
<nav>	Contains the navigation section of a web page with primary navigation links to other pages or to content within the page
<output>	Contains the result of a calculation
<progress>	Represents the completion progress of a task
<rp>	Ruby parentheses hide ruby text <rt> from browsers that do not support the <ruby> element
<rt>	Contains ruby text, used with the <ruby> element

Continued on next page...

ELEMENT	DESCRIPTION
<ruby>	Allows markup of text content with ruby annotations. Ruby annotations are descriptive strings of text presented alongside base text, primarily used in East Asian typography as a guide for pronunciation or to include other annotations. In Japanese, this form of typography is also known as *furigana*. Used with the <rp> and <rt> elements.
<section>	Contains a generic section of a web page, usually with a related grouping of content, typically with its own heading
<source>	Specifies multiple media resources for media elements
<time>	Contains a date or time
<video>	Contains video content

Table 1-2: New elements in HTML5
© 2015 Cengage Learning®

Attributes in HTML5

Elements can contain attributes that set properties for an element. In the following code sample, the <header> element has a class attribute with a value of *main*.

```
<header class="main">
```

In earlier versions of HTML, a wide variety of attributes contained presentation information, such as the size, color, or alignment of text. In HTML5, all display information is specified with CSS, so far fewer attributes are necessary. Some elements have specific attributes, while other attributes are global and can be applied to any element. Some of the more important global attributes include style, title, and class. You will find a complete list of HTML5 attributes in Appendix A.

Obsolete Elements in HTML5

Many elements have been removed from HTML5, most of which were used for presentation effects that are better handled with a CSS style. Examples of elements that are obsolete in HTML5 include some that are commonly avoided in web design, such as <font>. Also, the <frameset> and <frames> elements are no longer available, so frame-based sites are obsolete. The <iframe> element is still available to embed a page within a page. Appendix A provides a complete list of obsolete HTML5 elements.

Using HTML5 Elements for Page Structure

Generally, all web pages share some common characteristics. For example, most web pages have some type of header, navigation, article, and figure content, footers, and possibly sidebars for related content. Until recently, most web pages were marked up using a combination of <div> elements and id or class names as shown in Figure 1-16.

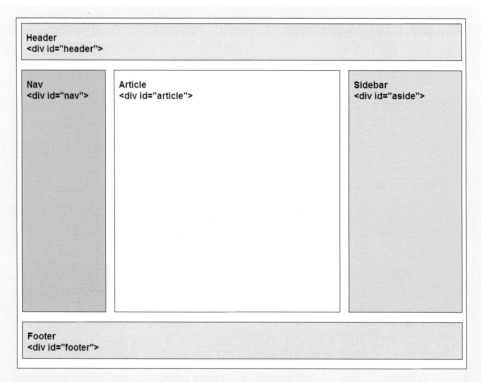

Figure 1-16: Five page sections using <div> elements and id names
© Cengage Learning®

The id names shown in Figure 1-16 may vary, but generally all of the page components shown occur in one form or another on every web site. HTML5 standardizes the names of each of these common web page sections and provides an element for each section, and for other document components as well.

HTML5 now offers a new set of elements for describing document structure. In the past, HTML authors used the division element, or <div>, to structure the page. The <div> element is designed expressly for this purpose. It is a neutral element and is intended only as a container for content. You name <div> elements with an id or class attribute, such as:

```
<div id="article">This is an article on my web page</div>
```

HTML5 replaces the use of <div> with named elements to structure the page. The <article> element can be used instead of the <div> element, as in the following example:

```
<article>This is an article on my web page</article>
```

Using HTML5, the web page shown in Figure 1-16 can now be marked up as shown in Figure 1-17.

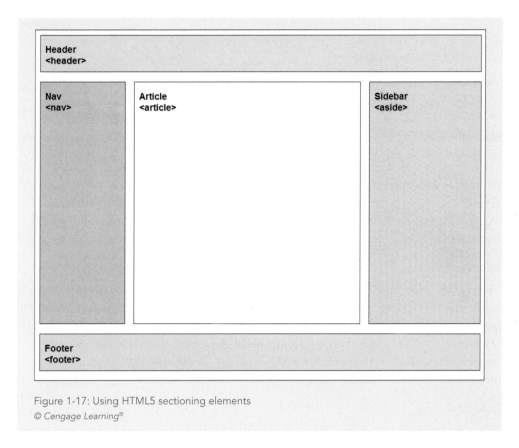

Figure 1-17: Using HTML5 sectioning elements
© Cengage Learning®

The HTML5 elements that are designed for page layout include the following:

> <header>—Contains the page header content

> <nav>—Contains the navigation elements for the page

> <article>—Contains the primary page content. This element is also used to designate content designed for syndication or redistribution.

> <section>—Defines sections or groupings of the page content, typically with its own heading

> <aside>—Contains additional content such as a quote or sidebar

> <figure>—Contains images for the article content

> <footer>—Contains the page footer content, typically information such as copyrights, policies and legal information, and contact information

These elements offer benefits for building page layouts. They standardize the naming conventions for parts of a web page, allowing software tools to apply consistent rules for content management, presentation, and processing. Using the <article> element, you can designate content for redistribution through news services, RSS feeds, aggregators, and other content aggregation systems.

The <section> element is for thematic groupings of content, each with its own heading structure. This means that each section can have up to six headings (<h1> through <h6>), which can create more complex page structures. The <section> element also allows automatically generated tables of content or outlines of page content. You will learn more about how to use these elements when building page layouts in Chapter 7.

Interactive Capabilities in HTML5

HTML5 supports a number of new features for applications and interaction with users. Browser support varies for these new features, so evaluate and test them carefully before implementation.

Audio and Video

The <audio> and <video> media elements let developers embed audio or video streams into a web page. Until HTML5, web designers had no standard way to embed media without using third-party software such as QuickTime or Flash. With these new elements, HTML5 offers a standardized method of embedding media. Support for both of these elements varies widely across browsers and operating systems. Fallback methods and workarounds are available to make sure that your multimedia content is viewable for different users.

Drawing Canvas

The <canvas> element provides a bitmap drawing area for displaying graphs, drawings, games, or other visual elements dynamically in the browser. The canvas element lets you specify a rectangle on your page within which you can use a JavaScript application to create 2-D drawings.

Background Application Processing

"Web workers" are background scripting processes that can run in the browser while the user is performing other actions. This means that calculations, data transfers, and other background processing are available to support more complex applications. These are JavaScript applications that run in the background, independent of what else the user might be doing on a web page.

Local Data Storage

As browser-based applications become more complex, they need to be able to store data locally on the user's machine, rather than having to interact with the server each time data needs to be read or written. This task is currently handled by cookies, small pieces of text-based data that are stored on the user's machine. Cookies transfer only small pieces of information with every request to the web server. Part of the HTML5 effort is a recommendation called Web Storage that specifies how larger amounts of data can be stored and retrieved from the user's computer by web applications.

Using Good Coding Practices

In the past, web designers wrote nonstandard code, employing a "whatever works" mentality to trick the browser into presenting the results they wanted. Some examples of this are using the heading tags <h1> through <h6> solely for their font sizes rather than as logical headings, or manipulating the <table> elements into a layout tool instead of a container for data as they were intended.

These are bad habits that are best left behind. This section provides the following guidelines for creating code that ensures the greatest standards-compliance, presentation, and usefulness of your content:

> Stick to the standards.

> Use semantic markup.

> Validate your code.

Stick to the Standards

The best way to create well-coded web sites is to strictly follow the standards set by the W3C. This approach provides the greatest acceptance and most uniform display of your content across multiple browsers and operating systems. This "best practices" method of coding is widely supported among sites that are interested in the widest accessibility. Reliable visual and information design techniques, along with the use of CSS, can help you overcome many functional limitations.

Skills at Work | Good Coding Is Good for Your Career

If you develop web sites on your own or on the job, let your client or employer know that you are coding with standards and respecting the W3C mandate to separate content structure from presentation information. Doing so makes your content more accessible and portable to different devices and destinations, which makes your employer's web site more durable and flexible. Who would have envisioned that, at the outset of the web, content would be delivered on smartphones or tablet computers? Who can imagine what devices will be used in the future? Content that is designed to standards is more meaningful to search engines, has better accessibility, is displayed more consistently in multiple browsers, and has a longer life and greater chance of being accessible in future applications. Those advantages position your web sites as practical and useful, and position you as a forward-thinking professional, which can only be good for your career.

Use Semantic Markup

Semantic markup is descriptive markup that identifies the intended use of document sections. Semantic markup accurately describes each piece of content. Although this may sound like an obvious use of markup elements, until recently this logical use of HTML elements was largely ignored by the web development community. For example, HTML authors know that an <h1> element signifies a block of text as a first-level heading, but many times this element is used simply for its ability to increase the font size of text. The <ul> element, which indicates a bulleted list, was used for its indenting characteristics. When you use semantic markup, the document elements match the meaning and usage of the document sections; a <p> signifies a paragraph, a <blockquote> is for a lengthy quotation, and so on. Semantically correct markup is readable not only by humans but by software as well, lending itself to improved recognition by search engines, news agents, and accessibility devices.

The use of semantic markup goes hand in hand with the new sectioning elements offered in HTML5. Elements such as <article>, <section>, and <aside> let HTML authors specifically mark up elements for reuse and sharing. Each of these has a specific meaning for the use of content. You will read more about the sectioning elements in Chapter 7.

> **Note**
>
> Semantic markup is the basis for the evolution of the web into a universal medium for data, information, and knowledge exchange as described by the W3C in their Semantic Web Activity group (www.w3.org/2001/sw). Although this vision of the web is still in early development, the emphasis on correct usage of markup elements benefits the accessibility and longevity of your web content.

Validate Your Code

Another step towards standards compliance is to validate your code. **Valid code** conforms to the usage rules of the W3C. The lack of valid code is a major problem for the future of a standards-based web. A recent survey of 2.4 million web pages found that 99 percent did not meet W3C standards. Although this number may have decreased since the study, a quick survey of almost any web site shows that few have valid code.

Valid code enhances browser compatibility, accessibility, and exchange of data. Whether you write HTML or XHTML code, you should validate your code to make sure it conforms to W3C standards. Validation is so easy to perform, it is hard to understand why many web designers apparently ignore it. To validate your code, use a software program called a validator to read your code and compare it to the rules in the DTD. The validator generates a list of validation errors. Many HTML editors contain built-in validators, or you can use a web-based validator such as the W3C validation service at *http://validator.w3.org*, shown in Figure 1-18, which can validate HTML5.

Figure 1-18: The W3C markup validation service checks your code for errors

validator.w3.org/unicorn

Using a validator is an eye-opening experience for any Web designer. The most common mistakes that make your code invalid include:

> No doctype declaration

> Missing closing tags

> Missing alt attributes in <img> elements

> Incorrect tag nesting

> Unquoted attributes

If you compare this list to the XML syntax rules listed earlier in this chapter, you can see how moving to standardized coding practices helps clean up most of these common coding errors.

Chapter Summary

Many variables affect the way users view your web pages. As an HTML author, your goal should be to code pages that are accessible to the largest audience possible. As you plan your web site, make the following decisions before implementing your site:

⟩ Make sure to check for support of new HTML5 elements, and test carefully before adding them to your web site.

⟩ Use Cascading Style Sheets. The style enhancements and control offered by this style language are impressive, but they are not evenly supported by older browsers. Implement CSS gradually, testing for browser compatibility as you go.

⟩ Decide whether to code to the stricter HTML standard. If you are starting a new web site, your best choice is to code to this standard. If you are working with an existing web site, decide on the most expedient method for upgrading your existing code to these XML standards to ensure future compatibility with new tools and browsers.

⟩ Use good coding practices by writing standards-based markup that always includes a document type and content type and is correctly validated.

⟩ Use semantic markup, especially the HTML5 sectioning elements, to mark up your page correctly. This makes your content shareable across search engines, news agents, and accessibility devices.

Key Terms

attribute—Code added to an element to provide more information about the element.

Cascading Style Sheets (CSS)—A style language, created by the W3C, that allows complete specifications of style for HTML documents. CSS allows HTML authors to write style rules that affect the display of web pages. CSS style information is contained either within an HTML document or in external documents called style sheets.

cookie—A small piece of text-based data that a web page stores on the user's machine. Cookies transfer small pieces of information with every request to the web server.

deprecated element—An element that the W3C has identified as obsolete.

Document Type (doctype)—The section of an HTML document that specifies the rules for the document language so the browser knows how to interpret the HTML code and display it properly.

Document Type Definition (DTD)—A set of rules that contains all the elements, attributes, and usage rules for the markup language you are using.

element—A pair of HTML tags containing content. An <h1> element looks like this: <h1>Heading</h1>.

Extensible Hypertext Markup Language (XHTML)—HTML 4.01 reformulated as an application of XML.

Extensible Markup Language (XML)—A markup language with capabilities that are essential to software developers creating applications for the web.

hypertext—A nonlinear way of organizing information. When you are using a hypertext system, you can skip from one related topic to another, find the information that interests you, and then return to your starting point or move on to another related topic of interest.

Hypertext Markup Language (HTML)—The markup language that defines the structure and display properties of a web page. HTML code is interpreted by the browser to create the displayed results. HTML is an application of SGML. *See also* Standard Generalized Markup Language.

markup language—A structured language that lets you identify common elements of a document such as headings, paragraphs, and lists.

metadata—Information about the document itself, such as how to present the document, or what other documents are related to the current one, such as style sheets.

Multipurpose Internet Mail Extensions (MIME)—Originally a standard for email, MIME now defines content types for the web. It determines the type of document presented in an HTML file.

rendering engine—A program contained in every browser that interprets the markup tags in an HTML file and displays the results in the browser.

root element—The container element for all other elements in the document. In an HTML document, the root element is <html>.

semantic markup—Descriptive markup that identifies the intended use of document sections. Semantic markup accurately describes each piece of content.

single-source—To create content that can serve multiple purposes and be distributed to different users or devices.

Standard Generalized Markup Language (SGML)—A standard system for specifying document structure using markup tags.

style rule—In CSS, text that expresses the style characteristics for an HTML element.

style sheet—A set of style rules that describes a document's display characteristics. There are two types of style sheets: internal and external.

tag—An HTML tag includes an opening bracket (<), an element name such as h1, and a closing bracket (>). An h1 tag looks like this: <h1>.

valid code—Markup code that conforms to the usage rules of the W3C.

validator—A software program that checks an HTML document for syntactical errors.

void element—An HTML element that contains only a single tag and no content.

web page—A text document that is interpreted and displayed by web browser software.

well-formed document—A syntactically correct XML or XHTML file.

World Wide Web Consortium (W3C)—Founded in 1994 at the Massachusetts Institute of Technology to standardize web markup languages. The W3C, led by Tim Berners-Lee, sets standards for markup languages and provides an open, nonproprietary forum for industry and academic representatives to add to the evolution of HTML.

Review Questions

1. What does the <!DOCTYPE> statement specify?

2. What is the function of the root element?

3. What are the main sections of an HTML document?

4. Why is the content of the <title> element important?

5. How should display information be expressed for a web page?

6. What function does the browser's rendering engine perform?

7. What are the advantages of using an external style sheet?

8. What feature distinguishes XML from HTML?

9. What are the two HTML5 syntaxes?

10. What is a well-formed document?

11. What is document metadata?

12. Where is metadata stored?

13. List three new HTML5 elements that are designed for sectioning.

14. What is the function of the new HTML5 <canvas> element?

15. What does *semantic markup* mean?

Hands-On Projects

1. Download and install the latest versions of the following browsers onto your computer as necessary:
   - Internet Explorer
   - Firefox
   - Opera
   - Safari
   - Google Chrome

2. Visit the World Wide Web Consortium web site, and find the web-based validator at http://validator.w3.org. Validate the code from the two chapter activities. Interpret any error messages you receive from the validator, and make changes to your code as needed to complete an error-free validation.

3. Convert a text document to HTML from scratch. Open a text file, save it as an HTML file, and then add all markup elements to create a basic web page. View the browser result, and then validate the file.

4. Download and install at least two different HTML-editing programs that have code-based editing abilities. Write a short report detailing the capabilities of each. Create an HTML document that contains your findings and is viewable in the browser.

5. In this project, you mark up a basic HTML file and test it in the browser.
   a) Copy the **ch1project5.html** file from the Chapter01 folder provided with your Data Files to the Chapter01 folder in your work folder. (Create the Chapter01 folder, if necessary.)
   b) In your HTML editor, open **ch1project5.html** and examine the code. Replace "Your Name" in the comment at the bottom of the page with your first and last name. Notice that only the basic HTML elements are included to create the head and body sections of the document. It is your job to mark up the rest of the document sections to look like the result in Figure 1-19.
   c) Validate your results using the W3C validator to make sure your code is correct.

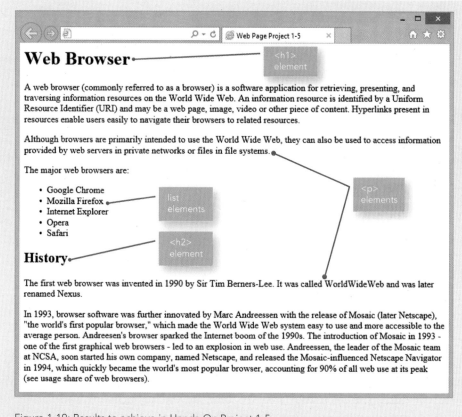

Figure 1-19: Results to achieve in Hands-On Project 1-5
Microsoft product screenshots used with permission from Microsoft Corporation.

6. In this project, you add CSS to a basic HTML file and test it in the browser.
   a) Copy the **ch1project6.htm** file from the Chapter01 folder provided with your Data Files to the Chapter01 folder in your work folder. (Create the Chapter01 folder, if necessary.)
   b) In your HTML editor, open **ch1project6.html** and examine the code. Replace "Your Name" in the comment at the bottom of the page with your first and last name. Notice that the document is marked up with HTML, but it does not contain style information. It is your job to add the style sheet rules so the page looks like the result in Figure 1-20.
   c) Make sure to add a <style> element within the <head> element to contain your style rules.
   d) Validate your results using the W3C validator to make sure your code is correct.

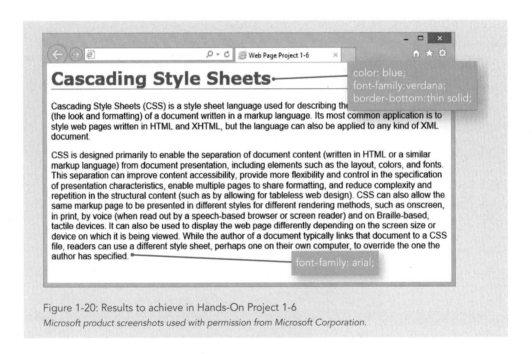

Figure 1-20: Results to achieve in Hands-On Project 1-6
Microsoft product screenshots used with permission from Microsoft Corporation.

Individual Case Project

To complete the ongoing Individual Case Project for this book, you must create a complete stand-alone web site. The site must have 6–10 pages that display at least three levels of information. You can choose your own content. For example, you can focus on a work-related topic, create a personal interest site, or design a site for your favorite nonprofit organization.

The site will be evaluated for cohesiveness, accessibility, compliance with W3C standards, and visual design. At the end of each chapter, you will complete a different section of the project. For Chapter 1, get started by creating a project proposal, using the outline shown in the "Project Proposal" section. As you progress through the chapters of the book, you will complete different facets of web site construction, resulting in a complete web site.

Project Proposal

Create a one- or two-page HTML document listing the basic elements you will include in your web site. Create this document using your favorite HTML editor or Notepad. At this stage, your proposal is primarily a draft. At the end of Chapter 2, you will have a chance to modify the proposal and supplement the design details.

Include the following items, if applicable:

> **Site title**—Specify the working title for the site.

> **Developer**—Identify yourself and anyone else who will work on the site.

> **Rationale or focus**—Explain the content and goals of the site, such as billboard, customer support, catalog/e-commerce, informational, or resource. Refer to Chapter 3, "Planning the Site," for help on content types.

> **Main elements outline**—Describe the main features of the site.

> **Content**—Estimate the number of individual web pages.

> **Target audience**—Describe the typical audience for the site.

> **Design considerations**—List the design goals for the site.

> **Limiting factors**—Identify the technical or audience factors that could limit the design goals of the site.

Team Case Project

To complete the ongoing Team Case Project for this book, you and your team must create a complete stand-alone web site. Your team should ideally consist of 3–4 members assigned by your instructor. The site must contain between 16 and 20 pages that display at least three levels of information. You will choose your own topic. For example, you can focus on a work-related topic, create a personal interest site, or develop a site for a fictional organization. The site will be evaluated for cohesiveness, accessibility, compliance with W3C standards, and visual design. At the end of each chapter, you will complete a different section of the project. For Chapter 1, get started by creating a project proposal, using the outline shown in the "Project Proposal" section. As you progress through the remaining chapters of the book, you will complete different facets of web site construction, resulting in a complete web site.

Project Proposal

Collaborate to create a one- or two-page HTML document stating the basic elements you will include in your web site. Create this document using your favorite HTML editor or Notepad. At this stage, your proposal is primarily a draft. At the end of Chapter 2, you will have a chance to modify the proposal and supplement the design details.

Include the following items, if applicable:

> **Site title**—Specify the working title for the site.

> **Development roles**—Identify each team member and individual responsibilities for the project.

> **Need**—Describe the need the web site will satisfy. What is the purpose of the site? Is there an interest group whose needs are not satisfied? Is there a target niche you are trying to fill?

> **Rationale or focus**—Explain the content and goals of the site such as billboard, customer support, catalog/e-commerce, informational, or resource. Refer to Chapter 3, "Planning the Site," for help on content types.

> **Main elements outline**—Describe the main features of the site.

> **Content**—Estimate the number of individual web pages.

> **Target audience**—Describe the typical audience for the site.

> **Design considerations**—List the design goals for the site.

> **Limiting factors**—Identify the technical or audience factors that could limit the design goals of the site.

> **Development schedule, milestones, and deliverables**—Using the dates in your class syllabus as a basis, build a development schedule that indicates milestones and deliverables for each team member.

CHAPTER

2

WEB SITE DESIGN PRINCIPLES

When you complete this chapter, you will be able to:

> Understand the web design environment

> Design for multiple screen resolutions

> Craft the look and feel of the site

> Create a unified site design

> Design for the user

> Design for accessibility

This chapter covers the design principles that you will apply to your web page design as you work through this book. By examining current web design theories and viewing a variety of web sites, you learn to focus on both the user's needs and the requirements of the content you want to deliver.

The sample web pages in this chapter come from a wide range of sites. The web is so far-reaching in content and design that no collection of pages can represent what is typical. Most of the samples illustrate good design principles, although some contain design defects as well. In truth, almost every site has one flaw or another, whether it is a confusing interface, overambitious design, or poor accessibility. Judge the samples with a critical eye. Look for elements of design that you can transfer to your own work. As you progress through the book, you will practice and apply these principles to your own web design efforts.

Understanding the Web Design Environment

In this section, you will learn about the external factors that affect your web design efforts. Even though web coding and design standards have progressed significantly in recent years, many variables still affect how your web page designs appear to users. As browsers have become more standardized, other more recent factors continue to change and pose challenges for web designers. These challenges include new screen resolutions based on popular widescreen monitor formats and new devices such as tablets, smartphones, e-readers, and other handheld devices. At the same time, not all users have the latest technology or fastest Internet access. You do not want to leave these users behind.

To be successful, your web site design must be portable and accessible by users who have a variety of browsers, operating systems, device platforms, and physical abilities. Many designers make the mistake of testing in only one environment, assuming that their pages look the same to all of their users. No matter how much web design experience you gain, always remember to test in different environments and with different users, even when you feel confident of your results.

You can avoid portability problems by coding to standards as described in Chapter 1 and testing for compatibility. Viewing your pages in multiple browsers, testing on the available operating systems, and viewing on all possible devices ensure that your site is accessible to the greatest number of users. Consider analyzing your audience and building a profile of your average user. You will read more about analyzing your audience in Chapter 3.

Browser Compatibility Issues

One of the greatest challenges facing web designers is designing pages that multiple browsers can display properly. As discussed in Chapter 1, every browser contains a program called a rendering engine that interprets the markup tags in an HTML file and displays the results in the browser. The logic for interpreting the HTML tags varies from browser to browser, resulting in potentially conflicting interpretations of the way the HTML file is displayed. As a web page designer, you must test your work in as many browsers as possible to ensure that the work you create appears as you designed it. You might be surprised to see that the results of your HTML code can look different when viewed with various browsers.

Often, web designers do not have the luxury of knowing the user's operating system or the age and type of browser that will be used to view their web pages. Browser and version choices can vary widely based on a number of variables. The widespread use of mobile browsers adds to the complexity of the designer's task. Many people and organizations are reluctant to upgrade software simply because a new version has been released. Although it is a good idea to test with the latest browsers, it also is prudent to test your work in older browsers when possible to maximize the number of people your web pages can reach.

> **Note** You can find complete browser compatibility charts at http://caniuse.com and www.quirksmode.org/compatibility.html.

You may never be able to achieve the exact same look across all the browsers that are available, but you should try to minimize differences as much as possible so that the greatest number of users experience your design as you intended. The more you work with HTML and CSS, the more you will realize that slight differences inevitably occur from browser to browser, though they may not matter to the user. The advances in browser technologies and their adherence to standards, combined with the greater acceptance of standards-based design, now make it easier to build well-designed sites that are displayed consistently from one browser to another, and can adapt to the broad number of devices people use to access the web.

> **Note** To download a particular browser, or find out which browser is currently the most popular, visit one of these web sites:
>
> > BrowserNews at www.upsdell.com/BrowserNews
> > CNET Browser Info at http://download.cnet.com/windows/browsers/
> > Internet Browser Review at http://internet-browser-review
> > .toptenreviews.com
>
> You can keep up with the latest browser market share statistics at http://gs.statcounter.com.

As discussed earlier, not only are new browsers released frequently, but many web users still use older browsers. Including newly supported features in your page design may significantly affect the way your page is viewed if the older browsers cannot interpret the latest enhancements. Browsers exhibit subtle differences across computing platforms as well.

The newer browsers offer much better support for the standards released by the W3C. Browser software companies have found that, as part of the web development community, they can benefit from the increased support of the standards. Standards-compliant browsers allow better visual design and a more consistent experience for all users.

To ensure the greatest compatibilities of your web pages across multiple browsers, follow these guidelines:

> **Follow W3C standards**—Use HTML and CSS correctly and consistently.

> **Validate your code**—Test for syntactical correctness and coding errors.

> **Know your audience**—Create designs that are accessible, readable, and legible.

> **Test your work in multiple browsers and devices**—Test and retest as you develop to mitigate problems as they occur.

Connection Speed Differences

The user's Internet connection speed has traditionally been a variable that web designers could not ignore. If pages download slowly because they contain large, detailed graphics or complicated animations, users may click to go to another site before they see even a portion of content. In the developed world, the number of people who can use broadband access to the web has steadily increased, which makes connection speeds less of an issue. Figures 2-1 and 2-2 show the total number of subscribers for both fixed and wireless broadband service.

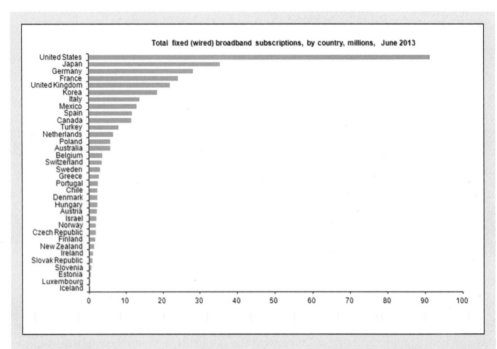

Figure 2-1: Total number of wired broadband subscribers, by country, millions, June 2013
Courtesy of oecd.org/sti/ict/broadband

Chapter 2 **Web Site Design Principles**

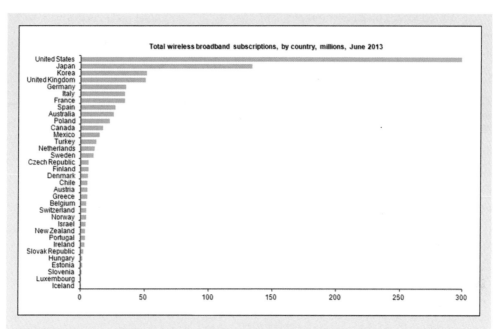

Figure 2-2: Total number of wireless broadband subscribers, by country, millions, June 2013
Courtesy of oecd.org/sti/ict/broadband

If you are building web sites for a worldwide audience, you still must plan your pages so they are accessible at a variety of connection speeds. As Figures 2-1 and 2-2 show, broadband access is not universal, and many users around the world connect at speeds slower than broadband. Smartphones and tablets often have lower bandwidth than home or business computers. You want to consider all possible users when you design the look and feel of your site. Many designers make the mistake of not testing their pages at different connection speeds. If you do not test, you cannot appreciate what it is like for users to connect at different speeds to your site, and you may lose valuable visitors or potential customers.

Browser Cache and Download Time

All web pages are stored on computers called web servers. When you type a Uniform Resource Locator (URL) address in your browser, it connects to the appropriate web server and requests the file you specified. The server serves up the file so your browser can download it. The first time you visit a site, the entire contents of the HTML file (which is plain text), every image referenced in the HTML code, and any CSS style sheets are downloaded to your hard drive. The next time you visit the web site, your browser downloads and parses the HTML file from the site. The browser checks to see if it has any of the specified images stored locally on the computer's hard drive in the cache. The cache is the browser's temporary storage area for web pages and images. The browser always tries to load images from the cache rather than downloading them again from the web.

You can take advantage of the browser's caching capabilities by reusing graphics as much as possible throughout your site. Once an image is downloaded, it remains in your user's cache for the number of days specified in the user's preference settings. Most users do not change the settings, so there is a good chance your graphics will remain on the user's hard drive for as long as a month, or until the storage space fills up. Every time the user revisits your site, the cached graphics load locally rather than from the web server. The browser's caching capability is a great argument for standardizing the look of your site by using the same navigation, branding, and background graphics throughout. Not only does the visual consistency increase the usability of your site, but your pages also load faster.

> **Note**
>
> As a web designer, you will be testing and retesting your site. As you do, the browser's caching behavior can work against you. Because the browser stores and reloads files from the cache, your latest changes may not be loaded, especially if filenames match for graphics or style sheets. If you make changes to a web page but don't see the results in the browser, it is probably because your browser is reading from the cache rather than loading the changes you made. To clear the cache in most browsers, press the Ctrl+Shift+Del key combination on a Windows PC or hold down the Shift key and click the Reload button in the browser. In Firefox, press Ctrl+F5. Most browsers, including mobile browsers, also let you clear the cache using their menu system.

Device and Operating System Issues

The user's computer system or mobile browsing device is the variable over which you have the least control. People use endless combinations of monitors, computers, and operating systems on desktops and laptops. Smartphones and tablets are available in a multitude of configurations and screen sizes. The best method for dealing with this variety is to test your content on as many devices as possible. Remember the following points about different computer systems:

> **Screen sizes and color depth**—Because of many technical and physical reasons, the colors you choose and images you prepare for your site can look significantly different on different devices. Screen resolutions and sizes, color depth, and video hardware and software all affect the look of your web pages.

> **Browser type and version**—The web is a very nonstandard software environment, and to create web pages that look the best on the most browsers is a constant challenge for web designers. Browsers are available for every computing device ranging from the traditional browsers for the PC and Mac, to newer browsers for tablets and smartphones, and to device-specific and more obscure browsers, such as those bundled with e-readers and gaming stations. The release version of the browser also affects the way your pages appear. Each release of Microsoft Internet Explorer has major differences from its previous version, causing web developers to retest existing content. Other vendors release many updates a year, but users may not always upgrade to the latest release of a browser. In the past, web designers struggled with the different ways that browsers interpreted HTML and CSS. Now that desktop browsers are more consistent, mobile devices introduce a whole new range of browsers to contend with. Always test your work on as many devices as possible, from phone to desktop.

> **Font choices**—Installed fonts vary widely from one computer to another. Choose fonts that are commonly used for the web; otherwise, if a font you choose is not installed on the user's device, it will appear in a default typeface. Choose fonts for legibility and ease of use on different devices. You will also want to use CSS to style your fonts so they resize progressively based on the user's screen size. Chapter 6 provides more information on web typography.

Designing for Multiple Screen Resolutions

No matter how carefully you design pages, you can never know how users view your work because you do not know the screen resolution of their computer or handheld device. A device's screen resolution is the width and height of the screen in pixels. Most desktop and laptop computer monitors can be set to a number of different resolutions. Mobile devices such as tablets and smartphones generally have fixed resolutions that cannot be changed by the user. User screen resolution is a factor over which you have no control.

Desktop and Laptop Displays

Desktop and laptop displays have been the dominant browsing device for most of the history of the web. Web designers have adapted their content to the changing and improving technology of computer display devices, using different design techniques to present their content in the best possible way across different screen sizes and graphics technologies.

As Figure 2-3 shows, currently the most popular computer screen resolution is 1366 x 768, a common laptop computer resolution. The second most common screen resolution is 1024 x 768, a default setting for a majority of 15- and 17-inch monitors that still exist in many workplaces and public spaces such as libraries.

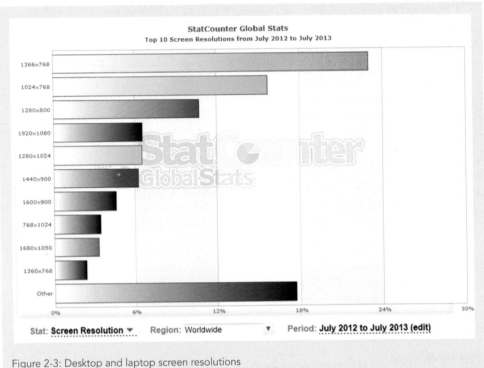

Figure 2-3: Desktop and laptop screen resolutions
http://gs.statcounter.com/#resolution-ww-monthly-201207-201307-bar

Widescreen monitors have become so inexpensive that many users now have these larger
screens on their home computers. The wider screen real estate offers a challenge for
designers building their page layouts, because flexible layouts that can adapt to different
screen resolutions can spread too wide and add too much white space to the content. If
a web browser is maximized on a wide landscape-mode screen, you must account for a
tremendous amount of horizontal layout space in your web design. To solve this problem,
many designers now limit the horizontal width of their designs so they appear as a centered
page on larger monitors.

To accommodate a range of screen sizes and resolutions, Amazon uses a flexible layout in
their page designs. Figure 2-4 shows the Amazon.com web site (*www.amazon.com*) in a
1366 x 768 resolution, and Figure 2-5 shows the same page in 1920 x 1080, a typical
widescreen format. As you can see, this page is designed to be flexible and fill the screen at
different screen resolutions. In Figure 2-5, you can see that additional white space fills areas
in the layout that are flexible to accommodate the wider screen resolution. On very wide

displays, this additional space can become so noticeable that it can detract from the layout of the page. The navigation menu on the left also appears only in the wider screen resolutions. Objects can be displayed or hidden using CSS style rules with media queries. In CSS, media queries let you customize web page designs for different devices based on attributes such as screen width, resolution, and orientation. You will read more about media queries in Chapter 12. By specifying a style sheet based on device characteristics, you can customize the page layout by designing the content to appear in a single column or providing navigation customized for smaller screens. You can also hide elements that will not be displayed properly, such as animated or overly large graphics and JavaScript elements.

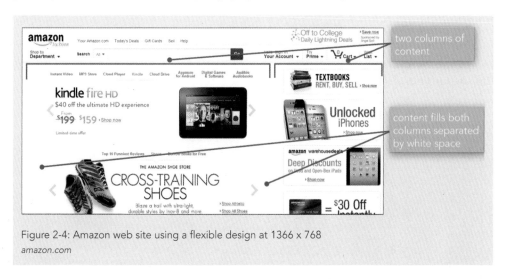

Figure 2-4: Amazon web site using a flexible design at 1366 x 768

amazon.com

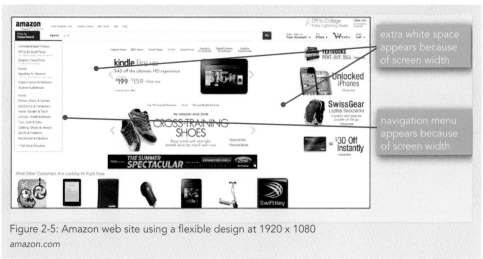

Figure 2-5: Amazon web site using a flexible design at 1920 x 1080

amazon.com

In contrast, the National Park Service (*www.nps.gov*) uses a fixed design that does not change based on user screen resolution. Fixed designs allow the designer to control the look of the web pages as if it were a printed page, with consistent width and height. Fixed-width page layouts are a popular choice because of the increasing variety of screen sizes and resolutions and the relative ease of constructing fixed-width designs compared to flexible designs. Most current fixed-width layouts are designed to stay centered in the browser window, regardless of the user's screen resolution. Figure 2-6 shows the National Park Service web site at 1024 x 768. Notice that the page fills the screen. The designers built the site with this resolution as the base for their design. If the user chooses to use a smaller browser window, or displays the site on older monitors that have a lower resolution, then the user will only see a portion of this screen and will have to scroll both horizontally and vertically to see the rest. If you refer back to Figure 2-3 (chart of screen resolutions), you can see that most users have resolutions that are at least 1024 x 768, so the designers are basing their design on this lowest resolution.

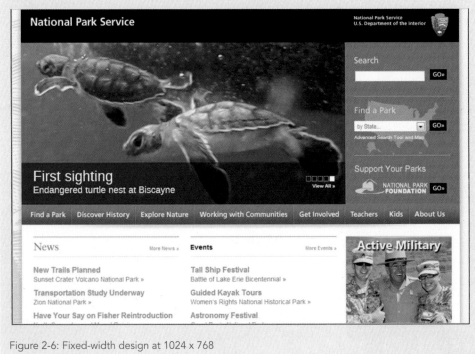

Figure 2-6: Fixed-width design at 1024 x 768
www.nps.gov

As the screen resolution changes, a web page with a fixed design stays centered in the browser window, splitting the remaining space into equal amounts on the left and right side of the browser window. Figure 2-7 shows the same National Park Service page at 1920 x 768. The benefit of centering a fixed-width page is that the layout of the content remains unchanged no matter what the user's screen resolution. Additionally, the designers have added a background graphic that enhances the page layout at higher resolutions.

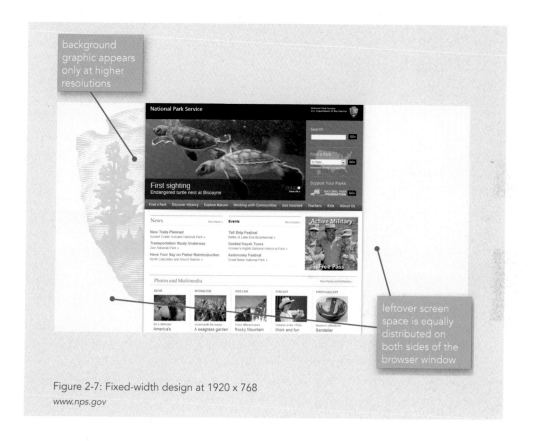

Figure 2-7: Fixed-width design at 1920 x 768
www.nps.gov

Mobile Devices

In addition to widescreen and standard monitors, mobile device usage has exploded in the last few years, adding to the number of screen sizes and resolutions web designers must contend with. Smartphones and tablets running the Apple iOS and Android operating systems come in a multitude of sizes that complicate the web designer's job.

Figure 2-8 shows popular mobile screen resolutions that designers must take into account when creating and testing their web site designs.

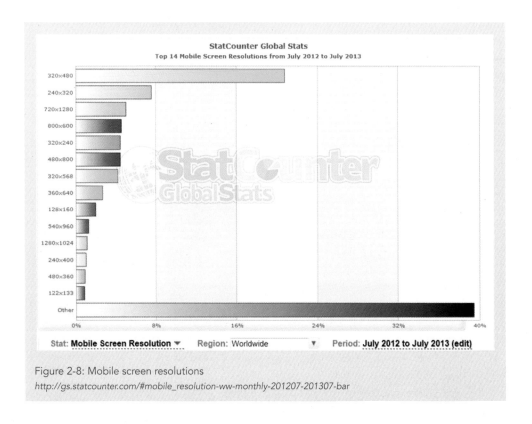

Figure 2-8: Mobile screen resolutions
http://gs.statcounter.com/#mobile_resolution-ww-monthly-201207-201307-bar

Even at their small size, many mobile devices have screens that are capable of incredibly high resolutions to create a sharper picture and richer color, as shown in Table 2-1. To achieve a 2048 x 1536 resolution, the pixels on an iPad retina display are smaller than those even on widescreen monitors, resulting in text and images that are incredibly detailed. However, the larger number of pixels make your images and fonts appear smaller. Although tablet and phone users can always zoom in to view images and text in more detail, the designer can make the decision to customize fonts and sizing using CSS media queries. You will learn more about this in Chapter 12.

DEVICE	SCREEN SIZE (INCHES)	SCREEN RESOLUTION
iPad (retina display)	9.7	2048 x 1536
iPad Mini	7.9	1024 x 768
Kindle Fire HD	7	1280 x 800
iPhone 5	4	1136 x 640
Microsoft Surface	10.5	1366 x 768
Samsung Galaxy	4.8	1280 x 720

Table 2-1: Screen size and resolution of popular mobile devices
© 2015 Cengage Learning®

The ever-expanding array of screen sizes means that web designers have to decide how to serve their content to both desktop and mobile users. Designers can use two strategies to serve their content: a separate mobile site or a responsive design.

Separate Mobile Site

Following this strategy, you can offer two versions of your site, one for desktop computers and one for mobile devices. The web server can detect the type of device that is requesting the web page and redirect the user's browser to the mobile or desktop web site. This method can maximize the user's mobile experience because the site is expressly designed to present content in that format, offering web pages that fit the device and use appropriate fonts, colors, and applications.

Although these two presentations usually draw from a single source of content using a content management system (CMS), maintenance of two sites doubles the work. A CMS is software that allows editing and publishing of content to different formats, such as a desktop and mobile web site. Having separate sites does complicate maintenance and ongoing updates of the page designs because there are duplicates of everything.

Figure 2-9 shows a portion of the main page that Amazon presents for mobile devices. This page is designed to fit the portrait orientation of most mobile device screens, which allows one column of content. The expandable content links let users quickly search for an item or check their shopping cart.

Amazon.com is serving pages that are appropriate for the user's device type. When a mobile user enters the Amazon web address, the Amazon server can detect the mobile request and respond with the appropriate page.

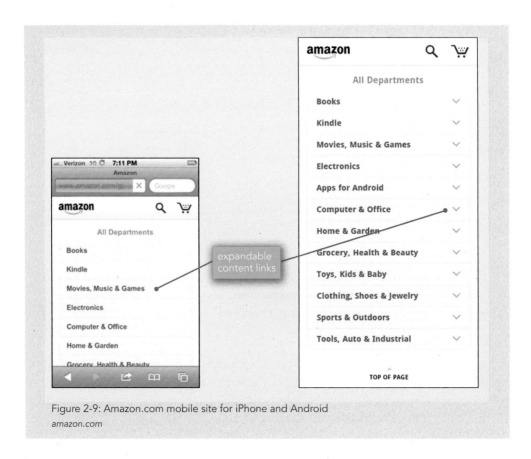

Figure 2-9: Amazon.com mobile site for iPhone and Android
amazon.com

Responsive Design

Using a responsive design approach, you design your web pages to adapt to different screen sizes—from smartphone to desktop—using CSS styles and media queries. You will learn more about these techniques throughout the book and in Chapter 12 in particular. The major benefit of this strategy is that maintenance and updates are limited to a single set of content and web pages. The challenge is refining the design and creating the style code so that the pages render appropriately across different devices. This technique is often called responsive design, a method of designing web sites that are adaptable to a wide range of devices from mobile phones to desktop monitors.

The Mashable web site (*www.mashable.com*) is an excellent example of responsive design. Using media queries and CSS style sheets, the site is designed for a range of screen sizes that include phones, tablets (in both landscape and portrait orientations), laptops, and widescreen monitors. In Figure 2-10, notice that as the screen size shrinks to accommodate different devices, certain articles are dropped from the display or repositioned on the page.

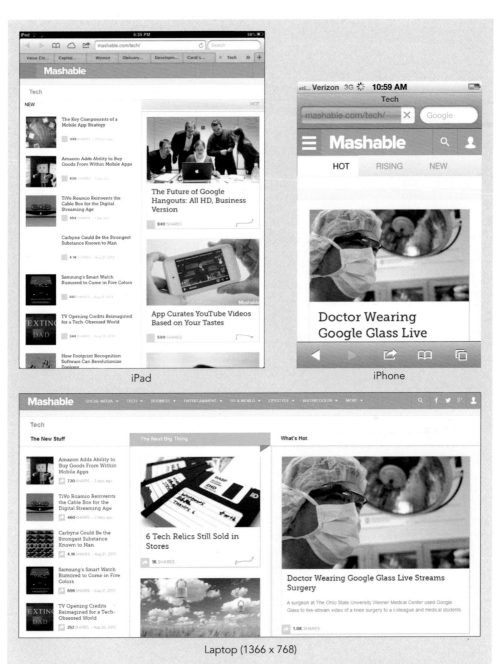

iPad

iPhone

Laptop (1366 x 768)

Figure 2-10: Using responsive design, columns expand to fit the screen and resolution

mashable.com

Continued on next page...

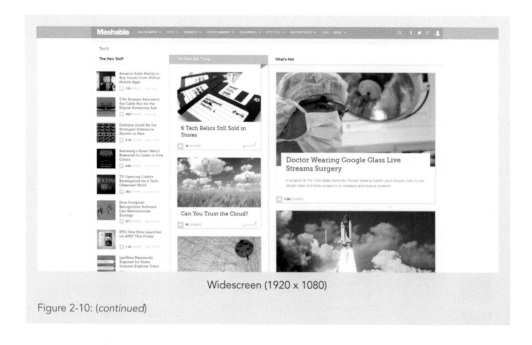

Widescreen (1920 x 1080)

Figure 2-10: (*continued*)

Suggestions for Solving the Screen Resolution Dilemma

Which of the two layout types—fixed or flexible—is right for your design? Currently, many mainstream sites still use fixed designs, but mobile devices require either a separate mobile site or a move to a more responsive design. Fixed designs require mobile users to pan, zoom, and scroll to read content, so designs that are flexible are more adaptable for the user and to multiple devices. Consider the following advantages of each type of design when you determine which approach is right for you.

Flexible/responsive design advantages:

> User controls the view of the content

> Less chance of horizontal scrolling

> More flexibility for multiple devices

> Better suited to text-based layouts and simpler designs

Fixed-width design advantages:

> Designer controls the view of the content

> Allows more complex page layouts

> More control over text length

As a web designer, you will find yourself busy with multiple projects and a full plate of meetings and other work commitments. You will need to make time in your busy schedule to keep up with design trends and keep in touch with what other designers are doing. You want to keep your skills fresh and your familiarity with industry trends and standards current. Follow your favorite designers and design web sites through social media. Keep up with the latest from the World Wide Web Consortium standards and coding recommendations. Sign up to attend local or national web design conferences, if possible. Many larger corporations offer conference attendance or classes to keep their staff up to date; always accept these opportunities when offered to you. Web design is a constantly changing field, and it is crucial for your career to keep educating yourself as the industry evolves.

Crafting the Look and Feel of the Site

The interface that the user must navigate is often called the look and feel of a web site. Users look and feel when they explore your site. They read text, make associations with links, view multimedia, and, depending on the freedom of your design, create their own path through your information. The look and feel is both the way your web site works and the personality it conveys to the user. Not only should you plan for a deliberate and consistent look and feel, but as mentioned earlier in this chapter, you must test your designs against the variable nature of the web and the many devices people use to access it. You want to ensure that the greatest number of users can navigate your site successfully.

Balance Design and Content

When planning the design of a web site, access to your content and the needs of your users should always guide your design decisions. As you will read in Chapter 3, web development teams often comprise many people, each with their own idea of what is important in the current web site project. Within your company or design team, various stakeholders contribute to the design of the site. The customer has their vision of the finished web site they are paying your company to design. The designers want to build a site that showcases their design skills. The development team wants to include the latest technologies. The publishing and editorial teams want to highlight their content. Advertising revenues may determine placement and design of ad space on the page.

These varied stakeholders vie for positioning and exposure to their content and content depth, and the larger the site project, the more interests are involved. Everyone wants to contribute their own ideas to the design process. The emphasis on the look of the site can overwhelm the needs of the user, for example, when sites have unnecessary entry pages, too many images, layers that add extra clicks to uncover content, and overdone technology—scrolls, news banners, cycling images, and complicated navigation. All of these factors can distract the user from their search for information.

A web site's design should complement the content and support the reader. The information design should be logically divided and structured to expose similar groupings of content, and then provide access to the content through designed navigation. When in doubt, always choose simple and direct designs that showcase content and allow easy access, and set aside unneeded technology and complex visual designs that can frustrate and misdirect your user.

Plan for Easy Access to Your Information

Your information design is the single most important factor influencing the success of your site because it determines how easily users can access your web content. The goal is to organize your content and present it as a meaningful, navigable set of information. Your navigation options should present a variety of choices to users without detracting from their quests for information.

A visitor to your site may choose to browse randomly or look for specific information. Often users arrive at a page looking for data that is low in the hierarchy of information. Sometimes users arrive at your site seeking a specific piece of information, such as contact information, product support, or files they want to download. Anticipate and plan for the actions and paths that users are likely to choose when they traverse your site. Provide direct links to the areas of your site that you find or expect to be in the greatest demand. Offer search and site map functions to allow users different ways to find the content they want. Ask your server administrator for web server reports to determine which pages are in highest demand, and feature those pages in your design and navigation to allow users easy access. Remember that users want to get to your site, retrieve their desired information, and move on.

Plan for Clear Presentation of Your Information

Even with the current move to higher resolutions and crystal-clear displays, the computer monitor or mobile device can be a poor reading medium. Environmental factors such as glare or physical distance from the screen can make reading difficult. To counter these problems, design your information so it is easy to read and legible on the screen. Many web sites fail these criteria by using too many fonts, colors, and lengthy passages of text. Break text into reasonable segments that make for easier onscreen reading. Think about providing contrasting colors that enhance the legibility of your text, such as dark colors against a light or white background. Use plenty of white space to accent specific areas of content and provide separation and structure to your information.

Keep in mind that readers have different habits when reading online. Compared to how they read printed text, online visitors scan more and read less, skimming long pages quickly as they scroll through the text. Include plenty of headings so users can find content quickly. Control the width of your text to provide complete, easy-to-read columns. Rather than presenting long scrolling pages, break information into smaller chunks and link them with hypertext.

The Pew Research Center site (*www.pewresearch.org*) offers both clear presentation and easy access to information, as shown in Figure 2-11. The navigation links on the top of the page are organized and offer clear descriptions of their destinations. A search text box is located at the top of the page for quick and easy access. The text used throughout the site is legible and easy to read online. Plenty of active white space between the page elements adds to the readability of the page. (You'll learn more about white space later in this chapter.)

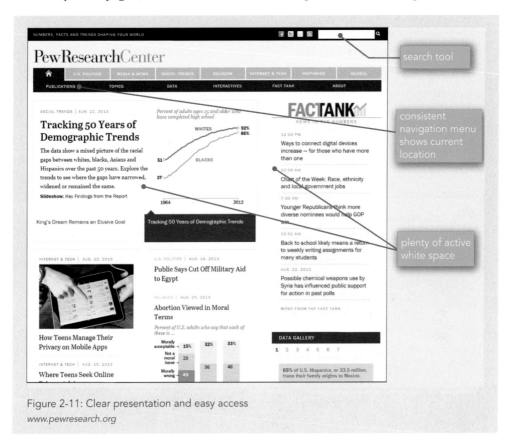

Figure 2-11: Clear presentation and easy access
www.pewresearch.org

Creating a Unified Site Design

When designing your site, plan the unifying themes and structure that will hold the pages together. Your choices of colors, fonts, graphics, and page layout should communicate a visual theme to users that orients them to your site's content. The theme should reflect the impression that you or your organization want to convey.

When you design a site, you must consider more than each page. For a well-integrated, unified site, plan smooth transitions, use a grid to provide visual structure, and include active white space. Each of these techniques is explained in the following sections.

Plan Smooth Transitions

Plan to create a unified look among the sections and pages of your site. Reinforce the identifying elements of the site and create smooth transitions from one page to another by repeating colors and fonts and by using a page layout that allows you to organize information in a hierarchy. Avoid random, jarring changes in your format, unless this is the effect you want to achieve. Consistency and repetition create smooth transitions from one page to the next, reassuring viewers that they are traveling within the boundaries of your site, and helping them find information.

Provide grounding for the user by placing navigation elements in the same position on each page. Users will orient themselves quickly to your navigation structure. Use the same navigation graphics throughout the site to provide consistency and avoid the need to download many graphics.

Think of users turning the pages of a periodical when they browse from web page to web page. Although each page should be a complete entity, it also is a part of the whole site. The overall design of a page at any information level should reflect the identity of the site as a whole. For example, Figure 2-12 and Figure 2-13 show the main page and a secondary-level page from the Los Angeles Zoo web site (*www.lazoo.org*).

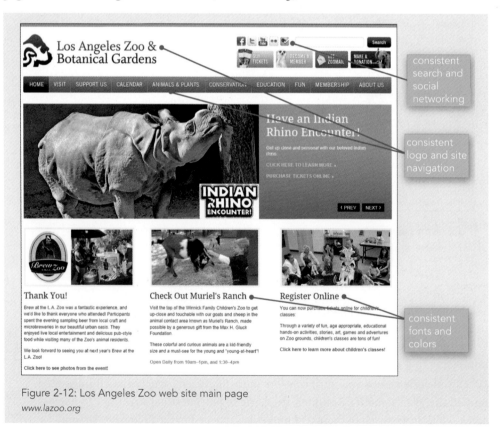

Figure 2-12: Los Angeles Zoo web site main page
www.lazoo.org

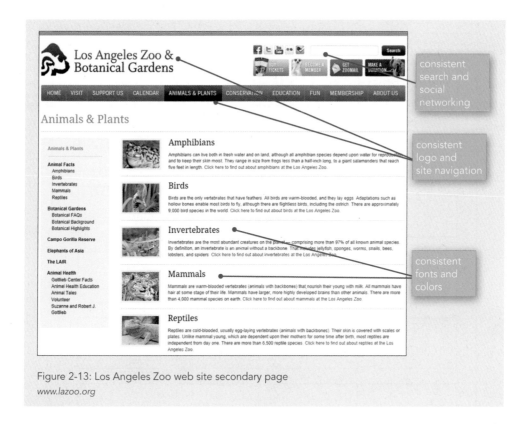

Figure 2-13: Los Angeles Zoo web site secondary page
www.lazoo.org

Because these pages share the same color scheme, logo, fonts, and navigation, the web site offers a smooth transition from the main page to the secondary page and presents a unified look and feel.

Use a Grid to Provide Visual Structure

The structure of a web page is imposed by the grid or page template you choose for your page design. The **grid** is a conceptual layout device that aligns your page content into columns and rows. You can impose a grid to provide visual consistency throughout your site. Use the grid to enforce structure, but you also can break out of the grid to provide variety and highlight important information. Figure 2-14 shows a web page divided into four columns and eight rows. These grid sections provide placement guidelines for page elements, each of which can cover multiple rows and columns of the grid as needed, as shown in Figure 2-15.

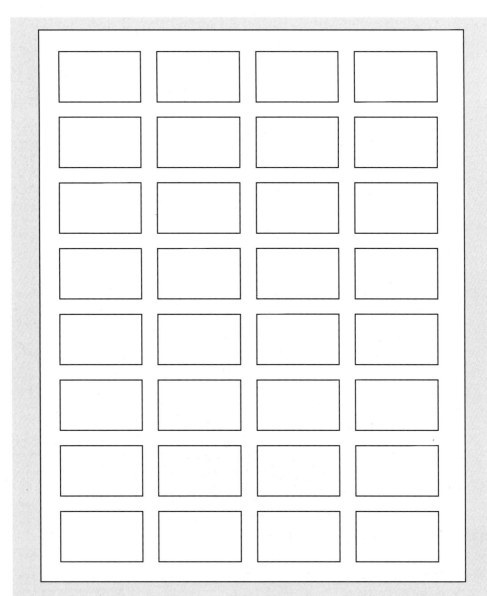

Figure 2-14: Four-column grid
© Cengage Learning®

Figure 2-15: Four-column grid with layout elements
© Cengage Learning®

Notice that the grid also provides a page margin around the content and gutters of white space between elements on the page. This white space actively separates the content and provides structure for the users' eye to follow. Web pages that respect the grid and consistently align text and graphic elements have a more polished look than pages that have scattered alignments.

The *Guardian* site's main page (*guardian.co.uk*) in Figure 2-16 has a six-column grid. All of the text and graphic elements on the page align within the grid to create an orderly layout.

Figure 2-16: Grid provides visual structure

guardian.co.uk

Note

The 960 grid system (www.960.gs) has become a commonly accepted standard for many web designers. The "960" refers to the width in pixels of the page design, which can easily be divided into multiple columns and fits screen resolutions from 1024 pixels wide and up. The web site has CSS files that let you build grid page designs that can become the basis for your own page designs.

Use Active White Space

White spaces are the blank areas of a page, regardless of the color you choose to give them. Use white space deliberately in your design, rather than as an afterthought. Good use of white space guides the reader and defines the areas of your page. White space that is used deliberately is called active white space and is an integral part of your design because it structures and separates content. Sometimes the strongest part of a design is the active white space. Passive white space includes the blank areas that border the screen or are the result of mismatched shapes. Figure 2-17 illustrates active versus passive white space.

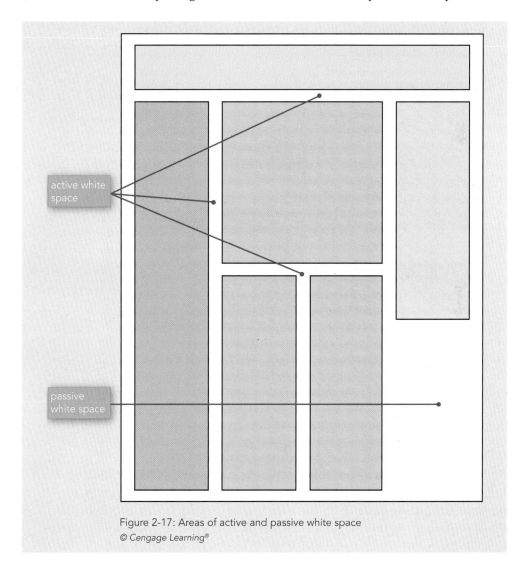

Figure 2-17: Areas of active and passive white space
© Cengage Learning®

Content presentation can become confused when designers do not use enough active white space to separate and define content. A lack of active white space creates the impression that a page contains too much information and that it will be difficult to find the piece of information you want. The Smithsonian Air and Space Museum home page (*www.airandspace .si.edu*) in Figure 2-18 shows effective use of active white space, making the content easy to read. Plenty of active white space reduces clutter and clarifies the organization of your ideas.

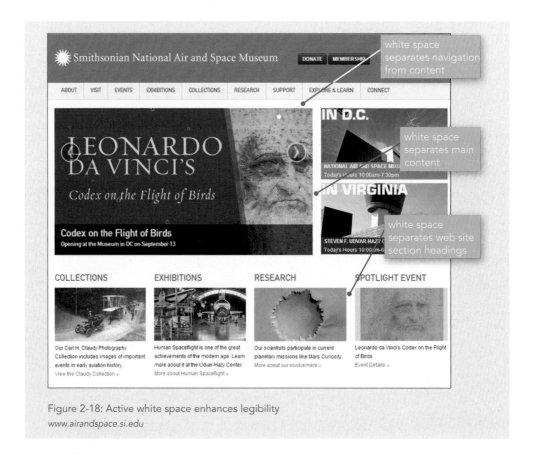

Figure 2-18: Active white space enhances legibility
www.airandspace.si.edu

Designing for the User

Keep your design efforts centered solely on your user. Knowledge of your audience can help you answer almost all design questions—if it serves the audience, keep it; if it is potentially distracting or annoying, eliminate it. Find out what users expect from your site. If you can, survey them with an online form. Create a profile of your average user by compiling responses to basic questions. What do users want when they get to your site?

Are they trying to find customer support and troubleshooting help, or do they want to buy something? Do they want to read articles or search for information? Once you know what your users want from your site, you can evaluate how the design reflects the audience's profile and needs. Consider the main page for the Internal Revenue Service (*www.irs.gov*), shown in Figure 2-19. Users who come to this web site are looking for a range of specific topics. The navigation links, column headings, and feature items are all designed to let users get information as quickly as possible.

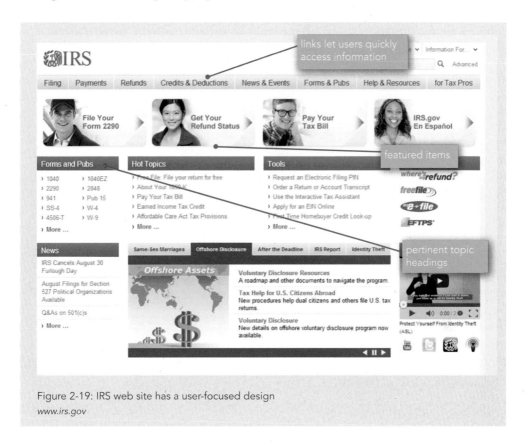

Figure 2-19: IRS web site has a user-focused design
www.irs.gov

In contrast, the web site for the *Wall Street Journal* (*www.wsj.com*) in Figure 2-20 projects a strong periodical-like image that will resonate with its audience. The main page components are textual. Even though the page has a lot of content, it is well organized with clear headings and readable text in well-defined columns. The design uses just enough active white space to clearly separate each element on the page. The overall effect evokes the look of a printed page while using the color, linking, and design flexibility that the web offers.

Figure 2-20: Paper-based design for *The Wall Street Journal's* audience
www.wsj.com

These two examples demonstrate how the design suits the audience's visual expectations—the look of the site. However, you also should consider the ways in which users interact with the content—the feel of the site.

Design for Interaction

Think about how the user wants to interact with the information on your web page. Design for your content type, and decide whether the user is likely to read or scan your pages.

For example, suppose your page is a collection of links, such as a main page or section page. Users want to interact with these types of pages by scanning the content, scrolling if necessary, pointing to graphics to see if they are hyperlinked, and clicking linked text. Design for this type of user interaction by using meaningful column headings, linked text, and short descriptions. Organize links into related topic groups, and separate groupings with white space, graphics, or background color.

Suppose the page is an article that contains large blocks of text. Your user is accustomed to interacting with pages of text by scrolling and possibly clicking hyperlinked words of interest. The links may be in the body of the article or contained in a sidebar. Design your pages for this text-oriented content by keeping paragraphs short for online consumption. Make reading easier by using a text column that is narrower than the width of the screen. Keep your text legible by providing enough contrast between foreground and background colors. Provide links that allow the user to jump quickly to related content.

Two screens from the Boston Globe web site (*www.bostonglobe.com*) illustrate the difference between designing for reading and designing for scanning. Figure 2-21 shows the site's main page. Three columns of content present a variety of information, with plenty of active white space to separate features and allow easy reading. Users can scan links to find a topic of interest, read article abstracts, or choose one of the featured main sections.

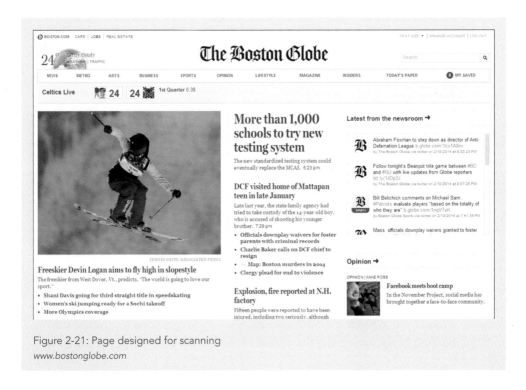

Figure 2-21: Page designed for scanning
www.bostonglobe.com

When users choose a link, they jump to a page designed for reading, as illustrated in Figure 2-22, which shows a secondary page from the Boston Globe web site. This page has a two-column layout, with a more generous right column that contains the main article text. Featured main sections are provided in the banner at the top of the page. An article sidebar provides links to related content.

Figure 2-22: Page designed for reading
www.bostonglobe.com

Design for Location

The user can traverse a page in a variety of ways. Human factors studies show a wide range of results when tracking a user's eye movements. As you plan your design to guide the user through your content, consider the different ways your user could be viewing your web pages.

Fixed-width designs tend to have the same proportions as the printed page, which enforces scanning the page using paper-based reading habits. In this reading pattern, the user's eye moves from left to right and back again, as shown in Figure 2-23.

Figure 2-23: Paper-based reading pattern
© Cengage Learning®

In contrast, when viewing flexible layouts that fill the screen, users may scan information following a clockwise pattern, as shown in Figure 2-24.

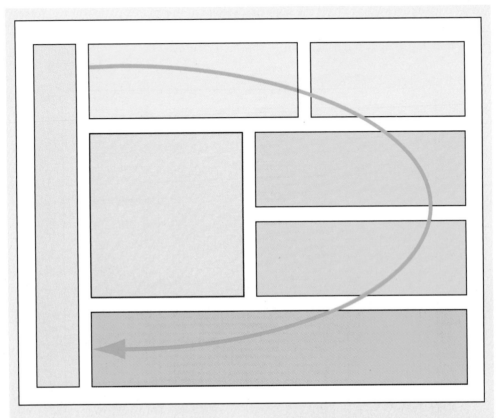

Figure 2-24: Landscape-based viewing pattern
© Cengage Learning®

A third pattern, found in eye-tracking studies performed by Jakob Nielsen, shows that "users often read web pages in an F-shaped pattern: two horizontal scans followed by a vertical scan." (*www.useit.com/alertbox/reading_pattern.html.*) The F-shaped pattern, shown in Figure 2-25, is dominated by the upper-left part of the page, where users look for the most important information and navigation on the page. According to Nielsen, users' dominant reading patterns tend to follow this sequence:

> ⟩ Users first read across the top of the page.

> ⟩ Next, users move down the page a bit and scan across the page again. This scan is typically shorter than the first.

> ⟩ Finally, users scan the content's left side in a vertical movement. Sometimes this is a fairly slow and systematic scan of the content.

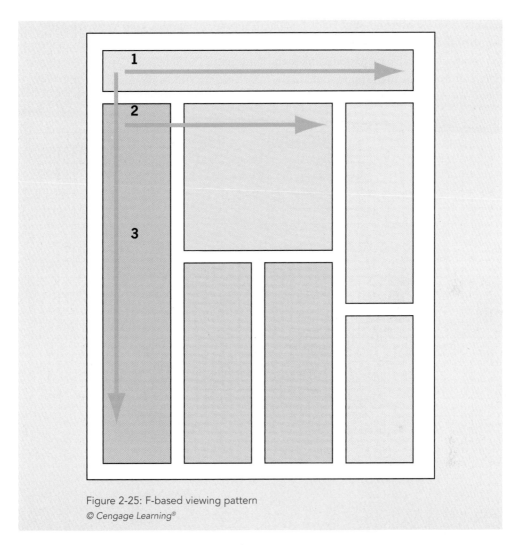

Figure 2-25: F-based viewing pattern
© Cengage Learning®

In addition to knowing how the user views your pages, you should also know what expectations he or she might have about your navigation and content. Users have come to expect common elements of a web page in certain locations. These conventions have evolved because of usage by popular web sites as well as basic page design criteria. Eye-tracking studies cited by Patrick J. Lynch and Sarah Horton in the *Web Style Guide, Third Edition,* (*http://webstyleguide.com/wsg3/3-information-architecture/4-presenting-information.html*) shows how users, when asked to identify where they expected to find certain elements, more or less agreed on the relative positioning on a web page grid. In Figure 2-26, the top rows of grids show different element expectations, with the deeper colors indicating higher preference. The page mockup below the grids shows the aggregate of the results positioned on a web page design. These expectations reflect many web sites and would look familiar to anyone who has browsed the web for any length of time. For example, the Home link graphic shows that most users look to the upper-left corner of the web page to find a link to the home page. The Shopping Cart element shows that most users look to the upper-right or the middle-right to find a shopping cart link. Keep these expectations in mind to satisfy the needs of the user and help solve design problems.

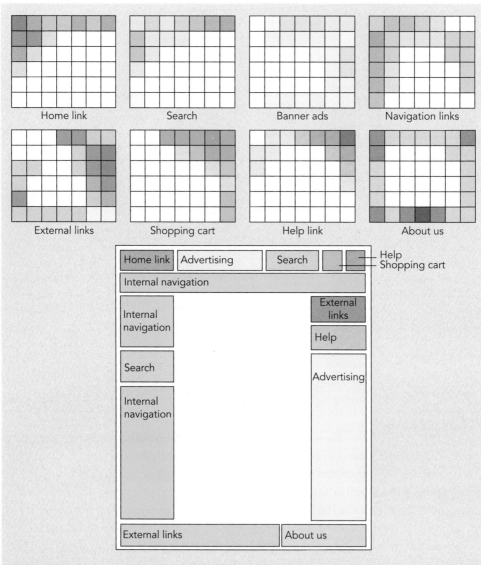

Figure 2-26: User expectations of web page element locations
Courtesy of Patrick J. Lynch and Sarah Horton

Remember that these studies and theories are guidelines for design, not hard and fast rules. They suggest general user tendencies rather than specific habits. Knowing these common user tendencies is one more way to help you decide where to focus the user's attention by object placement, text weight, and color use. Keep the following points in mind:

> Think about your grid structure and how you want to break out of it to attract attention.
> Use text weight and size to communicate relative importance of information.
> Use meaningful headings to help users navigate through your content.
> Divide content into sections with rules or active white space.
> Use shapes and color to reinforce location or topic.

Keep a Flat Hierarchy

Do not make users navigate through too many layers of your web site to find the information they want. Structure your web site to include section- or topic-level navigation pages that let users find their desired paths quickly. Create content sections organized logically by theme.

Try to follow the three clicks rule; that is, don't make your users click more than three times to get to the content they desire. Provide prominent navigation cues that enable quick access. For example, a standard navigation bar consistently placed on every page reassures users that they will not get lost, and it lets them move through the site with flexibility. Think about the primary tasks the user wants to accomplish at your web site, and design accordingly to make it easy for the user to accomplish those tasks.

Consider providing a site map that graphically displays the organization of your web site. Figure 2-27 shows a site map from the Scholastic web site (*www.scholastic.com*). This graphical view of the web site shows all the individual pages and the sections in which they reside. Clear headings organize the content. Users can click to go directly to a page or orient themselves to the site's structure.

Scholastic.com

Shop

The Teacher Store
The Scholastic Store Online
Scholastic Book Fairs
Scholastic Book Clubs
• Club Ordering Online
• Check Order Status
• Request a Catalog
Printables
Klutz
Back To Basics Toys
The Scholastic Store SoHo
Scholastic Library Publishing
(Librarian's Toolkit)

Education Materials

After School Learning Program
Products by State
Classroom Magazines
Classroom Libraries
Guided Reading
Literacy Place
Read 180
Scholastic Red
Scholastic Reading Counts!
Scholastic Reading Inventory
Grant and Funding Connection
Professional Development
Lectorum
Weston Woods
Tom Snyder Productions
Request a Catalog
For Customers Outside the U.S.
Parent & Child Magazine
Coach & Athletic Director
Early Childhood Today
Administr@tor Magazine
Instructor

Parents

Books & Reading
Life & Learning
School Success
Activities & Printables
Blogs

Book Fairs

Parent's Guide
Featured Books
Chairperson's Guide

Book Clubs

Kids

Ages 0-6 (Family Playground)
Games
Printables
Favorites
• Clifford the Big Red Dog
• I Spy
• The Magic School Bus
• Maya & Miguel
• PLAY! Scholastic
• WordGirl

Ages 7-14 (THE STACKS)
Books & Authors
Games
Blog
Videos
Message Boards
Your Profile
Favorites
• Allie Finkle's Rules for Girls
• Animorphs

Teachers

Teaching Resources
Lesson Plans
Teaching Strategies
Timesaving Tools
Class Homepage Builder
Printables
New Teachers
Professional Development Programs
Scholastic School Jobs Now

Student Activities
Language Arts
Social Studies
Science
Math
Scholastic News Online
Activities by Grade

Books & Authors
New & Noteworthy
Teacher Book Wizard
List Exchange
All About Authors
Teaching with Books
Flashlight Readers
Book Fairs' Featured Books

Connect

Class Homepage Builder (Teachers)
Class Homepage (Parent/Student Sign-in)
Teacher Communities
Student Communities
Teacher Planning Calendar
Scholastic's Grant and Funding Connection
State Home Pages

Figure 2-27: Scholastic.com site map
www.scholastic.com

Use Hypertext Linking Effectively

Unlike paper-based authors, as an HTML author you have the luxury of adding clickable text and images where necessary to guide users through your information. This powerful ability comes with a measure of responsibility. You make the decisions that determine how users move through your site and process information. Readers browsing through magazines can flip to any page in any order they desire. You can replicate this nonlinear reading method on your web site with links that let users move from page to page or section to section. With thoughtful hypertext writing, you can engage readers in a whole new way.

Many sites have separate columns of links and topics, but not enough sites provide links within the text. Weave links into your prose to offer a variety of paths. Avoid using the meaningless phrase "Click Here" as the hypertext link. Instead provide a helpful textual clue to the destination of the link.

Figure 2-28 shows a page from the Wikipedia web site (*www.wikipedia.org*). Note how the hypertext links are worked directly into the text. When users click a link, they move to another page of information; from that page they can either go back or move to another page of information, and so on. The abundant hypertext links allow users to create a view of the site's information that is uniquely their own.

Provide plenty of links to let the user get around quickly. Use links to let the user return to the navigation section of your page, to a site map, or to the main page. Do not make the user scroll through lengthy columns. Provide links that let users jump down the page, return to the top of the page, or navigate a clear path back to higher levels of your content.

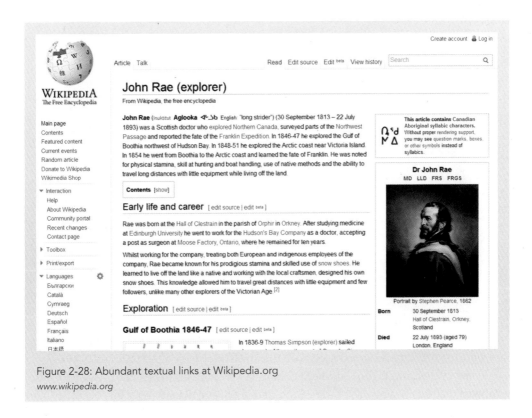

Figure 2-28: Abundant textual links at Wikipedia.org
www.wikipedia.org

How Much Content Is Too Much?

You can crowd only so much information onto a web page. Be conscious of overloading your user with too much information, making it hard for them to find content or complete tasks. ESPN's web site (*www.espn.com*) in Figure 2-29 offers a vast array of content choices. For some users this visual clutter of information is hard to absorb, making it difficult to find and process information.

Figure 2-29: Vast array of choices
www.espn.com

Resist the temptation to overload users with too much information. According to a study conducted by the University of Southern California Marshall Business school, "By 2015, it is estimated that Americans will consume both traditional and digital media for over 1.7 trillion hours, an average of approximately 15 and a half hours per person per day. The amount of media delivered will exceed 8.75 zettabytes annually, or 74 gigabytes—9 DVDs worth—of data sent to the average consumer on an average day." That equals thousands of words, images, and multimedia cascading from a variety of sources. Users quickly learn to screen out the "noise" of banner and animated ads, images, videos and blocks of undistinguishable text. To make your content stand out and have impact, carefully divide it into smaller sections and present it in a structured manner with lots of white space and meaningful navigation cues.

Reformat Content for Online Presentation

Although tempting, it often is a poor choice to take documents that are formatted for print and post them online without considering the destination medium. In most cases, a document that is perfectly legible on paper is hard to negotiate online. The text length, font, and content length do not transfer successfully to the computer screen. Figures 2-30 and 2-31 show the same section of text from Edgar Allen Poe's "The Tell-Tale Heart." Figure 2-30 is formatted as if it were a page from a book. The text is dense and fills the screen in large blocks, with no margins to relieve the reader's eye.

Figure 2-30: Content formatted for print
www.literature.org

In contrast, Figure 2-31, from the Readprint web site (*www.readprint.com*), shows text that has been designed for online display. The text width is short and easy to read without horizontal scrolling. The font is designed for online reading. The white space on the left creates a text column that enforces the vertical flow of the page. The differences between these two pages show that text must be prepared thoughtfully for online display.

Figure 2-31: Content formatted for the web
www.readprint.com

Designing for Accessibility

Any large audience for a web site includes users who want to access your content despite certain physical challenges. Designing for accessibility means developing web pages that remain accessible despite any physical, sensory, and cognitive disabilities; work constraints; or technological barriers on the part of the user. As Tim Berners-Lee said, "The power of the web is in its universality. Access by everyone, regardless of disability, is an essential aspect." Most mainstream web sites are so heavily image- and media-intensive that they are not suitable for adaptive devices such as screen readers, voice browsers, and Braille translators.

Many web sites employ at least some accessibility features, while others are more aggressive about conforming to the standards set by the W3C, which maintains the Web Content Accessibility Guidelines (WCAG) recommendation. Many of these features can be helpful for any visitor to your site. For example, allowing the user to change the font size on a web page (rather than using the browser zoom function) would possibly be used by people with a sight disability and people who have high-resolution monitors where the text appears much smaller. Offering more accessibility features makes your content available to a wider audience.

Building more accessible content does not mean that you have to forgo interesting web designs. Many of the guidelines necessary for developing accessible content naturally lend themselves to creating good design. Common accessibility features can be unobtrusive additions to your site design. For example, the Langdon College site (Figures 2-32 and 2-33) includes the following among its accessibility features:

> **Optional navigation links**—Lets users with screen readers skip repetitive navigation links and jump directly to the page content

> **High-contrast version**—Lets users switch to a legible alternate page version to make text easier to read

> **User-controlled font size**—Lets users adjust the font size for optimal legibility

> **Access keys**—Lets users access sections of the site with keystrokes, which are listed on the Accessibility page.

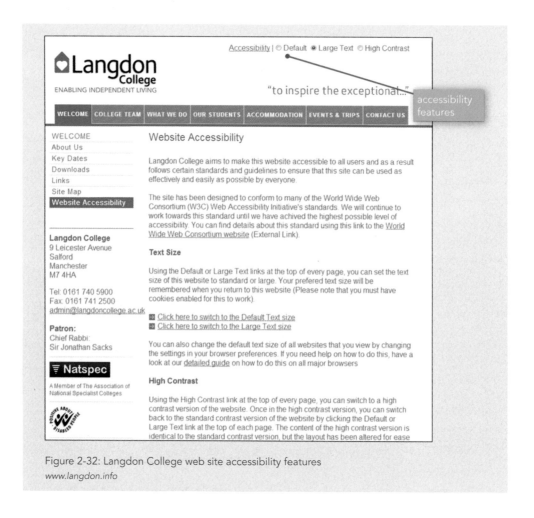

Figure 2-32: Langdon College web site accessibility features
www.langdon.info

Two current sets of accessibility guidelines are available to web designers. The W3C's Web Accessibility Initiative publishes the WCAG 2.0. The U.S. government has its own set of guidelines, which are part of the Rehabilitation Act Amendments of 1998 called Section 508. The law requires federal agencies to provide information technology that is accessible to federal employees and citizens who have disabilities. Both sets of guidelines help you create more accessible web content, so which should you use? If you are designing a web site for the federal government, you must follow the 508 guidelines, but for general public web sites, the W3C guidelines will suffice. The next section examines the WCAG 2.0 guidelines.

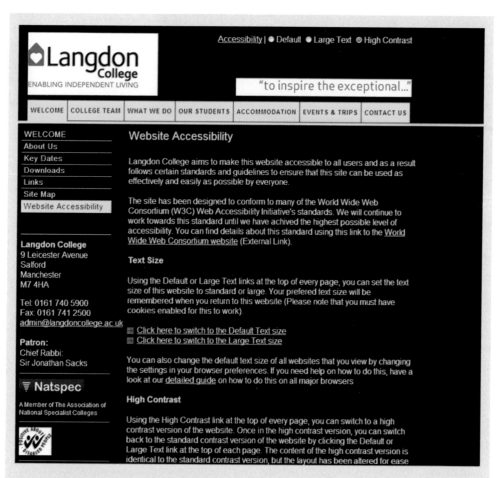

Figure 2-33: Langdon College web site high-contrast version
www.langdon.info

Note

To find out more about the W3C's Web Accessibility Initiative, go to www.w3.org/WAI/. The site includes many guidelines and standards to build accessible web content and explains the release of WCAG 2.0 in detail. You can learn more about the adaptive devices and assistive technologies for accessible browsing at www.w3.org/WAI/intro/people-use-web/Overview .html. Finally, you can read the Section 508 guidelines at www.section508.gov.

WCAG 2.0 Guidelines

WCAG 2.0 consists of four main guidelines, which state that web content must be:

> **Perceivable**—Information and user interface components must be perceivable by users.

> **Operable**—User interface components must be operable by users.

> **Understandable**—Information about the user interface and its operation must be understandable by users.

> **Robust**—Content must be robust enough to be interpreted reliably by a wide variety of user agents, including assistive technologies.

A number of tips, summarized in the following sections, help define the goal of each guideline. Each tip is followed by a detailed explanation.

> **Note** To find a quick reference guide to the new WCAG 2.0, see www.w3.org/WAI/WCAG20/quickref.

Perceivable Content

WCAG 2.0 includes the following tips to help you provide perceivable content in your web pages:

> Provide text alternatives for any nontext content so that it can be changed into other forms people need, such as large print, Braille, speech, symbols, or simpler language.

> This guideline ensures that all nontext content is available as electronic text. For example, use the alt attribute to describe the function of each visual element. You will learn about using the alt attribute in Chapter 8.

> Provide synchronized alternatives for multimedia.

> This guideline ensures that users can access multimedia content. For example, provide captioning and transcripts of audio and descriptions of video as alternatives to the multimedia content.

> Create content that can be presented in different ways (for example, spoken aloud, in a simpler layout, and so on) without losing information or structure.

> This guideline ensures that information is available in a form that all users can perceive. For example, the best way to meet this guideline is to build well-structured content with separate presentation information (as you learned in Chapter 1). This practice ensures that the structure and relationship of the content does not change, no matter what assistive device or software the user chooses.

> Make it easier for people with disabilities to see and hear content, including separating foreground from background.

This guideline ensures that the default presentation is as usable as possible to people with disabilities, making it easier for users to separate foreground information from the background. This basic tenet of web design, often ignored, is to make sure that information presented on top of a background contrasts sufficiently with the background. You will learn more about this principle in Chapter 8. This guideline also applies to spoken text, so that background sounds do not interfere with understanding the spoken text.

Operable Content

WCAG 2.0 includes the following tips to help you provide operable content in your web pages:

> Make all functionality available from a keyboard.

You should ensure that all actions that can be performed with a mouse or other input device can also be performed with a keyboard.

> Provide users who have disabilities enough time to read and use content.

Many users with disabilities take longer to complete tasks than the average user. For example, some text scrolls animate text across the page faster than users with disabilities can read the text. This guideline ensures that these users can complete tasks within their comfort zone.

> Do not create content that is known to cause seizures.

Some users with seizure disorders can have a seizure triggered by flashing visual content. The purpose of this guideline is to avoid content that flashes or blinks quickly enough to cause a seizure—for example, avoid the deprecated <blink> element that causes text to flash on and off.

> Provide ways to help users with disabilities navigate, find content, and determine where they are.

This guideline ensures that users can find the content they need and keep track of their location, as you read previously in the "Plan for Clear Presentation of Your Information" section in this chapter. This is a sound and essential design principle when planning for the general public as well as for users who have disabilities.

Understandable Content

WCAG 2.0 includes the following tips to help you provide understandable content in your web pages:

> Make text content readable and understandable.

This guideline ensures the greatest legibility and readability of text. Many characteristics of this guideline are simple, sound design techniques that you will read about in Chapter 7. These techniques include limiting the line length of text, providing appropriate white space, and avoiding large chunks of italic text.

> Make web pages appear and operate in predictable ways.

The purpose of this guideline is to help users with disabilities by presenting content and navigation options in a predictable order from web page to web page, as you learned in the "Creating a Unified Site Design" section earlier in this chapter. Users who employ screen magnifiers see only part of the screen at one time. A consistent page layout makes it easier for them to find navigation bars and other repeated components. Placing page elements in the same relative order within a web site allows users with reading disabilities to focus on the desired area of the screen, rather than spending additional time looking for what they want.

> Help users avoid and correct mistakes that do occur.

This guideline ensures that users can detect when they have made an error—for example, when entering data into a form. Typical error indicators, such as color-coded text or an icon, may not be enough to alert the user. Additional indicators such as sound or highlighted text can aid the user in identifying incorrect entries.

Robust Content

WCAG 2.0 includes the following tips to help you provide robust content in your web pages:

> Maximize compatibility with current and future user agents, including assistive technologies.

This guideline ensures compatibility with current and future browsers, especially assistive technology browsers. To meet this guideline, use standards-compliant markup and validated code, as described in Chapter 1. Present content in standard ways that assistive technology software can recognize and with which it can interact.

Note *You can check your web site for web accessibility compliance by using www.achecker.ca.*

Chapter Summary

Web sites have a wide variety of looks. It is easy to see why so many web designers get caught up in the medium and forget their message. The lure of technology makes it easy to overlook that you are still trying to communicate with words and pictures, just as humans have for centuries. Adapting those elements to online display for effective communication is the challenge.

Plan a site that stands out and delivers its message. If you stick with the principles you learned in this chapter, you can present information that is both accessible and engaging.

> Craft an appropriate look and feel, and stick with it throughout your site. Test and revise your interface by paying close attention to the demands of online display.

> Make your design portable by testing it in a variety of devices, screen resolutions, browsers, operating systems, computing platforms, and connection speeds.

> Plan for easy access to your information. Provide logical navigation tools, and do not make users click through more than two or three pages before they reach the information they are seeking.

> Design a unified look for your site. Strive for smooth transitions from one page to the next. Create templates for your grid structure, and apply them consistently.

> Use active white space as an integral part of your design. Use text, color, and object placement to guide the user's eye.

> Know your audience, and design pages that suit their needs, interests, and viewing preferences.

> Leverage the power of hypertext linking. Provide enough links for users to create their own paths through your information.

> Design your text for online display, considering the differences between formatting for the screen and formatting for the printed page.

> Choose the suite of devices, browsers and operating systems you will use to test your site. Although you will include the latest versions of Firefox, Safari, Opera, Internet Explorer, and Google Chrome, consider testing in older versions of each browser as well.

> Decide how browser specific your site will be. In most cases, your goal is to create a site that is widely accessible to multiple browsers. To ensure the greatest compatibility with a variety of browsers, be sure to follow W3C coding standings, validate your code, know your audience, and test your work.

> Resolve to test your work continually as you build your site. Test with multiple browsers at different screen resolutions and at different connection speeds and on different devices.

⟩ Remember to build in accessibility from the beginning of your design efforts to make sure your content is available to everyone.

Key Terms

active white space—White space used deliberately as an integral part of your design that provides structure and separates content.

cache—The browser's temporary storage area for web pages and images.

content management system (CMS)—Software that allows editing and publishing of content to different formats, such as a desktop and mobile web site.

grid—A layout device that organizes the web page, providing visual consistency.

look and feel— The overall character of the interface the user must navigate on a web site.

media queries—CSS statements that let you specify different style rules for different media destinations. For example, an HTML document could be displayed with different fonts for print or screen.

passive white space—The blank area that borders the screen or is the result of mismatched shapes in a layout.

responsive design—A method of designing web sites that are adaptable to a wide range of devices from mobile phones to desktop monitors.

screen resolution—The width and height of the computer screen in pixels.

Review Questions

1. Make a list of human factors to consider when building a web site.

2. Make a list of technical factors to consider when building a web site.

3. What design guidelines will you follow to ensure compatibility?

4. How does browser caching affect web design?

5. How do multiple screen resolutions affect web design?

6. Name three ways to create a unified look for your site.

7. Describe two methods of designing for multiple screen resolutions. Note the advantages and disadvantages of each method.

8. How does a grid layout enhance web design?

9. Explain active versus passive white space.

10. List three ways to create a smooth transition between pages of a web site.

11. List two benefits of consistently placing navigation tools.

12. Describe the difference between reading and scanning a page.

13. Describe three web page viewing patterns.

14. Name three ways to focus a user's attention.

15. Describe why using "Click Here" as link text is ineffective.

16. Describe the benefits of textual links.

17. Name three differences between paper-based and screen-based design.

18. Describe a good strategy to format text for online display.

19. Describe the four main guidelines in the WCAG 2.0 for designing accessible web sites.

Hands-On Projects

1. Browse the web for examples of web sites that exhibit good web design.
    a. Using a screen-capture program, such as the snipping tool in Windows, capture web pages from a web site that show two levels of information. For example, capture the main page of a web site and a secondary page. Describe how the layouts for the two pages suit their information types and the needs of their users.
    b. Use the graphic tools in a word-processing program or presentation program to include screen callouts with the web page images you capture. The callouts should indicate the unifying characteristics of the pages, such as shared colors, fonts, graphics, and page layout. (A callout is an arrow or line that connects to explanatory text. Many figures in this book have callouts, including Figure 2-5.) For example, Microsoft Word includes a callout tool in its collection of shapes.
    c. Indicate the areas of active white space and passive white space.
    d. Describe whether the design of the site is appropriate for the content.

2. Browse the web for examples of poor web design on mainstream web sites.
    a. Using a screen-capture program, capture web pages from the web site that show two levels of information. For example, capture the main page of a web site and a secondary page.
    b. Indicate with screen callouts the jarring or distracting inconsistencies of the site, such as abrupt changes in any design elements, including theme and layout.
    c. List detailed recommendations for improving the site design.

3. Write a short essay critiquing a web site's design. Describe the structural layout of the site, and determine whether information is presented clearly and is easily accessible.

4. Browse the web for sites that use unique navigation methods. Write a short essay describing why the method is or is not successful, or prepare a short slide presentation that you can present to your class.

5. Test cross-browser compatibility.
    a. Make sure you have recent versions of at least two current browsers installed on your computer. (See "Hands-On Project 1" in Chapter 1 if you need to download and install a browser.) If possible, have a smartphone or tablet available as well.

b. Browse a variety of web sites. Make sure to view various pages of the sites in different browsers and on different devices.

   c. Write a detailed description of how the various sites appear in the browsers you have chosen. Look for text, layout, and graphic inconsistencies.

6. Test accessibility software. Download a trial version of one of the following screen-reading programs. Navigate to different web sites, and use the tool to read the site. Close your eyes while listening. Write a short essay describing your experience.

   › Jaws (*www.freedomscientific.com/downloads/jaws/jaws-downloads.asp*)

   › Window Eyes (*www.gwmicro.com/Window-Eyes/Demo*)

Individual Case Project

Visualize the page design for your site by sketching a number of page layouts for different information levels of the site. Figure 2-34 shows a sample page sketch. For example, sketch the main page, a secondary page, and a content page. You do not have to be concerned with the exact look of the elements, but be prepared to indicate the main components of the pages, such as headings, navigation cues, link sets, text areas, and so on.

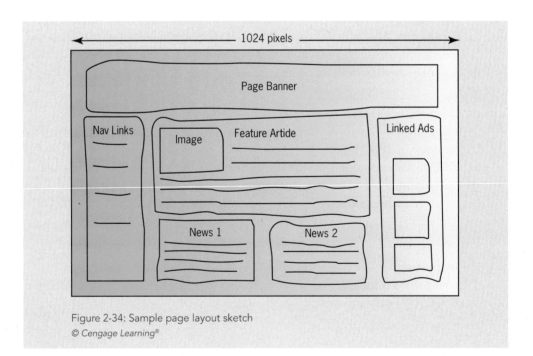

Figure 2-34: Sample page layout sketch
© *Cengage Learning®*

Start to organize your site. Create a visual diagram that indicates the main page, section pages, content pages, and so on. Indicate the links between the pages. Indicate whether you will provide alternate navigation choices such as a table of contents and site map.

Team Case Project

Work individually to create your view of the page designs for your site. Sketch a number of page layouts for different information levels of the site. For example, sketch the main page, a secondary page, and a content page, similar to the example shown in Figure 2-34. You do not have to be concerned with the exact look of the elements, but be prepared to indicate the main components of the pages, such as headings, navigation cues, link sets, text areas, and so on.

Next, meet and work as a team to create the team's page layouts by combining the best ideas from the individual page designs. Organize your site. Create visual diagrams that indicate the main page, section pages, content pages, and so on. Indicate the links between the pages. Indicate whether you will provide alternate navigation choices such as a table of contents and site map.

SITE PLANNING

When you complete this chapter, you will be able to:

> Understand the web site development process

> Create a site specification

> Identify the content goal

> Analyze your audience

> Build a web site development team

> Create conventions for filenames and URLs

> Set a directory structure

> Create a site storyboard

> Publish your web site

> Test your web site

A good web site design requires a detailed initial planning phase. Before starting to code your site, pick up a pencil and paper and sketch out your site design. Creating the stylistic conventions and conceptual structure of your site beforehand saves time during development. Whether you are creating a single personal web site or working on a professional web development team, you save time and improve quality by thoroughly planning the site design and development process before you start creating it. This chapter walks you through planning and building a framework for your site, resulting in more efficient development when you build your web site.

Understanding the Web Site Development Process

What are your objectives for building a web site? You may want to gain visibility, provide a service, sell a product, create a community, attract new customers, or disseminate information. Although the content may vary, a good project outcome requires a sound development process to ensure that you have valid and achievable goals for your site.

A good project plan encompasses all stages of the project and is accessible to everyone involved. The complexity and depth of each stage of the planning process can vary based on the complexity of the site. In commercial web site development, a project manager controls and disseminates the project plan using tools such as Microsoft Project to create charts and track all phases of production.

You can choose from many types of models of the web site development process and use one as a framework for planning your site development. Figure 3-1 shows a typical high-level project plan. The stages in this illustration would match scheduled calendar dates that are milestones in the project plan. The lifecycle of the project is the complete project plan from inception to completion. Stages can overlap at different points in the process. Most design experimentation should occur at the beginning of the project; as the project evolves, design changes must decrease and the design must become stable to ensure a successful implementation. Major design changes cannot be introduced late in the project without significant rework and risk of extending the project schedule.

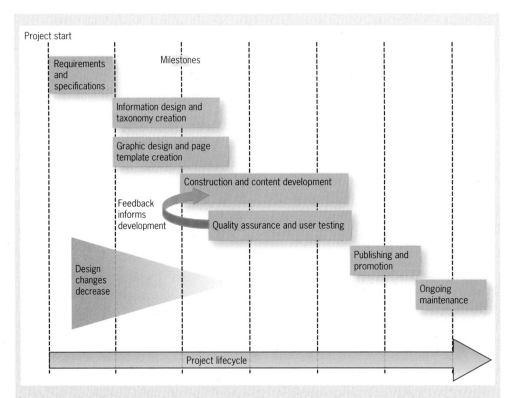

Figure 3-1: Web development project lifecycle
© Cengage Learning®

Requirements and Specifications

In this stage of a web development project, the client presents the requirements for the web site. Requirements are the list of customer needs, such as search capability, tabbed menu navigation, branding requirements, mobile site design, integration with a content management system, and anything else that will create the desired outcome for the site. The web project team must analyze these requirements for viability and then break them down into tasks. This is a good time to assess the talents of the team members to make sure all requirements can be met.

If programming is needed for the site, those tasks should be separated into their own software development life cycle. Applications have special needs, such as quality assurance and security, that are best addressed in their own project plan. Development of software applications and web site design can occur concurrently and then be integrated for user testing.

The web project team works with the client during the requirements and specifications stage to analyze and define the audience. After analyzing and defining requirements and determining the user profile, the team prepares a project specification that contains the design requirements, page layout sketches, audience definition, and technical requirements. The specification will guide you to the next stages of the project.

Information Design and Taxonomy Creation

In this stage, user analysis guides the designers as they prepare and test different organizations of the site content. The goal of this stage is to structure the site content in a way that is the most meaningful and easiest to navigate by the intended user. During this stage, the taxonomy of the site information is developed. A *taxonomy* classifies and names content in a hierarchical structure. The taxonomy of the site directly translates to the navigation through the top-level content topics down to individual pieces of information that the user is looking for. The taxonomy is often reflected in topic section names and in the navigation and menu system of the site.

Graphic Design and Page Template Creation

At the same time designers are testing the organization of the site information, they prepare design sketches and page mockups to represent page layouts that will be used in the site. All page layouts start with a mockup that is usually just a sketch of the desired design. Designers can submit the page layout mockups to the web site stakeholders for discussion and critique. Generally, you create a mockup for each page layout in the web site. A sketch of a proposed design, as shown in Figure 3-2, indicates the general layout of a web site home page.

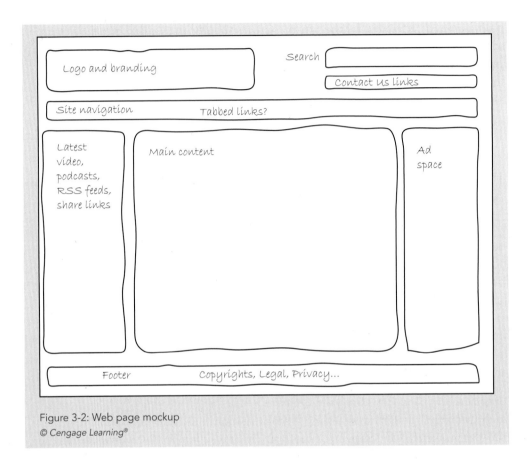

Figure 3-2: Web page mockup
© Cengage Learning®

These mockups can be easily edited and changed based on feedback and input from the design team. As the design becomes more stable, the mockup can evolve to a more refined state, often called a **wireframe**. Wireframes show a more complete version of the page designs, often including navigation elements, search functions, advertising space, and other similar elements. The wireframes offer stakeholders a more complete view of what the final design will look like. Designers also use wireframes to gain insight and reactions from content developers and software engineers and to test design changes. Remember that it is always easier to make changes to a page mockup or wireframe than it is to a web site once you have started coding it.

Figure 3-3 shows a wireframe that builds on the page design articulated in the mockup sketch in Figure 3-2.

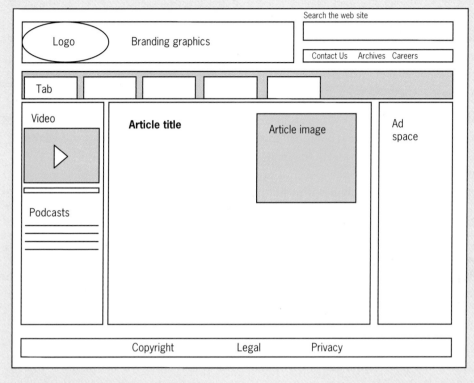

Figure 3-3: Sample wireframe for page layout
© Cengage Learning®

Note You can find freeware wireframe software tools at the following web sites:

Pencil (http://pencil.evolus.vn)

Gliffy (www.gliffy.com/wireframe-software)

Construction and Content Development

When the design stage is mostly complete and page designs are stable, the construction stage can begin. This stage encompasses all of the technical development of the site, including page coding and validation, application development, and content preparation. Some testing occurs during this stage of loading content in page templates and evaluating the performance of applications or multimedia.

Quality Assurance and User Testing

As the site construction nears completion, the quality assurance and user testing phase validates the design of the site. The development team performs various tests for cross-browser and device compatibility, accessibility to all users, and connectivity at different bandwidths. They test links and all user interfaces, data forms, and multimedia technologies. Usability testing ensures that users can access content, navigate through the site, and understand the taxonomy.

Publishing and Promotion

During this stage, the site is published to the web or the organization's intranet, and the client begins to publicize and promote the site. This includes making the web site address available in all collateral media, such as print and broadcast; advertising on other web sites; registering with search engines; distributing press releases; and starting publicity campaigns.

Ongoing Maintenance

This stage begins the moment the site goes live, as web content must be updated and kept fresh to remain vital. New sections of content may be added that restart certain phases of the project lifecycle, such as new audience definitions, designs for new content areas, or the design and development of new interface elements or interactive features.

Creating a Site Specification

Start your planning by creating a site specification; this is the design document for your site. If you completed the Individual or Team Case Project at the end of Chapter 1, you created a basic draft of a project proposal. You can use some of that information in your site specification. After you read this chapter, you will be able to answer additional questions about your site. You can return to the site specification as you build your site to help maintain your focus. If you are providing a web site design to a client, the site specification is the first document the client sees that establishes the basic site design.

Answer the following questions in your site specification:

> Who is the client for the web site? This is not the user, but the person who has employed you to build a web site. Are you creating a personal site (in which case, you are the client), or are you part of a design team working independently or for a corporation or nonprofit organization? What do you or the client company or organization hope to gain from creating and maintaining a web site?

> Can you write a mission statement that succinctly states the site's focus and goals?

> What are the requirements for the web site? Look to your client for their list of wants. Explicitly state the required functions that you want the site to contain.

> Are the requirements feasible? Do you or your team have the necessary technical and editorial skills to build the site that the client requires?

> How will you judge the success of the site? What are the factors you can use to assess the effectiveness of the site?

> Who is the target audience? What are some of their common characteristics? How can you find out more about your target audience?

> What are the limiting technical factors affecting your site?

> What is the budget? What are the schedule or target milestone dates? Are the dates realistic and achievable?

> Is this a new site or an upgrade to an existing site? If this is a site upgrade project, what can you learn from the first version of the site?

> What hardware and software are needed to complete the project?

> Have you thought about maintenance, which is an everyday aspect of the web site life cycle? Consider how much maintenance the design will require and how easy these tasks will be to perform.

Identifying the Content Goal

Consider carefully the type of site you are building. What you and the design team want the web site to accomplish and what your users want from your site may differ. For example, designers and other stakeholders are often more concerned with the look than the feel. Don't let this deter you from advocating for the user. Your users probably care more about how quickly they can find information. Adopt your user's perspective, and let your user analysis guide your content decisions. Think about the type of content the web site will provide and what will give the greatest value to your user. Look at your search and navigation capabilities carefully to ensure easy and direct access. Look to the web for examples of how best to present, organize, and focus your content. The following types of web sites demonstrate ways to focus your content.

> **Billboard**—These sites establish a web presence for a business or commercial venture. In many cases, they are informational and offer limited content, acting as an online business card or brochure rather than offering web-based interaction. Many smaller businesses build this type of site first and then expand as necessary, adding functions when needed.

> **Publishing**—Every major newspaper and periodical publishes both to print media and to the web. These web sites are some of the most ambitious in breadth and depth of content, often containing multiple levels of information with many page designs. Many publishing sites use a content management system (CMS) to dynamically create web pages, drawing content from the same databases that produce their paper-based versions. This allows their authors to write the article once, but have it published to multiple destinations, such as the daily newspaper and the web site.

> **Portal**—Portals act as gateways to the web and offer an array of services including searching, email, shopping, news, and organized links to web resources. Many major search engines have been converted into portals to attract more users. These sites are often heavy with advertising content, which is their main source of revenue.

> **Special interest, public interest, and nonprofit organization**—These sites include news and current information for volunteers, enthusiasts, novices, a specific audience, or the general public. Public-service web sites contain links, information, downloadable files, addresses, and telephone numbers that can help you solve a problem or find more resources. Nonprofit organizations can state their manifestos, seek volunteers, and foster grassroots virtual communities.

> **Blog**—Short for *weblog*, a blog is a personal web page that reflects the personality and interests of the author. No matter what your interest, a community of bloggers (blog authors) on the web is devoted to it. Many blogs are personal diaries or commentaries on life. Most blogs are published with tools that can archive content, provide comment threads that allow visitors to comment on blog posts, and offer built-in page designs. WordPress (*www.wordpress.com*) is a popular example of this type of software. There are literally millions of blogs on the web. You can find listings at *www.blogcatalog.com* and *www.blogarama.com.*

> **Social networking**—Sites such as Twitter, Facebook, Google+, and LinkedIn are the most visible of these types of virtual communities, which allow users to post profiles and connect with friends, family, and professional contacts. Users can share comments and exchange messages with their friends, play games, take surveys, and post photos, videos, and links to interesting sites. Social networking sites are the reason many people use the Internet.

> **Wikis**—A wiki is a type of online database that accepts contributions from multiple authors. Wikipedia is the most visible example of a wiki. Wikis are collaborative web sites that allow contributors to use wiki software to easily edit information and create linked web pages. Wikis allow any user to comment on or change another user's entries. Appropriate anywhere that collaboration and sharing of content is needed, wikis are used in both academic and commercial environments.

> **RSS (Real Simple Syndication)**—This is a syndication service provided by web sites that automatically distribute content. RSS is a format for web feeds that update users who subscribe to this service. RSS feeds usually contain headlines or summaries of content, which users read with a software tool called an RSS reader. RSS readers are built into the major browsers. With RSS feeds, any author updates to a web site are automatically transmitted to subscribers.

> **Virtual gallery**—The web is a great place to show off samples of all types of art and design. Photographers and artists can display samples of their work; musicians and

bands can post audio files of their songs; writers can offer sections of text or complete manuscripts. However, keep in mind that any copyrighted material you display on a web site can be downloaded to a user's machine without your permission. As a solution to this problem, software companies such as Digimarc (*www.digimarc.com*) offer digital watermarking technology that lets artists embed digital copyright information in their electronic files as a deterrent to piracy of proprietary content. This information cannot be seen or altered by the user.

> **E-commerce, catalog, and online shopping**—The web as shopping medium continues to expand as more users improve their Internet access and learn to trust the security of online commerce. Web commerce competes successfully with traditional retailing, offering many advantages over mail-order shopping, such as letting the customer know immediately whether an item is in stock. Other types of commerce on the web include stock trading, airline ticketing, online banking, auctions, and more. Many software vendors offer turnkey systems that can be integrated with existing databases to speed the development of a commerce site. A good electronic commerce (e-commerce) site provides users with quick access to the items they want, shopping carts and wish lists to store their choices, detailed product descriptions, and easy, secure ordering and checkout.

> **Product support**—The web is a boon to consumers who need help with a product. Manufacturers can disseminate information, upgrades, troubleshooting advice, documentation, and online tutorials through their web sites. Companies that provide good product support information on the web typically find that the volume of their telephone-based customer support calls decreases. Software companies especially benefit from the web; users can download patches and upgrades and use trial versions of software before they buy. Companies may also provide a forum for users of their products to discuss issues, tips, and other information.

> **Intranet and extranet**—Private web sites are often hosted on a company intranet or extranet. An intranet is a smaller, limited version of the Internet on a company's private local area network (LAN), accessible only to those who are authorized to use their network. Many companies have telecommuting employees who need access to company policies, documentation, parts lists, pricing information, and other materials. These employees can be reached via an extranet, which is a part of the private intranet extended outside the organization via the Internet. Web sites on an intranet or extranet are typically developed by companies for use by employees, customers, and suppliers.

Analyzing Your Audience

If possible, analyze your audience and produce an audience definition, a profile of your average user. If you are building a new site, work from your market research, look at sites with content similar to yours, and try to characterize your average user.

If you have an existing user base, contact your typical users and try to answer the following questions:

> What do users want when they come to your site? Can they easily find desired content?
> What initially attracts your visitors? What brings them back for multiple visits to your site?
> What type of computer and connection speed does your typical visitor have?

Though your users may fit no common profile, you can gather information about them in a few ways. One way is to include an online feedback form in your site. Figure 3-4 shows an online survey from the State of Maine web site (*www.maine.gov/portal/survey.html*).

The survey asks users about their experiences visiting the web site. Some questions restrict responses to a list of choices, while others pose open-ended questions to elicit a variety of responses from the user concerning the visual and information design of the site.

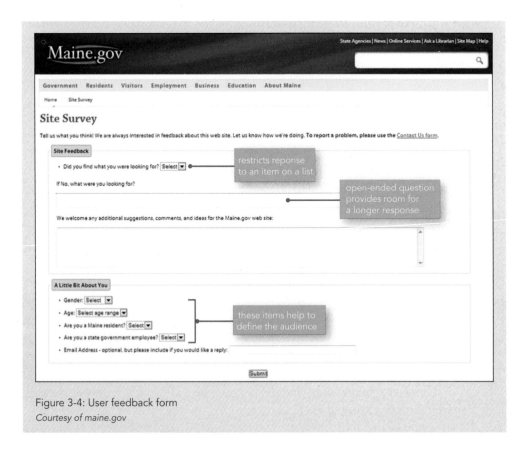

Figure 3-4: User feedback form
Courtesy of maine.gov

If you cannot survey your users, or if you feel you are not getting good survey results, try to adopt a typical user's perspective as you define your audience. Here are some questions to consider:

> Who are the typical members of your audience? Are they male or female? Do they have accessibility issues? What is their level of education? What is their reading and vocabulary level? What is their level of technical aptitude?

> Why do people come to your site? Do they want information? Do they want to download files? Are they looking for links to other web sites?

> Do you have a captive audience, such as a base of loyal customers that want up-to-date information? Are you designing for an intranet, where users are employees of an organization?

> If users are unfamiliar with the site, will they know what you offer?

> How often will users return to your site? Why would they come back?

> What computing platform do your users have? What is their typical connection speed? What type of browser do they use? If you are on an intranet, does it use standards for browsers, connection, and screen resolution?

> Whose skills do you need to build the site? Who will create the graphics, code the pages, and write the text? Do you have the talent, software, and economic resources that you need? Will the results meet the expectations of your users?

Refine your content and presentation even after your site is built and running. Continue soliciting user feedback to keep your site focused and the content fresh.

Note | *You can set up a free web-based survey with SurveyMonkey (www.surveymonkey.com).*

Using Web Analytics

Web analytics are statistics that are gathered by web servers and then analyzed. Web servers track and record various usage and traffic statistics in files called server logs. Reporting tools can aggregate and analyze the data in these files to help you learn about your users and their activity on your web site. The data gathered by the web servers contains relevant details about your visitors, including how they came to your site, whether by bookmark, search engine, or a link on another web site. If visitors used a search engine, you can see what term they entered to find your site. You can see what pages are most visited, and even see an approximate view of where your users are geographically located, based on their identifying Internet address.

Figure 3-5 shows statistics from W3 Counter (*www.w3counter.com*), a free web analytics tool that you can add to any web site. This figure shows two important web log statistics: page views and unique visitors. A page view is the number of times a page is viewed by a user, which could be multiple times by the same user. The unique visitor statistic tracks the number of unique visitors to a site, no matter how many times they access the same page. So the page views tell you which pages are the most popular with your users, while the unique visits tell you how many different users are visiting your site.

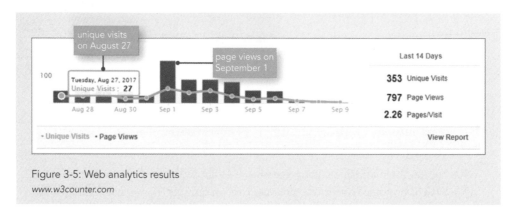

Figure 3-5: Web analytics results
www.w3counter.com

In addition to viewing how many times users accessed your pages and visited your site, you can also see which browsers they used, as shown in Figure 3-6.

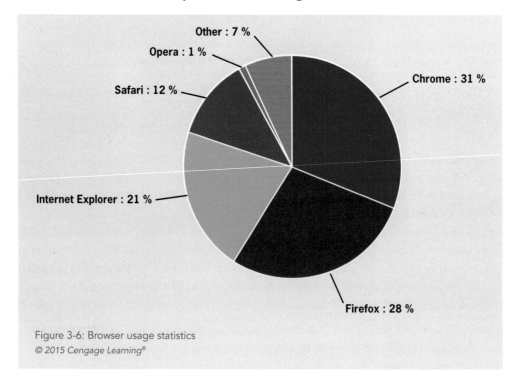

Figure 3-6: Browser usage statistics
© 2015 Cengage Learning®

Web analytics are an important method of determining details about your users and how they interact with and traverse the content areas of your site. Use web analytics as a guide to enhancing your content and making important pages accessible, but remember that they are not flawless. Many factors can affect the results you receive. Statistics are just one method of determining user preferences.

Identifying Technology Issues and Accessibility Constraints

Make your best effort to identify any technological limitations or advantages that members of your audience share. As you read in Chapter 2, you have to make assumptions about the user's browser, connection speed, device type, and screen resolution. Users in developed countries have greater access to the latest hardware technologies and consistent high-speed Internet connections. Many other users throughout the world may be using older equipment. Think about where your users are located and what their technology level might be. Are they using mobile devices to access your site? Test in different environments and with different technologies to make sure these users can view your site.

You also need to consider the physical capabilities of users that are visiting your site. How do they interact with your content? Are they older users with sight or dexterity issues? Will they need to magnify your pages to read your text? Many types of physical limitations can affect the way people interact with a computer.

When planning a web site, you can identify accessibility constraints in the following ways:

> Review the WCAG 2.0 and Section 508 accessibility guidelines as needed.

> If you are building a new web site, plan for accessibility.

> If you have an existing web site, assess the current accessibility of your content.

> Review case study examples of real-life accessibility implementations. You can find case studies at *www.w3.org/WAI/bcase/resources.html.*

> Discuss accessibility solutions, authoring tools, and evaluation tools with other web professionals.

Study your web statistics and user feedback. If you think your user is the average person browsing the web, you may have to adopt settings that represent the lowest common denominator to satisfy the widest audience. If you find that your users are savvy about technology and use the latest computer hardware and software, higher resolution and connection speeds may apply. If you are designing an intranet site, you may have the luxury of knowing your users' exact operating systems and browser versions. Whatever the particulars, make sure to design at an appropriate level, or you risk losing visitors.

Identifying Software Tools

Determining the software requirements for your web site is important during the planning process. Try to choose software that matches the complexity and needs of your site so that you do not end up with a tool that is either underequipped or overspecialized. Simple web sites, including many student sites, can be built with one of the many shareware and freeware tools (see Table 3-1) that are available on the web. As your site and skills grow, you might choose to move up to more robust tools such as Adobe Creative Cloud or individual Adobe tools such as Dreamweaver (*www.adobe.com*). Microsoft offers Visual Studio as its web site design tool. These tools offer complete coding, design, and site management capabilities. You may also need graphics tools (discussed in Chapter 8), database software, and online credit and shopping programs, based on the skills and talents of the members of your web site team, as described in the next section.

One popular type of software is shareware, programs that you can download and use for a trial period. After the trial period, users can register the software for a relatively small fee compared to commercially produced software. Another type of software already mentioned in this chapter is freeware, which is available free of charge or with an optional donation fee if you want to contribute to support the software developers' efforts. Table 3-1 lists freeware HTML development tools.

DEVELOPMENT TOOL	PLATFORM	URL
Amaya	Windows, Macintosh, Linux	www.w3.org/Amaya
BBEdit	Macintosh	www.barebones.com
Bluefish	Windows, Macintosh, Linux	bluefish.openoffice.nl
Firebug Firefox add-on	Windows, Macintosh, Linux	addons.mozilla.org/en-US/firefox/addon/1843
Kompozer	Windows, Macintosh, Linux	www.kompozer.net
SeaMonkey	Windows, Macintosh, Linux	www.seamonkey-project.org
Trellian	Windows	www.trellian.com/webpage

Table 3-1: Freeware Web Site Development Tools
© 2015 Cengage Learning®

Building a Web Site Development Team

Although one person can maintain small web sites, larger sites require groups of people filling a variety of roles. Of course, these roles can overlap, and many aspects of site design require collaboration to solve a problem. The following are examples of the types of talent necessary to build a larger, well-conceived site.

> **Project management**—The project management team is responsible for planning, scheduling, and integrating the many tasks that it takes to create a web site. They create the milestones for deliverables and balance the staffing resources to keep the project on schedule and within budget. The project manager coordinates communication among team members and keeps the focus on the deliverables promised to the client.

> **HTML developers**—These are the people responsible for creating the HTML code, conforming to standards, validating code, troubleshooting the site, and testing the site across different operating systems and web browsers.

> **Designers**—Designers are the graphic artists responsible for the look of the site. They use graphic design software such as Adobe Photoshop or Adobe InDesign. Designers are responsible for the wireframes, page template design, navigation icons, color scheme, and logos. If your site uses photographic content, the designers are called upon to prepare the photos for online display. They might also create animations and interactive content.

> **Writers and information designers**—Writers and information designers prepare content for online display, including taxonomies, hypertext linking conventions, and navigation paths. In addition, writers may be responsible for creating a site style guide and defining typographic conventions, as well as consistency, grammar, spelling, and tone. They also work closely with the information and graphic designers to develop page templates and interactive content.

> **Application developers**—Developers write the software programs and scripts you need to build interaction into your site. They may write a variety of applications in different programming languages for user interaction or write back-end applications that interact with a database. Application developers are also responsible for the security of the site and use these skills to help prevent attacks on the site's databases and customer information.

> **Database administrators**—The people who are responsible for maintaining the databases play an important role in commercial web sites. Databases store all the information for customer transactions and e-commerce. Database administrators, application developers, and HTML developers work together when designing front-end forms used

to collect data from the user. Database administrators are also responsible for data security backup and data recovery.

> **Server administrators**—Get to know and appreciate the technical people who run your web server. They take care of the sticky technical issues such as firewalls, ports, internal security, file administration, and backup procedures. Consult with them to determine your web site's default filename and directory structure. They also can manage the server logs that contribute to your web analytics reporting to determine how many visitors your site is attracting, where the visitors are coming from, and what pages they like best.

Skills at Work | *Effective Stakeholder Communication*

As a member of a web development team, you might find yourself debating design elements for the web site of a client or employer. Be aware that you are not making the decision on your own—you are solving a problem for people who have a stake in the success or failure of the site. Identify who these stakeholders are, and ask for their advice and recommendations. As you work on the site design and run into problems, be sure to let the stakeholders know you need to make a decision so they can contribute ideas and solutions. If possible, provide options and ask stakeholders to select one or two. Clear, frequent (though not overwhelming) communication avoids surprises and disappointments.

Creating Conventions for Filenames and URLs

Before you sit down at the keyboard, plan the filename conventions for your site. Find out from your system administrator what type of operating system your web server uses. Typically you develop your web site locally on a PC or Macintosh and upload the files to the web server as the last step in the publishing process. If the web server runs a different operating system from your local development system, any filename or directory structure inconsistencies encountered in transferring your files to the server may break local URL links.

Naming Files

A filename's maximum length, valid characters, punctuation, and sensitivity to uppercase and lowercase letters vary among operating systems, as described in Table 3-2. Note that the ISO 9660 Standard is the base file-naming convention designed to work across all operating systems.

OPERATING SYSTEM AND FILE SYSTEM	FILENAME CONVENTIONS
ISO 9660 Standard	Maximum of eight letters followed by a period and a three-letter extension; allowed characters are letters, numbers, and the underscore (_)
Newer PCs: Windows 8, Windows 7, Windows Vista, Windows XP (NTFS), Windows 2000 (NTFS), Microsoft Windows/NT (NTFS)	Maximum of 255 letters; all characters allowed except \ / * " < > | : ?
Older PCs: Windows 98 (FAT32), Windows 95 (VFAT), DOS, and Windows 3.× (FAT file system)	The same as ISO 9660 but with the following additional characters allowed: $ % ' ` - @ ^ ! & [ ] ( ) # This format is also compatible with newer PC operating systems
Newer Macintosh: O/S 8.1 to OS X	Maximum of 255 characters; all characters allowed except the colon (:)
Older Macintosh: Operating systems released before O/S 8.1	Maximum of 31 letters; all characters allowed except the colon (:) This format is also compatible with newer Macintosh operating systems
UNIX	Maximum of 255 letters; all characters allowed except the forward slash (/) and spaces

Table 3-2: File Naming Conventions
© 2015 Cengage Learning®

Case Sensitivity

If you have an image file named Picture.gif, for example, and you reference that file as <img src="picture.gif">, the image is displayed properly on a Macintosh or Windows machine. On a UNIX server, however, the image does not load properly because UNIX is case sensitive; Picture.gif and picture.gif are recognized as two different files. It is best to use lowercase letters for all filenames, including filenames in your HTML code.

Character Exceptions

As shown in Table 3-2, it is best when naming your files to leave out special characters such as <, >, /, \, &, *, and blank spaces to ensure cross-platform compatibility. Some special characters that may be valid on one operating system will not work on another.

File Extensions

You must use the correct file extensions to identify your file to the browser. HTML text files created in HTML-editing programs commonly end in .htm or .html unless they are generated dynamically by an application. In this case, they may have extensions such as .asp, .php, or others. You also must use the correct filename extensions to identify image file formats. For example, Joint Photographic Experts Group (JPEG) files must end in .jpg or .jpeg; Graphics Interchange Format (GIF) files must end in .gif; and Portable Network Graphic (PNG) files must end in .png.

Choosing the Correct File-Naming Conventions

It is best to set conventions for your filenames right from the beginning of the web development process. Create a list of conventions and refer to it frequently. Here are some guidelines to remember:

> Don't use spaces in your filenames; use underscores instead. Instead of *about web design.html*, use *about_web_design.html*.

> Avoid all special characters. Stick to letters, numbers, dashes, and underscores.

> Use all lowercase letters for your filenames.

Default Main Page Name

Every web site has a default main page that appears when the browser requests the main URL of the site, such as *www.google.com* rather than a specific file. In this instance, the web server must decide which file to provide, which is usually the home page of the site. The default is generally index.html, but others may apply based on site particulars. Always check with your system administrator to verify the correct main page filename.

Using Complete or Partial URLs

Although you may know that URLs are the addresses you type into your browser to access a site, you may not realize that there are two types of URLs: complete and partial.

Complete URLs

A Uniform Resource Locator (URL) is the unique address of a file's location on the World Wide web. A complete URL includes the protocol the browser uses, the server or domain name, the path, and the filename. Figure 3-7 shows an example of a complete URL.

Figure 3-7: Parts of a complete URL
© Cengage Learning®

In this example, *http* is the protocol, and *www.yoursite.com* is the domain name. The path shows that the destination file, *mobility.html,* resides in the *business/trends* folder. Use complete URLs in your HTML code when linking to another web site.

Partial URLs

Use a partial URL when you are linking to a file that resides on your own computer or server. Partial URLs omit the protocol and domain or server name, and specify the path to the file on the same server. Files that reside in the same directory (or folder) need no path information other than the filename. The following code shows an example of a partial URL.

```
<a href="mobility.html">link text</a>
```

Setting a Directory Structure

You will probably build your web site on a computer that is different from the computer that hosts your site. Keep this in mind when you are designing the directory and file structure. All of the files for your web site will need to be transferred from your computer to the web server that will be hosting your site. Because your files will be transferred to another computer, any URLs you specify to link to other pages in your site must include paths that are transferable. This is why you should never specify an absolute path in your partial URLs. An absolute path points to the computer's root directory, indicated by a leading (forward) slash in the file path:

```
/graphics/logo.gif
```

If you include the root directory in your partial URLs, you are basing your file structure on your development machine's file system. If the files are moved to another machine, the path to your files will not apply, and your site will include links that do not work because the browser cannot find the files.

To avoid this problem, use relative paths. Relative paths tell the browser where a file is located relative to the document the browser currently is viewing. Because relative paths are not based on the root directory, they are transferable to other computers.

Using a Single Folder Structure

One easy way to ensure that all your path names are correct is to keep all of your HTML and image files in the same directory. Because all files are kept together, the only information you need to put in the src or href attribute is the filename itself. In Figure 3-8, User2 has a simplified directory structure. To reference the file logo.gif, User2 adds the following code in one of the HTML files:

```
<img src="logo.gif">
```

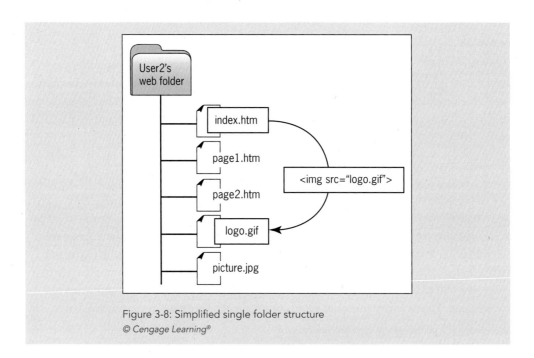

Figure 3-8: Simplified single folder structure
© Cengage Learning®

Using a Hierarchical Folder Structure

The simple directory structure shown in the preceding example is fine for a small web site, but as your site grows, you may want to separate different types of content into separate folders for ease of maintenance. Take a look at the relative file structure for User2's web site as depicted in Figure 3-9. Notice that User2's web folder contains three HTML files and one subfolder named images, which contains the graphics and pictures for the web site.

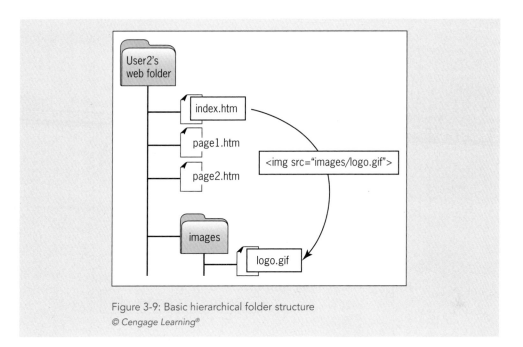

Figure 3-9: Basic hierarchical folder structure
© Cengage Learning®

To include the image file logo.gif in index.htm, User2 adds the following code to index.htm:

```
<img src="images/logo.gif">
```

The path in the src value tells the browser to look down one level in the directory structure for the images folder and find the file logo.gif. The path to the file is relative to the file the browser is viewing. This type of relative file structure can be moved to different machines; the relationship between the files does not change, because everything is relative within the web folder.

User2's web site may need a more refined directory structure, as shown in Figure 3-10. In this example, common files such as the index (the home page) and site map reside in the top-level folder. Multiple subfolders contain chapter and image content. Two linking examples are illustrated in this figure:

> **Example 1**—To build a link from page1.htm (in the chapter1 folder) to index.htm, use ../ in the path statement to indicate that the file resides one level higher in the directory structure, as shown in the following code:

```
<a href="../index.htm">Home</a>
```

> **Example 2**—To include the image file logo.gif in page1.htm, use ../ to indicate that the file resides in the images folder, which is one level higher in the directory structure, as shown in the following code:

```
<img src="../images/logo.gif">
```

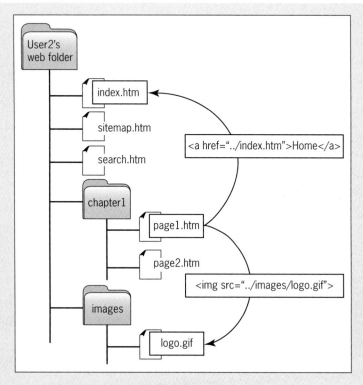

Figure 3-10: More segregated hierarchical folder structure
© Cengage Learning®

Creating a Site Storyboard

Plan your site by creating a storyboard flowchart that shows the structure, logic, and taxonomy behind the content presentation and navigation choices you offer. You can sketch your site with paper and pencil or create it using flowchart diagramming software such as Microsoft Visio. Sometimes it is helpful to use sticky notes or cards to plan the structure visually. This method lets you easily move pages from one section or level to another. Whichever method you choose, this preliminary planning step is one of the most important in planning your site. You can move pages and whole sections of content freely, plan navigation paths, and visualize the entire site. This is the stage at which to experiment and refine your designs. Once you have started coding the site, it is much more difficult and time consuming to go back and make major changes. Remember to adhere to the file-naming conventions for each of your pages.

Organizing the Information Structure

Think about your users' information needs and how they can best access the content of your site. How should your information design map look? Review the sample structures provided in this section, and judge how well they fit your information. Your design may incorporate several structures, or you may have to adapt the structures to your content. Each sample structure is a template; you may have more or fewer pages, sections, topics, or links. You may choose to use bidirectional links where only single-direction links are indicated. Use these examples as starting points and design from there.

Linear Structure

The linear information structure, illustrated in Figure 3-11, guides the user along a straight-forward path. This structure lends itself to booklike presentations; once into the content, users can navigate backward or forward. Each page can contain a link back to the main page if desired. Pages may also contain links to a related subtopic. If the users jump to the subtopic page, they only can return to the page that contains the subtopic link. This structured navigation returns them to the same point in the content path.

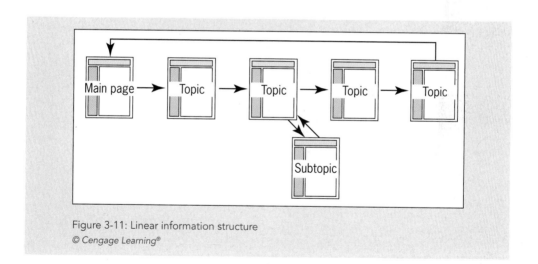

Figure 3-11: Linear information structure
© Cengage Learning®

Tutorial Structure

The tutorial structure illustrated in Figure 3-12 is perfect for computer-based training content such as lessons, tutorials, or task-oriented procedures. The tutorial structure builds on the simple linear structure in Figure 3-11. The user navigates the concept, lesson, and review pages in order. Because the lessons use hypertext, users can leave the lesson structure and return at any time. They also can choose the order of lessons and start anywhere they want. Notice that the table of contents, index, and site map pages are linked to—and from—all pages in the course. Within each lesson users can navigate as necessary to familiarize themselves with the content before they review. This structure can be adapted to fit content needs; for example, the group of pages in the illustration could be one section of a larger training course.

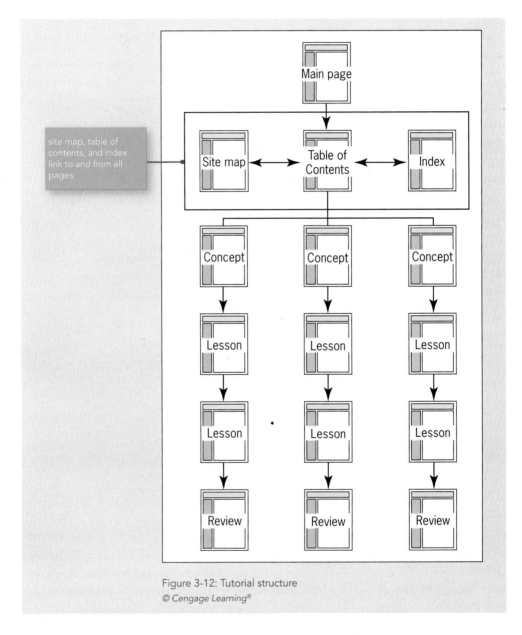

Figure 3-12: Tutorial structure
© Cengage Learning®

Web Structure

Many smaller sites follow the web content structure illustrated in Figure 3-13, which is nonlinear, allowing the user to jump freely to any page from any other page. If you choose to use this type of content structure, make sure that each page includes clear location information and a standardized navigation bar that not only tells users where they are, but where they can go.

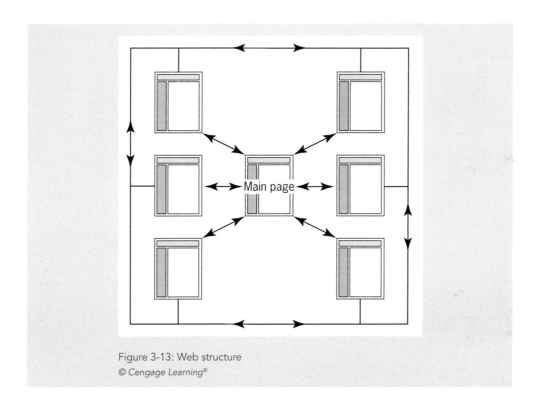

Figure 3-13: Web structure
© Cengage Learning®

Hierarchical Structure

The hierarchical structure illustrated in Figure 3-14 is probably the most common information design. It lends itself to larger content collections because the section pages break up and organize the content at different levels throughout the site. Navigation is primarily linear within the content sections. Users can scan the content on the section page and then choose the content page of their choice. When they finish reading the content, they can return to the section page. The site map allows users to navigate freely throughout the site. A navigation bar on each page lets the user jump to any section page, the main page, and the site map.

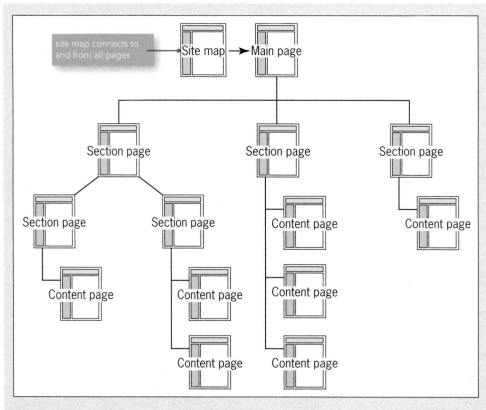

Figure 3-14: Hierarchical structure
© Cengage Learning®

Cluster Structure

The cluster structure illustrated in Figure 3-15 is similar to the hierarchical structure, except that every topic area is an island of information, with all pages in each cluster linked to each other. This structure encourages exploration within a topic area, allowing the user to navigate freely through the content. All pages contain a navigation bar with links to the section pages, main page, and site map.

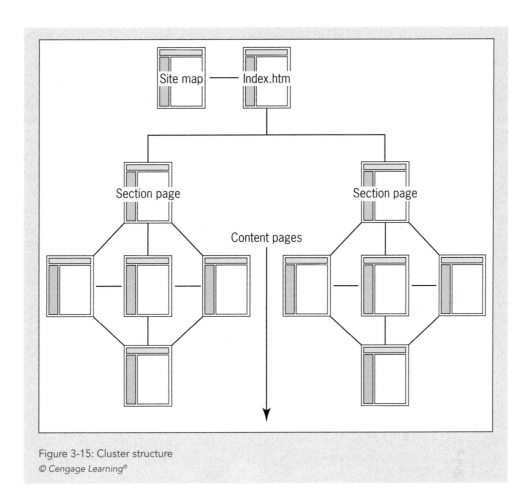

Figure 3-15: Cluster structure
© Cengage Learning®

Catalog Structure

The catalog structure illustrated in Figure 3-16 is ideally suited to online shopping. The user can browse or search for items and view specific information about each product on the item pages. Users can add items to their shopping cart as they shop. When they are finished, they can review the items in their shopping cart and then proceed to checkout, where they can enter payment information and finalize the order.

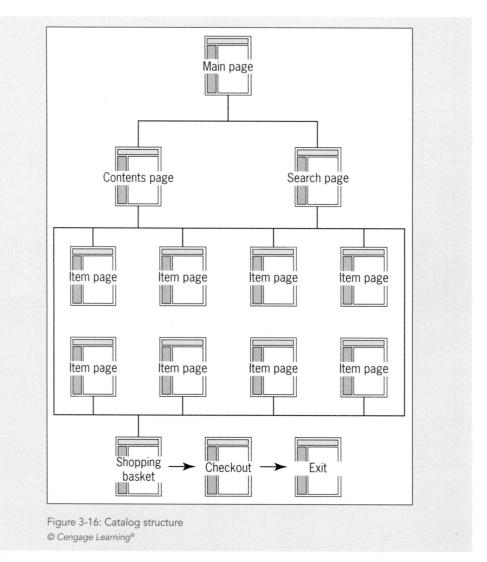

Figure 3-16: Catalog structure
© Cengage Learning®

This type of web site requires back-end data transaction processing to handle the shopping cart tally, process credit card information, and generate an order. Businesses that want to set up an e-commerce site can purchase ready-made commerce software packages or develop their own from scratch.

Publishing Your Web Site

To make your web site live, you transfer your web site files to a **web server**, a computer connected to the Internet and running server software. The software lets the computer use the Hypertext Transfer Protocol (HTTP) to serve HTML files to web browser clients. Unless your company or organization has a web server and hosts its own content, you must use the services of a web hosting provider. After you choose a server to host your files, you need to select file transfer software and upload the web site files from your development machine to the web server.

Choosing a Web Hosting Service Provider

One of the most important choices you will make is your web hosting service. This is the company that hosts your web pages on a web server, making them available to anyone who knows your URL. Most web hosting companies offer hosting services for both personal and business use. The web host provides you with Internet access, email accounts, and space for a personal or business web site. If you are building a web site for business use, your web host can register a personalized domain name for your web site.

Small web sites (around 15–20 pages of content) do not need much more than 1 or 2 MB of server space to hold all of the HTML pages and graphics. Your web hosting package should provide at least 10 MB of space so your web page has room to grow. Many personal web sites can be hosted on the free server space that comes with many cable and digital subscriber line (DSL) modem connection packages. Check with your service provider to see if this feature is available.

Larger or more complex sites need more server space, especially if you have downloadable files, archives, lots of graphic content, or databases. If you are building a business web site, seek out larger hosting services that are more appropriate for hosting a complex commercial site.

Shopping for a web hosting service can be a confusing experience, as no two are exactly alike. Do some research and learn about offerings from different vendors. The following sections discuss the features you should seek in a hosting service.

> **Note**
>
> Some web hosting services offer proprietary design tools and templates to assist you in building a web site. It's best to avoid these types of tools as they tend to tie you to one vendor and make it difficult to switch hosting services and post your web site elsewhere.

Accessible Technical Support

Technical support is not a feature—it is an absolute necessity. Make sure that your web hosting service has competent, accessible customer service. When you are checking into web hosting services, call and talk with the companies' customer service representatives. Tell them how experienced you are with computers, and let them know what you hope to accomplish (such as the type of web site you want to build). Note how long you are on hold when waiting to speak with customer service. Make sure that you are comfortable with the level of service you receive on these initial inquiries.

Email Addresses

All web hosting accounts come with a variable number of email addresses that you can assign to yourself and anyone else you want to have an email address that uses your domain name. If you are part of a group, multiple mailbox accounts let each person receive his or her own email. You can also set up a catchall email address that will accept any email sent to your web site regardless of whether it is addressed to you.

SQL Database Support

If you are planning on any type of electronic commerce or customized data presentation, you need database support. Databases that understand Structured Query Language (SQL), a programming language that lets you select information from a database, are the most common and powerful type of database.

Secure Socket Layer (SSL) Support

The Secure Socket Layer (SSL) is an Internet communications protocol that allows encrypted transmission of data between the user and the server. SSL is necessary if you are planning to set up an electronic commerce site or transmit other sensitive data. Encrypting the data ensures the information cannot be read if the transmission is intercepted.

Registering a Domain Name

A domain name is an alias that points to your actual location on the web server, as shown in Figure 3-17. User2 has purchased the domain name *www.mysite.com*. The actual path to User2's content is hidden, and the visitor to the site sees only the domain name.

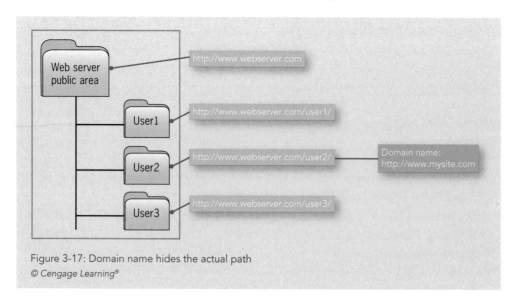

Figure 3-17: Domain name hides the actual path
© Cengage Learning®

Domain names are managed by the Internet Corporation for Assigned Names and Numbers (ICANN). ICANN has agreements with a number of vendors to provide domain name registration services. You can purchase a domain name through a vendor, and they will register it with ICANN. Current popular domain name registration services include Go Daddy (*www.godaddy.com*), Register.com (*www.register.com*), and Dotster (*www.dotster.com*).

Web Hosting Service Comparison Checklist

Use the following checklist when you compare web hosting services:

> Is the web host local or national?

> What are the details of the different hosting packages? How much server space comes with each? What are the limits (if any) on uploads and downloads?

> Are there bandwidth limits for the number of visitors your site receives per month?

> Does the web host offer technical support? When are support staff available?

> How many email addresses do you get with an account?

> Does the web host provide software, such as a File Transfer Protocol (FTP) client to transfer files over the Internet?

> Does the web host support the latest connection technologies?

> Does the web host offer enhanced services, such as SQL database support, SSL, a scripting language environment, and support for streaming audio and video?

Uploading Files with the File Transfer Protocol

To publish your pages on the web, you must send your HTML code, images, and other files to the web server. To do this, you need File Transfer Protocol (FTP) software, often called an FTP client. Some HTML-authoring software, such as Microsoft Visual Studio and Adobe Dreamweaver, include built-in software packages that let you upload files to your web server. You also can choose from many shareware and freeware FTP programs to upload your files. Table 3-3 lists some popular FTP clients available as freeware and shareware. Visit a shareware site to search for other FTP clients.

FTP CLIENT	WEB SITE
Cute FTP—Shareware	*www.cuteftp.com*
Filezilla—Freeware	*http://filezilla-project.org*
FireFTP (Firefox plug-in)—Freeware	*http://fireftp.mozdev.org*

Table 3-3: Freeware and Shareware FTP Clients
© 2015 Cengage Learning®

When you have decided which FTP software to use, verify the FTP address from your web host. You also need your account name and password, which in most cases automatically points your FTP client to the proper directory on the server.

To upload your files, start your FTP program and connect to your web server using the FTP information provided by your web host. Your password allows you write access to your directory on the web server, which means you can copy files to and from the directory. Once the FTP client has connected to the web server, you can choose the files you want to transfer.

> **Note** As discussed earlier in this chapter, make sure that you maintain the exact directory structure on the web server that you used on your development computer to ensure that all relative file paths are correct.

Select the files that you want to upload in your local directory listing and transfer them to the web server. The first time you go live with your web site, you must transfer all the files. Later you upload only the files that you have updated. After the files reach the web server, they are available for access immediately on the web.

After you find a web hosting service and publish your web site to the web, it is time to test your web site in the real-life Internet environment.

Testing Your Web Site

Even though you performed tests throughout the development of your web site, you need to continue testing after you post your files live on the web. If possible, load your files to the web server and test them before making your URL available for users to access the web site. If you have enough server space, you may want to establish a testing area on the web site. You can do this by creating a subdirectory in your public HTML directory. Do not publicize the URL so that your testing area can remain private.

Testing Considerations

Always test in as many different environments as possible. Remember to test for the following web design variables:

> **Multiple browsers**—Test your site using as many browsers as you can to make sure your work is portable and is displayed consistently.

> **Multiple operating systems**—If you can, test your site from different operating systems. If you have a PC as a development machine, use a Macintosh for testing, and vice versa. You even can run different versions of UNIX on a single PC, if necessary.

Because computer chip development moves at a lightning pace, machines become outdated quickly. You can often find discounted and used machines that are Internet capable as long as they have a good Internet connection. Because you won't use these machines to *develop* web sites (only to *view* them), you do not need the latest or most powerful hardware. You can also use a virtual machine for testing. A virtual machine is a software emulator that acts like a physical computer, allowing you to test different operating systems no matter what type of computer you have. Subscription services are available on the web, such as *www.browserstack.com*, that emulate Windows, Mac OS X, and Linux operating systems.

› **Connection speeds**—Do not rely on the same connection speed when testing your web site, especially if you work in a corporate environment where the connection to the Internet usually is faster than the average user's. Go to a friend's house, library, or Internet café and access your web site from there. Test for download times at different connection speeds.

› **Device types**—Test at different screen resolutions and device types to make sure your pages are displayed consistently on all screen sizes.

› **Links**—Use a link validation tool to ensure that all of your links connect to a live page. Link validation tools are built into many HTML editors and are available as stand-alone tools. Many web sites also offer validation, including the W3C's link validator at *validator.w3.org/checklink*. Any pages that link outside of your web site need to be tested on a regular basis to make sure that the destination site has not moved, shut down, or posted content different from what you expect.

› **Security testing**—A critical step in the testing process is finding security vulnerabilities in applications running on your web site. Although this is usually the responsibility of web application developers, security testing is an important part of any web development plan. You can read more about this at the Open Web Application Security Project at *https://www.owasp.org/*.

Usability Testing

Usability testing can be as simple as asking a few colleagues to look at your web site, or as complex as conducting extensive formalized testing. Some companies invest in special user testing labs with videotaping and one-way mirrors to record user behavior, or software that can track users' mouse movements and eye coordination as they look at their web site. Even if you do not need this level of sophisticated testing, you should perform some type of user assessment of your work. The goal of user testing is to determine whether your web site is easy to navigate with easy access to content. Consider the following points when planning for user testing of your site.

Vary Your Subjects

Draw your test subjects from a variety of backgrounds, if possible. Gather test subjects who are representative of your target audience. Find users with varying computing skills and familiarity with the information. Avoid using friends as test users, as they may only compliment your work. You might choose to let users look at the web site on their own time, but you can learn a lot by watching users interact with your web site. Make sure to let them navigate and use the web site without any outside help from you. Just stand back and watch.

Formalize Your Testing

Formalize your testing by creating repeatable methods of testing your web site. Prepare a series of questions for users to answer after viewing the web site. Give users a specific task to complete or have them find a particular piece of information. Let them rate the ease of completing such tasks. Compare the results from different users to find any problem areas in navigation. Administer the same testing methods to a variety of users, and watch for trends and consistencies. This lets you compare results or focus on a particular feature of the web site.

Develop a Feedback Form

Develop a feedback form that users can fill out after they have tested the web site. Include a set of criteria, and let them rate the web site on a progressive scale, or ask them a series of open-ended questions. You also may want to provide the feedback form online, allowing users to offer feedback directly from the web site. Here are some sample questions you might ask:

> Did you find the information you needed?

> Was it easy or difficult to access the information you needed?

> Did you find the web site visually attractive?

> Did you find the content easy to read?

> Did you find the web site easy to navigate?

> Did you think the information was presented correctly?

> Did the information have enough depth?

> What area of the web site did you like the best? Why?

> What area of the web site did you like the least? Why?

> Would you recommend the web site to others?

Chapter Summary

A successful web site is the result of careful planning. The steps you take before you actually start coding the site save you time, energy, and expenses in the long run. Remember these guidelines for successful planning:

> Become familiar with the stages in the web site development cycle.

> Start with pencil and paper; your ideas are less restricted and you can easily revise and recast without recoding. Follow a development process to ensure fewer revisions and design reworking.

> Write a site specification document. You will find it invaluable as a reference while building your site.

> Identify the content goal by adopting your users' perspective and learning what they expect from your site.

> Analyze your audience, and create an audience profile. Focus your site on the users' needs, and continue to meet those needs by adapting the site based on user feedback.

> An effective site is most commonly the result of a team effort. Leverage different skill sets and experience to build a web site development team.

> Plan for successful implementation of your site by creating portable filename conventions. Build a relative file structure that can be transferred to your web server without a hitch.

> Select a basic information structure for your site, and then manually diagram it, customizing it to the needs of your site.

> Shop carefully and compare features when you are looking for an ISP or web host. Consider the future disk space and technology needs of your content.

> Download and learn to use an FTP client for the often-repeated task of transferring files to your web site.

> After your web site is live, test it against the basic web variables of browser, operating system, display resolution, device type, and connection speed.

> Test your web site with a variety of users. Listen carefully to their feedback to identify trouble spots in your information design.

> Plan for the maintenance, upkeep, and redesign of your web site. Keep your content up to date. Let users know when you have made updates to the web site.

Key Terms

audience definition—A profile of your average user.

complete URL—An address of documents and other resources on the web that includes the protocol the browser uses to access the file, service, domain name, the relative path, and the filename.

extranet—A private part of a company's intranet that uses the Internet to securely share part of an organization's information.

File Transfer Protocol (FTP)—A standard communications protocol for transferring files over the Internet.

freeware—Programs available free of charge or with an optional donation fee.

Internet service provider (ISP)—A company that provides Internet access and web site hosting services to individuals and organizations.

intranet—A private collection of networks contained within an organization. Intranet users gain access to the Internet through a firewall that prevents unauthorized users from getting into the intranet.

ISO 9660 Standard—A file system standard published by the International Organization for Standardization (ISO) that supports computer operating systems such as Windows, classic Mac OS, and UNIX-like systems, to exchange data.

page view—The number of times a web page is viewed by a user.

partial URL—A Uniform Resource Locator (URL) that omits the protocol and server name and only specifies the path to the file relative to one another on the same server.

requirements—The list of customer needs for a web site, such as search capability, tabbed menu navigation, specific color and branding requirements, or anything else that will create the desired outcome for the site.

Secure Socket Layer (SSL)—Communications software that allows transmission of encrypted secure messages over the Internet.

shareware—Software that is distributed free so users can try it before they buy it. Users then can register the software for a relatively small fee compared to software produced commercially. Shareware usually is developed by individuals or very small software companies, so registering the software is important.

site specification—The design document for your web site.

Structured Query Language (SQL)—A programming language that lets you select information from a database.

taxonomy—A classification and naming of content in a hierarchical structure.

Uniform Resource Locator (URL)—The global address of documents and other resources on the web.

virtual machine—A software emulator that acts like a physical computer.

web analytics—The analysis of statistics that are gathered by web servers.

web server—A computer connected to the Internet that runs server software. The software lets the computer use the Hypertext Transfer Protocol (HTTP) to serve HTML files to web browser clients.

wireframe—Web page mockups that represent page layouts for a web site.

Review Questions

1. List three technology constraints that can affect the way a user views your web site's content.

2. Consult your web server administrator when you need to determine the _____ and _____ for your site.

3. Name two inconsistencies that can cause broken links when you upload your files to a web server.

4. List three characteristics of filenames that vary by operating system.

5. The international standard for filenames is often called _____.

6. Which computer operating system is case sensitive?

7. Rename the following files so that they are compatible across all operating systems:

   My file.html _____

   case:1.html _____

   #3rdpage.html _____

8. What is the default main page filename for a web site?

9. What are the two types of URLs?

10. What are the four parts of a complete URL?

11. What type of URL links to another server?

12. What type of URL links within a server?

13. What affects the format of the URL for your web site?

14. What is the benefit of purchasing a domain name?

15. Why should you never specify an absolute path in partial URLs?

16. What is the benefit of building a site with relative paths?

17. Files that reside in the same directory need only the _____ to refer to each other.

18. List two benefits of diagramming your site before you start coding.

19. How does a web site become live?

20. List the six variables to consider when testing your web site.

Hands-On Projects

1. Browse the web, and find a site you like. Write a brief statement of the web site's goals.

2. Browse the web, and find web sites that fit the following content types:
   a. Billboard
   b. Publishing
   c. Special interest
   d. Product support

   Write a short summary of how the content is presented in each web site, and describe how each site focuses on its users' needs.

3. Browse the web, and find a site that does not contain a user survey form. Write a user survey with 10–15 questions that you would use on the site. Tailor the questions to the site's content and goals.

4. Browse the web to find examples of the following site structures, and describe how the content fits the structure. Think about how the chosen structure adds to or detracts from the effectiveness and ease of navigation of the site. Determine whether the site provides sufficient navigation information. Print examples from the site, and indicate where the site structure and navigation information is available to the user.
   a. Linear
   b. Hierarchical

5. Browse the web to find a site that uses more than one structure type, and describe why you think the site's content benefits from multiple structures. Consider the same questions as in Project 3-4.

6. Are there other structure types that are not described in this chapter? Find a site that illustrates a structure content not covered in this chapter. Create a flowchart for the site, and determine how it benefits from the different structure type.

7. Write a test plan for your web site.
   a. Create a section for each design variable.
   b. Spell out the exact steps of the test and the different variables to be tested. State explicitly which browsers and versions should be used, and on which operating system. Detail the different screen resolutions and connection speeds. List the exact pages that should be tested.
   c. Walk through the test procedure to test its validity.

8. Write a sample user feedback questionnaire.

9. Write a maintenance plan for your web site.
    a. Include a schedule of content updates for the different sections of the web site.
    b. Include a schedule of design reviews.
    c. Plan for link maintenance.

Individual Case Project

Write a site specification for the site you defined in Chapters 1 and 2. Include as much information as possible from the project proposal you completed at the end of Chapter 1. Make sure to include a mission statement. Determine how you will measure the site's success in meeting its goals. Include a description of the intended audience. Describe how you will assess user satisfaction with the site. Include technological issues that may influence the site's development or function.

Prepare a detailed flowchart for your site using the preliminary flowchart you created at the end of Chapter 2. Create a filename for each page, using a consistent naming standard. Indicate all links between pages. Write a short summary that describes the flowchart. Describe why you chose the particular structure, how it suits your content, and how it benefits the user.

Use the page layouts you sketched in Chapter 2 to create wireframes. Download one of the free wireframe tools listed in this chapter, or use a drawing program to create the wireframes.

Team Case Project

Collaborate to write a site specification for the site you defined in Chapters 1 and 2. Include as much information as possible from the project proposal you completed at the end of Chapter 1. Make sure to include a mission statement. Determine how you will measure the site's success in meeting its goals. Include a description of the intended audience. Describe how you will assess user satisfaction with the site. Include technological issues that may influence the site's development or function.

Work individually to determine the information structure you think is optimal for the type of content your site will contain. Then meet and work as a team to determine the information structure using the best pieces of each team member's information structure plan. Prepare a detailed flowchart for your site using the preliminary flowchart you created at the end of Chapter 2. Create a filename for each page, using a consistent naming standard. Indicate all links between pages. Write a short summary that describes the flowchart. Describe why you chose the particular structure, how it suits your content, and how it benefits the user.

Use the page layouts you sketched in Chapter 2 to create wireframes. Download one of the free wireframe tools listed in this chapter, or use a drawing program to create the wireframes.

CHAPTER

4

CASCADING STYLE SHEETS

When you complete this chapter, you will be able to:

> Recognize the benefits of using CSS

> Build a basic style sheet

> Use inheritance to write simpler style rules

> Examine basic selection techniques

> Apply basic selection techniques

> Use class and id selectors

> Use the <div> and <span> elements

> Use other selectors

Cascading Style Sheets (CSS) let you control the display characteristics of your web site. In this chapter, you examine the syntax of CSS and learn how to combine CSS rules with your HTML code. You start by examining the CSS style rules, and then you apply them to build a basic style sheet. You learn selection techniques to apply a particular style declaration to an element in your document. You learn about inheritance and how it affects your styles. The <div> and <span> elements let you apply styles to groups of elements or sections of text. More specific techniques include using the class attribute and id attribute to provide customized naming for your styles and applying the styles consistently across an entire web site. You learn about using pseudo-selectors and pseudo-elements to select and apply CSS styles to links and to create special effects such as hovers, generated content, drop caps, and typographic effects.

Recognizing the Benefits of Using CSS

Recall from Chapter 1 that Cascading Style Sheets were developed to standardize display information for web pages and to enhance the separation of style and content. The first version of CSS, named CSS 1, was released in December 1996. CSS 1 contained properties to control fonts, color, text spacing and alignment, margins, padding, and borders. CSS 2, released in May 1998, added positioning, media types, and other enhancements. Even though CSS offered web designers an easy-to-use and powerful method of controlling display properties, spotty browser support became a serious obstacle to the widespread adoption of the new style language. Finally, in May 2000, Internet Explorer (IE) 5 for the Macintosh became the first browser to fully support CSS 1.

Later, as CSS became more fully supported, inconsistencies across different browsers still made web development a matter of testing and retesting to make sure that CSS style rules were implemented correctly. It was only with the release of Internet Explorer 8 that all major browsers supported CSS 2.1, which was released in 2005.

The latest release of CSS is CSS level 3 (CSS3). Although work started on CSS3 in 1998, this version is still not a complete recommendation from the W3C in 2013. (In this context, a recommendation is the final stage of development by the World Wide Web Consortium (W3C), and means the release has been reviewed and tested extensively.) In CSS3, the W3C has broken CSS into modules, each of which contains a specific set of CSS properties. Although many features of CSS3 are now supported by the major browsers, always make sure to test for compatibility. You may decide to implement CSS3 features realizing that some browsers do not offer users the same result that they may see in other browsers. In some cases, these differences are negligible, so you can include the CSS3 feature without seriously affecting the user's view of your content. CSS3 properties are always indicated as such throughout this book so you can make informed decisions about which properties to implement.

> **Note** Web sites such as www.caniuse.com and www.quirksmode.org offer browser support cross-reference charts to help you determine which CSS properties are supported by different browser versions.

CSS Style Rules

In CSS, **style rules** express the style characteristics for an HTML element. A set of style rules is called a **style sheet**. Style rules are easy to write and interpret. For example, the following style rule sets all <p> elements in the document to blue text.

```
p {color: blue;}
```

A style rule is composed of two parts: a selector and a declaration. The style rule expresses the style information for an element. The **selector** determines the element to which the rule is applied. Selection is the key to working with CSS. As you will learn later in this chapter, CSS contains a variety of powerful selection techniques. By using the different types of selectors available, you build styles that affect an entire web site or you can drill down to one specific paragraph or word in a web page. The **declaration**, contained within curly brackets, details the exact property values. Figure 4-1 shows an example of a simple style rule that selects all <h1> headings and sets their color to red.

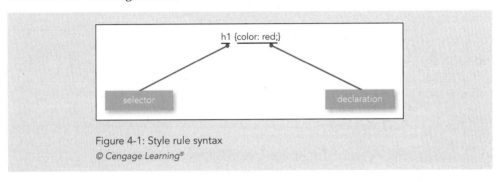

Figure 4-1: Style rule syntax
© Cengage Learning®

As illustrated in Figure 4-2, the declaration contains a property and a value. The **property** is a quality or characteristic, such as color, font size, or margin, followed by a colon (:). The **value** is the precise specification of the property, such as blue for color, 125% for font size, or 30px (pixels) for margin, followed by a semicolon (;). CSS contains a wide variety of properties, each with a specific list of values. As you will see later in this chapter, you can combine selectors and property declarations in a number of ways.

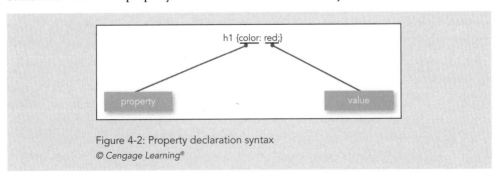

Figure 4-2: Property declaration syntax
© Cengage Learning®

This chapter uses a variety of CSS style rules as examples. Although you have not yet learned about their properties in detail, you will see that the CSS property names express common desktop publishing characteristics such as font-family, margin, text-indent, and so on. The property values sometimes use abbreviations such as *px* for pixel, percentages such as 200%, or keywords such as *bold*. You will learn about these properties and values in detail as you progress through this book.

Combining CSS Style Rules with HTML

You can combine CSS rules with HTML code in the following three ways:

> Inline style

> Internal style sheet

> External style sheet

Figure 4-3 shows the code for a single web page with all three methods of combining CSS style rules with the HTML.

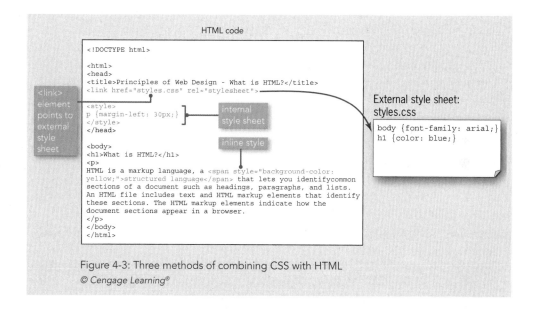

Figure 4-3: Three methods of combining CSS with HTML
© Cengage Learning®

Note
You can find all of the example files for this chapter at www.joelsklar.com/pwd6. You can use these files for practice, testing, and as inspiration for your project web sites.

As you review Figure 4-3, keep the following principles in mind:

> The <link> element in the document's <head> section points to an external style sheet named styles.css, which contains rules that set the body text to Arial and the <h1> heading to the color blue. This external style sheet can be linked from other documents as well, meaning these styles will be applied across multiple pages within the web site.

> The internal style sheet affects only the one document in which it is contained, applying a 30-pixel left margin to all paragraph elements within the document.

> The inline style within the paragraph affects only the span of words it surrounds, applying a yellow background to the words *structured language*.

In this example, the style rules from all three sources—external, internal, and inline—combine to create the finished look for this web page. This flexibility in the application of style rules is an enormous benefit to web designers, who can use external style sheets to set styles that apply across an entire web site while maintaining control over individual pages and elements as necessary. Each method is discussed in detail in the following sections.

Using External Style Sheets

Placing style sheets in an external document lets you specify rules for multiple web pages. This is an easy and powerful way to use style sheets because it lets you control the styles for an entire web site with one style sheet file. Additionally, external style sheets are stored in the user's cache, so once downloaded, they are referenced locally for every file on your web site, saving time for your user.

An external style sheet is simply a text document that contains the style rules. External style sheets have a .css extension. Here's an example of a simple external style sheet named styles.css:

```
h1 {color: white; background-color: green; }
h2 {color: red; }
```

The style sheet file does not contain any HTML code, just CSS style rules, because the style sheet is not an HTML document. It is not necessary to use the <style> element in an external style sheet.

Linking to an External Style Sheet

The <link> element lets you establish document relationships. It can only be used within the <head> section of a document. To link to an external style sheet, add the <link> element, as shown in the following code:

```
<head>
<title>Sample Document</title>
<link href="styles.css" rel="stylesheet">
</head>
```

The <link> element in this code tells the browser to find the specified style sheet. The href attribute states the relative URL of the style sheet. The rel attribute specifies the relationship between the linked and current documents. The browser displays the web page based on the CSS display information.

The advantage of the external style sheet is that you can state the style rules in one document and affect all the pages on a web site. When you want to update a style, you only have to change the style rule once in the external style sheet to automatically update all the pages that use it.

Using Internal Style Sheets

Use the <style> element to create an internal style sheet in the <head> section of the document. Style rules contained in an internal style sheet affect only the document in which they reside. The following code shows a <style> element that contains a single style rule:

```
<head>
<title>Sample Document</title>
<style>
h1 {color: red;}
</style>
</head>
```

Note

Older HTML code often includes a type attribute in the <style> element:

```
<style type="text/css">
```

The value "text/css" defines the style language as Cascading Style Sheets. In HTML5, the type attribute is not required, but it is often included because earlier versions of HTML required it.

Using Inline Styles

You can define the style for a single element using the style attribute, which is called an inline style.

```
<h1 style="color: blue;">Some Text</h1>
```

You generally use the style attribute to set a unique style for a single element or to override a style that was set at a higher level in the document, such as when you want a particular heading to be a different color from the rest of the headings on the page. (You'll learn more about overriding a style later in this chapter.) The style attribute is also useful for testing styles during development. You will probably use this method of styling an element the least, because it only affects one instance of an element in a document.

Writing Clean CSS Code

When you are creating external or internal style sheets, it is best to write CSS code that is consistent and easy to read. The flexibility of CSS syntax lets you write style rules in a variety of ways. For example, you've already seen style rules in this chapter that combine multiple declarations on the same line, as in the following code:

```
h1 {color: white; background-color: green;}
```

This technique is fine if you have simple styles, but style rules often contain many declarations that would be too hard to read in this format, especially when styles grow more complex, as shown in the following code:

```
p {font-family: arial, helvetica, sans-serif; font-size: 85%;
line-height: 110%; margin-left: 30px;}
```

This style rule is easier to read and maintain if you use a cleaner, more organized format as shown in the following code:

```
p {
    font-family: arial, helvetica, sans-serif;
    font-size: 85%;
    line-height: 110%;
    margin-left: 30px;
}
```

This format makes it easier to read the style rules, because all properties are consistently left-aligned with their values on the right.

Using Comments

CSS allows comments within the <style> element or in an external style sheet. CSS comments begin with the forward slash and asterisk characters (/*) and end with the asterisk and forward slash characters (*/). You can use comments in a variety of ways, as shown in the following code:

```
<style>
/* This is the basic style sheet */
h1 {color: gray;} /* The headline color */
h2 {color: red;} /* The subhead color */
</style>
```

Comments provide documentation for your style rules. Because they are embedded directly in the style sheet, they provide immediate information to anyone who needs to understand how the style rules work. Comments are always useful, and you should consider using them in all of your code, whether as a simple reminder to yourself or as an aid to others with whom you work.

Activity: Building a Basic Style Sheet

In the following steps, you build and test a basic style sheet. Save your file, and test your work in your browser as you complete each step. The new code to add is displayed in blue text. Refer to Figure 4-4 as you progress through the steps to see the results.

To build a basic style sheet:

1. Copy the **ch4activity1.html** file from the Chapter04 folder provided with your Data Files to the Chapter04 folder in your work folder. (Create the Chapter04 folder, if necessary.)

2. In your browser, open **ch4activity1.html**. When you open the web page, it looks like Figure 4-4.

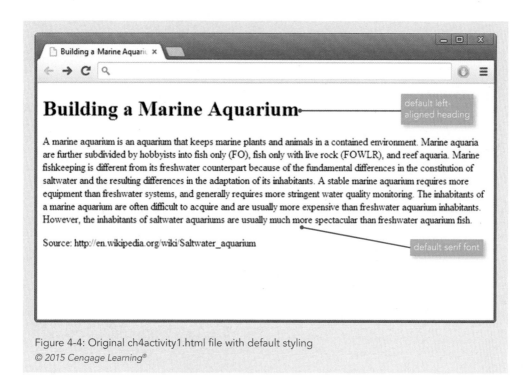

Figure 4-4: Original ch4activity1.html file with default styling
© 2015 Cengage Learning®

3. Open the **ch4activity1.html** file in your HTML editor, and examine the code. Notice that the file contains basic HTML code with no style information.

4. Add a <style> element in the <head> section to contain your style rules, as shown in blue in the following code. Leave a line or two of white space between the <style> tags to contain the style rules.

```
<head>
<title>Building a Marine Aquarium</title>
<meta http-equiv="Content-Type" content="text/html; charset=UTF-8">
<style>

</style>
</head>
```

5. Add a style rule for the <h1> element, as shown in blue in the following code. This style rule uses the text-align property to center the heading.

```
<style>
h1 {text-align: center;}
</style>
```

6. Save the file as **ch4activity1.html** in the Chapter04 folder in your work folder, and then reload the file in the browser. The <h1> element is now centered.

7. Add a style rule for the <p> element, shown in blue in the following code. This style rule uses the font-family property to specify a sans-serif font for the paragraph text. You will learn more about the font-family property in Chapter 5.

```
<style>
h1 {text-align: center;}
p {font-family: sans-serif;}
</style>
```

8. Save the file, and then reload it in the browser. Figure 4-5 shows the finished web page. Notice that the <p> element is now displayed in a sans-serif typeface and the <h1> heading is centered.

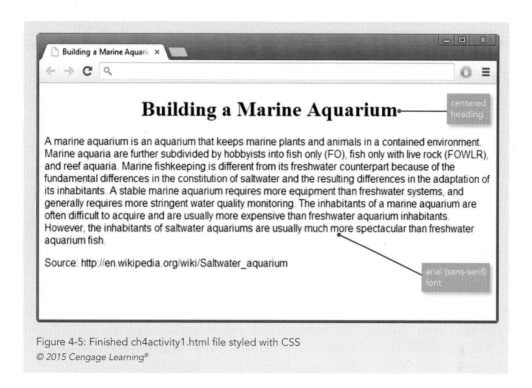

Figure 4-5: Finished ch4activity1.html file styled with CSS
© 2015 Cengage Learning®

Using Inheritance to Write Simpler Style Rules

The elements in an HTML document are structured in a hierarchy of parent and child elements. Figure 4-6 represents the structure of a simple HTML document.

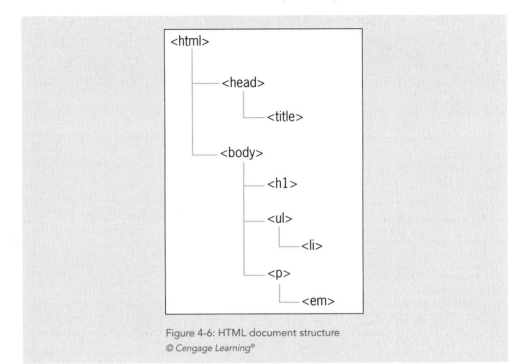

Figure 4-6: HTML document structure
© Cengage Learning®

Note the hierarchical structure of the elements. At the top, <html> is the parent element of the document. **Parent elements** contain nested elements called **child elements**. Both <head> and <body> are immediate child elements of <html>. Yet, <head> and <body> are parent elements as well, because they contain other nested elements. As you travel further down the document hierarchy, you find additional elements that are both parent and child elements, such as <p> and <ul>.

By default, most CSS properties inherit from parent elements to child elements, which is called **inheritance**. The CSS property descriptions in the following chapters and Appendix B list whether a property is inherited. Therefore, if you set a style rule for <ul> elements in the document shown in Figure 4-6, the <li> elements inherit the style rules for <ul>, unless you specifically set a rule for <li>.

You can style multiple document elements with just a few style rules if you let inheritance work for you. For example, consider the following set of style rules for a document.

```
<style>
h1 {color: red;}
p {color: red;}
```

```
ul {color: red;}
em {color: red;}
li {color: red;}
</style>
```

This style sheet sets the color to red for five elements in the document. Inheritance lets you write a far simpler rule to accomplish the same results:

```
<style>
body {color: red;}
</style>
```

This rule works because all of the elements are children of <body> and because all the rules are the same. It is much more efficient to write a single rule for the parent element and let the child elements inherit the style. Because <body> is the parent element of the content area of the HTML file, it is the selector to use whenever you want to apply a style across the entire document.

Examining Basic Selection Techniques

In this section, you review style rule syntax and learn about the following basic selection techniques:

› Using type selectors

› Grouping selectors

› Combining declarations

› Using descendant selectors

Using Type Selectors

As you learned previously, the selector determines the element to which a style declaration is applied. To review, examine the syntax of the style rule shown in Figure 4-7. This rule selects the <h1> element in the document and sets the text color to red.

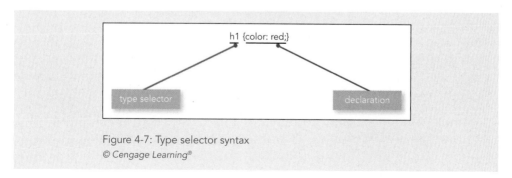

Figure 4-7: Type selector syntax
© Cengage Learning®

This rule uses a *type selector* to apply the rule to every instance of the element in the document. This is the simplest kind of selector, and many style sheets are composed primarily of type selector style rules, as shown in the following code:

```
body {color: gray;}
h2 {color: red;}
p {font-size: 85%;}
```

Grouping Selectors

To make your style rules more concise, you can group selectors to which the same rules apply. For example, the following style rules set the same declaration for two elements— they set the color of <h1> and <h2> elements to red:

```
h1 {color: red;}
h2 {color: red;}
```

These two style rules can be expressed in a simpler way by separating the selectors with commas and using one declaration for both elements:

```
h1, h2 {color: red;}
```

Combining Declarations

In many instances, you want to state multiple property declarations for the same selector. The following style rules set the <p> element to blue text and the size to 125% of the default font size:

```
p {color: blue;}
p {font-size: 125%;}
```

These two style rules can be expressed in a simpler fashion by combining the declarations in one rule. The declarations are separated by semicolons:

```
p {
    color: blue;
    font-size: 125%;
}
```

Using Descendant Selectors

A descendant selector (sometimes known as a contextual selector) is based on the hierarchical structure of the elements in the document tree. This selector lets you select elements that are the descendants of other elements. For example, the following rule selects only <em> elements that are contained within <p> elements. None of the other <em> elements in the document are affected.

```
p em {color: blue;}
```

Notice that the selector contains two elements, separated only by white space. You can use more than two elements if you prefer to choose more specific selection characteristics. For example, the following rule selects <em> elements within <li> elements within <ul> elements only:

```
ul li em {color: blue;}
```

Using the Universal Selector

The universal selector lets you quickly select groups of elements and apply a style rule. The symbol for the universal selector is the asterisk (*). For example, to set a default color for all elements within a document, use the following rule:

```
* {color: purple;}
```

You can also use the universal selector to select all children of an element. For example, the following rule sets all elements within a <div> element to a sans-serif typeface:

```
div * {font-family: sans-serif;}
```

The universal selector is always overridden by more specific selectors. The following style rules show a universal selector along with two other rules that have more specific selectors. In this example, the <h1> and <h2> rules override the universal selector for the <h1> and <h2> elements.

```
* {color: purple;}
h1 {color: red;}
h2 {color: black;}
```

Activity: Applying Basic Selection Techniques

In the following steps, you will build a style sheet that uses basic selection techniques. Save your file, and test your work in your browser as you complete each step. The new code to add is displayed in blue text. Refer to Figure 4-9 as you progress through the steps to see the results.

To build the style sheet:

1. Copy the **ch4activity2.html** file from the Chapter04 folder provided with your Data Files to the Chapter04 folder in your work folder.

2. Open the file **ch4activity2.html** in your HTML editor.

3. In your browser, open the file **ch4activity2.html**. When you open the file, it looks like Figure 4-8.

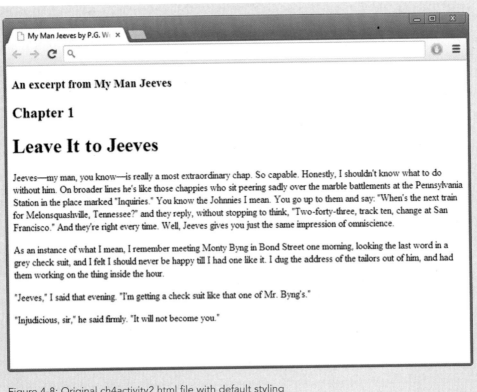

An excerpt from **My Man Jeeves**

Chapter 1

Leave It to Jeeves

Jeeves—my man, you know—is really a most extraordinary chap. So capable. Honestly, I shouldn't know what to do without him. On broader lines he's like those chappies who sit peering sadly over the marble battlements at the Pennsylvania Station in the place marked "Inquiries." You know the Johnnies I mean. You go up to them and say: "When's the next train for Melonsquashville, Tennessee?" and they reply, without stopping to think, "Two-forty-three, track ten, change at San Francisco." And they're right every time. Well, Jeeves gives you just the same impression of omniscience.

As an instance of what I mean, I remember meeting Monty Byng in Bond Street one morning, looking the last word in a grey check suit, and I felt I should never be happy till I had one like it. I dug the address of the tailors out of him, and had them working on the thing inside the hour.

"Jeeves," I said that evening. "I'm getting a check suit like that one of Mr. Byng's."

"Injudicious, sir," he said firmly. "It will not become you."

Figure 4-8: Original ch4activity2.html file with default styling
© 2015 Cengage Learning®

4. In your text editor, examine the page code. Notice that the file contains basic HTML code with no style information.

5. Add a <style> element in the <head> section to contain your style rules, as shown in blue in the following code. Leave a line or two of white space between the <style> tags to contain the style rules.

```
<head>
<title>My Man Jeeves by P.G. Wodehouse</title>
<meta http-equiv="Content-Type" content="text/html; charset=UTF-8">
<style>

</style>
</head>
```

6. Write a style rule for the body element to set the default page font to arial.

```
<style>
body {font-family: arial;}
</style>
```

7. Write the style rule for the <h3> element. Align the heading to the right, and set the font family to georgia. The style rule looks like this:

```
<style>
body {font-family: arial;}
h3 {
    text-align: right;
    font-family: georgia;
}
</style>
```

8. Write the style rules for the <h1> and <h2> elements, which share a common property value. Both elements have a left margin of 20 pixels (abbreviated as 20px). Because they share this property, group the two elements to share the same style rule, as shown in the following code:

```
<style>
body {font-family: arial;}
h3 {
    text-align: right;
    font-family: georgia;
}
h1, h2 {
    margin-left: 20px;
}
</style>
```

9. Write an additional rule for the <h1> element. The <h1> element has two style properties that it does not share with <h2>, so a separate style rule is necessary to express the border and the padding white space within the border. This rule uses the border shortcut property to specify multiple border characteristics—a 1-pixel border weight and solid border style. The padding-bottom property sets the border 5 pixels below the text.

```
<style>
body {font-family: arial;}
```

```
h3 {

    text-align: right;

    font-family: georgia;

}

h1, h2 {

    margin-left: 20px;

}

h1 {

    border-bottom: 1px solid;

    padding-bottom: 5px;

}

</style>
```

10. Write a style rule for the <p> elements so they have a 20-pixel left margin (to line up with the other elements on the page), and a font size of 110%.

```
<style>

body {font-family: arial;}

h3 {

    text-align: right;

    font-family: georgia;

}

h1, h2 {

    margin-left: 20px;

}

h1 {

    border-bottom: 1px solid;

    padding-bottom: 5px;

}

p {

    margin-left: 20px;

    font-size: 110%;

}

</style>
```

Save the HTML document and then view it in the browser. Figure 4-9 shows the finished document with the style properties.

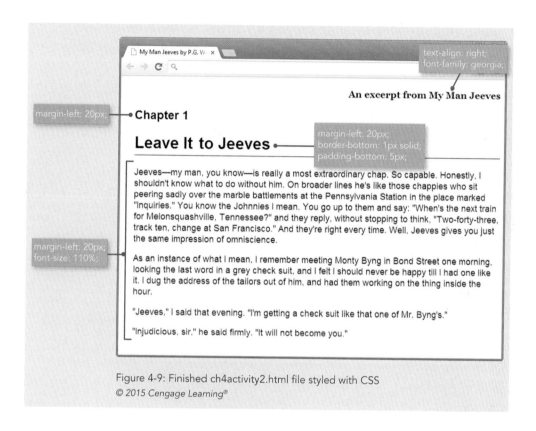

Figure 4-9: Finished ch4activity2.html file styled with CSS
© 2015 Cengage Learning®

Using class and id Selectors

This section describes CSS selection techniques that allow more than the basic element-based selection capabilities described in the previous section. You will learn to select elements of an HTML document using the following methods:

> The class selector

> The id selector

> The <div> and <span> elements

> The pseudo-class and pseudo-element selectors

Using the class Selector

The class selector lets you write rules, give each a name, and then apply that name to any elements you choose. You apply the name using the class attribute, which is a common attribute that applies to any HTML element. Refer to Appendix A for descriptions of the common attributes. To apply a style rule to an element, you can add the class attribute to the element and set it to the name you specified.

To create a class, declare a style rule. The period (.) flag character indicates that the selector is a class selector. Figure 4-10 shows an example of a rule with a class selector named *special*.

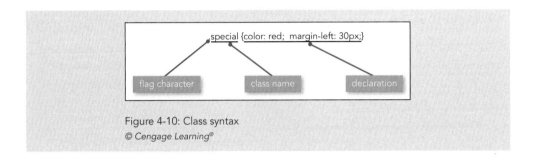

Figure 4-10: Class syntax
© Cengage Learning®

After writing the style rule, add it to the document by using the class attribute, as shown in the following code:

```
<h1 class="special">This heading will be red with a 30-pixel left
margin.</h1>
```

The class attribute lets you select elements with greater precision. For example, read the following style rule:

```
p {font-size: 125%;}
```

This rule sets all <p> elements in the document to a font size of 125%. Suppose that you want only one <p> element in your document to have larger text. You need a way to specifically select that one paragraph. To do this, use a class selector. The following style rule sets the style for the class named *intro*:

```
.intro {font-size: 125%;}
```

The class selector can be any name you choose as long as it has no spaces. In this instance, the class name *intro* denotes a special paragraph of the document. Now apply the rule to the <p> element in the document using the class attribute:

```
<p class="intro">This is the first paragraph of the
document. It has a different style based on the "intro"
class selector.</p>
<p>This is the second paragraph of text in the document. It is a
standard paragraph without a class attribute.</p>
```

Figure 4-11 shows the result of the style rule.

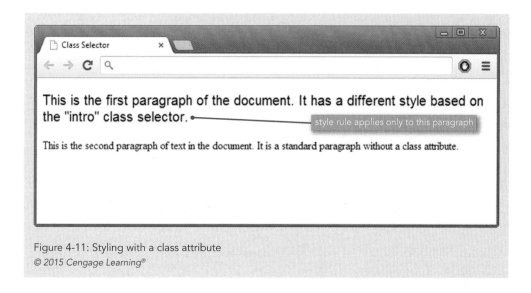

Figure 4-11: Styling with a class attribute
© 2015 Cengage Learning®

Note | You have a chance to practice using a class selector in Hands-on Project 4-4.

Making Class Selectors More Specific

Using the class attribute is a powerful selection technique because it allows you to write style rules with names that are meaningful to your organization or information type. The more specific your class names become, the greater control you need over the way they are applied. In the preceding example, you saw a style rule named *intro* that was applied to a <p> element. However, the intro style can be applied to any element in the document, not just <p>. To solve this problem, you can restrict the use of the class attribute to a single element type.

For example, your organization might use a special style for a procedure heading, the heading that appears before steps in a training document. The style is based on an <h1> element, with a sans-serif font and left margin of 20 pixels. Everyone in your organization knows this style is named *procedure*. You can use this same style name in your style sheet, as shown in the following style rule:

```
.procedure {
    font-family: sans-serif;
    margin-left: 20px;
}
```

To use these rules in the document, you apply the class attribute, as shown in the following code:

```
<h1 class="procedure">Procedure Heading</h1>
```

This works well, but what happens if someone on your staff neglects to apply the classes properly? For the style rule to work, it must be applied to an <h1> element. To restrict the use of the class to <h1> elements, include a prefix for the class selector with the element to which you want it applied:

```
h1.procedure {
    font-family: sans-serif;
    margin-left: 20px;
}
```

These style rules restrict the use of the procedure style to <h1> elements only. If this style is applied to other elements, it will not work.

Using the id Selector

The id attribute, like the class attribute, is an HTML common attribute. The difference is that the id attribute should refer to only one occurrence within a web page. The id attribute has become the selector of choice when identifying layout sections of the page. The id attribute is perfect for this because generally only one layout section such as a footer or sidebar occurs per page. For example, you might want to specify that only one <p> element can have the id *copyright* and its associated style rule. Figure 4-12 shows a style rule that uses the id of copyright as a selector.

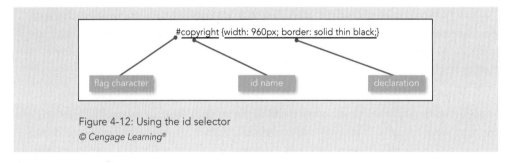

Figure 4-12: Using the id selector
© Cengage Learning®

Notice that the id selector uses a pound sign (#) flag character instead of the period you used with the class selector. You can apply the id value to the appropriate element in the document, which in this example is a <p> element:

```
<p id="copyright">This is the copyright information for
the page.</p>
```

The id value uniquely identifies this one <p> element as containing copyright information. For consistency in design, no other element in the document should share this exact id value.

Just like classes, you can make id selectors more specific by adding an element selector before the flag character, as shown in the following code:

```
p#copyright {
    font-family: times;
    text-align: center;
}
```

This style rule will only apply to a <p> element with the id set to copyright.

> **Note** | You have a chance to practice using an id selector in Hands-on Project 4-5.

Using the <div> and <span> Elements

The <div> (division) and <span> (span of words) elements are designed to be used with CSS. They let you specify logical divisions within a document that have their own name and style properties. The difference between <div> and <span> is their element display type, which is described in more detail in Chapter 6. Essentially, <div> is a block-level element, and <span> is its inline equivalent. Used with the class and id attributes, <div> and <span> let you effectively create your own element names for your HTML documents.

Working with <div> Elements

The <div> element is a generic element that you can use with the class and id attributes to create content containers on a web page. The <div> element does not represent anything by itself. Instead, the <div> element is commonly used to represent page sections such as headers and footers, but it is being replaced by the HTML5 sectioning elements (discussed in Chapters 1 and 7).

To create a customized division, declare it with a class or id selector in the style rule. The following example specifies a division with an id named *column* as the selector for the rule:

```
div#column {
    width: 200px;
    height: auto;
    padding: 15px;
    border: thin solid;
}
```

To apply this rule, specify the <div> element in the document. Then use the id attribute to specify the exact type of division you want to insert. In the following example, the code defines the <div> element with the id of column:

```
<div id="column"><p>This division is displayed as a column of text
in the browser window. This is one of the uses of the division
element as a page layout tool with CSS. You will learn more about
this in later chapters of this book.</p>
<p>Lorem ipsum...</p>
</div>
```

Figure 4-13 shows the result of the style rule.

Figure 4-13: Using the <div> element to create a column of text
© 2015 Cengage Learning®

Working with <span> Elements

The <span> element lets you specify inline elements within a document that have their own name and style properties. Inline elements reside within a line of text, like the <strong> or <em> element. You can use <span> with a class or id attribute to create customized inline elements.

To create a span, declare it within the <style> element first. The following example specifies a span named *logo* as the selector for the rule:

```
span.logo {
    color: blue;
    font-family: verdana;
    letter-spacing: 2px;
}
```

Next, specify the <span> element in the document. Use the class attribute to specify the exact type of span. In the following example, the code defines the <span> element as the class named *logo*.

```
<p>Welcome to the <span class="logo">Wonder Software</span>
web site.</p>
```

Figure 4-14 shows the result of the style rule.

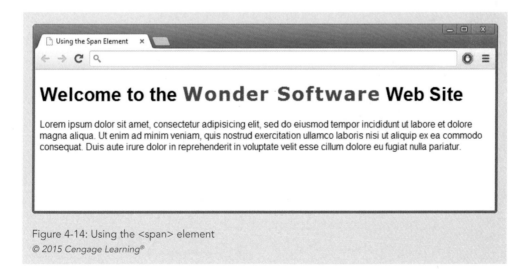

Figure 4-14: Using the <span> element
© 2015 Cengage Learning®

Using Other Selectors

Besides class and id selectors, you can use attribute selectors, pseudo-class and pseudo-element selectors, and CSS3 selectors.

Using Attribute Selectors

Attribute selectors let you select an element based on whether the element contains an attribute. You can also choose an element based on a specific value the attribute contains.

Attribute selectors make selections by matching attributes and their values. In the following code, the <img> element has three attributes: src, title, and alt.

```
<img src="images/home.gif" title="home" alt="Home navigation
button">
```

Using attribute selectors, you could choose this element based on the presence of the title attribute, as in the following code:

```
img[title] {border-color: red;}
```

Or, you could choose this element based on the value that the title attribute contains, as shown:

```
img[title=home] {border-color: red;}
```

Attribute selectors come in handy when multiple elements share the same characteristics, sometimes differing only by the values of the attributes they contain. Table 4-1 lists the CSS attribute selectors that were introduced in CSS 2.1.

SYNTAX	DESCRIPTION	EXAMPLE
[attribute]	Select when the element contains the named attribute; the attribute value is not matched	p[title] {color: blue;} matches: <p title="opening"> <p title="closing">
[attribute=value]	Select when the element contains the named attribute and specific value	p[title=footer] matches: <p title="footer">
[att~=val]	Select when the attribute contains the value in a list of values separated by white space	p[att~=copyright] matches: <p type="copyright trademark">
[att|=val]	Select when an attribute contains the exact value or begins with the value	p[att|=en] matches: <p lang="english">

Table 4-1: CSS 2.1 Attribute Presence and Value Selectors
© 2015 Cengage Learning®

CSS 3 added three selectors that let you match parts of an attribute value, such as the beginning or ending of a string of text. Table 4-2 lists the syntax and description for the CSS3 substring matching attribute selectors.

SELECTOR SYNTAX	DESCRIPTION
p[att^=val]	Matches any p element whose att attribute value begins with *val*
p[att$=val]	Matches any p element whose att attribute value ends with *val*
p[att*=val]	Matches any p element whose att attribute value contains the substring *val*

Table 4-2: CSS3 Substring Matching Attribute Selectors
© 2015 Cengage Learning®

For example, the following rule selects div elements whose class attribute begins with the word *content*:

```
div[class^="content"]
```

Using Pseudo-Class and Pseudo-Element Selectors

Pseudo-class and pseudo-element selectors let you express style declarations for characteristics of a document that are not signified with the standard HTML elements. Pseudo-classes select elements based on characteristics other than their element name. For example, assume that you want to change the color of a new or visited hypertext link. No HTML element lets you directly express these characteristics of the <a> element. With CSS, you can use the pseudo-class selector to change the link color.

Pseudo-elements let you change other aspects of a document that are not classified by elements, such as applying style rules to the first letter or first line of a paragraph. For example, you might want to create a drop initial or drop capital that extends below the line of type, or make the first line of a paragraph all uppercase text. These are common publishing design techniques that are not possible with standard HTML code. With CSS you can use the :first-letter and :first-line pseudo-elements to add these two style characteristics to your documents.

Using the Link Pseudo-Classes

The link pseudo-classes let you change the style characteristics for four hypertext link states, as described in Table 4-3.

PSEUDO-CLASS	DESCRIPTION
:link	Selects any unvisited link that the user has not clicked or is not hovering over with their pointer
:visited	Selects any link that your user has already visited
:hover	Selects any link that your user is hovering over with the pointer
:active	Selects a link for the brief moment that your user is actually clicking the link

Table 4-3: Link Pseudo-Classes
© 2015 Cengage Learning®

The following rules change the colors of the hypertext links in a web page:

```
a:link {color: red;}
a:visited {color: green;}
```

Note that the colon (:) is the flag character for a pseudo-class.

Note

Because of the specificity of the pseudo-class selectors, you should always place your link pseudo-class in the following order:

1. Link
2. Visited
3. Hover
4. Active

You do not have to use all of the different link states, so if you skip one, make sure the others follow the correct order. You will learn about specificity later in this chapter.

Whether you choose to change your hypertext link colors depends on the design of your site and the needs of your users. Remember that many web users are comfortable with the default underlining, and that color alone may not be enough to differentiate links from the rest of your text.

Using the :hover Pseudo-Class

The :hover pseudo-class lets you apply a style that appears when the user hovers over an element with a pointer. This is a useful navigation aid to add to the <a> element, with the result that the link appears highlighted when the user points to it. The following style rule shows the :hover pseudo-class with the <a> element as the selector.

```
a:hover {background-color: yellow;}
```

This style rule changes the background color of the link to yellow, which is an effective highlight color. Figure 4-15 shows the results of this style rule.

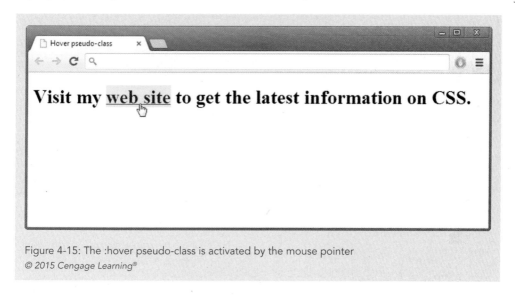

Figure 4-15: The :hover pseudo-class is activated by the mouse pointer
© 2015 Cengage Learning®

You can also use :hover to have underlines appear or change the color of text. Additionally, you can use the :hover pseudo-class with the new CSS3 transition properties to add color changes and animations to menu bars and other objects. You can read about these properties in Appendix C.

Using the :first-letter Pseudo-Element

Use the :first-letter pseudo-element to apply style rules to the first letter of any element. This lets you create interesting text effects, such as initial capitals and drop capitals, which are usually set in a bolder and larger font. Initial capitals share the same baseline as the rest of the text, while drop capitals extend down two or more lines below the text baseline. To apply :first-letter to build an initial capital, specify a style rule like the following:

```
p:first-letter {
    font-weight: bold;
    font-size: 200%;
}
```

This creates a first letter that is bold and twice the size of the <p> font. For example, if the <p> element has a font size of 12 points, the initial cap will be 24 points.

To make sure that this rule applies only to one paragraph, rather than every paragraph in the document, a class name needs to be added to the style rule. To solve this problem, add a class name, such as *initial*, to the rule, as shown in Figure 4-16.

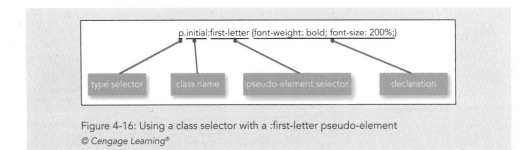

Figure 4-16: Using a class selector with a :first-letter pseudo-element
© Cengage Learning®

This style rule affects only <p> elements with the class value of initial, as shown in the following code:

```
<p class="initial">From the far north they heard a low wail of the
wind, and Uncle Henry and Dorothy could see where the long grass
bowed in waves before the coming storm. There now came a sharp
whistling in the air from the south, and as they turned their eyes
that way they saw ripples in the grass coming from that direction
also.</p>
```

Figure 4-17 shows the result of the style rule.

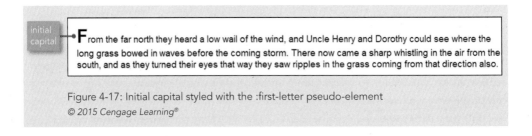

Figure 4-17: Initial capital styled with the :first-letter pseudo-element
© 2015 Cengage Learning®

You can make the initial capital a drop capital by adding the float property to the rule, which allows the letter to extend downward. The float property is described in Chapter 6. Here is a :first-letter style rule with the float property added:

```
p.dropcap:first-letter {
    font-weight: bold;
    font-size: 200%;
    float: left;
}
```

Notice that the class has been changed to signify that this first letter is a drop capital. Remember, you can set the class attribute to any naming value that makes sense to you.

This style rule affects only <p> elements with the class value of *dropcap*, as shown in the following code:

```
<p class="dropcap">From the far north they heard a low wail of the
wind, and Uncle Henry and Dorothy could see where the long grass
bowed in waves before the coming storm. There now came a sharp
whistling in the air from the south, and as they turned their eyes
that way they saw ripples in the grass coming from that direction
also.</p>
```

Figure 4-18 shows the result of the new style rule.

From the far north they heard a low wail of the wind, and Uncle Henry and Dorothy could see where the long grass bowed in waves before the coming storm. There now came a sharp whistling in the air from the south, and as they turned their eyes that way they saw ripples in the grass coming from that direction also.

Figure 4-18: Drop capital using the :first-letter pseudo-element
© 2015 Cengage Learning®

The :first-letter pseudo-element can only be applied to a block-level element. In addition, only the following properties can be applied to the :first-letter selector:

- Font properties
- Color properties
- Background properties
- Margin properties
- Padding properties
- Word-spacing
- Letter-spacing
- Text-decoration
- Vertical-align

> Text-transform

> Line-height

> Text-shadow

> Clear

Using the :first-line Pseudo-Element

The :first-line pseudo-element works in much the same way as :first-letter, except for the obvious difference that it affects the first line of text in an element. For example, the following rule sets the first line of every <p> element to uppercase letters:

```
p:first-line {text-transform: uppercase;}
```

The problem with this code is that it affects every <p> element in the document. As you saw in the preceding :first-letter selector, you can add a class attribute to more narrowly define the application of the :first-line style:

```
p.introduction:first-line {text-transform: uppercase;}
```

This rule transforms to uppercase the first line of the <p> element that contains the following code:

```
<p class="introduction">From the far north they heard a low wail
of the wind, and Uncle Henry and Dorothy could see where the long
grass bowed in waves before the coming storm. There now came a sharp
whistling in the air from the south, and as they turned their eyes
that way they saw ripples in the grass coming from that direction
also.</p>
```

Figure 4-19 shows the results of the style rule.

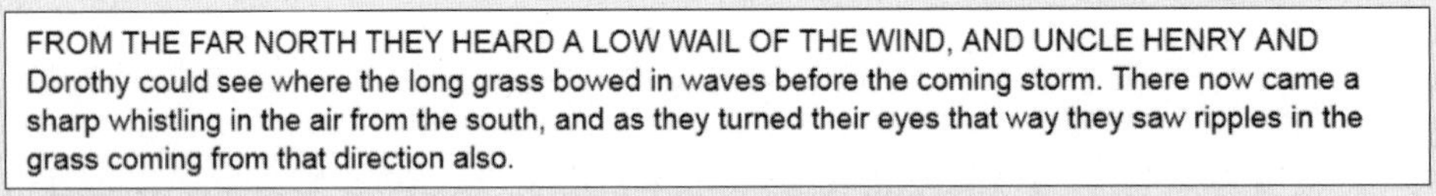

FROM THE FAR NORTH THEY HEARD A LOW WAIL OF THE WIND, AND UNCLE HENRY AND Dorothy could see where the long grass bowed in waves before the coming storm. There now came a sharp whistling in the air from the south, and as they turned their eyes that way they saw ripples in the grass coming from that direction also.

Figure 4-19: First line transformation using the :first-line pseudo-element
© 2015 Cengage Learning®

The :first-line pseudo-element can only be applied to a block-level element. In addition, only the following properties can be applied to :first-line. Notice that :first-line does not support padding, margin, or border properties:

> Font properties
> Color properties
> Background properties
> Word-spacing
> Letter-spacing
> Text-decoration
> Text-transform
> Line-height
> Text-shadow
> Clear

Using the :before and :after Pseudo-Elements

The :before and :after pseudo-elements let you insert content in your web page that is created by the style sheet rather than provided in your document text. Your web page content may include terms that must be used repeatedly. These can be inserted by a style sheet so that you do not have to enter them repeatedly. A good example is including the word *Figure* in the title of all of your figures. For example, the following style rule inserts the word *Figure* followed by a colon before any <p> text that has the class figtitle:

```
p.figtitle:before {content: "Figure: ";}
```

The :before pseudo-element places generated content before the selected element, and the :after pseudo-element places generated content after the selected element. The following example uses :before to add generated content to a glossary. Style rules select the elements and apply generated content based on the class name.

```
p.term:before {content: "Term: "; font-weight: bold;}
p.definition:before {content: "Definition: "; font-weight: bold;}
```

These style rules apply to the following HTML code. Figure 4-20 shows the results.

```
<p class="term">Quasar</p>
<p class="definition"> A quasi-stellar radio source (quasar) is a
very energetic and distant galaxy with an active galactic nucleus.
They are the most luminous objects in the universe.</p>
```

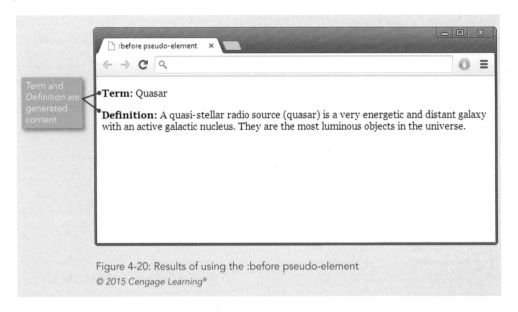

Term and Definition are generated content

Term: Quasar

Definition: A quasi-stellar radio source (quasar) is a very energetic and distant galaxy with an active galactic nucleus. They are the most luminous objects in the universe.

Figure 4-20: Results of using the :before pseudo-element
© 2015 Cengage Learning®

Understanding How the Cascade Affects Style Rules

One of the fundamental features of CSS is that style sheets cascade. This means that multiple style sheets and style rules can apply to the same document. HTML authors can attach a preferred style sheet, while the reader might have a personal style sheet to adjust for preferences such as human or technological handicaps. However, only one rule can apply to an element. The CSS cascading mechanism determines which rules are applied to document elements by assigning a weight to each rule based on the following three variables:

> Specificity of the selector

> Order of the rule in the style sheet

> Use of the !important keyword

Determining Rule Weight by Specificity

Another method of determining style rule weight is the specificity of the rule's element selector. Specificity determines which rule, if there is a conflict, applies to your HTML elements. Rules with more specific selectors take precedence over rules with less specific selectors.

Specificity is actually a complex calculation that is performed by the browser to determine which rule takes precedence, based on adding the weight values of the possible style rules that affect an element.

Specificity conflicts normally occur when multiple style sheets affect a web page, which is common in larger content management systems, and when compounded selectors are used to narrowly target a specific element on a page. For example, the following style rules target a <p> element. The first applies to all <p> elements on the page, and the second applies to <p> elements that are specifically within a <div> element. The more specific descendant selector determines the outcome, so the <p> elements contained within a <div> will be blue.

```
p {color: red;}
div p {color: blue;}
```

This is a very simple example of specificity to illustrate the concept. The following general rules make it easier to understand which style rule takes precedence.

> Inline styles, using the style attribute, have the greatest weight.

> Styles with id selectors override styles with class selectors.

> Class selectors override simple type selectors.

Determining Rule Weight by Order

CSS applies weight to a rule based on its order within a style sheet. Rules that are included later in the style sheet order take precedence over earlier rules. Examine the following style rules for an example:

```
body {color: black;}
h1 {color: red;}
h1 {color: green;}
```

In this example, <h1> elements in the document appear green because the last style rule specifies green as the color. This also applies to internal and external style sheets. Internal style sheet rules have greater weight than external style sheet rules.

Determining Rule Weight with the !important Keyword

A conflict can arise when multiple rules apply to the same element. By default, rules that are closest to the element, or more specific, always take precedence. The !important keyword ensures that a particular rule will always apply. The following style sheet states a rule for <p> elements that sets the font family to arial, regardless of other rules that might apply to the element:

```
<style>
p {font-family: arial !important;}
</style>
```

The !important keyword also allows you to specify that a rule should take precedence no matter what order the rules are listed in the style sheet. Examine the following style rules for an example:

```
body {color: black;}
h1 {color: red !important;}
h1 {color: green;}
```

In this example, <h1> elements in the document will appear red, even though the rule that sets the color to green would normally take precedence because of its order in the document.

However, it is always best to use the !important keyword sparingly since it defeats the flexible nature of CSS.

Advanced Selectors

CSS3 adds advanced selectors that let you narrow down the exact element you want to select with even greater precision. Many of the new selectors let you choose elements based on where they reside in the document structure, letting you make selections such as the first or last paragraph on every page, or setting different styles for odd or even rows of a table or list. Most browsers support these selectors, but make sure to test carefully for compatibility.

CSS3 includes a number of new types of selectors, including the following:

> Structural pseudo-class

> UI element states

Structural Pseudo-Class Selectors

Earlier in this chapter you read how an HTML document is a tree structure of parent and child elements. The structural pseudo-classes let you select elements based on where they reside in the document tree. Table 4-4 lists the syntax and description for structural pseudo-class selectors.

SELECTOR SYNTAX	DESCRIPTION
:root	Matches the document's root element; in HTML, the root element is always the HTML element
p:nth-child(n)	Matches any <p> element that is the *n*th child of its parent
p:nth-last-child(n)	Matches any <p> element that is the *n*th child of its parent, counting from the last child
p:nth-of-type(n)	Matches any <p> element that is the *n*th sibling of its type
p:nth-last-of-type(n)	Matches any <p> element that is the *n*th sibling of its type, counting from the last sibling
p:last-child	Matches any <p> element that is the last child of its parent
p:first-of-type	Matches any <p> element that is the first sibling of its type
p:last-of-type	Matches any <p> element that is the last sibling of its type
p:only-child	Matches any <p> element that is the only child of its parent
p:only-of-type	Matches any <p> element that is the only sibling of its type
p:empty	Matches any <p> element that has no children (including text nodes)

Table 4-4: Structural Pseudo-Class Selectors
© 2015 Cengage Learning®

For example, if you want to style the last <p> element on a web page, you can use this style rule:

```
p:last-child {border-bottom: solid thin black;}
```

You can see an example of structural selector usage in Chapter 10.

UI Element States Selectors

The UI element states selectors let you choose an element based on its state of user interaction. Table 4-5 lists the syntax and description of UI element states selectors.

SELECTOR SYNTAX	DESCRIPTION
:enable	Matches any interface element, such as a form control, that is in an enabled state
:disabled	Matches any interface element, such as a form control, that is in a disabled state
:checked	Matches any option button or check box that is in a selected state

Table 4-5: UI Element States Selectors
© 2015 Cengage Learning®

For example, you could highlight a selected option button with the following style rule:

```
input:checked {background-color: yellow;}
```

Skills at Work | *Set Coding Conventions*

Once you learn to use CSS effectively, you will see that the flexibility of the language's syntax can also be a drawback. Two designers can write very different style sheets that create the same output. Whether you are working by yourself or with a team, you need to establish coding standards that everyone agrees on and consistently applies to their work. You can create a style book or sample web page that shows how different style rules are used. This can be a great job aid for both experienced and new designers on your team.

Good standards include a requirement for plenty of comments to explain what the code does. Comment on each section of your style sheets as needed so that other developers have a clear idea of your intent. Stick to the standards, and include good communication within your code to support consistency in your teamwork and your design.

Chapter Summary

This chapter presents the basic syntax of the CSS language. You learned about the different methods of selecting elements and applying style rules in a variety of ways. You saw that the CSS basic selection techniques are often powerful enough to handle most document styling. You learned that the class and id attributes let you create naming conventions for styles that are meaningful to your organization or information type. As you will see in the upcoming chapters, CSS is an easy-to-use style language that lets you gain visual control over the display of your web content.

> CSS rules can be combined with your HTML code in a number of ways. CSS rules are easy to write and read.

> CSS uses inheritance and cascading to determine which style rules take precedence.

> Basic style rules let you apply style rules based on standard element selectors. You can combine the selectors and declarations to create more powerful style expressions. You can also select elements based on the contextual relationship of elements in the document tree.

> You can use the class and id attribute selectors to further customize elements. You can create rules, name them, and apply them to any element or group of elements you choose.

> The pseudo-class and pseudo-element selectors let you change the color and styling of hypertext links and affect elements of a document, such as first line and first letter, that are not signified with the standard HTML elements.

> Advanced selectors let you narrow down the exact element you want to select with even greater precision. Many of the new selectors let you choose elements based on where they reside in the document structure, make selections such as the first or last paragraph on every page, or set different styles for odd or even rows of a table or list.

Key Terms

!important—A CSS keyword that lets the user override the author's style setting for a particular element.

cascade—Style sheets originate from three sources: the author, the user, and the browser. The cascading feature of CSS lets these multiple style sheets and style rules interact in the same document.

child element—An HTML element contained within another element.

declaration—The declaration portion of a style rule consists of a property name and value. The browser applies the declaration to the selected element.

inheritance—The order of CSS rules dictating that child elements inherit rules from parent elements.

\<link\> element—An HTML element that lets you establish document relationships, such as linking to an external style sheet.

parent element—An HTML element that contains child elements.

property—A quality or characteristic stated in a style rule, such as color, font-size, or margin. The property is a part of the style rule declaration.

pseudo-class—An element that selects elements based on characteristics other than their element name.

pseudo-element—An element that lets you change other aspects of a document that are not classified by elements, such as applying style rules to the first letter or first line of a paragraph.

recommendation—The final stage of development by the W3C, indicating that a technology release has been reviewed and tested extensively.

selector—The part of a style rule that determines which HTML element to match. Style rules are applied to any element in the document that matches the selector.

style rule—The basic unit of expression in CSS. A style rule is composed of two parts: a selector and a declaration. The style rule expresses the style information for an element.

style sheet—A set of style rules that describes a document's display characteristics. There are two types of style sheets: internal and external.

type selector—A CSS selector that applies a rule to every instance of the element in a document.

universal selector—A selector that lets you quickly select groups of elements and apply a style rule.

value—The precise specification of a property in a style rule, based on the allowable values for the property.

Review Questions and Exercises

1. What are the two parts of a style rule?

2. What are the three ways to combine CSS rules with your HTML code?

3. List two reasons to state a style using the style attribute.

4. What are the advantages of using an external style sheet?

5. What is the inheritance default for CSS rules?

6. What is the benefit of the !important declaration?

7. Write a basic style rule that selects \<h1\> elements and sets the color property to red.

8. Add the \<p\> element as an additional selector to the rule you created for Question 7.

9. Add a font-size property to the rule, and set the size to 120%.

10. Write a style rule that selects \<ul\> elements only when they appear within \<p\> elements and set the color property to red.

11. Write the style rule for a class selector named note. Set the font-weight property to bold.

12. Restrict the rule you developed for Question 11 so it can be used only with <p> elements.

13. What is the difference between <div> and <span>?

14. Write a style rule that sets the default document text color to red.

15. What is the advantage of working with the class attribute?

16. What element does this selector choose?

```
p ul li
```

17. What element does this selector choose?

```
article p *
```

18. What element does this selector choose?

```
p.warning
```

19. What is the advantage of working with the id attribute?

20. Write a style rule that applies a yellow background color to <a> elements when the user points the mouse to a hypertext link.

Hands-On Projects

1. By yourself or with a partner, choose a mainstream publishing web site, such as a newspaper or periodical site. Examine the style characteristics of the site. What common styles can be applied across the site, such as headings, paragraphs, and bylines? Write an analysis of the site's style requirements, and list the styles you would include in the site's style sheet.

2. In this project, you have a chance to test a few simple style rules on a standard HTML document and view the results in your browser.
   a. Copy the **ch4project2.html** file from the Chapter04 folder provided with your Data Files to the Chapter04 folder in your work folder.
   b. Open the file **ch4project2.html** in your text editor, and examine the code.
   c. Add a <style> element to the <head> section, as shown in the following code.

```
<head>
<title>Cascading Style Sheets</title>
<meta http-equiv="Content-Type" content="text/html; charset=UTF-8">
<style>

</style>
</head>
```

d. Add a style rule that uses *body* as a selector and sets the color property to blue, as shown in the following code:

```
<style>
body {color: blue;}
</style>
```

e. Save **ch4project2.html**, and view it in the browser. All of the document text should now be blue.

f. Add a style rule that sets <h1> elements to be displayed in black:

```
<style>
body {color: blue;}
h1 {color: black;}
</style>
```

g. Save **ch4project2.html**, and view the results in the browser.

h. Finally, add a style rule that sets a left margin for <p> elements to 30 pixels:

```
<style>
body {color: blue;}
h1 {color: black;}
p {margin-left: 30px;}
</style>
```

i. Save **ch4project2.html**, and view the results in the browser.

3. In this project, you have a chance to test a few basic selection techniques on a standard HTML document and view the results in your browser. Save the file and view it in your browser after completing each step.

   a. Copy the **ch4project3.html** file from the Chapter04 folder provided with your Data Files to the Chapter04 folder in your work folder. Save the file in the Chapter04 folder in your work folder as **ch4project3.html**.

   b. Open the file **ch4project3.html** in your text editor, and examine the code.

   c. Add a <style> element to the <head> section, as shown in the following code:

```
<head>
<title>Cascading Style Sheets </title>
<meta http-equiv="Content-Type" content="text/html; charset=UTF-8">
<style>

</style>
</head>
```

d. Write a style rule that uses *body* as a selector and sets the left margin to 20 pixels.

e. Write a single style rule that applies to both <h1> and <h2> elements. Set the color property to blue.

f. Write a descendant selector rule that affects the <em> element that is contained within the <p> element, and set the font-weight property to bold.

4. In this project, you have a chance to apply CSS class selectors to a standard HTML document and view the results in your browser. Save the file and view it in your browser after completing each step.

a. Copy the **ch4project4.html** file from the Chapter04 folder provided with your Data Files to the Chapter04 folder in your work folder. Save the file in the Chapter04 folder in your work folder as **ch4project4.html**.

b. Open the file **ch4project4.html** in your text editor, and examine the code.

c. Add a <style> element to the <head> section.

d. Write a rule for a class selector named *heading*. Set the color property to red and the font-family property to arial. Apply the heading class to the <h1> element in the document.

e. Write a rule for a class selector named *emphasis*. Set the color property to blue and the background-color property to yellow. In the document, apply the emphasis class to the <em> element within the paragraph.

5. In this project, you have a chance to apply CSS id selectors to a standard HTML document and view the results in your browser. Save the file and view it in your browser after completing each step.

a. Copy the **ch4project5.html** file from the Chapter04 folder provided with your Data Files to the Chapter04 folder in your work folder. Save the file in the Chapter04 folder in your work folder as **ch4project5.html**.

b. Open the file **ch4project5.html** in your text editor, and examine the code.

c. Add a <style> element to the <head> section.

d. Write a rule for an id selector named *heading*. Set the color property to blue and the font-family property to georgia. Apply the heading class to the <h1> element in the document.

e. Write a rule for an id selector named *subheading*. Set the border-bottom property to solid 1px and the font-family property to arial. Apply the heading class to the <h2> element in the document.

Individual Case Project

Revisit your project proposal and the site specifications you created in Chapter 3. How will you implement Cascading Style Sheets into your project web site? In the next few chapters, you will learn how to control typography, white space, borders, colors, and backgrounds with CSS. Think about each of these style characteristics and how you will apply them to your page designs. In addition, make a list of possible class names you might use to identify your content.

For example, consider using class names for the following page characteristics, as well as creating some of your own:

> Body copy

> Header (possibly different levels)

> Footer

Team Case Project

Revisit your project proposal and the site specifications you created in Chapter 3. Each team member is responsible for individual templates, such as the home page template, the section page template, and the article-level page template.

In the next few chapters, you will learn how to control typography, white space, borders, colors, and backgrounds with CSS. Decide how you will handle these style characteristics in your web site. Each team member should create a suggested list of styles and naming conventions for use in your site.

For example, you might have top-level, secondary-level, and tertiary-level headings. What names will you use for consistency throughout the site? You might want to name these *A-head*, *B-head*, and so on. Also, you will need to segregate and name the different copy styles in your site. For example, you might have a different body copy style for the main page than you have on a secondary section or on reading-level pages. Think about the different style properties that you will be able to manipulate (you can look these up in Appendix B) and how you will consistently use, manage, and name these style characteristics for your project web site. Meet as a team to review each member's ideas, and come to an agreement on the proposed styles and naming conventions.

CHAPTER 5

WEB TYPOGRAPHY

When you complete this chapter, you will be able to:

> Understand type design principles
> Understand Cascading Style Sheets (CSS) measurement units
> Use the CSS font properties
> Use the CSS text properties
> Build a font and text properties style sheet
> Customize bulleted and numbered lists

The type choices you make for your site provide the foundation for the clear communication of your content. The consistent use of type to express the hierarchy of your content provides valuable information cues to the reader, and the choices you make to enhance text legibility affect the usability of your web site. Cascading Style Sheets offers a potent style language, allowing you to manipulate a variety of text properties to achieve professional, effective results, all without resorting to graphics that add download time. New type properties and more new fonts are available for designers, providing more typographic choices and control over type characteristics. New applications and web font tools let you test and manipulate fonts so your content is readable across multiple devices.

Understanding Type Design Principles

Type can flexibly express emotion, tone, and structure. As more users access the web through smaller devices, type becomes even more important. To reduce web pages to fit on smartphones, most images are usually hidden or decreased in size so that mostly text remains.

> **Note** In strict typography terms, a *typeface* is the name of the type, such as Times New Roman or Futura Condensed. A *font* is the typeface in a particular size, such as Times Roman 24 point. For the most part on the web, the two terms are interchangeable.

Figure 5-1 shows sample pages from *The New Yorker* and *The Washington Post* that are designed for display on smartphones. *The Washington Post* uses a clean, legible font combined with a descriptive headline and synopsis sentence. *The New Yorker* uses its own distinctive font to reinforce its brand on the small smartphone screen. Your choices of page fonts have a major impact on the way users react to your site and navigate through it.

For Romo, one mistake is too many

Kent Babb

The Dallas quarterback's interception in the final minutes of a shootout leads to the winning field goal for unbeaten Denver.

NFC East is still up for grabs

Sally Jenkins

COLUMN | The Eagles and Giants play an ugly game while the Cowboys lose during the Redskins' bye week.

Porter forced to wait his turn

Michael Lee

A strained right hip flexor has kept rookie Otto Porter Jr. from Wizards practice.

Petty settling in, again, at linebacker

Alex Prewitt

After providing emergency relief at quarterback last season, Shawn Petty is back at linebacker.

AMERICAN CHRONICLES
HIPPIES, HIPSTERS, ENTREPRENUERS
BY NATHAN HELLER

In San Francisco, again, the new mode of American success is being borne out.

THE FINANCIAL PAGE
THE BUSINESS END OF OBAMACARE
BY JAMES SUROWIECKI

The Affordable Care Act may well be the best thing Washington has done for small businesses in decades...

WORK FOR HIRE
MY FIRST SUMMER JOB
BY AMY POEHLER

Standing on a chair and singing "Happy Birthday," I was reminded of things I already secretly knew about myself: I wasn't shy, I liked to be looked at...

VIDEO FESTIVAL 2013
THE CHANGING TIMES

Jill Abramson, executive editor of the New York *Times*, discusses how the paper has evolved under her leadership.

The Washington Post   The New Yorker

Figure 5-1: Text dominates on web pages designed for smartphones
Courtesy of The Washington Post, Courtesy of The New Yorker

Most of the type principles that apply to paper-based design apply to the web as well. For example, it is possible to go overboard by using too many typefaces and sizes. Just because you have many typefaces at your disposal does not mean you should use them all. As you work with type, consider the following principles for creating an effective design:

> Choose fewer fonts and sizes.

> Use available fonts.

> Design for legibility.

> Avoid using text as graphics.

Choose Fewer Fonts and Sizes

Your pages will look cleaner when you choose fewer fonts and sizes of type. Decide on a font for each type of content, such as page headings, section headings, and body text. Communicate the hierarchy of information with changes in the size, weight, or color of the typeface.

For example, a page heading should have a larger, bolder type, while a section heading would appear in the same typeface, only lighter or smaller.

Pick a few sizes and weights in a type family. For example, you might choose three sizes: a large one for headings, a smaller size for subheadings, and your body text size. You can vary these styles by changing the weight; for example, bold type can be used for topic headings within text. Avoid making random changes in your use of type conventions. Consistently apply the same fonts and the same combination of styles throughout your web site; consistency develops a strong visual identity. The *Time* magazine web site (*www.time.com*) shown in Figure 5-2 is a good example of effective type usage. The site has a strong typographic identity, yet it uses only two typefaces. The designers of this site built a visually interesting page simply by varying the weight, size, white space, and color of the text.

Figure 5-2: Effective typographic design
Courtesy of Time.com

Use Common Web Fonts

Fonts often are a problem in HTML because font information is client based. The user's browser and operating system determine how a font is displayed, or if it is displayed at all. If you design your pages using a font that your user does not have installed, the browser defaults to Times on a Macintosh or Times New Roman on a PC. To make matters worse, even the most widely available fonts appear in different sizes on different operating systems. Unfortunately, the best you can do about this is to test on multiple platforms to judge the effect on your pages.

To control more effectively how text appears on your pages, think in terms of font families, such as serif and sans-serif typefaces (see Figure 5-3), rather than specific styles. Notice that serif fonts have strokes (or serifs) that finish the top and bottom of the letter. Sans-serif fonts consist of block letters without serifs.

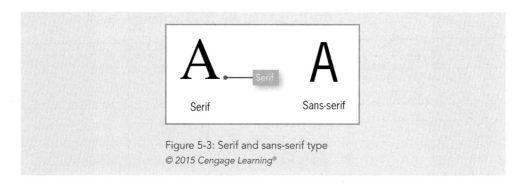

Figure 5-3: Serif and sans-serif type
© 2015 Cengage Learning®

Because of the variable nature of fonts installed on different computers, you never can be sure the user will see the exact font you have specified. You can, however, use font fallback values (described later in this chapter), which let you specify a variety of fonts within a font family, such as the common sans-serif fonts, Arial and Helvetica.

Table 5-1 lists the most common installed fonts on the PC, Macintosh, and Linux operating systems.

COMMON PC FONTS	COMMON MACINTOSH FONTS	COMMON LINUX FONTS
Arial	Helvetica	Helvetica
Courier New	Courier	Times
Times New Roman	Times	URW Chancery L
Trebuchet MS	Trebuchet MS	Century Schoolbook
Verdana	Verdana	URW Gothic L
Tahoma	Arial	URW Bookman L
Comic Sans MS	Geneva	Nimbus Mono L
Lucida Console	Lucida Grande	URW Palladio L
Georgia	Monaco	DejaVu Sans Mono

Table 5-1: Common Installed Fonts
© 2015 Cengage Learning®

The fonts that become the most common for the web are the result of the Core Fonts for the web initiative started by Microsoft in 1996. Their font pack, which was freely distributed, contained Arial, Georgia, Verdana, and Times New Roman. As Table 5-1 shows, Times (or Times New Roman) is available on all three operating systems; it is the default browser font. Courier is the default monospace font, and Arial or Helvetica is usually the default sans-serif font. Arial, Trebuchet, and Verdana come with Internet Explorer, so many Macintosh and PC users have these fonts installed. Because some Macintosh users only have Helvetica, it is a good idea to specify this font as an alternate choice when you are using sans-serif fonts.

Proprietary Web Fonts

Web designers have traditionally been limited to choosing fonts that are installed on users' systems. The CSS3 font-face property lets you link to a font, download it, and use it in style rules as if it were installed on the user's computer. The common browsers support the font-face property, though they each implement it differently. Internet Explorer uses its proprietary Embedded Open Type format, while the other major browsers use TrueType or Open Type formats. This inconsistency means that if you use the font-face property, you need to specify multiple fonts to satisfy the needs of different browsers. To solve this problem, Microsoft, Mozilla, and Opera have collaborated on a new type format named the Web Open Font Format (WOFF). WOFF became a W3C Recommendation in 2012. Even though WOFF offers a single interoperable format for web fonts, you still need to consider many browser incompatibilities. Several web-based tools and services offer generated code to control how the different browsers implement web fonts. Also, many web fonts are freely available from providers such as Adobe and Google. Not only do these providers offer free fonts, they can generate the code to add to your web page and display the fonts properly in different browsers. Google has a Google Fonts service that offers a variety of interesting fonts. As shown in Figure 5-4, the One Million Trees web site (*milliontrees.ca*) uses three Google fonts—Cabin Sketch, Cabin, and Neucha—in an attractive layout that would not have the same distinctive look using the standard browser fonts.

Figure 5-4: Using Google web fonts
Courtesy of milliontrees.ca

The font-face property opens a new range of fonts to make web pages more attractive and legible, but in many instances web designers or their clients must be prepared to pay licensing fees for the fonts they want to use. Commercial web sites that license fonts include Typekit (*www.typekit.com*) and Typotheque (*www.typotheque.com*). Other sources for fonts include the Open Font Library (*openfontlibrary.org/media*) and Font Squirrel (*www.fontsquirrel.com*). Tools such as Typecast (*www.typecast.com*) and Typetester (*www.typetester.org*) let you test, preview, and organize web fonts in your browser.

Design for Legibility

Figure 5-5 shows the same paragraph in Times, Trebuchet, Arial, Verdana, and Georgia at the default browser size in Internet Explorer and Chrome. Although these two examples look almost identical, remember that browser versions, operating systems, and video capabilities can produce variations in the weight, spacing, and rendering of font families to individual users.

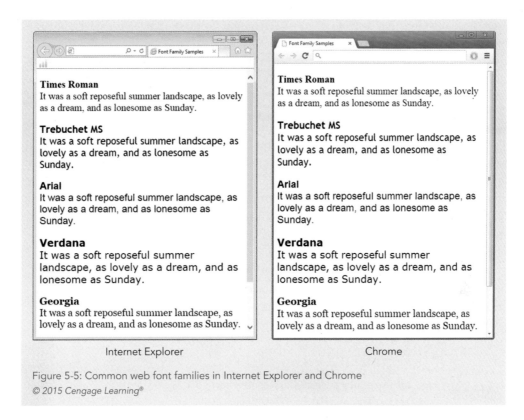

Internet Explorer

Chrome

Figure 5-5: Common web font families in Internet Explorer and Chrome
© 2015 Cengage Learning®

These examples show that where the text wraps at the end of each line depends on the font and the display characteristics of the browser. Because its x-height (the height of the letter *x* in the font) is smaller than that of other fonts, Times Roman can be hard to read, even though it is a serif typeface. This makes it a poor choice for a default font. Georgia is a good replacement for Times Roman because its expanded font width and larger x-height makes it easier to read. Trebuchet is a sans-serif face that has a large x-height and rounded letter forms for easy screen legibility. Arial is widely available and is the most commonly used sans-serif font. Verdana is an expanded font—each letter takes up more horizontal space than letters in the other font families. This makes the text easier to read online, but takes much more space on the page.

The size and face of the type you use on your pages determines the legibility of your text. The computer screen has a lower resolution than the printed page, making fonts that are legible on paper more difficult to read on screen. Keep fonts big enough to be legible, and avoid specialty fonts that degrade when viewed online. To aid the reader, consider adding more white space to the page around your blocks of text and between lines as well. Test your content with both serif and sans-serif body text. Finally, make sure that you provide enough contrast between your text color and the background color; in general, dark text on a light background is easiest to read.

Avoid Creating Text as Graphics

The increased number of common fonts and the availability of web fonts mean that fewer web designers must resort to creating graphics simply to present text. This technique used to be common in the earlier days of web design when font choices were more restricted. Still, most web sites use text graphics in one form or another, whether for a main logo, banner, or advertisement. Some sites still use images for navigation graphics, which can be easily substituted with CSS. Additional graphics mean additional download time, so save text graphics for important purposes, as described here. Remember that including text as graphics means users cannot search for that text, and that your content will not be accessible to users with screen readers and other adaptive devices. Whenever possible, use HTML-styled text on your pages and create HTML and CSS-based navigation, which you will learn about in Chapter 9.

> **Note** You can use a print style sheet to control how your web pages look when they are printed, as described in Appendix D.

Understanding CSS Measurement Units

CSS offers a variety of measurement units, including absolute units, such as points, and relative units, such as ems. The measurement values you choose depend on the destination medium for your content. For example, if you are designing a style sheet for printed media, you can use absolute units of measurement, such as points or centimeters. (See Appendix D for more information.) When you are designing a style sheet for a web page, you can use relative measurement values that adapt to the user's display type, such as ems or percentages. In this section, you will learn about the CSS measurement units. These units are detailed in Table 5-2.

UNIT	UNIT ABBREVIATION	DESCRIPTION
ABSOLUTE UNITS		
Centimeter	cm	Standard metric centimeter
Inch	in	Standard U.S. inch
Millimeter	mm	Standard metric millimeter
Pica	pc	Standard publishing unit equal to 12 points
Point	pt	Standard publishing unit, with 72 points in an inch
Pixel	px	The size of a pixel on the current device
RELATIVE UNITS		
Em	em	The width of the capital M in the current font, usually the same as the font size; 1 em is the default font size, 1.5 em is one-and-one-half times the default font size, and so on. Em is relative to the current font size.
Ex	ex	The height of the letter x in the current font
Percentage	Example: 150%	Works exactly like em: 100% is the default font size, 150% is one-and-one-half times the default font size, and so on
Rem	rem	Works like em, but is relative to the root element of the document. This newer CSS3 measurement unit may not have consistent browser support.
Viewport Width	vw	Equal to 1% of the width of the initial containing block
Viewport Height	vh	Equal to 1% of the height of the initial containing block
Viewport Minimum	vmin	Equal to the smaller value of vw or vh
Viewpoint Maximum	vmax	Equal to the larger value of vw or vh

Table 5-2: CSS Measurement Units
© 2015 Cengage Learning®

Absolute Units

CSS lets you use absolute measurement values that specify a fixed value. The measurement values require a number followed by one of the unit abbreviations listed in Table 5-2. By convention, do not include a space between the value and the measurement unit. The numeric value can be a positive, negative, or fractional value. For example, the following rule sets margins to 1.25 inches:

```
p {margin: 1.25in;}
```

You generally want to avoid using absolute units for web pages because they cannot be scaled to an individual user's display type. Absolute units are appropriate when you know the exact measurements of the destination medium. For example, if you know a document will be printed on 8.5 × 11-inch paper, you can plan your style rules accordingly because you know the physical dimensions of the finished document. For this reason, absolute units are better suited to print destinations than web destinations. Although the point is the standard unit of measurement for type sizes, it is not the best measurement value for the web. Because device displays vary widely in size, they lend themselves better to relative units of measurement that can adapt to different sizes and screen resolutions.

Relative Units

The relative units are designed to let you build scalable web pages that adapt to different display types and sizes. This practice ensures that your type sizes are properly displayed relative to each other or to the default font size set for the browser.

Relative units are always relative to the inherited size of their containing element. For example, the following rule sets the font size for the <body> element to 1.5 times (150%) the size of the browser default:

```
body {font-size: 150%;}
```

Child elements inherit the percentage values of their parents. For example, a <p> element within this body element inherits the 150% sizing.

The em Unit

The em is a printing measurement, traditionally equal to the horizontal length of the capital letter *M* in any given font size. In CSS, the em unit is equal to the font size of an element. It can be used for both horizontal and vertical measurement. In addition to stating font sizes, em is useful for padding and margins. You can read more about this in Chapter 6.

The size of the em is equivalent to the font size of the element. For example, if the default paragraph font size on a device is 12-pixel text, the em equals 12 pixels. Stating a text size of 2em creates 24-pixel text—two times the default size. This is useful because it means that measurements stated in em are always relative to their environment. For example, assume that you want a large heading on your page. If you set the <h1> element to 24 points, it always remains that size. If a user sets his or her default font size to 24 points, the headings are the same size as the text. However, if you use the relative em unit, the size of the heading is always based on the size of the default text. The following rule sets h1 elements to twice the size of the default text:

```
h1 {font-size: 2em;}
```

Remember that em units are relative only to their parent element, in contrast to the rem element described below, which is relative to the root element container of the document.

Percentage

Percentage values for fonts work exactly the same as ems, as described earlier. For example, if the default paragraph font size is 12-point text, a 100% font size equals 12 points. A font size set to 125% based on a 12-point default would be 15 points.

The ex Unit

The **ex unit** is equal to the height of the lowercase letter *x* in any given font. As shown in Figure 5-6, the height of the lowercase letter *x* varies widely from one typeface to another.

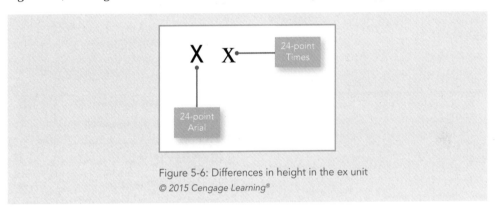

Figure 5-6: Differences in height in the ex unit
© 2015 Cengage Learning®

Ex is a less reliable unit of measurement than em because the size of the letter *x* changes in height from one font family to another, and the browser cannot always calculate the difference correctly. Most browsers simply set the ex value to one-half the value of the font's em size. Ex is not commonly used to set font sizes.

The rem Unit

The rem unit works exactly like the em unit described above. The only difference is that rem is relative only to the root element of the document; hence, the *r* in the name distinguishes it from the em measurement. Rems are useful because all measurements are independent of the parent element in which they are contained. Rems are a new unit and may not have complete browser support.

Viewport Percentage Units

The viewport percentage lengths are relative to the size of the device viewport window used to display your web page. These lengths are similar to percentage lengths, except that they are based on the root container rather than their immediate parent container. The vw and vh elements are equal to 1% of the width or height of the viewport. The vmin value is equal to the smaller measurement when vw and vh are compared. The vmax unit is equal to the larger measurement of vw or vh. The viewport percentage units are newer CSS measurement values and may not be supported in all browsers.

CSS Property Descriptions

The property descriptions on the following pages and in other chapters provide key information about each CSS property. A property description looks like the following:

border-width property description	
Value:	thin	medium	thick	<length>
Initial:	medium
Applies to:	all elements
Inherited:	no
Percentages:	N/A

Table 5-3 lists the five property description categories.

CATEGORY	DEFINITION
Value	The valid keyword or variable values for the property; variable values are set between angle brackets; for example, <length> means enter a length value (Table 5-4 lists the value notation symbols)
Initial	The initial value of the property
Applies to	The elements to which the property applies
Inherited	Indicates if the property is inherited from its parent element
Percentages	Indicates if percentage values are allowed

Table 5-3: Property Description Categories
© 2015 Cengage Learning®

Table 5-4 lists the value category notation.

NOTATION	DEFINITION
< >	Words between angle brackets specify a variable value; for example, <length>
		A single vertical bar separates two or more alternatives, one of which must occur; for example, thin	medium	thick
||	Two vertical bars separate options; one or more of the values can occur in any order; for example, underline || overline || line-through
[]	Square brackets group parts of the property value together; for example, none	[underline || overline || line-through] means that the value is either none or one of the values within the square brackets
?	A question mark indicates that the preceding value or group of values is optional

Table 5-4: Value Category Notation
© 2015 Cengage Learning®

Using the CSS Font Properties

The CSS font properties allow you to control the appearance of your text. These properties describe how the form of each letter looks. The CSS text properties, covered later in this chapter, describe the spacing around the text rather than the actual text itself. In this section, you will learn about the following properties:

> font-family

> font-face

> font-size

> font-style

> font-variant

> font-weight

> font (shorthand property)

Note	You can find all of the example files for this chapter at www.joelsklar.com/pwd6. You can use these files for practice, testing, and as inspiration for your project web sites.

Specifying Font Family

font-family property description	
Value:	<family-name>	<generic-family>
Initial:	depends on user agent
Applies to:	all elements
Inherited:	yes
Percentages:	N/A

The font-family property lets you state a generic font-family name, such as sans-serif, or a specific font-family name, such as Arial. You can also string together a list of font families, separated by commas, supplying a selection of fonts that the browser can attempt to match. Font names containing more than one word must be quoted.

When considering fonts for your web designs, start by thinking in terms of font families, such as serif and sans-serif typefaces, rather than specific styles. If you are not using licensed fonts, be aware of the variable nature of fonts installed on different computers.

You can never be sure that the user will see the exact font you have specified. You can, however, use font fallback values to specify a variety of fonts within a font family, such as Arial or Helvetica, which are both common sans-serif fonts.

Generic Font Families

You can use the following generic names for font families:

> Serif fonts are the traditional letter form, with strokes (or serifs) that finish off the top and bottom of the letter. The most common serif font is Times.

> Sans-serif fonts have no serifs. They are block letters. The most common sans-serif fonts are Helvetica and Arial.

> Monospace fonts are fixed-width fonts. Every letter has the same horizontal width. Monospace is commonly used to mimic typewritten text or for programming code. The style rules and HTML code in this book are printed in Courier, a monospace font.

> Cursive fonts are designed to resemble handwriting. This font is often displayed as Comic Sans, but be aware that this choice can provide inconsistent results.

> Fantasy fonts are primarily decorative. Fantasy is not a widely used choice.

The practice of using generic names ensures greater portability across browsers and operating systems because it does not rely on a specific font being installed on the user's computer. The following rule sets <p> elements to the default sans-serif font:

```
p {font-family: sans-serif;}
```

Of course, if you don't specify a font family, the browser displays the default font, usually some version of Times. Figure 5-7 shows the generic font families in Chrome, Internet Explorer, Firefox, and Safari. Notice the difference in the display size of the monospace font. Also notice that the cursive font is actually Comic Sans, except in Internet Explorer, where it does not resemble handwriting. If a certain font is not available, a different font will be substituted, based on the user's operating system.

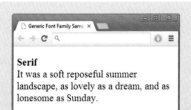

Serif
It was a soft reposeful summer landscape, as lovely as a dream, and as lonesome as Sunday.

Sans-serif
It was a soft reposeful summer landscape, as lovely as a dream, and as lonesome as Sunday.

Monospace
It was a soft reposeful summer landscape, as lovely as a dream, and as lonesome as Sunday.

Cursive
It was a soft reposeful summer landscape, as lovely as a dream, and as lonesome as Sunday.

Chrome

Serif
It was a soft reposeful summer landscape, as lovely as a dream, and as lonesome as Sunday.

Sans-serif
It was a soft reposeful summer landscape, as lovely as a dream, and as lonesome as Sunday.

Monospace
It was a soft reposeful summer landscape, as lovely as a dream, and as lonesome as Sunday.

Cursive
It was a soft reposeful summer landscape, as lovely as a dream, and as lonesome as Sunday.

Internet Explorer

Serif
It was a soft reposeful summer landscape, as lovely as a dream, and as lonesome as Sunday.

Sans-serif
It was a soft reposeful summer landscape, as lovely as a dream, and as lonesome as Sunday.

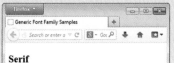

Monospace
It was a soft reposeful summer landscape, as lovely as a dream, and as lonesome as Sunday.

Cursive
It was a soft reposeful summer landscape, as lovely as a dream, and as lonesome as Sunday.

Firefox

Serif
It was a soft reposeful summer landscape, as lovely as a dream, and as lonesome as Sunday.

Sans-serif
It was a soft reposeful summer landscape, as lovely as a dream, and as lonesome as Sunday.

Monospace
It was a soft reposeful summer landscape, as lovely as a dream, and as lonesome as Sunday.

Cursive
It was a soft reposeful summer landscape, as lovely as a dream, and as lonesome as Sunday.

Safari

Figure 5-7: Generic font families in Chrome, Internet Explorer, Firefox, and Safari
© 2015 Cengage Learning®

Specific Font Families

In addition to generic font families, the font-family property lets you declare a specific font family, such as Futura or Garamond. The user must have the font installed on his or her computer or have downloaded it as a web font; otherwise, the browser uses the default font. If the font family name contains white space, such as "lucida console," the font name must be contained within quotes.

The following rule specifies Lucida Console as the font family for the <p> element:

```
p {font-family: "lucida console";}
```

Font Fallbacks

You can specify a list of alternate fonts using a comma as a separator. The browser attempts to load each successive font in the list. If no fonts match, the browser falls back to the default font. The following code tells the browser to use Arial; if Arial is not present, the browser uses Helvetica.

```
p {font-family: arial, helvetica;}
```

Note *You should always include a default generic font, such as sans-serif, as the last choice in your font fallback choices. Doing so makes sure that the browser does not use its default font.*

This font substitution string produces a sans-serif font on PCs that have Arial installed and on Macintosh computers that have Helvetica installed. To further ensure the portability of this rule, add a generic font family name to the list, as shown in the following rule:

```
p {font-family: arial, helvetica, sans-serif;}
```

This rule ensures that the <p> element is displayed in some type of sans-serif font, even if it is not Arial or Helvetica.

Using the @Font-Face Rule

The @font-face rule lets you specify a font to be downloaded and displayed in the browser, overcoming the limitations of only using fonts that reside on a user's computer. The font-face property lets you define the name and location of the desired font. Fonts are usually specified in the TrueType format (TTF). The following code shows an example of the @font-face rule:

```
@font-face {font-family: generica;
src: url(http://www.generic.com/fonts/generica.ttf)}
h1 {font-family: generica, serif;}
```

Remember to always include fallback values in case the browser has a problem downloading the primary font.

Specifying Font Size

font-size property description	
Value:	<absolute-size>	<relative-size>	<length>	<percentage>
Initial:	medium
Applies to:	all elements
Inherited:	the computed value is inherited
Percentages:	refer to parent element's font size

The font-size property gives you control over the specific sizing of your type. You can choose from length units, such as ems or pixels, or a percentage value that is based on the parent element's font size.

The following rule sets the <blockquote> element to 1.5em Arial:

```
blockquote {font-family: arial, sans-serif; font-size: 1.5em;}
```

To specify a default size for a document, use *body* as the selector. This rule sets the text to .85em Arial:

```
body {font-family: arial, sans-serif; font-size: .85em;}
```

You can also choose from a list of absolute size and relative size keywords, as described in the following sections.

Absolute Font Size Keywords

These keywords refer to a table of sizes that is determined by the browser. The keywords are:

> xx-small

> x-small

> small

> medium

> large

> x-large

> xx-large

The CSS specification recommends a scaling factor of 1.2 between sizes for the computer display. Therefore, if the medium font is 10 points, the large font would be 12 points (10 × 1.2 = 12).

Solving the Font Size Dilemma

Figure 5-8 shows a variety of font size samples in the Google Chrome browser. With so many methods of font sizing available, which should you use? The designers of CSS, Hakon Lie and Bert Bos, recommend always using relative sizes (specifically, the em value) to set font sizes on your web pages. Here are some reminders about each relative measurement value:

> **Ems or percentage**—These are the best choice for fonts because ems and percentages are scalable based on the user's default font size. For the same reason, padding and margins specified in ems are another way to make web pages more adaptable.

> **Pixels**—Pixel values entirely depend on the user's screen resolution, making it very difficult to ensure consistent presentation. Pixels are a good choice for borders and other design elements, but not a good choice for fonts.

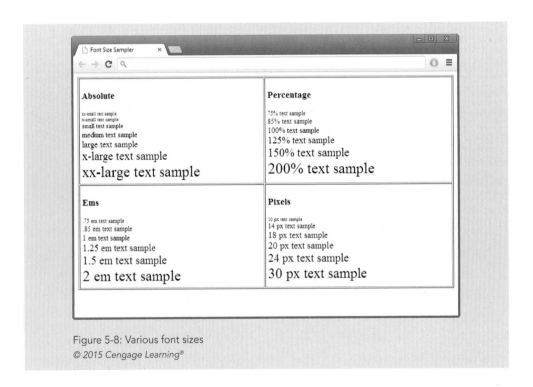

Figure 5-8: Various font sizes
© 2015 Cengage Learning®

Specifying Font Style

font-style property description	
Value:	normal | italic | oblique
Initial:	normal
Applies to:	all elements
Inherited:	yes
Percentages:	N/A

The font-style property lets you specify italic or oblique text. The difference between italic and oblique text is subtle. The italic form of a typeface is designed with different letter forms to create the slanted font, while the oblique form is simply normal text slanted to the right. In print-based typography, oblique text is considered inferior to italic. On the web, however, current browsers cannot make the distinction between the two—either value creates slanted text. The following example sets italicized text for the note class.

```
.note {font-style: italic;}
```

Here is the note class applied to a <p> element:

```
<p class="note">A note to the reader:</p>
```

The text contained in the <p> appears italicized in the browser. Remember that italic text is hard to read on a computer display. Use italics for special emphasis rather than for large blocks of text.

Specifying Font Variant

font-variant property description	
Value:	normal | small-caps
Initial:	normal
Applies to:	all elements
Inherited:	yes
Percentages:	N/A

The font-variant property lets you define small capitals, which are often used for chapter openings, acronyms, and other special purposes. Small capitals are intended to be a different type style from regular capital letters, but this feature is not supported in all browsers. In fact, some simply downsize the regular capital letters. Figure 5-9 shows an example of small capitals.

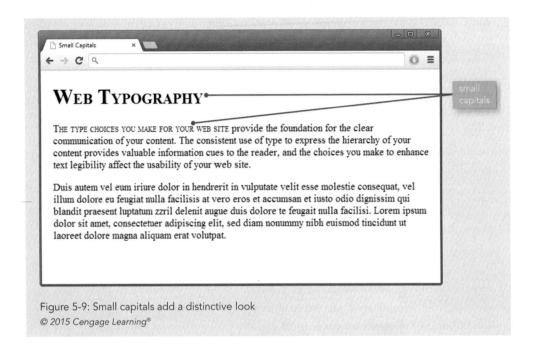

Figure 5-9: Small capitals add a distinctive look
© 2015 Cengage Learning®

In this example, a style rule specifies a class named *small* to be used with a <span> element. The <span> element in the HTML code contains the text that is converted to small capitals.

```
span.small {font-variant: small-caps}
<p><span class="small">The type choices you make for your web
site</span> provide the foundation for...</p>
```

Specifying Font Weight

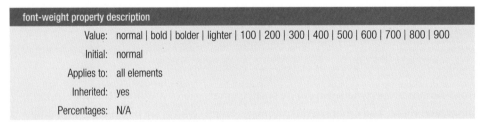

font-weight property description	
Value:	normal | bold | bolder | lighter | 100 | 200 | 300 | 400 | 500 | 600 | 700 | 800 | 900
Initial:	normal
Applies to:	all elements
Inherited:	yes
Percentages:	N/A

The font-weight property lets you set the weight of the typeface. The numeric values express nine levels of weight from 100 to 900, although most browsers and fonts do not support such a wide range of weights. The default type weight is equal to 400, and bold text is equal to 700. Bolder and lighter are relative weights based on the weight of the parent element.

Using the bold value produces the same weight of text as the <strong> element. The following style rule sets the class named *warning* to bold:

```
.warning {font-weight: bold;}
```

Using the Font Shortcut Property

font property description	
Value:	[[<'font-style'> || <'font-variant'> || <'font-weight'>]? <'font-size'> [/ <'line-height'>]? <'font-family'>]
Initial:	see individual properties
Applies to:	all elements
Inherited:	yes
Percentages:	allowed on 'font-size' and 'line-height'

The **font property** is a shortcut that lets you specify the most common font properties in a single statement. The syntax of this property is based on a traditional typographical short-hand notation to set multiple properties related to fonts.

As shown in the value listing for the font shortcut property, the font property lets you state the font-style, font-variant, font-weight, font-size, line-height, and font-family in one statement. The only two required values are font-size and font-family, which must be in the correct order for the style rule to work. The following rules are basic examples of using the font property:

```
p {font: 12pt arial, sans-serif;}
h1 {font: 2em sans-serif;}
```

The font properties other than font-size and font-family are optional and do not have to be included unless you want to change their default. If you want to include line-height, note that it must always follow a slash after the font-size. The following rule sets .85em Arial text on 1em line height:

```
p {font: .85em/1em arial;}
```

The font shortcut property lets you abbreviate the more verbose individual property listings. For example, both of the following rules produce the same result:

```
p {font-weight: bold;
font-size: .85em;
line-height: 1em;
font-family: arial;
}
```

```
p {font: bold .85em/1em arial;} /* Same rule as above */
```

Although the font shortcut property is a convenience, you may prefer to state explicitly the font properties as shown in the more verbose rule, because they are easier to understand. It is also a good idea to choose a convention of using either the individual property names or the shortcut notation, and then to use the convention consistently throughout your web site.

Using the CSS Text Properties

The CSS text properties let you adjust the spacing around and within your text and add text decorations. The properties in this section let you create distinctive text effects. In this section, you will learn about the following properties:

> text-indent
> text-align
> line-height
> vertical-align
> letter-spacing
> word-spacing
> white-space
> text-decoration
> text-transform
> text-shadow

Specifying Text Indents

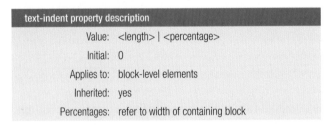

text-indent property description	
Value:	<length> | <percentage>
Initial:	0
Applies to:	block-level elements
Inherited:	yes
Percentages:	refer to width of containing block

Use the text-indent property to set the amount of indentation for the first line of text in an element, such as a paragraph. You can specify a length or percentage value. The percentage is relative to the width of the containing element. If you specify a value of 15%, the indent will be 15% of the width of the element. Negative values let you create a hanging indent. Figure 5-10 shows two text-indent effects.

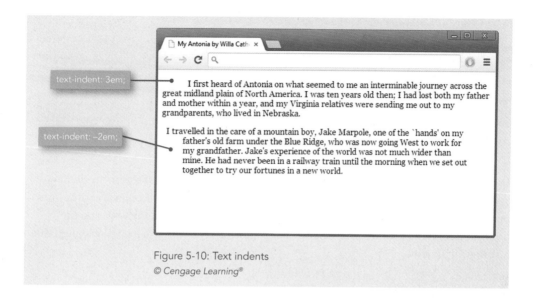

Figure 5-10: Text indents
© Cengage Learning®

The following rules set an indent of 2em for the <p> element and -2em for the <blockquote> element:

```
p {text-indent: 2em;}
blockquote {text-indent: -2em;}
```

Indents are sensitive to the language specification for the document. You can specify the document language with the lang attribute in the opening <html> tag, such as <html lang="en">. In left-to-right reading languages (such as English), the indent is added to the left of the first line; in right-to-left reading languages (such as Hebrew), the indent is added to the right of the first line.

Indents are inherited from parent to child elements. For example, the following rule sets a 2em text indent to an <article> element:

```
article {text-indent: 2em;}
```

Any block-level elements, such as <p>, that are contained within this article element have the same 2em text indent specified in the rule for the parent <article>.

Note | You can find a complete list of the standard language codes here: www.loc.gov/standards/iso639-2/php/code_list.php.

Specifying Text Alignment

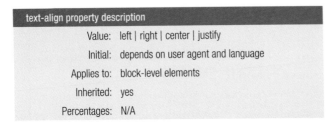

text-align property description	
Value:	left | right | center | justify
Initial:	depends on user agent and language
Applies to:	block-level elements
Inherited:	yes
Percentages:	N/A

Use the text-align property to set horizontal alignment for the lines of text in an element. You can specify four alignment values: left, center, right, and justify. The justify value lines up the text on both horizontal margins, adding white space between the words on the line, like a column of text in a newspaper. The following style rule sets the <p> element to justified alignment:

```
p {text-align: justify;}
```

Figure 5-11 shows a sample of all four alignment values.

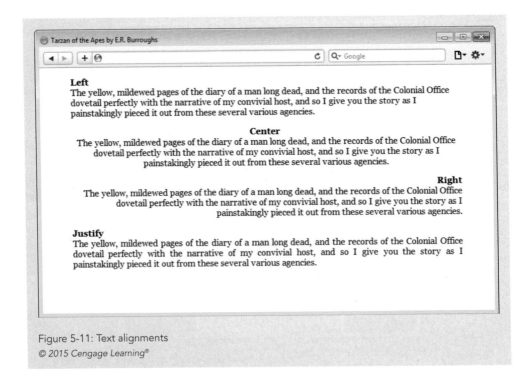

Figure 5-11: Text alignments

© 2015 Cengage Learning®

When choosing an alignment value, keep in mind the default settings for the language and the user's preferences. For example, most Western languages are read from left to right, and the default alignment is left. Unless you are trying to emphasize a particular section of text, use the alignment with which most readers are comfortable. Both right and center alignment are fine for short sections of text, but they make reading difficult for lengthier passages.

Justified text lets you create newspaper-like alignment where the lines of text all have the same length. The browser inserts white space between the words of the text so both margins of the text align, as shown in Figure 5-11. Justify is not supported by all browsers, and different browsers might justify text differently.

Specifying Line Height

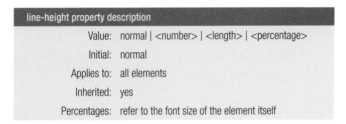

line-height property description	
Value:	normal | <number> | <length> | <percentage>
Initial:	normal
Applies to:	all elements
Inherited:	yes
Percentages:	refer to the font size of the element itself

CSS allows you to specify either a length or percentage value for the line height, which is also known as **leading**, the white space between lines of text. The percentage is based on the font size. Setting the value to 150% with a 1em font size results in a line height of 1.5em. The following rule sets the line height to 150%:

```
p {line-height: 150%;}
```

Figure 5-12 shows the default line height and various adjustments in line height. Notice that the line height is evenly divided between the top and bottom of the element.

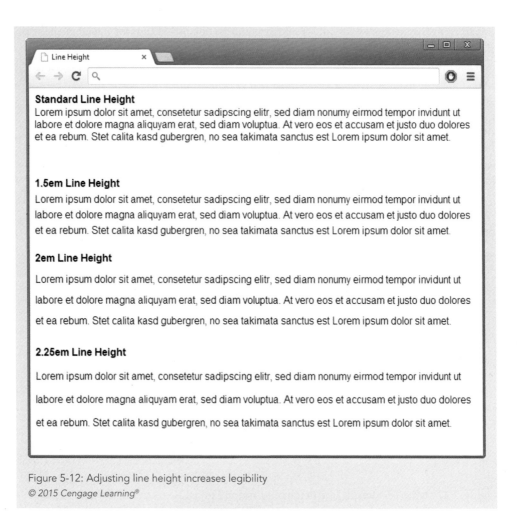

Figure 5-12: Adjusting line height increases legibility
© 2015 Cengage Learning®

The line-height property can increase the legibility of your text. Adding to the default line height inserts additional white space between the lines of text. On a display device, increasing the white space helps guide the user's eyes along the line of text and provides rest for the eye. As Figure 5-12 shows, increasing the line height adds to the legibility of the text.

Specifying Vertical Alignment

vertical-align property description	
Value:	baseline | sub | super | top | text-top | middle | bottom | text-bottom | \<percentage\> | \<length\>
Initial:	baseline
Applies to:	inline-level and 'table-cell' elements
Inherited:	no
Percentages:	refer to the 'line-height' of the element itself

The vertical-align property lets you adjust the vertical alignment of text within the line box. Vertical-align works only on inline elements. You can use this property to superscript or subscript characters above or below the line of text and to align images with text. Table 5-5 defines the different vertical-align values. The baseline, sub, and super values are the most evenly supported by the different browsers.

VALUE	DEFINITION
baseline	Align the baseline of the text with the baseline of the parent element
sub	Lower the baseline of the box to the proper position for subscripts of the parent's box; this value does not automatically create a smaller font size for the subscripted text
middle	The CSS2 specification defines *middle* as "the vertical midpoint of the box with the baseline of the parent box plus half the x-height of the parent;" realistically, this means the middle-aligned text is aligned to half the height of the lowercase letters
super	Raise the baseline of the box to the proper position for superscripts of the parent's box; this value does not automatically create a smaller font size for the superscripted text
text-top	Align the top of the box with the top of the parent element's font
text-bottom	Align the bottom of the box with the bottom of the parent element's content box
top	Align the top of the box with the top of the line box
bottom	Align the bottom of the box with the bottom of the line box

Table 5-5: vertical-align Property Values
© 2015 Cengage Learning®

The following rule sets superscripting for the superscript class:

```
.superscript {vertical-align: super;}
```

Figure 5-13 shows different types of vertical alignments.

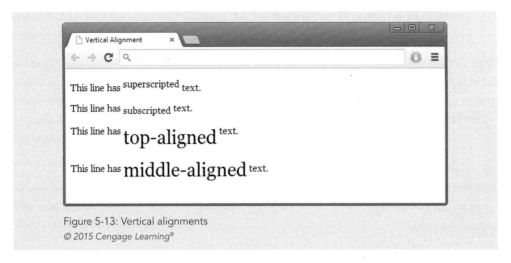

Figure 5-13: Vertical alignments
© 2015 Cengage Learning®

You can also use vertical alignment to align text with graphics. The following rule, added to the <img> element with the style attribute, sets the vertical alignment to top:

```
<img src="image.gif" style="vertical-align: text-top;">
```

Figure 5-14 shows various alignments of images and text. Note that the vertical alignment affects only the one line of text that contains the graphic, because the graphic is an inline element. If you want to wrap a paragraph of text around an image, use the float property, as described in Chapter 6.

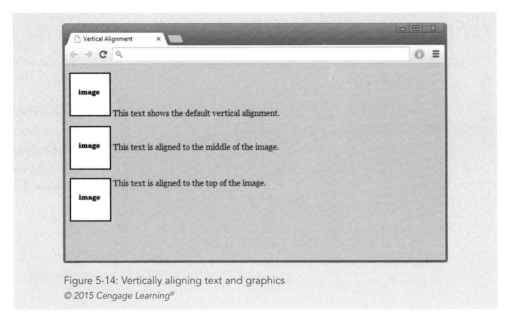

Figure 5-14: Vertically aligning text and graphics
© 2015 Cengage Learning®

Specifying Letter Spacing

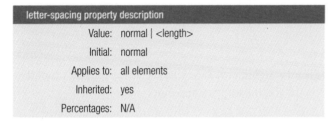

letter-spacing property description	
Value:	normal | <length>
Initial:	normal
Applies to:	all elements
Inherited:	yes
Percentages:	N/A

The letter-spacing property lets you adjust the **kerning**, the white space between letters. The length you specify in the style rule is added to the default letter spacing. The following code sets the letter spacing to 4 pixels:

```
h1 {letter-spacing: 4px;}
```

Figure 5-15 shows samples of different letter-spacing values. The letter-spacing property is an excellent method of differentiating headings from the rest of your text.

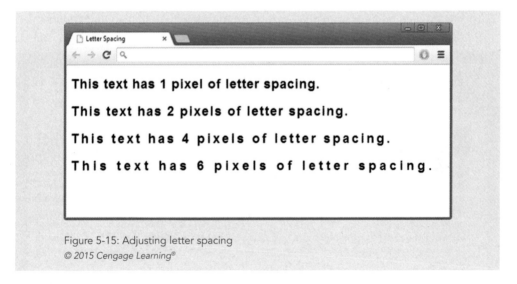

Figure 5-15: Adjusting letter spacing
© 2015 Cengage Learning®

Specifying Word Spacing

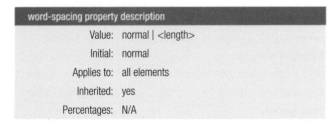

word-spacing property description	
Value:	normal | <length>
Initial:	normal
Applies to:	all elements
Inherited:	yes
Percentages:	N/A

The word-spacing property lets you adjust the white space between words in the text. The length you specify in the style rule is added to the default word spacing. The following code sets the word spacing to 2em:

```
h1 {word-spacing: 2em;}
```

Figure 5-16 shows the result of the word-spacing property. Like the letter-spacing property, word spacing is an effective way to make your headings stand out.

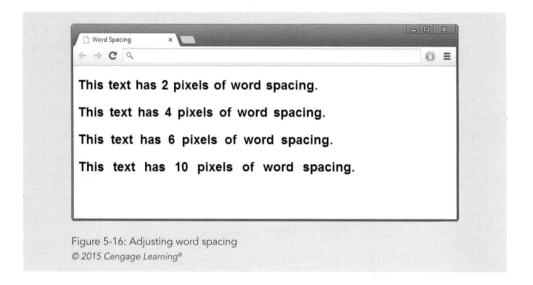

Figure 5-16: Adjusting word spacing
© 2015 Cengage Learning®

Controlling White Space

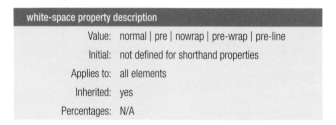

white-space property description	
Value:	normal	pre	nowrap	pre-wrap	pre-line
Initial:	not defined for shorthand properties
Applies to:	all elements
Inherited:	yes
Percentages:	N/A

The CSS3 white-space property controls how paragraph text wraps and whether to preserve white space. See Figure 5-17. Normally the browser ignores extra spaces between words; you can preserve this space using the *pre* value. This property is especially useful for representing indents or special spacing in computer code. Several values are available to let you control every aspect of line wrapping and white space. See Table 5-6. Reserve this property for special design needs; in general, you want to let the browser wrap the text normally within the columns and sections of your page layout.

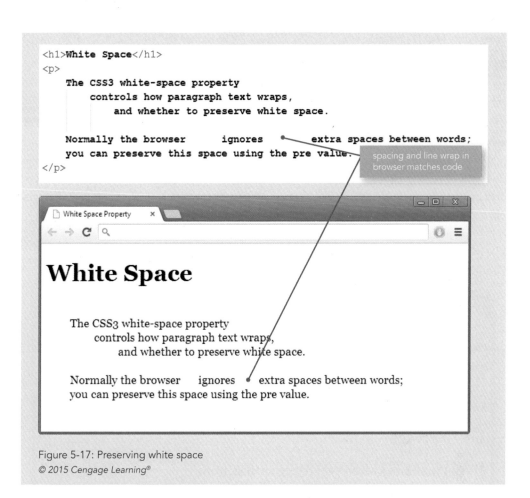

Figure 5-17: Preserving white space
© 2015 Cengage Learning®

VALUE	DESCRIPTION
normal	The browser collapses sequences of white space into a single space and wraps lines of text as needed
pre	This value preserves white space; lines of text will not wrap unless there is a element
nowrap	Like the normal value, this value collapses white space, but like pre, it does not allow wrapping
pre-wrap	Like pre, this value preserves white space, but like normal, it allows wrapping
pre-line	Like normal, this value collapses consecutive spaces and allows wrapping, but it preserves segment breaks in the source as forced line breaks

Table 5-6: white-space Property Values Description
© 2015 Cengage Learning®

Specifying Text Decoration

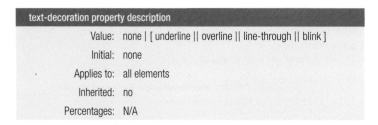

text-decoration property description	
Value:	none | [underline || overline || line-through || blink]
Initial:	none
Applies to:	all elements
Inherited:	no
Percentages:	N/A

Text decoration lets you underline text, an effect that has particular meaning in a hypertext environment. See Figure 5-18. Your users know to look for underlined words as the indicators for hypertext links. Any text you underline appears to be a hypertext link. Except for text links, underlining is an inappropriate text style for a web page.

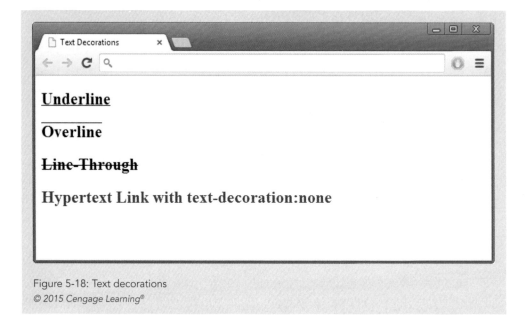

Figure 5-18: Text decorations
© 2015 Cengage Learning®

As Figure 5-18 shows, the text-decoration property lets you remove the underlining from the <a> element. As you read earlier, the user commonly relies on underlining to indicate a hypertext link. However, some web sites choose to remove link underlining, indicating links with a color different from the standard text color. You can remove the underlining from your anchor elements with the following rule:

```
a {text-decoration: none;}
```

Users with sight disabilities can have trouble finding the links in your content if you choose to remove the underlining. Alternately, users can override the author's style rules by setting preferences in their browsers or applying their own style sheets.

Specifying Capitalization

text-transform property description	
Value:	capitalize | uppercase | lowercase | none
Initial:	none
Applies to:	all elements
Inherited:	no
Percentages:	N/A

The text-transform property lets you change the capitalization of text. This property is useful for headings when you want to change their capitalization from the original format without actually editing the text.

The *capitalize* value capitalizes the first letter of every word. The values of *uppercase* and *lowercase* transform the case of an entire word. The following code transforms the case of an <h1> element to uppercase.

```
h1 {text-transform: uppercase;}
```

Specifying Text Shadow

text-shadow property description	
Value:	none | [<shadow>,] * <shadow>
Initial:	none
Applies to:	all elements
Inherited:	yes
Percentages:	N/A

The text-shadow property lets you define a shadow that is displayed behind text. You can specify the vertical and horizontal offset as well as the blur of the shadow. This property is ideal for adding depth and character to headings and other important typographic elements on your web page, although it is best used sparingly. The following code shows the text-shadow property syntax.

```
h1 {text-shadow: 2px 2px #666;}
```

The first two length values indicate the horizontal and vertical offset from direct alignment with the text. Positive values move to the right and down, and negative values move to the left and up.

The third length value specifies the blur amount, which determines how softly the edges of the shadow are displayed. The final value sets the color of the shadow. Figure 5-19 shows examples of different shadow values with and without blur.

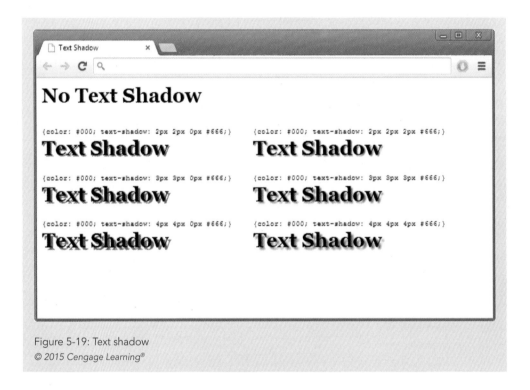

Figure 5-19: Text shadow
© 2015 Cengage Learning®

Remember to test the text-shadow property carefully. However, if text-shadow is not supported, the text is simply displayed without a shadow.

Currently Unsupported CSS3 Properties

The CSS3 recommendation contains some properties that are not supported evenly or at all by different browsers and devices. These properties may change, so check the latest CSS3 documentation at *www.w3.org* for the latest updates. As new versions of the browsers are released, these properties should gradually become supported. Table 5-7 contains descriptions of these properties.

PROPERTY	CHARACTERISTICS
text-wrap Controls text wrapping	Value: normal | unrestricted | none | suppress Initial: normal Applies to: all elements Inherited: yes Percentages: N/A
word-wrap Controls whether words can be broken to wrap a sentence	Value: normal | break-word Initial: normal Applies to: all elements Inherited: yes Percentages: N/A
text-align-last When text is set to justify, the last line in a paragraph may align unevenly; this property controls the alignment of the last line	Value: start | end | left | right | center | justify Initial: start Applies to: all elements Inherited: yes Percentages: N/A
text-emphasis Intended for Asian languages; adds accent marks above characters for emphasis	Value: none | [[accent | dot | circle | disc] [before | after]?] Initial: none Applies to: all elements Inherited: yes Percentages: N/A
text-outline Specifies a text outline's thickness and blur length	Value: none | [<color> <length> <length>? | <length> <length>? <color>] Initial: none Applies to: all elements Inherited: yes Percentages: N/A

Continued on next page...

PROPERTY	CHARACTERISTICS
font-stretch The font-stretch property lets you expand or compress the font face; not all forms of the font may be available, so the next closest choice is substituted: the closest condensed face substitutes for any condensed choice, and the closest expanded face for any expanded choice	Value: normal | wider | narrower | ultra-condensed | extra-condensed | condensed | semi-condensed | semi-expanded | expanded | extra-expanded | ultra-expanded | inherit Initial: none Applies to: all elements Inherited: yes Percentages: N/A
font-size-adjust For font sizes, the size of the actual characters varies by font—if you are using font substitution, one of the substituted fonts may be smaller and less legible than the primary font you specified; the font-size-adjust property lets you maintain the legibility of your text when substitution occurs. It affects the x-height of the font.	Value: <number> | none | inherit Initial: see individual properties Applies to: all elements Inherited: yes Percentages: N/A

Table 5-7: Currently Unsupported CSS3 Properties
© 2015 Cengage Learning®

Activity: Building a Font and Text Properties Style Sheet

In the following set of steps, you will build a style sheet that uses the typographic techniques you learned about in this chapter. Save your file, and test your work in the browser as you complete each step.

To build the style sheet:

1. Copy the **ch5activity1.html** file from the Chapter05 folder provided with your Data Files to the Chapter05 folder in your work folder. (Create the Chapter05 folder, if necessary.)

2. Open the file **ch5activity1.html** in your HTML editor, insert your name in the comment at the bottom of the file, and save the file in your Chapter05 folder with the same name.

3. In your browser, open the file **ch5activity1.html**. When you open the file, it looks like Figure 5-20.

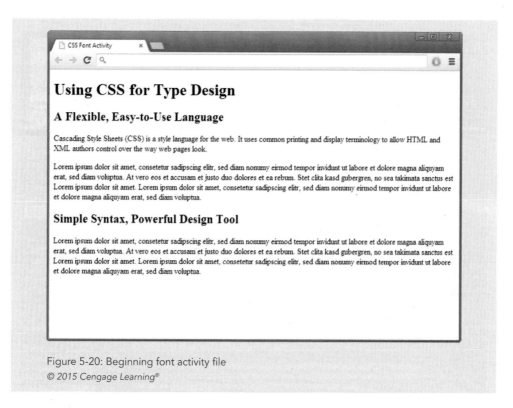

Figure 5-20: Beginning font activity file
© 2015 Cengage Learning®

Adding the <style> Section

Because you are working on a single document, you can use a <style> element in the <head> section to contain your style rules. In the steps throughout the chapter, enter the code shown in bold and blue.

To add the <style> section:

1. Using your text editor, add a <style> element in the <head> section to contain your style rules, as shown in the following code. Leave a few lines of white space between the <style> tags to contain the style rules.

```
<head>
<title>CSS Font Activity</title>
<style>



</style>
</head>
```

2. Save the file.

Styling the Headings

To style the headings:

1. Write a style rule that selects the <h1> element. Set the font-size to 3em and the font-family to georgia, with a fallback generic serif font, as shown in the following code:

```
h1 {
    font-size: 3em;
    font-family: georgia, serif;
}
```

2. Write a style rule that selects the <h2> element. Set the font-size to 1.5em and the font-family to arial. Add fallback values of helvetica and sans-serif to the font-family declaration.

```
h2 {
    font-size: 1.5em;
    font-family: arial, helvetica, sans-serif;
}
```

3. Save your file, and check your work in the browser. Figure 5-21 shows the changes from the style rules you added.

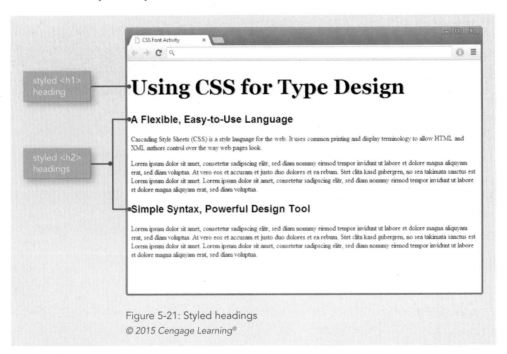

Figure 5-21: Styled headings
© 2015 Cengage Learning®

Styling the Paragraphs

Write a rule that makes the paragraph text easier to read by changing the font, increasing the white space between lines, and adding a left margin to move the paragraphs away from the edge of the browser window. This rule will also use a class name to apply the style rule to the paragraphs.

To style the paragraphs:

1. Write a style rule that uses a class selector and a class named *copy*. Set the font-family property to georgia, serif as you did for the <h1> element. Set the line-height property to 1.5em, and add a margin-left of 20 pixels (20px). You will learn more about margins in Chapter 6.

```
.copy {
    font-family: georgia, serif;
    line-height: 1.5em;
    margin-left: 20px;
}
```

2. Locate the first <p> element within the file and add class="copy" to the opening <p> tag as shown:

```
<p class="copy">Cascading Style Sheets (CSS) is a style language for
the web. It uses common printing and display terminology to allow
HTML and XML authors control over the way web pages look.</p>
```

3. Repeat Step 2 and add the class attribute to the remaining <p> elements. There are three in all.

4. Save your file, and check your work in the browser. Figure 5-22 shows the changes from the style rules you added.

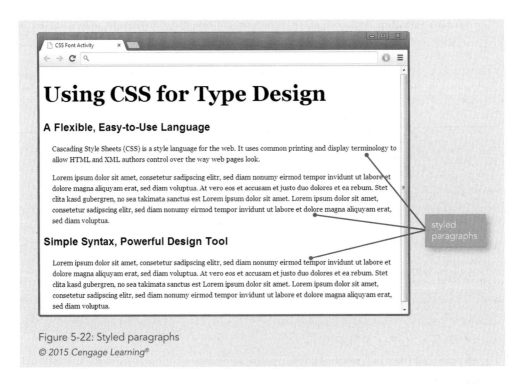

Figure 5-22: Styled paragraphs
© 2015 Cengage Learning®

Making the Second-Level Headings More Distinctive

The page is looking better with more legible text, but the second-level headings could stand out more. You will add a left margin and letter-spacing to the existing style rule.

To add styles to the <h2> elements:

1. Include a style rule in the existing h2 selector to add a left margin of 20 pixels that aligns the headings with the paragraphs.

```
h2 {
    font-size: 1.5em;
    font-family: arial, helvetica, sans-serif;
    margin-left: 20px;
}
```

2. Add one more style rule to set the letter-spacing to 4px.

```
h2 {
    font-size: 1.5em;
    font-family: arial, helvetica, sans-serif;
    margin-left: 20px;
```

```
        letter-spacing: 4px;
}
```

3. Save the file, and view your changes in the browser. It should look similar to Figure 5-23.

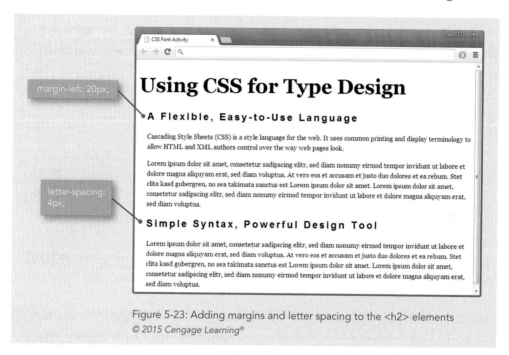

Figure 5-23: Adding margins and letter spacing to the <h2> elements
© 2015 Cengage Learning®

Capitalizing Key Words

You can use the text-transform property along with a <span> element and class selector to select the first few words in the first paragraph and capitalize them. This common printing technique adds a professional look to the page.

To select and capitalize the words:

1. Write a style rule that uses a class selector for a class named caps. Add the text-transform property set to uppercase.

```
.caps {
    text-transform: uppercase;}
```

2. Add another declaration to the rule, specifying a bold font-weight.

```
.caps {
    text-transform: uppercase;
    font-weight: bold;
}
```

3. Locate the text "Cascading Style Sheets (CSS)" in the first paragraph, and place span tags before and after this text.

```
<p class="copy"><span>Cascading Style Sheets (CSS)</span> is a
style language for the web. It uses common printing and display
terminology to allow HTML and XML authors control over the way web
pages look.</p>
```

4. Add the class attribute to the opening <span> tag and set the value to **caps**.

```
<p class="copy"><span class="caps">Cascading Style Sheets (CSS)
</span> is a style language for the web. It uses common printing and
display terminology to allow HTML and XML authors control over the
way web pages look.</p>
```

5. Save the file, and view your changes in the browser. Figure 5-24 shows the result of the style rule.

Figure 5-24: Transforming text to uppercase
© 2015 Cengage Learning®

Customizing Bulleted and Numbered Lists

The list-style properties let you control the visual characteristics of elements that have a display property value of list-item, which are the numbered and bulleted lists signified by the <ol> and <ul> elements. These properties let you set the appearance of the marker that indicates each item within the list. With CSS, the marker can be a symbol, number, or image. You can also determine the position of the marker next to the list content.

The two common elements that have a default display value of list-item are <ul> and <ol>, which generate a bulleted (unordered) and ordered list, respectively. The following code shows a sample of each type of list:

```
<!-- Bulleted List -->
<h3>Things to do...</h3>
  <ul>
   <li>Buy dog food</li>
   <li>Clean up the house</li>
   <li>Take a rest</li>
  </ul>
<!-- Ordered List -->
<h3>Places to go...</h3>
  <ol>
   <li>Paris</li>
   <li>Sydney</li>
   <li>Cairo</li>
  </ol>
```

Figure 5-25 shows the result of this code. Notice that the default markers are a solid bullet, called a disc for the <ul> list, and an Arabic numeral called decimal for the <ol> list. You can change these marker values with the CSS list-style properties.

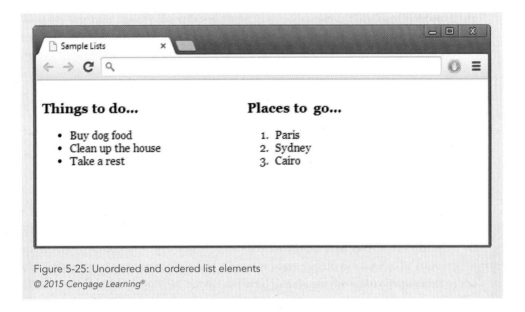

Figure 5-25: Unordered and ordered list elements

© 2015 Cengage Learning®

Specifying the list-style-type Property

The list-style-type property lets you customize the list marker to a variety of different values.

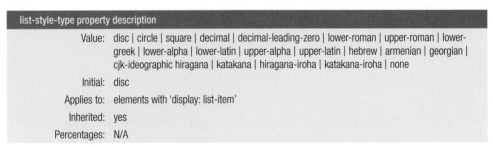

list-style-type property description	
Value:	disc | circle | square | decimal | decimal-leading-zero | lower-roman | upper-roman | lower-greek | lower-alpha | lower-latin | upper-alpha | upper-latin | hebrew | armenian | georgian | cjk-ideographic hiragana | katakana | hiragana-iroha | katakana-iroha | none
Initial:	disc
Applies to:	elements with 'display: list-item'
Inherited:	yes
Percentages:	N/A

The list-style-type property lets you specify one of three types of markers for a list. You can choose a symbol, a numbering system, or an alphabetical system. CSS allows a wide variety of marker values. Remember to test support for these markers in different browsers. Tables 5-8, 5-9, and 5-10 list the different values and their descriptions.

VALUE	DESCRIPTION
disc	Filled circle (see Figure 5-26)
circle	Hollow circle (see Figure 5-26)
square	Filled square (see Figure 5-26)

Table 5-8: Bulleted List Values
© 2015 Cengage Learning®

VALUE	DESCRIPTION
decimal	Decimal numbers, beginning with 1; this is the default numbering
decimal-leading-zero	Decimal numbers padded by initial zeros (01, 02, 03...)
lower-roman	Lowercase roman numerals (i, ii, iii...)
upper-roman	Uppercase roman numerals (I, II, III...)
hebrew	Traditional Hebrew numbering
georgian	Traditional Georgian numbering
armenian	Traditional Armenian numbering
cjk-ideographic	Plain ideographic numbers
hiragana	Japanese hiragana language characters
katakana	Japanese katakana language characters
hiragana-iroha	Japanese hiragana-iroha language characters
katakana-iroha	Japanese katakana-iroha language characters

Table 5-9: Numerical List Values
© 2015 Cengage Learning®

VALUE	DESCRIPTION
lower-alpha	Lowercase ASCII letters (a, b, c, ... z)
upper-alpha	Uppercase ASCII letters (A, B, C, ... Z)
lower-greek	Lowercase classical Greek

Table 5-10: Alphabetical List Values
© 2015 Cengage Learning®

Figure 5-26 shows the list types that most browsers support.

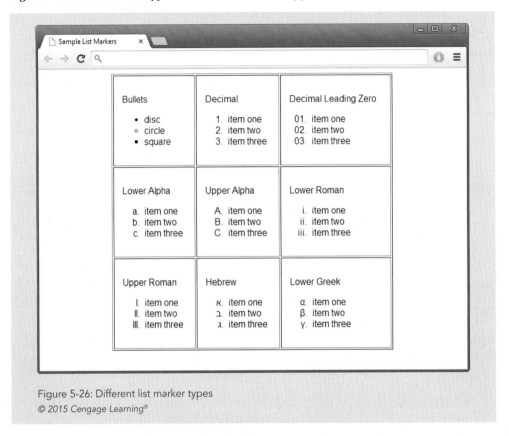

Figure 5-26: Different list marker types
© 2015 Cengage Learning®

To specify a list-style marker type, select the list container element, either ul or ol, and specify the value as shown in the following style rules:

```
ol {list-style-type: decimal-leading-zero;}
ul {list-style-type: circle;}
```

Sometimes, you might want to specify a list-style-type within an individual list. You can do this by using the style attribute within the <ul> or <ol> element, as shown in the following code:

```
<ol style="list-style-type: lower-alpha;">
<li>Item One</li>
<li>Item Two</li>
<li>Item Three</li>
</ol>
```

This style rule affects only this one instance of the list.

Specifying the list-style-image Property

The list-style-image property lets you easily attach an image to a list and have it repeated as the marker symbol.

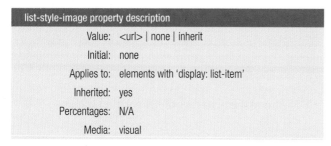

list-style-image property description	
Value:	<url> | none | inherit
Initial:	none
Applies to:	elements with 'display: list-item'
Inherited:	yes
Percentages:	N/A
Media:	visual

The list-style-image property lets you replace the standard symbol with an image of your choice. The following code shows the style rule that attaches an image to a bulleted list:

```
ul {list-style-image: url(pawprint.gif);}
```

Figure 5-27 shows the result of the style rule. The image is repeated whenever a list element is used.

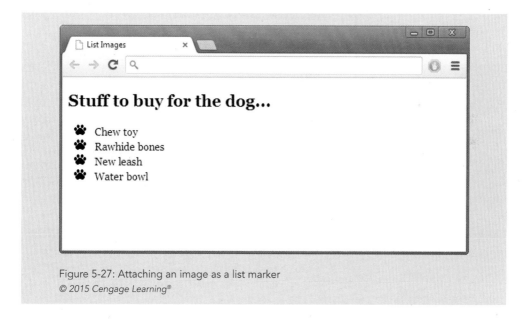

Figure 5-27: Attaching an image as a list marker
© 2015 Cengage Learning®

Specifying the list-style-position Property

The list-style-position property lets you determine the placement of the list marker, either inside or outside the list-item content box.

list-style-position property description	
Value:	inside | outside | inherit
Initial:	outside
Applies to:	elements with 'display: list-item'
Inherited:	yes
Percentages:	N/A
Media:	visual

The default value is outside. Figure 5-28 shows the two types of list position values.

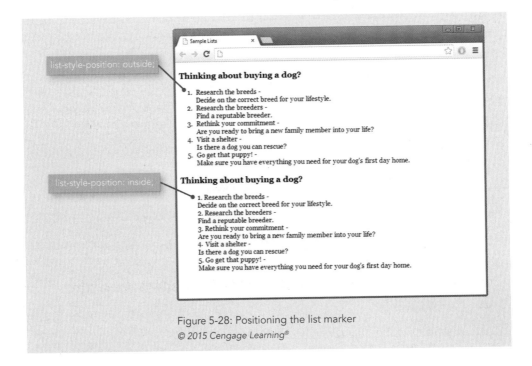

Figure 5-28: Positioning the list marker

© 2015 Cengage Learning®

This figure shows two <ol> lists. The style rules for this page use a class selector to differentiate between the two:

```
ol.outside {list-style-position: outside;}
ol.inside {list-style-position: inside;}
```

The class is then applied to each <ol> element, as shown in the following code fragment for the first list:

```
<ol class="outside">
```

The class is applied to the second list in the same way:

```
<ol class="inside">
```

Using the list-style Shorthand Property

Like the font shorthand property, the list-style property lets you write a single rule to specify all of the list-item properties.

list-style-shorthand property description	
Value:	[<list-style-type> || <list-style-position> || <list-style-image>] | inherit
Initial:	not defined for shorthand properties
Applies to:	elements with 'display: list-item'
Inherited:	yes
Percentages:	N/A
Media:	visual

The list-style shorthand property lets you state the following list-style properties in one concise style rule:

> list-style-type

> list-style-image

> list-style-position

You can specify values in any order. In the following style rule, the list is set to lowercase alphabetical letters that are inside the list box:

```
ol {list-style: lower-alpha inside;}
```

Skills at Work | *Cultivate Good Relationships*

When you work as a professional web designer in an organization, you encounter a wide variety of people in different roles. You work with graphic designers, software developers, project managers, and peers. These people are integral to the success of your project and your career. Always try to develop good working relationships with your coworkers. Build trust by delivering on your responsibilities and tasks. Stop what you are doing to answer questions, give advice, or assist a coworker. Contribute thoughtfully and respect the opinions of others. Be an active listener, and be willing to compromise. When projects are a success, be sure to credit coworkers, and when projects run into trouble, be prepared to shoulder part of the blame. Honesty and trust in the workplace will lead to your future success and enjoyment in your career.

Chapter Summary

You can use Cascading Style Sheets to manipulate a variety of text properties and achieve professional-quality typography on your web site. Keep the following points in mind:

> Use type to communicate information structure. Be sparing with your type choices; use fonts consistently and design for legibility.

> Remember that HTML text downloads faster than graphics-based text. Use HTML text whenever possible.

> Use fonts that appear as consistently as possible across operating systems.

> Standardize your styles by building external style sheets and linking them to multiple documents.

> Test your work. Different browsers and computing platforms render text in different sizes.

> Use type effectively by choosing available fonts and sizes. Design for legibility and use text to communicate information about the structure of your material.

> Choose the correct measurement unit based on the destination medium. Ems or percentage measurements can best scale the text to the user's device.

> Use font properties to control the look of your letter forms. Specify font-substitution values to ensure that your text is displayed properly across different platforms.

> Use the text spacing properties to create more visually interesting and legible text.

Key Terms

cursive—A generic value for the CSS font-family property. Cursive fonts are designed to resemble handwriting. Most browsers do not support this font family.

em unit—In CSS, a unit equal to the font size of an element.

ex unit—In CSS, a unit equal to the height of the lowercase letter x in any given font.

fantasy—A generic value for the CSS font-family property. Fantasy fonts are primarily decorative. Most browsers do not support this font family.

font—A typeface in a particular size, such as Times Roman 24 point.

font property—In CSS, a shortcut that lets you specify the most common font properties in a single statement.

kerning—The white space between characters.

leading—The white space between lines of text.

monospace—A generic value for the CSS font-family property. Monospace fonts are fixed-width fonts. Every letter has the same horizontal width.

sans-serif—A generic value for the CSS font-family property. Sans-serif fonts have no serifs. The most common sans-serif fonts are Helvetica and Arial.

serif—A generic value for the CSS font-family property. Serif is the traditional printing letter form, with strokes (or serifs) that finish off the top and bottom of the letter. The most common serif fonts on the web are Times and Times Roman.

text property—A CSS property that lets you adjust the spacing around and within your text.

typeface—The name of a type family, such as Times Roman or Futura Condensed.

x-height—The height of the letter *x* in a particular font.

Review Questions and Exercises

1. What is the default browser font?

2. What does the browser do if you specify a font that is not stored on a user's computer?

3. What are two drawbacks to the use of graphics-based text?

4. What are the three types of CSS measurement units?

5. What is the best destination for absolute units of measurement?

6. Why would you use relative or percentage values for a web page?

7. What is the size of the em?

8. What determines the size of a pixel?

9. What is the advantage of the generic font families?

10. Write a font-family substitution string that selects Arial, Helvetica, or any sans-serif font for a <p> element.

11. Write a style rule for an <h2> element that specifies bold text that is twice the size of the default font size.

12. Write a rule specifying that <p> elements appear as 1.5em text with 2em leading.

13. Write a rule specifying that <strong> elements are displayed in red only when they appear within <p> elements.

14. Write a rule defining a division named *note*. Specify 12-point bold Arial text on a yellow background.

15. What three typographic white-space areas can you affect with style rules?

16. Write a style rule for a <p> element with a 1.5 em hanging indent and a 30-pixel margin on the left and right sides.

17. Rewrite the following rule using the font shortcut property:

    ```
    blockquote {font-style: italic; font-size: 1.2em;
    line-height: 1.75em; font-family: times, serif;}
    ```

18. What is a benefit of increasing the standard text line height?

19. What is the size of the text indent and line height relative to the user's default font size in the following style rule?

```
p {text-indent: 3em; line-height: 150%;}
```

Hands-On Projects

1. In the following set of steps, you will learn how to style list-item elements with the list-style properties. As you work through the exercise, refer to Figure 5-30 to see the results you will achieve. Save your file and test your work in the browser as you complete each step.

   To apply the list-style properties:
   a. Open the file **ch5project1.html** in your HTML editor.
   b. Copy the image file **diamond.gif** into your work folder.
   c. In your browser, open the file **ch5project1.html**. When you open the file, it looks like Figure 5-29. Notice that the file contains three lists. You will apply a different list-style to each list.

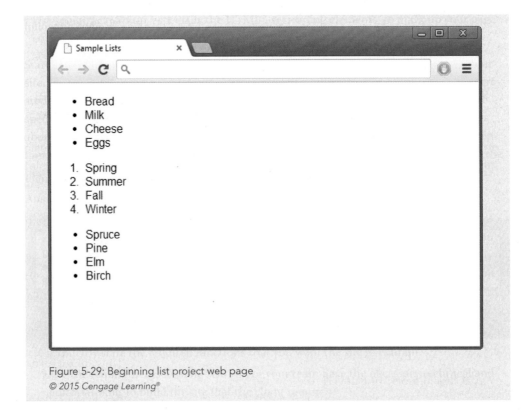

Figure 5-29: Beginning list project web page
© 2015 Cengage Learning®

d. The first list on the page is a bulleted list that currently displays the default disc (bullet) style. Write a style rule that uses a class selector circle to uniquely select the list. Set the list-style-type property to change the bullet style to circle.

```
ul.circle {list-style-type: circle;}
```

e. Now apply the style to the first list by adding the class attribute to the <ul> element.

```
<!-- Bulleted List -->
<ul class="circle">
<li>Bread</li>
<li>Milk</li>
<li>Cheese</li>
<li>Eggs</li>
</ul>
```

f. The second list on the page is an ordered list that currently displays the default decimal style. Write a style rule that uses a class selector alpha to uniquely select the list. Set the list-style-type property to change the style to upper-alpha.

```
ol.alpha {list-style-type: upper-alpha;}
```

g. Now apply the style to the second list by adding the class attribute to the <ol> element.

```
<!-- Alphabetical List -->
<ol class="alpha">
<li>Spring</li>
<li>Summer</li>
<li>Fall</li>
<li>Winter</li>
</ol>
```

h. The third list on the page is an unordered list that currently displays the default bullet style. Write a style rule that uses a class selector image to uniquely select the list. Set the list-style-image property to a URL value, using the image file **diamond.gif**.

```
ul.image {list-style-image: url(diamond.gif);}
```

i. Now apply the style to the third list by adding the class attribute to the `<ol>` element. Figure 5-30 shows the finished document.

```
<!-- List Image -->
<ul class="image">
<li>Spruce</li>
<li>Pine</li>
<li>Elm</li>
<li>Birch</li>
</ul>
```

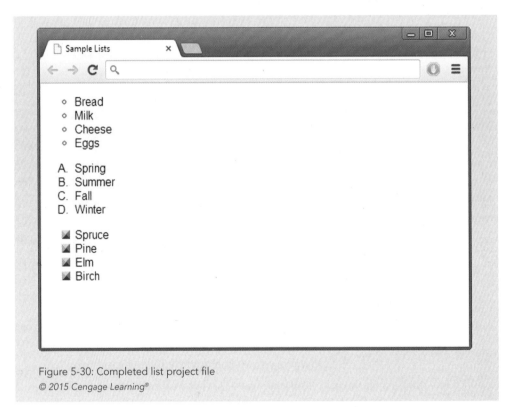

Figure 5-30: Completed list project file
© 2015 Cengage Learning®

2. Modify an existing HTML document to use Cascading Style Sheets font and text properties. You can download or copy the **ch5project2.html** file from the Chapter05 folder provided with your Data Files to the Chapter05 folder in your work folder. Use this as a practice file for this activity.

    a. Build styles using the existing standard HTML elements in the file.
    b. Test the work in multiple browsers to verify that all styles are portable.
    c. Remove the styles, and place them in an external style sheet.
    d. Link the HTML file to the style sheet. Test to make sure the file is displayed properly.

3. Browse the web for examples of good typography. Write a short design critique of why the type works effectively on the web sites you find. Save and print screen shots of the sample web pages to accompany your critique.

4. Browse the web for examples of poor typography. Write a short design critique of why the type is confusing or misleading to the user. Save and print screen shots of the sample web pages to accompany your critique.

5. In this project, you have a chance to test the font and text properties on paragraphs of text. Save and view the file in your browser after completing each step.

    a. Using your HTML editor, create a simple HTML file (or open an existing file) that contains multiple <p> elements and so on. Save the file in your Chapter05 folder as **ch5project5.html**.
    b. Add a <style> element to the <head> section, as shown in the following code:

```
<head>
<title>CSS Test Document</title>
<style>

</style>
</head>
```

    c. Write a style rule that uses p as a selector and sets the font-family to a sans-serif font. You can use a generic font family, or choose one of the fonts available on your computer.
    d. Specify a list of alternate fonts to ensure that your font choice is displayed properly across a range of computers.
    e. Specify a text indent for the <p> elements. Use the em value as the measurement unit.
    f. Add the line-height property to the style rule. Experiment with different line heights until you find one that you feel enhances the legibility of the paragraph text.

Individual Case Project

Design the type hierarchy for your Case Project web site. Create a type specification HTML page that shows examples of the different typefaces and sizes and how they will be used. This can be a mock-up page that uses generic content but demonstrates the overall typographic scheme. Consider the following questions:

> What will be the typefaces and styles for the body type and headings?

> How many levels of headings are necessary?

> What are the different weights and sizes of the headings?

> How will text be emphasized?

> Will hypertext links be standard or custom colors?

> How will you ensure the legibility and readability of your text?

> What will your line length be?

Team Case Project

Meet as a team and discuss the type hierarchy and options for your site. Each team member should bring a type specification HTML page with his or her ideas and examples of the different typefaces and sizes and how they can be used. This can be a mock-up page that uses generic content but demonstrates the overall typographic scheme. Consider the following questions:

> What will be the typefaces and styles for the body type and headings?

> How many levels of headings are necessary?

> What are the different weights and sizes of the headings?

> How will text be emphasized?

> Will hypertext links be standard or custom colors?

> How will you ensure the legibility and readability of your text?

> What will your line length be?

CHAPTER **6**

BOX PROPERTIES

When you complete this chapter, you will be able to:

> Understand the CSS visual formatting model

> Use the CSS box model

> Apply the margin properties

> Apply the padding properties

> Apply the border properties

> Use the page layout box properties

> Create a simple page layout

In this chapter, you will explore the CSS box properties. These properties let you control the margin, padding, and border characteristics of block-level elements. To understand how these properties work, you will first learn about the CSS visual formatting model and the box model. These models control the way content is displayed on a web page. Then you will learn about the margin, padding, and border properties and how you can use them to enhance the display of content in the browser. Finally, you will see how the special box properties—width, height, float, and clear—let you create containers for content that you can position on your web page. These box properties will become the basis for the page layout techniques you will learn about in the next chapter.

Understanding the CSS Visual Formatting Model

The **CSS visual formatting model** describes how the element content boxes should be displayed by the browser—for example, whether scroll bars appear and how text is wrapped based on the browser window size. The visual formatting model is based on the hierarchical structure of the HTML document and the element display type. In HTML, elements fall into two primary box types:

> **Block**—Block-level boxes appear as blocks such as paragraphs. Block elements can contain other block elements or inline boxes that contain the element content.

> **Inline**—Inline-level boxes contain the content within the block-level elements. They do not form new blocks of content.

Figure 6-1 shows three different block-level elements: <body>, <h1>, and <p>. The <h1> and <p> elements contain inline content boxes.

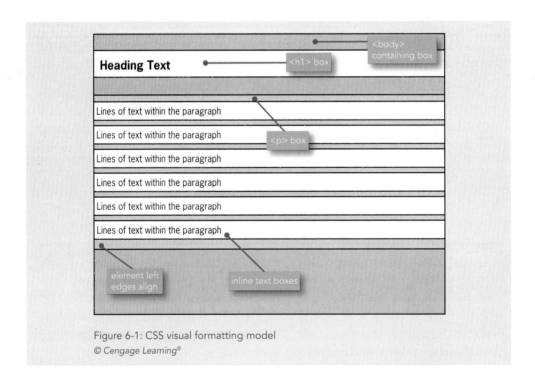

Figure 6-1: CSS visual formatting model
© Cengage Learning®

Figure 6-1 also shows that parent elements contain child elements. The parent element is called the containing box. You can see that <body> is the containing box for the elements of a web page. All other elements' boxes reside within <body>; some of these boxes may contain their own child boxes. In Figure 6-1, the <body> element is the containing box for the <h1> and <p> elements. The <p> element is the containing box for the inline text that comprises the paragraph text. Inline text boxes are split as necessary to fit the dimensions of the containing box and to wrap text to the next line.

CSS lets you specify margin, border, and padding values for all block-level elements. In some instances, the values you specify depend on the containing box that is the parent of the element you want to affect. For example, if you choose a percentage value for a margin, the percentage value is based on the containing box. In Figure 6-1, a 10% margin value for the <p> element would create margins that are 10 percent of the width of the containing box—in this case, the <body> element.

CSS lets you change the display type of any box, either block or inline, with the display property, which is described next.

Specifying the Display Type

display property description	
Value:	block | inline | list-item | none | run-in | inline-block | table | inline-table | table-row-group | table-header-group | table-footer-group | table-row | table-column-group | table-column | table-cell | table-caption | none
Initial:	inline
Applies to:	all elements
Inherited:	no
Percentages:	N/A

The CSS display property determines how the browser displays an element box. By default, elements are displayed either as block-level or inline elements, as described earlier.

The display property values let you change the display type of an element for special design situations. Most of the display property values are rarely used, but some are very handy. The inline value is often used to create horizontal navigation lists, which you will learn about in Chapter 9. Here is a simple example that uses the display property with an <li> selector to make the list items appear horizontally across the page:

```
li {
    display: inline;
    list-style-type: none;
}
```

The list-style-type property hides the bullets that are normally displayed with an unordered list, as you saw in Chapter 5. The style rule applies to the following HTML code for an unordered list:

```
<ul>
    <li><a href="url">Home</a></li>
    <li><a href="url">Search</a></li>
    <li><a href="url">Products</a></li>
    <li><a href="url">Contact Us</a></li>
    <li><a href="url">Support</a></li>
    <li><a href="url">Downloads</a></li>
</ul>
```

The result of this style rule is a series of list elements that can be used to create a navigation bar, as shown in Figure 6-2.

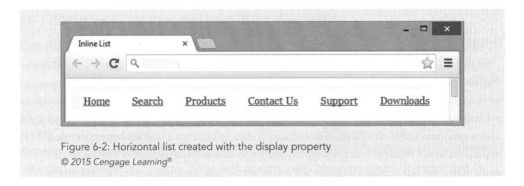

Figure 6-2: Horizontal list created with the display property
© 2015 Cengage Learning®

The display property also has a value of none, which completely removes an element from the browser window. The none value is not widely used; content marked as none cannot be indexed by search engines and cannot be read by screen readers.

Note You will find all of the example files for this chapter at www.joelsklar.com/pwd6. You can use these files for practice, testing, and as inspiration for your project web sites.

Using the CSS Box Model

The CSS box model describes the rectangular boxes that contain content on a web page. Each block-level element you create is displayed in the browser window as a box with content. Each content box can have margins, borders, and padding, as shown in Figure 6-3.

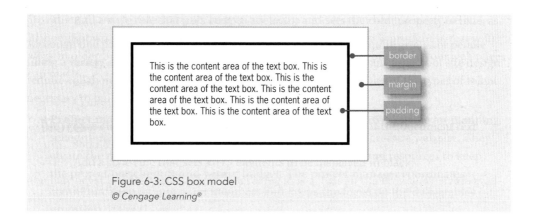

Figure 6-3: CSS box model
© Cengage Learning®

As Figure 6-3 illustrates, the content box is the innermost box, surrounded by the padding, border, and margin areas. The padding area has the same background color as the content element, but the margin area is always transparent. The border separates the padding and margin areas.

Figure 6-4 shows the box model areas in a paragraph element. This paragraph has 2em padding, a thin black border, and 2em margins. Notice that the margin area is transparent.

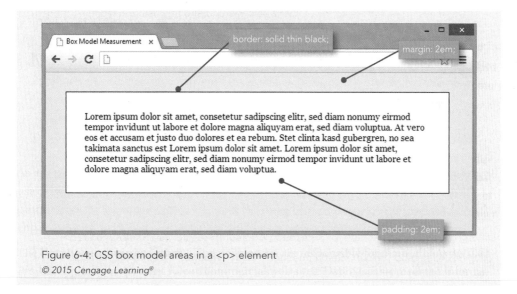

Figure 6-4: CSS box model areas in a <p> element
© 2015 Cengage Learning®

The following code shows the style rule for the paragraph in Figure 6-4:

```
p {
    margin: 2em;
    padding: 2em;
    border: solid thin black;
    background-color: white;
}
```

The margin and padding properties set the length to 2em for all four sides of the box. As you learned in Chapter 5, specifying padding and margins in ems is a good way to make web pages scalable to different devices. The border property sets the border-style to solid, the border-width to thin, and the border-color to black. The background-color property sets the paragraph background color to white.

CSS lets you specify margin, padding, and border properties individually for each side of the box. Figure 6-5 shows that each area has a left, right, top, and bottom side. Each one of the sides can be referred to individually. For example, you can select the padding-bottom, border-top, or margin-left properties if you prefer.

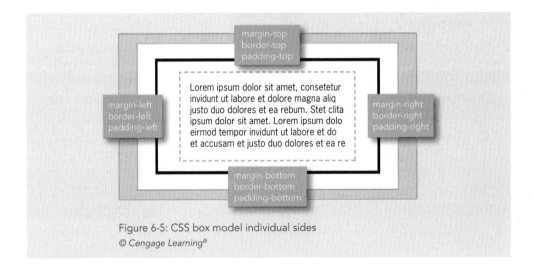

Figure 6-5: CSS box model individual sides
© Cengage Learning®

Figure 6-6 shows a paragraph with a variety of box property settings. As you can see, CSS gives you complete control over the individual white space areas and borders in block elements. The style rule for the paragraph is:

```
p {
    background-color: white;
    border-left: 6px solid;
    margin-left: 2em;
    margin-top: 3em;
    padding-top: 2em;
    padding-right: 2em;
    padding-bottom: 1em;
    padding-left: 1em;
}
```

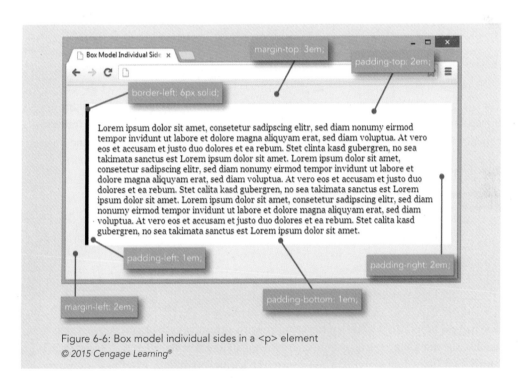

Figure 6-6: Box model individual sides in a <p> element
© 2015 Cengage Learning®

Measurement Values

The margin, border, and padding properties let you state two types of measurement values—either a length or a percentage. (For a full discussion of measurement values, see Chapter 5.) If you use a percentage value, the percentage is based on the width of the containing box, as described earlier. If you choose a length, you have to decide whether to use an absolute or relative value. As with font sizes, you are better off using relative units such as ems or percentages when you are stating margin, border, or padding sizes. The relative measurement values let you build scalable web pages. Pixel values for padding and margins are often specified in fixed page designs where the dimensions of the layout are constant. Many web designers prefer pixel measurements for certain properties such as borders when they know the size of the border line will remain constant across different monitors and devices.

> **Note** *Always use relative measurement values, such as ems or percentages, if you want your web pages to adapt to different browser sizes or user-applied font sizes.*

Applying the Margin Properties

The **margin properties** let you control the margin area of the box model. Margins are always transparent, showing the background of their containing element. You can use margins to enhance the legibility of text, create indented elements, and add white space around images.

Specifying Margins

margin, margin-top, margin-right, margin-bottom, margin-left property description	
Value:	<length> | <percentage>
Initial:	0
Applies to:	all elements
Inherited:	no
Percentages:	refer to width of containing block

The margin properties let you specify margins with either a length or percentage value. You can use the margin property to state one value for all four margin sides, or you can specify settings for individual margins. The following style rule sets all four margins in a paragraph to 2em.

```
p {margin: 2em;}
```

You can also choose to specify individual margin properties that let you control each margin: margin-left, margin-right, margin-top, and margin-bottom. The following style rules set the left and right margins for a paragraph element:

```
p {
    margin-left: 2em;
    margin-right: 3em;
}
```

Margin Property Shorthand Notation

The shorthand notation syntax lets you state individual margin settings within the same rule. The individual margin settings change based on the number of values and their order within the rule. Table 6-1 shows how the syntax works.

NUMBER OF VALUES	EXAMPLE	DESCRIPTION
1 value	p {margin: 1em;}	All four margins are 1em
2 values	p {margin: 1em 2em;}	Top and bottom margins are 1em Left and right margins are 2em
3 values	p {margin: 1em 2em 3em;}	Top margin is 1em Right and left margins are 2em Bottom margin is 3em
4 values	p {margin: 1em 2em 3em 4em;}	Top margin is 1em Right margin is 2em Bottom margin is 3em Left margin is 4em

Table 6-1: Shorthand Notation for the margin Property
© 2015 Cengage Learning®

It is your choice to use the shorthand notation or state the margin properties individually. Some designers prefer the more specific and easy-to-read individual margin properties rather than the shorthand notation. Others prefer the brief syntax of the shorthand notation. Either way, set a coding convention for your web site and use it consistently.

Figure 6-7 shows two paragraph elements. The first paragraph has the left and right margins set to 2em; the second has the left and right margins set to 4em. Notice that the increased margins enhance the legibility of the text.

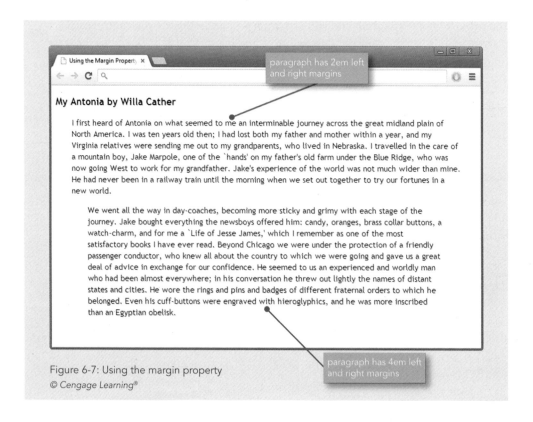

Figure 6-7: Using the margin property
© Cengage Learning®

Negative Margins

Margins are unusual because you can use negative values. You can set negative margin values to achieve special effects. For example, you can remove the default margins by setting a negative value or overlap elements on the page.

Figure 6-8 shows two <h1> elements, one with the default margins, and one with the bottom margin set to a negative value. The following rule sets a negative value of 20 pixels for the element's bottom margin:

```
h1 {margin-bottom:-20px;}
```

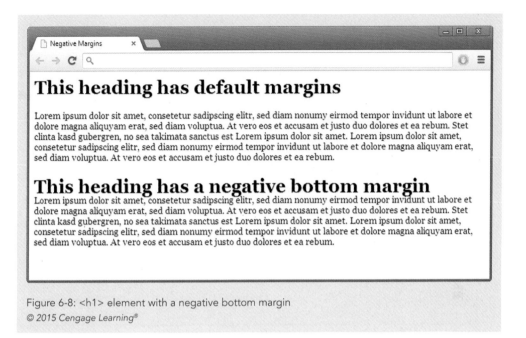

Figure 6-8: <h1> element with a negative bottom margin

© 2015 Cengage Learning®

Collapsing Margins

To ensure that the spacing between block-level elements is consistent, the browser collapses the vertical margins between elements. The vertical margins are the top and bottom element margins. The browser does not add the values of the two, but picks the greater value and applies it to the space between the adjoining elements. To illustrate this, consider the following rule:

```
p {
    margin-top: 15px;
    margin-bottom: 25px;
}
```

If the browser did not collapse the vertical margins, the web page would have 40 pixels of space between each paragraph. Instead, the browser collapses the margin. Following the CSS convention, the browser sets the vertical margin between paragraphs to 25 pixels, the greater of the two values. Figure 6-9 shows how the browser maintains the space between the paragraphs.

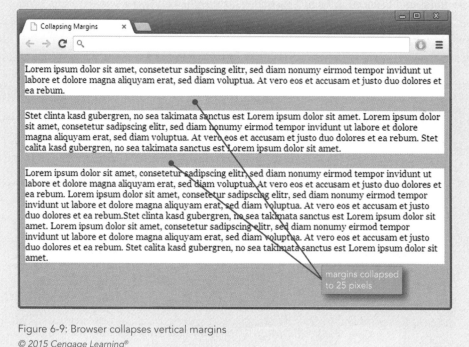

Figure 6-9: Browser collapses vertical margins
© 2015 Cengage Learning®

Zeroing Margins

You can set margin values to zero if you want to remove the default margin spacing that is built into the browser. This technique is useful if you have problems getting your page designs to look consistent across multiple browsers and display devices. By setting the values in the body section to zero, the settings are inherited for all elements on the page. Then you can set specific margin settings for each element as necessary for your design. The style rule for zeroing margins looks like this:

```
body {margin: 0; padding: 0;}
```

This technique is also handy when you want to place an image against the side of the browser window, as shown in Figure 6-10.

Figure 6-10: Zeroing margins to place images against the edge of the window
Seahorses courtesy of www.seascapesaquariums.com

Note | *If you zero margins for the entire page, you must explicitly set margins for any elements that you do not want to place against the edge of the browser window.*

Applying the Padding Properties

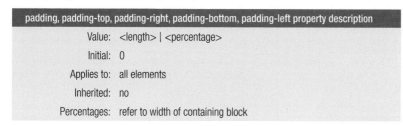

padding, padding-top, padding-right, padding-bottom, padding-left property description	
Value:	<length> | <percentage>
Initial:	0
Applies to:	all elements
Inherited:	no
Percentages:	refer to width of containing block

The CSS padding properties let you control the padding area in the box model. The padding area is between the element content and the border. The padding area inherits the background color of the element, so if a <p> element has a white background, the padding area will be white as well.

Figure 6-11 shows how adding padding to an element increases the space between the content and the edge of the element box. Notice the effect of the extra padding on the legibility of the text.

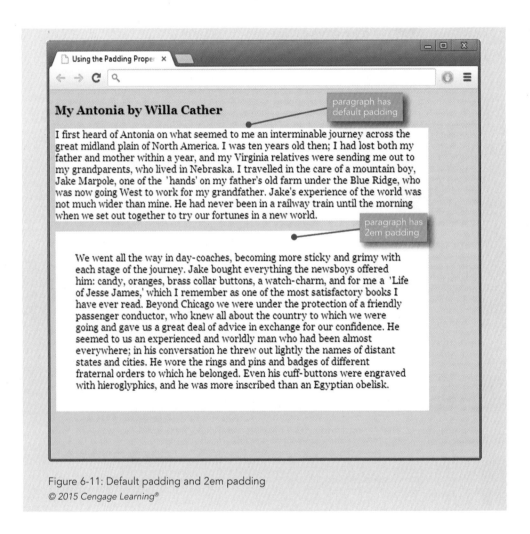

Figure 6-11: Default padding and 2em padding
© 2015 Cengage Learning®

Like the margin property, the padding property lets you state one value for all four padding sides, or you can specify settings for individual padding areas. You can specify either a length or a percentage value. Unlike margins, you cannot collapse the padding area or set negative padding values. The following style rule sets all four padding sides in a paragraph to 2em.

```
p {padding: 2em;}
```

You can also choose to specify individual padding properties, which let you control each padding area: padding-left, padding-right, padding-top, and padding-bottom. The following style rules set the left and right padding for a paragraph element:

```
p {
    padding-left: 2em;
    padding-right: 3em;
}
```

Padding Property Shorthand Notation

The shorthand notation syntax lets you state individual padding settings. Like the margin shorthand property described earlier, the individual padding settings change based on the number of values and their order within the rule. Table 6-2 shows how the syntax works.

NUMBER OF VALUES	EXAMPLE	DESCRIPTION
1 value	p {padding: 1em;}	Top, bottom, left, and right padding are 1em
2 values	p {padding: 1em 2em;}	Top and bottom padding are 1em Left and right padding are 2em
3 values	p {padding: 1em 2em 3em;}	Top padding is 1em Right and left padding are 2em Bottom padding is 3em
4 values	p {padding: 1em 2em 3em 4em;}	Top padding is 1em Right padding is 2em Bottom padding is 3em Left padding is 4em

Table 6-2: Shorthand Notation for the padding Property
© 2015 Cengage Learning®

The following style rule sets the top and bottom padding areas for a paragraph, along with complementing borders, a white background, and margins to offset the paragraph from the browser sides:

```
p {
    padding-top: 2em;
    padding-bottom: 2em;
    border-top: solid thin black;
    border-bottom: solid thin black;
    background-color: white;
    margin: 2em;
}
```

As Figure 6-12 shows, the paragraph now has the default left and right padding with 2em top and bottom padding.

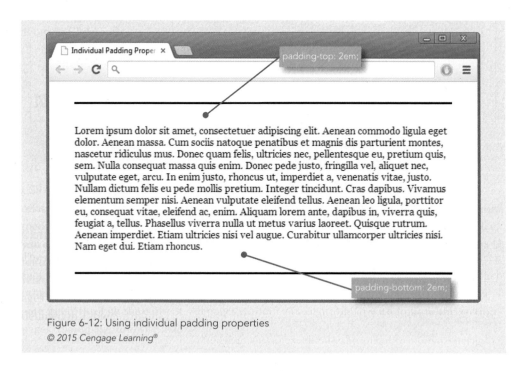

Figure 6-12: Using individual padding properties
© 2015 Cengage Learning®

Applying the Border Properties

The **border properties** let you control the appearance of borders around elements. The border area resides between the margin and padding. Border properties for each border side let you specify the style, width, and color of each border. You will most likely use the five border shorthand properties, which include:

> border

> border-left

> border-right

> border-top

> border-bottom

These shorthand properties let you state border-style, border-color, and border-width for all four borders or for any of the individual sides of the box. However, you can also state much more specific borders by using the border properties separately. Table 6-3 lists the entire range of 20 border properties.

DESCRIPTION	PROPERTY NAME		
Overall shorthand property	border		
Individual side shorthand properties	border-left, border-top, border-right, border-bottom		
Specific shorthand property	border-style	border-width	border-color
Individual properties	border-left-style	border-left-width	border-left-color
	border-right-style	border-right-width	border-right-color
	border-top-style	border-top-width	border-top-color
	border-bottom-style	border-bottom-width	border-bottom-color

Table 6-3: Border Properties
© 2015 Cengage Learning®

Before you can use the shorthand properties, you must first understand the three border characteristics—border-style, border-color, and border-width.

Specifying Border Style

border-style, border-top-style, border-right-style, border-bottom-style, border-left-style property description	
Value:	<border-style>
Initial:	none
Applies to:	all elements
Inherited:	no
Percentages:	N/A

The border-style property is the most important border property because it must be stated to make a border appear. The border-style property lets you choose from one of the following border style keywords:

> **none**—No border on the element; this is the default setting

> **dotted**—Dotted border

> **dashed**—Dashed border

> **solid**—Solid line border

> **double**—Double line border

> **groove**—Three-dimensional border that appears to be engraved into the page

> **ridge**—Three-dimensional border that appears to be embossed (or extend outward from the page)

> **inset**—Three-dimensional border that appears to set the entire box into the page

> **outset**—Three-dimensional border that appears to extend the entire box outward from the page

The following code shows an example of the border-style property in use:

```
p {border-style: solid;}
```

Figure 6-13 shows examples of the borders. As you can see, each browser displays the border styles differently. If a border you specify is not supported, the border defaults to solid.

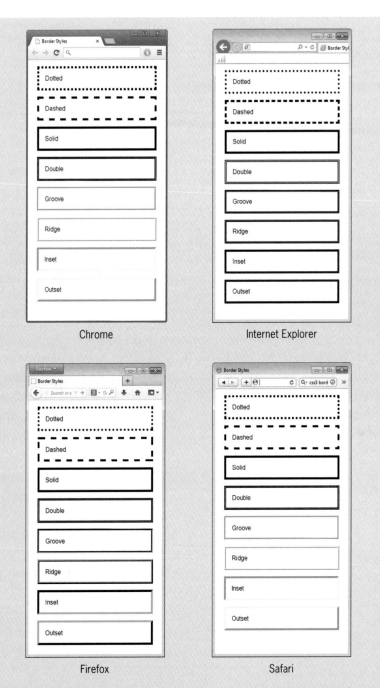

Figure 6-13: Border styles in Chrome, Internet Explorer, Firefox, and Safari

© 2015 Cengage Learning®

> **Note** When designing layouts, it is often handy to turn the borders on for an element, even though you may turn them off for the finished web page. The border lets you see the dimensions of the element on the page. Remember that adding borders to an element increases the element's width.

Individual Border Styles

You can also specify individual border styles with the following border-style properties:

> border-left-style

> border-right-style

> border-top-style

> border-bottom-style

These properties let you single out one border and apply a style. The following rule applies only to the left border of the element:

```
p {border-left-style: double;}
```

Border-Style Property Shorthand Notation

The shorthand notation syntax lets you state individual border-style settings. The individual border style settings change based on the number of values and their order within the rule. Table 6-4 shows how the syntax works.

NUMBER OF VALUES	EXAMPLE	DESCRIPTION
1 value	p {border-style: solid;}	All four borders are solid
2 values	p {border-style: solid double;}	Top and bottom borders are solid Left and right borders are double
3 values	p {border-style: solid double dashed;}	Top border is solid Right and left borders are double Bottom border is dashed
4 values	p {border-style: solid double dashed dotted;}	Top border is solid Right border is double Bottom border is dashed Left border is dotted

Table 6-4: Shorthand Notation for the border-style Property
© 2015 Cengage Learning®

Of course, if you examine the rules in Table 6-4, you can see they might create odd effects. For example, a paragraph with a different border style for each side is not a common design technique. Remember to use restraint, focus on your content, and keep the user in mind when working with border styles.

Specifying Border Width

border-width, border-top-width, border-right-width, border-bottom-width, border-left-width property description	
Value:	thin | medium | thick | <length>
Initial:	medium
Applies to:	all elements
Inherited:	no
Percentages:	N/A

The border-width property lets you state the width of the border with either a keyword or a length value. You can use the following keywords to express width:

> thin

> medium (default)

> thick

The width of the rule when you use these keywords is based on the browser. The length values let you state an absolute or relative value for the border; percentages are not allowed. Using a length value lets you create anything from a hairline to a very thick border. The following code shows an example of the border-width property in use:

```
p {border-width: 1px; border-style: solid;}
```

Remember that the border is not displayed unless the border-style property is stated. Figure 6-14 shows examples of different border widths.

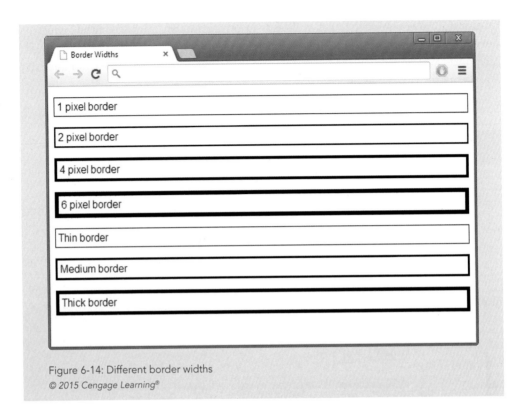

Figure 6-14: Different border widths
© 2015 Cengage Learning®

Individual Border Widths

You can also specify individual border widths with the following border-width properties:

> border-left-width

> border-right-width

> border-top-width

> border-bottom-width

These properties let you single out one border and apply a width. The following rule applies only to the left border of the element:

```
p {border-left-width: thin;}
```

Border-Width Property Shorthand Notation

The shorthand notation syntax lets you state individual border-width settings. The individual border-width settings change based on the number of values and their order within the rule. Table 6-5 shows how the syntax works.

NUMBER OF VALUES	EXAMPLE	DESCRIPTION
1 value	p {border-width: 1px;}	All four borders are 1 pixel wide
2 values	p {border-width: 1px 2px;}	Top and bottom borders are 1 pixel wide Left and right borders are 2 pixels wide
3 values	p {border-width: 1px 2px 3px;}	Top border is 1 pixel wide Right and left borders are 2 pixels wide Bottom border is 3 pixels wide
4 values	p {border-width: 1px 2px 3px 4px;}	Top border is 1 pixel wide Right border is 2 pixels wide Bottom border is 3 pixels wide Left border is 4 pixels wide

Table 6-5: Shorthand Notation for the border-width Property
© 2015 Cengage Learning®

Specifying Border Color

border-color, border-top-color, border-right-color, border-bottom-color, border-left-color property description	
Value:	<color>
Applies to:	all elements
Inherited:	no
Percentages:	N/A

The border-color property lets you set the color of the element border. The value can be either a hexadecimal value, RGB value, or one of the 16 predefined color names shown in the following list:

Aqua	Navy	Gray	Silver
Black	Olive	Green	Tea
Blue	Purple	Lime	White
Fuchsia	Red	Maroon	Yellow

Note | You can learn more about color values in Chapter 8.

To set a border color, use the property as shown in the following rule:

```
p {
    border-color: red;
    border-width: 1px;
    border-style: solid;
}
```

The default border color is the color of the element content. For example, the following style rule sets the element text color to red. The border is also red because a border color is not specified.

```
p {
    color: red;
    font-family: arial;
    border: solid;
}
```

Individual Border Colors

You can also specify individual border colors with the following border-color properties:

> border-left-color
> border-right-color
> border-top-color
> border-bottom-color

These properties let you single out one border and apply a color. The following property applies only to the left border of the element:

```
p {
    border-left-color: red;
    border-style: solid;
}
```

Border-Color Property Shorthand Notation

The shorthand notation syntax lets you state individual border-color settings. The individual border color settings change based on the number of values and their order within the rule. Table 6-6 shows how the syntax works.

NUMBER OF VALUES	EXAMPLE	DESCRIPTION
1 value	p {border-color: black;}	All four borders are black
2 values	p {border-color: black red;}	Top and bottom borders are black Left and right borders are red
3 values	p {border-color: black red green;}	Top border is black Right and left borders are red Bottom border is green
4 values	p {border-color: black red green blue;}	Top border is black Right border is red Bottom border is green Left border is blue

Table 6-6: Shorthand Notation for the border-color Property
© 2015 Cengage Learning®

Using the Border Shorthand Properties

The shorthand properties are the most common and easiest way to express border characteristics. When you use these shorthand properties, you are stating the style, color, and width of the border in one concise rule.

border, border-top, border-right, border-bottom, border-left property description	
Value:	<border-width>	<border-style>	<border-color>
Initial:	see individual properties
Applies to:	all elements
Inherited:	no
Percentages:	N/A

The border property lets you state the properties for all four borders of the element. You can state the border-width, border-style, and border-color in any order. Border-style must be included for the border to appear. If you do not include border-width, the width defaults to medium. If you do not include border-color, the border appears in the same color as the element. The following example rules show different uses of the border property.

The following rule sets the border-style to solid. The border-width defaults to medium. The border-color is the same as the color of the <p> element; because no color is stated, the border color is black.

```
p {border: solid; }
```

The following rule sets the border-style to solid. The border-width is 1 pixel. The border-color is red.

```
p {border: solid 1px red;}
```

The following rule sets the border-style to double. The border-width is thin. The border-color is blue. Notice that the order of the values does not matter.

```
p {border: double blue thin;}
```

The following rules let you state border-style, border-width, and border-color in one statement that selects particular element borders. For example, the following rule sets border-style to solid and border-width to thin for the left and right borders, respectively. Because no color is stated, the borders default to the element color.

```
p {border-left: solid thin; border-right: solid thin;}
```

The following rule sets border-style to double and border-color to red for the top border. Because no border-width is stated, the width defaults to medium.

```
p {border-top: double red;}
```

Specifying Rounded Borders

border-radius, border-top-right-radius, border-top-left-radius, border-bottom-right-radius, border-bottom-left-radius property description	
Value:	[*<length>*	*<percentage>*]
Initial:	0
Applies to:	all elements
Inherited:	no
Percentages:	N/A

The CSS 3 border-radius property lets you create rounded borders on block-level elements, an effect that now has widespread support across the major browsers.

The example in Figure 6-15 shows different uses of border-radius, including borders that are hidden or showing, and varying measurement values that create a variety of results.

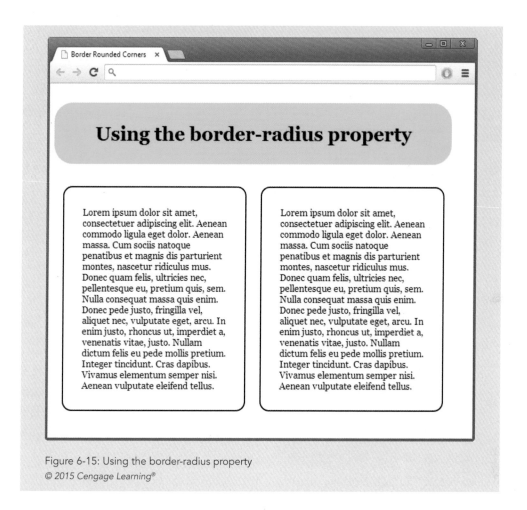

Figure 6-15: Using the border-radius property
© 2015 Cengage Learning®

The two length values determine the radius of each corner. The following rule sets the radius for all four corners to 1em:

```
border-radius: 1em;
```

The style rule for the <h1> element in Figure 6-15 uses the following code:

```
padding: 1em;
background-color: #ffcc33;
margin-top: 1em;
border-radius: 1em;
width: 625px;
text-align: center;
```

You can also use individual properties to set each corner, as shown in the bottom paragraph in Figure 6-16. When you use the individual properties, you can state one or two measurements for the radius. If you use two values, the first value is the horizontal measurement and the second value is the vertical measurement. The style properties for the box in Figure 6-16 look like this:

```
border-top-left-radius: 25px 50px;

border-top-right-radius: 50px 25px;

border-bottom-left-radius: 50px;

border-bottom-right-radius: 25px;
```

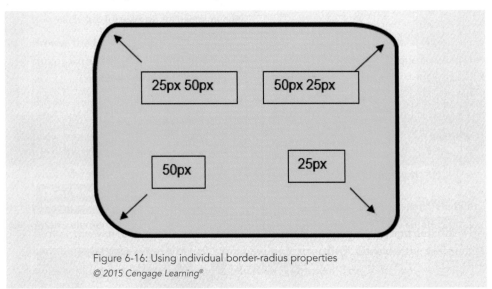

Figure 6-16: Using individual border-radius properties
© 2015 Cengage Learning®

You can create a variety of box shapes using border-radius combined with other box model properties, as shown in Figure 6-17.

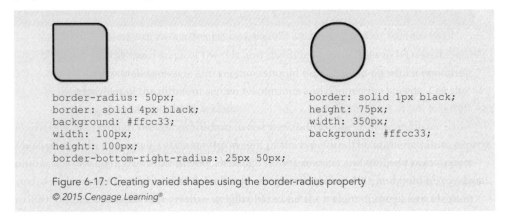

```
border-radius: 50px;                         border: solid 1px black;
border: solid 4px black;                     height: 75px;
background: #ffcc33;                          width: 350px;
width: 100px;                                 background: #ffcc33;
height: 100px;
border-bottom-right-radius: 25px 50px;
```

Figure 6-17: Creating varied shapes using the border-radius property
© 2015 Cengage Learning®

Using the Page Layout Box Properties

The **page layout box properties** let you control the dimensions and position of content boxes. These properties are essential to building CSS page layouts, which you will learn about in Chapters 7 and 12. Using these box properties, you can specify the exact shape of a content box and create columns and boxes of content. You can set minimum and maximum widths and heights as well as control how your boxes are resized based on the size of the browser window. You can also align boxes to the left or right of other elements using the float property and allow text to wrap around images.

In this section, you will learn about the following box properties:

> width, min-width, max-width

> height, min-height, max-height

> float

> clear

> overflow

Setting Element Width

width, min-width, max-width property description	
Value:	<length> | <percentage>
Initial:	auto
Applies to:	all elements but text inline elements, table rows, and row groups
Inherited:	no
Percentages:	refer to width of containing block

The width property lets you set the horizontal width of an element using either a length value or a percentage. The percentage value is based on the width of the containing element box. The following is an example of width property usage:

```
div {width: 200px;}
```

If you use percentages, the content boxes will adapt to the size of the browser or the containing element, allowing you to build flexible page layouts based on the browser size. If you are building fixed dimension layouts, use pixel values for width.

Figure 6-18 shows two <article> elements, one that is 200 pixels wide and one that is 50% wide. Each of the <article> elements in this example contains both headings and paragraphs. The left box is fixed at 200 pixels wide. Its height is determined by the content it contains. The right box is set to a percentage value, which means the box size will change based on the size of the browser window. This box's width will always be 50 percent of the current window size. If the user resizes the browser, the box width will change.

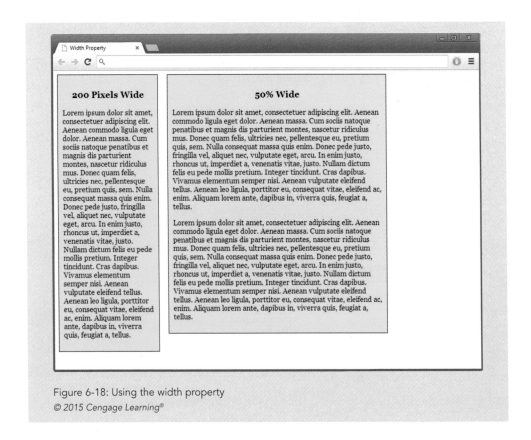

Figure 6-18: Using the width property
© 2015 Cengage Learning®

Calculating Box Model Width

When you specify a width, you are specifying the width of the content only, not of the entire element. In Figure 6-19, the paragraph width is 400 pixels as specified by the width property. The actual element width of 500 pixels is the result of adding the padding, border, and margin properties to the content width.

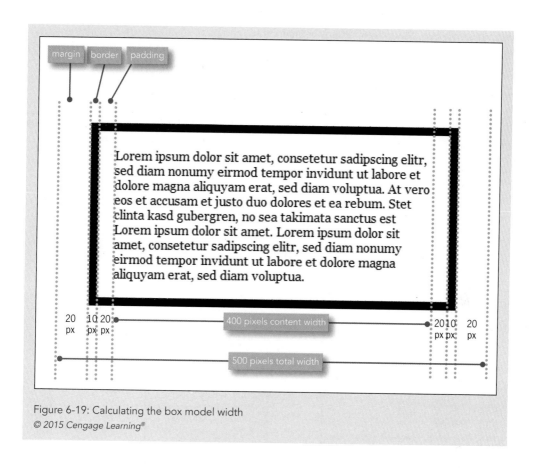

Lorem ipsum dolor sit amet, consetetur sadipscing elitr, sed diam nonumy eirmod tempor invidunt ut labore et dolore magna aliquyam erat, sed diam voluptua. At vero eos et accusam et justo duo dolores et ea rebum. Stet clinta kasd gubergren, no sea takimata sanctus est Lorem ipsum dolor sit amet. Lorem ipsum dolor sit amet, consetetur sadipscing elitr, sed diam nonumy eirmod tempor invidunt ut labore et dolore magna aliquyam erat, sed diam voluptua.

Figure 6-19: Calculating the box model width
© 2015 Cengage Learning®

The sizing illustrated in Figure 6-19 is the default element behavior, but you can change this behavior using the box-sizing property.

Setting Sizing Type

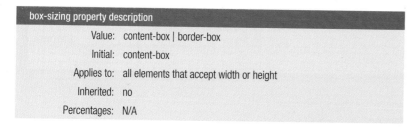

box-sizing property description	
Value:	content-box | border-box
Initial:	content-box
Applies to:	all elements that accept width or height
Inherited:	no
Percentages:	N/A

The box-sizing property lets you control whether element boxes shrink the content area to make room for the padding and borders or whether they add these dimensions to the outside of the box. Standard element behavior adds the padding and border measurements to the content width, as shown in Figure 6-19. By using the box-sizing property with a value of border-box, the box width will remain at the measurement you specify and decrease the content area to make room for the padding and border. In Figure 6-20, the box on the left is set to 200 pixels wide with a 2-pixel border and 20 pixels of padding. The total width of this box is 244 pixels (200+2+2+20+20=244). The box on the right is 200 pixels wide with a box-sizing property set to border-box. It has the same border and padding settings as the box on the left. It maintains a width of 200 pixels regardless of the border and padding measurements.

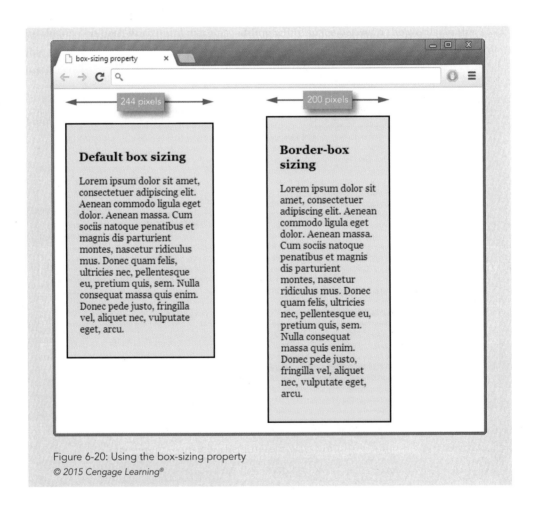

Figure 6-20: Using the box-sizing property
© 2015 Cengage Learning®

Setting Minimum and Maximum Widths

The min-width and max-width properties let you determine exactly how wide or narrow you want a box to be. This is helpful when building flexible layouts, as you will see in Chapters 7 and 12. In Figure 6-18, the content element on the right will always be 50 percent of the browser window, but the user may occasionally make a window very narrow or very wide, and you don't want the box to become either a skinny, narrow column or an overly wide column. You can control the width with min-width and max-width. In the following example, a page content box is set to 100%, which will fill the browser window. However, the box will not be allowed to shrink to less than 750 pixels or expand to more than 1280 pixels.

```
article.feature {
    width: 100%;
    min-width: 750px;
    max-width: 1280px;
}
```

Setting Element Height

height property description	
Value:	<length> | <percentage>
Initial:	auto
Applies to:	all elements but text inline elements, table columns, and column groups
Inherited:	no
Percentages:	N/A

The height property lets you set the vertical height of an element. Height should only be used in situations where you know the exact height of the element content, such as an image. At other times, you may need to create a box with specific dimensions for a design. It is a better practice to let the content determine the height of the element.

The height property accepts either a length value or a percentage. The percentage value is based on the height of the containing element box. The following is an example of height property usage:

```
div {height: 150px; width: 300px;}
```

Setting Minimum and Maximum Height

The min-height and max-height properties let you determine exactly how tall or short you want a box to be. These properties work exactly like the min-width and max-width properties described earlier.

Floating Elements

float property description

Value:	left | right | none
Initial:	none
Applies to:	all elements except positioned elements and generated content (see Appendix B)
Inherited:	no
Percentages:	N/A

The float property lets you position an element to the left or right edge of its parent element. You can float an image to the left or right of text, as shown in Figure 6-21.

Figure 6-21: Floating an image
© 2015 Cengage Learning®

The style rule for the floating image floats the image to the left and adds a margin to offset the text from the image. The style rule looks like this:

```
img {
    float: left;
    margin-right: 10px;
}
```

The float property can also be used to float a content box to the left or right of text. Used with the width element, you can create a content box as shown in Figure 6-22.

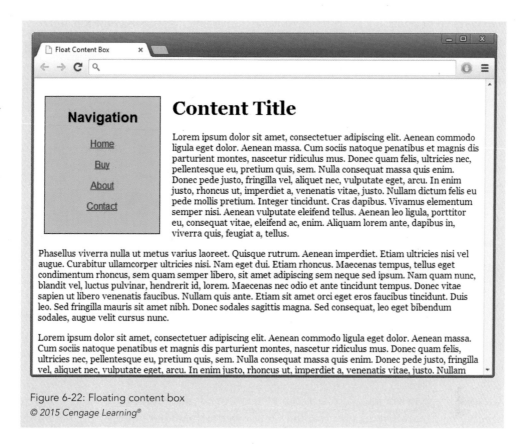

Figure 6-22: Floating content box
© 2015 Cengage Learning®

The rule for the left-floating content box looks like this:

```
#float {
    width: 200px;
    float: left;
    border: 1px solid black;
    padding-bottom: 20px;
    margin: 0px 20px 10px 10px;
    text-align: center;
    background-color: #fb6;
}
```

The style rule uses an id of *float* as the selector. The width property sets the width of the element to 200 pixels. The float property floats the box to the left of the page. Notice that the rule does not include a height property. The height of the box is determined by the content it contains and the padding values. The margin property states the top, right, bottom, and left margin values.

The floated content box is a <nav> element that gets the id value of *float*:

```
<nav id="float">
    <h2>Navigation</h2>
    <p><a href="url">Home</a></p>
    <p><a href="url">Buy</a></p>
    <p><a href="url">About</a></p>
    <p><a href="url">Contact</a></p>
</nav>
```

Clearing Elements

clear property description	
Value:	none | left | right | both
Initial:	none
Applies to:	block-level elements
Inherited:	no
Percentages:	N/A

The clear property lets you control the flow of text around floated elements. You only use the clear property when you are using the float property. Use the clear property to force text to appear beneath a floated element, rather than next to it. Figure 6-23 shows an example of normal text flow around an element.

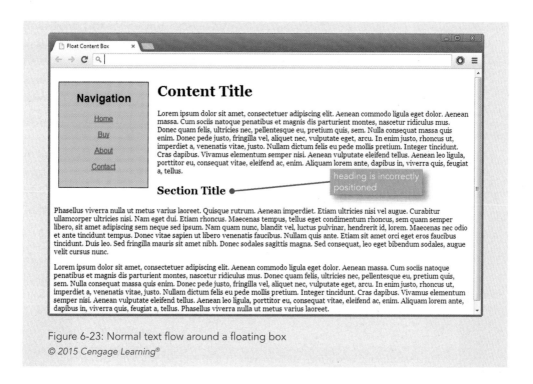

Figure 6-23: Normal text flow around a floating box

© 2015 Cengage Learning®

This figure shows the left floating content box from the previous example. The text flows down around the box on the right, which is the correct behavior. The second-level heading does not appear in the correct position. It should be positioned beneath the floating content box. To correct this problem, use the clear property. In this instance, the <h2> should be displayed clear of any left-floating images. Add this style rule directly to the <h2> element with the style attribute as follows:

```
<h2 style="clear: left;">
```

Figure 6-24 shows the result of adding the clear property.

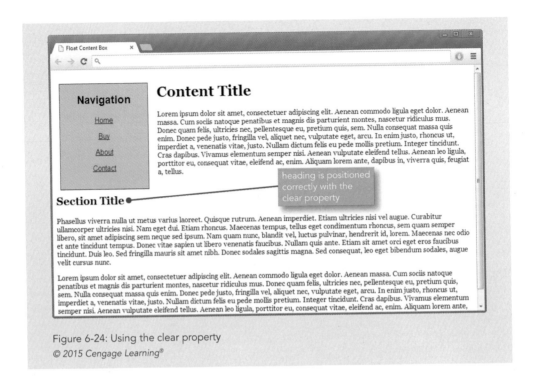

Figure 6-24: Using the clear property

© 2015 Cengage Learning®

Notice that the clear property lets you clear from either left- or right-floating images using the *left* and *right* values. The *both* value lets you control text flow if you have floating images on both the left and right sides of the text.

Controlling Overflow

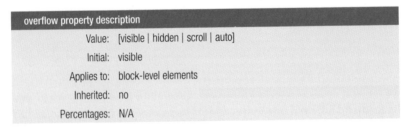

overflow property description	
Value:	[visible | hidden | scroll | auto]
Initial:	visible
Applies to:	block-level elements
Inherited:	no
Percentages:	N/A

The overflow property lets you control situations when content overflows its content box. This can happen when the content is larger than the area it is designed for, especially when a height property is set for a content element. Figure 6-25 shows text overflow in a content box with fixed width and height.

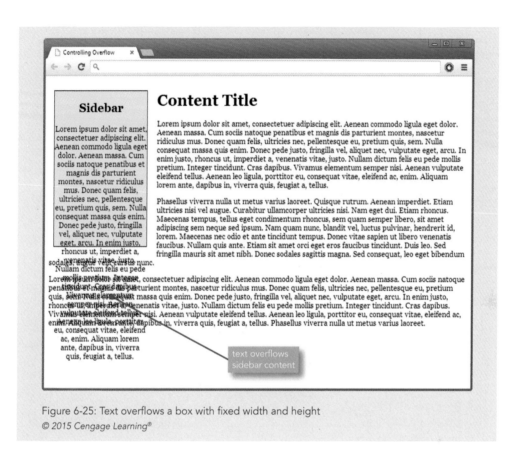

Figure 6-25: Text overflows a box with fixed width and height

© 2015 Cengage Learning®

To solve this problem, you can add an overflow property to the element. You can choose to show scroll bars or to hide the overflow content. In Figure 6-26, you can see the result of adding the overflow property set to auto, which automatically adds a scroll bar when the content overflows the box.

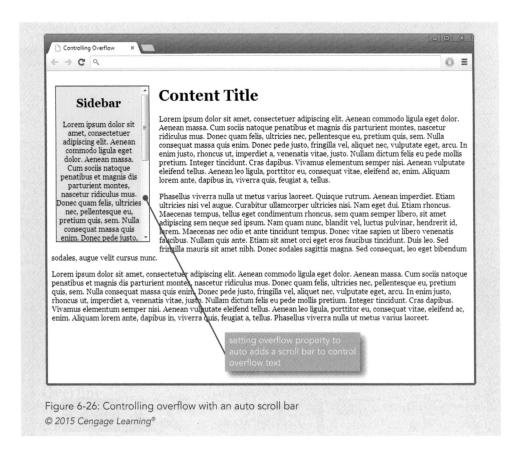

Figure 6-26: Controlling overflow with an auto scroll bar

© 2015 Cengage Learning®

Creating Box Shadows

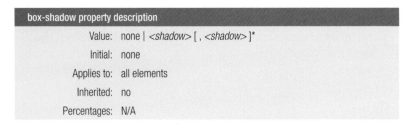

box-shadow property description	
Value:	none | *<shadow>* [, *<shadow>*]*
Initial:	none
Applies to:	all elements
Inherited:	no
Percentages:	N/A

The box-shadow property lets you add box shadows to an element to create a 3-D effect. This property is supported by all modern browsers. Figure 6-27 shows a paragraph element with a gray shadow, making the box appear to be floating on the page.

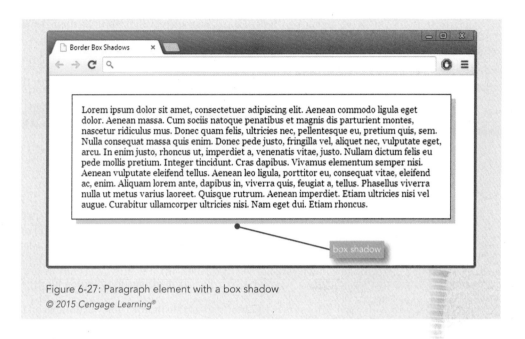

Figure 6-27: Paragraph element with a box shadow
© 2015 Cengage Learning®

The box-shadow property lets you set both the horizontal and vertical measurement and color for the shadowed edges of the paragraph box. The style rule for the paragraph in Figure 6-27 looks like this:

```
p {
    margin: 2em;
    border: thin solid;
    box-shadow: .5em .5em #ccc;
    padding: 1em;
}
```

The first value is the horizontal offset, and the second is the vertical offset. You can also use negative values to achieve results like the one shown in Figure 6-28.

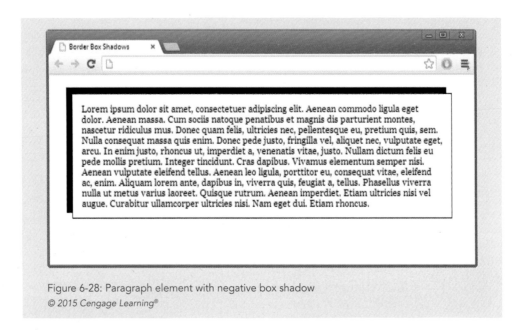

Figure 6-28: Paragraph element with negative box shadow
© 2015 Cengage Learning®

The style rule for the negative shadow looks like this:

```
p {
    margin: 2em;
    border: thin solid;
    box-shadow: -10px -10px #000;
    padding: 1em;
}
```

Activity: Creating a Simple Page Layout

In the following steps, you have a chance to apply some of the properties you learned about in this chapter to build a simple page layout. You will build on these skills in the next chapter to create more complex page designs. As you work through the steps, refer to Figure 6-32 to see the results you will achieve. New code that you will add is shown in **blue**. Save your file and test your work in the browser as you complete each step.

To apply the box properties:

1. Copy the **ch6activity1.html** file from the Chapter06 folder provided with your Data Files to the Chapter06 folder in your work folder. (Create the Chapter06 folder, if necessary.)

2. Open the file **ch6activity1.html** in your HTML editor.

3. In your browser, open the file **ch6activity1.html**. When you open the file, it looks like Figure 6-29.

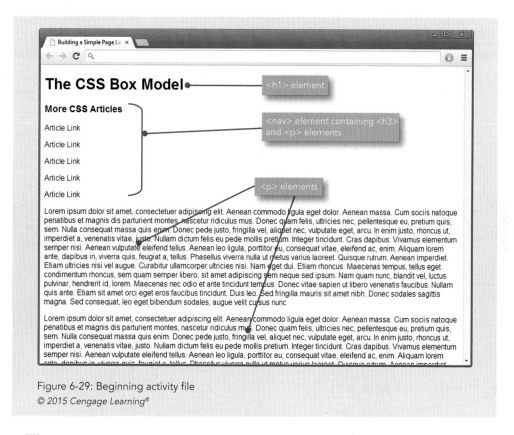

Figure 6-29: Beginning activity file
© 2015 Cengage Learning®

4. Examine the code. Notice the <style> section of the file. It contains one style rule to set the font-family for the page.

```
<style>
body {font-family: arial, sans-serif;}
</style>
```

As shown in Figure 6-29, the HTML code in the file consists of:

- <h1> element for the heading
- <nav> content container that has an <h3> heading and <p> elements that simulate links
- Two paragraph elements

5. Start by styling the <h1> element with a 20-pixel left and right margin, as shown in the following code:

```
h1 {
    margin-left: 20px;
    margin-right: 20px;
}
```

6. Add a border to the left and bottom sides of the <h1> for a distinctive look. Set the width of the border to 4 pixels.

```
h1 {
    margin-left: 20px;
    margin-right: 20px;
    border-bottom: solid 4px black;
    border-left: solid 4px black;
}
```

7. Add 5 pixels of padding to the left and bottom sides of the <h1> to offset the text from the border you just created.

```
h1 {
    margin-left: 20px;
    margin-right: 20px;
    border-bottom: solid 4px black;
    border-left: solid 4px black;
    padding-bottom: 5px;
    padding-left: 5px;
}
```

The finished <h1> element looks like Figure 6-30.

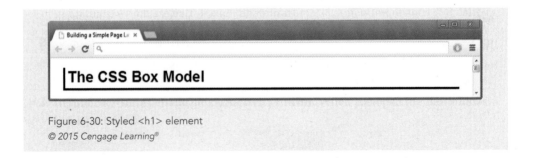

Figure 6-30: Styled <h1> element
© 2015 Cengage Learning®

8. Now you will create the floating content box that contains the "More CSS Articles" heading and links. Write a style rule that uses an id of *sidebar*. Add a width of 200 pixels and a solid 1-pixel border.

```
#sidebar {
    width: 200px;
    border: 1px solid black;
}
```

9. In the <body> section of the document, find the <nav> element that contains "More CSS Articles" and add the id attribute to apply the sidebar style as shown:

```
<nav id="sidebar">
<h3>More CSS Articles</h3>
<p>Article Link</p>
<p>Article Link</p>
<p>Article Link</p>
<p>Article Link</p>
<p>Article Link</p>
</nav>
```

10. Float the division to the left side of the page. Add a left margin of 20 pixels to align the box with the heading and a right margin of 20 pixels to offset the paragraph text from the box.

```
#sidebar {
    width: 200px;
    border: 1px solid black;
    float: left;
    margin-left: 20px;
    margin-right: 20px;
}
```

11. Finish the content box by centering the text and adding a background color (#cff).

```
#sidebar {
    width: 200px;
    border: 1px solid black;
    float: left;
    margin-left: 20px;
    margin-right: 20px;
```

```
text-align: center;
background: #cff;
}
```

Figure 6-31 shows the completed floating sidebar content box. Notice that the paragraph text is very close to the left and right sides of the browser window.

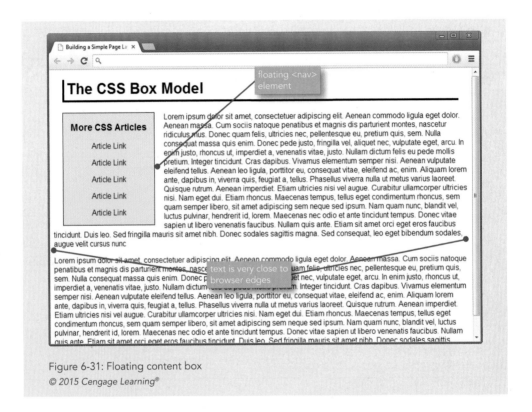

Figure 6-31: Floating content box
© 2015 Cengage Learning®

12. Finish the design by aligning the text properly using left and right margin properties. Write a rule that selects the <p> elements and sets the left margin to 20 pixels and the right to 40 pixels.

```
p {
    margin-left: 20px;
    margin-right: 40px;
}
```

Figure 6-32 shows the completed web page design.

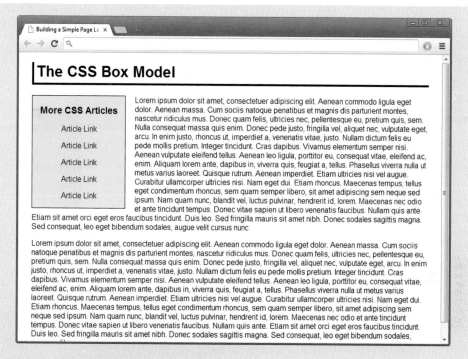

Figure 6-32: Completed web page design
© 2015 Cengage Learning®

Here is the finished style sheet code:

```
<style>
body {font-family: arial, sans-serif;}
h1 {
    margin-left: 20px;
    margin-right: 20px;
    border-bottom: solid 4px black;
    border-left: solid 4px black;
    padding-bottom: 5px;
    padding-left: 5px;
}
```

```
#sidebar {
    width: 200px;
    border: 1px solid black;
    float: left;
    margin-left: 20px;
    margin-right: 20px;
    text-align: center;
    background: #cff;
}
p {
    margin-left: 20px;
    margin-right: 40px;
}
</style>
```

Skills at Work | *Learning Public Speaking Skills*

Part of your work as a web designer will be to explain your designs and techniques to others during formal and informal presentations. To communicate successfully, you need to polish your public speaking skills. Speaking and presenting effectively is a talent anyone can learn and master. If you are still in school, take advantage of classes in oral communication and present your papers and work to your classmates whenever possible. If you are employed and out of school, join a public speaking club such as Toastmasters, or find out if your company sponsors classes in presentation skills. To take the fear out of public speaking, practice your presentations and know your content. Prepare by speaking in front of friends, or videotape yourself so you can honestly appraise your strengths and weaknesses. Speak slowly and clearly, and learn to communicate with your eyes and body language. If you are nervous, harness that energy to make your presentation better. Remember to smile, take a deep breath, and treat the audience as if they are friends. Audiences want speakers to do well and you want them on your side. Learning to present and communicate in a concise and authentic manner is one of the single most important skills you can gain to further your career.

Chapter Summary

In this chapter you learned about the concepts of the CSS box and visual formatting models. You saw how the margin, padding, and border properties let you control the space around block-level elements on a web page. By using these properties judiciously, you can enhance the legibility of your content. You also learned how the page layout box properties create boxes and columns for content, wrap text, and float images.

> The CSS box model lets you control spacing around the element content.

> You can state values of margin, border, and padding for all four sides of the box or individual sides.

> To build scalable web pages, choose relative length units such as ems or percentages.

> To build fixed pages, choose pixel measurements.

> The browser collapses vertical margins to ensure even spacing between elements.

> Margins are transparent, showing the color of the containing element's background color. Padding takes on the color of the element to which it belongs.

> The border properties let you add borders to all individual sides or all four sides of an element. The three border characteristics are style, color, and width. Style must be stated to make the border appear.

> The page layout box properties let you create floating content boxes and wrap text around images.

> Remember to use margin, border, and padding properties to enhance the legibility of your content.

Key Terms

border properties—CSS properties that let you control the appearance of borders around elements.

box model—A CSS element that describes the rectangular boxes containing content on a web page.

containing box—The containing rectangle, or parent element, of any child element. The absolute containing element is the window area of the browser. All other elements are displayed within this containing box, which equates to the <body> element of an HTML document. Within <body>, elements such as <div> or <p> are parents, or containing boxes, for their child elements.

CSS visual formatting model—A model that describes how CSS element content boxes should be displayed by the browser.

margin properties—CSS properties that let you control the margin area of the box model.

padding properties—CSS properties that let you control the padding area in the box model.

page layout box properties—CSS properties that let you control the dimensions and position of content boxes.

Review Questions and Exercises

1. What are the three space areas in the box model?

2. Which space area is transparent?

3. What does the visual formatting model describe?

4. What is the visual formatting model based on?

5. What are percentage measurement values based on?

6. What is the preferred length unit for margins and padding?

7. In the following rule, what is the size of the vertical margins between paragraphs?

   ```
   p {margin-top: 15px; margin-bottom: 10px;}
   ```

8. Where is the padding area?

9. What are the five most common border properties?

10. What is the default border style?

11. What is the default border width?

12. What is the default border color?

13. What does the float property let you do?

14. What does the clear element let you do?

15. Write a style rule for a <p> element that sets margins to 2em, padding to 1em, and a black, solid 1-pixel border.

16. Write a style rule for an <h1> element that sets top and bottom padding to .5em with a dashed thin red border on the bottom.

17. Write a style rule for a <p> element that creates left and right padding of 1em, a left margin of 30 pixels, and a left black medium double border.

Hands-On Projects

1. Browse the web and choose a site that you feel exhibits good use of white space to increase the legibility of the content. Write a short design critique of what the designers did well and why the white space works effectively.

2. Browse the web and choose a site that can benefit from the box properties available in CSS. Print a copy of the page and indicate where you would change the spacing and border properties. Write a short essay that describes the changes you want to achieve and how they would increase the legibility of the content.

3. In this project, you will create a floating text box.

   a. Copy the **ch6project3.html** file from the Chapter06 folder provided with your Data Files to the Chapter06 folder in your work folder. (Create the Chapter06 folder, if necessary.)

   b. Open the file **ch6project3.html** in your HTML editor.

   c. In your browser, open the file **ch6project3.html**. When you open the file, it looks like Figure 6-33.

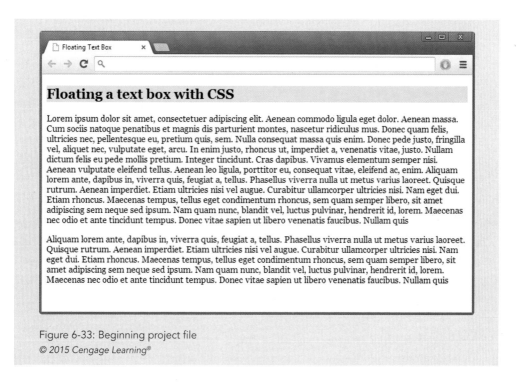

Figure 6-33: Beginning project file
© 2015 Cengage Learning®

   d. Examine the page code. Notice that an existing style rule sets a background-color for a floatbox class, as shown in the following code fragment:

```
.floatbox {background-color: #ccddee;}
```

e. This class is applied to the first <p> element in the document, as shown in Figure 6-33. Your goal is to use a variety of box properties to create a finished page that looks like Figure 6-34.

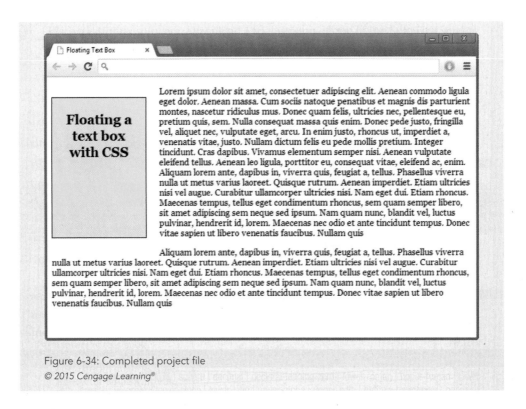

Figure 6-34: Completed project file
© 2015 Cengage Learning®

f. Use the following properties to create the finished floating text box:
- width
- height
- float
- padding
- margin-right
- border
- text-align

Experiment with the different properties until you achieve results that look as close to the finished page as possible.

4. In this project, you will have a chance to test the border properties. Save and view the file in your browser after completing each step.

    a. Copy the **ch6project4.html** file from the Chapter06 folder provided with your Data Files to the Chapter06 folder in your work folder. (Create the Chapter06 folder, if necessary.)

    b. Open the file **ch6project4.html** in your HTML editor.

    c. Add a <style> element to the <head> section as shown in the following code:

```
<head>
<title>CSS Borders Practice File</title>
<meta http-equiv="Content-Type" content="text/html;
charset=UTF-8">
<style>
</style>
</head>
```

    d. Experiment with the different border styles. Start by applying any of the following style rules to your document's elements:

```
h1 {border: solid 1px black;}
h2 {border-top: solid 1px; border-bottom: solid 3px;}
p {border-left: double red; border-right: solid 1px;}
```

    e. Experiment with adding padding properties to your style rules to offset the borders from the text. The following style rules have sample padding properties to try:

```
h1 {border: solid 1px black; padding: 20px;}
h2 {border-top: solid 1px; border-bottom: solid 3px;
    padding-top: 15px; padding-bottom: 30px;}
p {border-left: double red; border-right: solid 1px;
    padding-left: 30px; padding-right: 20px;}
```

    f. Continue to experiment with the border and padding properties. Try adding color and margin properties to see how the elements are displayed.

Individual Case Project

Create the box model conventions for your web site. Build on the typographic classes you created in Chapter 5. Think about the different spacing requirements for your content, and decide how the legibility can be enhanced using the box properties. Add this information to the type specification HTML page that shows examples of the different typefaces and sizes and how they will be used. Decide on margins, padding, and borders, and select the elements that will benefit from their use. Create before-and-after sample HTML pages that reflect the enhanced design.

Team Case Project

Work with your team to decide on the box model conventions for your project web site. These conventions include any spacing specifications for your content that will increase legibility and clarity.

You may need to create sample mock-up HTML pages to present your ideas on these characteristics to your team members. Decide on margins, borders, and padding and how you will use these in your web site. Think about creating floating boxes within sections for text highlights, how to standardize the look of different sections of your site with increased white space, and how borders can help to emphasize headings and columns.

After you have reached a general consensus, go back to work on your page template. Create more finished mock-ups of your page design. Trade the page layout examples with your team members to reach consensus.

CHAPTER 7

PAGE LAYOUTS

When you complete this chapter, you will be able to:

> Understand the normal flow of elements
> Create content containers using the division element and sectioning elements
> Create floating layouts
> Build a flexible page layout
> Build a fixed page layout

In a standard HTML document, the default positioning of elements is generally top to bottom and left to right. In the past, web designers used tables to create multiple-column layouts and gain more control of their page designs. HTML tables are not intended for page layout and are no longer in favor, although they still exist on many web pages.

Modern web designs are built using the CSS layout capabilities. As you saw in Chapter 6, you can use floats to position content elements on a web page and move them out of the normal flow of elements. In this chapter, you will learn how to expand on this concept by using floats to create multicolumn web pages that can either be flexible based on the browser size and screen resolution or fixed to a definite width. You will see how to resolve common float problems, and you will get a chance to build both a flexible layout and a fixed page layout. In Chapter 12, you will learn to use these techniques with media queries to build responsive web page designs that adapt to different device types, including smartphones, tablets, and desktop monitors.

Understanding the Normal Flow of Elements

By default, the browser normally displays elements on the page one after the other, depending on whether the elements are block-level or inline elements. Some elements float to the left or right of other elements on the page, as you saw in Chapter 6. Element position can be affected by margin or padding properties, but generally the browser lays out element boxes from top to bottom and left to right until all elements that make up the web page have been displayed.

In the normal flow for block-level elements, boxes are laid out vertically one after the other, beginning at the top of the containing block. Each box horizontally fills the browser window. The space between boxes is determined by the margin settings. The normal flow determines the sequence of element display with which you are familiar in standard HTML. For an example of normal flow, examine the following HTML code and the resulting normal flow diagram in Figure 7-1:

```
<body>
    <h1>The Document Title</h1>
    <p>Lorem ipsum...</p>
    <p>Duis autem...</p>
    <p>Ut wisi enim...</p>
</body>
```

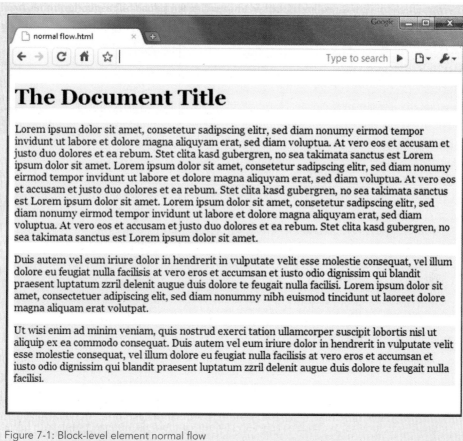

Figure 7-1: Block-level element normal flow
© 2015 Cengage Learning®

The <body> element is the containing element for the content section of the web page. The elements within the <body> element are displayed exactly in the order they appear in the code from top to bottom, which in this example is an <h1> element followed by three <p> elements. Elements do not appear next to each other unless they are floated (see Chapter 6) or have a display type of *inline*.

In the normal flow for inline elements, boxes are laid out horizontally, beginning at the top left of the containing block. The inline boxes comprise the lines of text within—for example, a <p> element. The browser flows the text into the inline boxes, wrapping the text to the next line box as determined by the constraints of the containing box or the browser window size.

When you float, or position an element, you take it out of the normal flow. Other elements that are not floated or positioned will still follow the normal flow, so you should check the results frequently as you are designing your layout using floats. Figure 7-2 shows a floated element on the left side of the page. Notice that the two other nonfloating elements remain in the normal flow and still span the width of the browser window, even extending behind the floating elements. As you can see in the example, the text in the normal flow boxes appears in the correct position to the right of the floated element. This behavior allows text to wrap around floated elements such as images, which is a basic advantage of floats. However, when you start to use floats to build page layouts, the behavior of floats can cause problems. As you gain more experience working with floating layouts, you will be able to anticipate and correct problems with floats as you code your page designs.

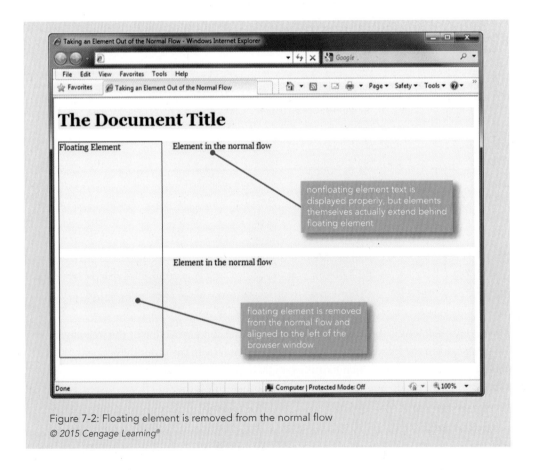

Figure 7-2: Floating element is removed from the normal flow
© 2015 Cengage Learning®

Creating Content Containers

You use the sectioning elements described in Chapter 1 as well as occasionally using the <div> element to create content sections in your web page designs. Using the box properties you learned about in Chapter 6, you can create containers that are any shape you need to contain and segregate sections of content. You can create vertical columns containing content and control the white space between and within the columns. You can nest content elements within containers and create interesting content presentations. Finally, you can create a division element to contain an entire web page, often called a **wrapper**, which centers the web page within the browser window, regardless of screen resolution.

Figure 7-3 shows a web page created with a <div> element that has an id named wrapper. The wrapper division, outlined in red, contains the entire content of the web page. The wrapper has three child elements: header, nav, and article. Each of these elements will contain page content.

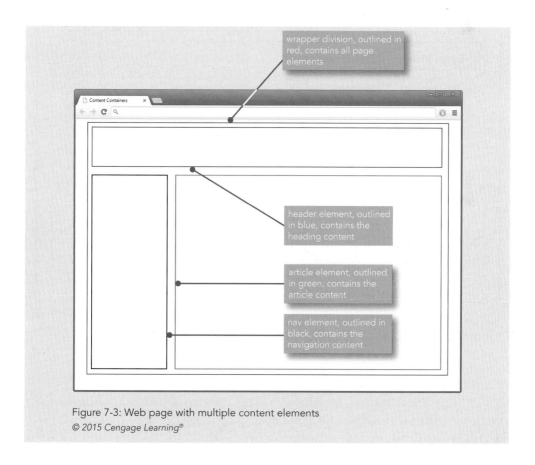

Figure 7-3: Web page with multiple content elements
© 2015 Cengage Learning®

In Figure 7-4, you can see these same elements with sample content. The header element contains an <h1> element. The nav element contains an <h2> heading and links. The article element contains an <h2> heading, an image, and paragraph elements. Various margin and padding settings offset the content from the sides of the container elements. The wrapper element holds all the pieces together and allows the page to be centered in the browser window.

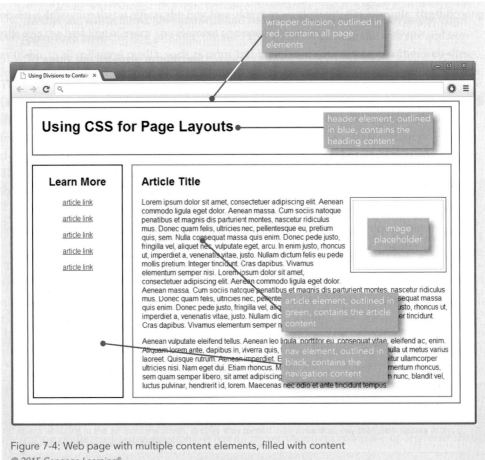

Figure 7-4: Web page with multiple content elements, filled with content
© 2015 Cengage Learning®

Choosing the Correct Content Element

HTML5 has several sectioning elements, such as the <header> and <footer> elements, which were described in detail in Chapter 1; their usage is obvious based on their element name. However, the use of three sectioning elements, <div>, <article>, and <section>, is not readily apparent and can cause confusion. When you are designing a page of content, as shown in Figure 7-4, which of these elements should you use to contain your content?

As described in Chapter 1, the <div> element is well known because it was used in place · of elements like <article> or <section> prior to HTML5. Now that elements are specifically designed for semantic representation of page content, <div> will not be used as often.

The <div> element has no special meaning; use it only as a container for a block of content, especially for style purposes, such as the wrapper example shown in Figures 7-3 and 7-4.

```
<div class="wrapper"> child content... </div>
```

The <article> and <section> elements are new in HTML5, and their general acceptance and usage across the web development community is not consistent. Both can be used to contain content, and they can be interchangeably nested within each other, so articles can contain sections and sections can contain articles.

The <section> element represents a thematically grouped section of a document, and should contain a heading element to describe its contents. A section can represent a chapter or any other cohesive grouping of content on your web site, as in the following example:

```
<section>
<h1>Contact Us</h1>
<p>You can reach us at 555-410-4224</p>
</section>
```

In most cases, other elements can represent most parts of a web page, so the <section> element might not be used much.

The <article> element also contains a themed group of content, but it is different from <section>, as described by the W3C:

"The article element is a complete self-contained composition in a document, page, application, or site and that is, in principle, independently distributable or reusable, e.g. in syndication. This could be a forum post, a magazine or newspaper article, a blog entry, a user-submitted comment, an interactive widget or gadget, or any other independent item of content."

If you follow this description for usage, then an article must stand on its own and as a complete piece of content, even if it is removed from its web site.

Articles can contain sections, so the two elements could be used like this:

```
<article>
  <section>
    <h1>Using the Sectioning Elements</h1>
    <p>Content...</p>
  </section>
  <section>
    <h1>Chapter 1</h1>
    <p>Content...</p>
  </section>
  <section>
    <h1>Chapter 2</h1>
    <p>Content...</p>
  </section>
</article>
```

Articles can contain any content, so you can add footers, asides, and other content elements to your articles. Be consistent, and apply the same usage across your web site content.

Creating Floating Layouts

The float property lets you build columnar layouts by floating content elements to either the right or left side of the browser window. A typical web page design can contain both floating and nonfloating elements. For example, Figure 7-5 shows a web page layout with a header, three columns of content, and a footer. The three columns are floating elements, while the header and footer are nonfloating. The nav and article columns are floating to the left, while the sidebar is floating to the right. All of the page elements are separated from each other with margin settings to provide gutters between the columns.

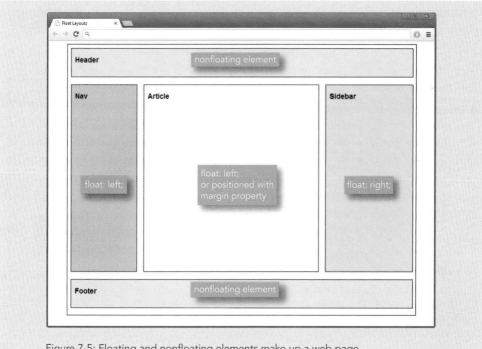

Figure 7-5: Floating and nonfloating elements make up a web page
© 2015 Cengage Learning®

Building floating layouts requires that you choose a method for containing the floating elements. Floats are designed to extend outside of their containing element because the original concept of floating was to allow text to wrap around images, as you saw earlier in this chapter. When you start to build floating layouts, you will often see that the floating elements extend beyond their containing elements, which will result in a "broken" layout, as illustrated in Figure 7-6.

Note | *Floating elements must always have a specified width or they will expand to the size of the browser window.*

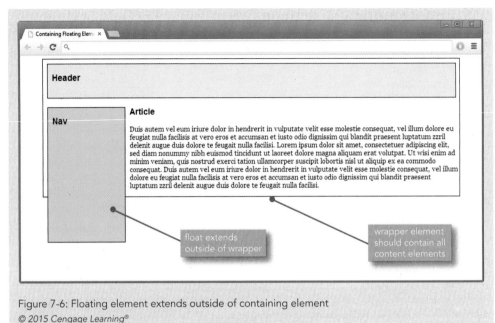

Figure 7-6: Floating element extends outside of containing element

© 2015 Cengage Learning®

You can use two methods to fix this problem.

Solution 1: Using a Normal Flow Element

If you have multiple columns, at least one needs to be nonfloating (in the normal flow), and positioned with margin properties, as shown in Figure 7-7.

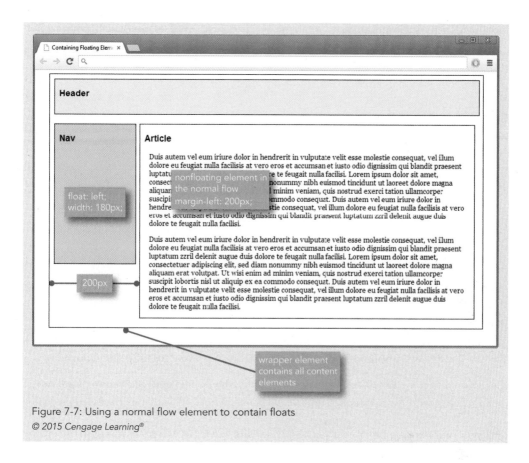

Figure 7-7: Using a normal flow element to contain floats
© 2015 Cengage Learning®

In this example, the article element is nonfloating and has a 200-pixel left margin to position the element to the right of the floating nav element. The style rule for the nav and article elements looks like this:

```
nav {
    width: 180px;
    height: 300px;
    float: left;
    border: solid thin black;
    margin-top: 20px;
    margin-left: 10px;
    margin-right: 10px;
    background-color: #fabf8f;
}
```

```
article {
    width: 740px;
    margin-left: 200px;
    border: solid thin black;
    background-color: #fff;
    margin-top: 20px;
    margin-bottom: 20px;
}
```

Solution 2: Using the Clear Property

If you use a nonfloating footer element (in the normal flow), with the clear property set to *both*, the containing wrapper will extend beyond the footer property to contain all content elements on the page, as shown in Figure 7-8.

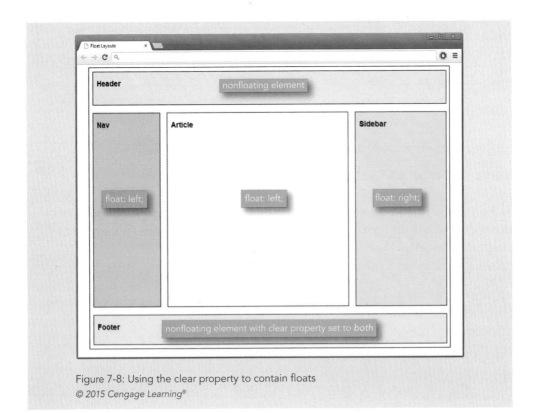

Figure 7-8: Using the clear property to contain floats
© 2015 Cengage Learning®

The style rule for the footer elements looks like this:

```
footer {
    width: 940px;
    height: 75px;
    margin-left: 10px;
    clear: both;
    border: solid thin black;
    background-color: #e5dfec;
}
```

Because some type of footer is a consistent design feature in most web sites, this second solution works very well. Your footer can be as simple as a horizontal rule <hr> element or a graphic contained with a footer element.

Floating Elements Within Floats

Using floating elements gives you a wide variety of options for building interesting page layouts. For example, you can float elements within floating elements, as shown in Figure 7-9.

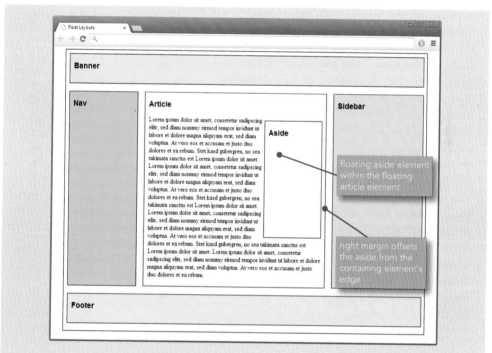

Figure 7-9: Floating element within a float
© 2015 Cengage Learning®

In this example, a floating element within the article element contains an aside, a quotation, or an excerpt from the main article that is used to draw the reader's attention to the article. This is a good example of using the aside element, which is designed for content that is tangentially related to the content around it. This element floats right within the article element, and it is offset from the border of the article element with a right margin. An image element can also be floated using this same method.

When you are floating an element within another element, the order of the elements is important. In the example in Figure 7-10, the floating aside element follows the heading element and precedes the paragraph content. If this order were not followed, the aside would appear at the bottom of the article rather than in its correct position. Figure 7-10 shows the order of the elements within the article element.

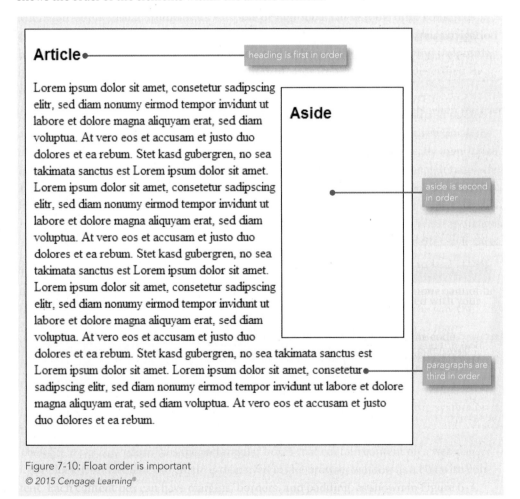

Figure 7-10: Float order is important
© 2015 Cengage Learning®

In contrast, Figure 7-11 shows what happens to the layout when the correct float order is not maintained. In this example, the order of the aside element and the paragraphs has been switched, with unintended results. The aside is pushed out of its container element because the paragraph elements take up all of the room in the article element.

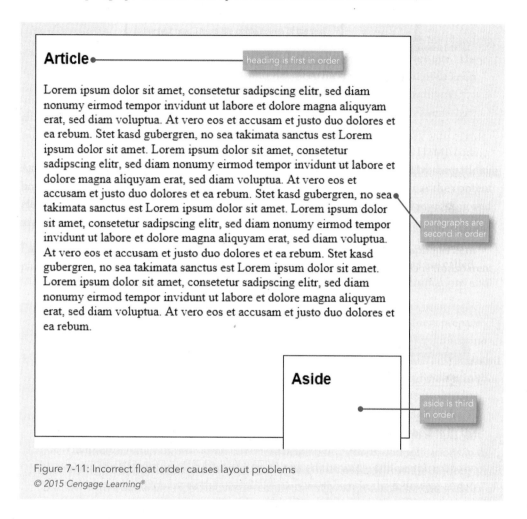

Figure 7-11: Incorrect float order causes layout problems
© 2015 Cengage Learning®

Fixing Column Drops

Column drops occur when the total width of the columnar elements in a page layout exceeds the width of their containing element. The width of a box element includes the total of its width value plus any left or right padding, border, and margins. Figure 7-12 shows an example of column drop caused by the total width of the contained columns being greater than the width of the containing wrapper element.

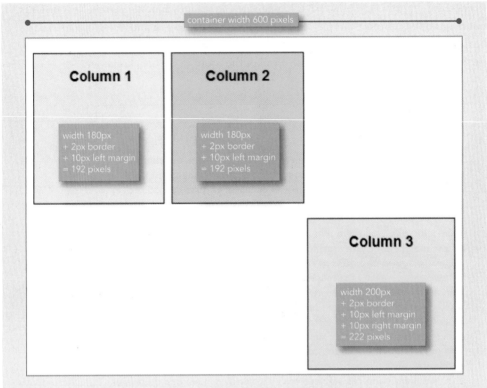

Figure 7-12: Column drop caused by combined element width being greater than container width
© 2015 Cengage Learning®

If you total the width of the three elements (192 + 192 + 222 = 606), the sum is greater than 600 pixels, the width of the containing element, forcing Column 3 to drop below the other columns because the layout does not provide enough horizontal width. To solve this problem, the width of Column 3 can be reduced to 180 pixels, reducing the overall width of the columns to 586 pixels. Another method of solving this problem is to use the box-sizing property to constrain the boxes' width so they always fit within the containing element, regardless of the border or padding size. Refer to "Setting Sizing Type" in Chapter 6 for details.

Clearing Problem Floats

When you are designing float-based layouts, floats occasionally do not appear exactly where you want them to appear. The clear property can help you solve this problem. For example, in Figure 7-13a, the footer element floats left and should appear below Column 1, but instead it floats in order after Column 2. To move it down the page to its correct position, add the clear property set to a value of left to move the footer down the page and align it with the next clear left edge of the browser window, as shown in Figure 7-13b.

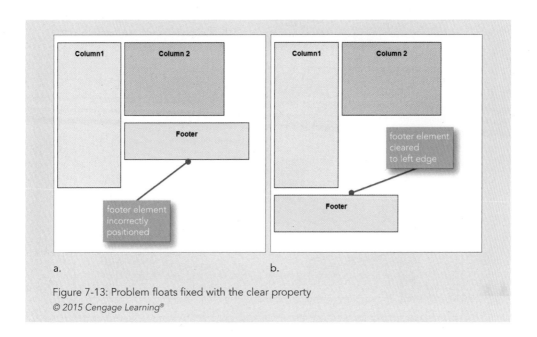

Figure 7-13: Problem floats fixed with the clear property
© 2015 Cengage Learning®

The style rule for the footer element looks like this:

```
footer {
    width: 350px;
    height: 100px;
    float: left;
    margin-top: 20px;
    margin-left: 10px;
    margin-right: 10px;
    border: solid 1px black;
    background-color: #c6d9f1;
    clear: left;
}
```

Building a Flexible Page Layout

Flexible layouts adapt to the size of the browser window. Flexible layouts shift as the user resizes the window, wrapping text or adding white space as necessary. In Figure 7-14, the flexible layout contains three elements. Flexible layouts are the basis for responsive layouts, which you will learn about in Chapter 12.

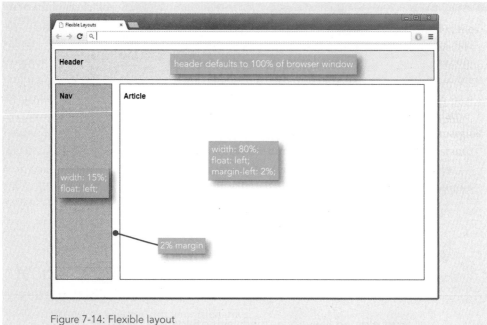

Figure 7-14: Flexible layout
© 2015 Cengage Learning®

The header element has no width set, so it defaults to the width of the browser window as
any normal flow element would. Below the header element are two floating elements, nav
and article. These elements have flexible widths set as well. The style rules for these three
elements follow:

```
header {
    height: 75px;
    margin-top: 1em;
    margin-bottom: 10px;
    border: solid thin black;
    background-color: #e5dfec;
}
nav {
    width: 15%;
    height: 500px;
    float: left;
```

```
        border: solid thin black;
        background-color: #fabf8f;
    }
    article {
        width: 80%;
        height: 500px;
        float: left;
        margin-left: 2%;
        border: solid thin black;
        background-color: #fff;
    }
```

> **Note** In the code example for Figure 7-14, the height property is used in both the nav and article elements. You normally want to avoid using height on elements that contain varying lengths of content, as too much content will overflow a fixed height.

Notice that the two widths for the floating elements do not equal 100% because the borders and margin contribute to the width of each element. Setting the values to equal 100% would overflow the layout window. The nav and article elements both float left. The article element has a 2% left margin, meaning that the margin changes size as the layout resizes to display a consistent gutter between the floating elements.

Flexible layouts offer the advantage of adapting to the user's browser size. From a design viewpoint, this can be less desirable because of the wide range of monitor sizes and resolutions. With a flexible layout, your content has to adapt and look good at a wide range of layout sizes, which can be difficult to achieve. (Refer to the Amazon web site in Figures 2-4 and 2-5 in Chapter 2 as an example.) Figure 7-15 shows a simple flexible layout at different screen resolutions. Notice how the content adapts to the different resolutions. With a simple layout, flexible web sites resize gracefully, but with more complex content and page designs, you may want to restrict your design with the min-width and max-width properties described in the next section.

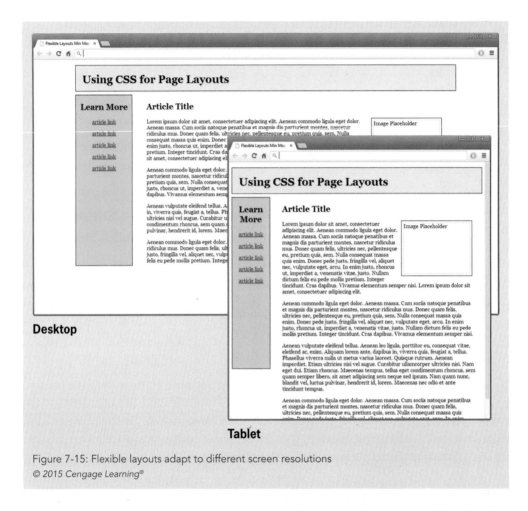

Desktop

Tablet

Figure 7-15: Flexible layouts adapt to different screen resolutions

© 2015 Cengage Learning®

Controlling Flexible Layout Width

You can control the compression and expansion of your content in a flexible layout by setting minimum and maximum widths for the content. As you saw in Chapter 6, you can set an element's min-width and max-width properties. You can add a wrapper element that contains the page elements, and then set the minimum and maximum sizes to control the boundaries of the page layout. This technique will come in handy when you are building responsive web pages that are designed for different device sizes, as described in Chapter 12.

In the following style rule for the wrapper, the min-width value stops the shrinking of the layout at 750 pixels, which is an optimum width for an 800 x 600 display; the max-width value stops the expansion of the layout at 1220 pixels, the optimum width for a 1280 x 1024 display. Any monitor with a higher resolution will display the layout at 1220 pixels wide, maintaining the integrity of the layout. The margin-left and margin-right properties are set to auto, which centers the layout in the browser at higher resolutions.

```
div.wrapper {
    width: 100%;
    min-width: 750px;
    max-width: 1220px;
    margin-left: auto;
    margin-right: auto;
}
```

You would then apply the wrapper to a <div> element that contains all other elements in your page layout. The following code shows a simplified version of what the wrapper <div> looks like in HTML:

Note To avoid guessing screen measurements, use a tool such as Screen Ruler, available from www.microfox.com, to easily measure pixels on your computer monitor.

```
<div id="wrapper"> <!-opens wrapper -->
<header> header content... </header>
<nav> nav content... </nav>
<article> article content... </article>
</div> <!-closes wrapper -->
```

You will build a wrapper division to contain a page layout like this in the Hands-On Projects later in the chapter.

Activity: Creating a Flexible Layout

In the following steps, you will build a flexible two-column layout to practice using floating elements within a flexible design. As you work through the steps, refer to Figure 7-19 to see the results you will achieve. New code that you will add is shown in blue. Save your file and test your work in a browser as you complete each step.

To create the flexible layout:

1. Copy the **ch7activity1.html** file from the Chapter07 folder provided with your Data Files. Open the file **ch7activity1.html** in your HTML editor.

2. In your browser, open the file **ch7activity1.html**. When you open the file, it looks like Figure 7-16.

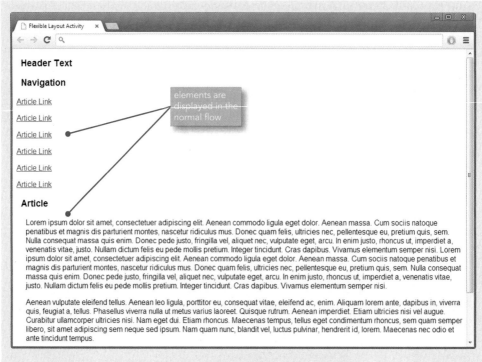

Figure 7-16: Flexible layout activity beginning web page
© 2015 Cengage Learning®

When you first look at the style rule, you see only the basic formatting properties:

```
<style>
body {font-family: arial;}
h3 {
    font-family: arial;
    margin-left: 10px;
}
.copy {margin-left: 20px}
</style>
```

There are no style rules for any of the content elements, so all are displayed in the normal flow, top to bottom in order and left-aligned to the browser window.

Styling the Header

Begin by formatting the header element with margins, a border, and a background color.

1. Within the <style> element, add a style rule that selects the header element and sets the height to 80 pixels.

```
header {
    height: 80px;
}
```

2. Add margins to offset the header from the top of the browser window and the content below by 10 pixels.

```
header {
    height: 80px;
    margin-top: 10px;
    margin-bottom: 10px;
}
```

3. Align the text to the center of the header, add a solid thin black border, and apply light purple as the background color (#e5dfec).

```
header {
    height: 80px;
    margin-top: 10px;
    margin-bottom: 10px;
    text-align: center;
    border: solid thin black;
    background-color: #e5dfec;
}
```

4. Save your file, and preview the work in the browser. The header element is now formatted, as shown in Figure 7-17.

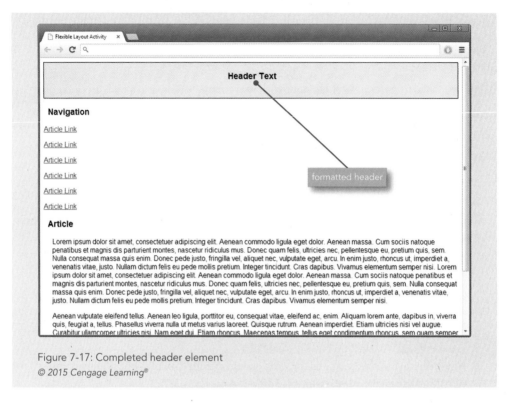

Figure 7-17: Completed header element
© 2015 Cengage Learning®

Styling the Nav Element

Format the nav element so it floats to the left of the page.

1. Add a new selector for the nav element, and set the element to float left with a width of 15%.

```
nav {
    float: left;
    width: 15%;
}
```

2. Set the height to 500 pixels, and align the text to center.

```
nav {
    float: left;
    width: 15%;
    height: 500px;
    text-align: center;
}
```

3. Add a solid thin black border, and set the background color to light orange (#fabf8f).

```
nav {
    float: left;
    width: 15%;
    height: 500px;
    text-align: center;
    border: solid thin black;
    background-color: #fabf8f;
}
```

4. Save your file, and preview the work in the browser. The nav element is now formatted, as shown in Figure 7-18. The article element needs some work, which you will do in the next set of steps.

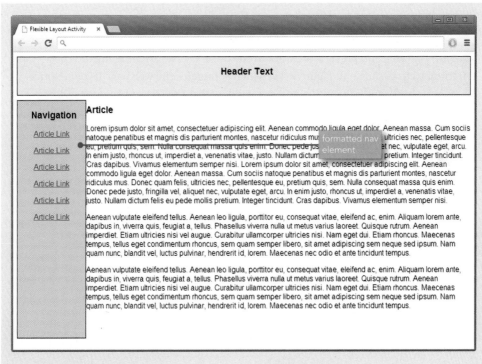

Figure 7-18: Completed nav element
© 2015 Cengage Learning®

Styling the Article Element

Format the article element to complete the flexible layout.

1. Within the <style> element, add a style rule that selects the article element and sets it to float left with a width of 80%.

```
article {
    float: left;
    width: 80%;
}
```

2. Set a left margin of 2%. This allows the margin to adapt to different browser widths. Also set a background-color of white (#fff).

```
article {
    float: left;
    width: 80%;
    margin-left: 2%;
    background-color: #fff;
}
```

3. Save your file, and preview the work in the browser. The article element is now formatted, as shown in Figure 7-19, which completes the web page layout. Notice as you shrink and expand the browser window that the content adapts to fill the window.

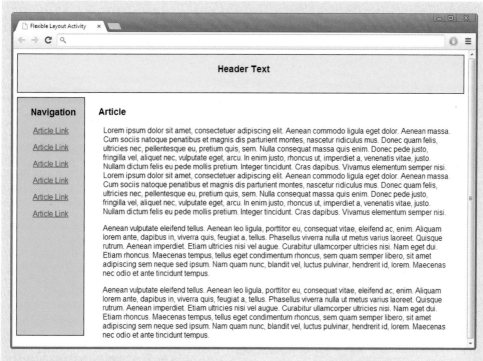

Figure 7-19: Completed flexible layout
© 2015 Cengage Learning®

The complete style sheet for the web page in Figure 7-19 is as follows:

```
<style>
body {font-family: arial;}
h3 {
    font-family: arial;
    margin-left: 10px;
}
.copy {margin-left: 20px}
header {
    height: 80px;
    margin-top: 10px;
    margin-bottom: 10px;
    text-align: center;
```

```
      border: solid thin black;
      background-color: #e5dfec;
   }
   nav {
      float: left;
      width: 15%;
      height: 500px;
      text-align: center;
      border: solid thin black;
      background-color: #fabf8f;
   }
   article {
      float: left;
      width: 80%;
      margin-left: 2%;
      background-color: #fff;
   }
   </style>
```

Building a Fixed Page Layout

Fixed layouts remain constant despite the resizing of the browser in different screen resolutions and monitor sizes. Many designers prefer fixed layouts because they have more control over the finished design. They can also build more complex layouts because they can be fairly sure of consistent results. Fixed layouts are normally contained by a wrapper element that controls the page width and centers the page in the browser window. Within the wrapper, you can choose whether to contain only fixed-size elements, percentage elements, or a combination of the two. Because the outside width of the page is fixed, the design is more precise, and content can flow down the page as necessary. Pixel measurements are favored by many designers when creating fixed designs.

Note | *Refer to Figures 2-6 and 2-7 in Chapter 2 for fixed layout examples.*

Figure 7-20 shows a two-column layout that contains four elements.

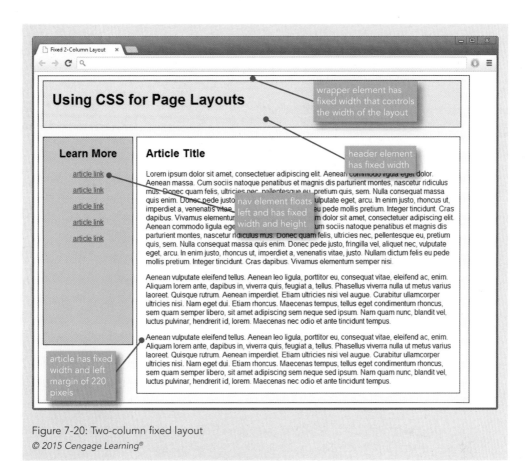

Figure 7-20: Two-column fixed layout
© 2015 Cengage Learning®

A wrapper division element contains the other content elements and sets the fixed width for the layout. Header, nav, and article elements contain the page content. The nav element floats to the left and has a fixed width and height. The article element has a margin-left property that positions it on the page.

The style rules for these four elements follow:

```
#wrapper {
    width: 960px;
    margin-right: auto;
    margin-left: auto;
    border: thin solid black;
    background-color: #ffc;
}
```

```
header {
    width: 930px;
    height: 100px;
    margin-top: 10px;
    margin-left: 10px;
    border: thin solid black;
    background-color: #e5dfec;
}
nav {
    width: 200px;
    height: 450px;
    float: left;
    border: thin solid black;
    margin: 20px 0px 10px;
    text-align: center;
    background-color: #fabf8f;
}
article {
    width: 718px;
    border: thin solid black;
    margin: 20px 8px 20px 220px;
    background-color: #fff;
}
```

Notice that the wrapper element has a fixed width, but no fixed height, allowing content to flow down the page as necessary. The 960-pixel value for the width reflects the base screen resolution of 1024 x 768; this may change based on your user's needs.

The header is in the normal flow and has a fixed width and height. The nav element floats left and has a fixed width and height as well. This element can be made more flexible by removing the height property and letting the content determine the height of the element.

The article element has a fixed width but no height, allowing the height of the element to be based on the amount of its content. The article element has a left margin (the last value in the margin property) that offsets the article 220 pixels from the left side of the browser window.

Controlling Fixed Layout Centering

Another benefit of using a wrapper division to contain your layout is the ability to automatically center the layout horizontally in the browser. This is a great solution for wide-screen monitors, as your layout will always be centered regardless of the screen resolution. Automatic centering is a simple use of the margin property. In the following style rule for the wrapper division in Figure 7-20, the margin-left and margin-right properties are set to *auto*, telling the browser to automatically proportion the extra space in the browser window, resulting in a centered layout.

```
#wrapper {
  width: 960px;
  margin-left: auto;
  margin-right: auto;
  border: thin solid black;
  background-color: #ffc;
}
```

Figure 7-21 shows the centered two-column fixed layout in a 1366 x 768 screen resolution.

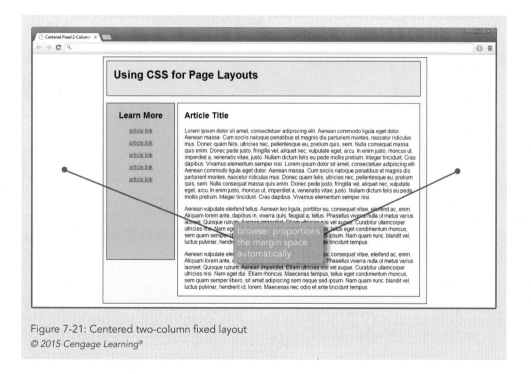

Figure 7-21: Centered two-column fixed layout
© 2015 Cengage Learning®

Activity: Creating a Fixed Layout

In the following steps, you will build a fixed three-column layout to practice using floating elements within a fixed design. As you work through the steps, refer to Figure 7-28 to see the results you will achieve. New code that you will add is shown in blue. Save your file and test your work in a browser as you complete each step.

To create the fixed layout:

1. Copy the **ch7activity2.html** file from the Chapter07 folder provided with your Data Files.

2. Open the file **ch7activity2.html** in your HTML editor.

3. In your browser, open the file **ch7activity2.html**. When you open the file, it looks like Figure 7-22.

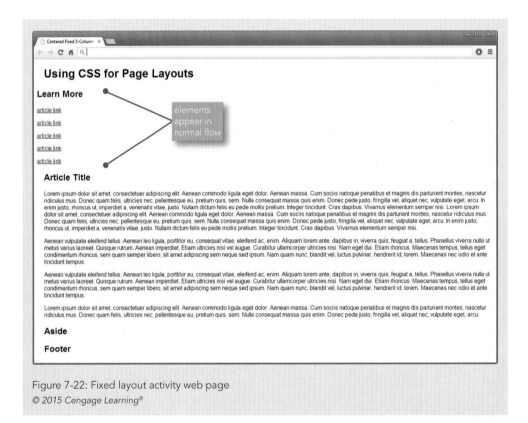

Figure 7-22: Fixed layout activity web page
© 2015 Cengage Learning®

When you first look at the CSS style rules, you see only the basic formatting rules:

```
<style>
body {font-family: arial;}
h1 {margin-left: 20px;}
.copy {
    margin-left: 20px;
    margin-right: 10px;
}
.title {margin-left: 20px;}
</style>
```

None of the content elements have float properties, so all are displayed in the normal flow, top to bottom in order and left-aligned to the browser window.

Creating the Wrapper Division

Start the project by creating the wrapper division element that will contain the web page content.

1. Add a style rule that selects an id named *wrapper*. Set the width of the element to 1220 pixels, appropriate for a 1280 x 1024 resolution or greater.

```
#wrapper {
    width: 1220px;
}
```

2. Add margin-right and margin-left properties, and set these to *auto* so the page is automatically centered in the browser window.

```
#wrapper {
    width: 1220px;
    margin-right: auto;
    margin-left: auto;
}
```

3. Add a thin solid border and a background color of light yellow (#ffc) to complete the wrapper style rule.

```
#wrapper {
    width: 1220px;
    margin-right: auto;
    margin-left: auto;
    border: thin solid;
    background-color: #ffc;
}
```

4. Save your work, and view it in the browser. Figure 7-23 shows the completed wrapper division.

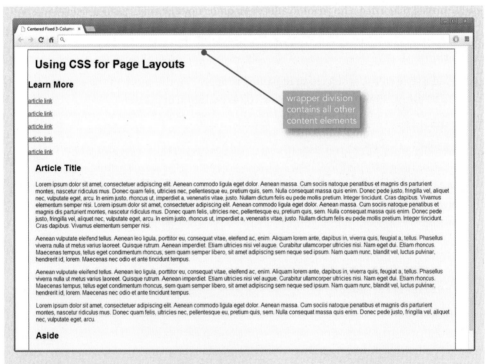

Figure 7-23: Completed wrapper division

© 2015 Cengage Learning®

Styling the Header Element

Format the header element by specifying the width, height, margins, border, and background color.

1. Set the width to 1200 pixels and the height to 100 pixels.

```
header {
    width: 1200px;
    height: 100px;
}
```

2. Add a top margin of 10 pixels and a left margin of 10 pixels.

```
header {
    width: 1200px;
    height: 100px;
    margin-top: 10px;
    margin-left: 10px;
}
```

3. Finish the header element by adding a solid thin border and a background color of light purple (#e5dfec).

```
header {
    width: 1200px;
    height: 100px;
    margin-top: 10px;
    margin-left: 10px;
    border: thin solid;
    background-color: #e5dfec;
}
```

4. Save your work, and view it in the browser. Figure 7-24 shows the completed header element.

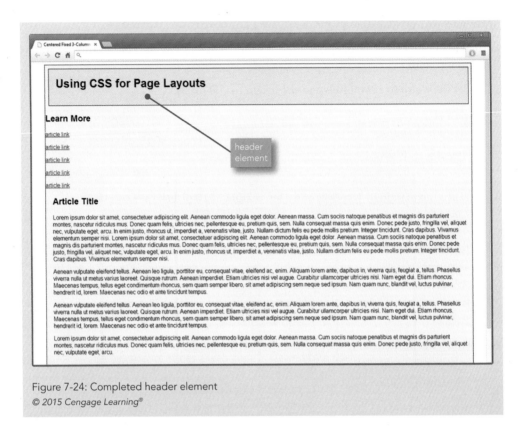

Figure 7-24: Completed header element

© 2015 Cengage Learning®

Styling the Nav Element

Format the nav element to float on the left side of the page.

1. Add a style rule that selects the nav element. Set the width to 200 pixels and the height to 600 pixels.

```
nav {
    width: 200px;
    height: 600px;
}
```

2. Float the nav element to the left. Use the margin shorthand properties to set the following margin values:

> Top margin: 20 pixels

> Right margin: 14 pixels

> Bottom margin: 0 pixels

> Left margin: 10 pixels

```
nav {
    width: 200px;
    height: 600px;
    float: left;
    margin: 20px 14px 0px 10px;
}
```

3. Complete the nav element by aligning the text to the center, adding a thin solid border, and setting the background color to light orange (#fabf8f).

```
nav {
    width: 200px;
    height: 600px;
    float: left;
    margin: 20px 14px 0px 10px;
    text-align: center;
    border: thin solid;
    background-color: #fabf8f;
}
```

4. Save your work, and view it in the browser. Figure 7-25 shows the completed nav element.

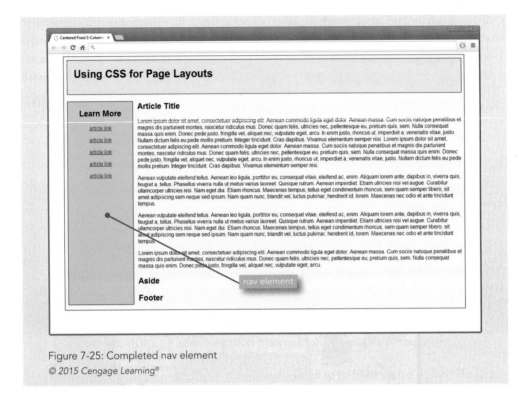

Figure 7-25: Completed nav element
© 2015 Cengage Learning®

Styling the Article Element

Write style rules for the article element to set the width, float, and border properties.

1. Add a style rule that selects the article element. Set the width to 770 pixels, and float the division to the left.

```
article {
    width: 770px;
    float: left;
}
```

2. Use the margin shorthand properties to set the following margin values:

> Top margin: 20 pixels

> Right margin: 0 pixels

> Bottom margin: 20 pixels

> Left margin: 0 pixels

```
article {
    width: 770px;
```

```
    float: left;
    margin: 20px 0px 20px 0px;
}
```

3. Add a thin solid border and a background color of white (#fff) to complete the article element.

```
article {
    width: 770px;
    float: left;
    margin: 20px 0px 20px 0px;
    border: thin solid;
    background-color: #fff;
}
```

4. Save your work, and view it in the browser. Figure 7-26 shows the completed article element.

Notice that the floating elements are no longer properly contained within the wrapper division. You will fix this when you create the footer element at the end of this activity.

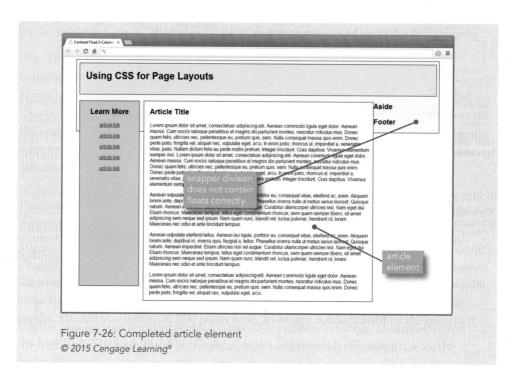

Figure 7-26: Completed article element
© 2015 Cengage Learning®

Styling the Aside Element

Format the aside element to float to the right side of the page.

1. Add a style rule that selects an id named *aside*. Set the width to 200 pixels and the height to 600 pixels.

```
aside {
    width: 200px;
    height: 600px;
}
```

2. Float the aside division to the right.

```
aside {
    width: 200px;
    height: 600px;
    float: right;
}
```

3. Use the margin shorthand properties to set the following margin values:

  › Top margin: 20 pixels

  › Right margin: 8 pixels

  › Bottom margin: 0 pixels

  › Left margin: 0 pixels

```
aside {
    width: 200px;
    height: 600px;
    float: right;
    margin: 20px 8px 0px 0px;
}
```

4. Add a thin solid border and a background color of light blue (#c6d9f1) to complete the aside division.

```
#aside {
    width: 200px;
    height: 600px;
    float: right;
    margin: 20px 8px 0px 0px;
    border: solid thin;
    background-color: #c6d9f1;
}
```

5. Save your work, and view it in the browser. Figure 7-27 shows the completed aside element.

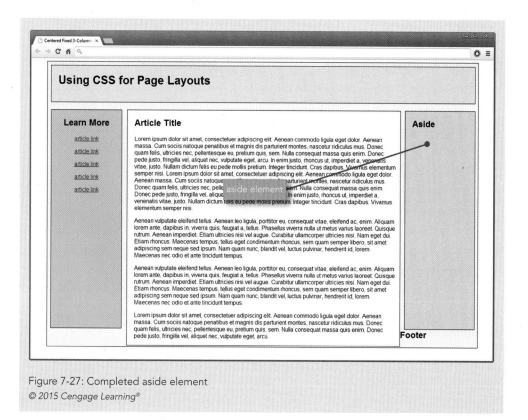

Figure 7-27: Completed aside element
© 2015 Cengage Learning®

Styling the Footer Element and Containing the Floats

Write style rules for the footer element to fix the floating problem and finish the layout.

1. Add a style rule that selects the footer element. Set the width to 1200 pixels and the height to 75 pixels.

```
footer {
    width: 1200px;
    height: 75px;
}
```

2. Add the clear property and set the value to *both*. This will fix the float containment problem you have seen in the previous steps.

```
footer {
    width: 1200px;
    height: 75px;
    clear: both;
}
```

3. Finish the footer by adding a solid thin border, setting the left and bottom margins to 10 pixels, and adding a background color of pink (#efdfec).

```
footer {
    width: 1200px;
    height: 75px;
    clear: both;
    border: solid thin;
    margin-left: 10px;
    margin-bottom: 10px;
    background-color: #efdfec;
}
```

4. Save your work, and test the file in the browser. You will see that the wrapper now contains all of the floating elements, as shown in Figure 7-28.

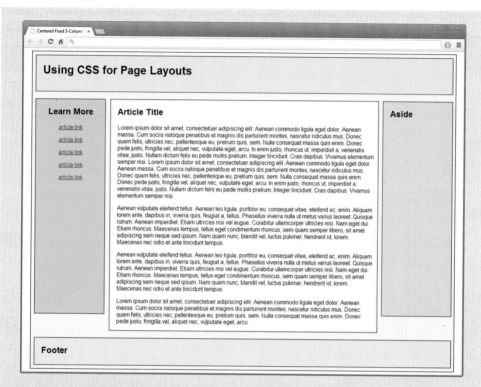

Figure 7-28: Completed fixed layout
© 2015 Cengage Learning®

Skills at Work | *Learn from Criticism*

As you read in Chapter 3, an integral part of any sound web design project is soliciting feedback from peers and stakeholders. Soliciting feedback from coworkers should be the first level of user testing that you perform. Look for people who are unfamiliar with your project to get the most authentic responses. Be open to new ideas and suggestions. Your team members and coworkers can provide a unique perspective on the features and design of your site—often noticing elements that you might have missed.

Project stakeholders and clients will tell you exactly what they like and don't like about your designs. There are times when you will want to defend your work because you think it is ideal, but other times you will be wrong. Gracefully accepting feedback and learning from it enhances your relationship with your peers and clients and will help your career.

Chapter Summary

In this chapter, you learned to apply the CSS page layout features to web page design. You learned about the normal flow of elements in the document and how the float property lets you remove elements from the normal flow. You learned how to create both flexible and fixed layouts, as well as how to resolve problems such as dropped columns and incorrectly positioned floats. Finally, you applied what you learned by building two complete page layouts using the techniques described in this chapter.

> The normal flow dictates the way in which elements normally are displayed in the browser window.

> When you remove an element from the normal flow, you may see unexpected behavior from other elements that are following the normal flow.

> Always use a width property for floating elements; otherwise, the element will extend across the page like elements in the normal flow.

> Avoid using the height property unless you are containing elements such as images that do not change size.

> For fixed layouts, content elements are usually contained with a wrapper element that sets the width for the page layout.

Key Terms

column drop—A layout error that occurs when the total width of the columnar elements in a page layout exceeds the width of their containing element.

fixed layout—A layout that remains constant despite the resizing of the browser in different screen resolutions and monitor sizes.

flexible layout—A layout that shifts as the user resizes the window, wrapping text or adding white space as necessary to adapt to the size of the browser window.

float—To position an element by taking it out of the normal flow of the web page layout.

normal flow—The sequence of element display in standard HTML from top to bottom and left to right until all elements that make up the web page have been displayed.

wrapper—A division element designed to contain an entire web page.

Review Questions

1. What is the normal flow for block-level elements?
2. Which element is the containing element for the content section of the web page?
3. What is the common name for the content container for a web page?
4. Would you normally use the height property when designing web pages? Why or why not?
5. What property would you use to add gutters between columns of text?
6. What are the two methods of properly containing floats on a web page?
7. Can you float elements within floating elements?
8. What causes column drops?
9. What property can be used to help position floating elements properly on a web page?
10. What are the three possible values of the clear property?
11. What is the benefit of flexible layouts?
12. What is the benefit of a fixed layout?
13. What are the properties and values you would use to control flexible layout width?
14. What are the properties and values you would use to automatically center a fixed layout?

Hands-On Projects

1. Create a fixed three-column web page with a header and a footer, as shown in Figure 7-29. This page is designed for a 1024 x 768 resolution.
   a. Copy the **ch7project1.html** file from the Chapter07 folder provided with your Data Files to the Chapter07 folder in your work folder. (Create the Chapter07 folder, if necessary.)
   b. Open the file **ch7project1.html** in your HTML editor.
   c. In your browser, open the file **ch7project1.html** and examine the page layout.
   d. Your goal is to use the values shown in Figure 7-29 to create a finished page with a fixed three-column layout, a header, and a footer.

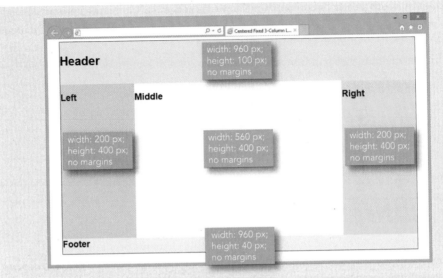

Figure 7-29: Fixed three-column web page with a header and a footer
© 2015 Cengage Learning®

2. Fix the column drop shown in Figure 7-30. The completed web page should look like Figure 7-31.
   a. Copy the **ch7project2.html** file from the Chapter07 folder provided with your Data Files to the Chapter07 folder in your work folder. (Create the Chapter07 folder, if necessary.)
   b. Open the file **ch7project2.html** in your HTML editor.
   c. In your browser, open the file **ch7project2.html** and examine the page layout.
   d. Your goal is to adjust the values used for the columns to create the web page shown in Figure 7-31.

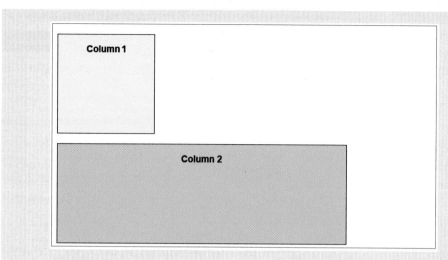

Figure 7-30: Column drop problem
© 2015 Cengage Learning®

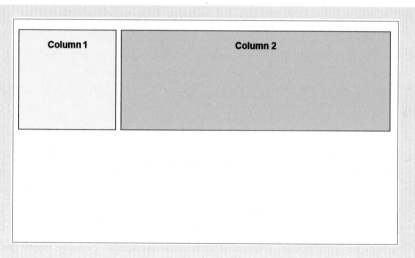

Figure 7-31: Column drop solution
© 2015 Cengage Learning®

3. Fix the float problem shown in Figure 7-32. The completed web page should look like Figure 7-33.
   a. Copy the **ch7project3.html** file from the Chapter07 folder provided with your Data Files to the Chapter07 folder in your work folder. (Create the Chapter07 folder, if necessary.)
   b. Open the file **ch7project3.html** in your HTML editor.
   c. In your browser, open the file **ch7project3.html** and examine the page layout.
   d. Your goal is to use floating and nonfloating elements to create the web page shown in Figure 7-33.

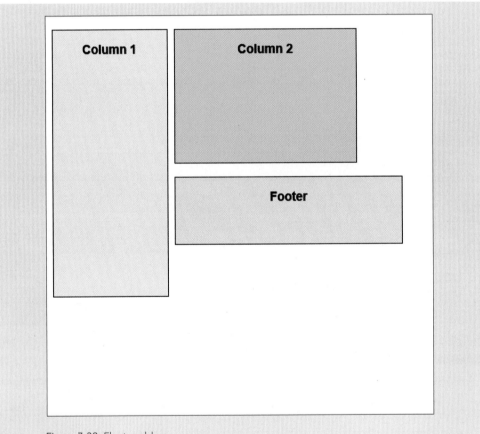

Figure 7-32: Float problem
© 2015 Cengage Learning®

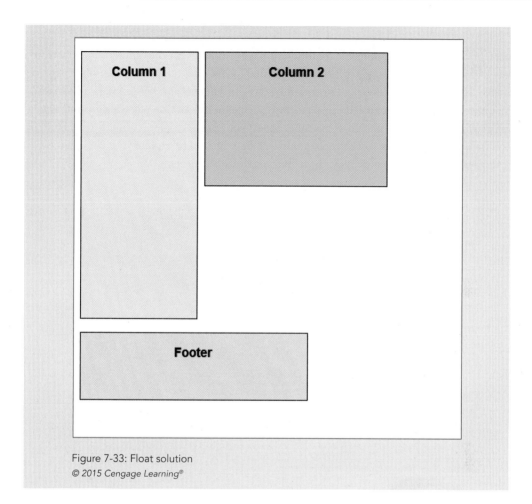

Figure 7-33: Float solution
© 2015 Cengage Learning®

Individual Case Project

Use your design sketches from Chapter 6 and start to build wireframe page mock-ups for the different page levels of your site. Decide whether you will build a fixed or flexible design. Using the skills you learned in this chapter, build and submit page layouts for the different levels of information your site will contain. For example, you need to build a home page mock-up, an article page mock-up, and a section page mock-up. Remember to test your page mock-ups with some text content and at different browser sizes and screen resolutions. Be prepared to explain your choices for your page layouts, such as why you chose fixed or flexible layouts.

Team Case Project

Each team member is responsible for different page templates for the different information levels of your web site. Using the skills you learned in this chapter, build and submit page layouts for the different levels of information your site will contain. For example, one team member is responsible for the home page design, one for the section page design, and one for the article-level page design. Remember to test your page template using the text content at different browser sizes and screen resolutions. Be prepared to explain your choices for your page layouts, such as why you chose fixed or flexible layouts.

GRAPHICS AND COLOR

When you complete this chapter, you will be able to:

> Understand graphics file formats

> Choose a graphics tool

> Use the image element

> Control image properties with CSS

> Create web site color schemes

> Control color properties with CSS

> Control background images with CSS

The ability to freely combine graphics, text, and color into page-type layouts is one feature that makes the web attractive and popular, but it also can be the undoing of many web sites. When you combine these elements wisely, you can produce an attractive and engaging site. Conversely, the use of too many large or complex images, poor color choices, or complicated backgrounds forces users to endure long download times and wade through unreadable text and confusing navigation choices.

Find a good balance between images and text. Use CSS to control image characteristics, such as spacing and text alignment. CSS background images let you enhance page layouts and brand your site.

Use color carefully to communicate, to guide the reader, or to create branding for your site. Test your color choices carefully to make sure they appear properly across different browsers. Also, test at a variety of connection speeds, especially on mobile devices to make sure the time needed to download your graphics does not discourage your readers.

Understanding Graphics File Formats

Currently you can use four image file formats on the web: GIF, JPG, PNG, and SVG. Choosing the right file format for an image is important. If you choose the wrong file type, your image will not compress or appear as you expect.

GIF

The Graphics Interchange Format (GIF) is designed for online delivery of graphics. GIF uses a lossless compression technique, meaning that no color information is discarded when the image is compressed.

The color depth of GIF is 8-bit, allowing a palette of no more than 256 colors. The fewer colors you use, the greater the compression and the smaller the file size. The GIF file format excels at compressing and displaying flat (unshaded) color areas, making it the logical choice for line art (simple drawings) and color graphics. Because of its limited color depth, however, GIF is not the best file format for photographs or more complex graphics that have gradations of color, such as shadows and feathering.

GIF Transparency

With GIF files you can choose one color in an image to appear as transparent in the browser. The background color or pattern of the page will show through the areas in the image that you have designated as transparent. Using transparent areas allows you to create graphics that appear to have an irregular outside shape, rather than a rectangular shape. Figure 8-1 shows the same shape with and without transparency.

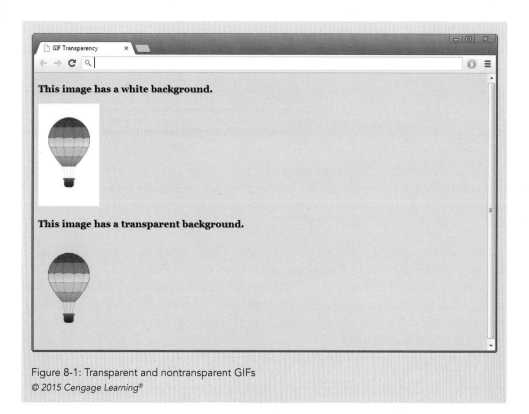

Figure 8-1: Transparent and nontransparent GIFs
© 2015 Cengage Learning®

You can create transparent areas using a graphics editor. When you choose the transparent color, all pixels of that color in the image let the background color show through. In Figure 8-1, the top image has no transparency. In the bottom image, the white background has been made transparent in an image-editing program, and the page color shows through the transparent areas of the graphic.

GIF Animation

The GIF format lets you store multiple images and timing information about the images in a single file. This means that you can build animations consisting of multiple static images that change continuously, creating the illusion of motion. You can create animated GIFs by using a variety of shareware and commercial software. Animated GIFs were very popular in the earlier days of the web, but they have gone out of favor in modern web design.

When you create a GIF animation, you can determine the time between frames and the number of times the animation plays. Figure 8-2 shows a series of individual GIFs combined to play as one animated GIF. The final GIF animation file is a single file whose name ends in the .gif extension.

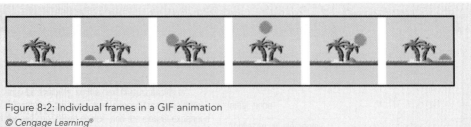

Figure 8-2: Individual frames in a GIF animation
© Cengage Learning®

GIF animation is somewhat limited when compared with the results of proprietary animation tools, which can play synchronized sounds and allow web users to interact with the animation. Animated GIFs do not require any special plug-ins for viewing and will play in any browser.

Use restraint when adding animated GIFs such as blinking icons and scrolling banners to your pages; users may find them annoying because they are repetitive and distract from the page content. Consider choosing to play an animation a limited number of times rather than letting it loop endlessly. Creating animated images with GIF animation software streamlines the process of setting the timing, color palette, and individual frame effects. See Table 8-1 for a list of GIF animation tools.

GIF ANIMATION TOOL	URL
GIF Construction Set Professional	*www.mindworkshop.com/gifcon.html*
GIFMaker	*gifmaker.me*
Advanced GIF Animator	*www.gif-animator.com*

Table 8-1: GIF Animation Tools
© 2015 Cengage Learning®

JPG

The **Joint Photographic Experts Group** format (**JPG**, sometimes called **JPEG**) is best for photographs or continuous-tone images. JPGs are 24-bit images that allow millions of colors. Unlike GIFs, JPGs do not use a palette to display color.

JPGs use a *lossy* compression routine specially designed for photographic images: when the image is compressed, some color information is discarded, resulting in a loss of quality from the original image. Because the display device is a low-resolution computer monitor, the loss of quality is not usually noticeable. Furthermore, JPG's faster download time compensates for its loss of image quality.

You can manipulate JPG images using Adobe Photoshop or other imaging software. You can balance the amount of compression versus the resulting image quality manually. Figure 8-3 shows the Photoshop Save for Web & Devices dialog box, which is the tool you use in Adobe Photoshop to adjust quality and find the estimated download time.

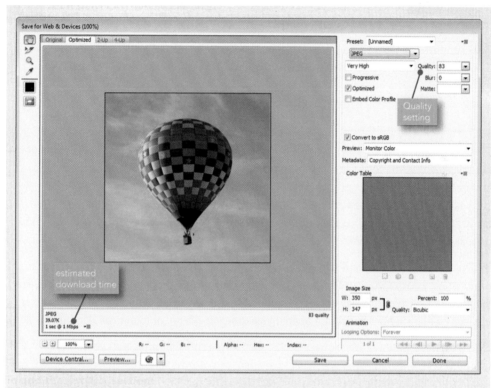

Figure 8-3: Photoshop Save for Web & Devices dialog box
Adobe product screenshot reprinted with permission from Adobe Systems Incorporated

Using the Quality setting, you can adjust the quality of the file; the higher the quality, the lower the file compression. You can experiment with this setting to create good-looking files that are as small as possible. Many photos can sustain quite a bit of compression and still maintain image integrity. The Preview window shows the result of your changes, allowing you to experiment with the image quality before saving the file. Photoshop displays the estimated download time based on the file size.

PNG

The Portable Network Graphics (PNG) format is designed specifically for the web. PNG is a royalty-free file format that replaces GIF. This lossless format compresses 8-bit images to smaller file sizes than GIF. PNG supports greater color depths than GIF, so it supports 8-bit indexed color, 16-bit gray scale, and 24-bit true-color images. Even though PNG supports 24-bit color, its lossless compression routine does not compress as efficiently as JPG, so it is not the best choice for photographic images.

PNG supports transparency and interlacing, but not animation. (Interlacing is the gradual display of a graphic in a series of passes as the data arrives in the browser.) One useful feature of PNG is its built-in text capabilities for image indexing, allowing you to store a string of identifying text within the file itself.

SVG

The Scalable Vector Graphics (SVG) format is a language for describing two-dimensional graphics using XML. SVG files can contain shapes such as lines and curves, images, text, animation, and interactive events. SVG is compatible with common web technologies such as HTML, XML, JavaScript, and Cascading Style Sheets (CSS). Tools such as Adobe Illustrator let you create SVG graphics. For more information on SVG, visit the W3C's SVG page at *www.w3.org/Graphics/SVG*.

SVG graphics are scalable to different display resolutions and can be printed on high-resolution printers. An SVG graphic can be reused at different sizes throughout a web site without downloading multiple files to the user. SVG graphics can also be viewed at different sizes based on user needs, allowing magnification of an image to see fine detail or to increase legibility.

SVG is a vector graphics file format. Vector graphics represent images as geometrical formulas, as compared with the raster graphics format, which represents images pixel by pixel for the entire image. GIF, PNG, and JPG are raster formats. The vector graphics format allows SVG graphics to be scalable and cross-platform compatible.

> **Note** Although SVG is the most underused image file format, it is supported by all major desktop browsers and most mobile browsers. You can check SVG browser compatibility at http://caniuse.com/svg.

Using Interlacing and Progressive Display

Most web-capable graphics editors let you save images in an interlaced (progressive) format. You can choose this display option when creating GIF, PNG, and JPG files. GIF and PNG files use an interlacing format, while JPG files use a progressive format. Interlacing and progressive formats generally are the same thing—the gradual display of a graphic in a series of passes as the data arrives in the browser. Each additional pass of data creates a clearer view of the image until the complete image is displayed. Figure 8-4 shows three rendering passes to display a complete image.

Figure 8-4: Three passes complete this progressive JPG image
© Cengage Learning®

The only real advantage to displaying graphics in the interlaced or progressive method is that users immediately see at least a blurred view of the complete image, giving them something to look at while waiting for the entire graphic to download. The disadvantage of choosing this display method is that older browsers may not display the graphic properly, and more processing power is needed on the user's machine to render the image. The use of these methods has declined as increased connection speeds have become more widespread.

Where You Can Find Images

You can acquire images from a variety of sources, including from a graphics professional you hire to create and prepare your images. If your budget does not allow for funding this service, consider one of the following resources:

> **Stock photo collections**—Stock photo collections can cost anywhere from thousands of dollars for a few images to under $20 for hundreds of images at your local retail store or web site retailer. These collections contain royalty-free images that you can use for any web site. You can manipulate the graphics to add or delete text or images, change the color, or make any other modifications. Most stock photo collections include a built-in browsing program that lets you search for a particular image, and some also provide image-editing software.

> **Digital camera**—A digital camera lets you take your own photos and use them on the web. These cameras store photos in JPG format, so you do not have to convert them. Most also provide image-cataloging software, and some include basic image-editing software. The price of digital cameras continues to drop, while the quality of the images gets better and better.

> **Scanner**—Good scanners are available for under $100. You can scan your own photos or images and save them as GIF, JPG, or PNG files for use on your web site.

> **Public domain web sites**—Many web sites maintain online catalogs of images that are available for download. Some of these sites charge a small membership fee, so you can download as many images as you want. Other public domain web sites are completely free. Most U.S. government web site images are public domain and can be freely used. Wikipedia maintains a list of public domain stock photo web sites at *http://en.wikipedia.org/wiki/Public_domain_image_resources*.

> **Create your own**—If you need a basic image or if you have graphic design skills, you can download a shareware or freeware graphics tool and learn to use it. Keep your custom image simple, such as text on colored backgrounds, and use fundamental shapes and lines. Look at graphics on other web sites; many are simple but effective and may provide a useful model for your own images.

Note | *Do not borrow images from other web sites for use in your own site. Although your browser allows you to copy graphics, you should never use someone else's work unless it is from a public domain web site and is freely available for use.*

Choosing the Right Format

The following list summarizes the advantages and disadvantages of each graphic file format for the web.

> **GIF**—Once the most common format for all types of simple colored graphics and line art, GIFs have been overtaken by the PNG format described below.

> **JPG**—Use JPG for all 24-bit full-color photographic images. This format is designed expressly for photos and results in the smallest file size.

> **PNG**—This nonproprietary format is now used more commonly than GIF. PNG provides greater compression and color depth, and it offers a variety of transparency options. Because PNG does not compress your 24-bit images as well as JPG does, do not use it for photos.

> **SVG**—This format offers many advantages, but its lack of acceptance in the web development community means SVG is not a common image format.

Choosing a Graphics Tool

As a web designer, you may be in the enviable position of having a complete staff of graphic design professionals preparing graphics for your site. Most web designers, however, do not have this luxury. If you are working on web page designs, you will eventually use a graphics tool. Many of your graphics tasks are simple, such as resizing an image or converting an image from one file format to another. More complex tasks often include changing color depth or adding transparency to an image. Anyone can learn these tasks using a popular graphics software application.

When it comes to creating images, you may want to enlist professional help. Your web site will not benefit if you choose to create your own graphics and you are not up to the task.

Professional-quality graphics can greatly enhance the look of your web site. Take an honest look at your skills and remember that the best web sites usually are the result of collaboration.

You use graphics software to create or manipulate graphics. Most web designers use Adobe Photoshop, which is an expensive and full-featured product that takes time to master. Adobe Illustrator, a high-end drawing and painting tool, also is available. A lower-priced option and an established tool is Paint Shop Pro. This tool is reasonably priced and contains a full range of image-editing features. Like most other shareware, this tool can be downloaded and used for a trial period. You can also find excellent freeware tools such as Paint.net and Pixlr. In general, look for a tool that meets your needs and will not take a long time to learn. Table 8-2 shows a list of web sites for the graphics tools mentioned in the text.

GRAPHICS TOOL	URL
Adobe Photoshop and Illustrator	www.adobe.com
Adobe Fireworks	www.adobe.com
Corel Paint Shop Pro	www.corel.com
Paint.net	www.getpaint.net
Pixlr	www.pixlr.com

Table 8-2: Graphics Tools Web Sites
© 2015 Cengage Learning®

Using the Image Element

The <img> element represents an image in the web page. It must have a src attribute to reference an image file. The browser treats the image as it treats a character; normal image alignment is to the baseline of the text. Images that are within a line of text must have spaces on both sides or the text will touch the image.

The <img> element only needs the src attribute for the image to be displayed in the browsers, though using only the src attribute is not good coding practice. The <img> tag should always contain the additional attributes shown in the following code sample and described in Table 8-3.

```
<img src="logo.gif" width="258" height="130" alt="Company logo
graphic" title="Click the logo to view the company home page">
```

ATTRIBUTE	USE
alt	Displays an alternate string of text if an image cannot be displayed, and provides a description of the image for users with visual impairments
height	Specifies the height of the image in pixels
src	The only required attribute, src specifies the URL of the graphic file you want to display; as with any URL, the path must be relative to the HTML file
title	A string of text that provides information about the image; visual browsers display the contents of the title attribute as a ToolTip or ScreenTip (a pop-up window that appears when the user pauses the pointer over an object); an audio browser could speak the title information
width	Specifies the width of the image in pixels

Table 8-3: <img> Element Attributes
© 2015 Cengage Learning®

Specifying alt and title Attribute Text

The alt attribute provides a description of the image if it cannot be viewed by the user because of physical or technical limitations. Proper use of the alt attribute improves web accessibility by describing the function of each image in your web site. This information can be used by screen readers and other adaptive devices.

The title attribute contains information about the element, as you would see in a ScreenTip or pop-up help window. This is usually a description, such as identifying the target of a link, providing copyright or identifying information about an image, or other comments or notations. The following code shows an example of the title attribute used with an <img> element.

```
<img src="balloons_sm.jpg" width="200" height="267" alt="Hot Air
Balloon image" title="Colorful Balloon in a Blue Sky">
```

Figure 8-5 shows the pop-up text that appears as a result of using the title attribute.

Hot Air Ballooning

The first modern hot air balloon was designed and built in 1960 by Ed Yost. He made the first free flight of such an aircraft in Bruning, Nebraska on 22 October 1960. Initially equipped with a plastic envelope and kerosene fuel, Yost's designs rapidly moved onto using a modified propane powered "weed burner" to heat the air and lightweight nylon fabric for the envelope material.

Today, hot air balloons are used primarily for recreation. There are some 7,500 hot air balloons operating in the United States. Since piloting a balloon requires some effort (licensing and purchase of equipment), many people opt to purchase a balloon flight from a company offering balloon rides. Balloon rides are available in many locations around the world and are especially popular in tourist areas.[5] Balloon festivals are a great way to see hot air balloons close up, and are an enjoyable family outing. Colorful Balloon in a Blue Sky stivals usually include other activities like live entertainment, amusement rides, etc.[6] Hot air balloons in flight

Hot air balloons are able to fly to extremely high altitudes. On November 26 2005, Vijaypat Singhania set the world altitude record for highest hot air balloon flight, reaching 21,290 meters (69,852 feet). He took off from downtown Bombay, India and landed 240 km (150 miles) south in Panchale. The previous record of 19,811 meters (64,980 ft) had been set by Per Lindstrand on June 6, 1988 in Plano, Texas. However, like all registered aircraft, oxygen is needed for all crew and passengers for any flight that reaches and exceeds an altitude of 12,500 feet.

On January 15, 1991, a balloon carrying Per Lindstrand (born in Sweden, but resident in the UK), and Richard Branson of the UK flew from Japan to Northern Canada, completing 7,671.91 km. This record was shattered on March 21 1999

Figure 8-5: Using the title attribute
© 2015 Cengage Learning®

Specifying Image Width and Height

Every <img> element on your web site should contain width and height attributes. These attributes provide important information to the browser by specifying the amount of space to reserve for the image. This information dramatically affects the way your pages download, especially at slower connection speeds. If you have included the width and height, the browser reserves the space on the page without waiting for the image to download, and displays the rest of your text content. If the browser does not know the width and height values, it must download the image before displaying the rest of the page. At slower connection speeds, the user will be looking at a blank page while waiting for the image to download.

You should set the width and height to preserve the look of your layout, whether the images are displayed or not. In Figure 8-6, the width and height have been omitted. Notice that if the browser does not know the width and height, the text wrapping and appearance of the page change dramatically when the image is not displayed.

Hot Air Ballooning

Hot Air Balloon image The first modern hot air bal
Bruning, Nebraska on 22 Oc
moved onto using a modified propane powered "w

Today, hot air balloons are used primarily for recr
balloon requires some effort (licensing and purcha
rides. Balloon rides are available in many locations
to see hot air balloons close up, and are an enjoyab
amusement rides, etc.[6] Hot air balloons in flight

Hot air balloons are able to fly to extremely high a
air balloon flight, reaching 21,290 meters (69,852
Panchale. The previous record of 19,811 meters (6
registered aircraft, oxygen is needed for all crew a

On January 15, 1991, a balloon carrying Per Linds
Northern Canada, completing 7,671.91 km. This re
circumnavigated the globe and set records for dur

Figure 8-6: Browser unable to reserve image size
© 2015 Cengage Learning®

The following code shows the width and height attributes for the image. It indicates that the browser should reserve a 200 × 267-pixel space for the balloons_sm.jpg image and should display the alternate text "Hot Air Balloon image" if it cannot display the image.

```
<img src="balloons_sm.jpg" width="200" height="267" alt="Hot Air
Balloon image" title="Colorful Balloon in a Blue Sky" >
```

In Figure 8-7, the width and height have been specified and the image size is reserved by the browser, retaining the look of the page layout.

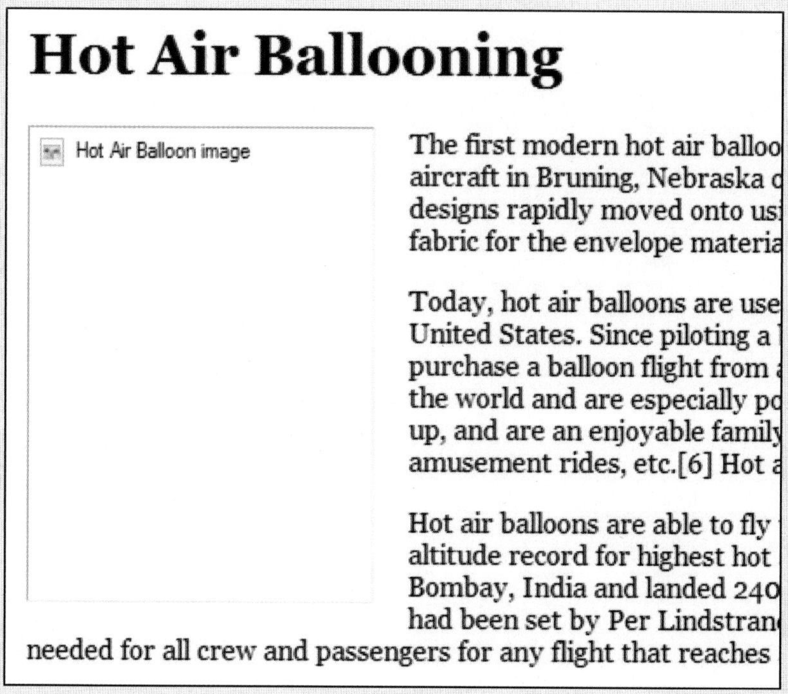

Hot Air Ballooning

Hot Air Balloon image

The first modern hot air balloo
aircraft in Bruning, Nebraska o
designs rapidly moved onto usi
fabric for the envelope materia

Today, hot air balloons are use
United States. Since piloting a
purchase a balloon flight from
the world and are especially po
up, and are an enjoyable family
amusement rides, etc.[6] Hot a

Hot air balloons are able to fly
altitude record for highest hot
Bombay, India and landed 240
had been set by Per Lindstran

needed for all crew and passengers for any flight that reaches

Figure 8-7: Image size reserved in the browser
© 2015 Cengage Learning®

You may notice that you can manipulate the width and height of the image itself using the width and height attributes in the <img> element. While it is tempting to use these attributes to change a graphic's size without using a graphics program, it is not a good idea. If the original graphic's area is too large and you reduce the size using the width and height attributes, you are not changing the file size of the image—only the area that the browser reserves for the graphic. The user is still downloading the original graphic file; no time is saved. Also, if you do not maintain the ratio of width to height, called the aspect ratio, you distort the image. Figure 8-8 shows an image in its actual size, the size after changing the width and height values in proportion to one another, and the distortion caused by incorrect width and height values.

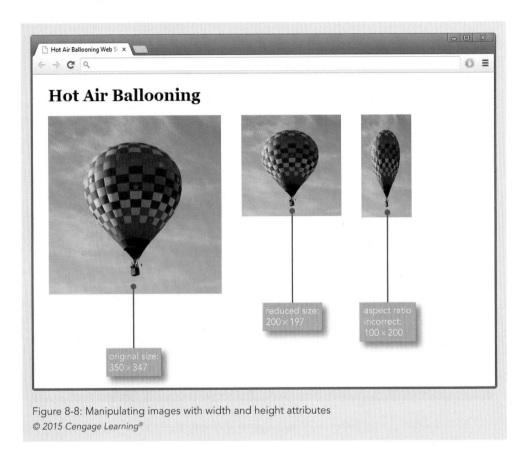

Figure 8-8: Manipulating images with width and height attributes
© 2015 Cengage Learning®

In the following code for the three images, the width and height attributes appear in bold, colored text:

```
<-- Original size -->
<img src="balloon-image.png" alt="Colorful Balloon in a Blue Sky"
title="Colorful Balloon in a Blue Sky" width="350" height="347">
<-- Reduced size -->
<img src="balloon-image.png" alt="Colorful Balloon in a Blue Sky"
title="Colorful Balloon in a Blue Sky" width="200" height="197">
```

```
<-- Incorrect Aspect Ratio -->
<img src="balloon-image.png" alt="Colorful Balloon in a Blue Sky"
title="Colorful Balloon in a Blue Sky" width="100" height="200">
```

However, the ability to manipulate image size using the width and height attributes comes in handy in certain circumstances. When creating a layout mock-up, you can test different image sizes by manipulating the width and height values.

Sizing Graphics for the Page

One way to keep file sizes small is to size graphics appropriately. Few experiences are more annoying than opening a web page you haven't visited before and waiting to download an overly large image. One of the easiest ways to make your graphics download quickly is to keep their dimensions small and appropriate to the size of the page. Figure 8-9 shows a variety of image sizes at 1024 × 768 screen resolution.

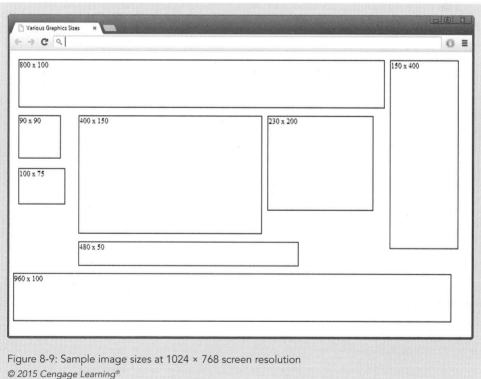

Figure 8-9: Sample image sizes at 1024 × 768 screen resolution
© 2015 Cengage Learning®

These sample sizes are guidelines to help you visualize your images as a part of your layout. It is also useful to think of image size in relation to the number of columns in your layout; size your graphics to occupy one, two, or more columns of the page.

> **Note**
> If you are building flexible pages that need to respond to the size of the device screen, you can use percentage values to specify image size. The image percentage width is always relative to the image's containing element, so if you create a column that is 25 percent of the page width, you can set the image to always be 75 percent of the width of that column. As the browser displays the column on different screen sizes, the proportional width of the column and the image will always be maintained. The browser will maintain the aspect ratio of the image and display it correctly based on the browser window size. You will read more about this in Chapter 12.

Using the Figure Element

The HTML5 <figure> element should not be confused with the <img> element. The <figure> element is a semantic element intended to represent content that is self-contained (like an image). You can include a caption with the <figure> element, but typically it is referenced as a single unit. For example, a figure can contain an image and a caption, or any other piece of content that stands alone from the main content, such as a code sample, graph, chart, or table. The <figure> element syntax looks like the following:

```
<figure>
<img src="balloons.png"
    alt="Colorful balloons in a blue sky">
<figcaption>Hot Air Balloon Festival</figcaption>
</figure>
```

The <figcaption> element is optional; if you use it, you will need to add CSS style properties to style the caption. The use of <figure> is optional as well, but it is valuable for correctly representing the document structure. Using it is a good step toward creating more semantic markup, which results in documents that are easier to search and index.

Using the Canvas Element

The <canvas> element is used to contain JavaScript animations and interactions. You can specify the width and size of the <canvas> element, but all content displayed in the canvas space on the web page is created with JavaScript. You can write your own basic JavaScript animations, but probably you will use an HTML5 animation application to create content.

These applications use SVG graphics, CSS, and HTML to create the type of content usually designed with Adobe Flash. Adobe is gradually withdrawing support for Flash because it is being supplanted by applications that run in the <canvas> element, such as Adobe's own Edge animation program, which is described as being able to create applications in HTML5, JavaScript, jQuery, and CSS3. At the time of this writing, <canvas> is supported by all modern browsers, but its use is not yet widespread.

Controlling Image Properties with CSS

In this section, you will use Cascading Style Sheet properties to control the following image characteristics:

> Removing the hypertext border

> Aligning text and images

> Floating images

> Adding white space around images

> **Note** | You will find all of the example files for this chapter at www.joelsklar.com/pwd6. You can use these files for practice, testing, and as inspiration for your project web sites.

Removing the Hypertext Border from an Image

When you create a hypertext image, the browser's default behavior is to display the hypertext border around the image, as shown in Figure 8-10. This border appears blue before you click the image and purple afterward. In a well-designed site, this border is unnecessary because users often use their mouse to point to each image and see whether the hypertext pointer appears. Another reason to abandon the display of hypertext borders is that their color may not complement your graphic.

To remove the hypertext border, add a style attribute with the border property set to *none*. Here is the code for the second balloon in Figure 8-10, which has the hypertext border turned off:

```
<img src="balloon.jpg" width="100" height="100" alt="balloon"
style="border: none">
```

You can read more about the border property in Chapter 6.

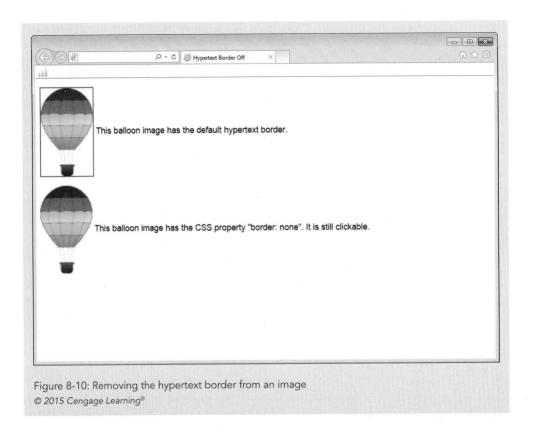

Figure 8-10: Removing the hypertext border from an image
© 2015 Cengage Learning®

Aligning Text and Images

You can align text along an image border using the vertical-align property, which is described in Chapter 5. The default alignment of the text and image is bottom-aligned, which means the bottom of the text aligns with the bottom edge of the image. You can change the alignment by using either the top or middle values. Figure 8-11 shows all three alignment values.

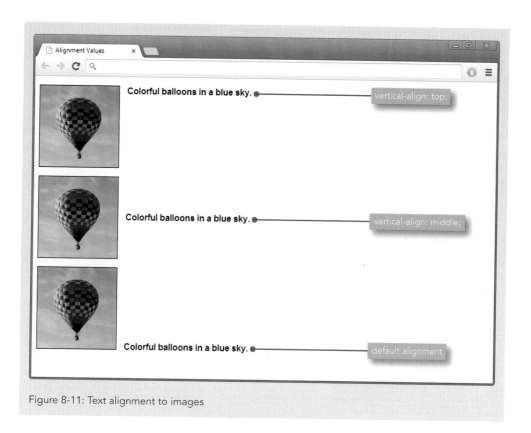

Figure 8-11: Text alignment to images

Floating Images

float property description	
Value:	left | right | none
Initial:	none
Applies to:	all elements except positioned elements
Inherited:	no
Percentages:	N/A

The float property can be used to float an image to the left or right of text. The following style rules create two classes of <img> elements; one floats to the left of text and the other floats to the right:

```
img.left {float: left;}
img.right {float: right;}
```

You can apply these rules to an image using the class attribute within the <img> element, as shown in the following code fragment:

```
<img src="sample.png" class="left">
```

Figure 8-12 shows two floating images within a page.

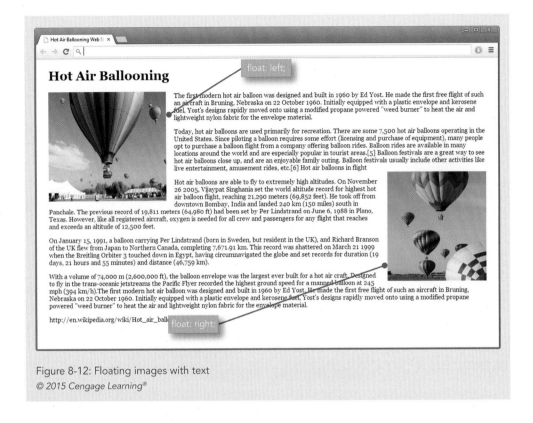

Figure 8-12: Floating images with text
© 2015 Cengage Learning®

Adding White Space Around Images

Add white space around your images to reduce clutter and improve readability. As shown in Figure 8-13, the default spacing places the text very close to the image.

Hot Air Ballooning

The first modern hot air balloon was designed and built in 1960 by Ed Yost. He made in Bruning, Nebraska on 22 October 1960. Initially equipped with a plastic envelope rapidly moved onto using a modified propane powered "weed burner" to heat the air envelope material.

Today, hot air balloons are used primarily for recreation. Th hot States. Since piloting a balloon requires some effort (licensing and purchase of equip balloon flight from a company offering balloon rides. Balloon rides are available in ma especially popular in tourist areas.[5] Balloon festivals are a great way to see hot air family outing. Balloon festivals usually include other activities like live entertainmen balloons in flight.

Hot air balloons are able to fly to extremely high altitudes. On November 26 2005, altitude record for highest hot air balloon flight, reaching 21,290 meters (69,852 feet India and landed 240 km (150 miles) south in Panchale. The previous record of 19,8

Per Lindstrand on June 6, 1988 in Plano, Texas. However, like all registered aircraft, oxygen is needed for all crew and passengers for altitude of 12,500 feet.

default image spacing

Hot Air Ballooning

Today, hot air balloons are used primarily for recreation. There are some 7,500 hot air balloons Since piloting a balloon requires some effort (licensing and purchase of equipment), many people from a company offering balloon rides. Balloon rides are available in many locations around the w in tourist areas.[5] Balloon festivals are a great way to see ho an er festivals usually include other activities like live entertainmer

different image with top and right margin added

Hot air balloons in flightHot air balloons are able to fly to extr mber set the world altitude record for highest hot air balloon flight, 52 fee Bombay, India and landed 240 km (150 miles) south in Panchale. The previous record of 19,811 set by Per Lindstrand on June 6, 1988 in Plano, Texas. However, like all registered aircraft, oxy passengers for any flight that reaches and exceeds an altitude of 12,500 feet.

On January 15, 1991, a balloon carrying Per Lindstrand (born in Sweden, but resident in the UK UK flew from Japan to Northern Canada, completing 7,671.91 km. This record was shattered on Breitling Orbiter 3 touched down in Egypt, having circumnavigated the globe and set records for and 55 minutes) and distance (46,759 km).

With a volume of 74,000 m³ (2,600,000 ft³), the balloon envelope was the largest ever built for in the trans-oceanic jetstreams the Pacific Flyer recorded the highest ground speed for a manned km/h).

http://en.wikipedia.org/wiki/Hot_air_ballooning

Figure 8-13: Image spacing
© 2015 Cengage Learning®

Use the CSS margin property to increase the white space around an image. You can read more about the margin property in Chapter 6. The margin property lets you add margins on all four sides of an image or to individual sides. The following code shows an image with a 20-pixel margin on the top and right sides, floating to the left of text:

```
img.left {
    float: left;
    margin-top: 20px;
    margin-right: 10px;
}
```

You also can add white space into the graphic itself using graphic-editing software.

Creating Web Site Color Schemes

The color scheme used on a web site can be the result of many factors, including the company's branding colors, designer preferences, and usability studies. Colors convey important meanings to the user and set the tone for a web site. Think of the types of colors a designer might choose for a site that promotes ecology and conservation versus those for a site that celebrates spicy foods. The color choices that come to mind would certainly be different—possibly cool greens and blues for the ecology site, and hot yellows and reds for the spicy foods site. Colors affect the mood and tone of your web site. Blues and greens are calming, and are associated with the ocean and forest. Reds and yellows are exciting, and are associated with fire and heat. In Figure 8-14, the Chile Pepper Institute web site (*www.chilepepperinstitute.org*) uses shades of red to match the appearance and heat of chile peppers. In contrast, the Manna Food Bank site (*http://mannafoodbank.org*) uses a soothing shade of green to promote philanthropy. The National Oceanic and Atmospheric Administration site (*noaa.gov*) uses shades of blue to reflect its association with the oceans and sky, while the DogsTrust site (*www.dogstrust.org.uk*) uses yellow to create a playful, lively impression. Keep in mind that colors and combinations of colors can symbolize many different cultural and political meanings for various users around the world.

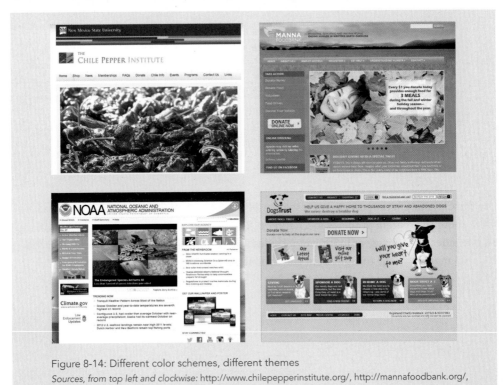

Figure 8-14: Different color schemes, different themes
Sources, from top left and clockwise: http://www.chilepepperinstitute.org/, http://mannafoodbank.org/, www.dogstrust.org.uk/, *and* noaa.gov

The scheme of colors you choose should work together to create a distinctive look for your site without detracting from your content's legibility. Choosing colors for your site can be difficult, so having a basic understanding of color theory helps you make choices that suit your site's needs.

The study of color theory began with Isaac Newton's series of experiments with prisms published in 1672. Newton found that with a prism, he could separate white light into its component colors: red, orange, yellow, green, blue, and violet. Newton created a wheel that arranged these colors logically, as shown in Figure 8-15.

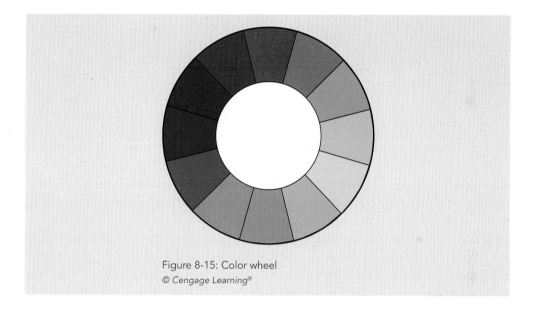

Figure 8-15: Color wheel
© Cengage Learning®

In Newton's color wheel, the primary colors—red, yellow, and blue—are arranged opposite their complementary colors; for example, red is opposite green. The primary colors are basic colors of light that cannot be created by mixing other colors. The secondary colors are combinations of primary colors. White, black, and gray are neutral and not included in the wheel. For example, Figure 8-16 shows how the color wheel arranges various relationships between colors.

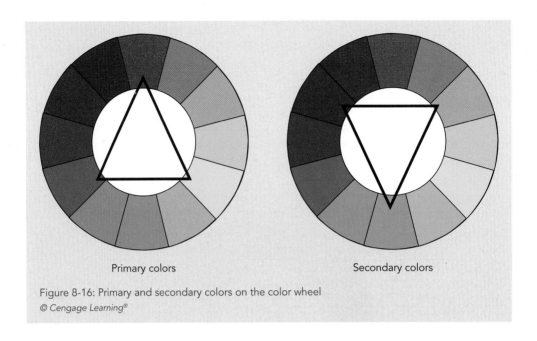

Primary colors   Secondary colors

Figure 8-16: Primary and secondary colors on the color wheel
© Cengage Learning®

Warm and Cool Colors

The color wheel is often divided into warm and cool colors. The warm colors include those that are normally seen in daylight or sunsets, including red through yellow, brown, and tan. The cool colors are associated with water, clouds, and overcast days, and include blue through green and violet. Although these perceptions are culturally dependent, they provide a broad characterization of color usage. The warm colors are generally seen as vivid and energetic, while cool colors are calming and relaxing.

Tints and Shades

In color theory, a pure color is called a hue, a color without a tint or shade. If a color is made lighter by adding white, the result is called a tint. If black is added, the darker version is called a shade. The result of adding these neutral colors to a pure color is shown in Figure 8-17.

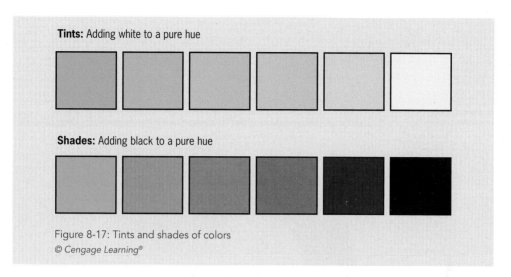

Tints: Adding white to a pure hue

Shades: Adding black to a pure hue

Figure 8-17: Tints and shades of colors
© Cengage Learning®

Types of Color Schemes

When using color for web sites, the color wheel can guide your color choices.

Complementary color schemes use the complementary colors that are always arranged opposite of each other on the color wheel. Complementary colors are vivid opposites and do not always go well together, despite their name. Complementary colors are a poor choice for text and backgrounds (for example, yellow text on a violet background) because of their high contrast. Using a complementary color scheme brings high contrast and excitement to your content. See Figure 8-18.

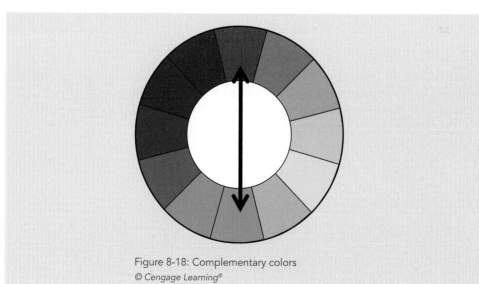

Figure 8-18: Complementary colors
© Cengage Learning®

Analogous color schemes use the analogous colors that are located next to each other on the color wheel, as shown in Figure 8-19. Analogous colors match well and create designs that are harmonious and pleasing to the eye. One color is usually dominant while the other colors are used to enhance the color scheme. Analogous schemes sometimes need the addition of a more contrasting color to add interest or highlight sections of a layout.

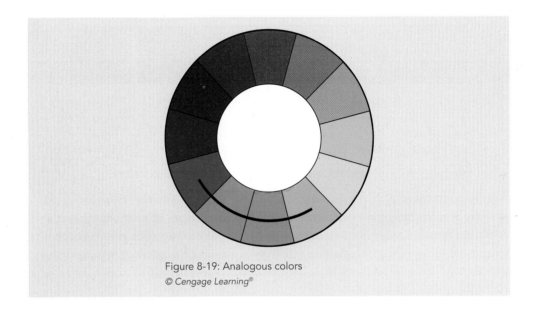

Figure 8-19: Analogous colors
© *Cengage Learning*®

Monochromatic color schemes use tints and shades of a single hue, as shown in Figure 8-20. This scheme looks unified and clean. Monochromatic colors go well together and are easy on the eyes, especially with cool colors. This scheme is a common choice for web designers who want to create a dignified, understated look. The primary color can be integrated with the neutral colors black, white, and gray. Like the analogous scheme, it can be difficult to highlight the most important elements because of a lack of color contrast.

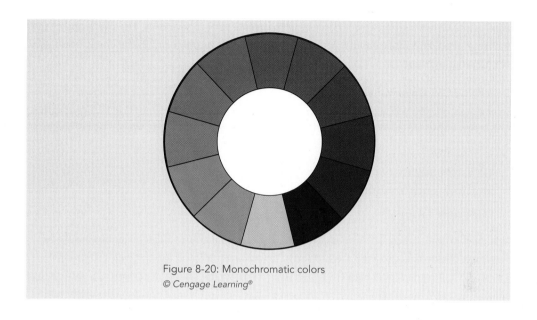

Figure 8-20: Monochromatic colors
© Cengage Learning®

Note The Color Wizard (www.colorsontheweb.com/colorwizard.asp) and the color scheme designer (http://colorschemedesigner.com/) are easy-to-use color matching tools that can help you choose colors for your web site designs.

Using Color Wisely

Because of the variable nature of color on the web, be sure to test the colors you choose, and use restraint when adding color to your design. Colors do not look the same on different types of devices. Even the latest high-definition tablet and phone displays use different ranges of colors, called color gamuts, that are a subset of all the available colors viewable by the human eye. This means that your design colors will always vary slightly based on the user's device.

When used properly, color can enhance the presentation of your information, providing structural and navigation cues to your user. Conversely, poor use of color distracts from your content and can annoy your users. Dark backgrounds, clashing colors, and unreadable links are just a few examples of unrestrained use of the HTML color attributes that are common on the web. Just because CSS allows you to easily apply color to any element does not mean that you should apply color haphazardly. Remember that many of your users might have accessibility issues that prevent them from seeing color the way you do. According to the Web Content Accessibility Guidelines, which are described in Chapter 2, color should not be used as the only visual means of conveying information or interaction. The user's ability to navigate, read, and interact with your content should always determine the choices and use of color in a web site.

Specifying CSS Color Values

In this section, you will learn about the different ways to express color using CSS properties. CSS lets you specify color values in one of four ways:

> Color names

> RGB color values

> Hexadecimal color values

> HSL color values

Which color value method should you use? Hexadecimal color values probably should be your first choice because they are supported by all browsers and are the web's color language. Both hexadecimal and RGB values are more specific and let you express a wider range of color than the color names. Regardless of which method you choose, make sure to use that method consistently throughout your entire web site.

Using Color Names

The color name values let you quickly state color using common names. You can use lists of 16 basic color names and of extended color names to select color in your CSS style rules. The 16 basic colors are listed in Table 8-4. You can view the list of extended colors at *http://en.wikipedia.org/wiki/X11_color_names*.

COLOR NAME	HEX	COLOR NAME	HEX
Aqua	00FFFF	Navy	000080
Black	000000	Olive	808000
Blue	0000FF	Purple	800080
Fuchsia	FF00FF	Red	FF0000
Gray	808080	Silver	C0C0C0
Green	008000	Teal	008080
Lime	00FF00	White	FFFFFF
Maroon	800000	Yellow	FFFF00

Table 8-4: Color Names Recognized by Most Browsers
© 2015 Cengage Learning®

Although the color names are easy to use and remember, they allow only a small range of color expression. To use a wider variety of available color, you must use a more specific value, such as RGB or hexadecimal. Use any of these 16 names in your CSS style rules, as shown in the following code:

```
p {color: aqua;}
```

Using RGB Colors

The RGB color model is used to specify numeric values that express the blending of the red, green, and blue color channels. When you specify RGB values, you are mixing the three basic colors to create a fourth color. Each of the three color channels can be specified in a range from 0 to 100%, with 0 representing the absence of the color, and 100% representing the full brilliance of the color. If all three values are set to 0, the resulting color is black, which is the absence of all color. If all three color values are set to 100%, the resulting color is white, which is the inclusion of all colors.

The syntax for specifying RGB is the keyword *rgb* followed by three numerical values in parentheses—the first for red, the second for green, and the third for blue. The following rule states a percentage RGB value:

```
p {color: rgb(0%, 100%, 100%);}
```

RGB color values can be specified as an integer value as well. The integer scale ranges from 0 to 255, with 255 equal to 100%. The following rules specify the same color:

```
p {color: rgb(0%, 100%, 100%);} /* percentages */
p {color: rgb(0, 255, 255);} /* integers */
```

Using Hexadecimal Colors

HTML uses hexadecimal numbers to express RGB color values, and you can use them in CSS as well. Hexadecimal numbers are a base-16 numbering system, so the numbers run from 0 through 9, and then A through F. When compared to standard base-10 numbers, hexadecimal values look strange because they include letters in the numbering scheme. Hexadecimal color values are six-digit numbers; the first two define the red value, the second two define the green, and the third two define the blue. The hexadecimal scale ranges from 00 to FF, with FF equal to 100%. Hexadecimal values are always preceded by a pound sign (#). The following rules specify the same color:

```
p {color: #00ffff;} /* hexadecimal */
p {color: rgb(0%, 100%, 100%);} /* percentages */
p {color: rgb(0, 255, 255);} /* integers */
```

Using HSL colors

This group of colors is specified by hue, saturation, and lightness (HSL). The hue value is a color that represents an angle on the color circle, which corresponds to a numerical value from 0 to 360. The value 0 is red, 120 is green, and 240 is blue.

Saturation and lightness are represented as percentages. 100% is full saturation, and 0% is a shade of gray. 0% lightness is black, 100% lightness is white, and 50% lightness is normal. HSL is considered a more intuitive color numbering system because you start by picking the hue you want and then adjust the saturation and lightness as necessary. Here is an example of HSL color values in CSS:

```
body {background-color: hsl(120, 100%, 50%);}
```

This represents color #120, set to 100% saturation and 50% lightness.

Understanding Element Layers

The color and background properties you will learn about in this chapter let you control three different layers of any element. You can imagine these layers as three individual pieces of tracing paper laid over each other to complete the finished web page. Each layer is transparent until you add a color or an image. These are the three layers listed in order from back to front:

- **Background color layer**—The back or bottom layer, specified by the background-color property
- **Background image layer**—The middle layer, specified by the background-image property; this layer can contain multiple images
- **Content layer**—The top layer; this is the color of the text content, specified by the color property

Figure 8-21 shows the three layers and their order from front to back. The background color layer (colored sky blue) lies behind the other layers. The background image layer displays the balloon image, which overlays the background color. The top layer contains the content. Notice that the content layer overlays both the background image and background color layers.

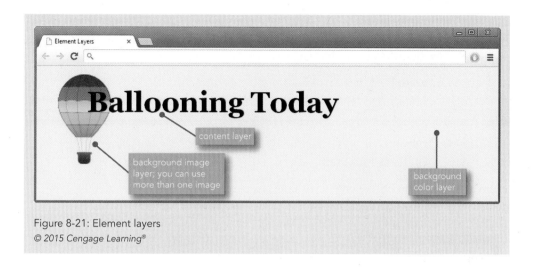

Figure 8-21: Element layers
© 2015 Cengage Learning®

Controlling Color Properties with CSS

In this section you will use Cascading Style Sheet properties to control the following color characteristics:

> Specifying color values

> Specifying opacity

> Setting default text color

> Changing link colors

> Specifying background color

> Setting the page background color

> Creating a text reverse

Specifying Color Values

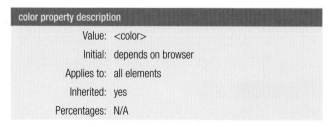

color property description	
Value:	<color>
Initial:	depends on browser
Applies to:	all elements
Inherited:	yes
Percentages:	N/A

The color property lets you specify the foreground color of any element on a web page. This property sets the color for both the text and the border of the element unless you have specifically stated a border color with one of the border properties (see Chapter 6).

The value for the color property is a valid color keyword or numerical representation, either hexadecimal or RGB (as described earlier in the "Using RGB Colors" section). The following style rules show the different methods of specifying the same color:

```
p {color: blue;} /* color name */
p {color: #0000ff;} /* hexadecimal value */
p {color: rgb(0,0,255);} /* RGB numbers */
p {color: rgb(0%,0%,100%);} /* RGB percentages */
p {color: hsl(240,100%,100%);} /* HSL percentages */
```

Figure 8-22 shows an <h1> element with the color set to red (hexadecimal #f90000). By default, the element's border is the same color as the element content.

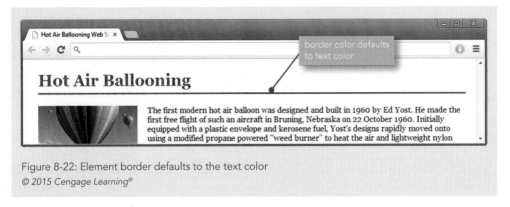

Figure 8-22: Element border defaults to the text color
© 2015 Cengage Learning®

Here is the style rule for the heading. Notice that the border color is not specified, so the element's border is the same color as the element text.

```
h1 {
    color: #f90000;
    border-bottom: 3px solid;
    padding-bottom: 6px;
}
```

Specifying Opacity

opacity property description	
Value:	<alphavalue>	inherit
Initial:	1
Applies to:	all elements
Inherited:	no
Percentages:	N/A

The opacity property lets you set the transparency of a text or image element. The value is a percentage expressed as a decimal, so 75 percent opacity is stated as .75 in the following style rule:

```
img {opacity: .75;}
```

Figure 8-23 shows samples of both text and images at different opacity values. You can choose any percentage from 0 to 100 to set the opacity of an element.

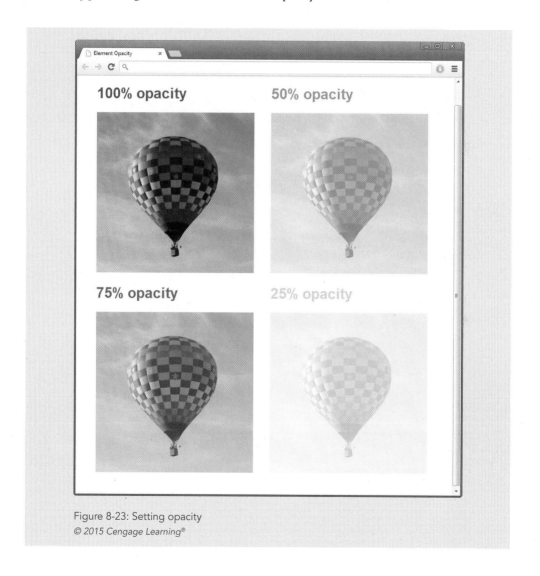

Figure 8-23: Setting opacity
© 2015 Cengage Learning®

Setting the Default Text Color

Color is inherited from parent to child elements. If you set the color for <body>, all elements on the page inherit their color from the <body> element, effectively setting the default text color for the entire web page. The following rule sets the color for the <body> element:

```
body {
    color: #006633;}
```

Changing Link Colors

You can change the colors of hypertext links by using the link pseudo-classes:

> **link**—The unvisited link color; the default is blue.

> **active**—The active link color; this color is displayed when the user points to a link and holds down the mouse button. The default is red.

> **visited**—The visited link color; the default is purple.

The following code shows the link pseudo-classes in use:

```
a:link {color: #cc0033;} /* new links are red */

a:active {color: #000000;} /* active links are black */

a:visited {color: #cccccc;} /* visited links are green */
```

Figure 8-24 shows a text-based navigation bar where the links have been colored red to match the design of the heading.

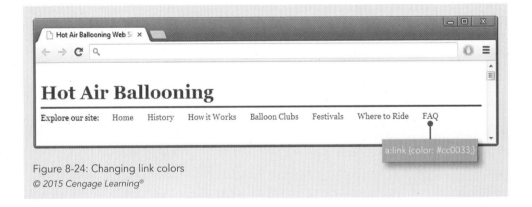

Figure 8-24: Changing link colors
© 2015 Cengage Learning®

Note

Remember to place your link pseudo-class in the following order:

1. Link

2. Visited

3. Hover

4. Active

Refer to Chapter 4 for more information on link pseudo-classes.

The familiar blue for new links and purple for visited links are among the most recognizable navigation cues for users visiting your site. Keep in mind that some users might have sight disabilities, such as color blindness, that could prevent them from seeing your web pages in the way you intend. However, many sites do change their links to match their design color scheme. Changing link colors is acceptable as long as you maintain color consistency and preserve the contrast between the new and visited link colors to provide a recognizable difference to the user.

Specifying Background Color

The background-color property lets you set the background color of any element on a web page. The background color includes any padding area (explained in Chapter 6) that you have defined for the element. Figure 8-25 shows an <h1> element with background color, border, and padding. The style rule looks like this:

```
h1 {
    color: #f90000;
    background-color: #fec893;
    border-bottom: 3px solid #191970;
    padding-top: 20px;
    padding-bottom: 6px;
    padding-left: 20px;
}
```

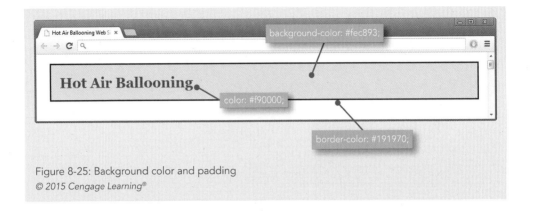

Figure 8-25: Background color and padding
© 2015 Cengage Learning®

The background-color property can be applied to both block-level and inline elements. To apply a background image color to inline text, use the <span> element to select the text. The following style rule selects a span element to apply a background color with 4 pixels of padding:

```
span.bgeffects {
    background-color: #add8e6;
    padding: 4px;
    border: 3px solid #191970;
}
```

This span element with class="bgeffects" selects the words "Hot Air" in the heading:

```
<span class="bgeffects">Hot Air</span> Ballooning
```

The result is shown in Figure 8-26.

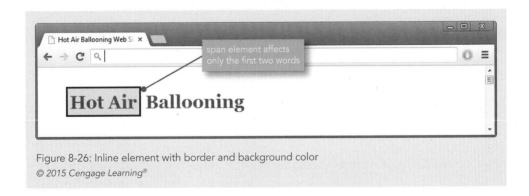

Figure 8-26: Inline element with border and background color
© 2015 Cengage Learning®

Setting the Page Background Color

To set the page background color, use *body* as the selector. This sets the background color for the content area of the web page. By default, the background color of any element is transparent. Therefore, all elements show the page background color unless the background-color property is specifically stated. The following rule sets a background color for the <body> element, as shown in Figure 8-27.

```
body {background-color: #add8e6;}
```

Notice in Figure 8-27 that the navigation links at the top of the page have a white background because the element that contains the navigation links has a background color set to white.

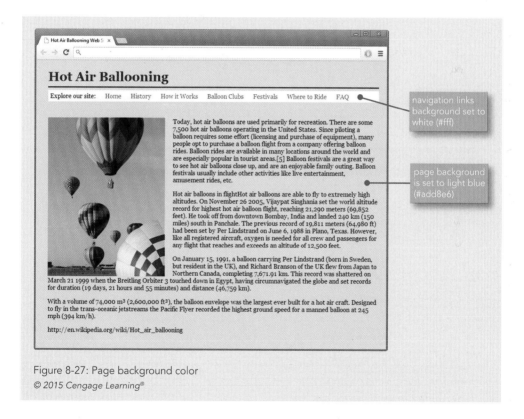

Figure 8-27: Page background color
© 2015 Cengage Learning®

It is always a good practice to include a page background color because some users might have a default background color that is different from the color you chose in your design. Even if you plan on a white page background, you can never be sure that all users have their default set to white, so include the background-color property rather than relying on the user's settings.

Creating a Text Reverse

A reverse is a common heading effect in which the normally white background color is reversed with the text color, which is usually black. On the web you can use this effect in your choice of color. Reverses are usually reserved for headings rather than the regular body text. You can easily create a reverse with a style rule. The following rule sets the background color of the <h1> element to blue and the text color to white:

```
h1 {
    background-color: #191970;
    padding: 10px;
    color: #fff;
}
```

The element padding is set to 10 pixels to increase the background color area. Figure 8-28 shows the result of the style rule.

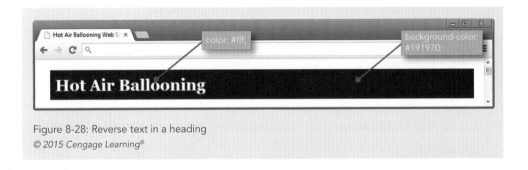

Figure 8-28: Reverse text in a heading
© 2015 Cengage Learning®

Controlling Background Images with CSS

In this section, you will use Cascading Style Sheet properties to control the following background characteristics:

> Specifying a background image

> Creating a page background

> Specifying background repeat

> Creating a vertical and horizontal repeat

> Creating a nonrepeating background image

> Specifying background position

> Positioning repeating background images

> Using multiple images in the background

The CSS background image properties let you use background images for a whole web page or within individual elements. Using a background image lets you easily insert text over an image, create background textures on a page, or gracefully adapt to different screen resolutions. You can also build interesting backgrounds for navigation or other sections of your pages. Using the background image layer, as described earlier in this chapter in the "Understanding Element Layers" section, you can place an image between the color layer and content layer. The NOAA web site uses this technique with a full-page background image, as shown in Figure 8-29.

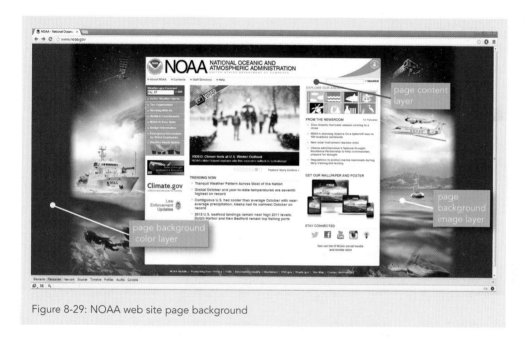

Figure 8-29: NOAA web site page background

In this figure, the screen resolution is 1920 x 1040. At lower resolutions or screen sizes, more or less of the background color and background image is visible in the browser window. Remember that when you place images in the background layer, you are using them only for presentation; the images are not considered part of the page content, as they would be if you used the <img> tag to display them.

Specifying a Background Image

background-image property description	
Value:	<url>, <url>
Initial:	none
Applies to:	all elements
Inherited:	no
Percentages:	N/A

The background-image property lets you specify which image to display. Other CSS background properties control how the image is displayed. The default behavior for the CSS background-image property is to repeatedly tile the image across the background of a web page in both horizontal and vertical directions. Figure 8-30 shows a document with an image tiled across the background.

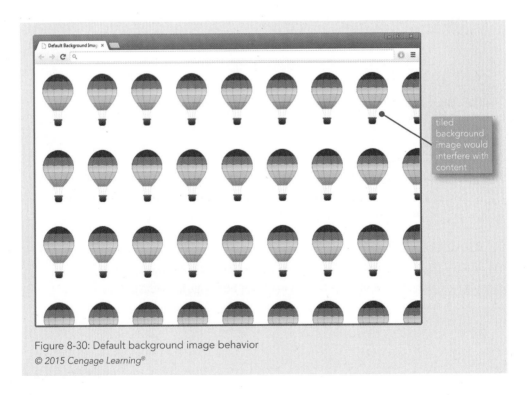

tiled background image would interfere with content

Figure 8-30: Default background image behavior
© 2015 Cengage Learning®

In Figure 8-30, the background would obviously detract from the legibility of any web page text. When choosing page or element backgrounds, keep the legibility of your text in mind. Avoid overly busy and distracting backgrounds that make your content difficult to read.

Specifying the Background Image URL

To specify a page background image, use the <body> element as the selector, because <body> is the parent element of the content area. To use an image in the background, you must specify the relative location of the image file in the style rule. CSS has a special notation for specifying a URL, as shown in Figure 8-31.

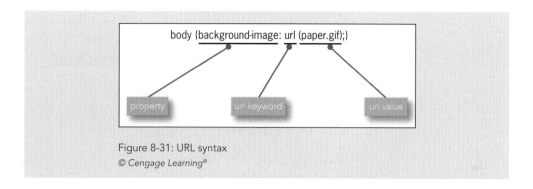

Figure 8-31: URL syntax
© Cengage Learning®

> **Note** If you are using external style sheets, the URL of the background image is relative to the location of the style sheet, not the HTML file to which the style sheet is applied.

You can specify multiple URLs to have more than one background image in an element, each on its own layer within the background layer. The first image on the list is in the front or the foreground, closest to the user, with successive values in order behind. The following style rule shows an example of multiple background images:

```
body {background-image: url (balloon.jpg), url(clouds.jpg);}
```

In this example, the image balloon.jpg would appear in front of the image clouds.jpg. Any image you use in front of another image should have the correct transparency, as described earlier in the chapter, to blend seamlessly with the background.

Creating a Page Background

To tile an image across the entire background of the web page, use body as the selector, as shown in the following rule. This style rule was used to create the background in Figure 8-32.

```
body {background-image: url(clouds.jpg);}
```

In this example, a seamless background graphic tiles repeatedly across the page background, and behind the wrapper <div> element that contains the page content. This technique lets you frame your content on the left and right margins with a background color that integrates with your design. This also fills the browser window regardless of the user's resolution, so your pages are always framed by an active part of the design, rather than passive screen space.

Figure 8-32: Repeating page background
© 2015 Cengage Learning®

Figure 8-33 shows the seamless graphic that was used to create the page background in Figure 8-32.

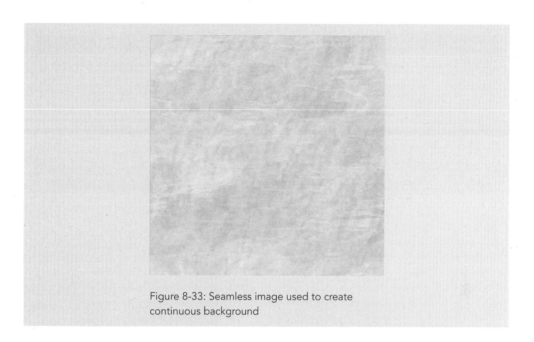

Figure 8-33: Seamless image used to create continuous background

Specifying Background Repeat

background-repeat property description	
Value:	repeat | repeat-x | repeat-y | no-repeat | space | round | inherit
Initial:	repeat
Applies to:	all elements
Inherited:	no
Percentages:	N/A

The background-repeat property lets you control the tiling of background images across the document or element background.

A background image must be specified for this property to work, so you always use the background-image property with the background-repeat property. Table 8-5 lists the background-repeat values.

VALUE	BACKGROUND IMAGE BEHAVIOR
repeat	The image is repeated across the entire background of the element; this is the default behavior
repeat-x	The image is repeated across the horizontal (x) axis of the document only
repeat-y	The image is repeated across the vertical (y) axis of the document only
no-repeat	The image is not repeated; only one instance of the image is shown in the background
space	The image is repeated as often as it will fit within the background positioning area without being clipped, and then the images are spaced out to fill the area.
round	The image is repeated as often as it will fit within the background positioning area; if it doesn't fit a whole number of times, it is rescaled until it does

Table 8-5: Background-Repeat Property Values
© 2015 Cengage Learning®

Note

The space and round values in Table 8-5 let you control the way images repeat in the background. Using space lets the browser fit enough repeating images so that the image is not "clipped," or partially cut off at the edge of the browser window. Browser support for these two values is not consistent, so test to make sure your background images appear correctly.

Creating a Vertical Repeat

The repeat-y value of the background-repeat property lets you create a vertical repeating background graphic. Figure 8-34 shows an example of this effect. The background graphic shown in Figure 8-34 is a 200-pixel wide by 50-pixel high JPG file.

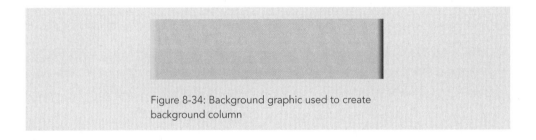

Figure 8-34: Background graphic used to create background column

This property lets you easily create columns with image or color backgrounds because the graphic is repeated vertically. You can then align content or division elements over the background image columns, as shown in Figure 8-35.

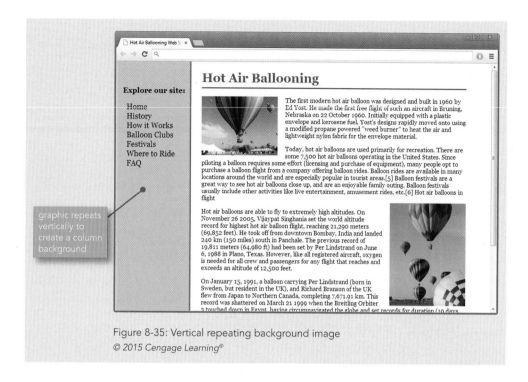

Figure 8-35: Vertical repeating background image
© 2015 Cengage Learning®

The web page in this figure has a two-column layout, as you saw in Chapter 7. The navigation content is contained in a division that is the same width as the background graphic behind it. The background graphic is repeated only on the y-axis to create a vertical column. The style rule for the background uses body as the selector with background-repeat set to repeat-y:

```
body {
    background-image: url(column.jpg);
    background-repeat: repeat-y;
}
```

Creating a Horizontal Repeat

The repeat-x value of the background-repeat property lets you create a horizontal repeating background graphic. Figure 8-36 shows an example of this effect. The background graphic shown in this figure is a 50-pixel wide by 110-pixel high graphic.

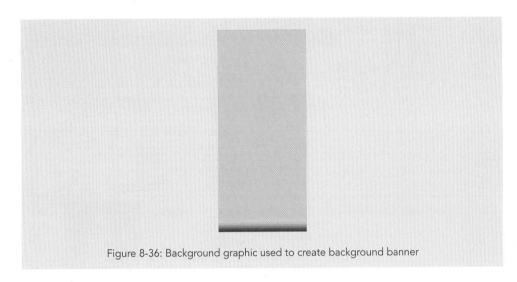

Figure 8-36: Background graphic used to create background banner

This property lets you easily create a background banner with a graphic that is repeated horizontally, as shown in Figure 8-37.

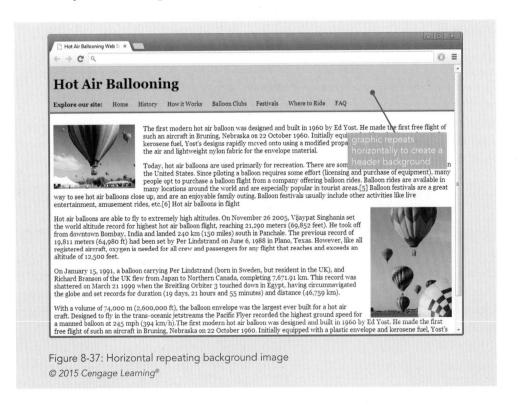

Figure 8-37: Horizontal repeating background image

© 2015 Cengage Learning®

The style rule for the background uses body as the selector with background-repeat set to repeat-x:

```
body {
    background-image: url(header.jpg);
    background-repeat: repeat-x;
}
```

Creating a Nonrepeating Background Image

The no-repeat value of the background-repeat property lets you create a single instance of an image in the background. This is a great way to add images to your site that appear consistently as part of your layout or branding.

The following style rule shows the use of the no-repeat value:

```
body {
    background-image: url(balloon_sm.jpg);
    background-repeat: no-repeat;
}
```

The background position property is used to position the image within the column. Figure 8-38 shows a single balloon image centered at the bottom of a division element.

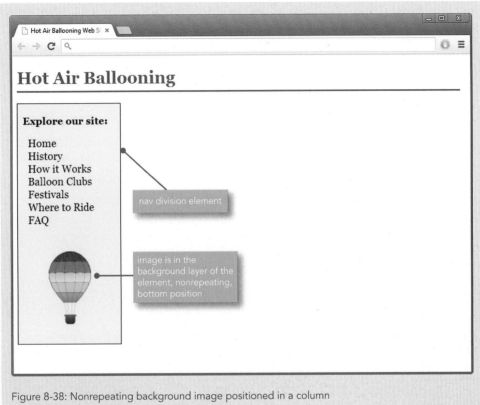

Figure 8-38: Nonrepeating background image positioned in a column
© 2015 Cengage Learning®

Specifying Background Position

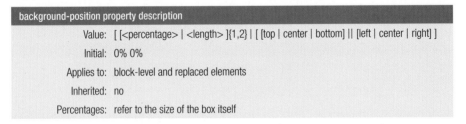

background-position property description	
Value:	[[<percentage> | <length>]{1,2} | [[top | center | bottom] || [left | center | right]]
Initial:	0% 0%
Applies to:	block-level and replaced elements
Inherited:	no
Percentages:	refer to the size of the box itself

The background-position property lets you use three types of values: percentage, length, or keywords. Table 8-6 lists the values and their meanings. Figure 8-39 shows the keyword positions in the element box and their equivalent percentage values.

You can use the keywords in Table 8-6 alone (*left*) or in combination (*left top*) to position the background image. Figure 8-39 shows the nine keyword positions and their percentage equivalents. The keywords can be used interchangeably, so the values *left top* and *top left* are the same.

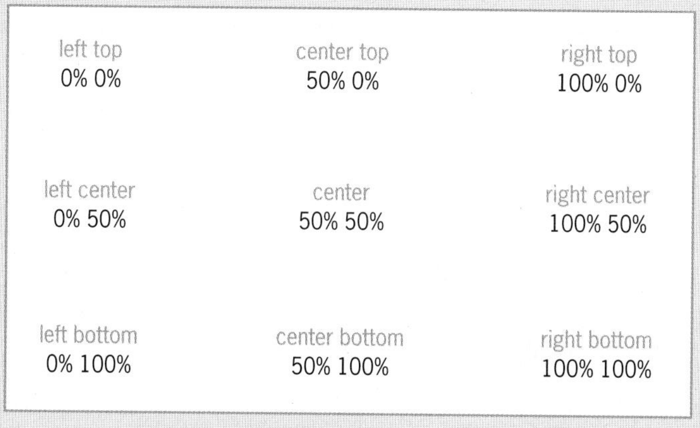

left top	center top	right top
0% 0%	50% 0%	100% 0%
left center	center	right center
0% 50%	50% 50%	100% 50%
left bottom	center bottom	right bottom
0% 100%	50% 100%	100% 100%

Figure 8-39: Keyword and percentage background positions
© Cengage Learning®

VALUE	BACKGROUND IMAGE BEHAVIOR
percentage	The percentage values are based on the starting point of the upper-left corner of the containing element's box. The first percentage value is horizontal; the second is vertical. For example, the value *45% 30%* places the background image 45% from the left edge and 30% from the top edge of the containing box.
length	Length values work in much the same way as percentages, starting from the upper-left corner of the element's containing box. The first length value is horizontal; the second is vertical. For example, the value *100px 200px* places the background image 100 pixels from the left edge and 200 pixels from the top edge of the containing box.
keywords	The keywords are: ⟩ Left ⟩ Right ⟩ Center ⟩ Top ⟩ Bottom

Table 8-6: Background-position Property Values
© 2015 Cengage Learning®

Positioning Repeating Background Images

You can also position images that repeat on either the horizontal or vertical axis of the web page. The following style rule positions the vertical repeating background image along the right side of the element:

```
#right {
    background-image: url(rightgradient.gif);
    background-repeat: repeat-y;
    background-position: right;
}
```

Figure 8-40 shows the four different alignments of repeating images. For repeat-y, the default is left. For repeat-x, the default is top.

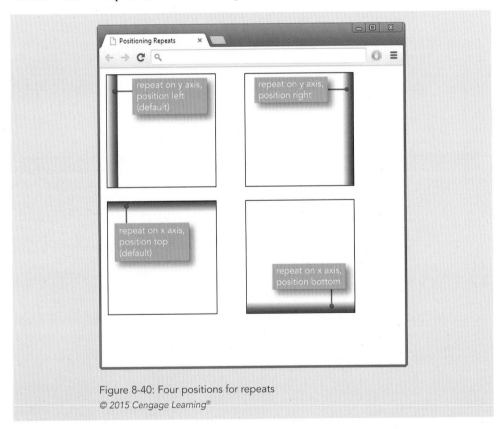

Figure 8-40: Four positions for repeats
© 2015 Cengage Learning®

Again, these repetitive borders are composed from a single image; in this case, a small gradient box was rotated with an image-editing program for the four different positions. The graphic is shown in Figure 8-41.

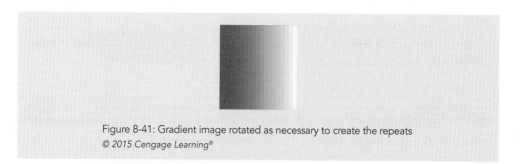

Figure 8-41: Gradient image rotated as necessary to create the repeats
© 2015 Cengage Learning®

Using Multiple Images in the Background

CSS3 offers the capability of layering multiple images in the background of an element. This feature is supported by all modern browsers. Figure 8-42 shows a page with both a sky image and a balloon image in the background layer of the element. The balloon image has a transparent background, as described earlier in the chapter, allowing the image to integrate seamlessly with the background.

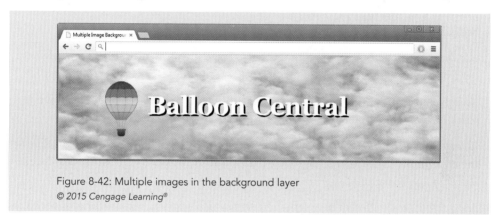

Figure 8-42: Multiple images in the background layer
© 2015 Cengage Learning®

The style rules for the background let you position and control the repeat properties for multiple images, with each value separated by commas. The first image on the following list is in the front or foreground, closest to the user, with successive values in order behind. This principle applies to all of the rule values. In other words, for the background-position property, the *100px 40px* value affects the image closest to the user, which is balloon_art_trans.png.

```
body {
    background-image: url(balloon_art_trans.png),
    url(clouds-and-sky.jpg);
    background-repeat: no-repeat, no-repeat;
    background-position: 100px 40px, top left;
}
```

Chapter Summary

To create an engaging, accessible, and informative web site, you must use graphics wisely. Keep the following points in mind:

> The four popular image file formats for the web are GIF, JPG, PNG, and SVG. The first three formats compress images to create smaller files. Unless you choose the appropriate file format, your image will not compress and appear as you expect. As a vector graphics format, SVG graphics are scalable and cross-platform compatible.

> Your computer monitor displays color by mixing the three basic colors of light: red, green, and blue (RGB). Colors vary widely from one monitor to another, based both on the user's preferences and the particular brand of equipment.

> Reduce image size to the appropriate dimensions for a web page.

> The color scheme you choose for a web site should work to create a distinctive look without detracting from your content's legibility. Use hexadecimal values when specifying colors for your web site. Color names are not always the best way to specify color values because of their variable nature.

> Use the color property to set foreground colors for elements. Remember that the element border defaults to the element color unless you specifically state a border color.

> Background colors affect any padding areas in the element. They can be applied both to block-level and inline elements.

> Choose background images that do not detract from the legibility of your content. Use the background-repeat and background-position properties to control the appearance of images in the background.

> Test your work on different browsers and computing platforms, because they render colors differently.

Key Terms

analogous color scheme—A scheme that uses adjacent colors on the color wheel.
aspect ratio—The ratio of width to height in an image or shape.
color gamut—A range of colors that contains a subset of all the available colors viewable by the human eye; used on high-definition tablet and phone displays.
complementary color scheme—A scheme that uses colors opposite of each other on the color wheel.

Graphics Interchange Format (GIF)—A file format designed for online delivery of graphics. The color depth of GIF is 8-bit, allowing a palette of no more than 256 colors. The GIF file format excels at compressing and displaying flat color areas, making it the logical choice for line art and graphics with simple colors.

hue—A pure color in color theory.

interlacing—The gradual display of a graphic in a series of passes as the data arrives in the browser. Each additional pass of data creates a clearer view of the image until the complete image is displayed. You can choose an interlacing process when creating GIFs.

Joint Photographic Experts Group (JPG or JPEG)—A file format, commonly shortened to JPG, designed for the transfer of photographic images over the Internet. JPGs are best for photos and images that contain feathering, complex shadows, or gradations.

lossless—A compression technique that does not discard color information from image files when the image is compressed.

lossy—A compression technique designed for photographic images; when the image is compressed, some color information is discarded, resulting in a loss of quality from the original image.

monochromatic color scheme—A color scheme that uses tints and shades of a single hue.

Portable Network Graphics (PNG)—A graphics file format for the web that supports many of the same features as GIF.

raster graphics—Images represented pixel by pixel for the entire image. GIFs and JPGs are raster formats.

Scalable Vector Graphics (SVG)—A language for describing two-dimensional graphics using XML. SVG files can contain shapes such as lines and curves, images, text, animation, and interactive events.

shade—A color made darker by adding black.

tint—A color made lighter by adding white.

vector graphics—Images represented as geometrical formulas, as compared with a raster graphics format, which represents images pixel by pixel for the entire image. SVG is a vector graphic format. Vector graphics are scalable and cross-platform compatible.

Review Questions

1. What are the four image file formats you can use on a web site?

2. Which file formats support 24-bit color?

3. How many colors does GIF support?

4. What is lossless file compression?

5. Which file formats support transparency?

6. What are the drawbacks of using animated GIFs?

7. Explain lossy image compression.

8. What image characteristics can you control using the JPG format?

9. What are some options for acquiring images for your site?

10. Which image format is best for a two-color company logo?

11. Which image format is best for a photograph?

12. What three attributes should you always include in the image tag? Why?

13. How many layers can you work with when designing pages?

14. What are the four different ways to express color values in CSS?

15. How is the default border color of an element determined?

16. What are the three special selectors that let you change link colors?

17. To what type of elements can you apply a background color?

18. What is the default background image behavior?

Hands-On Projects

1. Practice using the CSS float property.
   a. Download an image from the Online Companion web site, or find an image of your own.
   b. Add text around the image. Experiment with the float property and its values to view the way text wraps.
   c. Test the work in multiple browsers to verify that the text wraps consistently.

2. Practice using the CSS margin property attributes with images.
   a. Download an image from the Online Companion web site, or find an image of your own.
   b. Add text around the image. Experiment with the margin property to add white space around the image.
   c. Test the work in multiple browsers to verify that the text spacing is consistent.

3. Practice using width and height image attributes.
   a. Download an image from the Online Companion web site, or find an image of your own.
   b. Build a simple page that contains text and multiple images. Do not include the width and height attributes in the <img> tag.
   c. With the images turned off in your browser, view the page.
   d. Add the appropriate width and height information to the <img> tag for each image.
   e. Again, turn the images off in your browser and view the page. Note the differences between the two results and the way your layout is affected.

4. In this project, you add an image and color information to a web page. The code you will add to the file appears in blue.

   a. Copy the **ch8project4.html** file and the **daisy.jpg** file from the Chapter08 folder provided with your Data Files to the Chapter08 folder in your work folder. (Create the Chapter08 folder, if necessary.)

   b. Start your text editor, and open the file **ch8project4.html**.

   c. Add an <img> element to the page immediately after the opening <p> tag, as shown in the following code in blue text:

```
<html>
<head>
<title>Growing Wildflowers</title>
</head>
<body>
<h1>Growing Wildflowers</h1>
<p> <img src="daisy.jpg"> Lorem ipsum dolor sit
    amet, consectetuer adipiscing elit, sed diem
    nonummy nibh euis mod tincidunt ut lacreet
    dolore magna aliguam erat volutpat.
...body text...
    adipiscing elit, sed diem nonummy nibh euismod
    tincidunt ut lacreet dolore magna aliguam erat
    volutpat. Ut wisis enim ad minim veniam, quis
    nostrud exerci tution ullamcorper suscipit lobortis
    nisl ut aliquip ex eacommodo consequat.
</p>
</body>
</html>
```

   d. Save the file, and view it in the browser. It should look like Figure 8-43.

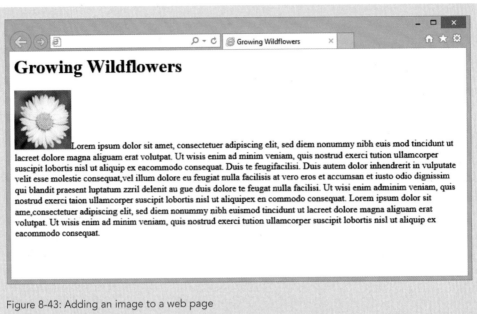

Figure 8-43: Adding an image to a web page
© 2015 Cengage Learning®

e. Add attributes to the image to provide size and alternate text information. The image width and height are both 100 pixels. The alt and title attributes can contain any text you choose to describe the image, such as *daisy image*. The following code fragment shows the attribute additions:

```
<img src="daisy.jpg" width="100" height="100"
     alt="daisy image" title="The Wild Daisy">
```

f. Wrap the text around the image by adding a CSS style rule to the image. Use the style attribute with the float property set to *left*, as shown in the following code fragment:

```
<img src="daisy.jpg" width="100" height="100"
     alt="daisy image" title="The Wild Daisy"
     style="float: left;">
```

g. Save the file, and view it in the browser. The file looks like Figure 8-44.

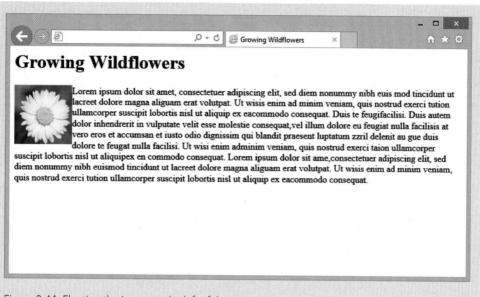

Figure 8-44: Floating the image to the left of the text

h. Adjust the right margin of the image by adding a margin-right property to the style attribute. Set the measurement value to 20px, as shown in the following code:

```
<img src="daisy.jpg" width="100" height="100"
    alt="daisy image" title="The Wild Daisy"
    style="float: left; margin-right: 20px;">
```

i. Save the file, and view it in the browser. It should look like Figure 8-45.

Figure 8-45: Adding a right margin to the image

© 2015 Cengage Learning®

j. Add a style attribute to the <h1> element to change the color to forest green. The hexadecimal code is 006633. The following code fragment shows the <h1> element with the style attribute.

```
<h1 style="color: #006633">Growing Wildflowers</h1>
```

k. Finish the page by setting the background color to a light green. Add a style attribute to the body element, and set the background color to light green, hexadecimal value 99cc99, as shown in the following code fragment:

```
<body style="background-color: #99cc99">
```

1. Save the file, and close the editor. Then view the finished page in the browser. It should look like Figure 8-46, with a deep green heading and light green page background. The complete code for the page follows.

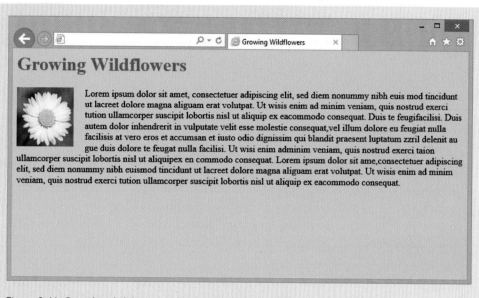

Figure 8-46: Completed ch8project4.html web page
© 2015 Cengage Learning®

```html
<html>
<head>
<title>Growing Wildflowers</title>
</head>
<body style="background-color: #99cc99">
<h1 style="color: #006633">Growing Wildflowers</h1>
<p><img src="daisy.jpg" width="100" height="100"
    alt="daisy image" title="The Wild Daisy"
    style="float: left; margin-right: 20px;"> Lorem
    ipsum dolor sit amet, consectetuer adipiscing
    elit, sed diem nonummy nibh euis mod tincidunt
    ut lacreet dolore magna aliguam erat volutpat.
```

```
...body text...
        adipiscing elit, sed diem nonummy nibh euismod
        tincidunt ut lacreet dolore magna aliguam erat
        volutpat. Ut wisis enim ad minim veniam, quis
        nostrud exerci tution ullamcorper suscipit
        lobortis nisl ut aliquip ex eacommodo consequat.
    </p>
    </body>
    </html>
```

5. Browse the web, and choose a site that you feel exhibits positive use of color, in both content and backgrounds. Write a short design critique that describes how the use of color enhances the legibility of the site and improves user access to information.

6. Browse the web, and choose a mainstream (not amateur) site that can benefit from a change in color scheme. Look for problems with legibility of text over background colors, use of nonstandard linking colors, and so on. Write a short essay that describes the changes you would implement to improve the use of color on the site.

Individual Case Project

Gather or create the graphics to use on the different pages of your site. These include any banner, navigation, section, or identifying graphics. Add these graphics to the test pages of your site. Test the images in multiple browsers to make sure they are displayed properly.

Think about the different color requirements for your content, and decide how you can enhance the legibility of the content. Can color help communicate the structure of your information?

Determine the color choices for your web site. Pick the colors for text, table backgrounds, and page backgrounds.

Establish graphics standards for your web site, including but not limited to the following:

> Decide whether you will use a standard amount of white space around each graphic.

> Determine exactly which img attributes should be included in all <img> tags.

> Formulate a standard for all alt and title attributes.

> Formulate a basic set of image standards for your site. Use this as the display standard for testing your graphics.

> Determine colors of links and visited links.

> Write a short standards document that can be provided to anyone who contributes to the site.

Team Case Project

Work with your team to decide on the graphics and color choices for your project web site. These include any banner, navigation, section, or identifying graphics, and the colors for text, table backgrounds, and page backgrounds.

You may need to bring sample graphics or mock-up HTML pages to present your ideas on these characteristics to your team members.

Establish graphics standards for your web site, including but not limited to the following:

> Decide whether you will use a standard amount of white space around each graphic.

> Determine exactly which img attributes should be included in all <img> tags.

> Formulate a standard for all alt and title attributes.

> Formulate a basic set of image standards for your site. Use this as the display standard for testing your graphics.

> Determine colors of links and visited links.

Write a short standards document that can be submitted to the instructor and provided to the team members.

After you have reached a general consensus, go back to work on the page template you adopted in Chapter 7. Create more finished mock-ups of your page design. Trade the page layout examples with your team members. Look for unifying characteristics that give your site a unique identity. Make sure the colors and graphics flow through the different page levels on the site. Work toward smooth transitions between your pages. You want all the pages to exhibit a graphic identity that connects them together.

CHAPTER

9

SITE NAVIGATION

When you complete this chapter, you will be able to:

> Create usable navigation
> Design navigation for mobile devices
> Use graphics for navigation and linking
> Build text-based navigation
> Use lists for navigation
> Build horizontal navigation bars
> Build vertical navigation bars
> Use background color and graphics to enhance navigation
> Create hover rollovers

The free-flowing nature of information in a nonlinear hypertext environment can be confusing to navigate. Help your users find content easily rather than making them hunt through a maze of choices. Let your users know where they are at all times and where they can go within your web site. In this chapter, you learn to build user-focused navigation to accomplish these goals.

Creating Usable Navigation

Webopedia (*www.webopedia.com*) defines hypertext as "a system in which objects (text, pictures, music, programs, and so on) can be creatively linked to each other. ... You can move from one object to another even though they might have very different forms." Hypertext was envisioned in the 1960s by Ted Nelson, who described it as nonsequential writing in his book *Literary Machines*. Nelson's basic idea of connecting content through hypertext linking influenced the creators of the web. With hypertext-linked content, users can traverse information in any order or method they choose, creating their own unique views.

Hypertext is a distinctly different environment in which to write and structure information. In traditional paper-based media, users navigate by turning pages or by referring to a table of contents or an index separate from the information they are reading. In a hypertext document, users can connect instantly to related information. The hypertext forms of traditional navigation devices, such as tables of contents and cross-references, can be displayed constantly alongside related content. The user can explore at will, jumping from one point of interest to another. Of course, the ease of navigation depends on the number of links and the context in which they were added by the hypertext author.

Planning Site Navigation

When planning your site navigation, do not skimp on navigation cues, options, and contextual links. You can use the CSS style properties you have learned about to create attractive navigation elements. Most modern web sites use primarily text-based graphics styled with CSS. Text-based navigation does not add download time. Furthermore, it is displayed consistently across devices and can be styled in limitless ways with the CSS3 properties you have studied so far. If you choose to use graphics for navigation, remember to keep them simple and reuse the same graphics throughout your web site. Once the navigation graphics are loaded in the user's cache, the server does not have to download them again. You can also use images in the background layer, as described in Chapter 8. Use an alternate set of text links in case the user cannot view your graphics, and to meet accessibility guidelines. You will learn more about text linking later in this chapter.

Orienting the User

Figure 9-1 shows four web sites and their navigation designs. Even though their look may vary, common items appear, such as search tools in the upper-right corner, some form of "about us" link, and links that guide users to frequently accessed or top levels of information. As you read in Chapter 2, users are accustomed to finding certain features in the main navigation section of the page. In mobile sites, the same conventions are offered in a more concise fashion, as you will read later.

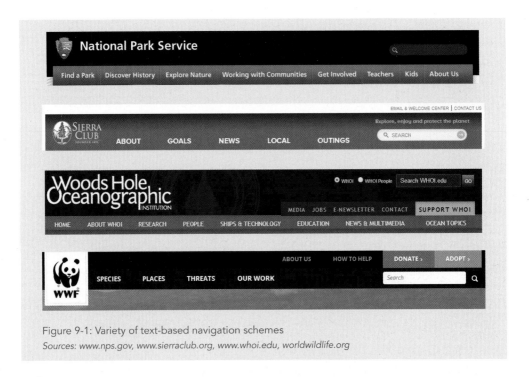

Figure 9-1: Variety of text-based navigation schemes
Sources: www.nps.gov, www.sierraclub.org, www.whoi.edu, worldwildlife.org

In addition to providing links to other sections in the web site, effective navigation includes providing cues to the user's location. Users should be able to answer the following navigation questions:

> Where am I?

> Where can I go?

> How do I get there?

> How do I get back to where I started?

To allow users to answer these questions, provide the following information:

> The current page and the type of content they are viewing

> Where they are in relation to the rest of the web site

> Consistent, easy-to-understand links

> Alternatives to the browser's Back button that let users return to their starting point

In Figure 9-2, the web site for the UK's *Guardian* newspaper uses colorful text-based navigation plus search features and breadcrumbs to orient the user. The linked breadcrumb path at the top of the page shows the user's location within the site hierarchy. Users can click any link in the path to move through the content structure. This location device is especially effective in guiding users who may have arrived at the page from outside the web site. Using these navigation devices, users can jump directly to a page, search for information, or move back up through the information hierarchy.

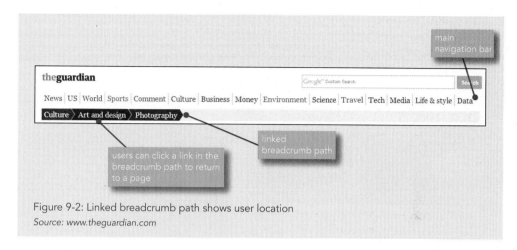

Figure 9-2: Linked breadcrumb path shows user location
Source: www.theguardian.com

Limiting Information Overload

Many web sites present too much information at one time. Lengthy files that require scrolling or have arrays of links and buttons can frustrate and overwhelm the user. You can limit information overload in the following ways:

> **Create manageable information segments**—Break your content into smaller files, and then link them together. Provide logical groupings of choices. Keep a flat hierarchy. Users should not have to click more than two or three times to see the information they desire.

> **Control page length**—Do not make users scroll through never-ending pages. Large files also can mean long downloads. Provide plenty of internal links to help users get around, and keep the pages short. You can judge your page length by pressing the Page Down key; if you have to repeat the action more than two or three times to move from the top of the page to the bottom, break up the content. On a mobile device, the display column width is much narrower, so longer scrolling is more common.

> **Use hypertext to connect facts, relationships, and concepts**—Provide contextual linking to related concepts, facts, or definitions, letting the users make the choices they want. Know your material, and try to anticipate the user's information needs.

Designing Navigation for Mobile Devices

Limiting information overload in navigation is especially important for mobile web sites and the smaller sizes of most handheld displays. When designing your navigation structure, try to limit the layers of navigation needed for users to reach the content they desire.

On mobile devices, minimize the number of clicks or taps the user has to make. Users will quickly leave your mobile site if they cannot easily find what they want. The limited screen space means your links must clearly tell users where they are going in as few words as possible. Many mobile web designs use navigation symbols that have become universal, such as a magnifying glass for the search function, a shopping cart, and stacked lines (often called the hamburger icon) to represent a menu, as shown in Figure 9-3.

Figure 9-3: Common navigation icons for mobile devices
Sources: www.bestbuy.com, www.ebay.com, www.yahoo.com, www.sears.com

Some mobile sites use fewer navigation cues based on their functions, as shown in Figure 9-4. In these examples, the user interface focuses on the most important features for the site. Wikipedia offers only a search bar for its search-driven content, while Slate offers only a menu icon to access the major sections of its site. For each of these sites, the designers are presenting just what the user needs—and no more—to access content quickly.

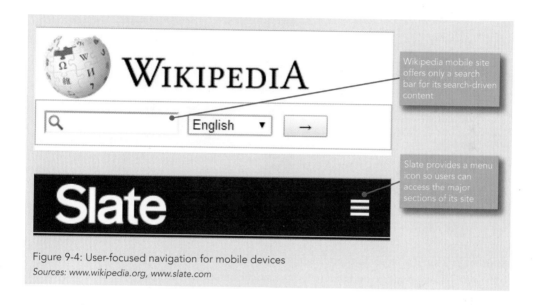

Figure 9-4: User-focused navigation for mobile devices
Sources: www.wikipedia.org, www.slate.com

By offering a menu of deeper navigation choices, usually for the top-level sections of the site, the designer simplifies the user's choices. With an open menu, more screen real estate is available, but navigation must still be clear and direct. Figure 9-5 shows Slate's menu, which opens when the user selects the Menu icon, and the open menu on the Salvation Army's mobile site.

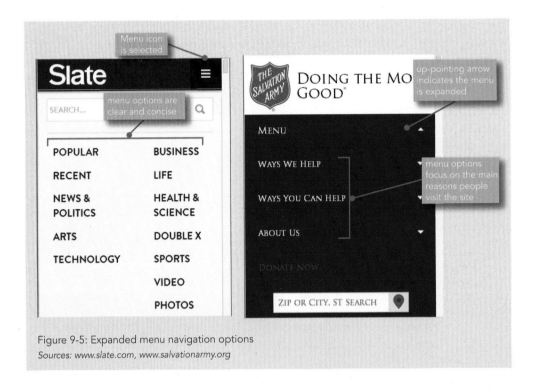

Figure 9-5: Expanded menu navigation options
Sources: www.slate.com, www.salvationarmy.org

Whether you build a separate mobile site for your content or a responsive site that adapts to the smaller screen size, you need to focus navigation options around your users' needs. Remember that mobile devices often have slower connection speeds, so using text-based navigation and consistent graphics helps your pages load more quickly.

Note | *You will learn more about responsive web design in Chapter 12.*

Using Graphics for Navigation and Linking

Although current web design trends favor text-based navigation, creating a clickable graphic for a link is often still desirable. To make sure your navigation graphics help users rather than hinder them, use the same graphics consistently throughout your web site, for the following reasons:

> **To provide predictable navigation cues**—After users learn where to find navigation icons and how to work with them, users expect them on every page. Consistent placement and design also build users' trust and help them feel confident that they can find the information they want.

> **To minimize download time**—After a graphic is downloaded, the browser retrieves it from the cache for subsequent pages rather than downloading it every time it appears.

Note	*Remember that linked graphics are the result of placing an <img> element within a set of <a> tags. For example:*

```
<a href="index.html"><img src="home.gif"
alt="home page image" width="50" height="20"></a>
```

Refer to Chapter 8 for more information on working with images.

Using the alt Attribute

As you read earlier, you should provide alternate text-based links in addition to graphical links. You can do so by including an alt attribute in the <img> tag of the HTML code for the graphic. Repeating navigation options ensures that you meet the needs of a wide range of users. Some sites choose not to offer a text-based alternative, which makes it difficult for users who cannot view graphics in their browsers. The alt attribute is highlighted in the following code:

```
<a href="index.html"><img src="home.gif"
alt="home page image" width="50" height="20"></a>
```

Users can still use image-based navigation by reading the alt text and pointing to image areas to find the clickable spots. Accessibility devices can use the alt attribute to provide navigation information as spoken content or in other media. The inclusion of alt attributes is very important to the accessibility of your web site.

Note	*Remember that the alt attribute is different from the title attribute. Alt is designed to provide the alternate text, while the title attribute text is displayed in a ToolTip or ScreenTip, a pop-up window that appears when the user points to an object. You can read more about these attributes in Chapter 8.*

Using Meaningful Images

No matter what types of navigation graphics you use, make sure that your users understand their meaning. Test navigation graphics on users in your target audience, and ask them to interpret the icons and directional graphics you want to use. The most obvious graphics to avoid are culturally specific symbols, especially hand gestures (such as thumbs up), which may be misinterpreted in other cultures. Other graphics, such as directional arrows or accepted representational graphics, are more likely to be interpreted correctly.

Activity: Building Navigation Structures

Text-based linking is often the most effective and accessible way to provide navigation on your site. In the following set of steps, you will link a series of sample web pages using lists for navigation menu choices. Figure 9-6 shows the content structure of the collection of sample HTML documents you will use, including the Home page, Table of Contents page, Site Map page, and individual chapter pages.

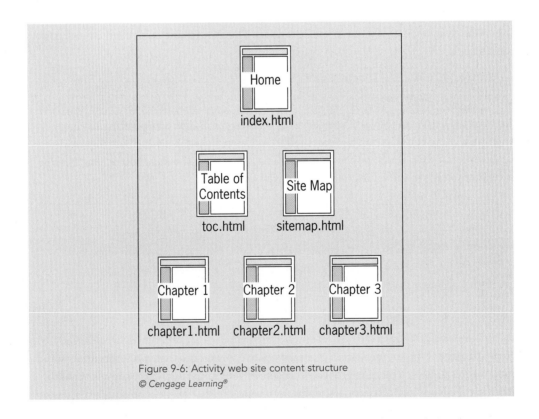

Figure 9-6: Activity web site content structure
© Cengage Learning®

In the following steps, you will add a variety of linking options that produce different paths through the information. The focus for these steps is the Table of Contents page, toc.html, and how it relates to the rest of the content in the collection. You will also add navigation options to the individual chapter pages. The Home and Site Map pages are included to complete the sample web site, and will be target destinations for some of the links you will build. This activity demonstrates a wide variety of linking options; you can use some or all of them based on the navigation needs for your web site.

To complete the steps in this activity, you need to work on a computer with a browser and an HTML editor or simple text editor, such as Notepad or TextEdit.

To prepare for linking the web pages:

1. Copy the following files from the Chapter09 folder provided with your Data Files:
   - index.html
   - toc.html
   - sitemap.html
   - chapter1.html
   - chapter2.html
   - chapter3.html
   - styles.css

2. Save the files using the same filenames in the Chapter09 folder within your work folder. (Create the Chapter09 folder, if necessary.) Make sure to save all the files in the same folder.

> **Note** In the following set of steps, you use basic HTML coding techniques. If necessary, review your basic HTML knowledge before proceeding.

Linking with a Text Navigation Bar

The Table of Contents page must link to the other main pages of the web site and allow users to go directly to the pages they want. You can create these links by adding a simple text-based navigation bar.

To build the navigation bar:

1. From the Chapter09 folder in your work folder, open the file **toc.html** in your browser. It should look like Figure 9-7.

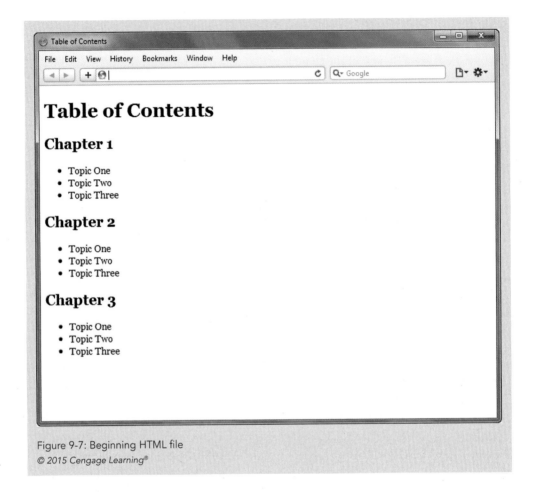

Figure 9-7: Beginning HTML file
© 2015 Cengage Learning®

2. Open the file in your HTML editor, and examine the code. Notice that the file contains a link to an external style sheet that controls the basic styles for the site.

```
<!DOCTYPE html>
<html>
<head>
<title>Table of Contents</title>
<meta content="text/html; charset=utf-8" http-equiv="Content-Type" />
<link href="styles.css" rel="stylesheet">
</head>
```

3. Add a <nav> element to place the navigation bar immediately following the opening <body> tag. Set the id attribute to *headernav*, as shown in the following code. (The new code you should add appears in blue in this step and the following steps.)

```
<body>
<nav id="headernav"> </nav>
```

4. Add a <p> element with text, as shown in the following code.

```
<nav id="headernav">
<p>Home | Table of Contents | Site Map</p>
</nav>
```

5. Add <a> tags with href attributes that link to the home page and the site map.

```
<nav id="headernav">
<p><a href="index.html">Home</a> | Table of Contents |
<a href="sitemap.html">Site Map</a></p>
</nav>
```

6. Add a span element with a class attribute to contain the Table of Contents text. Because the Table of Contents page is the current page, the text "Table of Contents" is not a hypertext link, but is bold to designate the user's location. The code looks like this:

```
<nav id="headernav">
<p><a href="index.html">Home</a> |
<span class="current">Table of Contents</span> |
<a href="sitemap.html">Site Map</a></p>
</nav>
```

7. Save the file, and view it in your browser. It should look like Figure 9-8. Now that you have created a simple text menu, you will add CSS style rules to enhance the menu's look.

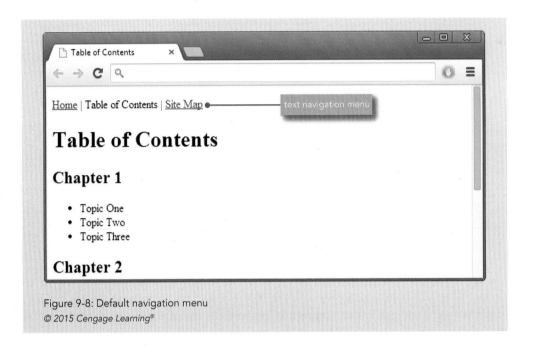

Figure 9-8: Default navigation menu
© 2015 Cengage Learning®

8. In styles.css, add a style for the id *headernav* that specifies a width, automatic margins, a border, padding, text alignment, font family, and padding. Use a comment to describe the style rule.

```
/* Navigation Header */
#headernav {
    width: 320px;
    margin-left: auto;
    margin-right: auto;
    border: solid 1px black;
    padding-top: 10px;
    padding-bottom: 10px;
    text-align: center;
    font-family: arial, sans-serif;
}
```

9. Add another style for the *current* class that indicates which page the user is currently viewing.

```
/* Current Page Indicator */
.current {
```

```
    font-weight: bold;
}
```

10. Save and close the style sheet file, and then view the Table of Contents page in your browser. It should look like Figure 9-9. Test your hypertext links in the navigation bar to make sure they point to the correct pages.

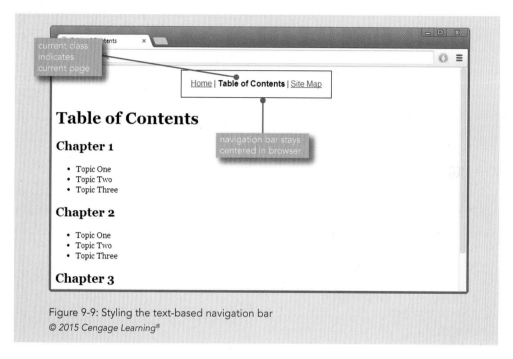

Figure 9-9: Styling the text-based navigation bar
© 2015 Cengage Learning®

11. Add this navigation bar to all of the sample pages. Remember to change the links and placement of the <span class="current"> element to reflect the current page. For example, the Site Map page would include the text "Site Map" in <span> and links to the Table of Contents and Home pages. The chapter pages (chapter1.html, chapter2. html, and chapter3.html) do not need a span element, just links to the Home, Table of Contents, and Site Map pages.

12. Save **toc.html** in the Chapter09 folder of your work folder, and leave it open in your HTML editor for the next steps.

Linking to Chapter Pages

While the navigation bar lets users access the main pages in the web site, the table of contents lets users access the exact content pages they want. Therefore, the Table of Contents page needs links to the individual chapter files in the web site. In this set of steps, you will add links to the individual chapter files listed in the table of contents.

To build page links:

1. Continue working in the file **toc.html**. Add the following <a> element around the text "Chapter 1":

```
<h2><a href="chapter1.html">Chapter 1</a></h2>
```

> **Note** As this example shows, always make <a> the innermost set of tags to avoid extra space in the hypertext link.

2. Add similar <a> elements around the text "Chapter 2" and "Chapter 3" that point to the files chapter2.html and chapter3.html, respectively.

3. Save **toc.html**, and view the finished Table of Contents page in your browser. It should look like Figure 9-10. Test your hypertext links to make sure they point to the correct page.

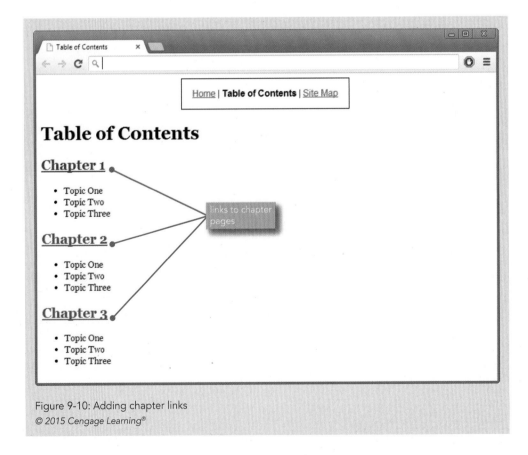

Figure 9-10: Adding chapter links
© 2015 Cengage Learning®

This linking method lets users scroll through the table of contents, scan the chapters and topics, and then jump to the chapter they want. The link colors—by default, blue for new and purple for visited—allow users to keep track of which chapters they have already visited.

Adding Internal Linking

In addition to linking to external documents, you can add internal links for navigating within the table of contents itself. In the Table of Contents page illustrated in Figure 9-11, you will add a Back to Top link that lets users return to the top of the page when they reach the bottom.

This link requires two <a> anchor elements: one uses the name attribute to name a fragment identifier in the document, and the other targets the fragment name in the href attribute. A *fragment identifier* names a segment of an HTML file that you can reference in a hypertext link.

To add an internal link:

1. Continue working with the file **toc.html** in your editor. Add a new <a> element at the top of the page, immediately after the <body> tag. Add a name attribute, and set the value to *top* as shown.

```
<body>
<a name="top"></a>
<nav id="headernav">
<p><a href="index.html">Home</a> |
<span class="current">Table of Contents</span> |
<a href="sitemap.html">Site Map</a></p>
</nav>
```

Notice that this <a> element is empty. The name attribute identifies this location in the document as "top." You can then refer to this name as an href target elsewhere in the document. The value of the name attribute can be any combination of alphanumeric characters.

2. Add an <a> element at the bottom of the page, after the listing for Chapter 3 and just before the closing </body> tag. Reference the target fragment *top* by using the number sign (#) in the href attribute, as shown in the following code.

```
<h2><a href="chapter3.html">Chapter 3</a></h2>
  <ul>
  <li>Topic One</li>
```

```
<li>Topic Two</li>
<li>Topic Three</li>
</ul>
<a href="#top">Back to Top</a>
</body>
```

3. Add a `<p>` element around the `<a>` element.

```
<p><a href="#top">Back to Top</a></p>
```

4. Save the **toc.html** file, and view the Table of Contents page in your browser. Resize your browser to show only a portion of the page, as shown in Figure 9-11.

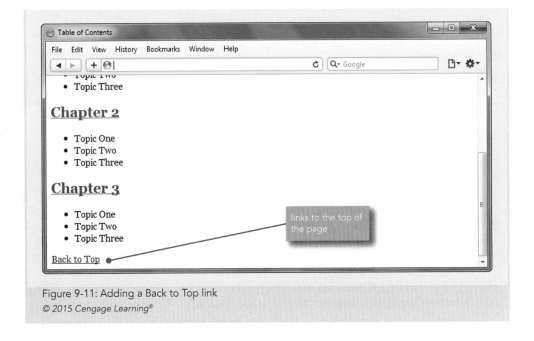

Figure 9-11: Adding a Back to Top link
© 2015 Cengage Learning®

5. Test the link to make sure it opens the browser window at the top of the page, as shown in Figure 9-12.

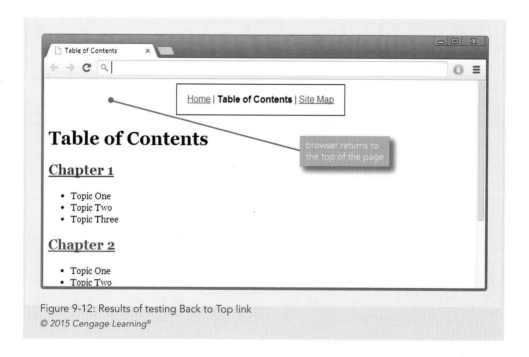

Figure 9-12: Results of testing Back to Top link
© 2015 Cengage Learning®

Adding a Page Navigation Bar

You can use additional fragment identifiers in the table of contents to add more user-focused navigation choices. Figure 9-13 shows the addition of a page navigation bar. When users click one of the linked chapter numbers, they jump to the specific chapter information they want to view within the table of contents further down the page.

To add a page navigation bar:

1. Continue working with the file **toc.html** in your HTML editor. Add a <nav> element immediately after the <h1> element, and set the id attribute to pagenav, as shown in the following code. Even though you will not write any style rules for this navigation bar now, it is still a good idea to add a class name for future use.

```
<h1>Table of Contents</h1>
<nav id="pagenav"> </nav>
```

2. Add a <p> element with text, as shown in the following code.

```
<nav id="pagenav">
<p>Jump down this page to Chapter... 1 | 2 | 3</p>
</nav>
```

3. Add <a> elements around each chapter number. Insert href attributes that point to a named fragment for each chapter.

```
<nav id="pagenav">
<p>Jump down this page to Chapter...
<a href="#chapter1">1</a> |
<a href="#chapter2">2</a> |
<a href="#chapter3">3</a>
</p>
</nav>
```

4. Add the name attribute to each chapter link's <a> element. These are the fragment names you referred to in Step 3. The following code shows the new name attributes in the <a> element for each chapter.

```
<h2><a href="chapter1.html" name="chapter1">Chapter 1</a>
</h2>
    <ul>
      <li>Topic One</li>
      <li>Topic Two</li>
      <li>Topic Three</li>
    </ul>
<h2><a href="chapter2.html" name="chapter2">Chapter 2</a>
</h2>
    <ul>
      <li>Topic One</li>
      <li>Topic Two</li>
      <li>Topic Three</li>
    </ul>
<h2><a href="chapter3.html" name="chapter3">Chapter 3</a>
</h2>
    <ul>
      <li>Topic One</li>
```

```
<li>Topic Two</li>

<li>Topic Three></li>

</ul>
```

5. Save the **toc.html** file in the Chapter09 folder in your work folder, and then close the file. View the Table of Contents page in your browser. Resize your browser to show only a portion of the page, as shown in Figure 9-13.

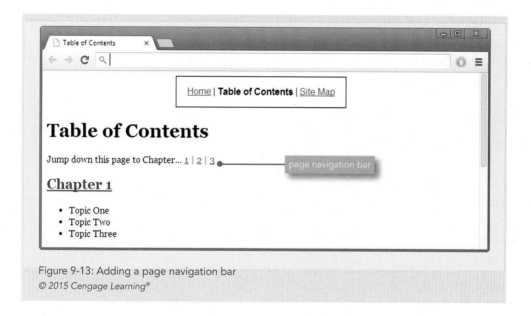

Figure 9-13: Adding a page navigation bar
© 2015 Cengage Learning®

6. Test the navigation bar links by selecting a chapter number and making sure the browser window opens to the correct place in the file. Figure 9-14 shows the result of selecting the Chapter 2 link.

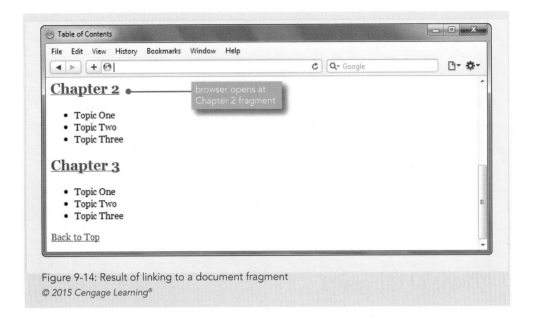

Figure 9-14: Result of linking to a document fragment
© 2015 Cengage Learning®

Linking to External Document Fragments

Now that you have completed internal linking in the table of contents, reexamine how the table of contents is linked to each chapter file. Currently, each chapter has one link in the table of contents; users click the chapter link, and the browser opens the chapter file at the top. However, each chapter also contains multiple topics, which can be linked as external fragments. You can let users jump from the table of contents to the exact topic they want within each chapter. This requires adding code to the Table of Contents page and each individual chapter page.

To add links to external fragments:

1. In your HTML editor, open the file **chapter1.html** from the Chapter09 folder in your work folder.

2. Find the topic headings within the file. For example, the following code creates the topic heading for Topic 1:

```
<h2>Topic 1</h2>
```

3. Add an <a> element around the text "Topic 1." Set the name attribute value to *topic1* for this heading, as shown in the following code.

```
<h2><a name="topic1">Topic 1</a></h2>
```

4. Add the same code to each of the other topic headings in the file, using *topic2* and *topic3* as the name attribute values for the Topic 2 and Topic 3 headings, respectively.

5. Save **chapter1.html** in the Chapter09 folder of your work folder, and then close the file.

6. In your HTML editor, open the files **chapter2.html** and **chapter3.html** from the Chapter09 folder of your work folder. Repeat Steps 2 through 5 for both files, adding appropriate name attribute values for each topic in each file.

7. In your HTML editor, open the file **toc.html** from the Chapter09 folder of your work folder. (This is the toc.html file you saved in the last set of steps.)

8. Find the topic links for each chapter within the file. For example, the following code contains three topic links for Chapter 1:

```
<h2>
<a href="chapter1.html" name="chapter1">Chapter 1</a>
</h2>
    <ul>
      <li>Topic One</li>
      <li>Topic Two</li>
      <li>Topic Three</li>
    </ul>
```

9. Add <a> elements for each topic. The href value is the filename combined with the fragment name. The following code shows the <a> element for the Chapter 1, Topic 1 link.

```
<h2>
<a href="chapter1.html" name="chapter1">Chapter 1</a>
</h2>
    <ul>
      <li><a href="chapter1.html#topic1">Topic One</a></li>
      <li>Topic Two</li>
      <li>Topic Three</li>
    </ul>
```

10. Continue to add similar links for each topic listed in the table of contents. When you are finished, your chapter navigation section should look like the following example. The link code is shown in color. (The location of your line breaks might differ.)

```
<h2>
<a href="chapter1.html" name="chapter1">Chapter 1</a>
</h2>
    <ul>
      <li><a href="chapter1.html#topic1">Topic One</a></li>
      <li><a href="chapter1.html#topic2">Topic Two</a></li>
      <li><a href="chapter1.html#topic3">Topic Three</a></li>
    </ul>
<h2>
<a href="chapter2.html" name="chapter2">Chapter 2</a>
</h2>
    <ul>
      <li><a href="chapter2.html#topic1">Topic One</a></li>
      <li><a href="chapter2.html#topic2">Topic Two</a></li>
      <li><a href="chapter2.html#topic3">Topic Three</a></li>
    </ul>
<h2>
<a href="chapter3.html" name="chapter3">Chapter 3</a>
</h2>
    <ul>
      <li><a href="chapter3.html#topic1">Topic One</a></li>
      <li><a href="chapter3.html#topic2">Topic Two</a></li>
      <li><a href="chapter3.html#topic3">Topic Three</a></li>
    </ul>
```

11. Save the **toc.html** file in the Chapter09 folder of your work folder, and view it in your browser. Test the topic links by selecting a chapter topic and making sure the browser window opens to the correct place in the correct file. Figure 9-15 shows the result of selecting the Chapter 2, Topic 2 link.

When users click the topic links in the table of contents, the browser opens the destination file and displays the fragment.

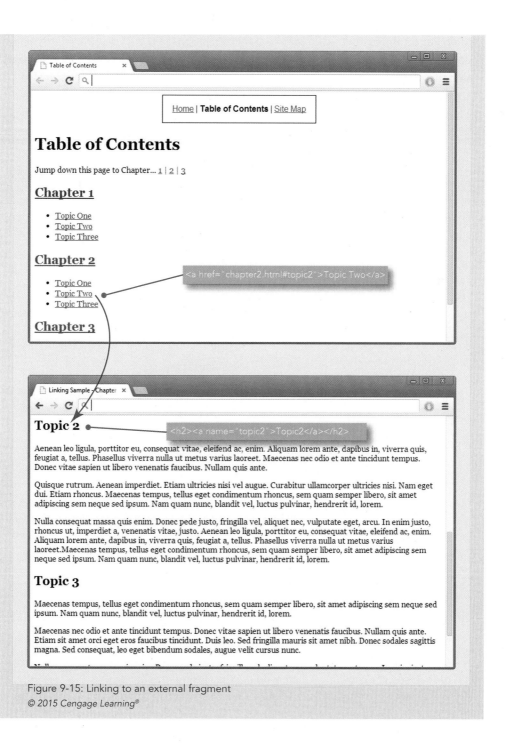

Figure 9-15: Linking to an external fragment
© 2015 Cengage Learning®

Adding Page Turners

Each chapter file currently contains a navigation bar and fragment identifiers for each topic within the chapter. In this page collection, the user can jump to any file and topic within a file, though some users may want to read the pages sequentially. You can offer this sequential function by adding page-turner links. Page turners let you move to the previous or next page or section in the collection. They work well in a linear structure of pages, for computer-based learning, or where users read pages or sections in order, as shown in Figure 9-16.

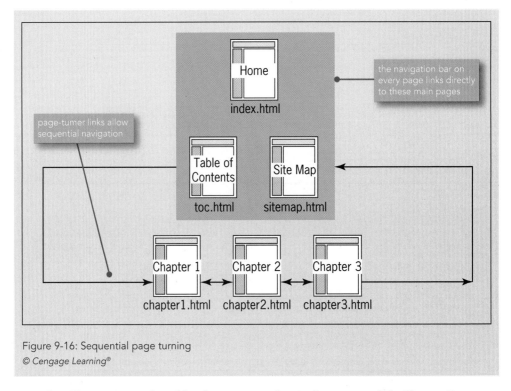

Figure 9-16: Sequential page turning
© Cengage Learning®

Note that Chapter 1 uses the table of contents as the previous page, while Chapter 3 uses the site map as the next page.

To add page-turner links:

1. In your editor, open the file **chapter1.html** from the Chapter 09 folder of your work folder.

2. Add a footer element and set the id attribute to footernav, as shown in the following code. Insert the code immediately before the closing </body> tag.

```
<footer id="footernav"> </footer>
</body>
```

3. Add a <p> element with text, as shown in the following code:

```
<footer id="footernav"><p>Previous | Chapter 1 |
Next</p></footer>
```

4. Add an <a> element for the previous page. Because this is Chapter 1, make the previous page destination toc.html, as shown in the following code. Refer to Figure 9-16 to see how the pages are connected.

```
<footer id="footernav"><p><a href="toc.html">Previous</a> |
Chapter 1 | Next</p></footer>
```

5. Add an <a> element for the next page. Because this is Chapter 1, make the next page destination chapter2.html, as shown in the following code.

```
<footer id="footernav"><p><a href="toc.html">Previous</a> |
Chapter 1 |
<a href="chapter2.html">Next</a></p></footer>
```

6. Add a span element with a class attribute to contain the Chapter 1 text. Because this is the Chapter 1 page, the text "Chapter 1" is not a hypertext link, but is bold to designate the user's location. You will reuse the *current* style you used previously when building the header navigation bar to indicate the current page. The code looks like this:

```
<footer id="footernav"><p><a href="toc.html">Previous</a> |
<span class="current">Chapter 1</span> |
<a href="chapter2.html">Next</a></p></footer>
```

7. Save the **chapter1.html** file in the Chapter09 folder of your work folder.

8. Now that the HTML code is complete, you need to add the *footernav* style to the CSS style sheet. Open the style sheet file **styles.css** in your editor. Locate the headernav style:

```
/* Navigation Header */
#headernav {
    width: 300px;
    margin-left: auto;
    margin-right: auto;
    border: solid 1px black;
    padding-top: 10px;
    padding-bottom: 10px;
    text-align: center;
    font-family: arial, sans-serif;
}
```

9. You can easily match the style of the header navigation bar for the footer by adding the footernav id selector to the existing style rule:

```
/* Navigation Header */
#headernav, #footernav {
    width: 300px;
    margin-left: auto;
    margin-right: auto;
    border: solid 1px black;
    padding-top: 10px;
    padding-bottom: 10px;
    text-align: center;
    font-family: arial, sans-serif;
}
```

10. Save and close the **styles.css** file. Save the **chapter1.html** file, and then view it in your browser. Your file should now look like Figure 9-17. Test the page-turner links to make sure they point to the correct files.

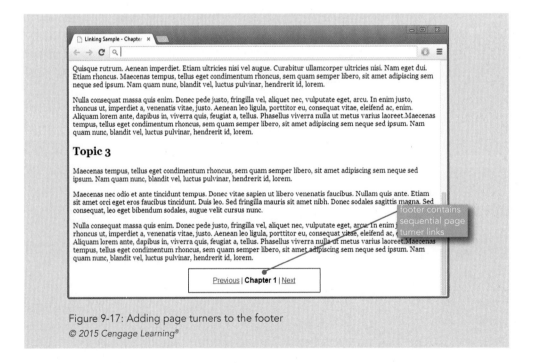

Figure 9-17: Adding page turners to the footer
© 2015 Cengage Learning®

11. Add the page-turner links to chapter2.html and chapter3.html, changing the Previous and Next links to point to the correct files. Test all your links to make sure they work properly. When you are finished, save and close all the .html files in the Chapter09 folder of your work folder.

Adding Contextual Linking

One of the most powerful hypertext capabilities is contextual linking. Contextual links allow users to jump to related ideas or cross-references by clicking the word or item that interests them. You can embed these standard hypertext links directly in the flow of your content by choosing key terms and concepts you anticipate your users will want to follow. Figure 9-18 shows a page from the Wikipedia web site (www.wikipedia.org) that contains contextual linking.

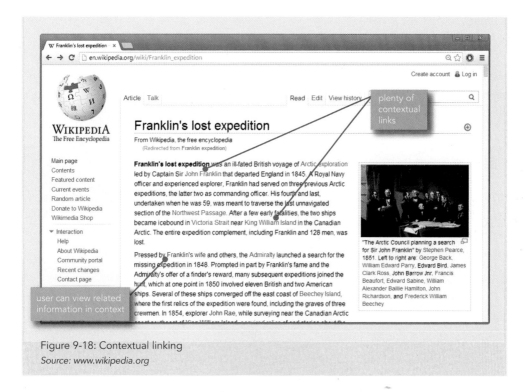

Figure 9-18: Contextual linking
Source: www.wikipedia.org

Note the links within the lines of text, which let the user view related information in context. Including the link within a line of text is more effective than including a list of keywords, because users can see related information within the context of the sentence they are reading. Users also can see that repeated words are linked no matter how many times they appear within the browser window, offering users the opportunity to access additional information at any time.

Navigation Summary

You can choose from a variety of navigation options to link a collection of pages. The sample web pages in this section demonstrated the following text-based linking actions:

> To main pages (Home, Table of Contents, Index)

> To the top of each chapter

> Within the Table of Contents page to chapter descriptions

> From the Table of Contents page to specific topics within each chapter

> Between previous and next chapters

> To related information by using contextual links

Use as many of these options as necessary, but remember to view your content from the user's perspective. Provide enough navigation options to allow easy and clear access to your content.

Using Lists for Navigation

The HTML list elements are the preferred elements for containing navigation links. Lists provide an easy way to create navigation that can be styled with CSS. They are adaptable to different devices, and are accessibility compatible.

Note | *Refer to Chapter 5 for more information on list elements.*

The HTML list elements are commonly used to create bulleted and numbered lists. The following code shows <ul> and <li> elements used conventionally to create a bulleted list. This list has an id of *navlist* that will be used for applying style rules.

```
<ul id="navlist">
    <li><a href="index.html">Home</a></li>
    <li><a href="history.html">History</a></li>
    <li><a href="how.html">How it Works</a></li>
    <li><a href="clubs.html">Balloon Clubs</a></li>
    <li><a href="festivals.html">Festivals</a></li>
    <li><a href="rides.html">Where to Ride</a></li>
    <li><a href="faq.html">FAQ</a></li>
</ul>
```

This code results in the default bulleted list shown in Figure 9-19.

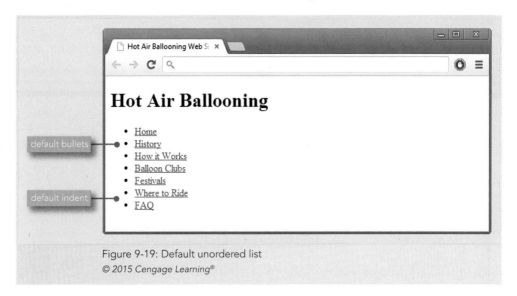

Figure 9-19: Default unordered list
© 2015 Cengage Learning®

Removing Default Padding and Margin

The bulleted list in Figure 9-19 has built-in spacing that indents the list from the left side of the browser window. Depending on the browser, this built-in spacing is applied using either padding or margins. In most instances you must remove this default spacing before creating navigation lists. Set both the margin and padding properties to zero for the <ul> element, as shown in the following code, which selects a <ul> element with an id of *navlist*.

```
ul#navlist {
    padding: 0;
    margin: 0;
}
```

Removing Default Bullets

HTML lists come with built-in bullets, which are useful when you are creating standard lists. When you are building lists for navigation, you can remove the default bullets with the list-style-type property. You can add this property to the same style rule you use to remove the default padding and margin, as shown below:

```
ul#navlist {
    padding: 0;
    margin: 0;
    list-style-type: none;
}
```

Removing the default bullets and indenting results in the list shown in Figure 9-20. This list is ready to be turned into a horizontal or vertical navigation bar.

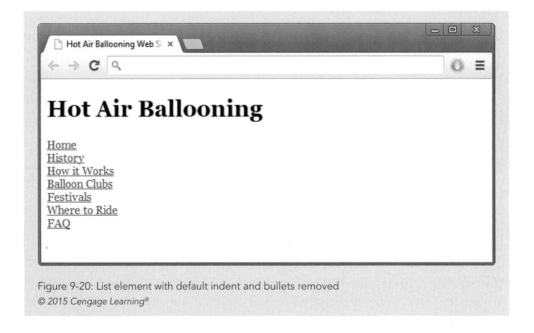

Figure 9-20: List element with default indent and bullets removed
© 2015 Cengage Learning®

Building Horizontal Navigation Bars

To create a horizontal navigation bar, you need to add one more style rule. In a standard list element, the list items are block-level elements. A line break separates each item on its own line. To create a horizontal navigation bar using a list, you need to set each list item's display setting to *inline*, which allows the list to be displayed without line breaks. You can do this with the display property. The following style rule uses an id selector and descendant selection to select the <li> elements within a <ul> element with an id of *navlist*. The style rule sets the display property to *inline*:

```
ul#navlist li{
    display: inline;
}
```

The result of adding this style is shown in Figure 9-21. The list is now displayed on a single line.

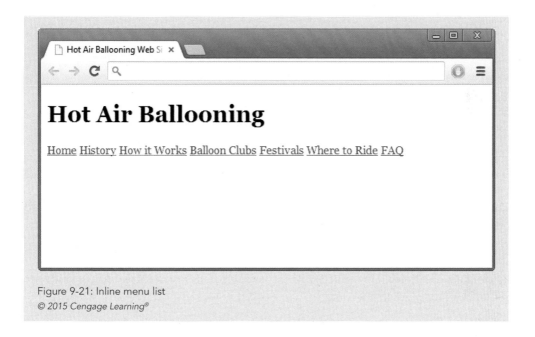

Figure 9-21: Inline menu list
© 2015 Cengage Learning®

Note | Refer to Chapter 6 for more information on the display property and Chapter 4 for more information on CSS selectors and descendant selection.

The horizontal navigation bar in Figure 9-21 requires three style rules: one that styles the <ul> container, one that sets the <li> elements to inline, and a third that styles the <a> elements that create the hypertext links.

The first style rule removes the default spacing and bullets from the unordered list:

```
ul#navlist {
    padding: 0;
    margin: 0;
    list-style-type: none;
}
```

The second style rule sets the <li> elements to inline display:

```
ul#navlist li{
    display: inline;
}
```

The third style rule styles the <a> elements that contain the link text. In this example, a right margin is added to each link to provide some white space between the links in the horizontal list.

```
ul#navlist a{
    margin-right: 20px;
}
```

Customizing the Horizontal Navigation Bar

Once you have created the basic list, you can customize it using different CSS style properties. You can remove underlining, add borders and background colors or images, and set space between buttons, all with a few style rules. For example, you can build on the basic horizontal navigation bar in Figure 9-21, which was created with the three style rules shown at the end of the preceding section.

Add a border and background color to the <a> element that contains the link text, and set the right margin from 20px to 5px, bringing the link elements closer together.

```
ul#navlist {
    padding: 0;
    margin: 0;
    list-style-type: none;
}
ul#navlist li{
    display: inline;
}
```

```
ul#navlist a{
    margin-right: 5px;
    border: solid 1px;
    background-color: #ccccff;
}
```

Add 5 pixels of top and bottom padding and 10 pixels of left and right padding. Set the text decoration to *none* to remove the underlining from the links.

```
ul#navlist {
    padding: 0;
    margin: 0;
    list-style-type: none;
}
ul#navlist li{
    display: inline;
}
ul#navlist a{
    margin-right: 5px;
    border: solid 1px;
    background-color: #ccccff;
    padding: 5px 10px 5px 10px;
    text-decoration: none;
}
```

Finally, add a top margin to the <ul> element to offset the entire navigation bar from the heading above.

```
ul#navlist {
    padding: 0;
    margin: 10px 0px 0px 0px;
    list-style-type: none;
}
ul#navlist li{
    display: inline;
}
ul#navlist a{
```

```
    margin-right: 5px;

    border: solid 1px;

    background-color: #ccccff;

    padding: 5px 10px 5px 10px;

    text-decoration: none;

}
```

This code results in the enhanced navigation bar shown in Figure 9-22.

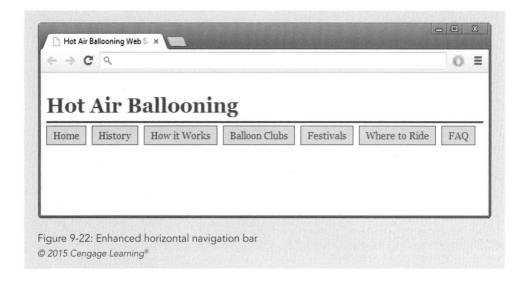

Figure 9-22: Enhanced horizontal navigation bar
© 2015 Cengage Learning®

Controlling Navigation Bar Width

Your horizontal navigation bar will wrap if a user makes his browser window small enough, as shown in Figure 9-23. To keep this from happening, add a width property to the <ul> element style rule, as shown in the following code:

```
ul#navlist {

    padding: 0;

    margin: 10px 0px 0px 0px;

    list-style-type: none;

    width: 700px;

}
```

Figure 9-23: Undesirable wrapping can be fixed with the width property
© 2015 Cengage Learning®

Controlling Navigation Button Width

In the previous example, the widths of the horizontal navigation bar buttons are based on the size of the text they contain. You may want to make all navigation buttons the same width. To create same-size buttons, change the display type of the <a> elements to *block* to set a consistent width, and then float the boxes so they will align next to each other. The result is the navigation bar shown in Figure 9-24.

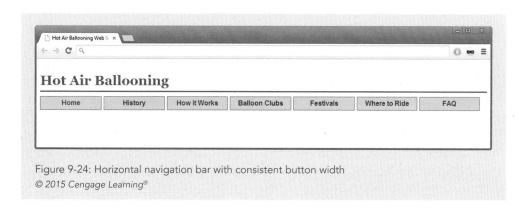

Figure 9-24: Horizontal navigation bar with consistent button width
© 2015 Cengage Learning®

To create buttons of uniform width, add a float property to the <li> elements within the list:

```
ul#navlist {
    padding: 0;
    margin: 10px 0px 0px 0px;
    list-style-type: none;
}
ul#navlist li{
    display: inline;
    float: left;
}
```

Set properties for the <a> elements that contain the hypertext links. Set the display property to *block* so you can set a width for the buttons. Choose a width that will contain the longest piece of text in your link buttons—in this case, 7em. Align the text to center with the text-align property.

```
ul#navlist a{
    margin-right: 5px;
    border: solid 1px;
    background-color: #ccccff;
    padding: 5px 10px 5px 10px;
    text-decoration: none;
    display: block;
    width: 7em;
    text-align: center;
```

Note | *Ems are a good measurement choice when designing for multiple screen sizes; the buttons will adjust accordingly to the default font size of the device.*

Building Vertical Navigation Bars

When you are building a vertical navigation bar, you can use a standard list structure without changing the display type, as you did for a horizontal navigation bar. The common style of vertical navigation bars usually includes buttons that are clickable links to different areas of a web site. These can be styled in an endless variety of ways.

As you saw in the example of the horizontal navigation bar, the <a> elements are contained within <li> elements to create the clickable hypertext links. Because <a> elements are inline by default, you need to set each <a> element's display setting to *block*, which lets you create clickable buttons of any width you choose.

This example uses the same HTML list elements you saw in the horizontal example. The interesting thing about these examples is that you can produce two very different results—a horizontal and vertical navigation bar with the same HTML code—just by varying the CSS style rules.

```
<ul id="navlist">
    <li><a href="index.html">Home</a></li>
    <li><a href="history.html">History</a></li>
    <li><a href="how.html">How it Works</a></li>
    <li><a href="clubs.html">Balloon Clubs</a></li>
    <li><a href="festivals.html">Festivals</a></li>
    <li><a href="rides.html">Where to Ride</a></li>
    <li><a href="faq.html">FAQ</a></li>
</ul>
```

To create a vertical navigation bar, start by setting the margin and padding to zero and removing the default bullet:

```
ul#navlist {
    margin: 0;
    padding: 0;
    list-style-type: none;
}
```

Now style the <a> elements that reside within the <li> elements. Set the display to *block* for the links. Remove the underlining from the link text with the text-decoration property. Set a width of 140 pixels, and add a border that is 2 pixels wide and solid blue (#0033cc).

```
ul#navlist li a {
    text-decoration: none;
    display: block;
    width: 140px;
    border: 2px solid #0033cc;
}
```

This style rule results in the incomplete navigation bar in Figure 9-25. You can see the basic structure, but it needs more style rules to look better.

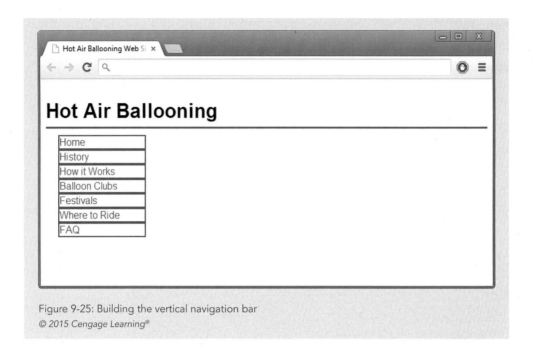

Figure 9-25: Building the vertical navigation bar
© 2015 Cengage Learning®

To finish the navigation bar, add 5 pixels of padding to offset the link text from the borders of the button. Set the background color to a light blue (#ccccff), and change the text color to black (#000). Finally, add 5 pixels of top margin to separate the buttons vertically.

```
ul#navlist li a {
    text-decoration: none;
    display: block;
    width: 140px;
    border: 2px solid #0033cc;
    padding: 5px;
    background-color: #ccccff;
    color: #000;
    margin-top: 5px;
}
```

Adding this code results in the finished navigation bar shown in Figure 9-26.

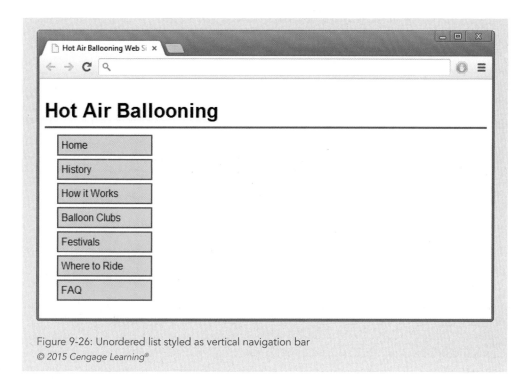

Figure 9-26: Unordered list styled as vertical navigation bar
© 2015 Cengage Learning®

Using Background Color and Graphics to Enhance Navigation

You can use background colors and graphics in a variety of ways to enhance your navigation. For example, you can indicate the user's location in the web site with a graphic or by changing a background color. You can also create an interactive "hover" effect that changes a color or background when the user points to a navigation link.

Note | *Refer to Chapter 8 for more information on background graphics.*

Indicating History

You can use the link pseudo-classes (described in Chapter 4) along with CSS background images to show users where they have been on your web site. Figure 9-27 shows a simple table of contents where the user's visited links are indicated with a red check mark.

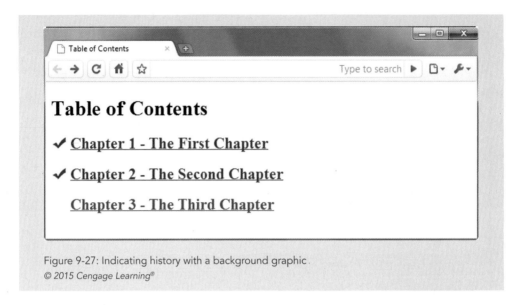

Figure 9-27: Indicating history with a background graphic.
© 2015 Cengage Learning®

To create this effect, you must leave enough room in the background area of the element to display the image. In this example, the <a> element content needs to be moved in from the left margin by 30 pixels, which you accomplish using the following style rule. Note that this style rule affects only <a> elements with a *class="chapter"* attribute, so that other <a> elements on the page are not affected.

```
a.chapter {padding-left: 30px;}
```

The result of this rule is that 30 pixels of white space are added to the left of the text, leaving room for the check mark to be displayed, as illustrated in Figure 9-28.

Figure 9-28: Using padding-left to make room for the check mark

The selector in the following style rule applies the background graphic only to <a> elements that have a state of *visited* and a class="chapter" attribute.

```
a:visited.chapter { }
```

You can then specify the background graphic's location, repetition, and positioning. The background image property points to the location of the file. The background-repeat property specifies that the image should only appear once. Finally, the background-position property states that the image is aligned horizontally to the left and vertically to the center height of the element.

```
a:visited.chapter {
    background-image: url(redcheck.jpg);
    background-repeat: no-repeat;
    background-position: left center;
}
```

The result of these styles is that the user will see a check mark next to any visited pages.

Indicating Location

The user's location in the web site can be indicated by a change in text weight, text color, background color, or with an indicating graphic commonly found on the web. Indicating location can be as simple as using bold text instead of a link in a navigation bar, as shown in Figure 9-29.

Figure 9-29: Indicating location with bold text
© 2015 Cengage Learning®

This is easy to accomplish with a style named *current*, for example, which is applied to the link text for the current page:

```
#current {
    font-weight: bold;
}
```

The *current* style rule can then be applied with a <span> element, identifying the current page in the code for the navigation bar as shown:

```
<ul id="navlist">
    <li><a href="index.html">Home</a></li>
    <li><span id="current">History</span></li>
    <li><a href="how.html">How it Works</a></li>
    <li><a href="clubs.html">Balloon Clubs</a></li>
    <li><a href="festivals.html">Festivals</a></li>
    <li><a href="rides.html">Where to Ride</a></li>
    <li><a href="faq.html">FAQ</a></li>
</ul>
```

The same type of style rule can be used to change any number of characteristics for the current page text. For example, to change the background color for the current page text, use the background-color property as shown:

```
#current {
    background-color: #f90000;
}
```

Creating Hover Rollovers

You can use the CSS :hover pseudo-class with a variety of effects to add interactivity when users scroll over a list of navigation links or buttons. You can change text colors, background colors, and background images based on user actions.

Changing Text Color and Background Color on Hover

Figure 9-30 shows an interactive hover that changes the text color and background color when the user hovers the mouse pointer over any of the links in the navigation bar.

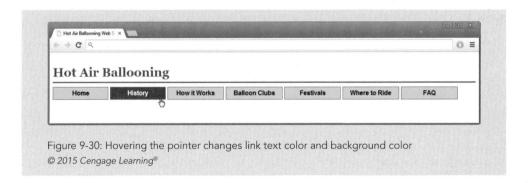

Figure 9-30: Hovering the pointer changes link text color and background color
© 2015 Cengage Learning®

Here are the style rules for the navigation bar. You saw very similar code used for the horizontal navigation bar in Figure 9-24.

```
ul#navlist {
    padding: 0;
    margin: 10px 0px 0px 0px;
    list-style-type: none;
}
ul#navlist li{
    display: inline;
    float: left;
}
ul#navlist a{
    font-family: arial, sans-serif;
    font-weight: bold;
    margin-right: 5px;
    border: solid 1px;
    padding: 5px 10px 5px 10px;
    text-decoration: none;
    color: #000;
    background-color: #ccccff;
    width: 125px;
    text-align: center;
    display: block;
}
```

The hover effect is created with the following style rule. Note that this rule selects only <a> elements within the <ul> element that have an *id="navlist"* element; otherwise, it would affect all <a> elements on the page. When the user hovers the mouse over the link, the text color changes to white (#fff), and the background color changes to blue (#0033cc). The font-weight property makes the text bold.

```
ul#navlist a:hover {
    color: #fff;
    background-color: #0033cc;
    font-weight: bold;
}
```

Changing Background Images on Hover

You can change background images as easily as changing background colors. For example, Figure 9-31 shows a navigation bar composed of three-dimensional button graphics. When the user hovers the pointer over a navigation button, the button changes color from dark blue to light blue. The buttons are CSS background images that are displayed behind the link text and switch from dark blue to light blue based on the user action.

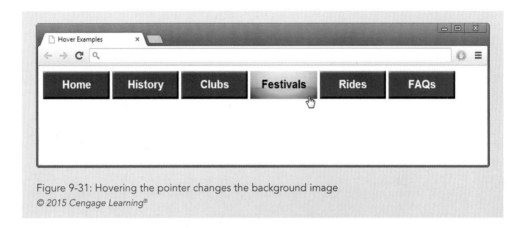

Figure 9-31: Hovering the pointer changes the background image
© 2015 Cengage Learning®

Figure 9-32 shows the two buttons used in this navigation bar.

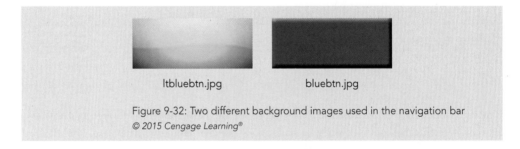

ltbluebtn.jpg   bluebtn.jpg

Figure 9-32: Two different background images used in the navigation bar
© 2015 Cengage Learning®

Here are the style rules that make up the navigation bar. Like the earlier example, the <a> element style rule includes the font characteristics for the link text, along with some padding and margin properties. The width and height of the <a> element matches the width and height of the button area, making the entire button clickable. Note that the background image specifies ltbluebtn.jpg.

```
ul#navlist {
    padding: 0;
    margin: 10px 0px 0px 0px;
```

```
        list-style-type: none;
    }
    ul#navlist li{
        display: inline;
        float: left;
    }
    a.navbutton{
        font-family: arial;
        font-size: 1.25em;
        font-weight: bold;
        padding-top: 12px;
        margin-right: 5px;
        text-decoration: none;
        width: 125px;
        height: 50px;
        text-align: center;
        display: block;
        color: #000;
        background-image: url(ltbluebtn.jpg);
        background-repeat: no-repeat;
    }
```

The hover effect is created with the following style rule. Note that this rule selects only <a> elements with a class="navbutton" attribute; otherwise, it would affect all <a> elements on the page. When the user hovers the pointer over the link, the background image changes from ltbluebtn.jpg to bluebtn.jpg.

```
    a.navbutton:hover {
        background-image: url(bluebtn.jpg)
        color: #fff;
    }
```

Underlining on Hover

Many web sites disable the default underlining of hypertext links. The CSS text-decoration property sets the value to *none*, which turns off hypertext linking, as shown in the following code:

```
    a {text-decoration: none;}
```

You can use the :hover pseudo-class to turn the underlining on when the user points to the link. The style rule looks like this:

```
a:hover {text-decoration: underline;}
```

> **Note**   *You can also use background colors to highlight links using the background-color property, as described in the Chapter 4 section titled "Using the :hover Pseudo-Class."*

You can create other linking effects by substituting a bottom border instead of the standard text underlining. In the following style rule, the border-bottom property is used to display a dashed blue line when the user points to the link, as shown in Figure 9-33.

```
a:hover {border-bottom: dashed blue;}
```

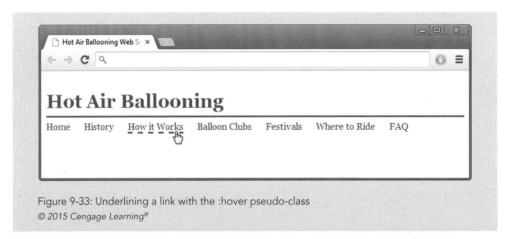

Figure 9-33: Underlining a link with the :hover pseudo-class
© 2015 Cengage Learning®

Skills at Work | Be a Champion for Accessibility

Whether you are designing navigation schemes for a web site or thinking about information architecture, keep in mind that many users come to the web with physical, cognitive, or technical barriers. You want to create web navigation designs that are legible and easy to access. When you are working with web site stakeholders, it is your job to advocate for the user and be a champion for accessible design. In your discussions with stakeholders and clients, remind them that accessibility is good for business because it attracts the most users to their site. Accessible navigation design leads to better design for all users.

Chapter Summary

Usable navigation is the result of working with the power of hypertext and designing for your users' needs. Keep the following points in mind:

> Work from the user's point of view. Think about where users want to go within your web site, and make it easy for them to get there.

> Add plenty of links to make all areas of your web site quickly accessible to users. Link to fragments as well as whole pages. Make it easy to get back to your navigation options.

> In addition to providing links, make sure you provide plenty of location cues to let users know where they are.

> Use text-based navigation bars to link users to other pages in your site. Use other text-based links to help users move through a long page of information or through a table of contents.

> Consider text as an alternative to graphical links. Every graphic adds to download time. When using graphics and icons as navigational links, make sure users can interpret these links correctly by including text as part of the images. Also, be sure to use navigation icons consistently throughout your web site to provide predictable cues for users and to minimize download time, especially for mobile users.

> Include alt values with your <img> tags to provide alternate navigation options for users.

> Use CSS to build attractive horizontal and vertical navigation bars using simple list elements.

> You can use background colors, text colors, and graphics to enhance navigation by indicating the user's history or location in the web site.

> You can use the :hover pseudo-class to add interactivity to navigation.

Key Terms

breadcrumb path—A series of links, usually at the top of a web page, that shows the user's location within the site hierarchy. Users can click any of the links in the path to move through the content structure.

contextual link—A link that allows users to jump to related ideas or cross-references by clicking the word or item that interests them. You can embed contextual links directly in your content by choosing the key terms and concepts you anticipate your users will want to follow.

fragment identifier—The use of the <a> element and name attribute to name a segment of an HTML file. You then can reference the fragment name in a hypertext link.

Review Questions

1. List three advantages of linking by using text instead of graphics.

2. What four navigation questions should the user be able to answer?

3. List three types of navigation cues.

4. List three ways to control information overload when designing a web site.

5. Explain why you would include both graphic and text-based links on a web page.

6. List two navigation cues you can add to a text-based navigation bar.

7. Why is it best to make <a> the innermost element to a piece of text?

8. What <a> tag attribute is associated with fragment identifiers?

9. List two ways to break up lengthy HTML pages.

10. What attribute do you use to make an <a> tag both a source and destination anchor?

11. How do you link to a fragment in an external file?

12. Page turners work best in what type of structure?

13. What are the benefits of contextual linking?

14. List two reasons for standardizing graphics.

15. What are the benefits of using navigation graphics?

16. What are the drawbacks of using navigation icons?

17. What are the benefits of using the alt attribute?

Hands-On Projects

1. This book's Online Companion web site contains all the HTML files for the sample web site illustrated in Figure 9-6. Use these sample HTML files to build an alternate navigation scheme. Refer to the information structure illustrations in Chapter 3 (Figure 3-8 through Figure 3-16) for examples of different navigation models. Choose a structure and code examples of usable navigation for the model.

2. In this project, you build a horizontal navigation bar. The code you add to the file in the following steps appears in blue.
   a. Copy the **ch9project2.html** file from the Chapter09 folder provided with your Data Files to the Chapter09 folder in your work folder. (Create the Chapter09 folder, if necessary.)

b.   Start your text editor, and open the file **ch9project2.html**. The HTML code is an unordered list with an id of navlist.

```
<ul id="navlist">
<li><a href=" ">Welcome</a></li>
<li><a href=" ">Services</a></li>
<li><a href=" ">Portfolio</a></li>
<li><a href=" ">About Us</a></li>
<li><a href=" ">Contact Us</a></li>
<li><a href=" ">FAQ</a></li>
</ul>
```

c.   Open the **ch9project2.html** file in a browser. The list should look like Figure 9-34.

Figure 9-34: Unstyled menu list
© 2015 Cengage Learning®

d.   In the style section, create a selector for the navigation list:

```
ul#navlist { }
```

e.   Add style properties to remove the default spacing and bullets from the unordered list:

```
ul#navlist {
    padding: 0;
    margin: 0;
    list-style-type: none;
}
```

f. Write another rule that selects the \<li\> elements and sets them to inline display:

```
ul#navlist li{
    display: inline;
}
```

g. Write a third style that selects the \<a\> elements containing the link text. Add a right margin to provide some white space between each link in the horizontal list:

```
ul#navlist a{
    margin-right: 20px;
}
```

h. Save your file, and view it in your browser. The finished navigation bar looks like Figure 9-35.

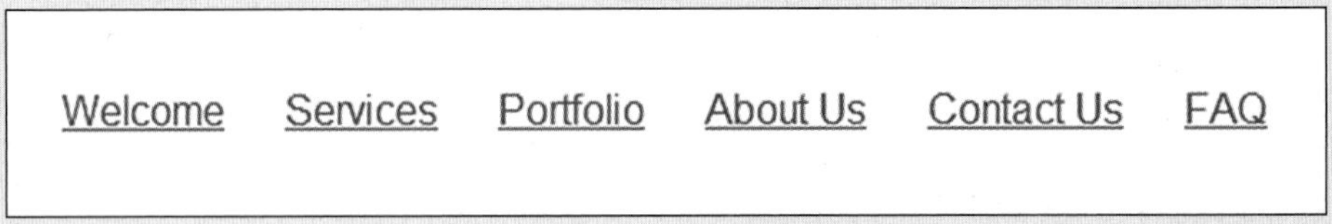

Welcome   Services   Portfolio   About Us   Contact Us   FAQ

Figure 9-35: Completed horizontal navigation bar
© 2015 Cengage Learning®

3. In this project, you build a vertical navigation bar. The code you add to the file in the following steps appears in blue.

a. Copy the **ch9project3.html** file from the Chapter09 folder provided with your Data Files to the Chapter09 folder in your work folder. (Create the Chapter09 folder, if necessary.)

b. Start your text editor, and open the file **ch9project3.html**. The HTML code is an unordered list with an id of navlist.

```
<ul id="navlist">
<li><a href=" ">Welcome</a></li>
<li><a href=" ">Services</a></li>
<li><a href=" ">Portfolio</a></li>
<li><a href=" ">About Us</a></li>
<li><a href=" ">Contact Us</a></li>
<li><a href=" ">FAQ</a></li>
</ul>
```

c. Open the **ch9project3.html** file in a browser. The list should look like Figure 9-36.

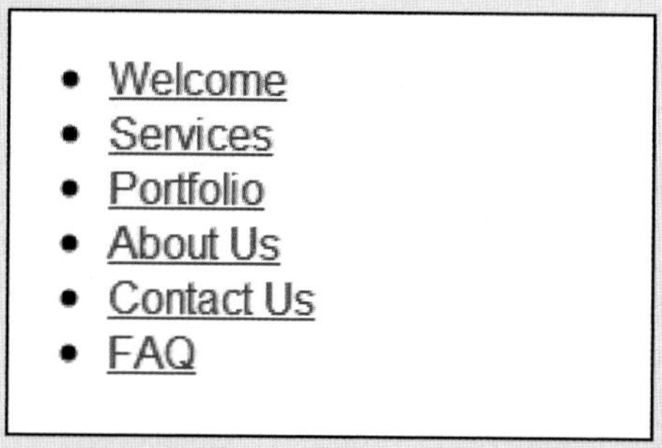

- Welcome
- Services
- Portfolio
- About Us
- Contact Us
- FAQ

Figure 9-36: Unordered list in the beginning
vertical navigation bar file
© 2015 Cengage Learning®

d. In the style section, create a selector for the navigation list:

```
ul#navlist { }
```

e. Add style properties to remove the default spacing and bullets from the unordered list:

```
ul#navlist {
    padding: 0;
    margin-left: 30px
    list-style-type: none;
}
```

f. Create a second rule that selects the `<a>` elements residing within the `<li>` elements:

```
ul#navlist li a { }
```

g. Add style rules that set the display to *block* for the links. Remove the underlining from the link text with the text-decoration property. Set a width of 140 pixels, and add a 2-pixel solid border.

```
ul#navlist li a {
    text-decoration: none;
    display: block;
    width: 140px;
    border: 2px solid;
}
```

h. Finish the navigation bar by adding 5 pixels of padding to offset the link text from the borders of the button. Also add 5 pixels of top margin to separate the buttons vertically.

```
ul#navlist li a {
    text-decoration: none;
    display: block;
    width: 140px;
    border: 2px solid;
    padding: 5px;
    margin-top: 5px;
}
```

i. Save your file, and view it in your browser. The finished navigation bar looks like Figure 9-37.

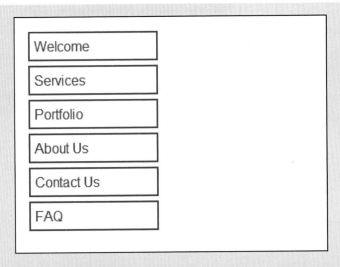

Figure 9-37: Completed vertical navigation bar
© 2015 Cengage Learning®

4. Browse the web and find a web site that has a successful navigation design. Write a short summary that explains why the navigation is effective and how it fits the user's needs. Consider the following criteria:
   a. Are the linking text and images meaningful?
   b. Is it easy to access the site's features?
   c. Can you easily search for content?
   d. Is there a site map or other site-orienting feature?

5. Find an online shopping web site.
   a. Examine the navigation options, and indicate whether you think the navigation adds to or detracts from the online shopping experience.
   b. Describe how to change the navigation to increase its effectiveness.

6. Find an online information resource likely to be used for research. Examine the navigation options, and describe how the navigation helps or hinders the user's information-searching process. Consider the following:
   a. How cluttered is the user interface? Does it deter finding information?
   b. Is navigation prominent or secondary to the page design? Does the user always know his or her location in the site? Is the linking text concise and easy to understand? Is the link destination easy to determine from the linking text?
   c. How deep is the structure of the site? How many clicks does it take to get to the desired information?

7. Browse the web to find examples of web sites that need better navigation options. Using examples from the web site, describe how you would improve the navigation choices.

8. Browse the web to find a web site that uses more than one navigation method. Describe whether this approach benefits the web site and why.

9. Find a site that illustrates a navigation method different from the ones described in this chapter. Describe the navigation method; state whether this approach benefits the web site and why.

Individual Case Project

Examine the flowchart you created for your web site. Consider the requirements of both internal and external navigation. Create a revised flowchart that shows the variety of navigation options you are planning for the web site.

Using your HTML editor, mark up examples of navigation bars for your content. Make sure your filenames are intact before you start coding. Save the various navigation bars as separate HTML files for later inclusion in your web pages.

Plan the types of navigation graphics you want to create. Sketch page banners, navigation buttons, and related graphics. Find sources for navigation graphics. For example, you can use public domain (noncopyrighted) clip art collections on the web for basic navigation arrows and other graphics.

Team Case Project

Work as a team to examine and discuss the flowchart you created for your web site. Consider the requirements of both internal and external navigation. Collaborating as a team, refine your work to create a revised flowchart that shows the variety of navigation options you are planning for the web site. Make sure you have standardized your filenames and that all team members agree on the naming conventions.

Work individually to create text-based navigation bars for your content. Use your HTML editor to mark up examples of navigation bars for site navigation. Save the various navigation bars as separate HTML files. Have a team meeting where all members can present their navigation schemes. Choose the best scheme or combine features from different schemes to create the navigation for the group's web site.

Work together to plan the types of navigation graphics you want to create. Assign team members to complete the remaining tasks, which include sketching page banners, navigation buttons, and related graphics, as well as finding sources for navigation graphics. For example, you can use public domain (noncopyrighted) clip art collections on the web for basic navigation arrows and other graphics.

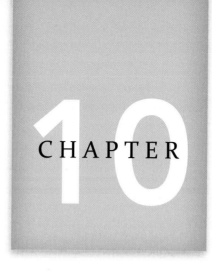

CHAPTER

DATA TABLES

When you complete this chapter, you will be able to:

> Use table elements

> Use table headers and footers

> Style table borders

> Apply padding, margins, and floats to tables

> Style table background colors

> Apply table styles

The 3.2 release of HTML in 1997 included table elements for the purpose of organizing tabular data in rows and columns. Web designers quickly realized they could use the table elements to build print-like design structures that allowed them to break away from the left-alignment constraints of basic HTML. With tables, web designers had the control and the tools to build columnar layouts, align text, add white space, and structure pages. This misuse of the table elements, although well intentioned, created problems with web site accessibility and compatibility. CSS has long offered the potential for an alternate page layout system, but browser support had to catch up before CSS could become a viable method. The flexibility, accessibility, and ease of maintaining layouts created with CSS makes them the clear choice for designing web pages, as detailed in Chapter 7. Now that CSS page layouts are broadly supported, tables should be used only to present data, as described in this chapter.

Using Table Elements

To build effective tables, you must be familiar with the HTML table elements. This section describes the most commonly used table elements.

HTML tables are designed not only to present data properly in the browser window, but to be read sequentially by screen readers and other assistive devices. Some of the table features available to web designers include the ability to span rows and columns and to create table header cells that declare the contents of a column of data.

The HTML table elements allow the arrangement of data into rows, cells, and columns. Table 10-1 lists the table elements and their usage.

ELEMENT	DESCRIPTION
table	Establishes the table; contains all other elements that specify caption, rows, and content
tr	Table row; contains the table cells
td	Table data cell; contains the table data
th	Table header cell; contains header information for a column of data
caption	Provides a short description of the table's contents
thead	Signifies table header
tbody	Signifies table body
tfoot	Signifies table footer
col	Specifies column properties
colgroup	Specifies multiple column properties

Table 10-1: HTML Table Elements
© 2015 Cengage Learning®

The HTML <table> element contains the table information, which consists of table header elements (<th>), table row elements (<tr>), and individual table data cells (<td>). These are the three elements used most frequently when you are building tables. Figure 10-1 shows a basic HTML table with a caption, headers, and rows of data. This table also has an accompanying style that sets a border for each of the cells. The style rule looks like this:

```
th, td {border: solid 1px black;}
```

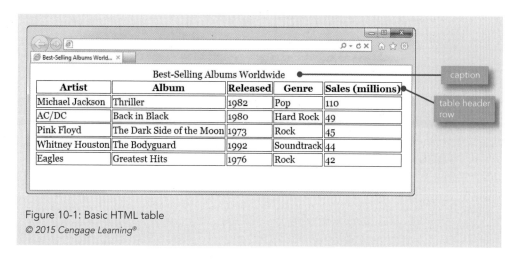

Figure 10-1: Basic HTML table

© 2015 Cengage Learning®

The basic table is the result of the following code:

```
<table>
<caption>Best-Selling Albums Worldwide</caption>
    <tr>
        <th>Artist</th>
        <th>Album</th>
        <th>Released</th>
        <th>Genre</th>
        <th>Sales (millions)</th>
    </tr>
    <tr>
        <td>Michael Jackson</td>
        <td>Thriller</td>
        <td>1982</td>
        <td>Pop</td>
        <td>110</td>
    </tr>
    <tr>
        <td>AC/DC</td>
        <td>Back in Black</td>
        <td>1980</td>
        <td>Hard Rock</td>
```

```
      <td>49</td>
   </tr>
   <tr>
      <td>Pink Floyd</td>
      <td>The Dark Side of the Moon</td>
      <td>1973</td>
      <td>Rock</td>
      <td>45</td>
   </tr>
   <tr>
      <td>Whitney Houston</td>
      <td>The Bodyguard</td>
      <td>1992</td>
      <td>Soundtrack</td>
      <td>44</td>
   </tr>
   <tr>
      <td>Eagles</td>
      <td>Greatest Hits</td>
      <td>1976</td>
      <td>Rock</td>
      <td>42</td>
   </tr>
</table>
```

> **Note**
>
> Table code can get complicated when you add content to your tables. One small error in your code can cause unpredictable results in the browser. You can simplify your table creation and maintenance tasks by writing clean, commented code. If you use plenty of white space in your code, you will find tables easier to access and change. Adding comments helps you quickly find the code you want.

The <table> element contains the rows and cells that make up the table. The <tr> tag marks the beginning and end of each of the five rows of the table. Notice that the <tr> tag contains the table cells, but no content of its own.

You may occasionally use the <caption> and <th> elements when creating tables. The <caption> element lets you add a caption to the table. By default, captions are displayed at the top of the table. The <caption> element must appear immediately after the opening table tag, as shown in the code sample for Figure 10-1. You will see how to use CSS to style the caption element later in this chapter.

The <th> element lets you create a table header cell that presents the cell content as bold and centered by default.

Collapsing Table Borders

Notice that each cell in the table shown in Figure 10-1 has its own border. This can make the data in the table difficult to read. The table will be more legible with the table borders collapsed. You can specify this setting with the CSS border-collapse property.

border-collapse property description	
Value:	separate | collapse
Initial:	separate
Applies to:	<table> element
Inherited:	yes

The following style rule collapses the borders for the table, as shown in Figure 10-2.

```
table {border-collapse: collapse;}
```

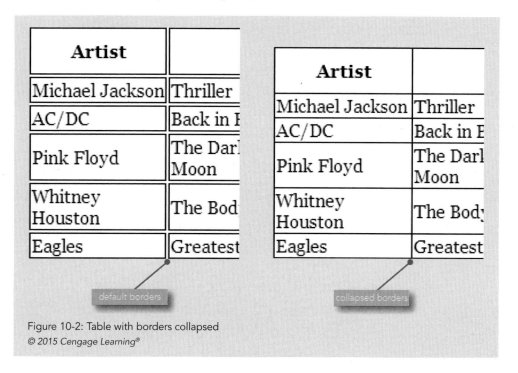

Figure 10-2: Table with borders collapsed
© 2015 Cengage Learning®

Spanning Columns

The **colspan** attribute lets you create cells that span multiple columns of a table. Column cells always span to the right. Figure 10-3 shows a table with a column span in the first row.

The following code fragment shows the colspan attribute in blue:

```
<tr>
    <td class="title" colspan="5">
    Best-Selling Albums Worldwide</td>
</tr>
```

Notice that this cell also contains a class="title" attribute, which is used to apply a CSS text-align property to center the text in the cell.

When you build column spans, make sure that all of your columns add up to the correct number of cells. In this code, because each row has five cells, the colspan attribute is set to five to span all columns of the table, as shown in Figure 10-3.

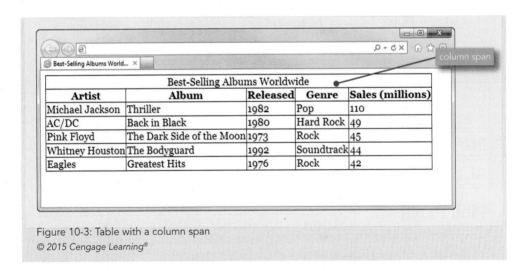

Figure 10-3: Table with a column span
© 2015 Cengage Learning®

Spanning Rows

The **rowspan** attribute lets you create cells that span multiple rows of a table. Rows always span down. Figure 10-4 shows a table with a row span added to the left of the data cells. Adding a row span usually means adding an extra cell to accommodate the span.

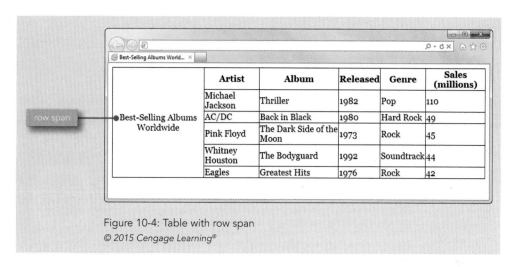

Figure 10-4: Table with row span
© 2015 Cengage Learning®

The following code shows the new cell that contains the rowspan attribute and the extra column cell in the table header row:

```
<table>
    <tr>
        <td class="title" rowspan="6">
        Best-Selling Albums Worldwide</td>
        <th>Artist</th>
        <th>Album</th>
        <th>Released</th>
        <th>Genre</th>
        <th>Sales (millions)</th>
    </tr>
... rest of the table code ...
</table>
```

The row span cell is the first cell in the first row of the table. It spans down through six rows of the table. Once again, note that a class="title" attribute is used to apply a text-align property to the text.

Using Table Headers and Footers

Rows can be grouped into head, body, and footer sections using the <thead>, <tbody>, and <tfoot> elements, as shown in the following code sample.

```
<table>
<thead>
```

```
        <tr><th>Header Cell 1</th>
            <th>Header Cell 2</th>
        </tr>
    </thead>
    <tbody>
        <tr><td>Body Cell 1</td>
            <td>Body Cell 2</td>
        </tr>
        <tr><td>Body Cell 3</td>
            <td>Body Cell 4</td>
        </tr>
    </tbody>
    <tfoot>
        <tr><td>Footer Cell 1</td>
            <td>Footer Cell 2</td>
        </tr>
    </tfoot>
</table>
```

The <thead> and <tfoot> elements can then be styled with style rules. Figure 10-5 shows an example of using CSS style rules to style the header and footer of a table.

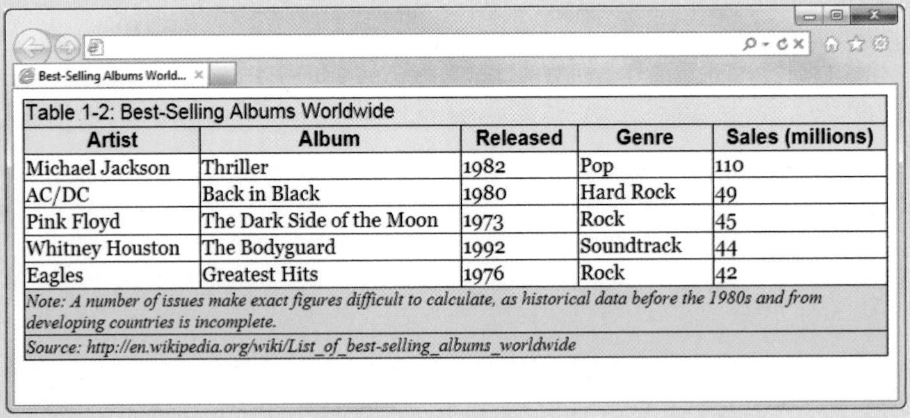

Figure 10-5: Table with styled headers and footers

```css
thead {
    font-family: arial;
    background-color: #ccddee;
}
tfoot {
    background-color: #ddccee;
    font-family: times, serif;
    font-size: .9em;
    font-style: italic;
}
```

```html
<table>
<thead>
    <tr>
    <td colspan="5">Table 1-2: Best-Selling Albums Worldwide
        </caption>
    </tr>
    <tr>
        <th>Artist</th>
        <th>Album</th>
        <th>Released</th>
        <th>Genre</th>
        <th>Sales (millions)</th>
    </tr>
</thead>
... rest of table code ...
<tfoot>
    <tr>
    <td colspan="5"> Note: A number of issues make exact figures
    difficult to calculate, as historical data before the 1980s
    and from developing countries is incomplete.</td>
    </tr>
    <tr>
    <td colspan="5"> Source: http://en.wikipedia.org/wiki/
    List_of_best-selling_albums_worldwide</td>
```

```
        </tr>
    </tfoot>
</table>
```

Grouping Columns

The <colgroup> and <col> elements allow you to apply style characteristics to groups of columns or individual columns in a table. The <colgroup> element has a span attribute that lets you set the number of columns specified in the group. Column groups are always applied left to right in the table. The only other available property is width, which lets you specify the width of a column or group of columns.

> **Note** Only the width property and the background properties, such as background-color and background-image, can be applied to the <colgroup> and <col> elements.

The <col> element lets you specify style characteristics for individual columns. It always appears within a set of <colgroup> tags. Both <colgroup> and <col> elements must appear immediately after the opening <table> element, or after the <caption> element if the table contains a caption.

Figure 10-6 shows the use of the <colgroup> element applied to the sample table. In this five-column table, the columns are organized into two column groups. The left column group contains two columns, and the right column group contains three columns.

Figure 10-6: Applying styles to column groups
© 2015 Cengage Learning®

The code for the table follows. Notice that each column group contains a class name, which is used to apply a CSS background color to the column group. The <colgroup> elements appear directly after the <caption> element.

```
<table>
<caption>Best-Selling Albums Worldwide</caption>
<colgroup span="2" class="left"></colgroup>
<colgroup span="3" class="right"></colgroup>
<tr>
    <th>Artist</th>
    <th>Album</th>
    <th>Released</th>
    <th>Genre</th>
    <th>Sales (millions)</th>
  </tr>
... rest of table code ...
```

You can use the <col> element to apply class names and style individual columns. The following HTML code in the table shows each column with a class name.

```
<colgroup>
    <col class="artist" />
    <col class="album" />
    <col class="released" />
    <col class="genre" />
    <col class="sales" />
</colgroup>
```

These class names can be used as selectors in the style sheet. The following style rule selects the column with the class name *artist* and applies a background color to the column, as shown in Figure 10-7.

```
col.artist {background-color: #ddeeff;}
```

Best-Selling Albums Worldwide				
Artist	**Album**	**Released**	**Genre**	**Sales (millions)**
Michael Jackson	Thriller	1982	Pop	110
AC/DC	Back in Black	1980	Hard Rock	49
Pink Floyd	The Dark Side of the Moon	1973	Rock	45
Whitney Houston	The Bodyguard	1992	Soundtrack	44
Eagles	Greatest Hits	1976	Rock	42

Figure 10-7: Selecting one column and applying a background color
© 2015 Cengage Learning®

Styling the Caption

You can style the caption with CSS to position the caption on the top or bottom of the table using the caption-side property. You can also choose from any of the other style properties to enhance the caption text.

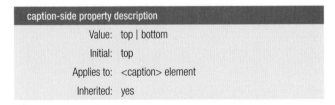

caption-side property description	
Value:	top | bottom
Initial:	top
Applies to:	<caption> element
Inherited:	yes

Figure 10-8 shows the caption left-aligned and italic. The style rule that follows shows the use of common CSS properties to specify text alignment, font style, and padding.

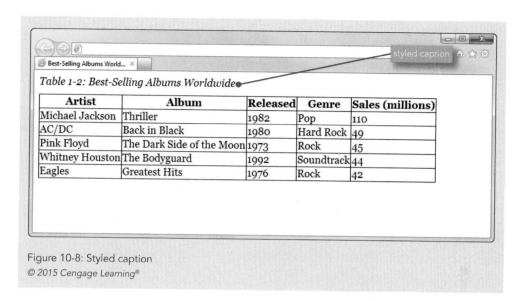

Figure 10-8: Styled caption
© 2015 Cengage Learning®

```
<style>
body {
    font-family: georgia;
}

table {
    border-collapse: collapse;
}

th, td {
    border: solid 1px black;
}

caption {text-align: left;
    font-style: italic;
    padding-bottom: 10px;
}
</style>
```

Styling Table Borders

By default, tables are displayed in the browser without borders. You can add borders to tables using CSS style rules. Borders can be applied to the whole table, to individual rows, and to individual cells. Using the table element as a selector applies the border only to the outside of the table, as shown in Figure 10-9.

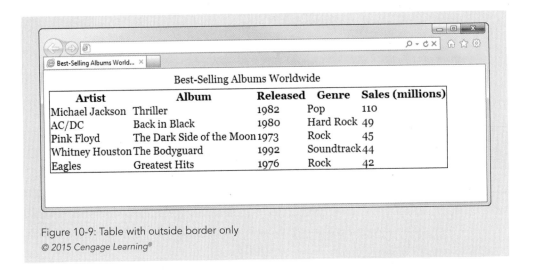

Figure 10-9: Table with outside border only
© 2015 Cengage Learning®

The style rule for this table looks like the following code. Note that the border-collapse property is used to remove the extra space between the borders.

```
table {
    border: solid 1px black;
    border-collapse: collapse;
}
```

Recall from Chapter 6 that borders do not inherit styles, so you can add borders for each cell by specifying them in a separate style rule. The sample table has two types of cells: table header cells <th> and table data cells <td>. These must each be added as selectors to make sure every cell has a border. The style rule looks like the following code, and the result is shown in Figure 10-10. Notice that the <th> and <td> elements share the same style declaration.

```
table {
    border: solid 1px black;
    border-collapse: collapse;
}
th, td {
    border: solid 1px black;
}
```

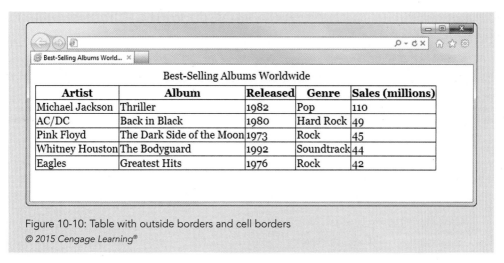

Figure 10-10: Table with outside borders and cell borders
© 2015 Cengage Learning®

You can also style individual row and cell borders using classes or ids to make specific selections in the table. For example, a row selector could look like the following:

```
tr.header {background-color: #ccddee;}
```

You would apply this rule using the class attribute in the specific row you want to have the background color:

```
<tr class="header">
```

Figure 10-11 shows a table that has the header row styled with a thick blue bottom border and light blue background color.

Figure 10-11: Table header row with custom bottom border
© 2015 Cengage Learning®

The style rule for this table shows the selector for the <th> elements with properties that set the border and background color.

```
table {
    border: solid 1px black;
    border-collapse: collapse;
}
th, td {
    border: solid 1px black;
}
th {
    border-bottom: solid thick blue;
    background-color: #ccddee;
}
```

Applying Padding, Margins, and Floats to Tables

The box properties can be applied to tables to increase spacing within cells, add white space around tables, and float them within blocks of text.

Note | *See Chapter 6 for more information on the box model properties.*

Using Padding

You can enhance the legibility of your table data by adding padding values for the entire table, or alternately adding padding values in individual rows or cells with class selectors. The <table> element does not accept the padding property, so you have to apply it to the <th> and <td> elements. This style rule adds 5 pixels of padding to both types of table elements:

```
th, td {padding: 5px;}
```

The table in Figure 10-12 uses this style rule to apply 5 pixels of padding to every cell.

Figure 10-12: Table with 5 pixels of padding in each cell
© 2015 Cengage Learning®

```
table {
    border: solid 1px black;
    border-collapse: collapse;
}
th, td {
    border: solid 1px black;
    padding: 5px;
}
```

You can also specify individual padding properties for each cell or row. For example, you might specify that <th> cells have extra padding on the bottom:

```
th {padding-bottom: 10px;}
```

Figure 10-13 shows a table with 10 pixels of padding in the header row, and 5 pixels of padding in the data cells.

Figure 10-13: Table with 5 pixels of padding in each data cell and 10 pixels in header cell
© 2015 Cengage Learning®

The style rule has separate selectors for the <th> and <td> elements.

```
table {
    border: solid 1px black;
    border-collapse: collapse;
}

th {
    padding: 10px;
}

td {
    border: solid 1px black;
    padding: 5px;
}
```

Using Margins and Floats

Tables can be floated like any other block-level element. When you float a table next to a block of text, you can provide white space around the table with the margin properties.

Figure 10-14 shows a table floated to the left, with right and bottom margin settings to offset the table from text.

The World's Best-Selling Albums

Lorem ipsum dolor sit amet, consectetur adipiscing elit. Nam blandit nisl mauris. Suspendisse vestibulum lorem non mauris blandit in pharetra dolor pellentesque. Nunc at posuere diam. Nam eleifend varius tincidunt. Nulla gravida mi a erat consectetur commodo. Ut aliquet suscipit nibh, ac viverra orci consectetur nec. Sed id diam arcu, ac tincidunt ligula. Cras ornare mi vel diam varius placerat. Vestibulum mollis auctor nulla, eu rhoncus arcu rutrum sed. Nulla eleifend semper erat, a viverra tortor porta nec. Phasellus velit augue, aliquet nec pellentesque eu, tempus non mi. Curabitur nec gravida elit. Quisque porttitor ultrices eros, sit amet rhoncus velit dictum nec. Morbi commodo euismod iaculis. Etiam euismod ullamcorper hendrerit. Nunc at orci et dui porta tempor at rhoncus massa. Vivamus aliquet, ligula ac semper commodo, diam mauris viverra turpis, non imperdiet nibh risus vel urna. Aliquam tincidunt iaculis interdum.

Table 1-1. Best-Selling Albums Worldwide

Artist	Album	Released	Genre	Sales
Michael Jackson	Thriller	1982	Pop	110 mil.
AC/DC	Back In Black	1980	Hard Rock	49 mil.
Pink Floyd	The Dark Side of the Moon	1973	Rock	45 mil.
Whitney Houston	The Bodyguard	1992	Soundtrack	44 mil.
Eagles	Greatest Hits	1976	Rock	42 mil.

Aliquam at porta nibh. Vestibulum mattis gravida nisi sit amet ornare. Praesent sed sem orci. Nulla magna augue, cursus ut tempus a, rutrum vitae mi. Quisque vel vehicula libero. Maecenas lorem velit, mattis id rutrum quis, elementum et metus. Aenean vestibulum convallis massa at consectetur. Maecenas eu dolor sem, at mattis lorem. Donec interdum mollis lacus, non vestibulum augue venenatis at. Cras eu lorem eget justo congue malesuada sed a urna. Maecenas sed sem a sapien sodales semper quis at urna. Donec hendrerit, sapien varius congue vulputate, velit urna eleifend erat, et tempus dolor mi tincidunt tortor.

Nulla facilisi. Duis iaculis feugiat nunc at iaculis. Suspendisse diam purus, tempor nec pretium in, ultrices at ligula. Integer rhoncus odio sit amet lectus porta lacinia. Curabitur dui massa, tincidunt eu hendrerit nec, volutpat sed diam. Class aptent taciti sociosqu ad litora torquent per conubia nostra, per inceptos himenaeos. Etiam dui mauris, blandit ac sollicitudin fermentum, rhoncus non mauris. Nulla mattis auctor lectus at molestie. Cras ante nunc, fermentum non luctus ac, aliquet non neque. Maecenas varius congue blandit. Nunc quam tellus, gravida quis vulputate vel, viverra dignissim sapien. Ut dictum placerat faucibus. Integer urna libero, tincidunt sed pharetra non, commodo sit amet justo. Etiam vitae mauris at dolor pulvinar vestibulum. Proin pulvinar enim interdum metus feugiat et sodales dolor blandit. Fusce placerat malesuada quam, sit amet feugiat velit convallis eget. Nam quam felis, condimentum ut lacinia dapibus, convallis sed quam. Nulla facilisi. Nulla porta, sapien in tristique varius, leo erat vehicula arcu, semper fermentum nunc orci congue leo. Cum sociis natoque penatibus et magnis dis parturient montes, nascetur ridiculus mus.

Donec lacus purus, dictum at ornare a, convallis ac elit. Vestibulum ac massa est, et euismod enim. Nam sed diam et ipsum placerat laoreet. Curabitur mauris arcu, sagittis a interdum at, cursus id tortor. Aliquam in accumsan nulla. Lorem ipsum dolor sit amet, consectetur adipiscing elit. Nunc vel blandit sapien. In elementum ipsum quis risus rutrum eget ultrices leo accumsan. Proin sodales pharetra metus quis pellentesque. Proin nec molestie arcu. Quisque in elit massa. Aliquam sed libero diam, eu ultrices turpis. Aliquam erat volutpat. Fusce dapibus imperdiet nulla non pellentesque. Praesent sit amet turpis lacus, eget mollis diam. Fusce mollis, risus non mollis hendrerit, magna dui placerat elit, sed suscipit purus tellus non mauris. Nullam euismod sem id quam porttitor condimentum. Lorem ipsum dolor sit amet, consectetur adipiscing elit. Vestibulum ante

Figure 10-14: Table floated to the left with right and bottom margins
© 2015 Cengage Learning®

The style rule for this table follows. Notice that the table has a class selector named *best* that specifies only this particular table for these style rules. The table has float and margin properties that position it on the page.

```
table.best {
    font-family: verdana;
    border: solid 1px black;
    border-collapse: collapse;
    float: left;
    margin-right: 20px;
    margin-bottom: 10px;
}
th, td {
    border: solid 1px black;
    padding: 5px;
}
```

```
caption {
    padding-bottom: 5px;
    text-align: left;
    font-style: italic;
}
```

> **Note** | Remember that you can select and style individual tables by giving them a class or id name to apply style rules only to the selected table.

Styling Table Background Colors

You can use the background color properties to add legibility to your table data. You can apply background colors to an entire table, single out rows and cells, or use the <colgroup> and <col> properties to highlight individual columns. You can alternate colors for different rows of data, or add hover interaction that highlights data when a user selects rows or cells.

Specifying Background Color

Background colors can make your tables easier to read by providing contrast. Figure 10-15 shows a table with different background colors for the column titles and data. Notice that the text in the column titles is white against the dark blue background.

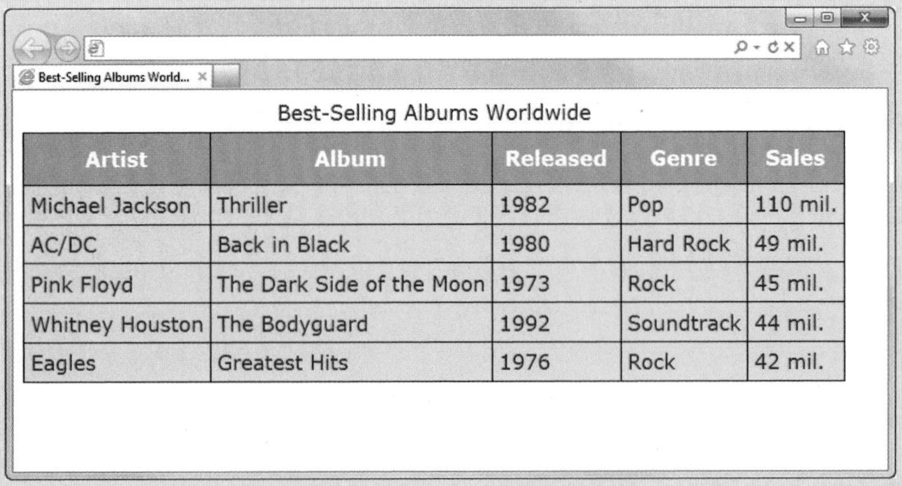

Best-Selling Albums Worldwide				
Artist	**Album**	**Released**	**Genre**	**Sales**
Michael Jackson	Thriller	1982	Pop	110 mil.
AC/DC	Back in Black	1980	Hard Rock	49 mil.
Pink Floyd	The Dark Side of the Moon	1973	Rock	45 mil.
Whitney Houston	The Bodyguard	1992	Soundtrack	44 mil.
Eagles	Greatest Hits	1976	Rock	42 mil.

Figure 10-15: Styling table background colors
© 2015 Cengage Learning®

The style rules for this table specify background and text colors for the <th> elements and a different background color for the <td> elements.

```
table {
    border: solid 1px black;
    border-collapse: collapse;
    color: #722750
}
td, th {
    border: solid 1px black;
    padding: 5px;
}
caption {
    padding-bottom: 5px;
}
th {
    padding: 10px;
    background-color: #7fa2c1;
    color: white;
}
td {
    background-color: #ccdae6;
}
```

Creating Alternate Color Rows

Table data becomes much easier to read when alternate rows have a distinguishing background color. This effect is easy to create with a structural pseudo-class (described in Chapter 4) that selects the alternate rows. Write a style rule for the odd (or even) row using a pseudo-class selector that specifies the *odd* class rows. The selector is *:nth-child(odd)* as shown:

```
tr:nth-child(odd) td {background-color: #eaead5;}
```

You can also select the even rows:

```
tr:nth-child(even) td {background-color: #eaead5;}
```

Notice in this style rule that a descendant selector, td, follows the pseudo-class selector. This syntax selects every other row and applies the background color to the child <td> elements in the selected rows.

```
tr:nth-child(odd) td {background-color: #eaead5;}
```

The result is shown in Figure 10-16.

> **Note** You can learn about the options for pseudo-class selectors at www.w3.org/TR/css3-selectors/#pseudo-classes.

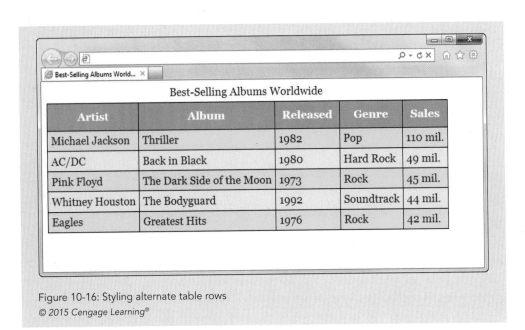

Figure 10-16: Styling alternate table rows
© 2015 Cengage Learning®

Creating Background Hover Effects

You can add interactivity to your table by adding hover effects. When a user hovers the pointer over a cell or row, the background, font, or formatting can change. Figure 10-17 shows a table with highlighted data activated by the pointer hovering over the cell.

Figure 10-17: Table cell hover
© 2015 Cengage Learning®

This effect uses the :hover pseudo-class described in Chapter 4. The following style rules state the default cell background color (#ccdae6) and the different background and text colors when the user hovers the pointer over a table cell.

```
td {
    background-color: #ccdae6;
}
td:hover {
    color: white;
    background-color: #722750;
}
```

This same effect can be used with a row of data by applying the hover to <tr> elements, as shown. These style rules show the default cell background and the alternate background and text colors when the user hovers the pointer over any row of data.

```
td {
    background-color: #ccdae6;
}
```

```
tr:hover td {
    color: white;
    background-color: #722750;
}
```

Figure 10-18 shows the result of the row hover.

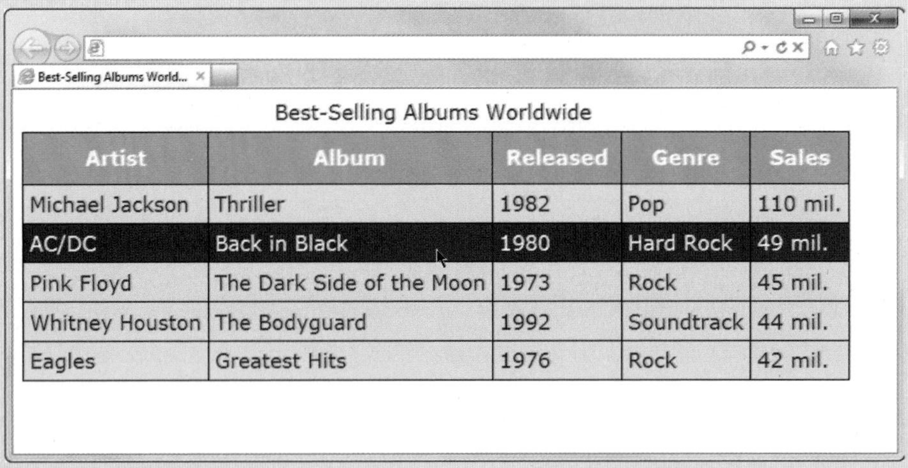

Figure 10-18: Table row hover
© 2015 Cengage Learning®

Activity: Applying Table Styles

In the following set of steps, you will style a table using CSS. Save your file, and test your work in the browser as you complete each step. Refer to Figure 10-22 as you progress through the steps to see the results. New code that you will add is shown in blue.

To style the table:

1. Copy the **ch10activity.html** file from the Chapter10 folder provided with your Data Files to the Chapter10 folder in your work folder. (Create the Chapter10 folder, if necessary.)

2. In your browser, open **ch10activity.html**. When you open the file, it looks like Figure 10-19.

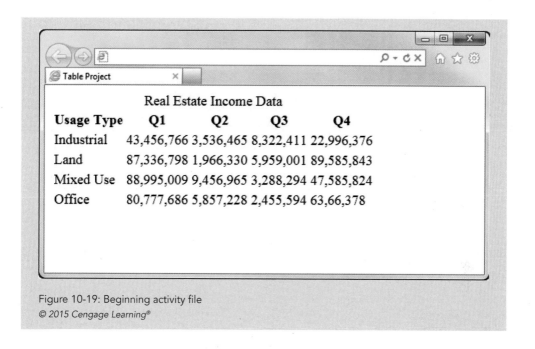

Figure 10-19: Beginning activity file
© 2015 Cengage Learning®

3. Start by setting a font family for the table. Use *table* as a selector, and specify Georgia as the font with an alternate generic font.

```
<style>
table {
    font-family: georgia, serif;
}
</style>
```

4. Specify a border for the outside of the table. Collapse the borders of the table as well.

```
table {
    font-family: georgia, serif;
    border: solid 1px black;
    border-collapse: collapse;
}
```

5. Specify a border and padding for both types of cell elements, <th> and <td>.

```
table {
    font-family: georgia, serif;
    border: solid 1px black;
```

```
      border-collapse: collapse;
}
th, td {
      border: solid 1px black;
      padding: 10px;
}
```

6. View the file in the browser. It should look like Figure 10-20.

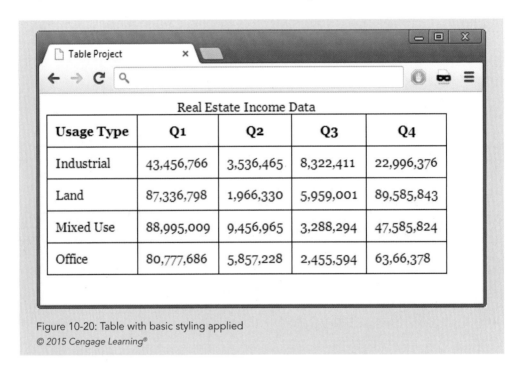

Real Estate Income Data

Usage Type	Q1	Q2	Q3	Q4
Industrial	43,456,766	3,536,465	8,322,411	22,996,376
Land	87,336,798	1,966,330	5,959,001	89,585,843
Mixed Use	88,995,009	9,456,965	3,288,294	47,585,824
Office	80,777,686	5,857,228	2,455,594	63,66,378

Figure 10-20: Table with basic styling applied
© 2015 Cengage Learning®

7. Add a background color for the header <th> cells.

```
th, td {
      border: solid 1px black;
      padding: 10px;
}
th {
      background-color: #d0dafd;
      color: #0070dd;
}
```

8. Prepare to add a background color to the far-left column by adding a <colgroup> element to the table code. Find the <caption> element in the table code, and add a <colgroup> element with class and span values as shown. These tags let you select the left column and apply a style to it.

```
<table>
<caption>Real Estate Income Data</caption>
<colgroup class="leftcol" span="1"></colgroup>
... rest of table code ...
```

9. Select the colgroup class, and apply a background color style as shown.

```
th {
    background-color: #d0dafd;
    color: #0070dd;
}
colgroup.leftcol {
    background-color: #d0dafd;
}
```

10. View the file in the browser. It should look like Figure 10-21.

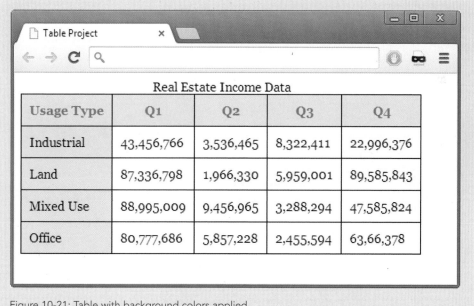

Figure 10-21: Table with background colors applied
© 2015 Cengage Learning®

11. Add a style for the caption that changes the font-family and adds some bottom padding to move it away from the table border.

```
colgroup.leftcol {
    background-color: #d0dafd;
}
caption {
    font-family: verdana, sans-serif;
    padding-bottom: 10px;
}
</style>
```

12. Finally, add a hover style that changes the background color when a user hovers over a cell.

```
caption {
    font-family: verdana, sans-serif;
    padding-bottom: 10px;
}
td:hover {
    background-color: #ff99ff;
}
</style>
```

13. View the file in the browser. It should look like Figure 10-22.

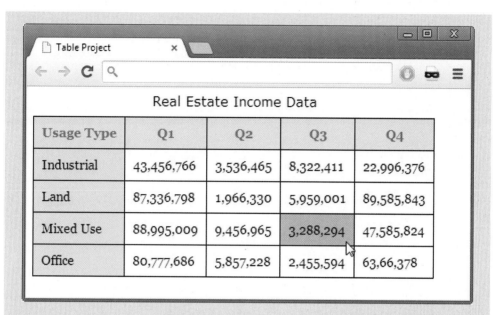

Figure 10-22: Finished styled table
© 2015 Cengage Learning®

Skills at Work | *Use Tables Effectively*

The purpose of a table on a web page is to organize related information. Usually, tables compare two or more categories of data, such as versions of HTML and the year each version was released. In some tables, the column headings list the categories, and the details in that category are listed in the column below the heading. In other tables, the row headings list the categories, with details listed in the row to the right of the heading. Tables are most valuable when they communicate a lot of information in a compact form. If you find yourself adding long explanations or even complete sentences to table cells, a table might not be the best format for that information. Instead, consider using a list with a short lead-in phrase followed by a longer explanation. Organize table data in a logical order. If you're ranking the top 10 movies of the last 25 years, list the movies in ascending or descending order. If the data doesn't lend itself to organization, list the categories in alphabetic order so the data is easy to reference.

Chapter Summary

⟩ Use tables for presentation of data, not for page layout.

⟩ To build effective data tables, you must be familiar with the HTML table elements, including the <table>, <caption>, <th>, <tr>, and <td> elements.

⟩ Use the grouping elements to apply styles to groups of rows or columns, or to the header, body, and footer of a table.

⟩ Apply borders to both the <table> and cell (<th> and <td>) elements to display a border on the entire table.

⟩ Use the border-collapse property to make table data more legible.

⟩ Always use CSS to add presentation style to tables.

⟩ Use padding to add space within your cells and make your data more legible.

⟩ You can float tables and add margins with the box model properties.

⟩ Specify background colors or hovers to aid in the legibility of your data.

Key Terms

<caption> element—An HTML element that lets you add a caption to a table.
colspan—An attribute that lets you create cells spanning multiple columns of a table.
rowspan—An attribute that lets you create cells spanning multiple rows of a table.
<table> element—An HTML element that contains table information.
table data cell (<td>)—An HTML element that contains the table data.
table header element (<th>)—An HTML element that contains the table header, which is the heading at the top of a column of data.
table row element (<tr>)—An HTML element that contains the table cells.

Review Questions

1. What are the three basic table elements?

2. What table element presents its content as bold and centered?

3. What table element lets you add a title for a table?

4. What CSS property can you use to change the alignment of the <caption> element?

5. What CSS property do you use to remove spacing between table cells?

6. What are the two table attributes that let you span columns and rows?

7. What value should colspan equal in the following code?

```
<tr><td>R1C1</td><td>R1C2</td><td>R1C3</td></tr>
<tr><td>R2C1</td><td colspan= >R2C2</td></tr>
```

8. What CSS property do you use to adjust spacing within table cells?

9. What HTML elements let you apply styles to table columns?

10. To which elements must you apply borders if you want to display them for an entire table?

11. Do border properties inherit from the <table> element to <td> elements?

12. What is one way to select a specific table row or cell?

13. What is a good way to add legibility to rows of data?

Hands-On Projects

1. In this project, you have a chance to apply some of the data table techniques you learned about in this chapter. As you work through the steps, refer to Figure 10-23 to see the results you will achieve. Save your file and test your work in the browser as you complete each step.

   a. Copy the **ch10project1.html** file from the Chapter10 folder provided with your Data Files to the Chapter10 folder in your work folder. (Create the Chapter10 folder, if necessary.)

   b. Open the file **ch10project1.html**. This is a blank HTML file with just the necessary structural elements, such as <head>, <body>, and so on.

   c. Build a simple table with four columns and five rows as shown. Copy the data shown in Figure 10-23 or use your own.

   d. Make sure you include the caption and header row.

   e. Display the results in a browser, and then compare them to Figure 10-23.

AFI Top 5 Movies			
#	Movie	Year	Director
1	Citizen Kane	1941	Orson Welles
2	The Godfather	1972	Francis Ford Coppola
3	Casablanca	1942	Michael Curtiz
4	Raging Bull	1980	Martin Scorsese
5	Singin' in the Rain	1952	Stanley Donen

Figure 10-23: Project 1 solution
© 2015 Cengage Learning®

2. In this project, you continue working in the **ch10project1.html** file from the previous exercise. As you work through the steps, refer to Figure 10-24 to see the results you will achieve. Save your file and test your work in the browser as you complete each step.

  a. Add the following style properties to the table in **ch10project1.html**:

   ◆ Font family: arial with a sans-serif fallback

   ◆ Table border: solid 4px blue

   ◆ All table borders collapsed

   ◆ Table cells border: solid 1px black

   ◆ Table cells padding: 10 pixels

  b. Display the results in a browser, and then compare them to Figure 10-24.

AFI Top 5 Movies			
#	Movie	Year	Director
1	Citizen Kane	1941	Orson Welles
2	The Godfather	1972	Francis Ford Coppola
3	Casablanca	1942	Michael Curtiz
4	Raging Bull	1980	Martin Scorsese
5	Singin' in the Rain	1952	Stanley Donen

Figure 10-24: Project 2 solution
© 2015 Cengage Learning®

3. In this project, you continue working in the file from the previous exercise. As you work through the steps, refer to Figure 10-25 to see the results you will achieve. Save your file and test your work in the browser as you complete each step.

    a. Style the table caption with the following properties:

         ◆ Alignment: left-aligned

         ◆ Font size: .85em

         ◆ Font style: italic

         ◆ Padding: 10 pixels on the bottom

    b. Display the results in a browser, and then compare them to Figure 10-25.

AFI Top 5 Movies

#	Movie	Year	Director
1	Citizen Kane	1941	Orson Welles
2	The Godfather	1972	Francis Ford Coppola
3	Casablanca	1942	Michael Curtiz
4	Raging Bull	1980	Martin Scorsese
5	Singin' in the Rain	1952	Stanley Donen

Figure 10-25: Project 3 solution
© 2015 Cengage Learning®

4. In this project, you continue working in the file from the previous exercise. As you work through the steps, refer to Figure 10-26 to see the results you will achieve. Save your file and test your work in the browser as you complete each step.

    a. Add a background color (#929292) and font-color (#fff) to the table header cells.

    b. Display the results in a browser, and then compare them to Figure 10-26.

AFI Top 5 Movies

#	Movie	Year	Director
1	Citizen Kane	1941	Orson Welles
2	The Godfather	1972	Francis Ford Coppola
3	Casablanca	1942	Michael Curtiz
4	Raging Bull	1980	Martin Scorsese
5	Singin' in the Rain	1952	Stanley Donen

Figure 10-26: Project 4 solution
© 2015 Cengage Learning®

5.   In this project, you continue working in the file from the previous exercise. As you
     work through the steps, refer to Figure 10-27 to see the results you will achieve. Save
     your file and test your work in the browser as you complete each step.
     a.   Add a background hover color (#66ccff) when the user points to a row of data.
     b.   Display the results in a browser, and then compare them to Figure 10-27.

AFI Top 5 Movies

#	Movie	Year	Director
1	Citizen Kane	1941	Orson Welles
2	The Godfather	1972	Francis Ford Coppola
3	Casablanca	1942	Michael Curtiz
4	Raging Bull	1980	Martin Scorsese
5	Singin' in the Rain	1952	Stanley Donen

Figure 10-27: Project 5 solution
© 2015 Cengage Learning®

Individual Case Project

Examine the content you are presenting in your project web site, and find data that would be enhanced by the use of a table. Write a single-page analysis or memo to your instructor that explains why you should or should not use tables to present your data. If your analysis warrants a table, then design and implement the table in the appropriate web page(s).

Team Case Project

As a team, examine the content you are presenting in your project web site, and find data that would be enhanced by the use of a table. Write a single-page analysis or memo to your instructor that explains why you should or should not use tables to present your data. If your analysis warrants a table, then design and implement the table in the appropriate web page(s).

WEB FORMS

When you complete this chapter, you will be able to:

> Understand how forms work

> Use the <form> element to create forms

> Create input objects

> Style forms with Cascading Style Sheets (CSS)

> Build a form

This chapter covers the HTML form elements. Forms let you build interactive web pages that collect information from a user and process it on the web server. You can use forms to gather information and create databases or to send customized responses to your users. Forms collect—but do not process—data. The data processing is performed by an application on the web server. Forms are the basis for online commerce; without them, users would not be able to enter their order choices, shipping address, and credit card information while shopping on the web.

Understanding How Forms Work

Figure 11-1 shows a typical form. You can use a variety of input elements for the form based on the type of information you want to gather from your user. Forms usually contain basic HTML formatting tags such as <p> and <br>. Forms can also be styled with CSS, which helps control their visual layout. Well-designed forms include active white space, aligned form elements, and clear labels. Use the design principles you have learned throughout this book to create forms that are legible and easy to use.

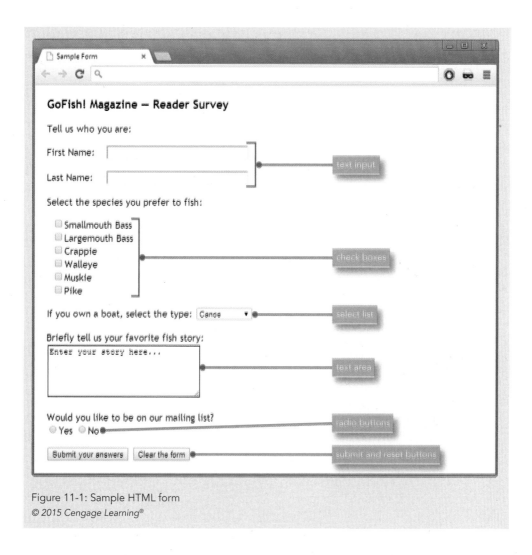

Figure 11-1: Sample HTML form
© 2015 Cengage Learning®

The HTML form itself is the interface for the user to enter data, but all of the actual data processing is performed on the server using applications that reside on the web server or in the Common Gateway Interface (CGI). The traditional method of processing forms input has been to use the Common Gateway Interface, which transfers data between the user and the server. Using programs called scripts, CGI can transfer the data sent by a user via the Hypertext Transfer Protocol (HTTP) and transfer it to a variety of data-processing programs, including spreadsheets, databases, or other software running on the server. The data-processing software can work with the data and send a response back to CGI, and then on to the user in the form of a web page generated by the application.

Although CGI is still in use, other alternatives are faster and more efficient. Most of the popular web server software, such as Apache on Linux web servers and Internet Information Service (IIS) on Windows web servers, have their own plug-in modules that run forms-processing software, while programming languages like Java, PHP, and PERL offer faster and more customizable options than the traditional CGI model.

The scripting language most often used with HTML forms is JavaScript, which was originally created for the Netscape browser in 1995. JavaScript is a client-side scripting language, which means that it runs on the user's computer, rather than on the server. JavaScript can enhance your web site with beneficial programming functions, including form field validation that checks a user's form entries for errors before the result is sent to a form script, which is a program that the data received from the form. As you will see later, validation is now more commonly performed by the browser, but scripting validation may still be necessary depending on the complexity of the data you are requesting and your security needs. A complete JavaScript tutorial is beyond the scope of this book, though many good references are available on the web.

Current trends in web development take advantage of the increased power in modern web browsers, which are more tightly integrated with HTML5 and CSS3 than earlier browsers. With the programming capabilities of JavaScript, web developers now have a more robust platform for building rich web-based applications.

Using the <form> Element to Create Forms

The <form> element is the container for creating a form, as the <table> element is the container for the elements that create a table. A form has several attributes that describe how the form data is handled, as shown in Table 11-1.

ATTRIBUTE	DESCRIPTION
action	The URL of the application that processes the form data; this URL points to a script file or an email address
enctype	The content type used to submit the form to the server (when the value of the method is *post*); most forms do not need this attribute
method	Specifies the HTTP method used to submit the form data; the default value is *get*
	> get—The form data is appended to the URL specified in the action attribute
	> post—The form data is sent to the server as a separate message
accept	A comma-separated list of content types that a server processing this form can handle correctly; most forms do not need this attribute
accept-charset	A list of allowed character sets for input data that is accepted by the server processing this form; most forms do not need this attribute

Table 11-1: Form Attributes
© 2015 Cengage Learning®

The <form> element by itself does not create a form. It must contain **form controls** (such as <input> elements) and structural elements such as <p> or <ul> to control the look of the form. CSS style classes let you select different form elements and control their look with style rules.

A variety of form controls are available for collection information, as described in the following sections. The following code shows a typical <form> element with some of the attributes listed in Table 11-1. This code specifies that the form data the user enters is being sent to a program named register.asp that resides on a web server.

```
<form method="post"
action="https://signup.website.com/register.asp">
```

Using get or post

The method you will specify in your form is often defined by the programmers who create the script that processes the form data. The difference between *get* and *post* is the way the data is sent to the server.

```
method="get"
```

The get method sends the form information by including it in the URL. The data is not secure and should not be used for passwords or other confidential information.

```
method="post"
```

The post method sends the form information securely to the server within the message body, so the data is not visible. This is the more common method for sending form data.

Using the mailto Action

With the mailto action, you can collect data from a form and send it to any email address. Although this method does not allow any data processing, it is fine for the occasional brief form or for simple web sites. The data is sent as a long string of text, which you can make easier to read by including the enctype="text/ plain" attribute. A <form> element with a mailto action looks like the following:

```
<form action="mailto:joel@joelsklar.com"
method="post" enctype="text/plain">
```

The data will be sent as an email message to the specified email address. For example, the data from an address form would look like this:

```
name=Joe User
street=3 Maple Lane
city=Smalltown
state=MA
zip=00000
```

The mailto action depends on whether users have email client software configured on their systems. If a mail client is configured, the user's email software will open when the user clicks the submit button. If no mail client is configured, the user will not be able to submit the form data.

Creating Input Objects

The <input> element defines many of the form input object types. Table 11-2 lists the available object types. You use the *type* attribute to specify the object type within the <input> element, such as:

```
<input type="text" name="firstname" id="First Name"
size="35" maxlength="35">
```

INPUT TYPE	DESCRIPTION
text	Creates a text entry field that lets the user enter a single word or a line of text; this is the default object type
password	Creates the same type of text entry field created by the value *text*, but the user's entry is masked by asterisks
checkbox	Provides on/off toggles that the user selects; check boxes are best used with multiple-answer questions, and multiple check boxes can contain the same name, which lets you group them together so users can select multiple values for the same property

Continued on next page...

INPUT TYPE	DESCRIPTION
radio	Lets a user choose one value from a range of values; when radio buttons are grouped together with the same name, only one choice can be selected
submit	Sends the form data to the server using the transmission method specified in the <form> element; every form needs a submit button
reset	Clears the form of any user-entered data and returns the form to its original state
hidden	Adds a control that is not displayed in the browser; the hidden type is useful for sending additional information with form data that may be needed for processing
image	Adds a graphic button to the form, rather than the default button
button	Creates a button that has no default behavior; the button's function is usually defined by a script; when the user pushes the button, the script function is triggered
file	Lets the user select a file that is submitted with the form

Table 11-2: <input> Element Types
Source: www.w3.org/TR/2011/WD-html5-20110525/the-input-element.html#attr-input-type

In addition to these 10 input types, which have been available since the inception of HTML, 13 new types are offered with HTML5. These new types are listed in Table 11-3. Make sure to test them carefully, as browser support is inconsistent. If your browser does not support one of the new input types, the <form> element will fall back to a type of *text*, so you can safely use the new types without worrying that your form will not work.

INPUT TYPE	DESCRIPTION
datetime	Global date and time with time zone information
datetime-local	A local date and time with no time zone information
date	A date only; in some browsers, this input type will open a calendar picker that lets the user choose a date
month	A calendar month
time	A time value
week	A calendar week
number	A number value; on mobile devices, this value can change the virtual keyboard to a number-entry keyboard, making it easier for the user to enter numbers. You can also add *min*, *max*, and *step* attributes to the <input> element to further describe the type of number allowed. For example: `<input type="number" min="0" max="10" step="2">` This element requires users to enter a value between 0 and 10. The step attribute means that the only acceptable values are 0, 2, 4, 6, 8, and 10.

Continued on next page...

INPUT TYPE	DESCRIPTION
range	A range of values. This input type is similar to the number type shown above. The difference is that the range of values is displayed in the browser as a slider control rather than a numeric text entry box. The code looks like this: `<input type="range" min="0" max="10" step="2">`
email	An email address. If the email address is not syntactically correct, some browsers will display an error message to the user. On mobile devices, this input type can change the virtual keyboard to include values that make it easier for the user to enter an e-mail address (for example, including a key for the @ symbol).
url	A URL value; this is an absolute URL, as described in Chapter 3. If the URL address is not syntactically correct, some browsers display an error message to the user. On mobile devices, this input type can change the virtual keyboard to include values that make it easier for the user to enter an URL (for example, including a key for the .com extension).
search	A search term
tel	A telephone number
color	A color name; if supported by the browser, this input type will display a color picker that lets the user choose a color value from a color wheel or color chart

Table 11-3: New HTML5 <input> Element Types
Source: www.w3.org/TR/2011/WD-html5-20110525/the-input-element.html#attr-input-type

The benefit of these new HTML5 input types is that they standardize much of the form entry data checking that previously was performed using JavaScript in the browser. In addition to server validation, Web developers now can rely on the browser to perform data validation with HTML5. For example, if a user enters an email address or date, the browser can validate the data to make sure it is in the correct format. If the data is incorrect, the browser can display a message asking the user to correct the data before the form is submitted to the server. Validation is automatic; if you do not want the form data to be validated, add the novalidate value to the opening form tag as shown:

```
<form method="post"
action="https://signup.website.com/register.asp" novalidate>
```

Creating Text Boxes

The text entry box is the most commonly used <form> input type. The default text box is 20 characters long, although you can change this value using the size attribute. The user can enter an unlimited number of characters in the text box, even if the visible length is exceeded. You can constrain the user's entry of text with the maxlength attribute and supply a default value for the text with the value attribute. The following code shows a simple form with two text boxes.

```
<form action=" action="http://someserver/script.php" method="post">
<p>Tell us who you are:</p>
<p>
    <label class="username" for="First Name">
    First Name: </label>
    <input type="text" name="firstname" id="First Name"
    size="35" maxlength="35"></p>
<p>
    <label class="username" for="Last Name">
    Last Name: </label>
    <input type="text" name="lastname" id="Last Name"
    size="35" maxlength="35"></p>
</form>
```

This code creates the two text box inputs shown in Figure 11-2.

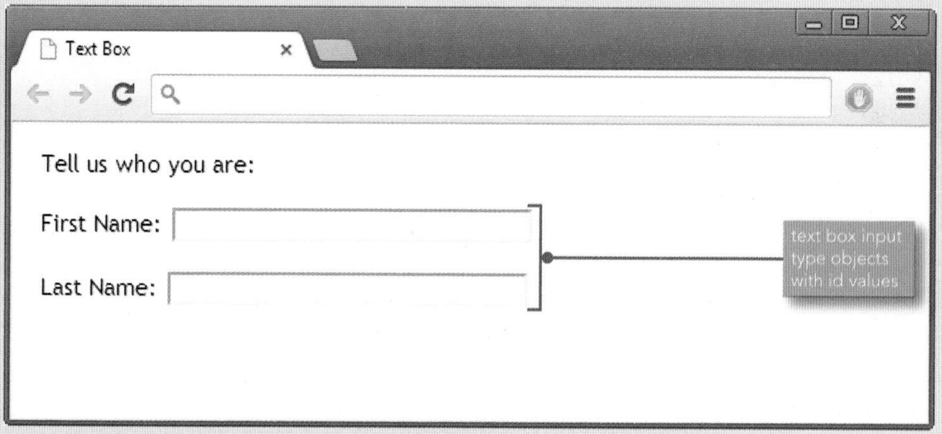

Figure 11-2: Text box input type
© 2015 Cengage Learning®

Creating Check Boxes

Check boxes are on/off toggles that the user can select. You can use the name attribute to group check boxes, allowing the user to select multiple values for the same property. Figure 11-3 shows an example of a group of check boxes.

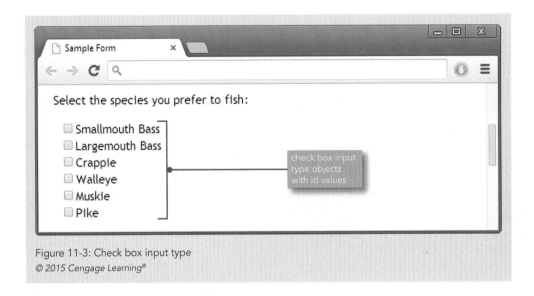

Figure 11-3: Check box input type
© 2015 Cengage Learning®

In the following code, the various fish species check boxes are grouped together with the name attribute set to *species*. Notice that the check boxes reside within a standard unordered list with the CSS list-style-type property set to none to remove the default bullet. Refer to Chapter 5 for more information on bulleted lists.

```
<p>Select the species you prefer to fish:</p>

<ul>
<li><input type="checkbox" name="species" value="smbass"
id="Smallmouth Bass">Smallmouth Bass</li>

<li><input type="checkbox" name="species" value="lgbass"
id="Largemouth Bass">Largemouth Bass</li>

<li><input type="checkbox" name="species" value="crappie"
id="Crappie">Crappie</li>
```

```
<li><input type="checkbox" name="species" value="walleye"
id="Walleye">Walleye</li>

<li><input type="checkbox" name="species" value="muskie"
id="Muskie">Muskie</li>

<li><input type="checkbox" name="species" value="pike"
id="Pike">Pike</li>
</ul>
```

To check a check box by default, you can use the checked attribute. The following code fragment shows the syntax for this attribute. Here, the Pike check box is checked by default.

```
<input type="checkbox" name="species" value="pike"
checked="checked">Pike
```

Creating Radio Buttons

Radio buttons are like check boxes, but only one selection is allowed. When radio buttons are grouped with the name attribute, only one value can be selected as "on," while all other values must be "off." To preselect one of the radio buttons, you use the checked attribute. Figure 11-4 shows the radio buttons input type.

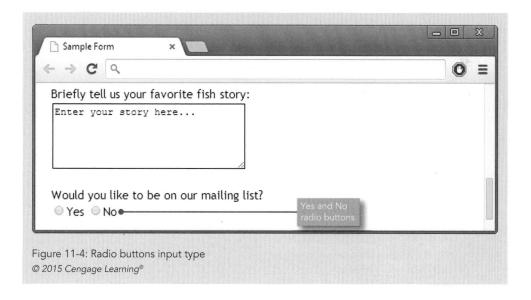

Figure 11-4: Radio buttons input type
© 2015 Cengage Learning®

In the following code, the Yes and No radio buttons are grouped together with the name attribute set to *list*. The user can choose only one of the two values.

```
<p>Would you like to be on our mailing list?<br>
<input type="radio" name="list" value="yes">Yes
<input type="radio" name="list" value="no">No
</p>
```

Note Use check boxes when you want to create a question to which multiple answers are allowed. Use radio buttons when you want users to choose only one answer.

Creating Submit and Reset Buttons
The submit and reset button input types let the user either send the form data to be processed or clear the form and start over. These are predefined functions that are activated by the button type. Set the input type to *submit* or *reset*. The default button text values are Submit Query and Reset. You can use the value attribute to customize the button text. Figure 11-5 shows the buttons.

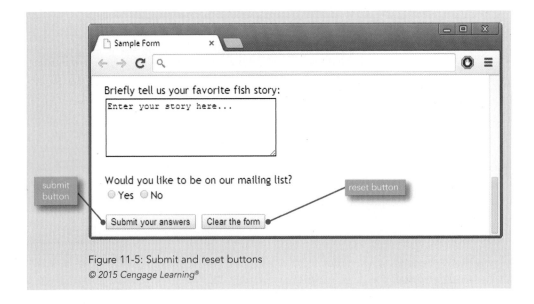

Figure 11-5: Submit and reset buttons
© 2015 Cengage Learning®

The following code shows the addition of submit and reset buttons with the customized button text shown in the figure.

```
<p>
<input type="submit" value="Submit your answers">
<input type="reset" value="Clear the form">
</p>
```

Creating an Image for the Submit Button

You can choose an image file and use it for the submit button instead of the default button image. The image type works only for the submit function. Make sure that the image you choose is an acceptable web file format (GIF, PNG, or JPG). The src attribute contains the location of the image file. Remember to include an alt attribute as you would with any other image. Figure 11-6 shows the use of an image (submit.jpg) for the submit button.

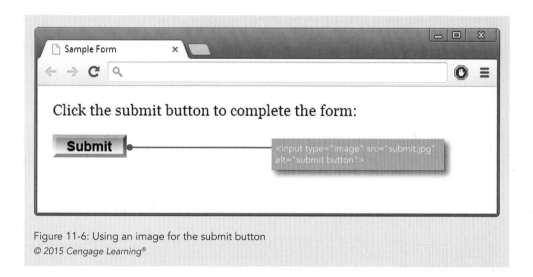

Figure 11-6: Using an image for the submit button
© 2015 Cengage Learning®

The following code shows the use of an image input type that specifies the image and the alt attribute.

```
<p>Click the submit button to complete the form:</p>
<p><input type="image" src="submit.jpg"
alt="submit button"></p>
```

Letting the User Submit a File

The file input type object lets users select a file on their own computers and send it to the server. For example, this option is useful when a user needs to upload an image or document. The file input type lets you create a text input area for the user to enter a filename. The length of the text input is specified with the size attribute. The file type automatically includes a browse button that lets users browse for a file on their computer. Figure 11-7 shows this input type with a selected file.

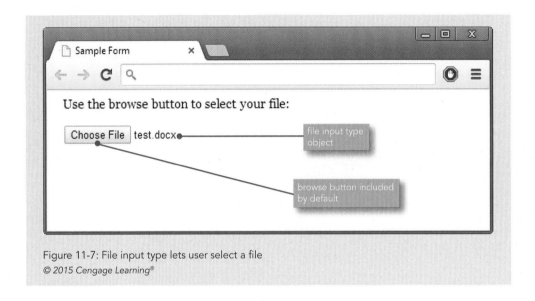

Figure 11-7: File input type lets user select a file
© 2015 Cengage Learning®

The following code shows the file input type. In this case, the text box accepts up to 30 characters.

```
<p>Use the browse button to select your file:</p>
<p><input type="file" size="30"></p>
```

Creating a Password Entry Field

The password input type object works like a text input box, with the additional feature that the entered text is masked by asterisks or bullets rather than shown on the screen. This is a very low level of password protection, as the password is only protected from unauthorized users looking at the screen. The password itself is sent to the server as plain text, and anyone with network access could read the password information.

If you use passwords, check with your system administrator to learn how to send passwords over a secure Internet connection. Figure 11-8 shows the password input type.

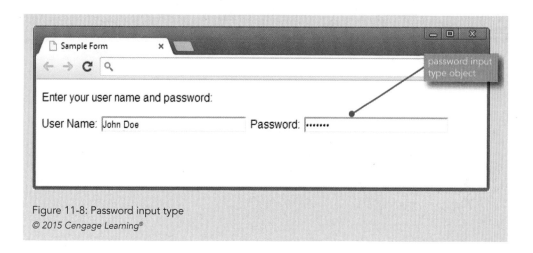

Figure 11-8: Password input type
© 2015 Cengage Learning®

The following code shows the use of the password input type. Both the user name and password text boxes accept up to 30 characters, as specified in the size attribute.

```
<p>Enter your user name and password:</p>
<p>
User Name: <input type="text" size="30">
Password: <input type="password" size="30">
</p>
```

Using the <select> Element

The <select> element lets you create a list box or scrollable list of selectable options. The <select> element is a container for the <option> element. Each <option> element contains a list value.

The following code shows the standard type of list box; the user can choose one value from the list. Figure 11-9 shows the result of the code.

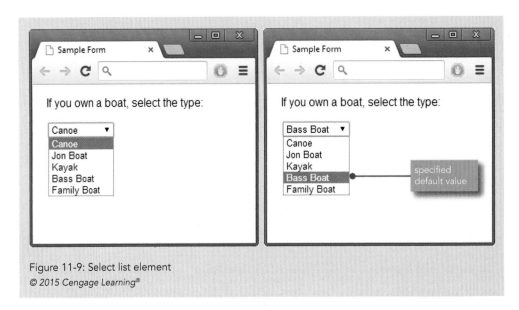

Figure 11-9: Select list element
© 2015 Cengage Learning®

Notice that the first option in the list is the default value that appears in the list box text area, as shown in the left screen in Figure 11-9.

```
<p>If you own a boat, select the type:</p>
<p>
<select name="boats">
    <option value="canoe">Canoe</option>
    <option value="jonboat">Jon Boat</option>
    <option value="kayak">Kayak</option>
    <option value="bassboat">Bass Boat</option>
    <option value="familyboat">Family Boat</option>
</select>
</p>
```

You can select the default value in a list by adding the *selected* attribute to an <option> element. In the following list, *Bass Boat* is the default value, as shown in the browser window on the right in Figure 11-9.

```
<p>If you own a boat, select the type:</p>
<p>
<select name="boats">
    <option value="canoe">Canoe</option>
    <option value="jonboat">Jon Boat</option>
```

```
<option value="kayak">Kayak</option>
<option value="bassboat" selected="selected">
Bass Boat</option>
<option value="familyboat">Family Boat</option>
</select>
</p>
```

You can also let the user pick multiple values from the list by adding the multiple attribute to the <select> element. The user can hold the Ctrl key and select multiple items in the list, or hold the Shift key to select contiguous options. Figure 11-10 and the following code show the use of the multiple attribute.

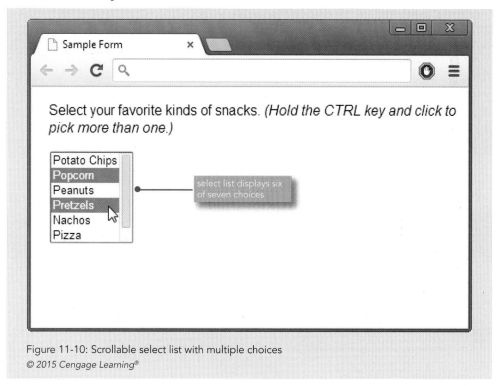

Figure 11-10: Scrollable select list with multiple choices
© 2015 Cengage Learning®

The size attribute specifies how many list options are visible at a time. The following list shows six options at once.

```
<p>Select your favorite kinds of snacks. <em>(Hold
the CTRL key and click to pick more than one.)</em></p>
<p>
<select name="snacks" multiple size="6">
    <option>Potato Chips</option>
```

```
<option>Popcorn</option>

<option>Peanuts</option>

<option>Pretzels</option>

<option>Nachos</option>

<option>Pizza</option>

<option>Fries</option>

</select>

</p>
```

Grouping List Options

You can group and label sets of list options with the <optgroup> element and label attribute. The result is a heading for a series of options within a list. Figure 11-11 shows the result of using the <optgroup> element.

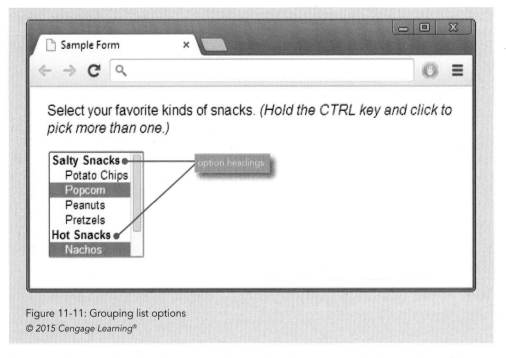

Figure 11-11: Grouping list options
© 2015 Cengage Learning®

The browser determines the format of the labels, but they are usually displayed in bold text. In the following code, the snack list is divided into two groups: salty snacks and hot snacks.

```
<p>
<select name="snacks" multiple size="7">
<optgroup label="Salty Snacks">
```

```
        <option>Potato Chips</option>
        <option>Popcorn</option>
        <option>Peanuts</option>
        <option>Pretzels</option>
    </optgroup>
    <optgroup label="Hot Snacks">
        <option>Nachos</option>
        <option>Pizza</option>
        <option>Fries</option>
    </optgroup>
    </select>
</p>
```

Using the <textarea> Element

The <textarea> element lets you create a text area for user input larger than the text input type object described previously. Figure 11-12 shows a sample of a <textarea> element.

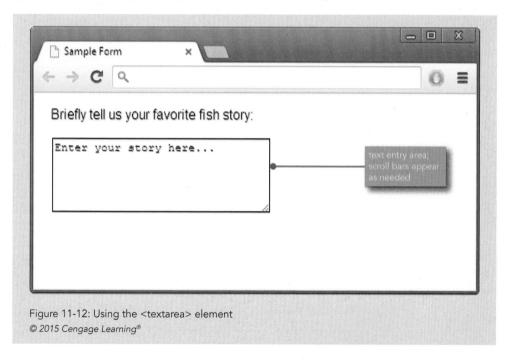

Figure 11-12: Using the <textarea> element
© 2015 Cengage Learning®

You can specify the width and height of the text area with the cols and rows attributes. If the text entered is longer than the height allotted, the browser adds scroll bars automatically.

Any text you enter in the <textarea> element appears as the default text in the user's browser. The following code shows a text area set to 30 columns wide by 5 rows high.

```
<p>Briefly tell us your favorite fish story:</p>
<p>
<textarea name="fishstory" rows="5" cols="30">
Enter your story here...
</textarea>
</p>
```

Creating Input Groupings

You can use the <fieldset> and <legend> elements to create groupings of different types of <input> elements. The <fieldset> element contains the <input> elements, and the <legend> element contains a label for the grouping. These two elements help make your forms more readable and increase their accessibility to screen readers and other accessibility devices. Figure 11-13 shows the use of the <fieldset> and <legend> elements. The code for the page follows.

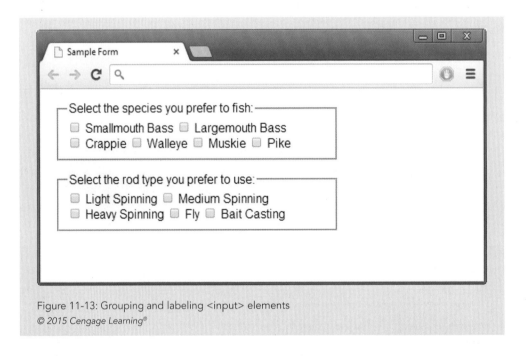

Figure 11-13: Grouping and labeling <input> elements
© 2015 Cengage Learning®

```
<fieldset>
<legend>Select the species you prefer to fish:
</legend>
```

```
<p>
<input type="checkbox" name="species"
value="smbass">
Smallmouth Bass
<input type="checkbox" name="species"
value="lgbass">
Largemouth Bass <br>
<input type="checkbox" name="species"
value="crappie">
Crappie
<input type="checkbox" name="species"
value="walleye">
Walleye
<input type="checkbox" name="species"
value="muskie">
Muskie
<input type="checkbox" name="species"
value="pike">
Pike
</p>
</fieldset>
<fieldset>
<legend>Select the rod type you prefer to use:
</legend>
<p>
<input type="checkbox" name="rod"
value="ltspin">
Light Spinning
<input type="checkbox" name="rod"
value="mdspin">
Medium Spinning <br>
<input type="checkbox" name="rod" value="hvspin">
Heavy Spinning
<input type="checkbox" name="rod"
value="fly">
```

```
Fly
<input type="checkbox" name="rod"
value="btcas">
Bait Casting
</p>
</fieldset>
```

Labeling Form Elements

The <label> element lets you create a caption for an <input> element. Although the user sees no visible difference when using the <label> element, it provides benefits both for accessibility and for applying style rules to form labels for greater control over their appearance.

The <label> element in the following code sample contains the caption text *First Name:*.

```
<p>
    <label class="username">First Name:</label>
    <input type="text" name="firstname"
    size="35" maxlength="35">
</p>
```

The <label> element lets you extend the clickable area of a form element to make these areas more accessible. For example, in addition to clicking the check box, users can also click the text caption to select the check box, as shown in Figure 11-14.

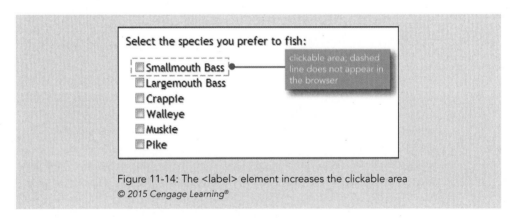

Figure 11-14: The <label> element increases the clickable area
© 2015 Cengage Learning®

To make the text clickable, you associate the <label> element with the <input> element by using the for and id attributes, as shown in the following code.

```
<p>
    <label class="username" for="First Name">
```

```
    First Name:</label>
    <input type="text" name="firstname" id="First Name"
    size="35" maxlength="35">
  </p>
```

The for attribute in the <label> element must match the *id* attribute in the <input> element
to associate the text with the <input> element. You will learn more about the <label>
element and its use in the next section.

Styling Forms with CSS

Most forms can benefit from CSS styling to increase their legibility and appeal. As you have seen
in the form samples in this chapter, forms need at least basic formatting elements, such as
and <p>, so you can place form elements on separate lines and add white space. Even with these
basic formatting elements, the look of your form may not be acceptable. Figure 11-15 shows a
typical form. Notice how the left justification of the elements gives the form a ragged look.

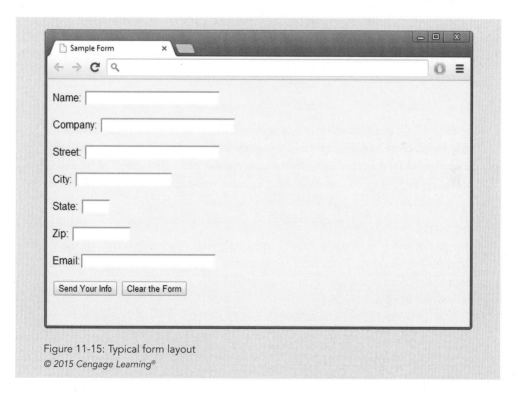

Figure 11-15: Typical form layout
© 2015 Cengage Learning®

In contrast to Figure 11-15, the form in Figure 11-16 has been styled with CSS, producing a
more visually appealing form that is easier for the user to follow when entering data.

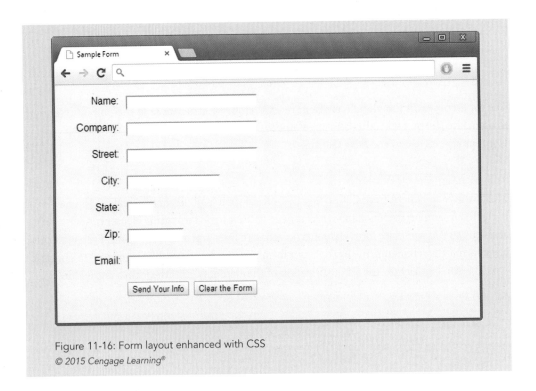

Figure 11-16: Form layout enhanced with CSS
© 2015 Cengage Learning®

Adding CSS to form elements is no different from adding styles to standard content elements. You can use many of the CSS properties to specify type styles, background colors, box properties, and colors that enhance the look of your forms. The grouping and labeling elements <fieldset>, <legend>, and <label> are useful when applying styles to forms. You can also use classes or ids to apply styles to specific form elements.

Aligning Form Elements

As shown in Figure 11-16, aligned form elements help you create forms that are more organized and easier to use. To create this alignment, you can set a width for the labels so they align in a column to the left of the form input elements. First, examine the code that creates the form in Figure 11-16.

```
<form method="post" action="http://someserver/script.php">
<p>
<label for="name">Name:</label>
<input type=text size=30 maxlength=256
name="name" id="name">
</p>
```

```
<p>
<label for="company">Company:</label>
<input type=text size=30 maxlength=256
name="company" id="company">
</p>
<p>
<label for="street">Street:</label>
<input type=text size=30 maxlength=256
name="street" id="street">
</p>
<p><label for="city">City:</label>
<input type=text size=20 maxlength=256
name="city" id="city">
</p>
<p>
<label for="state">State:</label>
<input type=text size=2 maxlength=256
name="state" id="state">
</p>
<p>
<label for="zip">Zip:</label>
<input type=text size=10 maxlength=256
name="zip" id="zip">
</p>
<p>
<label for="email">Email:</label>
<input type=text size=30 maxlength=256
name="email" id="email">
</p>
<p>
<input class="submit" type="submit"
value="Send Your Info">
<input type="reset" value="Clear the Form">
</p>
</form>
```

Notice that the label and each corresponding form element are contained within a <p> element. You can float the label to the left of the form element within each paragraph. Use the label element as the selector for the style rule. Float the label to the left, and set a width that fits the label content as shown:

```
label {
    float: left;
    width: 6em;
}
```

Figure 11-17 shows the result of this style rule. In this figure, a border shows the width and placement of the <label> element.

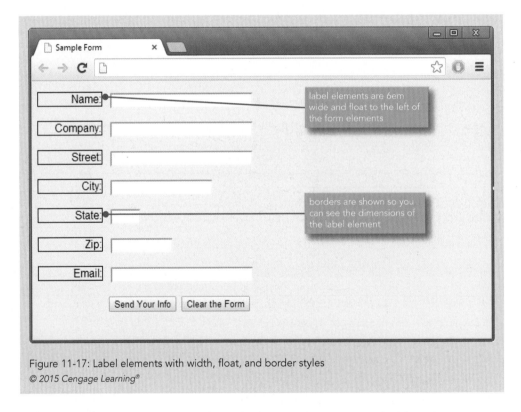

Figure 11-17: Label elements with width, float, and border styles
© 2015 Cengage Learning®

To complete the labels, add style properties to right-align the text and add a right margin to separate the label from the form input element.

```
label {
    float: left;
```

```
   width: 6em;
   text-align: right;
   margin-right: 10px;
}
```

Create a style for the paragraph that contains the submit and reset buttons. This rule uses *submit* as the class name and offsets the buttons from the left margin by 8ems.

```
.submit {margin-left: 8em;}
```

Next, apply this rule to the paragraph that contains the submit and reset buttons.

```
<p class="submit" >
<input type="submit" value="Send Your Info">
<input type="reset" value="Clear the Form">
</p>
```

These style rules result in the finished form shown in Figure 11-18.

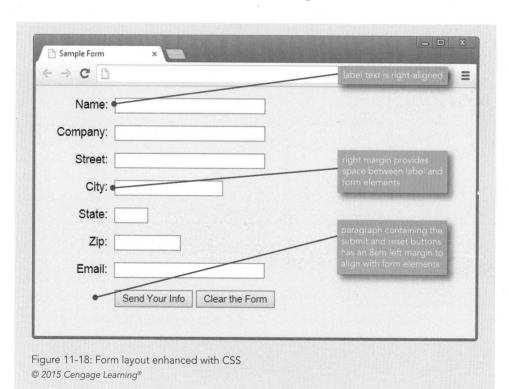

Figure 11-18: Form layout enhanced with CSS
© 2015 Cengage Learning®

Styling <Fieldset> and <Legend> Elements

The <fieldset> and <legend> elements are great for applying styles to make your forms
more attractive. Figure 11-19 shows the form with <fieldset> and <legend> elements in
their default display behavior. Notice that the fieldset border extends to the width of the
browser window.

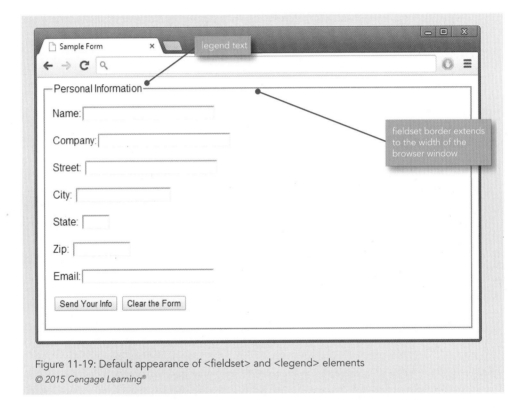

Figure 11-19: Default appearance of <fieldset> and <legend> elements
© 2015 Cengage Learning®

The fieldset can be set to a measured width to keep it from extending to the width of the
browser window. The following rule selects the <fieldset> element and applies a width
of 410px.

```
fieldset {
    width: 410px;
}
```

Adding a background color (#ddeeff) and a dark blue border (#053972) will help the form stand out on the page.

```
fieldset {
    width: 410px;
    background-color: #ddeeff;
    border: solid medium #053972;
}
```

The legend text can be styled to make it stand out. In this example, the legend has a 1px border that matches the color of the fieldset border. A white background and 2 pixels of padding help offset the text from the fieldset border.

```
legend {
    border: solid 1px #053972;
    background-color: #fff;
    padding: 2px;
}
```

Figure 11-20 shows the results of the fieldset and legend style rules.

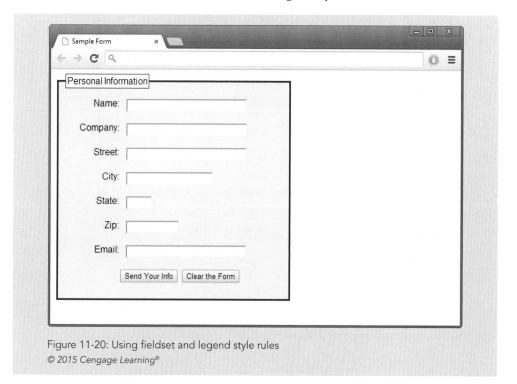

Figure 11-20: Using fieldset and legend style rules
© 2015 Cengage Learning®

Adding a Background Image

You can add a background image to a fieldset with the background-image property, as shown in Figure 11-21.

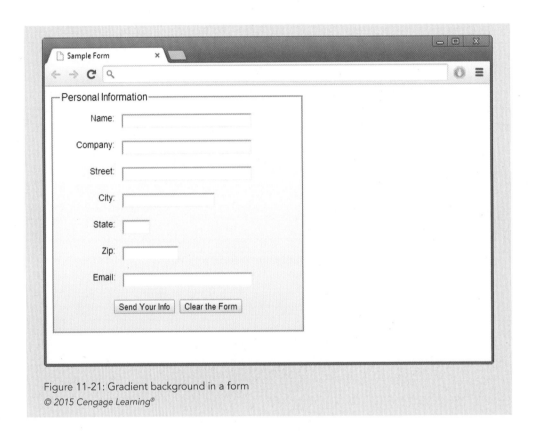

Figure 11-21: Gradient background in a form
© 2015 Cengage Learning®

In this example, the gradient image (formgradient.jpg) is specified with the background-image property. The background-position is set to bottom, and the background-repeat is set to repeat the graphic along the horizontal axis of the form.

```
fieldset {
    width: 410px;
    background-image: url(formgradient.jpg);
    background-position: bottom;
    background-repeat: repeat-x;
}
```

Activity: Building a Form

In the following set of steps, you will build a form for an online job search service. Users of the service will enter their addresses and personal information into the form.

To begin building the form:

1. Copy the file **ch11activity.html** from the Chapter11 folder provided with your Data Files to the Chapter11 folder in your work folder. (Create the Chapter11 work folder, if necessary.)

2. Open **ch11activity.html** in your HTML editor, and then examine the code. Note that a style section contains a body style that sets the font family and left margin for the page.

```
<!DOCTYPE HTML>
<html>
<head>
<title>Wonder Software Online Job Search Form</title>
<meta content="text/html; charset=utf-8"
    http-equiv="Content-Type">
<style>
body {font-family: arial, sans-serif; margin-left: 20px;}
</style>
</head>
<body>
<h1>Wonder Software<br>Online Job Search</h1>
<form action=" " method="post">
</form>
</body>
</html>
```

3. Begin building the form by adding three text <input> elements, one each for the user's name, email address, and telephone number. Set the size and name attribute values as shown in the following code. Make sure each <input> element is contained within a <p> element.

```
<form action=" " method="post">
<p>Name: <input size="30" name="name" id="name"></p>
<p>Email: <input size="30" name="email" id="email"></p>
<p>Phone: <input size="30" name="phone" id="phone"></p>
</form>
```

4. Add label elements for the label of each text box. Make sure to associate the label with the form element by adding the for attribute that matches the form input's id value.

```
<p><label for="name">Name:</label><input size="30"
   name="name" id="name"></p>
<p><label for="email">Email:</label><input size="30"
   name="email" id="email"></p>
<p><label for="phone">Phone:</label><input size="30"
   name="phone" id="phone"></p>
```

5. Group this set of fields with a <fieldset> and accompanying <legend> element, as shown in the following code.

```
<fieldset>
<legend>Contact Information</legend>
<p><label for="name">Name:</label><input size="30"
   name="name" id="name"></p>
<p><label for="email">Email:</label><input size="30"
   name="email" id="email"></p>
<p><label for="phone">Phone:</label><input size="30"
   name="phone" id="phone"></p>
</fieldset>
```

6. Save **ch11activity.html**, and leave it open for the next set of steps. Then view the file in the browser; it should now look like Figure 11-22.

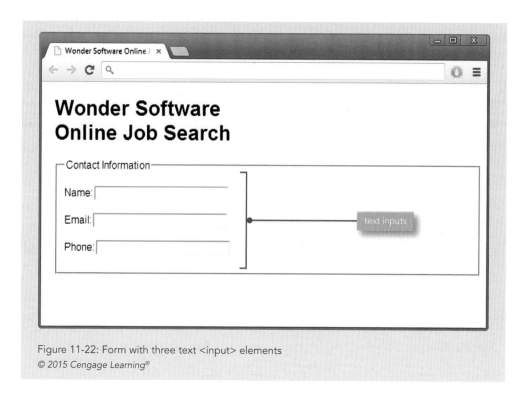

Figure 11-22: Form with three text <input> elements
© 2015 Cengage Learning®

Adding Check Boxes

Continue to build the form by adding check box <input> elements to collect information from the user. Later you will add a list box of job position options, where users can make only one selection from the list.

To continue building the form:

1. Continue working in the file **ch11activity.html**.

2. Add text to identify the check box inputs.

```
Select Your Area(s) of Interest:
```

3. Add the checkbox input elements as shown. The name attribute groups the check boxes together in the jobtitle category. Each check box is identified with a unique value. Contain the check boxes in two <p> elements, the first with two job titles and the second with three.

```
<p>
<input type="checkbox" name="jobtitle" value="ae">
Account Executive

<input type="checkbox" name="jobtitle" value="bd">
Business Development
</p>
<p>
<input type="checkbox" name="jobtitle" value="is">
Inside Sales

<input type="checkbox" name="jobtitle" value="sm">
Sales Manager

<input type="checkbox" name="jobtitle" value="vp">
VP Sales
</p>
```

4. Add label elements for each check box.

```
<p><input type="checkbox" name="jobtitle" value="ae">
<label>Account Executive</label>

<input type="checkbox" name="jobtitle" value="bd">
<label>Business Development</label></p>

<p><input type="checkbox" name="jobtitle" value="is">
<label>Inside Sales</label>

<input type="checkbox" name="jobtitle" value="sm">
<label>Sales Manager</label>
```

```
<input type="checkbox" name="jobtitle" value="vp">
<label>VP Sales</label></p>
```

5. Associate the labels with each checkbox input element by adding for and id attributes to the <label> and <input> elements.

```
<p><input type="checkbox" name="jobtitle" value="ae"
id="ae">
<label for="ae">Account Executive</label>

<input type="checkbox" name="jobtitle" value="bd"
id="bd">
<label for="bd">Business Development</label></p>

<p><input type="checkbox" name="jobtitle" value="is"
id="is">
<label for="is">Inside Sales</label>

<input type="checkbox" name="jobtitle" value="sm"
id="sm">
<label for="sm">Sales Manager</label>

<input type="checkbox" name="jobtitle" value="vp"
id="vp">
<label for="vp">VP Sales</label></p>
```

6. Group this set of fields with a <fieldset> and accompanying <legend> element, as shown in the following code.

```
<fieldset>
<legend>Select Your Area(s) of Interest:</legend>

<p><input type="checkbox" name="jobtitle" value="ae"
   id="ae"><label for="ae">Account Executive</label>

<input type="checkbox" name="jobtitle" value="bd"
   id="bd"> <label for="bd">Business Development</label></p>
```

```
<p><input type="checkbox" name="jobtitle" value="is"
    id="is"><label for="is">Inside Sales</label>

<input type="checkbox" name="jobtitle" value="sm"
    id="sm"><label for="sm">Sales Manager</label>

<input type="checkbox" name="jobtitle" value="vp"
    id="vp"><label for="vp">VP Sales</label></p>
</fieldset>
```

7. Save **ch11activity.html**, and leave it open for the next set of steps. Then view the file in the browser; it should now look like Figure 11-23.

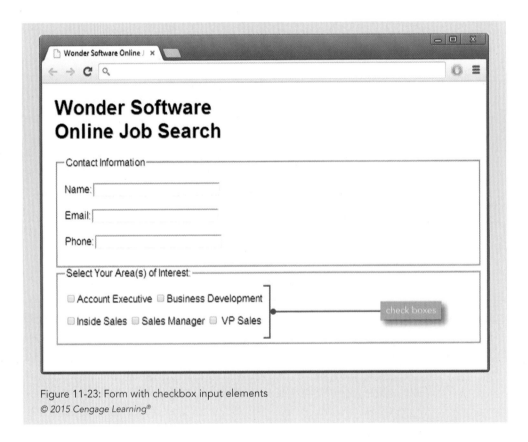

Figure 11-23: Form with checkbox input elements
© 2015 Cengage Learning®

Adding a List Box and Radio Buttons

Continue to build the form by adding two more input elements to collect information from the user. You will add a list box of job position options and a question with a yes or no answer.

To continue building the form:

1. Continue working in the file **ch11activity.html**.

2. Add a <select> element with four blank <option> tags, as shown in the following code. Place this code after the closing <fieldset> tag from the previous procedure.

```
<p>
Select the type of position you desire:
<select name="position">
<option> </option>
<option> </option>
<option> </option>
<option> </option>
</select>
</p>
```

3. Fill in a value for each option.

```
<p>
Select the type of position you desire:
<select name="position">
<option>Part-time contract</option>
<option>Full-time contract</option>
<option>Part-time permanent</option>
<option>Full-time permanent</option>
</select>
</p>
```

4. Below the select list, add the <p> element with the following question:

```
<p>
Are you willing to relocate?<br>
</p>
```

5. Add two <input> elements with the type set to *radio* to create radio buttons.

```
<p>
Are you willing to relocate?<br>
Yes <input type="radio">
No <input type="radio">
</p>
```

6. Add a value attribute for each element. Set the value for the Yes button to *yes*. Set the No button to *no*. Also, add a name attribute that groups the radio buttons together with a value of *relocate*.

```
<p>
Are you willing to relocate?<br>
Yes <input type="radio" value="yes" name="relocate">
No <input type="radio" value="no" name="relocate">
</p>
```

7. Add labels with for and id attributes.

```
<p>
Are you willing to relocate?<br>
<label for="yes">Yes</label><input type="radio"
   value="yes" name="relocate" id="yes">
<label for="no">No</label><input type="radio"
   value="no" name="relocate" id="no">
</p>
```

8. Save **ch11activity.html**, and leave it open for the next set of steps. Then view the file in the browser; it should now look like Figure 11-24.

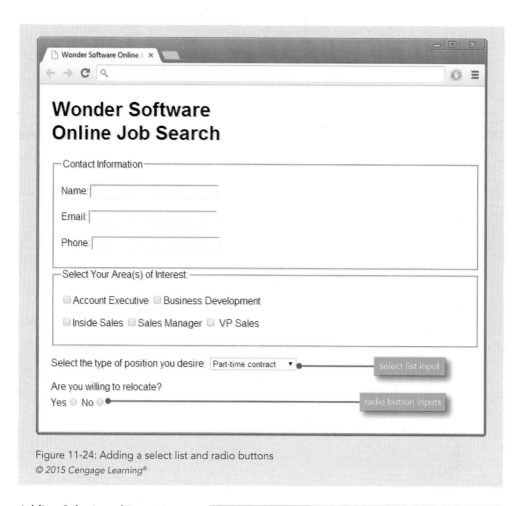

Figure 11-24: Adding a select list and radio buttons
© 2015 Cengage Learning®

Adding Submit and Reset Buttons

You finish the form by adding the submit and reset buttons.

To continue building the form:

1. Continue working in the file **ch11activity.html**.

2. Add submit and reset button element types, and set values for each button as shown.

```
<p>
<input type="submit" value="Submit">
<input type="reset" value="Clear">
</p>
```

3. Save **ch11activity.html**, and leave it open for the next set of steps. Then view the file in the browser; it should now look like Figure 11-25.

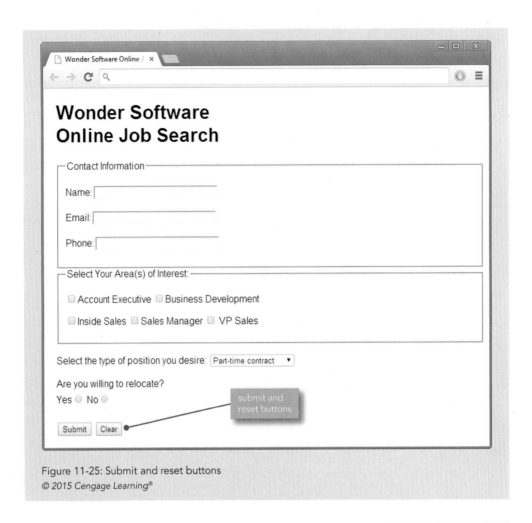

Figure 11-25: Submit and reset buttons
© 2015 Cengage Learning®

Styling the Labels

You will create two label styles, one for the Contact Information labels and one for the Areas of Interest labels.

To style the labels:

1. Continue working in the file **ch11activity.html**.

2. Create a style for contact labels, and use **contact** as the class name. Set the properties as shown to create floating labels with right-aligned text and a margin to offset the label from the input element.

```
label.contact {
    width: 80px;
```

```
    float: left;
    text-align: right;
    margin-right: 10px;
}
```

3. Apply the style by adding the class attribute to the contact labels.

```
<fieldset>
<legend>Contact Information</legend>
<p><label for="name" class="contact">Name:</label>
    <input size="30" name="name" id="name"></p>
<p><label for="email" class="contact">Email:</label>
    <input size="30" name="email" id="email"></p>
<p><label for="phone" class="contact">Phone:</label>
    <input size="30" name="phone" id="phone"></p>
</fieldset>
```

4. Create a style for the area labels using **area** as the class name. Set the properties as shown to add left and right margins that adjust the spacing of the labels for legibility.

```
label.area {
    margin-left: 2px;
    margin-right: 10px;
}
```

5. Apply the style by adding the class attribute to the area labels.

```
<fieldset>
<legend>Select Your Area(s) of Interest:</legend>
<p><input type="checkbox" name="jobtitle" value="ae"
    id="ae"><label for="ae" class="area">Account
    Executive</label>
<input type="checkbox" name="jobtitle" value="bd"
    id="bd"><label for="bd" class="area">Business
    Development</label></p>
<p><input type="checkbox" name="jobtitle" value="is"
    id="is"><label for="is" class="area">Inside
    Sales</label>
<input type="checkbox" name="jobtitle" value="sm" id="sm">
    <label for="sm" class="area">Sales Manager</label>
```

```
<input type="checkbox" name="jobtitle" value="vp" id="vp">
    <label for="vp" class="area">VP Sales</label></p>
</fieldset>
```

6. Save **ch11activity.html**, and leave it open for the next set of steps. Then view the file in the browser; it should now look like Figure 11-26.

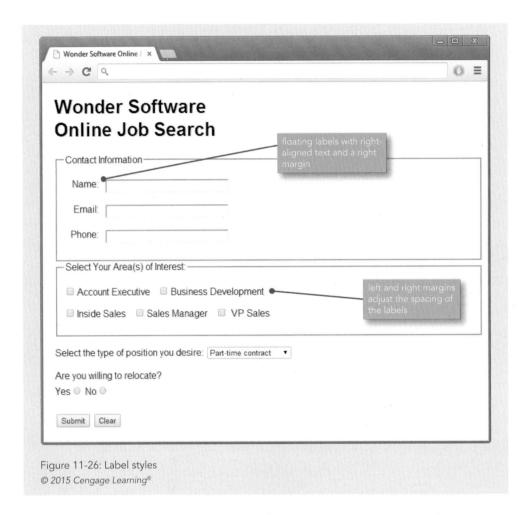

Figure 11-26: Label styles
© 2015 Cengage Learning®

Styling the Fieldsets and Legends

Finish the form design by styling the fieldsets and the legends.

To style the fieldsets and the legends:

1. Continue working in the file **ch11activity.html**.

2. Create a style that selects both fieldsets. Set the width to 410px.

```
fieldset {
    width: 410px;

}
```

3. Provide some white space between the two fieldsets by writing a rule that selects only the area fieldset and applying a top margin of 20px. Use area as the class name for this rule.

```
fieldset.area {
    margin-top: 20px;

}
```

4. Apply this rule to the area fieldset as shown.

```
<fieldset class="area">
<legend>Select Your Area(s) of Interest:</legend>
<p><input type="checkbox" name="jobtitle" value="ae"
    id="ae"><label for="ae">Account Executive</label>

<input type="checkbox" name="jobtitle" value="bd"
    id="bd"><label for="bd">Business Development</label></p>

<p><input type="checkbox" name="jobtitle" value="is"
    id="is"><label for="is">Inside Sales</label>

<input type="checkbox" name="jobtitle" value="sm"
    id="sm"><label for="sm">Sales Manager</label>

<input type="checkbox" name="jobtitle" value="vp"
    id="vp"><label for="vp">VP Sales</label></p>
</fieldset>
```

5. Create a style for the legends that will apply to the <legend> element in both fieldsets.

```
legend {
font-weight: bold;

}
```

6. Save **ch11activity.html**. Then view the file in the browser; it should now look like Figure 11-27.

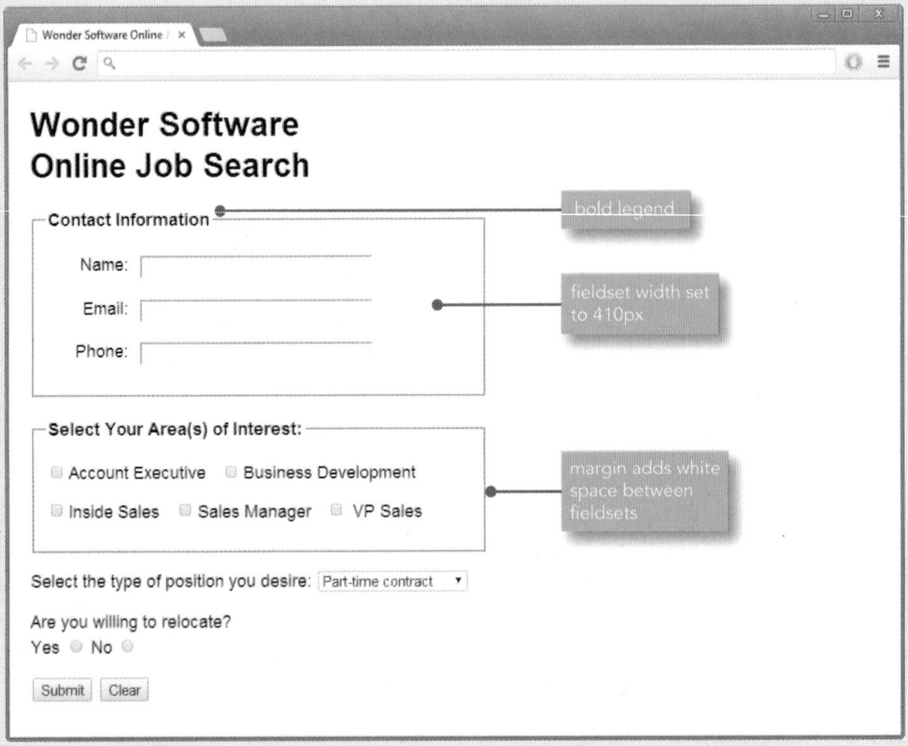

Figure 11-27: Completed form
© 2015 Cengage Learning®

Skills at Work | *Hold Productive Meetings*

Forms are usually the result of a team effort, one that demands collaboration with others and decision-making during meetings. As a professional web designer, you typically will attend one or more meetings a week. Effective meetings save time and make participants more productive, but they take planning. If you are in charge of a meeting, make sure you and everyone attending the meeting understands the purpose of the meeting and what you want to accomplish. If the purpose isn't clear, you might need to use a different form of communication, such as an exchange of email messages. Identify who should attend the meeting, including decision-makers and others who play an active role in achieving the meeting's goal. If anyone needs to present information, give them enough time to prepare it. Finally, create and distribute an agenda before the meeting so all participants know the topics you plan to discuss.

Chapter Summary

A usable form interface is the result of choosing the correct form elements for the type of data you are requesting and designing a clear and readable form. Keep the following points in mind:

› You need to work with some type of software program to process the data from your form. An HTML form is the interface for the user to enter data, and the data is processed using applications called scripts that run on the server.

› The <form> element is the container for creating a form. A form has a number of attributes that describe how the form data is handled, such as action, which often specifies the URL of a script file to process the form data.

› You have a variety of form elements to choose from when building a form. The <input> element defines many of the form input object types. Use the correct type of input object for the type of data you are gathering. For example, use check boxes for multiple-choice questions. For a long list of choices, use a select list.

› The <fieldset> and <legend> elements let you create more visually appealing forms that have logical groupings of <input> elements with a title.

› Most forms should be formatted to improve their legibility. The most basic formatting elements are <br> and <p>, which place form elements on separate lines and add white space. You can avoid the ragged look of forms by using CSS to align form elements; styling labels, legends, and fieldsets; or adding background colors or graphics.

Key Terms

Common Gateway Interface (CGI)—A communications bridge between the Internet and the server used as the traditional method of processing forms input. Using programs called scripts, CGI can collect data sent by a user via the Hypertext Transfer Protocol (HTTP) and transfer it to a variety of data-processing programs, including spreadsheets, databases, or software running on the server.

form control—An input element in an HTML form, such as a radio button, text box, or check box.

JavaScript—A client-side scripting language used with HTML forms.

script—A program that transfers form data to a server.

Review Questions

1. What are the five commonly supported form elements?

2. What does the action attribute in the <form> element contain?

3. What are the two possible values of the form method attribute?

4. How can you group multiple check boxes together?

5. How are radio buttons different from check boxes?

6. How do you control the length of a user's entry in a text <input> element?

7. How do you enter default text in a text <input> element?

8. How do you force a check box to be selected by default?

9. What button must be included with every form?

10. How do you change the default button image for the submit button?

11. What input type lets the user attach a file to the form data?

12. What is the security problem with the password input type?

13. What are the two types of select lists?

14. What attributes let you specify the width and height of the <textarea> element?

Hands-On Projects

1. In this project, you will build text box form elements.
   a. In your HTML editor, open the file **ch11project1.html** in the Chapter11 folder in your work folder.
   b. Save the file as **textbox.html** in the same location.
   c. Examine the code. The file contains only the default HTML elements and an empty <form> element.
   d. Build the form shown in Figure 11-28. Refer to Table 11-4 for each form element's attribute values.

NAME	SIZE	MAXLENGTH
Street	20	35
City	20	35
State	2	35
Zip	10	35

Table 11-4: Attribute Values for the Text Box Form
© 2015 Cengage Learning®

e. Use CSS style properties to align the labels, as shown in Figure 11-28.

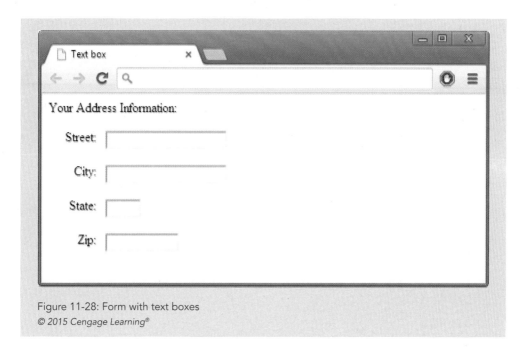

Figure 11-28: Form with text boxes
© 2015 Cengage Learning®

2. In this project, you will build check box form elements.
   a. In your HTML editor, open the file **ch11project2.html** in the Chapter11 folder in your work folder.
   b. Save the file as **checkbox.html** in the same location.
   c. Examine the code. The file contains only the default HTML elements and an empty <form> element.
   d. Build the form shown in Figure 11-29.
   e. Group the check boxes with a name attribute set to "flavor."
   f. Add labels that are associated with each input check box.

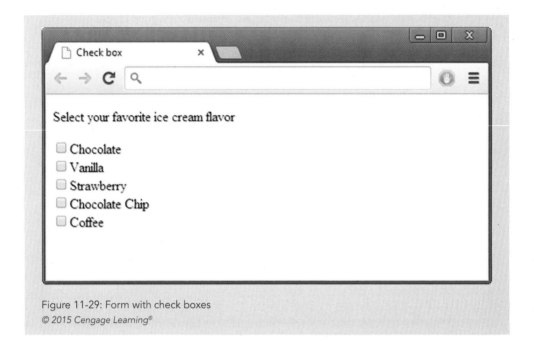

Figure 11-29: Form with check boxes
© 2015 Cengage Learning®

3. In this project, you build radio button form elements.
   a. In your HTML editor, open the file **ch11project3.html** in the Chapter11 folder in your work folder.
   b. Save the file as **radio.html** in the same location.
   c. Examine the code. The file contains only the default HTML elements and an empty <form> element.
   d. Build the form shown in Figure 11-30.
   e. Make sure that *Yes* is the selected option.
   f. Group the radio buttons with a name attribute set to *offer*.
   g. Add labels that are associated with each input radio button.

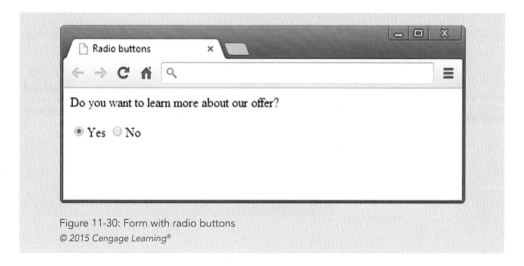

Figure 11-30: Form with radio buttons
© 2015 Cengage Learning®

4. In this project, you will build a text area form element.
   a. In your HTML editor, open the file **ch11project4.html** in the Chapter11 folder in your work folder.
   b. Save the file as **textarea.html** in the same location.
   c. Examine the code. The file contains only the default HTML elements and an empty <form> element.
   d. Build the form shown in Figure 11-31. The text area is 6 rows by 35 columns.

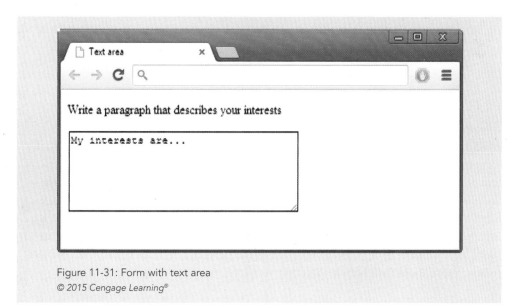

Figure 11-31: Form with text area
© 2015 Cengage Learning®

5. In this project, you will build a select form element.
   a. In your HTML editor, open the file **ch11project5.html** in the Chapter11 folder in your work folder.
   b. Save the file as **select.html** in the same location.
   c. Examine the code. The file contains only the default HTML elements and an empty <form> element.
   d. Build the form shown in Figure 11-32.

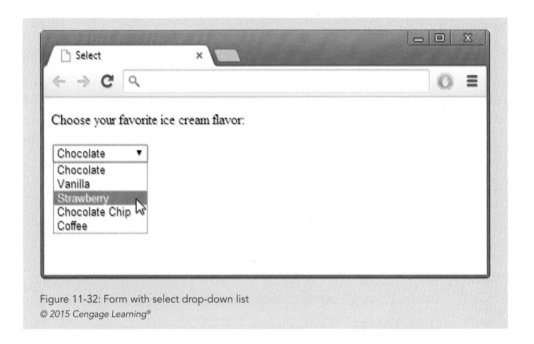

Figure 11-32: Form with select drop-down list
© 2015 Cengage Learning®

Individual Case Project

Build a user feedback form for your project web site. You can refer to the sample feedback form in Chapter 3 for ideas. Customize the types of questions you ask to match the content of your site. Create both scaled questions and open-ended questions for your users. For example, ask users to rate the navigation of your site on a scale of 1 to 5, and include a text area input where they can write about their experience of navigating your web site. Although you will not be able to activate the form because you don't have an appropriate script to process the data, you can demonstrate the types of questions you would ask users to learn more about their habits when they visit your site.

Team Case Project

Each team member creates his or her own feedback form and submits it to the instructor, as described in the preceding Individual Case Project. You are free to design the form as you choose, but it must include the navigation characteristics, typographic specifications, and design conventions of your project web site.

Then meet as a team and choose the best features, questions, and design characteristics from each member's submitted form. Create a new form that combines these features, and add it to your project web site.

CHAPTER 12

RESPONSIVE WEB DESIGN

When you complete this chapter, you will be able to:

> Recognize the need for responsive web design
> Use media queries to apply conditional styles
> Build a basic media query
> Create flexible responsive layouts
> Create responsive navigation schemes
> Use responsive images
> Build a responsive web page design for desktops, tablets, and smartphones

In this chapter, you will combine many of the techniques you have learned in this book to create responsive web page designs that seamlessly adapt to different screen sizes on the many devices used to browse the web, including desktop computers, tablets, and smartphones. You will learn how to use CSS3 media queries to apply conditional styles based on device properties such as browser width. You will build flexible pages that can adapt to a variety of devices using a single source of content and different style sheets. You will also learn to customize your images to flexibly adapt to screen sizes and build navigation schemes that let users quickly access desired content, no matter what type of device they use. Finally, you will have the chance to apply these new skills while converting a layout from a standard desktop design to a responsive design that adapts to different screen sizes.

Recognizing the Need for Responsive Web Design

Throughout the history of the web, the challenge for web designers has always been to adapt their page designs to a wide range of user needs and browsing devices. Traditionally, the variables have included browsers, connection speed, and device types, as you learned in Chapter 2. Web designers have tried many techniques to adapt to device specifications. For example, in the earlier days of the web, designers created browser-specific web pages to deal with different browser types, developed centered web pages to deal with different screen sizes, and used other ill-advised methods that defeat the accessible nature of the web. Ideally, no matter what device, connection speed, or browser type you design for, everyone should be able to access your web content. The temptation to design separate pages for different browsers or devices leads to maintenance problems because customized sites must be updated concurrently with the same content. Although many web-publishing software platforms can help support this multiple-site model, it is not ideal.

With the advent of smartphones and tablets in the last few years, the web developer's challenge to provide web sites that display content and perform correctly regardless of device has become even more complicated. As shown in Figures 12-1 through 12-3, and as you learned in Chapter 2, more device sizes, screen orientations, and screen resolutions are available now than ever before. The variety of screen formats is almost endless, and the challenge for web designers is growing as more new devices debut every day. You should design responsively for the needs of the content rather than those of the device, as you will learn in this chapter.

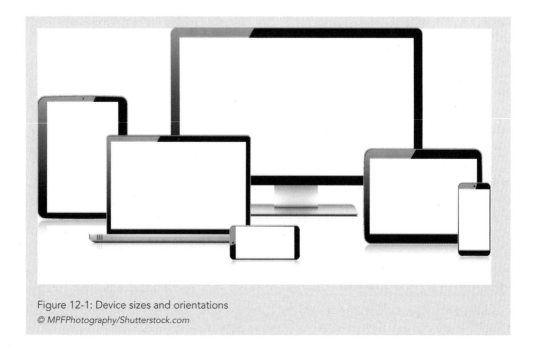

Figure 12-1: Device sizes and orientations
© MPFPhotography/Shutterstock.com

In the past, designers adapted their web sites by creating flexible designs that adjusted to different screen sizes or used fixed designs that always appeared in the center of the browser window. However, these techniques do not create suitable results in the many smaller devices that people now use to browse the web. The issue includes more than the inability to easily view a web site because of smaller screen size. Navigation is often a problem, especially on the smallest handheld devices. Users should be able to view your content without zooming or scrolling. Anyone with a smartphone is aware of such limitations, as many web sites designed for the large screens on desktop and laptop computers merely shrink their contents to fit on a smaller screen. The answer is to build a more flexible type of web page that responds to the varying size of displays used for online viewing. This new web design trend is called responsive design: building web sites to provide easier reading and navigation across a wide range of devices from mobile smartphones to desktop computer monitors. The best user experience, especially on smaller devices, minimizes resizing, panning, and scrolling. You can provide this experience with a variety of techniques, including redesigning pages to focus on content the user wants most and removing content that is not as important when displayed on smaller screens.

To create responsive web sites, web designers can call on a variety of techniques, many of which are a benefit of using CSS3 capabilities. In this chapter, you will learn to combine the three main elements of responsive design:

> **CSS media queries**: Using these expressions, you can apply styles based on display device characteristics.

> **Flexible images**: These images adapt to the parameters of the user's screen size.

> **Flexible layouts**: These layouts realign elements of your content structure based on the display device. For example, you can stack columns or minimize navigation so that the web site content is displayed in the most appropriate format based on the display size.

Figure 12-2 shows the responsive design of the World Wildlife Fund web site at five screen resolutions. The various resolutions represent typical devices used today. The 320-pixel width is a common smartphone size, 768 pixels represents tablets in landscape orientation, 1366 pixels is the most popular laptop width, and 1920 pixels represents the expansive screen real estate offered by inexpensive wide-screen desktop displays.

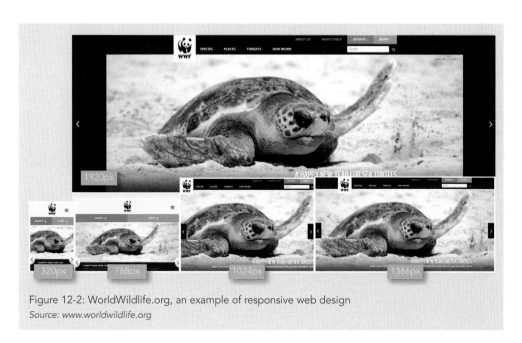

Figure 12-2: WorldWildlife.org, an example of responsive web design
Source: www.worldwildlife.org

Notice that the page design is similar for the smaller two screen resolutions with widths of 768 pixels or less. The three pages with widths of more than 768 pixels also share a design. Both page designs are flexible to adapt to sizes above or below the 768-pixel threshold. This threshold is called the breakpoint—the point at which design layouts change in responsive design schemes. You will learn more about choosing breakpoints later in this chapter.

Building this type of design does not mean you are building two separate page layouts. Instead, you are using CSS style rules to change the order, positioning, and other display characteristics of your page elements as they adapt to different user devices. You build one basic layout and then use style rules targeted to different screen sizes to build a page that offers the best user experience for a range of devices. As the layout changes, the images can also adapt to different page sizes—these responsive images are controlled with CSS to flexibly change size as needed based on the page width.

Figure 12-3 shows the range of sizes and the breakpoint used in the style of the World Wildlife site shown in Figure 12-2. The web site design adapts to larger screen sizes, expanding and adding more content and navigation as the browser widths increase. In this example, the breakpoint is set to 768 pixels. This value can change based on the needs of the design. In some cases, designers will add breakpoints to more specifically target multiple devices, but in general, anything that keeps your code simple, such as choosing only one breakpoint, is a better choice.

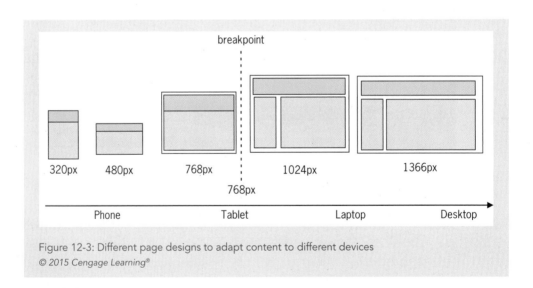

Figure 12-3: Different page designs to adapt content to different devices
© 2015 Cengage Learning®

By choosing a breakpoint and then designing for the devices above and below that point, you can adapt your design for optimal viewing in each range of screen sizes. The key concept to remember is that the content, not the device needs, should dictate when you add a breakpoint. You can control any number of style characteristics, including adding and removing entire columns, changing navigation, and stacking columns on top of each other to adapt the content as necessary. Figure 12-4 shows how the responsive page design for the Pittsburgh Children's museum adapts to different screen sizes.

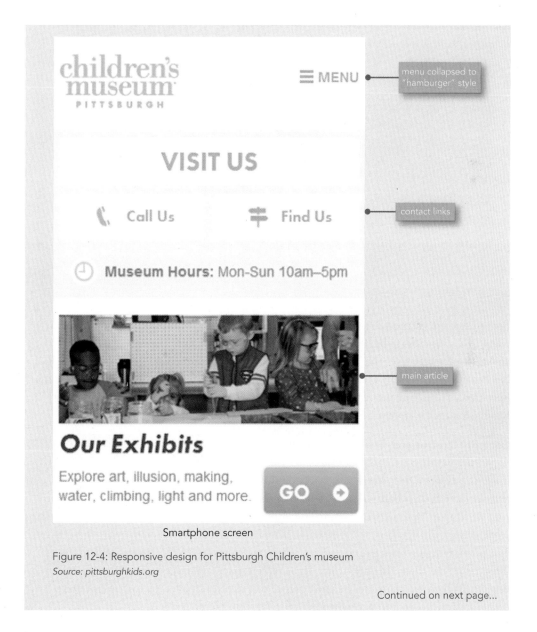

Smartphone screen

Figure 12-4: Responsive design for Pittsburgh Children's museum
Source: pittsburghkids.org

Continued on next page...

Desktop screen

Figure 12-4: (continued)

Both designs in Figure 12-4 contain the same elements; they are resized and rearranged using CSS style rules to be hidden or adapted to browser widths. The navigation in the smartphone screen uses the "hamburger" icon to represent a menu. This three-line symbol has become a universally accepted menu icon. The smartphone screen shows only the most important navigation and feature elements within the limited screen real estate. As the width expands for larger devices, more of these elements become available to the user.

Content-First Designs

As you are building responsive designs, you must think carefully about your content and users' needs when they come to your site on different devices. In some instances, such as the activity later in this chapter, you may be adapting an existing web page that was designed for a desktop or laptop device and making it responsive to smaller devices. Which elements of the design will you keep for the smaller screens? If you have the opportunity to build a responsive design from the ground up, where will you start? Will you create the mobile design first and then add enhancements as screen space increases for tablets and desktop devices? Which elements are the most crucial to a user on smaller devices? All of these considerations come into play when building for multiple devices.

As the idea of designing to adapt to multiple devices has evolved, the focus has changed from building the desktop design first and then paring down the content for mobile devices to focusing on the smaller design first and then adding more navigation and content choices as the screen size grows. Regardless of how you decide to work, look carefully at what users expect when they come to your site. Think about the following factors:

> Which content is valuable to the user of a smaller device? Which site functions (such as search or contact information) are important enough to include in your mobile site design?

> Think about how much content can be used effectively on each device. Do images need to be resized? Can users enter data into forms easily? Do font sizes need to be enlarged or reduced? Do site branding and colors need to be adapted for a range of device sizes?

> Will you have to edit or restructure content to make it useful on smaller devices?

Remember that redesigning the look of the site does not make your content instantly adaptable to multiple devices. You have to think about editing and restructuring your content to make it meaningful for the user.

Measurement Units in Responsive Designs

Previous examples showed the breakpoint measured in pixels to relate to typical device measurements. Breakpoints can also be measured in ems, which is a better choice. Pixels are easier to use when building responsive designs because they relate directly to screen resolutions, but ems are better because they are flexible, whereas pixels are a fixed measurement. If you set the breakpoint to a pixel width and users zoom their devices for better legibility, your design may not be displayed correctly. To solve this problem, you can use ems for measurements. It is easy to convert your measurements from pixels to ems by remembering that 1 em equals 16 pixels. You can also use a variety of converters on the web by searching for *em to pixel converter*. When you code measurements in CSS, add a comment to specify the equivalent value, as in the following code:

```
@media screen and (min-width: 21.25em)  /*340 px */
```

Using Media Queries to Apply Conditional Styles

CSS3 introduces media queries, an expansion on the concept of media types, which originated in CSS2. You can use **media types** to specify a style rule for each type of destination media, such as screen or print, without changing the content for each device. For example, the following link elements point to a specific style sheet based on the media destination.

```
<link rel="stylesheet" href="webstyle.css" media="screen">
<link rel="stylesheet" href="printstyle.css" media="print">
```

Using media types, you can apply conditional styles, styles that are applied only when the specified conditions are met. For example, if the browser detects a screen as the media device, it uses the webstyle.css style sheet. If the content's destination is a printer, the browser applies the printstyle.css style sheet rules. This simple style sheet switching technique can let web designers use one set of content for multiple destinations, as illustrated in Figure 1-8 in Chapter 1.

In CSS3, media types have been expanded into media queries, which let you create more precise rules for destination media. A media query contains both a media type and optional expressions that check conditions called media features, which include characteristics such as the width or height of the destination device.

In the example shown in Figure 12-5, the media type is *screen* and the media feature is *max-width*. The max-width value is 480 pixels. Note that the media feature is enclosed within parentheses.

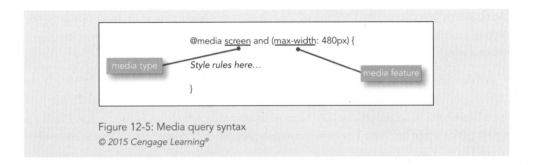

Figure 12-5: Media query syntax
© 2015 Cengage Learning®

With the addition of the following style rule, the browser will detect the maximum width of the screen. If it is 480 pixels or less, the header element will have a width of 90%.

```
@media screen and (max-width: 480px) {
header {width: 90%;}
}
```

You can add multiple media features with the *and* keyword.

```
@media screen and (min-width: 480px) and (max-width: 768px)
```

Any style rules that accompany this media query are applied when the width of the browser window falls between the stated minimum and maximum pixel values.

Applying Media Queries

You have three options for applying media queries to specify style rules. In the following three examples, the styles are applied if the device screen has a maximum width of

Chapter 12 Responsive Web Design

480 pixels. In the first method, the link element applies an external style sheet named mobiledevice.css if the device screen has a maximum width of 480 pixels. This link element resides in the head section of your document, as you read in Chapter 4.

```
<link rel="stylesheet" media="screen and (max-width: 480px)"
href="mobiledevice.css">
```

The next method uses an @import rule to apply an external style sheet named mobiledevice.css if the device has a screen with a maximum width of 480 pixels.

```
@import url("mobiledevice.css") screen and (max-width: 480px);
```

The third method uses the @media rule within a <style> element, as you saw earlier.

```
<style>
@media screen and (max-width: 480px) {
style rules here
    }
</style>
```

You can use multiple style rules if you want to have more than one breakpoint. For example, the following media queries let you apply different style rules for three browser sizes:

```
/* smaller than 1024 pixels */
@media screen and (max-width: 1024px) {
style rules here
}


/* smaller than 768 pixels */
@media screen and (max-width: 768px) {
style rules here
}
/* smaller than 480 pixels */
@media screen and (max-width: 480px) {
style rules here
}
```

Media Types

CSS3 supports the media types listed in Table 12-1. You can use these media types with media queries, as shown in the preceding examples and in Figure 12-5.

MEDIA TYPE	DESCRIPTION
all	Suitable for all devices
braille	Intended for Braille tactile feedback devices
embossed	Intended for paged Braille printers
handheld	Intended for handheld devices, typically those with small screens and limited bandwidth
print	Intended for paged material and for documents viewed in print preview mode
projection	Intended for projectors and other projected presentations
screen	Intended primarily for color desktop or handheld screens
speech	Intended for speech synthesizers; CSS2 had a similar media type called *aural*
tty	Intended for media that use a fixed-pitch character grid, such as teletypes, terminals, or portable devices with limited display capabilities. Authors should not use pixels as measurement units with this media type.
tv	Intended for television-type devices (low resolution, color, screens with limited scrollability, sound available)

Table 12-1: CSS3 Media Types
Source: www.w3.org/TR/css3-mediaqueries

Media Features

CSS3 supports the media features listed in Table 12-2. Notice that many of the features have *min-* and *max-* prefixes to express constraints.

FEATURE	DESCRIPTION	VALUE
width min-width max-width	The width of the output device's targeted display area. For print, this is the printable width of the page; for devices, it is the width of the viewport.	Length
height min-height max-height	The height of the output device's targeted display area. For print, this is the printable height of the page; for devices, it is the height of the viewport.	Length
device-width min-device-width max-device-width	The width of the output device screen. For print, this is the width of the page; for devices, it is the width of the viewport.	Length
device-height min-device-height max-device-height	The height of the output device screen. For print, this is the height of the page; for devices, it is the height of the viewport.	Length

Continued on next page...

FEATURE	DESCRIPTION	VALUE
orientation	The value is *portrait* when the length of the height media feature is greater than or equal to the length of the width media feature; otherwise, the value is *landscape*	Portrait | Landscape
aspect-ratio min-aspect-ratio max-aspect-ratio	The ratio of the value of the width media feature to the value of the height media feature	Ratio (for example, 16/9)
device-aspect-ratio min-device-aspect-ratio max-device-aspect-ratio	The ratio of the value of the device-width media feature to the value of the device-height media feature	Ratio
color min-color max-color	The number of bits per color component of the output device; if the device is not a color device, the value is zero	Integer
color-index min-color-index max-color-index	The number of entries in the color lookup table of the output device; if the device does not use a color lookup table, the value is zero	Integer
monochrome min-monochrome max-monochrome	The number of bits per pixel in a monochrome frame buffer; if the device is not a monochrome device, the output device value is 0	Integer
resolution min-resolution max-resolution	The screen resolution of the output device	Resolution (for example, 1024 x 768)
scan	Progressive | Interlace	Scanning process of "tv" output devices
grid	Query whether the output device is a grid or bitmap. If the output device is grid based (for example, a "tty" terminal or a phone display with only one fixed font), the value is 1; otherwise, the value is 0.	Integer

Table 12-2: CSS3 Media Features

Source: www.w3.org/TR/css3-mediaqueries/#media1

When building responsive web pages, you adapt the page to the width of the browser, which lets the user scroll to see the rest of the page content. As you saw in Chapter 7, the width is the dimension that most commonly needs to be constrained, while the height is based on the amount of content. It is always acceptable to let users scroll down the page to read more content, but making them scroll horizontally is unacceptable. On small devices like smartphones, horizontal scrolling is even more difficult. In Table 12-2, two media features address width: width and device-width. Device-width refers to the physical width of the device, while width refers to the browser width. Width is the more useful measurement when building responsive web pages, although developers occasionally use device-width to target a specific device like the Apple iPhone, which has a device width of 480 pixels. The examples in this chapter use width rather than device-width.

Table 12-2 lists other media features that you can use based on the specific needs of the web site or application. For example, the orientation feature can detect whether the device is in landscape or portrait mode, which is useful when you design content to adapt to tablets such as the iPad. Tablets can be viewed in either mode based on the user's preference. Other media features let you detect the color depth or device resolution. The best advice is to keep your designs and media queries as simple as possible, which results in easier maintenance.

Setting the Viewport Scale

In web design, the viewport is equal to the size of the browser window. In desktop devices the viewport can change based on the user's browser size, but on mobile devices the viewport is always the width of the device screen. The viewport on handheld devices is much narrower than a desktop browser window. The narrower viewport causes problems with responsive web pages that are designed to change based on the screen resolution. For example, some versions of the Apple iPhone report a screen width of 960 pixels when the physical device is actually much smaller. As a result, the device will automatically zoom the display so an entire web page fits on the screen. If you create a media query for smaller browser widths and the device does not report the correct width, the page design you want to display on the device will not render properly. You can solve this problem by including the following meta tag in the head section of your HTML page code.

```
<meta name="viewport" content="width=device-width, initial-scale=1.0">
```

This element tells the device to treat the actual device width as the screen width so pages you design for a certain size will render as expected.

Activity: Building a Basic Responsive Web Page

In the following set of steps, you will build a simple responsive web page that uses a style rule to change the display of the content when the browser width is greater than 480 pixels. In this example, the page is designed for a smaller device first, and then expands for a larger browser size. The breakpoint is 480 pixels. This is an approximate value that varies based on your design and device needs.

Save your file and test your work in the browser as you complete each step.

To build the responsive web page:

1. Copy the **ch12activity1.html** file from the Chapter12 folder provided with your Data Files to the Chapter12 folder in your work folder.

2. In your browser, open **ch12activity1.html**. The file looks like Figure 12-6, which shows a browser width of 320 pixels on the left. When you expand the browser window's width to 1024 pixels as shown on the right, the content fits, but it does not take advantage of the wider screen real estate. You will use an @media selector to adapt the content to the larger screen display.

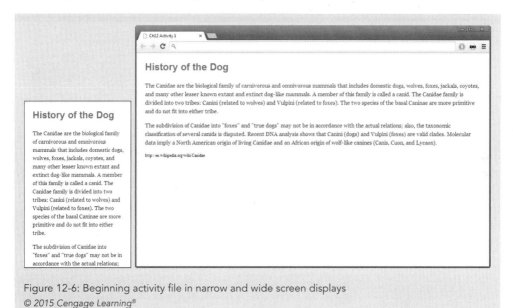

Figure 12-6: Beginning activity file in narrow and wide screen displays
© 2015 Cengage Learning®

3. Open the file in your HTML editor, and examine the code. This is a basic HTML file with <h1>, <p>, and <footer> elements. The style section contains basic style rules as shown.

```
<style>
body {
    font-size: 1em;
    line-height: 1.5em;
    margin-left: 1.5em;
    margin-right: 1.5em;
}
h1 {
    font-size: 1.75em;
    color: #008080;
    font-family: helvetica, arial, sans-serif;
}
```

```
p {
    font-family: georgia, serif;
    color: #3e3c3c;
}
footer {font-size: .75em;}
</style>
```

4. In the <head> section of the code, add the meta viewport element to set the viewport scale.

```
<html>
<head>
<title>Ch12 Activity 1</title>
<meta content="text/html; charset=utf-8" http-equiv="Content-Type">
<meta name="viewport" content="width=device-width,
initial-scale=1.0">
```

5. In the style section of the document, add a CSS comment to indicate where you will start the new code for the responsive style rule. Place this comment at the end of the existing style rules.

```
p {
    font-family: georgia, serif;
    color: #3e3c3c;
}
footer {font-size: .75em;}
/* Style rule for screens larger than 480 pixels */
```

6. Add an @media rule after the comment. Specify a media type of *screen* with a minimum width of 30em, which is equal to 480 pixels.

```
/* Style rule for screens larger than 480 pixels */
@media screen and (min-width: 30em) /* 480 px */ {       }
```

7. Add style rules only for the display characteristics you want to change for the larger screen display. In this example, you increase the body and h1 font sizes. Make sure to place your style rules within the existing @media curly brackets as shown.

```
@media screen and (min-width: 30em) /* 480 px */ {
body {
font-size: 1.5em;
}
```

```
h1 {
font-size: 2.5em;
}
}
```

8. Save your file, and view it in the browser. At widths below 480 pixels, the page looks like it did in Figure 12-7, but when you resize the browser to be more than 480 pixels, it has a larger heading and text size to fit the wider screen.

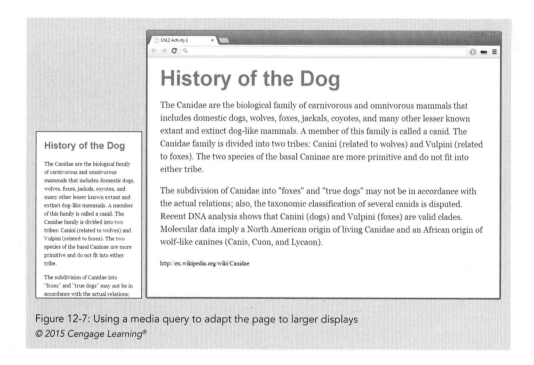

Figure 12-7: Using a media query to adapt the page to larger displays
© 2015 Cengage Learning®

In this activity, you learned how to use a style rule with an @media selector to change the display characteristics of a web page. This simple example demonstrated the concept of using breakpoints to adapt to different devices.

Creating Flexible Responsive Layouts

As you read in Chapter 7, flexible layouts are a good solution for adapting to different device sizes. However, this technique has limitations, so min-width and max-width style properties are often used to control the limits of the flexible design. By combining the techniques you learned in Chapter 7 with the power of media queries, you can extend the use of flexible layouts to adapt to any device size.

When you examine the code for the flexible layout you created in Chapter 7, you see it is limited to minimum and maximum widths of 750 pixels and 1220 pixels, respectively, as stated by the following style rule:

```
#wrapper {
    min-width: 750px;
    max-width: 1220px;
    margin-left: auto;
    margin-right: auto;
}
```

This code works well for any device with a width of 750 pixels and larger. At the larger display width, such as laptop or desktop size, the layout remains centered in the display, fixed at a width of 1220 pixels. At the lower end of the display width, the layout shrinks to fit. However, with any device less than 750 pixels wide such as a small tablet or smartphone, the user must scroll or pan to see the entire layout, as shown in Figure 12-8.

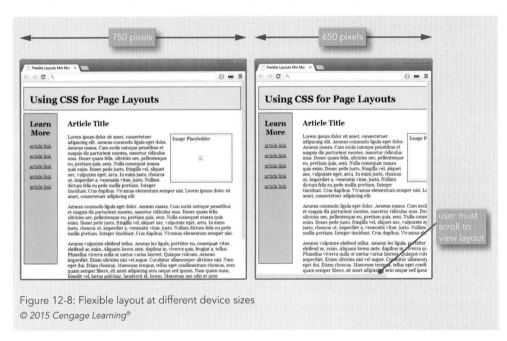

Figure 12-8: Flexible layout at different device sizes
© 2015 Cengage Learning®

To solve this problem, the layout's flexibility must be extended to include all screen sizes from smartphones to desktop displays. To visualize this idea, look at the design sketch in Figure 12-9. The sketch shows a design for smaller versions of the web page, which will accommodate both smartphones and smaller tablets.

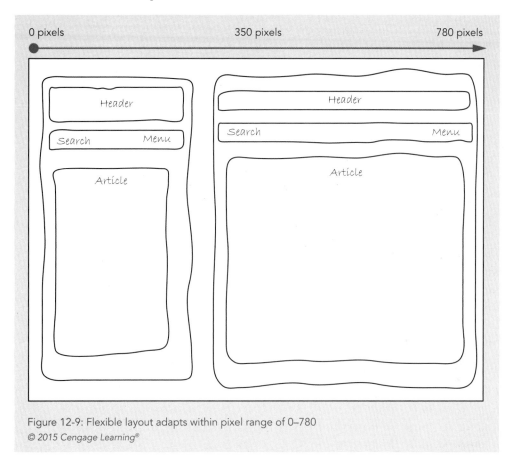

Figure 12-9: Flexible layout adapts within pixel range of 0–780
© 2015 Cengage Learning®

This proposed layout works well at any width between the smallest device and 780 pixels, a size that currently accommodates smartphones and many tablets. Once the design is expanded past 780 pixels, the content is spread too widely across the page. At this point, the page design can change to take advantage of the larger screen size, adding more navigation choices and content options for the user.

Once the browser width is increased, the layout can change to offer the user more options. Figure 12-10 shows the transition between widths of 780 pixels to 1220 pixels, the largest browser width. After 960 pixels, the page content stays fixed and centered in the browser window.

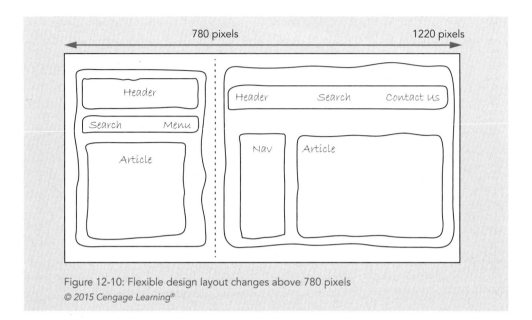

Figure 12-10: Flexible design layout changes above 780 pixels
© 2015 Cengage Learning®

The mockup in Figure 12-11 shows how the page design can adapt to different sizes within the ranges specified by the media queries. The page design changes when the width surpasses 780 pixels, and the layout stays centered in the browser window even at the largest browser width. At larger browser widths, the layout can adapt to the new usable area. More links, such as Search and Contact Us, can be included in the header. A full set of navigation links can be included in the left navigation column. The expanded article area has room for images or multiple columns of content or advertising space.

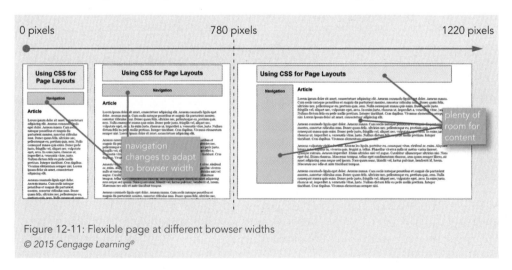

Figure 12-11: Flexible page at different browser widths
© 2015 Cengage Learning®

Examine the following code to see how the media queries and style rules work. Figure 12-12 shows the style rules of the page design for a width of less than 780 pixels.

```
/* below 780px   48.75em */
@media screen and (max-width: 48.75em)   {

div.wrapper {
    width: 100%;
    margin-left: auto;
    margin-right: auto;
}

header {
    width: 90%;
    border:   solid thin black;
    background-color: #e5dfec;
    text-align: center;
}


nav {
    border: solid thin black;
    background-color: #fabf8f;
    width: 90%;
    margin-top: 1em;
    text-align: center;
}

article {
    width: 90%;
    background-color: #fff;
}
}
```

max-width specified in ems

widths specified in percentages

margin settings will center the layout

margin specified in ems

Figure 12-12: Code for browser widths of less than 780 pixels
© 2015 Cengage Learning®

The section of style rules in Figure 12-12 shows the @media selector set to *screen* with a maximum width of 48.75em, or 780 pixels. These style rules apply only if the browser width is less than 780 pixels. The <head>, <nav>, and <article> elements will flow down the page in one column. Widths for each element are set to 90% of the available screen space, and the margin-left and margin-right properties are set to *auto* so the layout will automatically be centered in the browser window. Using ems for measurement ensures that the page is displayed correctly if the user zooms to enlarge or reduce the view.

The next set of style rules shown in Figure 12-13 controls browser widths greater than 780 pixels.

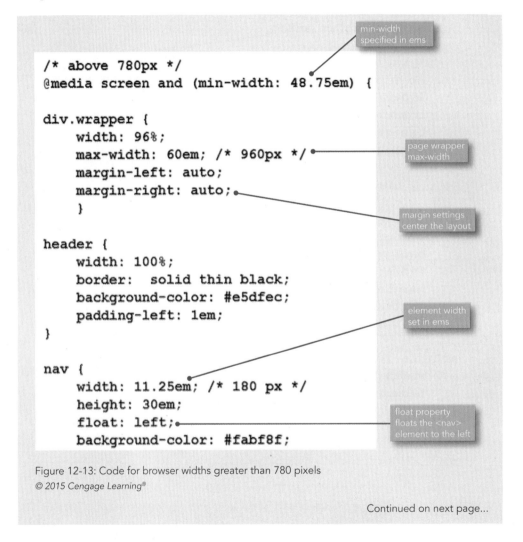

Figure 12-13: Code for browser widths greater than 780 pixels
© 2015 Cengage Learning®

Continued on next page...

```
        margin-left: auto;
        border: solid thin black;
        margin-top: .75em;
        text-align: center;
    }

    article {
        background-color: #fff;
        margin-left: 12.75em;  /* 204 px */
    }
    }
```

left margin set in ems

Figure 12-13: *(continued)*

The section of style rules in Figure 12-13 shows the @media selector set to *screen* with a minimum width of 48.75em, or 780 pixels. Now that the page is larger, the page wrapper has a fixed width of 960 pixels. The page design will be fixed at this width. The remaining background space will be evenly divided in the margins. The float property positions the <nav> element on the left side of the page. The width of the navigation column is set in ems. The <article> element has a left margin, also set in ems, that places it to the right of the <nav> element.

Using ems and percentages in this design creates a layout that is flexible across all devices, regardless of their physical screen size. The breakpoint is determined by the needs of the content, not by specific devices.

Another technique for adapting to different browser widths is to use the display property to remove or add content as needed. The page in Figure 12-14 shows an example of hiding or displaying content based on the browser width. The larger page design takes advantage of expanded screen space, while the smaller mobile design focuses on user navigation and content access. These designs adapt to their devices to make browsing easier. Besides using different sets of style rules for each page size, as you saw earlier, the <article> element is removed from the mobile display when the display property is used with a value of *none*.

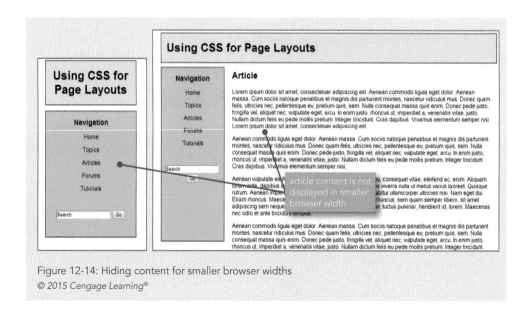

Figure 12-14: Hiding content for smaller browser widths
© 2015 Cengage Learning®

Examine the code in Figure 12-15 to see how the display property is used. You can read more about the display property in Chapter 6.

```
/* below 780px  48.75em */
@media screen and (max-width: 48.75em)  {

div.wrapper {
    width: 90%;
    margin-left: auto;
    margin-right: auto;
}


header {
    width: 90%;
    border:  solid thin black;
```

Figure 12-15: Code for a browser width of less than 780 pixels
© 2015 Cengage Learning®

Continued on next page...

```
        background-color: #e5dfec;
        text-align: center;
}


nav {
        border: solid thin black;
        background-color: #fabf8f;
        width: 90%;
        margin-top: 1em;
        text-align: center;
}

article {
        display: none;        ← display property hides <article>
}                                 element
}
```

Figure 12-15: (continued)

As you can see, when the browser width is less than 48.75em (780 pixels), the <article> element is set to a display value of *none*, which removes it from the browser display. When the browser width extends beyond 780 pixels, the rule is cancelled and the <article> element content will appear, as shown in Figure 12-14.

Creating Responsive Navigation Schemes

When readers access your content on a small device like a smartphone, they have different navigation motives than when using a larger screen. A site that is well designed for mobile users should offer the most popular links so they are readily available on the first page. Navigating on a small device is much easier when the navigation is direct and accessible, quickly getting users to the content they desire. Refer to Figure 9-3 in Chapter 9 to see samples of common navigation schemes for mobile devices.

As Figure 12-16 shows, you can change the navigation options to adapt to different device sizes and user expectations. With a larger browser width, a more traditional web page is available with familiar navigation options on the left side, header and footer information, and main article content. The interface for smaller browser widths offers navigation and search options; it is a single-page interface that provides access to the entire layout. Users can search or browse lists of content for quick access.

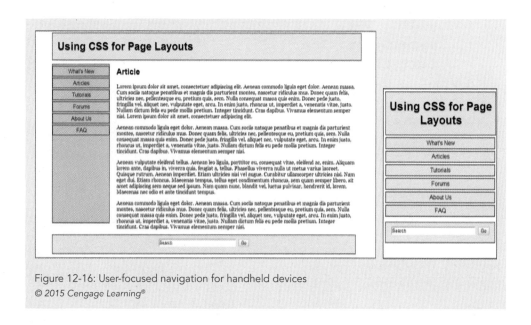

Figure 12-16: User-focused navigation for handheld devices
© 2015 Cengage Learning®

As you saw before, these two page layouts are derived from the same HTML code and use different styles depending on the width of the browser. The style sheet has three sections: one for common styles that are shared across both page layouts, and two other sections of style rules that the browser applies depending on whether the browser width is above or below 26.25em (420 pixels). The common styles, shown in Figure 12-17, apply to both sets of style rules. They include settings for the body and heading fonts, basic list settings for the navigation list, and style rules for the <footer> element that contains the search form. The <footer> element uses ems for measurement, so it adapts to either page layout because its measurements are flexible based on the browser width.

```
/* common styles */
body {font-family: georgia;}

h1, h2, h3 {font-family: arial;}

ul#navlist {
    margin:0;
    padding:0;
    list-style:none;
    font-family: arial, sans-serif;
}

footer.search {
    border:  solid thin black;
    background-color: #e5dfec;
    text-align: center;
    padding-top: .625em;
    padding-bottom: 1.25em;
    margin-top: 1em;
}
```

these styles are common to both page layouts

default settings for unordered navigation list

<footer> element styles are flexible based on ems for measurement; they adapt to either page style

Figure 12-17: Common layout styles
© 2015 Cengage Learning®

The next section of style rules, shown in Figure 12-18, sets the styles for the page when the width is less than 26.25em (420 pixels). The style for the <article> element sets the display property to *none*, hiding the article content from view and removing the space the element takes in the browser. The list styles that create the navigation for the handheld device select the <a> elements within the list. Refer to Chapter 9 to refresh your skills for creating navigation lists if necessary.

```
/* below 420px */
@media screen and (max-width: 26.25em)   {

header {
    width: 100%;
    border:  solid thin black;
    background-color: #e5dfec;
    text-align: center;
}

nav {
    width: 100%;
    text-align: center;
}

article {
    display: none;
}

ul#navlist li a {
    text-decoration:none;
    display:block;
    border: 2px solid #0033cc;
    padding: .31em;
    background-color: #e5dfec;
    color:#000;
    margin-top: .31em;
}
}
```

styles for layouts under 26.25em (420 pixels)

<article> element is hidden with the display property

unordered list styles for handheld device

Figure 12-18: Style rules for widths less than 26.25em
© 2015 Cengage Learning®

The final set of style rules, shown in Figure 12-19, is for browsers that have a width greater than 26.25em (420 pixels). The page now needs the wrapper to expand beyond a width of 60em (960 pixels). If the browser is wider, the page will remain centered in the window. The <nav> element is now a floating element that aligns to the left side of the browser window, while the article is positioned using a left margin.

```
/* above 420px */
@media screen and (min-width: 26.25em) {

div.wrapper {
    width: 96%;
    max-width: 60em; /* 960px */
    margin-left: auto;
    margin-right: auto;
    }
header {
    width: 100%;
    border:  solid thin black;
    background-color: #e5dfec;
    padding-left: 1em;
}
nav {
    width: 11.25em; /* 180 px */
    height: 30em;
    float: left;
    background-color: #fabf8f;
    margin-left: auto;
    border: solid thin black;
```

styles for layouts above 26.25em (420 pixels)

wrapper styles center page at widths above 60em (960 pixels)

<nav> element floats to the left and is 11.25em (180 pixels) wide

Figure 12-19: Style rules for widths greater than 26.25em
© 2015 Cengage Learning®

Continued on next page...

```
        margin-top: .75em;
        text-align: center;
}
ul#navlist li a {
        text-decoration: none;
        display:block;
        padding: .31em;
        border: solid 1px;
        color: #000;
        margin-top: 5px;
}
article {
        background-color: #fff;
        margin-left: 12.75em;   /* 204 px */
}
}
```

> <article> element is offset from the left using the margin-left property

Figure 12-19: (continued)

These style rules combine to create a web page that offers adaptive navigation based on the needs of the user. The smaller device has essential navigation and search features. The same content expands to adapt to tablets and larger devices, such as laptops, and offers a more full-featured interface.

Using Responsive Images

When building responsive layouts, you must consider the behavior of your images and how they react to changing browser widths across display devices. In Figure 12-20, the image expands to fit devices with widths of less than 48.75em (780 pixels). At larger browser widths, the image is fixed and floats to the left of the article content.

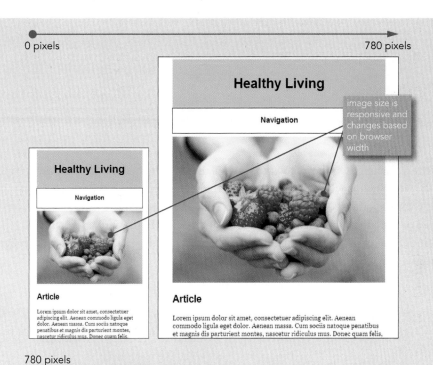

780 pixels

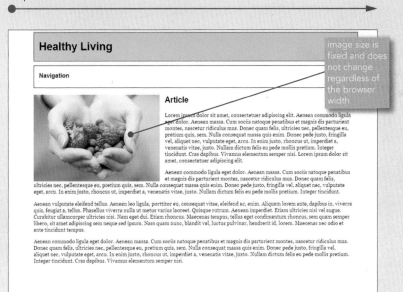

Figure 12-20: Responsive and fixed images in the browser

© iStockphoto.com/OlgaMiltsova

Creating responsive images is easy; just add a simple style rule to your code. For example, the style rule that creates the responsive image in Figure 12-20 uses the max-width property set to 100%:

```
img {
    max-width: 100%;
    height: auto;
}
```

By setting the height property to *auto*, you ensure that the image's aspect ratio is maintained when the image is scaled up or down to meet the needs of the responsive design. You can read about aspect ratios in Chapter 8. Remember that the width is based on the size of the containing element; you are not referring to the actual size, but its container. You leave out the actual image dimensions in the HTML code for the image, as shown:

```
<img src="freshberries.png" alt="Hands holding fresh berries">
```

You should use images that are larger than the container sizes to which you will adapt them. To maintain image quality, it is better to reduce an image rather than enlarge it from its original size.

With a style rule, you can choose to set a minimum fixed width for the image if necessary:

```
img {
    min-width: 240px;
}
```

In this example, you might decide that the image quality starts to degrade after a certain width is reached, or that the layout requires the image to maintain a minimum size. Either way, you have control over the image's adaptive behavior. In Figure 12-21, the image will stop being reduced at a width of 18.75em (240 px), regardless of the container size.

Healthy Living

Navigation

image centered, min-width restricted to 240 pixels

Article

Lorem ipsum dolor sit amet, consectetuer adipiscing elit. Aenean commodo ligula eget dolor. Aenean massa. Cum sociis natoque penatibus et magnis dis parturient montes, nascetur ridiculus mus. Donec quam felis, ultricies nec, pellentesque eu, pretium quis,

Figure 12-21: Image size restricted with min-width
© iStockphoto.com/OlgaMiltsova

You can wrap text around an image in a responsive column by floating the image and setting a width for the image that is a percentage of the containing column. Figure 12-22 shows an image floating within the column.

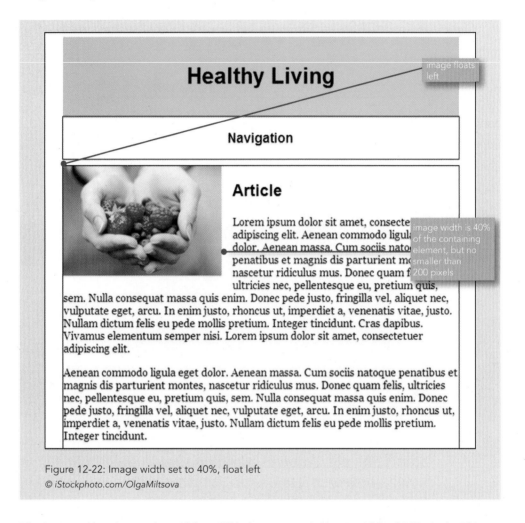

Figure 12-22: Image width set to 40%, float left
© iStockphoto.com/OlgaMiltsova

The image style rule sets the width at 40%, down to a minimum width of 200 pixels. This style rule keeps the image from becoming too small in relation to the surrounding text.

```
img {
    float: left;
    width: 40%;
```

```
    height: auto;
        min-width: 200px;
    margin: 0 1em 1em 0;
}
```

Remember that this style rule would be applied only when the browser requires a narrower width for a handheld device.

Responsive Images for High-Resolution Devices

As screen technologies improve, manufacturers can offer devices with super-high resolution displays. Images look incredibly sharp on these devices when displayed in high resolution. This causes a problem for designers who want to take advantage of high-resolution devices by using higher-definition images. Users with lower-resolution displays or slower connection speeds will have to download the larger files that accompany higher-resolution devices. Developers are trying to solve this problem in a variety of ways, including using JavaScript applications that switch images based on the device type. The W3C has a standards-based solution that is not currently supported by major browsers, but support may be available by the time you read this book. This solution is the srcset attribute of the <img> element, which supports the use of different files for the same image based on the device's needs. You can read more at *www.w3.org/html/wg/drafts/srcset/w3c-srcset/#adaptive-images*.

Building a Responsive Design

In the following activity, you will turn a typical web page design into a responsive web page that adapts to the screen sizes for different devices. You will examine the natural breakpoints in the content as it flows between screen dimensions and determine the best responsive content layouts. Using media queries, you will build a set of style rules that determines which set to apply to a single source of content. You will then create an external style sheet that contains style rules for the two content breakpoints.

Creating the Design

Figure 12-23 shows the Healthy Living web page, which is designed for a typical laptop or desktop monitor. The page contains a header, navigation, three columns of content, and a footer. The page is designed to be flexible within the range of most laptop and desktop computers.

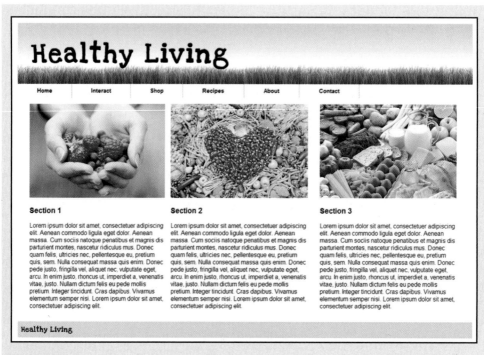

Figure 12-23: Healthy Living web page designed for laptop and desktop browser widths
© iStockphoto.com/OlgaMiltsova, © iStockphoto.com/aluxum, © iStockphoto.com/fcafotodigital,
© iStockphoto.com/fpm

Normally, such a web page has a minimum width property to keep the page design from collapsing if the browser width is too small for the content. For the purpose of determining the natural breakpoints in the content, examine what happens to the page content as the browser is resized to smaller widths. Figure 12-24 shows the page at two browser widths that are smaller than the designed layout.

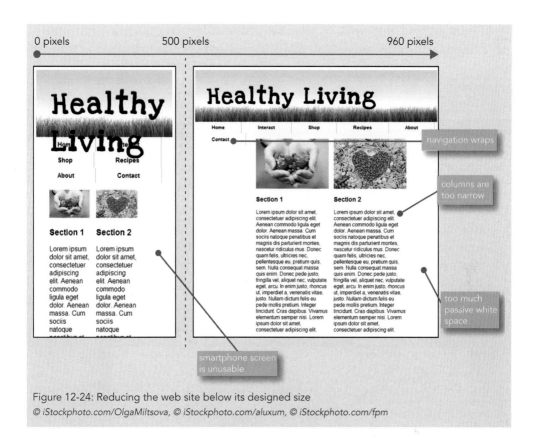

Figure 12-24: Reducing the web site below its designed size
© iStockphoto.com/OlgaMiltsova, © iStockphoto.com/aluxum, © iStockphoto.com/fpm

At just below 960 pixels, the layout starts to degrade. The navigation bar starts to wrap and the columns become too narrow. The margins of the columns contain too much passive white space. The layout breaks down at this width as the browser tries to wrap and fit all the content.

At less than 500 pixels, which is approaching smartphone size, the layout totally falls apart. The heading is too big for its space and interferes with the navigation. The two article images are too small to see and the narrow text column is unreadable.

Although the layout doesn't work at these sizes, the way the content responds helps determine where to build adaptations to the screen size. For this layout, you will create two breakpoints in the following activity: one at 960 pixels, where the content starts to break, and another at 500 pixels, to adapt to smartphone screens. Figure 12-25 shows a sketch of the two proposed layouts.

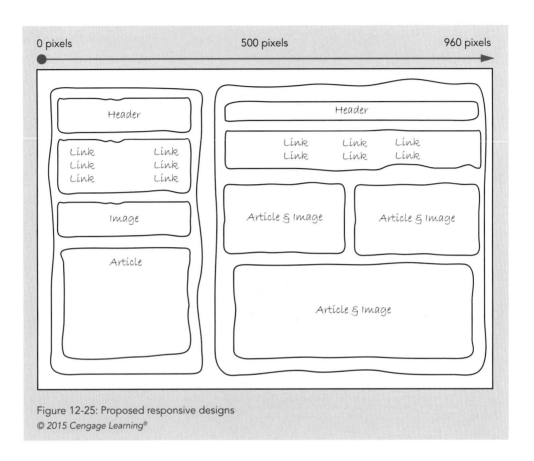

Figure 12-25: Proposed responsive designs
© 2015 Cengage Learning®

Activity: Creating a Responsive Style Sheet

As you work through this activity, remember to save your file and test your work in the browser as you complete each step. You should resize the browser so you can see the effect of the browser width on the responsive design.

Examining the HTML File

You will start by examining the structure of the HTML file.

1. Copy the **ch12activity2.html** file from the Chapter12 folder provided with your Data Files to the Chapter12 folder in your work folder. Repeat this step to copy the following image files and CSS files needed for the activity:

   > **freshberries.png**

   > **grasswithsky.png**

> **healthyfoods.png**

> **heartveggies.png**

> **main.css**

> **responsive.css**

2. In your browser, open **ch12activity2.html**, which looks like Figure 12-26.

3. Open the file in your HTML editor, and examine the code. In the head section, notice that the viewport meta element has already been included to set the viewport scale. A link element points to the style sheet file named **main.css**, the main file used for the layout's common styles.

```
<html>
<head>
<title>Chapter 12 Activity 2</title>
link for fonts
<meta content="text/html; charset=utf-8" http-equiv="Content-Type">
<meta name="viewport" content="width=device-width, initial-
scale=1.0">
<link href="main.css" rel="stylesheet">
```

4. Examine the rest of the HTML code, and notice that the page has a fairly simple three-column layout that uses the element floating techniques you learned about in Chapter 7. Figure 12-26 shows the structure of the page.

5. Compare the code in **ch12activity2.html** to the figure to understand the HTML structure of the page. Note the following:

> The <header> has a background image that tiles across the page and a child <h1> element that contains the web site title.

> The <nav> element contains a CSS-styled, unordered navigation list like the ones you learned about in Chapter 9.

> The three content columns float to the left, and each takes 30% of the browser width. Various margin settings on each column set the correct alignment. The footer element is set to clear both margins and keep the floating columns in line.

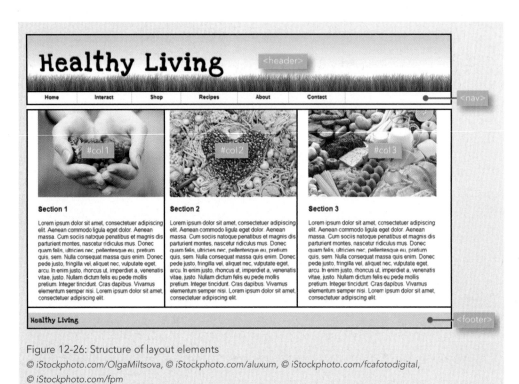

Figure 12-26: Structure of layout elements

© iStockphoto.com/OlgaMiltsova, © iStockphoto.com/aluxum, © iStockphoto.com/fcafotodigital,
© iStockphoto.com/fpm

Examining the Main CSS File

The file main.css is linked in the ch12activity2.html file as the default style sheet for the Healthy Living web page. The file contains style rules for the elements shown in Figure 12-26 and style rules to customize the navigation, fonts, and background image.

1. In your text editor, open the file **main.css**. Examine the style rule code to familiarize yourself with the style rules.

2. Notice the existing column id style rules. You will override these rules with responsive style rules later in this activity. The new style rules will help the page adapt to different screen widths as needed.

```
#col1 {
    float: left;
    width: 30%;
    margin: 1em 1em 1em 2em;
}
```

```
#col2 {
    float: left;
    width: 30%;
    margin: 1em 2em 0 0;
}


#col3 {
    float: left;
    width: 30%;
    margin-top: 1em;
}
```

3. Close the file.

Linking to the Responsive Style Sheet File

You will link to the style sheet file named responsive.css. This file will contain style rules that enable the page to adapt to smaller device sizes. You will use a media query to apply responsive.css only when the browser width is less than 960 pixels.

1. Continue working in the file **ch12activity2.html**, and add a new link element that points to the file **responsive.css**.

```
<meta content="text/html; charset=utf-8" http-equiv="Content-Type">
<meta name="viewport" content="width=device-width, initial-scale=1.0">
<link href="main.css" rel="stylesheet">
<link href="responsive.css" rel="stylesheet">
```

2. Add a condition to the link element using the media attribute. This condition states that the style sheet **responsive.css** will be used only when the browser width is less than 960 pixels. At widths of more than 960 pixels, the style rules default to the ones in **main.css**.

```
<link href="main.css" rel="stylesheet">
<link href="responsive.css" rel="stylesheet" media="screen and (max-width: 960px)">
```

3. Save the file, and keep it open in your text editor so you can refer to the HTML code when you create your style rules.

Building the 960-Pixel Breakpoint Styles

Create the alternate style sheet rules that are applied when the browser width is between 500 pixels and 960 pixels. Refer back to the sketch in Figure 12-25 to see the design.

1. Use your text editor to open the file **responsive.css**.

2. Add a media query that applies style rules when the browser width is 31.25em (500 pixels) or more. Add a comment to explain the rule. The style rules will be added between the curly brackets, as shown.

```
/* responsive.css */


/* 500 to 960 pixels */
@media screen and (min-width: 31.25em) {


}
```

3. Start by adding a rule to customize the navigation bar so that three links appear in a row. To add this rule, select the li elements and set their width to 33%. This selector uses descendant selection, which you learned about in Chapter 4.

```
/* responsive.css   */


/*  500 to 960 pixels */
@media screen and (min-width: 31.25em) {
nav ul li {
    width: 33%;
}
}
```

4. Save the file, and view **ch12activity2.html** in the browser. Make sure your browser is narrowed to a width of less than 960 pixels. The result should look similar to Figure 12-27. The navigation links line up nicely, but the third column has dropped in the layout.

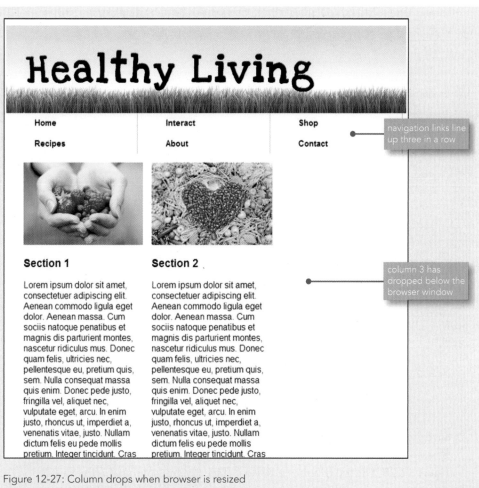

Figure 12-27: Column drops when browser is resized
© iStockphoto.com/OlgaMiltsova, © iStockphoto.com/aluxum, © iStockphoto.com/fpm

5. You will create a two-column layout from columns 1 and 2, and have column 3 appear below the two main columns. Examine the **ch12activity2.html** file, and note the three section elements that contain the column content with col1, col2, and col3 ids, such as the one for col1 shown below:

```
<section id="col1">
<img src="freshberries.png" alt="hands holding fresh berries">
<h3>Section 1</h3>
```

```
<p>
Lorem ipsum ...
</p>
</section>
```

6. In **responsive.css**, apply styles to create the new two-column layout. The columns are already floating, so you just need to adjust the width. Use the id selector to select columns 1 and 2, and set the width for each to 43%.

```
/* responsive.css */

/*  500 to 960 pixels */
@media screen and (min-width: 31.25em) {
nav ul li {
    width: 33%;
}
#col1 {
    width: 43%;
    }
#col2 {
    width: 43%;
}
}
```

7. Save the file, and view **ch12activity2.html** in the browser. Make sure your browser is narrowed to a width of less than 960 pixels. The result should look similar to Figure 12-28. The top columns now float correctly, but column 3 is floating to the right.

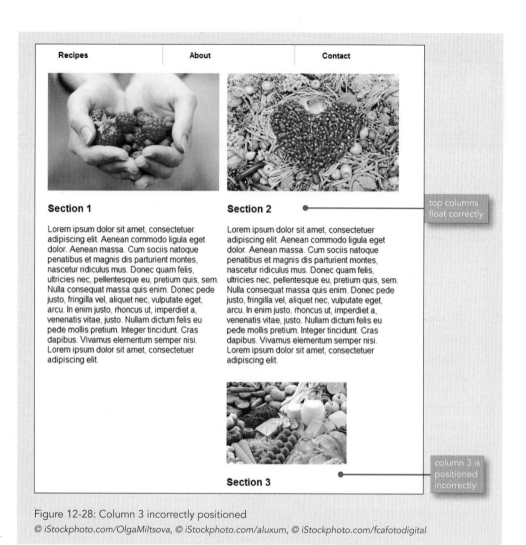

| Recipes | About | Contact |

Section 1

Lorem ipsum dolor sit amet, consectetuer adipiscing elit. Aenean commodo ligula eget dolor. Aenean massa. Cum sociis natoque penatibus et magnis dis parturient montes, nascetur ridiculus mus. Donec quam felis, ultricies nec, pellentesque eu, pretium quis, sem. Nulla consequat massa quis enim. Donec pede justo, fringilla vel, aliquet nec, vulputate eget, arcu. In enim justo, rhoncus ut, imperdiet a, venenatis vitae, justo. Nullam dictum felis eu pede mollis pretium. Integer tincidunt. Cras dapibus. Vivamus elementum semper nisi. Lorem ipsum dolor sit amet, consectetuer adipiscing elit.

Section 2

Lorem ipsum dolor sit amet, consectetuer adipiscing elit. Aenean commodo ligula eget dolor. Aenean massa. Cum sociis natoque penatibus et magnis dis parturient montes, nascetur ridiculus mus. Donec quam felis, ultricies nec, pellentesque eu, pretium quis, sem. Nulla consequat massa quis enim. Donec pede justo, fringilla vel, aliquet nec, vulputate eget, arcu. In enim justo, rhoncus ut, imperdiet a, venenatis vitae, justo. Nullam dictum felis eu pede mollis pretium. Integer tincidunt. Cras dapibus. Vivamus elementum semper nisi. Lorem ipsum dolor sit amet, consectetuer adipiscing elit.

top columns float correctly

Section 3

column 3 is positioned incorrectly

Figure 12-28: Column 3 incorrectly positioned

8. To fix the float problem, return to **responsive.css** and add a style rule for column 3 that uses the clear property, as described in Chapter 7. Set the float to *none* and the width to 90%, and then set the margins as shown.

```
/* responsive.css  */

/*  500 to 960 pixels */
@media screen and (min-width: 31.25em) {
nav ul li {
    width: 33%;
}
#col1 {
    width: 43%;
    }
#col2 {
    width: 43%;
}
#col3 {
    clear: both;
    float: none;
    width: 90%;
    margin: 0 1em 1em 1.5em;

}

}
```

9. Save the file, and view **ch12activity2.html** in the browser. Make sure your browser is narrowed to a width of less than 960 pixels. The result should look similar to Figure 12-29. The third column is now positioned under the two floating columns, but the image needs to be styled to fit the space better, and the text has to wrap around the image.

Section 1

Lorem ipsum dolor sit amet, consectetuer adipiscing elit. Aenean commodo ligula eget dolor. Aenean massa. Cum sociis natoque penatibus et magnis dis parturient montes, nascetur ridiculus mus. Donec quam felis, ultricies nec, pellentesque eu, pretium quis, sem. Nulla consequat massa quis enim. Donec pede justo, fringilla vel, aliquet nec, vulputate eget, arcu. In enim justo, rhoncus ut, imperdiet a, venenatis vitae, justo. Nullam dictum felis eu pede mollis pretium. Integer tincidunt. Cras dapibus. Vivamus elementum semper nisi. Lorem ipsum dolor sit amet, consectetuer adipiscing elit.

Section 2

Lorem ipsum dolor sit amet, consectetuer adipiscing elit. Aenean commodo ligula eget dolor. Aenean massa. Cum sociis natoque penatibus et magnis dis parturient montes, nascetur ridiculus mus. Donec quam felis, ultricies nec, pellentesque eu, pretium quis, sem. Nulla consequat massa quis enim. Donec pede justo, fringilla vel, aliquet nec, vulputate eget, arcu. In enim justo, rhoncus ut, imperdiet a, venenatis vitae, justo. Nullam dictum felis eu pede mollis pretium. Integer tincidunt. Cras dapibus. Vivamus elementum semper nisi. Lorem ipsum dolor sit amet, consectetuer adipiscing elit.

> column 3 image is too large and text needs to wrap around image

Section 3

Lorem ipsum dolor sit amet, consectetuer adipiscing elit. Aenean commodo ligula eget dolor. Aenean massa. Cum sociis natoque penatibus et magnis dis parturient montes, nascetur ridiculus mus. Donec quam felis, ultricies nec, pellentesque eu, pretium quis, sem. Nulla consequat massa quis enim. Donec pede justo, fringilla vel, aliquet nec, vulputate eget, arcu. In enim justo, rhoncus ut, imperdiet a, venenatis vitae, justo. Nullam dictum felis eu pede mollis pretium. Integer tincidunt. Cras dapibus. Vivamus elementum semper nisi. Lorem ipsum dolor sit amet, consectetuer adipiscing elit.

Healthy Living

Figure 12-29: Column 3 image does not fit the layout properly

© iStockphoto.com/OlgaMiltsova, © iStockphoto.com/aluxum, © iStockphoto.com/fcafotodigital

10. In **responsive.css**, add a style rule that selects the image in the column with the id #col3. This rule uses descendant selection, which was covered in Chapter 4.

```
/* responsive.css   */


/*  500 to 960 pixels */
@media screen and (min-width: 31.25em) {
```

```
nav ul li {
    width: 33%;
}
#col1 {
    width: 43%;
    }
#col2 {
    width: 43%;
}
#col3 {
    clear: both;
    float: none;
    width: 90%;
    margin: 0 1em 1em 1.5em;
}
#col3 img {
    float: left;
    width: 30%;
    margin: .5em 1em 1em 0;
}
}
```

11. Finally, add a style rule that restricts the layout from wrapping under 600 pixels before the transition to the next breakpoint, which you will add in the following section.

```
/* responsive.css   */

/*   500 to 960 pixels */
@media screen and (min-width: 31.25em) {
nav ul li {
    width: 33%;
}
```

```
#col1 {
   width: 43%;
   }
#col2 {
   width: 43%;
}
#col3 {
   clear: both;
   float: none;
   width: 90%;
   margin: 0 1em 1em 1.5em;
}
#col3 img {
   float: left;
   width: 30%;
   margin: .5em 1em 1em 0;
}

   div.wrapper {min-width: 600px;}{
}
```

12. Save the file, and view **ch12activity2.html** in the browser. Make sure your browser is narrowed to a width of less than 960 pixels. The result should look similar to Figure 12-30. This is the completed web page design for tablet-sized layouts that are approximately 500 to 960 pixels wide.

Healthy Living

Home	Interact	Shop
Recipes	About	Contact

Section 1

Lorem ipsum dolor sit amet, consectetuer adipiscing elit. Aenean commodo ligula eget dolor. Aenean massa. Cum sociis natoque penatibus et magnis dis parturient montes, nascetur ridiculus mus. Donec quam felis, ultricies nec, pellentesque eu, pretium quis, sem. Nulla consequat massa quis enim. Donec pede justo, fringilla vel, aliquet nec, vulputate eget, arcu. In enim justo, rhoncus ut, imperdiet a, venenatis vitae, justo. Nullam dictum felis eu pede mollis pretium. Integer tincidunt. Cras dapibus. Vivamus elementum semper nisi. Lorem ipsum dolor sit amet, consectetuer adipiscing elit.

Section 2

Lorem ipsum dolor sit amet, consectetuer adipiscing elit. Aenean commodo ligula eget dolor. Aenean massa. Cum sociis natoque penatibus et magnis dis parturient montes, nascetur ridiculus mus. Donec quam felis, ultricies nec, pellentesque eu, pretium quis, sem. Nulla consequat massa quis enim. Donec pede justo, fringilla vel, aliquet nec, vulputate eget, arcu. In enim justo, rhoncus ut, imperdiet a, venenatis vitae, justo. Nullam dictum felis eu pede mollis pretium. Integer tincidunt. Cras dapibus. Vivamus elementum semper nisi. Lorem ipsum dolor sit amet, consectetuer adipiscing elit.

Section 3

Lorem ipsum dolor sit amet, consectetuer adipiscing elit. Aenean commodo ligula eget dolor. Aenean massa. Cum sociis natoque penatibus et magnis dis parturient montes, nascetur ridiculus mus. Donec quam felis, ultricies nec, pellentesque eu, pretium quis, sem. Nulla consequat massa quis enim. Donec pede justo, fringilla vel, aliquet nec, vulputate eget, arcu. In enim justo, rhoncus ut, imperdiet a, venenatis vitae, justo. Nullam dictum felis eu pede mollis pretium. Integer tincidunt. Cras dapibus. Vivamus elementum semper nisi. Lorem ipsum dolor sit amet, consectetuer adipiscing elit.

Healthy Living

Figure 12-30: Responsive web page for tablet devices

© iStockphoto.com/OlgaMiltsova, © iStockphoto.com/aluxum, © iStockphoto.com/fcafotodigital, © iStockphoto.com/fpm

Building the 500-Pixel Breakpoint Styles

You will create a second set of alternate style sheet rules to apply when the browser width is less than 500 pixels. This design consists of a single column of content that fits most smartphone screens. The user will scroll up and down to read the content. Refer back to the sketch in Figure 12-25 to see the design.

1. Continue working in the file **responsive.css**. You will add a new media query that applies style rules when the browser width is 31.25em (500 pixels) or less. Add a comment to explain the query. You can place this rule immediately after the existing media query at the bottom of the file.

```
/* under 500 px */
@media screen and (max-width: 31.25em ) {

}
```

2. Refer back to Figure 12-24, and note that the heading is too large for the browser width. Add a style rule that will change the header size to 48 pixels, remove all of the padding, and center the text in the browser.

```
/*   under 500 px   */
@media screen and (max-width: 31.25em ) {
header h1 {
    font-size: 48px;
    padding: 0;
    text-align: center;
}

}
```

3. Save the file, and view **ch12activity2.html** in the browser. Make sure your browser is narrowed to a width of less than 500 pixels. The result should look like Figure 12-31. The heading is displayed correctly, but the navigation is misaligned and the columns are too narrow to read.

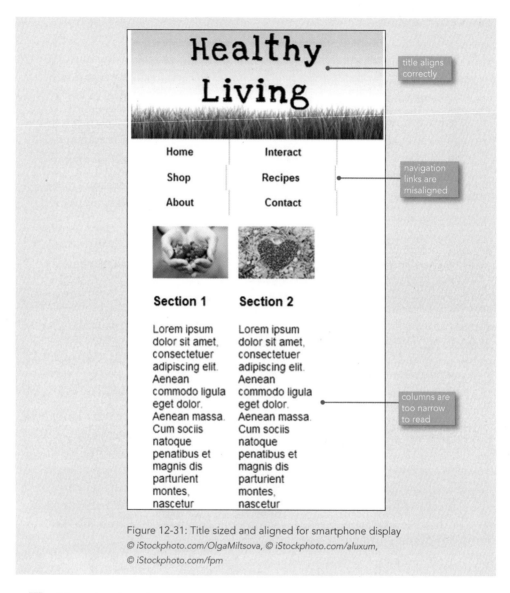

Figure 12-31: Title sized and aligned for smartphone display
© iStockphoto.com/OlgaMiltsova, © iStockphoto.com/aluxum,
© iStockphoto.com/fpm

Annotations in figure:
- title aligns correctly
- navigation links are misaligned
- columns are too narrow to read

4. Add a style rule to fix the navigation links so that they are displayed two per line. To add this rule, select the li elements and set their width to 50%.

```
/* under  500 px  */
@media screen and (max-width: 31.25em ) {
header h1 {
    font-size: 48px;
```

```
   padding: 0;
   text-align: center;
}
nav ul li {width: 50%}
}
```

5. Save the file, and view **ch12activity2.html** in the browser. Make sure your browser is narrowed to a width of less than 500 pixels. The result should look like Figure 12-32. The navigation links now align properly.

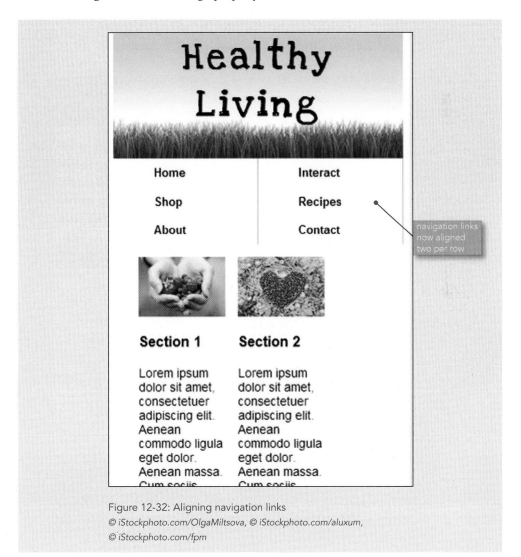

Figure 12-32: Aligning navigation links
© iStockphoto.com/OlgaMiltsova, © iStockphoto.com/aluxum,
© iStockphoto.com/fpm

6. To fix the columns so the content is legible, remove the floats and display the columns as a single column that fills the browser width. You can write one style rule that affects all three columns. Set the margin to zero, the float to none, and the width to 100%.

```css
/*  under 500 px  */
@media screen and (max-width: 31.25em ) {
header h1 {
    font-size: 48px;
    padding: 0;
    text-align: center;
}
nav ul li {width: 50%}
#col1, #col2, #col3 {
    margin: 0;
    float: none;
    width: 100%;
}
}
```

7. Save the file, and view **ch12activity2.html** in the browser. Make sure your browser is narrowed to a width of less than 500 pixels. The result should look like Figure 12-33. The column now fills the browser width.

Figure 12-33: Responsive web page for smartphones
© iStockphoto.com/OlgaMiltsova, © iStockphoto.com/fpm

8. Finally, add a style rule for the images that sets their display type to *block*, and add a margin property that sets the top and bottom margins to zero and the left and right margins to *auto*. These two properties ensure that the images remain centered in the column.

```
/*   under 500 px   */
@media screen and (max-width: 31.25em ) {
header h1 {
    font-size: 48px;
    padding: 0;
    text-align: center;
}
nav ul li {width: 50%}
#col1, #col2, #col3 {
    margin: 0;
    float: none;
    width: 100%;
}

img {
    display: block;
    margin: 0 auto;
}
}
```

Completed Responsive Design

You have created a responsive web page design for the Healthy Living web site. The design was based on natural breakpoints in the content, rather than for a particular type of device. The navigation, content, and images are flexible within ranges of browser widths, and they adapt as the browser sizes change to meet different device needs. Figure 12-34 shows the finished design at three screen widths.

Figure 12-34: Responsive web page design at three browser widths

© iStockphoto.com/OlgaMiltsova, © iStockphoto.com/aluxum, © iStockphoto.com/ fcafotodigital, © iStockphoto.com/fpm

When you finish your web design degree program, you will be qualified to apply for a variety of positions. The level at which you start in any of these positions depends on a number of factors: your degree, the quality of your portfolio, your interviewing style, and whether you have any experience in addition to your class experience. All of these positions may have "junior" or "associate" levels as entry-level titles. Listed below are some examples of job titles and duties. The descriptions here are general, and each position will have its own unique requirements and responsibilities:

> **Web designer**: Works independently or on a project team to design, develop, test, and deliver complete web sites. Designs web pages, graphics, multimedia, and user interfaces. Designs navigation branding. Performs user testing. Works with clients to meet web site requirements. Performs project management, and demonstrates creative, technical, and analytical skills.

> **Web production designer**: Populates web pages with content including copy, graphics, video, and animations. Performs the day-to-day tasks of updating web site content. Works with the content management system to archive, maintain, and update content. Maintains and updates the web site.

> **Web user interface (UI) designer**: Specializes in the user experience and web site interface and navigation. Performs usability testing to solve problems with interfaces, making them easier and more intuitive to navigate. Organizes information to make it more useful and retrievable through search applications. Creates accessible and standards-compliant designs that support ease of use and access to content, regardless of a user's physical or technological limitations.

Chapter Summary

In this chapter you learned how to use your web design skills to create responsive web pages. You learned how to use CSS3 media queries to apply conditional styles based on different device properties, such as browser width. You built flexible pages that can adapt to different devices using a single source of content and different style sheets, and you customized images to flexibly adapt to different screen sizes. You learned to build navigation schemes that let users quickly access desired content, no matter what type of device they use.

> Media queries let you apply conditional styles based on different device properties.

> Responsive web page designs let you create one source of content and use style sheets and media queries to adapt the page design to different devices.

> Design for the needs of the content, not the device. Remove or add content as necessary to provide the best experience for the user.

> Use the fewest breakpoints possible, and determine the breakpoints by examining how the content behaves at different browser widths.

Key Terms

breakpoint—The point at which design layouts change in responsive design schemes.
conditional style—A style that is applied only when specified conditions are met.
media feature—A characteristic of destination media, such as the width or height of the destination device.
media queries—A feature of CSS3 that expands on the concept of media types and lets you create more precise rules for different types of destination media.
media types—A feature of CSS3 that lets you specify different style rules for different types of destination media, such as screen or print, without changing the content for each device.
responsive design—Building web sites to provide easier reading and navigation across a wide range of devices.
viewport—The part of the screen dedicated to displaying a webpage.

Review Questions

1. What are the three main elements of responsive design?

2. What is the breakpoint in responsive design?

3. What is the best measurement value for responsive design?

4. What are the two parts of a media query?

5. When you build responsive web pages, are you adapting to the width or the height of the browser?

6. What is the viewport size equal to?

7. Which CSS property can be used to add or remove content based on the browser width?

8. Describe some navigation characteristics of a well-designed mobile site.

9. How can you ensure that an image's aspect ratio is maintained when the image scales up or down to meet the needs of the responsive design?

10. To maintain image quality, is it better to enlarge or reduce images from their original size?

Hands-On Projects

1. Write a media query for a screen with a maximum width of 480 pixels.

2. Write a media query for a screen with a minimum width of 480 pixels.

3. Write a style rule for a screen with a minimum width of 480 pixels and a maximum width of 1024 pixels.

4. Write a media query for a screen in landscape mode.

5. Build a different look for the Healthy Living home page, using the graphics and content provided. How else can you arrange the layout to create an interesting and accessible design? Once you have created a new layout design, create a responsive version that is displayed correctly on multiple devices.

6. Build a responsive secondary page for the Healthy Living layout that is designed for reading rather than scanning. (Refer to Chapter 2 if you need help.) Use the graphical elements and content from the main page. Make sure to design for a smooth transition between pages, using some of the same look and feel that the main page exhibits.

Individual and Team Case Project

Finalize your project web site by testing the finished design in multiple browsers and devices and making any necessary adjustments or changes to support compatibility. If available, post your web site to the class web hosting area for live testing on the Internet. If you cannot post your web site to the web, prepare a flash drive with your content to submit to your instructor or upload the site to the class FTP site if available.

If possible, enlist three to five people to review your web site and fill out either your online or paper-based user feedback form. Compile the results, and write a short paper detailing the results of your testing and what they indicate about the effectiveness of your design. Point out the areas that you feel could benefit from user recommendations. List any assumptions you made about the web site and how users either confirmed or denied these assumptions.

If the time and format allows, prepare to present and defend your web design to your fellow students. Prepare a short oral presentation (10–15 minutes) where you can present your design ideas and reasons for building the site. Be prepared to take questions and defend your design ideas.

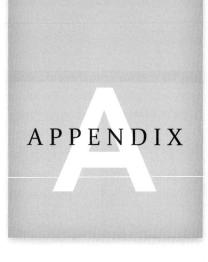

HTML5 REFERENCE

This appendix provides the following information:
- › Alphabetical HTML5 reference
- › Obsolete elements
- › Global attributes
- › Character and numeric entities

This appendix includes element descriptions sorted alphabetically. The elements listed in this appendix are the ones you will use most often, including a list of the global attributes allowed with all HTML5 elements and a complete list of character entities. Some elements are obsolete in HTML5 but are still in common use in many web sites. If you are creating HTML5-compliant web pages, you should not use these obsolete elements. For more detailed information, visit the World Wide Web Consortium web site at *www.w3.org*.

The HTML5 draft specification was published as a First Public Working Draft on January 23, 2008 and many updated Working Drafts of the specification have subsequently been published by the W3C HTML5 working group. Information about HTML5 elements may continue to change as the draft evolves until it becomes a complete W3C recommendation.

Alphabetical HTML5 Reference

Table A-1 lists the common HTML5 elements.

ELEMENT	DESCRIPTION	ATTRIBUTES
<!--comment text-->	Insert a comment in your code Browsers do not display comments in the Web page Place the comment within the tag. For example: <!-- This is a comment -->	None
<a>	Create a clickable hypertext anchor in a document; can be text or an image	Global attributes plus: *href* Target destination of the hyperlink *name* Name of a fragment of the document *target* Window or frame in which the linked document is displayed *hreflang* Language of the destination of the hyperlink *rel* Defines the relationship between the document and the destination *media* Valid media-query type *type* MIME type
<abbr>	Abbreviation or acronym	Global attributes
<address>	Contact information	Global attributes
<area>	Clickable area in an image map	Global attributes plus: *alt* Specify an alternate string of text if the image cannot be displayed by the browser *href* Target destination of the hyperlink *hreflang* Language of the destination of the hyperlink

Continued on next page...

ELEMENT	DESCRIPTION	ATTRIBUTES
		target Window or frame in which the linked document is displayed
		rel Defines the relationship between the document and the destination
		media Valid media-query type
		type MIME type
		shape Determines the shape of the clickable area, circle or poly and coordinates
<article>	A section of content that forms an independent part of a document or web site	Global attributes
<aside>	Content that is tangentially related to the main content	Global attributes
<audio>	Contains an audio stream	*src* URL of the radio stream content
		autoplay When set to *autoplay*, the video starts playing as soon as possible
		preload Indicates whether preloading is necessary
		controls When set to *controls*, displays playback controls
		loop When set to *loop*, the video plays repeatedly
<b>	Boldface text	Global attributes
	This element is redefined in HTML5 to have semantic meaning: "Bold text is offset from its surrounding content without conveying any extra emphasis or importance, and for which the conventional typographic presentation is bold text."	
<base>	Sets the base URL or target for a page	Global attributes plus:
	This is an empty element	*href* Absolute or relative original URL for the current document
		target Default window or frame in which links contained in the document are displayed
<blockquote>	Indents text on both the left and right margins	

Continued on next page...

ELEMENT	DESCRIPTION	ATTRIBUTES
\<body\>	Identifies the body section of the web page	
\<br\>	Inserts a line break, forcing text to the next line This is an empty element	
\<button\>	Creates a button outside of a form	Global attributes plus: *type* Values are button, reset, or submit *name* Name for the button *value* Initial value for the button; this can be changed by a script *disabled* When value is *disabled*, the button is not displayed *form* Value of the id attribute associated with the form
\<canvas\>	Used with scripting applications to dynamically render graphics, animations, or other visual images	Global attributes plus: *height* Height of the canvas, in pixels *width* Width of the canvas, in pixels
\<caption\>	Indicates that the text appears as the caption of a table	Global attributes
\<cite\>	Title of a cited work	Global attributes
\<code\>	Fragment of computer code	Global attributes
\<col\>	One or more columns in a column group within the \<colgroup\> element This is an empty element	Global attributes plus: *span* Number of columns spanned
\<colgroup\>	Group of columns within a table	Global attributes plus: *span* Number of columns spanned
\<command\>	Defines a command button within a \<menu\> element This is an empty element	Global attributes plus: *type* Command, checkbox, or radio
\<datalist\>	Defines a list of option values for a form input element The results of this element are not displayed in the browser window	Global attributes

Continued on next page...

ELEMENT	DESCRIPTION	ATTRIBUTES
<dd>	Definition for a term within a definition list <dl> element	Global attributes
<del>	Text that has been deleted from a document	Global attributes
<details>	Represents a control from which a user can request more information	Global attributes plus: *open* Specifies the contents should be shown to the user, value is *open* or *null*
<div>	Indicates a division within the document	Global attributes
<dt>	Term or name within a definition list <dl> element	Global attributes
<em>	Emphasizes text, usually as italic; browser determines the text style	Global attributes
<embed>	Contains content from an external source This is an empty element	*src* Address of the content being embedded *type* MIME type of the embedded content *height* Height of the embedded content, in pixels *width* Width of the embedded content, in pixels
<fieldset>	Container for form controls grouped under a heading	Global attributes
<figcaption>	Caption or legend for a figure	Global attributes
<figure>	Self-contained set of graphical or related content	Global attributes
<footer>	Contains footer content	Global attributes
<form>	Contains user-submittable form	*action* URL of the application that processes the form data; this URL points to a script file or an email address *enctype* Content type used to submit the form to the server (when the value of the method is "post"); most forms do not need this attribute *method* Specifies the HTTP method used to submit the form data; the default value is *get* ⟩ *get* Form data is appended to the URL specified in the action attribute ⟩ *post* Form data is sent to the server as a separate message

Continued on next page...

ELEMENT	DESCRIPTION	ATTRIBUTES
		accept Comma-separated list of content types that a server processing this form can handle correctly; most forms do not need this attribute
		accept-charset List of allowed character sets for input data that is accepted by the server processing this form; most forms do not need this attribute
		name Name of this form for data processing
\<h1\> to \<h6\>	Defines headings for six levels of content	Global attributes
\<head\>	Identifies the head section of the web page, which is reserved for metadata (information about the document)	Global attributes
\<header\>	Header of a section	Global attributes
\<hgroup\>	Group of headings \<h1\> through \<h6\>	Global attributes
\<hr\>	Inserts a horizontal rule on the page indicating thematic break in the content This is an empty element	Global attributes
\<html\>	Root element of an HTML file	Global attributes
\<i\>	Italicize text This element is redefined in HTML5 to have semantic meaning: "Italic text is offset from its surrounding content without conveying any extra emphasis or importance, and for which the conventional typographic presentation is italic text."	Global attributes
\<iframe\>	Creates an inline frame that contains a new content page	Global attributes plus: *src* Address of a page that the nested frame contains *name* Content name *width* Width of the iframe, in pixels *height* Height of the iframe, in pixels
\<img\>	Inserts an image into a web page This is an empty element	Global attributes plus: *width* Width of the image, in pixels *height* Height of the image, in pixels

Continued on next page...

ELEMENT	DESCRIPTION	ATTRIBUTES
		src URL that points to the image file; this attribute is required
		alt Specify an alternate string of text if the image cannot be displayed by the browser
<input>	Used in a <form> element to create a variety of input controls	Global attributes plus:
		text Text entry field where the user entry is masked by asterisks
		checkbox Provides on/off toggles that the user selects
		radio Lets a user choose one value from a range of values
		submit Sends the form data to the server
		reset Clears the form of any user-entered data and returns it to its original state
		hidden Adds a control that is not displayed in the browser
		image Adds a graphic button to the form, rather than the default button
		button Creates a button that has no default behavior
		file Lets the user select a file that is submitted with the form
		datetime Global date and time
		datetime-local Local date and time
		date Calendar date
		month Calendar month
		time Time value
		week Calendar week
		number Number value
		range Range of values
		email Email address
		url URL value
		search Search term
		tel Telephone number
		color Color name

Continued on next page...

Appendix A **HTML5 Reference**

ELEMENT	DESCRIPTION	ATTRIBUTES
`<ins>`	Text that has been added to a document	Global attributes plus:
		cite URL of a text citation for the document
		datetime Date and time when the text was added
`<kbd>`	Represents user input	Global attributes
`<keygen>`	Defines a key for secure communications	Global attributes plus:
		challenge Challenge text string that is submitted along with the key
		keytype Type of key, such as *rsa*
		autofocus Focuses on the textarea when the page loads
		name Name of this element for form processing
		form Value of the id attribute associated with the form
		disabled When value is *disabled*, the textarea is not displayed
`<label>`	Caption for a form control	Global attributes plus:
		for Reference the id of a form control to associate the label
		form Value of the id attribute associated with the form
`<legend>`	A title or explanatory caption for the parent element's content	Global attributes
`<li>`	Marks an individual list item This is an empty tag	Global attributes
`<link>`	Defines a relationship between the document and external resources, such as a style sheet	Global attributes plus:
		type Type of external resource
		href URL of the external resource
		rel Describes the relationship between the current document and the anchor specified by the href attribute
		hreflang Language of the destination link
		media Valid media-query type

Continued on next page...

ELEMENT	DESCRIPTION	ATTRIBUTES
<map>	Defines an image map	Global attributes plus: *name* Name for the map
<mark>	Text marked or highlighted for reference purposes	Global attributes
<menu>	Redefined in HTML5 to define a menu	Global attributes plus: *type* Type of menu to display; values are context, toolbar, or list; list is the default
<meta>	Used within the document head to provide information	*name* Meta information name, such as keyword or description *content* Content of the named information type
<meter>	Measurement or fractional value to measure data within a range	Global attributes plus: *value* Measured value shown by meter *min* Lower bound of the range for the meter *low* Point that marks the upper boundary of the *low* segment of the meter *high* Point that marks the lower boundary of the *high* segment of the meter *max* Upper bound of the range for the meter *optimum* Point that marks the *optimum* position for the meter
<nav>	Group of navigation links	Global attributes
<noscript>	Fallback content for scripts	Global attributes
<object>	Contains external content	Global attributes plus: *data* URL of the content *type* MIME type of the content *height* Height of the object, in pixels *width* Width of the object, in pixels *name* Name of the object
<ol>	Creates a numbered list	Global attributes
<optgroup>	Group of <option> elements with a common label	Global attributes plus: *label* Name of the group of options

Continued on next page...

ELEMENT	DESCRIPTION	ATTRIBUTES
<option>	Option choice in an <optgroup>	Global attributes plus: *label* Name of the group of options *value* Value for the option
<output>	Result of a calculation in a form	Global attributes plus: *name* Name of this element for form processing *form* Value of the id attribute associated with the form
<p>	Marks the beginning of a new block of text	Global attributes
<param>	Defines parameters for plug-ins in <object> elements	Global attributes plus: *name* Name of the parameter *value* Value of the parameter
<pre>	Preserves the formatting and spacing of text as typed in the source code; displays the text in a monospace font, different from the standard browser text	Global attributes
<progress>	Indicates the completion progress of a task Used with a scripting language	Global attributes plus: *max* Total value at completion. *value* How much of the task has been completed
<q>	Quoted text from another source	Global attributes plus: *cite* Contains the address of the source of the quoted text
<rp>	Inserts ruby parentheses to hide ruby text <rt> content from browsers that do not support the <ruby> element	Global attributes
<rt>	Marks ruby text	Global attributes
<ruby>	Marks spans of content as ruby annotations Ruby text is used to provide a short annotation of the associated base text Ruby annotations are used frequently in Japan in many kinds of publications, including books and magazines Ruby is also used in China, especially in schoolbooks	Global attributes

Continued on next page...

ELEMENT	DESCRIPTION	ATTRIBUTES
\<samp\>	Sample computer code	Global attributes
\<script\>	Contains dynamic script or data content	Global attributes plus:
		type MIME type of the script or data language
		src Address of the external script
		defer If set to *defer*, the script is executed after the page is loaded
		charset Character encoding of the external script
\<section\>	Section of a document typically including a title or heading	Global attributes
\<select\>	Form control for selecting from a list of options	Global attributes plus:
		name the name of this element for form processing
		form Value of the id attribute associated with the form
		disabled When value is *disabled*, the textarea is not displayed
		size Number of options to show
		multiple If set to *multiple*, user can select one or more options from the list
\<small\>	Contains legal, privacy, and other "fine-print" content	Global attributes
\<source\>	Allows specification for multiple media sources for audio and video elements	Global attributes plus:
		src Address of the media source
		type MIME type of the content
		media Valid media-query type
\<span\>	Serves as an inline division; used to apply a style class or rule to text	Global attributes
\<strong\>	Contains important text, usually displayed as boldface; browser determines the text style	Global attributes
\<style\>	Used in the \<head\> section to contain CSS style rules	*type* Valid MIME type that designates a styling language
		media Valid media-query type specifies to which media the style applies

Continued on next page...

ELEMENT	DESCRIPTION	ATTRIBUTES
<sub>	Subscripted text	Global attributes
<summary>	Summary, caption, or legend for a <details> element	Global attributes
<sup>	Superscripted text	Global attributes
<table>	Marks the beginning and end of a table	Global attributes plus: *summary* Description of the table
<tbody>	Block of rows in a table that contains the body content	Global attributes
<td>	Marks a data cell in a table	Global attributes plus: *colspan* Number of adjacent columns spanned by the <td> element *rowspan* Number of following rows spanned by the <td> element
<textarea>	Form control that lets users enter multiple lines of text content	Global attributes plus: *autofocus* Focuses on the textarea when the page loads *cols* Number of characters visible horizontally *disabled* When value is *disabled*, the textarea is not displayed *form* ID value defines the *form* the textarea belongs *maxlength* Defines the maximum number of characters *required* Element is a required part of the form submission *placeholder* Short text hint to aid the user when entering data *rows* Number of lines of text to display *wrap* When set to *hard*, the text wraps based on the *cols* value
<tfoot>	Block of rows in a table that contains the footer content	Global attributes

Continued on next page...

ELEMENT	DESCRIPTION	ATTRIBUTES
<th>	Forces the contents of a cell to be displayed as bold and centered	Global attributes
<thead>	Block of rows in a table that contains the header content	Global attributes
<time>	Contains a date or time value	Global attributes plus: *datetime* Specifies the date or time the element represents *pubdate* Indicates that the date or time given is a publication date or time
<title>	Specifies the title of the web page; title text appears in the browser title bar and as the bookmark or favorites text	Global attributes
<tr>	Marks a row of cells in a table	Global attributes
<tt>	Specifies monospace text, usually Courier	Global attributes
<ul>	Creates a bulleted indented list	Global attributes
<var>	Variable in a mathematical expression	
<video>	Video or movie content	Global attributes plus: *autoplay* When set to *autoplay*, the video starts playing as soon as possible *preload* Indicates whether preloading is necessary. *controls* When set to *controls*, displays playback controls *loop* When set to *loop*, the video plays repeatedly *poster* URL for an image displayed when the video is loading *height* Height of the video, in pixels *width* Width of the video, in pixels
<wbr>	Represents an approved linebreak location	Global attributes

Table A-1: Common HTML5 Elements
© 2015 Cengage Learning®

Obsolete Elements

Table A-2 lists the elements that are no longer supported in HTML5.

ELEMENT	HTML5 REPLACEMENT
<acronym>	<abbr>
<applet>	<object>
<basefont>	Use CSS
<big>	Use CSS
<center>	Use CSS
<dir>	<ul>
<font>	Use CSS
<frame>	No replacement
<frameset>	No replacement
<noframes>	No replacement
<s>	Use CSS
<strike>	Use CSS
<tt>	Use CSS
<u>	Use CSS
<xmp>	<pre>

Table A-2: Obsolete Elements
© 2015 Cengage Learning®

Global Attributes

Table A-3 lists the global attributes, which are allowed within all of the elements listed in the element tables.

ATTRIBUTE	DEFINITION
accesskey	Key label or list of key labels with which to associate the element; each key label represents a keyboard shortcut which browsers can use to activate the element or give focus to the element
class	Specifies a class name for an element; the class name can be used to specify style sheet rules

Continued on next page...

ATTRIBUTE	DEFINITION
contenteditable	Specifies whether the contents of the element are editable. Values are *true*, *false*, or empty
contextmenu	Use with the <menu> element to indicate that the element is part of a context menu
dir	Specifies the element's text directionality. Values are *ltr*, (left to right) or *rtl* (right to left)
draggable	Specifies whether the element is draggable. Values are *true* or *false*
hidden	Specifies that the element represents an element that is not yet, or is no longer, relevant
id	Specifies a document-wide unique identifier for an element. Multiple elements in the document cannot have the same id value
lang	Specifies the primary language for the contents of the element and for any of the element's attributes that contain text
spellcheck	Specifies whether the element represents an element whose contents are subject to spell checking and grammar checking. Values are *true*, *false*, or empty
style	Specifies a style sheet rule for the element
tabindex	Specifies whether the element represents an element that is focusable (that is, an element which is part of the sequence of focusable elements in the document), and the relative order of the element in the sequence of focusable elements in the document
title	Specifies a title for the element; the content of the title is displayed in the browser as a pop-up window or tooltip
translate	Specifies whether an element's attribute values and contents of its children are to be translated when the page is localized, or whether to leave them unchanged

Table A-3: HTML5 Global Attributes
© 2015 Cengage Learning®

Character and Numeric Entities

Table A-4 lists the HTML5 character and numeric entities.

CHARACTER	CHARACTER ENTITY	NUMERIC ENTITY	DESCRIPTION
"	&#123;	&quot;	Quotation mark
#	&#35;		Number sign
$	&#36;		Dollar sign

Continued on next page...

CHARACTER	CHARACTER ENTITY	NUMERIC ENTITY	DESCRIPTION
%	&#37;		Percent sign
&	&#38;	&amp;	Ampersand
'	&#39;		Apostrophe
(	&#40;		Left parenthesis
)	&#41;		Right parenthesis
*	&#42;		Asterisk
+	&#43;		Plus sign
,	&#44;		Comma
-	&#45;		Hyphen
.	&#46;		Period (full stop)
/	&#47;		Solidus (slash)
0	&#48;		Digit 0
1	&#49;		Digit 1
2	&#50;		Digit 2
3	&#51;		Digit 3
4	&#52;		Digit 4
5	&#53;		Digit 5
6	&#54;		Digit 6
7	&#55;		Digit 7
8	&#56;		Digit 8
9	&#57;		Digit 9
:	&#58;		Colon
;	&#59;		Semicolon
<	&#60;	&lt;	Less than sign
=	&#61;		Equals sign
>	&#62;	&gt;	Greater than sign
?	&#63;		Question mark
@	&#64;		Commercial at
A Z	A - Z		Uppercase letters A Z

Continued on next page...

CHARACTER	CHARACTER ENTITY	NUMERIC ENTITY	DESCRIPTION
[	&#91;		Left square bracket
\	&#92;		Reverse solidus (backslash)
]	&#93;		Right square bracket
^	&#94;		Caret
_	&#95;		Horizontal bar (underscore)
`	&#96;		Grave accent
a z	a - &#122		Lowercase letters a z
{	&#123;		Left curly brace
|	|		Vertical bar
}	&#125;		Right curly brace
~	&#126;		Tilde
			Nonbreaking space
¡	&#161;	&iexcl;	Inverted exclamation mark
¢	&#162;	&cent;	Cent sign
£	&#163;	&pound;	British Pound sign
$	&#164;	&curren;	Currency sign
¥	&#165;	&yen;	Yen sign
¦	&#166;	&brvbar;	Broken vertical bar
§	&#167;	&sect;	Section sign
¨	&#168;	&uml;	Spacing diaeresis
©	&#169;	&copy;	Copyright sign
a	&#170;	&ordf;	Feminine ordinal indicator
«	&#171;	&laquo;	Left-pointing double angle quotation mark
¬	&#172;	&not;	Not sign
	&#173;	&shy;	Soft hyphen
®	&#174;	&reg;	Registered trademark sign
¯	&#175;	&macr;	Macron overline
°	&#176;	&deg;	Degree sign

Continued on next page...

CHARACTER	CHARACTER ENTITY	NUMERIC ENTITY	DESCRIPTION
±	&#177;	&plusmn;	Plus-or-minus sign
2	&#178;	&sup2;	Superscript digit 2
3	&#179;	&sup3;	Superscript digit 3
´	&#180;	&acute;	Acute accent
µ	&#181;	&micro;	Micron sign
¶	&#182;	&para;	Paragraph sign
·	&#183;	&middot;	Middle dot
¸	&#184;	&cedil;	Cedilla
1	&#185;	&sup1;	Superscript digit 1
º	&#186;	&ordm;	Masculine ordinal indicator
»	&#187;	&raquo;	Right-pointing double angle quotation mark
¼	&#188;	&frac14;	Fraction one-quarter
½	&#189;	&frac12;	Fraction one-half
¾	&#190;	&frac34;	Fraction three-quarters
¿	&#191;	&iquest;	Inverted question mark
À	&#192;	&Agrave;	Capital letter A with grave
Á	&#193;	&Aacute;	Capital letter A with acute
Â	&#194;	&Acirc;	Capital letter A with circumflex
Ã	&#195;	&Atilde;	Capital letter A with tilde
Ä	&#196;	&Auml;	Capital letter A with diaeresis
Å	&#197;	&Aring;	Capital letter A with ring above
Æ	&#198;	&Aelig;	Capital letter AE
Ç	&#199;	&Ccedil;	Capital letter C with cedilla
È	&#200;	&Egrave;	Capital letter E with grave
É	&#201;	&Eacute;	Capital letter E with acute
Ê	&#202;	&Ecirc;	Capital letter E with circumflex
Ë	&#203;	&Euml;	Capital letter E with diaeresis
Ì	&#204;	&Igrave;	Capital letter I with grave

Continued on next page...

CHARACTER	CHARACTER ENTITY	NUMERIC ENTITY	DESCRIPTION
Í	&#205;	&Iacute;	Capital letter I with acute
Î	&#206;	&Icirc;	Capital letter I with circumflex
Ï	&#207;	&Iuml;	Capital letter I with diaeresis
Đ	&#208;	&ETH;	Capital letter ETH
Ñ	&#209;	&Ntilde;	Capital letter N with tilde
Ò	&#210;	&Ograve;	Capital letter O with grave
Ó	&#211;	&Oacute;	Capital letter O with acute
Ô	&#212;	&Ocirc;	Capital letter O with circumflex
Õ	&#213;	&Otilde;	Capital letter O with tilde
Ö	&#214;	&Ouml;	Capital letter O with diaeresis
×	&#215;	&times;	Multiplication sign
Ø	&#216;	&Oslash;	Capital letter O with stroke
Ù	&#217;	&Ugrave;	Capital letter U with grave
Ú	&#218;	&Uacute;	Capital letter U with acute
Û	&#219;	&Ucirc;	Capital letter U with circumflex
Ü	&#220;	&Uuml;	Capital letter U with diaeresis
Ý	&#221;	&Yacute;	Capital letter Y with acute
Þ	&#222;	&THORN;	Capital letter THORN
ß	&#223;	&szlig;	Sz ligature
à	&#224;	&agrave;	Small letter a with grave
á	&#225;	&aacute;	Small letter a with acute
â	&#226;	&acirc;	Small letter a with circumflex
ã	&#227;	&atilde;	Small letter a with tilde
ä	&#228;	&auml;	Small letter a with diaeresis
å	&#229;	&aring;	Small letter a with ring above
æ	&#230;	&aelig;	Small letter ae
ç	&#231;	&ccedil;	Small letter c with cedilla
è	&#232;	&egrave;	Small letter e with grave
é	&#233;	&eacute;	Small letter e with acute

Continued on next page...

CHARACTER	CHARACTER ENTITY	NUMERIC ENTITY	DESCRIPTION
ê	&#234;	&ecirc;	Small letter e with circumflex
ë	&#235;	&euml;	Small letter e with diaeresis
ì	&#236;	&igrave;	Small letter i with grave
í	&#237;	&iacute;	Small letter i with acute
î	&#238;	&icirc;	Small letter i with circumflex
ï	&#239;	&iuml;	Small letter i with diaeresis
d	&#240;	&eth;	Small letter eth
ñ	&#241;	&ntilde;	Small letter n with tilde
ò	&#242;	&ograve;	Small letter o with grave
ó	&#243;	&oacute;	Small letter o with acute
ô	&#244;	&ocirc;	Small letter o with circumflex
õ	&#245;	&otilde;	Small letter o with tilde
ö	&#246;	&ouml;	Small letter o with diaeresis
÷	&#247;	&divide;	Division sign
o/	&#248;	&oslash;	Small letter o with stroke
ù	&#249;	&ugrave;	Small letter u with grave
ú	&#250;	&uacute;	Small letter u with acute
û	&#251;	&ucirc;	Small letter u with circumflex
ü	&#252;	&uuml;	Small letter u with diaeresis
ý	&#253;	&yacute;	Small letter y with acute
þ	&#254;	&thorn;	Small letter thorn
ÿ	&#255;	&yuml;	Small letter y with diaeresis

Table A-4: Character and Numeric Entities
© 2015 Cengage Learning®

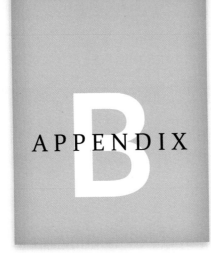

APPENDIX

CSS REFERENCE

This appendix provides the following information:

> CSS notation reference

> Alphabetical CSS property reference

> CSS measurement units

This appendix includes descriptions for all CSS properties used in this book, sorted alphabetically. For more detailed information, visit the World Wide Web Consortium web site at *www.w3.org*.

CSS Notation Reference

Table B-1 lists the notation symbols used in CSS properties.

NOTATION	DEFINITION
<>	Words between angle brackets specify a type of value; for example, <color> means to enter a color value such as red
|	A single vertical bar between values means one or the other must occur; for example, scroll | fixed means choose scroll or fixed
||	Two vertical bars separating values means one or the other or both values can occur; for example, <border-width> || <border-style> || <color> means any or all of the three values can occur
[]	Square brackets group parts of the property value together; for example, none | [underline || overline || line-through || blink] means the value is either none or one of the values within the square brackets

Table B-1: CSS Notations
© 2015 Cengage Learning®

Alphabetical CSS Property Reference

Table B-2 describes the CSS properties in alphabetical order.

PROPERTY	VALUES	DEFAULT	APPLIES TO	INHERITED
background	<background-color> || <background-image> || <background-repeat> || <background-attachment> || <background-position>	none	All elements	No
background-attachment	scroll | fixed	scroll	All elements	No
background-color	color name or hexadecimal value || transparent	transparent	All elements	No
background-image	<url> | none	none	All elements	No
background-position	[<percentage> | <length>] {1,2} | [top | center | bottom] || [left | center | right]	0% 0%	Block-level and replaced elements	No
background-repeat	repeat | repeat-x | repeat-y | no-repeat	repeat	All elements	No

Continued on next page...

PROPERTY	VALUES	DEFAULT	APPLIES TO	INHERITED
border	<border-width> || <border-style> || <color>	none	All elements	No
border-bottom	<border-bottom-width> || <border-style> || <color>	none	All elements	No
border-bottom-color	<color>	Value of the color property	All elements	No
border-bottom-left-radius	[<length> | <percentage>] [<length> | <percentage>]	0	All elements	No
border-bottom-right-radius	[<length> | <percentage>] [<length> | <percentage>]	0	All elements	No
border-bottom-style	none | dotted | dashed | solid | double | groove | ridge | inset | outset	none	All elements	No
border-bottom-width	thin | medium | thick | <length>	medium	All elements	No
border-collapse	separate | collapse	separate	<table> element	Yes
border-color	<color>	Value of the color property	All elements	No
border-left	<border-left-width> || <border-style> || <color>	none	All elements	No
border-left-color	<color>	Value of the color property	All elements	No
border-left-style	none | dotted | dashed | solid | double | groove | ridge | inset | outset	none	All elements	No
border-left-width	thin | medium | thick | <length>	medium	All elements	No
border-radius	[<length> | <percentage>] {1,4} [/ [<length> |<percentage>]{1,4}]	0	All elements	No
border-right	<border-right-width> || <border-style> || <color>	none	All elements	No
border-right-color	<color>	Value of the color property	All elements	No

Continued on next page...

PROPERTY	VALUES	DEFAULT	APPLIES TO	INHERITED
border-right-style	none | dotted | dashed | solid | double | groove | ridge | inset | outset	none	All elements	No
border-right-width	thin | medium | thick | <length>	medium	All elements	No
border-style	none | dotted | dashed | solid | double | groove | ridge | inset | outset	none	All elements	No
border-top	<border-top-width> || <border-style> || <color>	none	All elements	No
border-top-color	<color>	Value of the color property	All elements	No
border-top-left-radius	[<length> | <percentage>] [<length> | <percentage>]	0	All elements	No
border-top-right-radius	[<length> | <percentage>] [<length> | <percentage>]	0	All elements	No
border-top-style	none | dotted | dashed | solid | double | groove | ridge | inset | outset	none	All elements	No
border-top-width	thin | medium | thick | <length>	medium	All elements	No
border-width	[thin | medium | thick | <length>]	none	All elements	No
bottom	<length> | <percentage> | auto	auto	Positioned elements	
box-shadow	none | <shadow> [, <shadow>]*	none	All elements	No
caption-side	top | bottom	top	<caption> element	Yes
clear	none | left | right | both	none	All elements	No
color	<color>	Browser specific	All elements	Yes
display	inline | block | list-item | run-in | compact | marker | table | inline-table | table-row-group | table-header-group | table-footer-group | table-row | table-column-group | table-column | table-cell | table-caption | none	inline	All elements	No

Continued on next page...

PROPERTY	VALUES	DEFAULT	APPLIES TO	INHERITED
float	left | right | none	none	All elements	No
font	[\<font-style\> || \<font-variant\> || \<font-weight\>] \<font-size\> [/ \<line-height\>] \<font-family\>	none	All elements	Yes
font-family	Font family name (such as Times) or generic family name (such as sans-serif)	Browser specific	All elements	Yes
font-size	\<absolute-size\> | \<relative-size\> | \<length\> | \<percentage\>	medium	All elements	Yes
font-size-adjust	\<number\> | none | inherit	none	All elements	Yes
font-stretch	normal | wider | narrower | ultra-condensed | extra-condensed | condensed | semi-condensed | semi-expanded | expanded | extra-expanded | ultra-expanded	normal	All elements	Yes
font-style	normal | italic | oblique	normal	All elements	Yes
font-variant	normal | small caps	normal	All elements	Yes
font-weight	normal | bold | bolder | lighter | 100 | 200 | 300 | 400 | 500 | 600 | 700 | 800 | 900	normal	All elements	Yes
height	\<length\> | \<percentage\> | auto	auto	Block-level and replaced elements; also all elements except inline images	No
left	\<length\> | \<percentage\> | auto	auto	Positioned	No
letter-spacing	normal | \<length\>	normal	All elements	Yes
line-height	normal | \<number\> | \<length\> | \<percentage\>	normal	All elements	Yes
list-style	\<keyword\> || \<position\> || \<url\>	none	Elements with display value list-item	Yes
list-style-image	\<url\> | none	none	Elements with display value list-item	Yes

Continued on next page...

Appendix B **CSS Reference**

PROPERTY	VALUES	DEFAULT	APPLIES TO	INHERITED
list-style-position	inside | outside	outside	Elements with display value list-item	Yes
list-style-type	disc | circle | square | decimal | lower-roman | upper-roman | lower-alpha | upper-alpha | none	disc	Elements with display value list-item	Yes
margin	[<length> | <percentage> | auto]	none	All elements	No
margin-bottom	<length> | <percentage> | auto	0	All elements	No
margin-left	<length> | <percentage> | auto	0	All elements	No
margin-right	<length> | <percentage> | auto	0	All elements	No
margin-top	<length> | <percentage> | auto	0	All elements	No
max-width	<length> | <percentage> | auto	auto	All elements but inline text elements and table rows	No
min-width	<length> | <percentage> | auto	auto	All elements but inline text elements and table rows	No
opacity	<alphavalue> | inherit	1	All elements	No
overflow	[visible | hidden | scroll | auto]	visible	All elements	No
padding	<length> | <percentage>	0	All elements	No
padding-bottom	<length> | <percentage>	0	All elements	No
padding-left	<length> | <percentage>	0	All elements	No
padding-right	<length> | <percentage>	0	All elements	No
padding-top	<length> | <percentage>	0	All elements	No
position	static | relative | absolute | fixed	static	All elements except generated content	No
right	<length> | <percentage> | auto	auto	Positioned elements	No

Continued on next page...

PROPERTY	VALUES	DEFAULT	APPLIES TO	INHERITED
text-align	left | right | center | justify	Depends on browser and language direction	Block-level elements	Yes
text-decoration	none | [underline || overline || line-through || blink]	none	All elements	No
text-decoration-color	<color>	Current color	All elements	No
text-decoration-style	solid | double | dotted | dashed | wave	solid	All elements	No
text-indent	<length> | <percentage>	0	Block-level	Yes
text-outline	none | [<color> <length> <length>? | <length> <length>? <color>]	none	All elements	Yes
text-shadow	none | [<color> || <length> <length> <length>? ,]* [<color> ||<length> <length> <length>?]	none	All elements	Yes
text-transform	capitalize | uppercase | lowercase | none	none	All elements	No
text-wrap	normal | unrestricted | none | suppress	normal	All elements	Yes
top	<length> | <percentage> | auto	auto	Positioned	No
vertical-align	baseline | sub | super | top | text-top | middle | bottom | text-bottom | <percentage>	baseline	Inline elements	No
white-space	normal | pre | nowrap	normal	Block-level elements	No
width	<length> | <percentage> | auto	auto	All elements but inline text elements and table rows	No
word-spacing	normal | <length>	normal	All elements	Yes
word-wrap	normal | break-word	normal	All elements	Yes
z-index	auto | integer	auto	Positioned elements	No

Table B-2: CSS Properties
© 2015 Cengage Learning®

CSS Measurement Units

Table B-3 defines the CSS measurement units.

UNIT	CODE ABBREVIATION	DESCRIPTION
Centimeter	cm	Standard metric centimeter
Em	em	Width of the capital M in the current font, usually the same as the font size
Ex	ex	Height of the letter x in the current font
Inch	in	Standard U.S. inch
Millimeter	mm	Standard metric millimeter
Pica	pc	Standard publishing unit equal to 12 points
Pixel	px	Size of a pixel on the current display
Point	pt	Standard publishing unit; 72 points in an inch
Relative	For example: 50%	Sets a font size relative to the base font size; 150% equals 1.5 times the base font size
Rem	rem	Works like em, but is relative to the root element of the document.
Viewport Width	vw	Equal to 1% of the width of the initial containing block
Viewport Height	vh	Equal to 1% of the height of the initial containing block
Viewport Minimum	vmin	Equal to the smaller value of vw or vh
Viewpoint Maximum	vmax	Equal to the larger value of vw or vh

Table B-3: CSS Measurement Codes
© 2015 Cengage Learning®

APPENDIX C

PRINT STYLE SHEETS

This appendix provides the following information:

> Applying print styles

> Creating print styles

> Creating a print page layout

The print media type (described in Chapter 12) lets you add style sheet rules specifically for the printed page. Users may want to print your page for a variety of reasons, and complex web designs often do not print well. Link colors, background images, font sizes, and other web features do not translate well to the printed page. You can control how your printed pages look with a print style sheet.

Applying Print Styles

A print style sheet can be an external style sheet file, or the style rules can be embedded in the head section of a document. In the following code, the <link> element specifies the media type print and points to a style sheet named print_styles.css. The rules in this style sheet will apply to the printed version of the web page.

```
<link rel="stylesheet" media="print" href="print_styles.css">
```

Print style rules can also be embedded in the style section of the document using the @media keyword. Notice the additional external curly brackets (shown here in blue) that contain all of the style rules.

```
<style>
@media print {
body {
font-size: 12pt;
color: #000;}
}
</style>
```

The external style sheet method of applying print rules is the simplest way to manage print styles. If you have an external style sheet for both screen and print, only one will apply based on the destination media. If you have internal styles and use the <link> element only for a print style sheet, you may need to use the !important keyword (described in Chapter 4) to override style rules. For example, if your internal style sheet contains rules that specify a serif font-family, and you want to override those styles for printing, you would use the !important keyword in the external print style sheet as shown below:

```
body {font-family: serif !important;}
```

Creating Print Styles

With print style rules, you can change or remove any element on your web page. You can control fonts, colors, borders, and backgrounds. You can also hide elements that are not relevant on the printed page, such as navigation links.

Specifying Fonts and Color

Standard font sizes for printed text are different from what you would specify onscreen. Keep in mind that text also prints best in black. Two simple style rules accomplish this:

```
body {
    font-size: 12pt;
    color: #000;
}
```

In the following example, the style sheet specifies the arial font with a blue <h1> heading. The @media rule specifies print as the output and then sets the text to serif and the heading to black when the web page is printed.

```
body {
    font-family: arial, sans-serif;
}
h1 {
    color: #1e90ff;
}

@media print {
body {
    font-family: serif;
    color: #000;
}
h1 {
    color: #000;
}
}
```

Figure C-1 shows the resulting web page and print preview page with the results of the different styles.

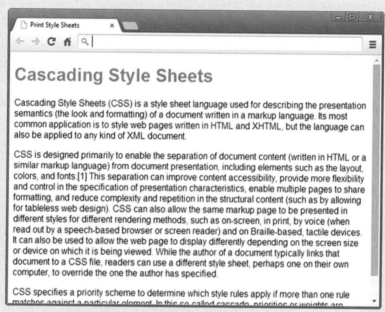

Browser output

Print output

Figure C-1: Using a print style sheet

© 2015 Cengage Learning®

Specifying Background Colors

When printing, you may also want to set background colors for the page to white for better legibility. This rule would also apply to the body selector.

```css
body {
    font-size: 12pt;
    color: #000;
    background-color: white;
}
```

Creating a Print Page Layout

As you saw in Chapter 12, you can customize a page layout so it appears in the best format for printing. You can remove navigation elements or reposition elements. For example, in the Healthy Living.com project page (see Figure 12-23) the navigation bar at the top of the page is not necessary when the page is printed. The three-column web layout is in landscape format for wider screens and does not fit the printed page. A print style rule can solve these problems by removing the navigation and reformatting the page for print. In the following print style rule, the display property is set to *none* for the <nav> element that contains the links. Page layout style rules for the different page elements create a two column layout. Figure C-2 shows the printed page result.

```css
@media print {
nav {
    display: none;
}

#col1 {
    width: 43%;
}

#col2 {
    width: 43%;
}

#col3 {
    clear: both;
    float: none;
    width: 90%;
    margin: 0 1em 1em 1.5em;
}
```

```
#col3 img {
    float: left;
    width: 30%;
    margin: .5m 1em 1em 0;
}
}
```

Healthy Living

page navigation removed

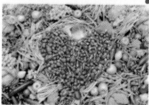

page layout designed to fit printed page

Section 1

Lorem ipsum dolor sit amet, consectetuer adipiscing elit. Aenean commodo ligula eget dolor. Aenean massa. Cum sociis natoque penatibus et magnis dis parturient montes, nascetur ridiculus mus. Donec quam felis, ultricies nec, pellentesque eu, pretium quis, sem. Nulla consequat massa quis enim. Donec pede justo, fringilla vel, aliquet nec, vulputate eget, arcu. In enim justo, rhoncus ut, imperdiet a, venenatis vitae, justo. Nullam dictum felis eu pede mollis pretium. Integer tincidunt. Cras dapibus. Vivamus elementum semper nisi. Lorem ipsum dolor sit amet, consectetuer adipiscing elit.

Section 2

Lorem ipsum dolor sit amet, consectetuer adipiscing elit. Aenean commodo ligula eget dolor. Aenean massa. Cum sociis natoque penatibus et magnis dis parturient montes, nascetur ridiculus mus. Donec quam felis, ultricies nec, pellentesque eu, pretium quis, sem. Nulla consequat massa quis enim. Donec pede justo, fringilla vel, aliquet nec, vulputate eget, arcu. In enim justo, rhoncus ut, imperdiet a, venenatis vitae, justo. Nullam dictum felis eu pede mollis pretium. Integer tincidunt. Cras dapibus. Vivamus elementum semper nisi. Lorem ipsum dolor sit amet, consectetuer adipiscing elit.

Section 3

Lorem ipsum dolor sit amet, consectetuer adipiscing elit. Aenean commodo ligula eget dolor. Aenean massa. Cum sociis natoque penatibus et magnis dis parturient montes, nascetur ridiculus mus. Donec quam felis, ultricies nec, pellentesque eu, pretium quis,

1/2

Figure C-2: Print layout for Healthy Living web page
© 2015 Cengage Learning®

INDEX

A

absolute font size keywords, 196–197
absolute path, 117
absolute units, 189–190
accept attribute, 495
accept-charset attribute, 495
accessibility
    access keys, 87
    alternate text-based links, 409
    clickable area, 512–513
    constraints, 111–112
    images, 351
    navigation links, 87
    operable content, 91
    Section 508, 88, 89
    understandable content, 91–92
    user-controlled font size, 87
    WCAG 2.0 guidelines, 90–92
    Web Content Accessibility Guidelines (WCAG), 87, 88
achecker.ca web site, 92
action attribute, 495
active class, 374
active links color, 374–375
:active pseudo-class, 164
active white space, 71–72, 94
Adobe Creative Cloud, 112
Adobe Edge, 357
Adobe Fireworks, 348
Adobe Flash, 357
Adobe Illustrator, 346, 348
Adobe InDesign, 113
Adobe Photoshop, 113, 345, 348–349
Adobe web fonts, 185
Advanced GIF Animator, 344
advanced selectors, 172–173
<a> element, 23, 31–32, 163–165, 416–417, 420, 422–423, 427, 432–433, 437–439, 442, 445–447, 567
:after pseudo-element, 169
all media type, 552
alt attribute, 350, 351, 409, 503
Amaya, 112
Amazon.com web site, 54–55, 59, 309
analogous color schemes, 366, 392
anchor elements, 212
and keyword, 550
Android operating system, 57
animated GIFs, 343–344
animation, 24, 165, 343–344, 356–357
Apache, 494
Apple iOS, 57
application developers, 113
area class, 531
Arial, 185–187, 194, 196

<article> element, 30–32, 34–36, 38, 295–297, 301, 304, 308–309, 316, 319–320, 328–329, 562–563, 565, 567
articles and sections, 297–298
artist class, 467
<aside> element, 32, 35, 38, 304–305, 330–331
aspect ratio, 354, 392, 572
.asp file extension, 116
<a> tags, 413
attributes, 4, 29–30, 33, 40, 162–163
attribute selectors, 162–163
audience, 50, 105
    See also users
    accessibility, 111–112
    analyzing, 107–112
    captive, 109
    feedback, 108
    software tools, 112
    technology issues, 111–112
    web analytics, 109–111
audience definition, 107–109, 134
audio, 36
<audio> element, 24, 31–32, 36

B

background color
    <body> element, 377
    columns, 467, 483
    complementary colors, 365
    elements, 375–377
    forms, 519
    header cells, 481–482
    hover rollovers, 444–445
    images, 342–343
    links, 165, 448
    navigation, 434, 440–444
    padding area, 250
    paragraphs, 242
    tables, 476–480
    web pages, 377
background color layer, 370
background-color property, 242, 370, 375–377, 448, 477
background graphics, 442–443
background image layer, 370, 379
background-image property, 370, 380–381, 383, 520
background images
    Cascading Style Sheets (CSS), 378–391
    fieldset, 520
    horizontal repeat, 385–387
    hover rollovers, 446–447
    multiple images, 391
    nonrepeating, 387
    positioning, 388–391
    properties, 378–391
    repeating, 383–384
    tiling, 380
    URLs (Uniform Resource Locators), 381
    vertical repeat, 384–385

background-position property, 388–391, 520
background-repeat property, 383–387, 520
BBEdit, 112
:before pseudo-element, 169
Berners-Lee, Tim, 19–20, 87
best class selector, 475
billboard sites, 105
block elements, 238, 243
block-level boxes, 238
block-level elements, 238–240, 292
    background-color property, 376
    borders, 239
    displaying, 240
    <div> element, 159
    :first-letter pseudo-element, 167
    :first-line pseudo elements, 169
    margins, 239
    padding values, 239
    rounded borders, 262–264
    spacing between, 247
<blockquote> element, 5, 30–31, 38
bloggers, 106
blogs, 106
Bluefish, 112
<body> element, 5–6, 31, 148, 153, 238–239, 293, 374, 377, 381, 463–466
body section, 5
body selector, 377
bold text, 183, 200–201
border-bottom-color property, 260
border-bottom-left radius property, 264
border-bottom property, 153–154, 253, 448
border-bottom-right radius property, 264
border-bottom-style property, 256
border-bottom-width property, 258
border-box value, 268
border-collapse property, 461, 470
border-color property, 242, 259–262
border-left-color property, 260
border-left property, 253
border-left-style property, 256
border-left-width property, 258
border properties, 242, 253–265, 285, 357
border-radius property, 262–264
border-right-color property, 260
border-right property, 253
border-right-style property, 256
border-right-width property, 258

borders
    block-level elements, 239, 243
    cells, 461, 470–471, 481
    color, 259–262
    content boxes, 240
    dashed, 254
    displaying, 257
    dotted, 254
    double line, 254
    element boxes, 268
    elements, 253–265
    header row, 471
    horizontal navigation bars, 434
    hypertext images, 357
    measurement values, 243
    paragraphs, 241–242
    removing extra space between, 470
    rounded, 262–264
    rows, 471
    shorthand properties, 261–262
    solid, 254, 262
    styles, 254–257
    tables, 461, 469–476, 481
    three-dimensional, 254
    width, 257–259
border-style property, 242, 254–257, 261–262
border-top-color property, 260
border-top-left radius property, 264
border-top property, 242, 253
border-top-right radius property, 264
border-top-style property, 256
border-top-width property, 258
border-width property, 192, 257–259, 261–262
Bos, Bert, 198
Boston Globe web site, 75–76
box model, 285
    calculating width, 266–268
    margin area, 243–249
    padding area, 250–252
box properties, 278–284
box-shadow property, 276–278
box-sizing property, 267–268, 306
braille media type, 552
breadcrumb path, 404–405, 449
breakpoints, 545–547, 576–577, 599
    measurement units, 549
    style rules, 551
browse button, 504
BrowserNews web site, 49
browsers
    borders, 257
    cache, 51–52
    Cascading Style Sheets (CSS) support, 139
    compatibility issues, 48–50, 92
    data validation, 498

element content boxes, 238–249, 292
elements, 11–13
Embedded Open Type format, 185
fonts, 183, 185
Hypertext Markup Language (HTML), 20–21
images, 350, 352–353
justifying text, 205
margins, 248–249
mobile devices, 48–49
Open Type format, 185
quirks mode, 28
rendering engines, **12**, 48
standards-compliant, 49
standards mode, 28
testing web pages, 13, 48–49, 130
TrueType format, 185
versions, 53
viewing web sites, 110–111
web fonts, 185
browser-specific web pages, 543
browser width, 566

 tag, 3
bulleted lists, 9, 38
bullets, 240, 431–432, 434
check boxes, 500
customizing, 223–229
default spacing, 434
images, 227
margins, 431
markers, 223–229
navigation, 430–432
padding, 431
vertical navigation bars, 438–440
button input type, 497
buttons, customizing text, 502–503

C

Cabin, 185
Cabin Sketch, 185
cable modems, 127
cache, 51–**52**, 94
caniuse.com web site, 49, 139
<canvas> element, 24, 32, 36, 356–357
<caption> element, 458, **460**–461, 486
captions
<input> element, 512–513
styling, 468–469, 484
caption-side property, 468–469
cascading, **170**–172, 174
Cascading Style Sheets (CSS), 5, **13**–18, 23, 40, 60, 170–172
background images, 378–391
browser support for, 139
class selector, 155–158
color properties, 368–378
CSS 1, 139
CSS 2, 139
CSS 2.1, 139
CSS3 (CSS level 3), 139
declaration, **140**
font properties, 193–202
forms, 513–521
HTML 4.01, 21
HTML5, 24

Hypertext Markup Language (HTML), 141–142
image properties, 357–361
measurement units, 188–192
media queries, **55**, 58, 60
properties, **140**–141, 148, 192
pseudo-class selectors, 163–165
pseudo-element selectors, 163, 165–169
selectors, **140**
style rules, 13–15, 55, **140**–144, 546
styles, 143
style sheets, 145–147
syntax, 15
text properties, **202**–214
values, **140**–141
writing clean code, 144–145
catalog structure, 125–126
cells
aligning text in, 462
background color, 479
borders, 461, 470–471, 481
padding, 472–473, 481
spanning columns and rows, 462–463
tables, 460
CERN (European Laboratory for Particle Physics), 19
CGI. *See* Common Gateway Interface (CGI)
character set, 5, 28
check boxes, 500–502, 523–526
checkbox input type, 496
checked attribute, 501
:checked selector, 173
child elements, **148**, 174, 239
Chile Pepper Institute web site, 362
Chrome. *See* Google Chrome
class attribute, 33–34, 155–158, 161, 167, 222, 360, 413, 427, 471, 531
classes, 157, 159, 161
class selectors, 155–158, 171, 219
clear property, 272–274, 302–303, 306–307, 332, 585
clients, 104
client-side scripting language, 494
closing tags, 29–30
cluster structure, 124
cm (centimeter) unit, 189
CMS. *See* content management system (CMS)
CNET Browser Info web site, 49
code, validating, 38–39, 50
coding
consistent practices, 27
good practices, 37–39
semantic markup, **38**
<col> element, 458, 466–467
<colgroup> element, 458, 466–467, 483
colspan attribute, **462**
colon (:) flag character, 164
color
analogous colors, 366
background color, 375–376, 377
borders, 259–262

complementary colors, 363, 365
cool colors, 364
hexidecimal colors, 369
HSL (hue, saturation, and lightness) colors, 370
hues, **364**
inheritance, 374
links, 374–375, 417
monochromatic colors, 366
name values, 368–369
opacity, 372–373
primary colors, 363
properties, 368–378
RGB color model, 369
rows, 477–478
secondary colors, 363
shades, **364**
text, 374
tints, **364**
values, 371–372
warm colors, 364
color gamuts, **367**, 392
color input type, 498
color picker, 370
color property, 370–372
color schemes, 362–370
color theory, 363
color wheel, 363–366
cols attribute, 509–510
colspan attribute, 486
column drops, 305–306, 334
columns, 462, 466–467, 483, 584
column selector, 159–160
Comic Sans, 194
<command> element, 32
comments (/* */), 10, 16, 144–145
commercial web sites, 186
Common Gateway Interface (CGI), **494**, 535
common web fonts, 183–185
complementary color schemes, 363, **365**, 392
complete URLs, **116**–117, 134
compression
lossless, **342**, 346
lossy, **344**
conditional styles, **550**, 599
connection speeds, 50–51, 131
containing box, **239**, 285, 572
content, 90–92, 105–107
borders, 268
development, 103
formatted for print, 85
hiding or displaying, 563–564
overflowing content box, 274–275
padding, 268
quickly finding information, 105
redistributing, 36
robust, 90, 92
RSS (Real Simple Syndication), 106
shrinking or enlarging area, 267–268
single-sourcing, **27**
style sheets, 169
thematic groupings, 36
too much, 84–85
understandable, 90–92

vertical columns, 295
width, 266–268, 310–311
content boxes, 240–241
adapting, 265
content overflowing, 274–275
floating to left or right of text, 271–272, 281
margins, 240
width, 268–269, 272
content containers, 159–160, 295–298
content elements
floating, 298–311
nesting within containers, 295
selecting, 296–298
content-first designs, 548–549
content layer, 370
content management system (CMS), **59**, 94, 105
context boxes, 265–278
contextual links, **429**, 449
contextual selectors, 150
continuous-tone images, 344
cookies, **36**, 40
cool colors, 364
copy class, 219
copyright selector, 158–159
Core Fonts for the web initiative, 185
Corel Paint Shop Pro, 348
Courier, 185, 194
CSS 1, 139
CSS 2, 139
CSS 2.1, 139, 162
CSS. *See* Cascading Style Sheets (CSS)
CSS box model, **240**–244
CSS3 (CSS level 3), 139
advanced selectors, 172–173
attribute selectors, 163
font-face property, 185–186
media queries, **550**–554
transition properties, 165
unsupported properties, 214–216
.css file extension, 142
CSS visual formatting model, **238**–249, 285
current style rule, 443–444
cursive fonts, **194**, 230
Cute FTP, 129

D

dashed keyword, 254
database administrators, 113–114
databases, 113, 128
<datalist> element, 32
data processing, 494
date input type, 497
datetime input type, 497
datetime-local input type, 497
declaration, **140**, 174
deprecated elements, **21**, 40
descendant selectors, 150–151, 432–433, 582, 587
designers, 113
desktop computers
resolution, 53–57, 545
viewport, 554
web site version, 59
<details> element, 32
development team, 113–114

devices
    color gamuts, **367**
    issues, 52–53
    screen width, 550–551
    testing web sites, 131
device-width media feature,
    553–554
<dialog> element, 32
Digimarc, 107
digital cameras, 348
digital subscriber line (DSL)
    modems, 127
directories, 117–118
:disabled selector, 173
display elements, 24
display property, 239–240,
    432–433, 438, 563–564
<div> element, 30, 33–34,
    159–160, 295–297, 311
doctype (Document Type), **4**, 40
<!DOCTYPE> statement,
    25, 28
documentation style rules, 145
document language, 203
documents
    default font size, 196
    inline elements, 161
    logical divisions, 159–161
    thematically grouped
        sections, 297
Document Type Definition. *See*
    DTD (Document Type
    Definition)
Document Type (doctype),
    4, 40
DogsTrust web site, 362
domain names, 116–117,
    128–129
Dotster, 129
dotted keyword, 254
double keyword, 254
download time, 51–52
drawing canvas, 36
Dreamweaver, 112, 129
dropcap class, 167
drop capitals, 165–168
DTD (Document Type
    Definition), **28**, 40

E

e-commerce, 107
element boxes, 292
    displaying in browser,
        238–249
    shrinking or enlarging
        content area, 267–268
elements, **3**, 30–32, 40
    attributes, **4**, 33, 162–163
    background color, 370,
        375–376, 377
    background image layer, 370
    block-level elements,
        239–240
    borders, 253–265, 268
    box shadows, 276–278
    child elements, **148**
    clearing, 272–274
    content layer, 370
    deprecated, **21**
    display type, 238
    first letter style rules,
        165–168
    first line of text, 168–169

floating, 272–274, 292, **294**,
    298–307
font size, 190
foreground color, 371–372
global attributes, 33
hierarchical structure, 148
horizontal width, 265
hovering over, 164–165
indented, 243
inline elements, 239–240
inline-level boxes, 238
margins, 247, 248–249
metadata content, 30
nesting, 29
nonfloating, 298
normal flow, **292–294**
obsolete, 33
padding, 250, 268
parent elements, **148,**
    270–272
root element, 5
sectioning elements, 31, 159
selecting, 156, 163–165
sharing characteristics,
    162–163
specificity of selector, 170–171
style characteristics, 13, 15,
    140–144
tags, 3
transparent content models,
    31–32
vertical height, 269
viewing in browser, 11–13
void, **3**
web page structure, 33–36
white space, 243
widths, 562
email addresses, 128
email input type, 498
Embedded Open Type format,
    185
<embed> element, 32
embossed media type, 552
<em> element, 31, 150–151
:empty selector, 172
em unit, 189, **190**, 230
:enable selector, 173
enctype attribute, 495
enctype="text/plain" attribute, 496
ESPN web site, 84
European Laboratory for
    Particle Physics. *See* CERN
    (European Laboratory for
    Particle Physics)
Extensible Hypertext Markup
    Language. *See* XHTML
    (Extensible Hypertext
    Markup Language)
Extensible Markup Language.
    See XML (Extensible
    Markup Language)
external style sheets, 141–145
extranets, **107**, 134
ex unit, 189, **191**, 230
eyedropper tool, 370

F

Facebook, 106
fantasy fonts, **194**, 230
feedback form, 132
<fieldset> element, 510–512,
    518–520, 525–526,
    532–533

fieldset style rule, 518
<figcaption> element, 356
figtitle class, 169
<figure> element, 32, 35, 356
figures, 356
file extensions, 116
file input type, 497, 504
filenames, 114–116, 120
File Transfer Protocol. *See* FTP
    (File Transfer Protocol)
Filezilla, 129
Firebug Firefox add-on, 112
Firefox, 12, 14
FireFTP, 129
:first-letter pseudo-element,
    163, 165–168
first letter style rules, 165–168
:first-line pseudo-element, 163,
    168–169
:first-of-type selector, 172
500-pixel breakpoint styles,
    591–596
fixed images, 570–571
fixed layouts, 56–57, 77,
    318, 334
    article element, 319, 328–329
    aside element, 330–331
    floats, 322, 332
    footer element, 332
    header element, 319, 325
    nav element, 319, 326–327
    wrapper division element,
        318–319, 323–324
Flash, 36
flexible images, 545
flexible layouts, 54–55, 269,
    307, 311–318, 334, 545
    adapting to browser size, 309
    article element, 316
    controlling width, 310–311
    header element, 313
    nav element, 314–315
    reading pattern, 77
    responsive layouts and, 307
flexible responsive layouts,
    557–565
    ems and percentages
        measurements, 562–563
    media queries, 557, 560–661
    screen sizes, 559–563
floating content boxes, 271–272,
    281–282
floating elements, 292, **294,**
    299, 334
    article element, 304
    content elements, 298–311
    fixed layouts, 322
    floats, 303–307
    image elements, 304
    nav element, 301
    normal flow element,
        300–302
    order of elements, 304–305
    tables, 474–476
    width, 299, 309
    wrapping text around,
        294, 299
floating images, 270–272,
    359–360
floating layouts, 298–307
float property, 166, 208, 270–272,
    298–307, 359–360, 438,
    475, 563, 585
float selector, 272

font and text properties style
    sheet, 216–222
<font> element, 33
font-face property, 185–186,
    196–197
@font-face rule, 196–197
font families, 184, 193–196, 481
font-family property, 18, 146,
    193–194, 196, 201, 218,
    279, 484
font properties, 193–202
font property, **201**–202, 230
fonts, 53, **181**, 230
    alternative, 196
    browsers, 183
    common web fonts, 183–185
    default, 185, 187
    downloading, 185, 196–197
    Embedded Open Type
        format, 185
    Hypertext Markup Language
        (HTML), 183
    legibility, 186–188
    linking to, 185
    monospace fonts, 185
    percentage, 191
    properties, 201–202
    proprietary web fonts,
        185–186
    sans-serif, 184–185
    serif, 184
    size, 196–198
    specialty, 188
    style, 199
    True Type format, 185, 196
    Web Open Font Format
        (WOFF), 185
    weight, 200–201
    x-height, **187**
font shortcut property, 201–202
font-size property, 154,
    196–198, 201, 218
Font Squirrel web site, 186
font-style property, 199
font-variant property, 199–200
font-weight property, 200–201,
    221, 445
<footer> element, 24, 30, 32,
    296, 302–303, 306–307,
    332, 426, 566, 579
footernav style, 427
footers, 463–466
for attribute, 512–513, 522,
    525, 528
foreground color, 371–372
form controls, **495**, 535
<form> element, 494–496
forms, 494–496, 521–533
    aligning elements, 514–517
    background color, 519
    background image, 520
    buttons, 517
    Cascading Style Sheets
        (CSS), 513–521
    check boxes, 500–501,
        523–526
    clearing, 502–503
    data entry, 498
    fieldset, 518–519, 532–533
    formatting elements, 513
    form controls, **495**
    gathering information,
        493–494
    grouping fields, 525–526

grouping list options, 508–509
input groupings, 510–512
input object types, 496–498
JavaScript, **494**
labeling elements, 512–513, 516, 522
labels, 516, 530–532
legends, 519, 532–533
list boxes, 505–508, 527–528
password entry field, 504–505
radio buttons, 501–502, 527–528
reset button, 502–503, 517, 529
scripts, **494**
scrollable lists, 505–508
structural elements, 495
submit button, 502–503, 517, 529
text areas, 504, 509–510
text boxes, 498–499
fragment identifier, **417**, 449
<frame> element, 33
frames, 24
<frames> element, 33
<frameset> element, 33
framesets, 24
freeware, **112**, 134
F-shaped pattern, 78
FTP (File Transfer Protocol), **129**–130, 134
Futura, 196

G

Garamond, 196
Gecko, 12
generic font families, 193–194
Georgia, 185–187
get method, 495
GIF. *See* Graphics Interchange Format (GIF)
GIF Construction Set Professional, 344
.gif files, 116, 343
GIFMaker, 344
Go Daddy, 129
Google+, 106
Google Chrome, 12, 14, 198
Google Fonts service, 185
graphic artists, 113
graphic design, 101–102
graphics
   See also images
   alternate text-based links, 409
   download time, 188, 409
   links, 408–410
   navigation, 408–410, 441–444
   professional-quality, 348
   representing text, 188
   reusing, 52, 403
   text and, 208
   text-based, 403
graphics file formats
   Graphics Interchange Format (GIF), **342**–344
   Joint Photographic Experts Group (JPG), **344**–345
   PNG (Portable Network Graphics), **346**
   SVG (Scalable Vector Graphics), **346**

Graphics Interchange Format (GIF), 116, **342**–344, 348, 393
graphics tools, 348
grid, **67**–70, 94
groove keyword, 254
gs.statcounter.com website, 49
Guardian newspaper web site, 404

H

handheld devices navigation, 544
handheld media type, 552
hanging indent, 202
<head> element, 148, 562
<header> element, 24, 30–33, 35, 295–296, 308–309, 313, 319–320, 325, 579
headers in tables, 463–466
headings, 2, 3, 5, 18, 31
<head> section, 5, 17, 28, 142–143, 146, 152, 217, 579
Healthy Living web page
   completed responsive design, 596
   examining HTML file, 578–579
   500-pixel breakpoint styles, 591–596
   head section, 579
   linking to responsive.css style sheet, 580
   main.css style sheet, 579–580
   960-pixel breakpoint styles, 582–590
   responsive design, 575–597
height attribute, 350, 352–355
height property, 269, 309, 572
<h1> element, 2–4, 6, 13–14, 18, 26, 31, 36–38, 142, 146–147, 149–151, 153, 218, 238, 280
<h2> element, 3, 150–151, 153, 218, 220–221
<h3> element, 153
<h6> element, 31, 36–37
Helvetica, 185, 194, 196
hexidecimal colors, 369
hidden input type, 497
hierarchical folder structure, 118–119
high-resolution devices, 575
horizontal navigation bars, 434–438
horizontal navigation lists, 239
Horton, Sarah, 79
hover effects, 478–480
:hover pseudo-class, 164–165, 444–448, 479
hover rollovers, 444–448
href attribute, 118, 143, 417, 420, 423
HSL (hue, saturation, and lightness) colors, 370
.htm file extension, 116
HTML 4.01, 21, 31
HTML5, 5–10
   animation, 24
   attributes, 33
   Cascading Style Sheets (CSS), 24
   categories of elements, 30–32

code shortcuts, 26
compatibility, 25
data validation, 498
<!DOCTYPE> statement, 25
elements, 24, 32–33
interactivity, 36–37
logical sectioning elements, 24
<meta> element, 25
obsolete elements, 33
proposal for, 23–24
rich media elements, 24
sectioning elements, 159, 296–297
strict syntax, 26–27
syntactically correct code, 29–30
unusable features, 24
HTML. *See* Hypertext Markup Language (HTML)
HTML developers, 113
HTML documents, 4–5
   blank template file, 29
   body section, 30
   character set, 28
   closing tags, 29–30
   comments, 16
   content type, 28
   display characteristics, 13
   doctype (Document Type), **4**
   editing, 16
   embedded content, 31
   headings, 3, 31
   head section, 30
   <html> tag, 5
   interactive content, 31
   metadata, **30**
   phrasing content, 31
   root element, 5
   sectioning content, 31
   sectioning root, 31
   structure, 147–148
   style rules, 156
   tags, 29
   well-formed, 29–30
<html> element, 148
.html file extension, 116
HTML files, 16–18, 116, 578–579
<html> tag, 5, 203
HTTP (Hypertext Transfer Protocol), 126, 494
hues, **364**, 393
hyperlinks, 19–20, 31, 75, 119, 164
   See also links
hypertext, **19**–20, 41, 403
   connecting facts, relationships, and concepts, 405
   contextual links, **429**
   image borders, 357
   links, 64, 82–83
   organizing information, 19
Hypertext Markup Language (HTML), **2**, 41
   browsers, 20–21
   coding errors, 21
   CSS style rules and, 141–142
   elements, **3**, 140–144
   font problems, 183
   history, 19–24
   HTML5 compatibility, 25
   markup elements, 4
   releases, 21

standards, 20–21
syntax, 3–4
tables, 20
tags, 3
Web page creation, 2–13
hypertext servers, 20
Hypertext Transfer Protocol (HTTP). *See* HTTP (Hypertext Transfer Protocol)

I

ICANN. *See* Internet Corporation for Assigned Names and Numbers (ICANN)
id attribute, 33–34, 158–160, 281, 413, 419, 426, 430, 512–513, 525, 528
id selectors, 171, 432, 584
element, 304, 359–360, 575
image input type, 497, 503
images, 3, 350–356
   See also graphics
   acquiring, 347–348
   aligning with text, 358
   aspect ratio, **354**, 572
   background color, 342–343
   background image, 380–381
   borrowing from other web sites, 348
   Cascading Style Sheets (CSS), 357–361
   continuous-tone, 344
   description, 351
   digital cameras, 348
   fixed, 570–571
   flexible, 545
   floating, 270–272, 359–360
   Graphics Interchange Format (GIF), **342**–344
   height, 352–355
   information about, 351
   interlacing, 346–347
   Joint Photographic Experts Group (JPG), **344**–345
   lists, 227
   lossless compression, **342**
   lossy compression, **344**
   margins, 361
   navigation, 188, 409–410
   normal alignment, 350
   opacity, 373
   percentage values, 356
   progressive format, 346–347
   public domain web sites, 348
   reducing, 572
   removing border, 357
   responsive, 570–575
   reusing, 52
   scanners, 348
   sizing, 355–356
   stock photo collections, 347
   submit button, 503
   transparency, 342–343
   user-created, 348
   vertical height, 269
   web file formats, 503
   white space, 243, 360–361
   width, 352–355
   wrapping text around, 574

<img> element, 3–4, 23, 31,
  349–356, 409
!important keyword, **171**–172,
  174
@import rule, 551
indented elements, 243
indenting text, 202–203
information
  catalog structure, 125–126
  clear presentation of, 64–65
  cluster structure, 124
  flat hierarchy, 81
  hierarchical structure, 66, 123
  hierarchy, 182–183
  instantly connecting to
    related, 403
  linear structure, 121
  organizing structure,
    121–126
  overloading user with, 84–85
  tutorial structure, 121–122
  web structure, 123
information design, 101
information designers, 113
information overload, 405
inheritance, **148**, 174
  color, 374
  indenting text, 203
  style rules, 147–149
in (inch) unit, 189
initial capitals, 165–168
initial class, 165–166
inline content boxes, 238
inline elements, 31, 159,
  161, 207, 239–240,
  293–294, 376
inline-level boxes, 238–239
inline styles, 141–144, 171
inline value, 239
<input> element, 496–498,
  510–513, 521, 523–525,
  528
input groupings, 510–512
input object types, 496–498
inset keyword, 254
interaction, 74–76
interactive content, 31
interactive elements, 31
interactivity, 36–37
interlacing, **346**–347, 393
internal links, 417–418
internal style sheets, 141–144
Internet Corporation for
  Assigned Names and
  Numbers (ICANN), 129
Internet Explorer (IE), 14, 53,
  139, 185
Internet Information Service
  (IIS), 494
Internet Service Provider (ISP),
  134
intranets, **107**, 111–112, 134
iPad resolution, 58
ISO 9660 Standard, **114**, 134
ISP. See Internet Service
  Provider (ISP)
italic text, 199

J

Jaffe, Jeff, 24
Java, 494
JavaScript, 36, 356–357, **494**,
  535

Joint Photographic Experts
  Group (JPEG). See JPEG
  (Joint Photographic
  Experts Group)
.jpeg file extension, 116
JPEG files, 116, **344**–345
JPEG (Joint Photographic
  Experts Group), **344**–345,
  348, 393
.jpg file extension, 116
JPG files, **344**–345
justifying text, 204–205

K

kerning, **209**, 230
<keygen> element, 32
keywords, 221–222
Kompozer, 112

L

label attribute, 508–509
<label> element, 512–513,
  516, 522
labels
  associating with input
    elements, 525
  form elements, 512–513, 516
  margins, 516
  styling, 530–532
lang attribute, 203
LANs. See local area networks
  (LANs)
laptops, 53–57, 544
large keyword, 196
:last-child selector, 172
:last-of-type selector, 172
layouts
  breakpoints, **545**–547
  fixed layouts, 56–57,
    318–333
  flexible layouts, 54–55, 269,
    307–318
  floating, 298–311
  multiple columns, 300–302
leading, **205**–206, 230
left-to-right reading languages,
  203, 205
<legend> element, 510–512,
  518–519, 525–526, 533
legends, 519, 532–533
legend style rule, 518–519
length value, 243, 265
letter-spacing property, 209
Lie, Hakon, 198
<li> element, 148, 239, 430,
  433–434, 438–439,
  582, 592
linear structure, 121
line height, 205–206
line-height property, 205–206
link class, 374
LinkedIn, 106
<link> element, **142**–143, 175,
  551, 579–580
linking
  to chapter pages, 415
  to external document
    fragments, 422–424
  with text navigation bar,
    411–415
:link pseudo-class, 164,
  374–375, 441–443

links
  See also hyperlinks
  alternate text-based, 409
  background color, 165
  building, 416–417
  changing color, 163–164,
    374–375
  characteristics for states,
    163–164
  colors, 417
  contextual links, **429**
  graphics, 408–410
  highlighting, 164–165
  internal, 417–418
  page-turner links, 426–429
  testing web sites, 131
  underlining, 165, 212–213
  user location in web site,
    443–444
  visited, 441–443
Linux operating systems, 184
Linux web servers, 494
list boxes, 505–509, 527–528
list container element, 226
list-item context box, 227–229
list-item property, 223
lists, 225–226
  horizontal navigation bars,
    432–438
  horizontal navigation lists,
    239
  images, 227
  inline list items, 432–434
  margins, 431
  markers, 224–226
  navigation, 430–432
  ordered, 223–229
  padding, 431
  removing bullets, 431–432
  scrollable lists, 505–508
  symbol markers, 224–226
  unordered, 223–229
  vertical navigation bars,
    438–440
list-style-image property, 227
list-style-position property,
  227–229
list-style property, 223
list-style shorthand property,
  229
list-style-type property, 224,
  240, 432, 500
Literary Machine (Nelson), 403
local area networks (LANs),
  107
local data storage, 36–37
long quotes, 5
look and feel, **63**–65, 94
lossless compression, **342**,
  346, 393
lossy compression, **344**, 393
lowercase value, 213
Lucida Console, 196
Lynch, Patrick J., 79

M

Macintosh operating systems,
  184
mailto action, 496
main.css style sheet, 579–580
maintenance, 104–105
Manna Food Bank web site, 362
margin-bottom property, 244

margin-left property, 153–154,
  242, 244, 282, 311, 319,
  321, 323, 475, 562
margin properties, **243**–249,
  285, 300
margin property, 242–244, 272,
  321, 361, 596
margin-right property, 244, 282,
  311, 321, 323, 475, 562
margins, 243–249
  block-level elements, 239
  collapsing, 247
  content boxes, 240
  default browser spacing,
    248–249
  explicitly setting, 248–249
  images, 361
  indented elements, 243
  labels, 516
  length value, 243–244
  lists, 431
  measurement values, 243
  negative values for, 246
  paragraphs, 241–242
  percentage value, 243–244
  tables, 474–476
  transparency, 243
  white space around images,
    243
  zeroing, 248–249
margin shorthand properties,
  327–328, 330
margin-top property, 244
<mark> element, 32
markup elements, 4
markup languages, **2**, 19, 22, 41
markup tags, 2
Mashable web site, 60
max-height property, 269
maxlength attribute, 498
max-width property, 269,
  309–311, 557–558, 572
measurement units, 189–191
media attribute, 580
media features, **550**, 552–554,
  599
media queries, **55**, 58, 60, 94,
  545, **550**–554, 557, 560–
  661, 580, 582, 591, 599
@media rule, 550–551
@media selector, 555–557,
  562–563
media types, **549**–552, 555, 599
medium keyword, 196, 257
menu bars, 165
metadata, **30**, 41
<meta> element, 5–6, 25, 28,
  579
meta tag, 554
<meter> element, 32
method attribute, 495
Microfox web site, 311
Microsoft, 185
Microsoft Project, 99
Microsoft Visio, 120
Microsoft Visual Studio, 129
MIME (Multipurpose Internet
  Mail Extension), **28**, 41
min-height property, 269
min-width property, 269,
  309–311, 557–558
mission statement, 104
MIT (Massachusetts Institute
  of Technology), 20